Comparative Politics

Domestic Responses to Global Challenges
Ninth Edition

Charles Hauss
Alliance for Peacebuilding

CENGAGE
Learning®

Australia • Brazil • Japan • Korea • Mexico • Singapore • Spain • United Kingdom • United States

CENGAGE Learning®

Comparative Politics: Domestic Responses to Global Challenges, 9th edition

Charles Hauss

Product Director: Suzanne Jeans

Product Team Manager: Carolyn Merrill

Associate Product Manager: Scott Greenan

Content Developer: Michael B. Kopf, S4Carlisle Publishing Services

Content Coordinator: Eireann Aspell

Senior Media Developer: Laura Hildebrand

Marketing Director: Michelle Williams

Marketing Manager: Valerie Hartman

Market Development Manager: Courtney Wolstoncroft

Senior Content Project Manager: Joshua Allen

Senior Art Director: Linda May

Manufacturing Planner: Fola Orekoya

Senior Rights Acquisition Specialist: Jennifer Meyer Dare

Production Service: Cenveo® Publisher Services

Cover Designer: Chris Miller

Cover Image: Glowimages/Getty Images; Bartosz Hadyniak/the Agency Collection/ Getty Images

Interior Credits: Comparative Emphasis: © Ohmega1982/Shutterstock.com; Profiles: Comstock Images/Getty Images

Compositor: Cenveo Publisher Services

For product information and technology assistance, contact us at
Cengage Learning Customer & Sales Support, 1-800-354-9706
For permission to use material from this text or product,
submit all requests online at **www.cengage.com/permissions.**
Further permissions questions can be emailed to
permissionrequest@cengage.com.

Library of Congress Control Number: 2013946616

Student Edition:
ISBN-13: 978-1-285-46550-0

ISBN-10: 1-285-46550-4

Cengage Learning
200 First Stamford Place, 4th Floor
Stamford, CT 06902
USA

Cengage Learning is a leading provider of customized learning solutions with office locations around the globe, including Singapore, the United Kingdom, Australia, Mexico, Brazil and Japan. Locate your local office at **international.cengage.com/region.**

Cengage Learning products are represented in Canada by Nelson Education, Ltd.

For your course and learning solutions, visit **www.cengage.com.**

Purchase any of our products at your local college store or at our preferred online store **www.cengagebrain.com.**

Instructors: Please visit **login.cengage.com** and log in to access instructor-specific resources.

Printed in the United States of America
1 2 3 4 5 6 7 17 16 15 14 13

Brief Contents

Contents

Chapter 3
THE UNITED STATES   51

Chapter 4
THE UNITED KINGDOM   73

Chapter 5
FRANCE   107

Chapter 9
RUSSIA   221

Chapter 10
CHINA   257

Part 4
THE GLOBAL SOUTH

Chapter 11
THE GLOBAL SOUTH   291

Chapter 12
INDIA   323

Chapter 13
IRAN   357

Part 6
CONCLUSION

Chapter 16
GLOBAL CHALLENGES AND DOMESTIC RESPONSES 459

Preface

This is the ninth edition of *Comparative Politics: Domestic Responses to Global Challenges*, which means I have revised it eight times. Never has it changed more from one edition to the next.

The book changed because of two phenomena, only the second of which was new.

First, the world keeps changing. That has been the backdrop to the entire history of this book, the first edition of which was written in the days after the Soviet Union collapsed.

Second, the two professions I am part of have also been changing in constructive ways that sent me back to the intellectual drawing boards. That is new, especially for comparative politics, which, frankly, has been stuck in many of the same intellectual ruts for more than a quarter century. But, it was also true of peacebuilding, where my colleagues and I are exploring more complex and—in academic terms—more interdisciplinary models.

As a result, I decided it was time to put everything in this book up for grabs. I initially considered changing the way it was structured, the countries it covered, and even the way the chapters on individual countries were organized.

In the end, I kept the basic structure of the book, but changed almost everything else. I thought twice before keeping even a single sentence from earlier editions. Concretely, that has resulted in a book that combines many features from earlier editions with new insights and features.

New to This Edition: Overarching Themes

To begin with, much of the book revolves around the "big questions" that are at the heart of political life in the first two decades of the twenty-first century. In the decades since my own student days in the 1960s and 1970s, comparativists did not spend much time on them. In recent years, they have become harder and harder for anyone interested in the social sciences to ignore. That said, we do not agree on what they are. I find four of them particularly useful and will focus on them, especially in the second half of the book:

- The overall pace of change in all areas of life.
- The impact of "identity politics" everywhere.
- Democratization and our difficulties in achieving it.
- New threats to security and political problem solving that at least in part are a reflection of globalization.

We are fortunate that political scientists and other observers *have* been addressing aspects of these and other overarching issues facing both political science and the world as a whole. Of those, the two most important conceptual and empirical breakthroughs have come, again, in the kinds of countries and regimes covered in Parts 3 and 4.

- Political scientists who focus on democratization have drawn our attention to what they often call hybrid regimes that combine elements of democratic and authoritarian rule, with the emphasis far too often on the latter.
- Other comparativists have begun to revise conventional interpretations of political and economic development. This new generation of analysts views development in broader and more historical terms that concentrate on both how states were formed and how they struggle with demands to include new groups in the social, political, and economic elites.

While I am delighted that political scientists are asking more of the tough questions that got me interested in the field forty years ago, my thinking has been reshaped even more by developments in peacebuilding and related disciplines. There, I am lucky to be part of a team of academic and "real world" analysts who are pushing the boundaries of political analysis in three main ways.

- In my work as a peacebuilder, I have been drawn to analyses of the increasingly widespread use of cooperative problem-solving techniques in most aspects of life *other than national politics*.

- Everyone from corporate executives to environmental scientists now increasingly relies on systems analysis and the insights it provides, which this edition uses to explore how countries and their states have evolved over time and may well do so even faster in the years to come.

- Last but by no means least, comparative political science researchers have done less than colleagues in most other fields in exploring the implications of globalization and the entangled and interconnected set of social, political, economic, and other relationships it has brought in its wake.

New to This Edition: Specific Changes

For good reason, American law requires textbook publishers to disclose specific changes an author makes in each new edition. This edition is so different from the first eight that this section could easily have been very long.

Chapter 1—Seeing with New Eyes. In addition to the four big questions, Chapter 1 presents systems theory in a deeper and more analytical way.

Chapter 2—Industrialized Democracies. This chapter has changed less than most. However, it does raise some new ideas about deepening or "thickening" our understanding of democracy.

Chapter 3—The United States. This chapter includes full coverage of the 2012 election and the emergence of the Tea Party and Occupy movements. It also uses that material to suggest that readers consider the possibility that the United States could and perhaps should consider profound changes to a system that, in the words of Thomas Mann and Norman Ornstein, is "worse than it looks."

Chapter 4—The United Kingdom. The UK has not had a national election since the eighth edition of *Comparative Politics* was published. Therefore, this chapter focuses on the continuing difficulties faced by the coalition government as it tries to dig the country out of its slump, while also suggesting the European Union could prove to be the most divisive issue in British politics in the next few years.

Chapter 5—France. The new material in this chapter not surprisingly focuses on François Hollande's election as president in 2012 and the policy changes that have followed in its wake. By considering the problems France faces economically, this chapter anticipates the next two in which European issues are on center stage.

Chapter 6—Germany. Like the UK, Germany has not had an election, although one will be held before this edition is published, which outgoing Chancellor Angela Merkel and her CDU seem almost certain to win. The most important theme in German politics, however, is the crisis in the eurozone, which only Germany has the resources to address. It also focuses on the ways in which German policy making has revolved around consensus building more than in any of the other countries covered in this book.

Chapter 7—The European Union. Because the EU and the uncertain future of the euro are both so important for all of the industrialized democracies, they have become increasingly the focus of this chapter. This chapter also anticipates some of the prospects for international regimes and other forms of cooperative problem solving that will be at the heart of Chapter 16.

Chapter 8—Current and Former Communist Regimes. This chapter begins for the first time with the question of whether or not textbooks like this one even need to have a section on states inspired by Marxist analysis. Because these countries still share a common historical bond that political scientists are actually stressing more and more in their research on "hybrid regimes," this chapter has been retained. Like Chapter 2, it has not changed all that much other than to consider some new conceptual breakthroughs on transitional regimes and democratization.

Chapter 9—Russia. Not surprisingly, this chapter focuses on President Putin's return to power and its implications for democratization and other potential liberalizing trends in Russia, all of which are in more jeopardy than they were when the eighth edition of *Comparative Politics* was published. The emphases of the chapter remain the same, but the authoritarian aspects of the regime get even more attention.

Chapter 10—China. This chapter also focuses on the leadership transition, in this case to a new team of leaders in China. It also draws more attention to the growing tensions between a society that is more open economically and a political system that remains almost as closed as ever.

Chapter 11—The Global South. Unlike Chapters 2 and 8 that begin Parts 2 and 3, Chapter 11 has changed dramatically largely because our analyses of the Global South continue to expand in two different ways. First, we have a better understanding of the historical roots of development, especially in dynamics that made societies more inclusive. Second, political scientists and economists are paying more attention to the BRICS and other countries that have made unexpected developmental progress in the twenty years since the first edition of *Comparative Politics* was written.

Chapter 12—India. This chapter concentrates on India as a BRIC, beginning with a discussion of two neighborhoods— a slum on the outskirts of Mumbai and a toney enclave near the government offices in New Delhi. It updates information about economic as well as political changes and points toward the generational change that will almost certainly follow the next legislative election that will occur shortly after this book is published.

Chapter 13—Iran. Like Iranian politics as a whole, this chapter concentrates on two interconnected themes—the standoff with the international community on nuclear and other issues and the transitional period after Rouhani took office as president. Even more than in the eighth edition, this one concentrates on the longer-term potential for change unleashed in the Green Movement and beyond.

Chapter 14—Nigeria. This chapter begins with a play on the name of President Goodluck Jonathan who has not had much good luck. The chapter continues to stress the overlapping problems of failed development and failing state whoever is in charge in Nigeria. Unlike earlier editions, however, this version includes more material from anthropologists and students of religion, especially to help explain the emergence of Boko Haram.

Chapter 15—Mexico. Here, too, the text focuses on a new administration and the return of the PRI to power. Although some analysts stress the fact that Mexico seems poised for an economic boom and might be a candidate for the "next generation" of BRICS, this chapter concentrates on the country's continuing burden of problems both domestically and in its relationship with the United States. Even more than in previous editions, it draws the reader's attention to the fact that political life in Mexico is increasingly shaped by decisions and trends originating in Washington and beyond.

Chapter 16—Global Challenges and Domestic Responses. I have changed this chapter completely. It returns to the four big questions and systems analysis but revisits them in ways that lay out important political choices readers of this book will face in the rest of their lives as citizens— even if they don't ever take another course in comparative politics.

Supplements for Students and Instructors

Online PowerLecture with Cognero®

ISBN-10: 1285775023 | ISBN-13: 9781285775029

This PowerLecture is an all-in-one online multimedia resource for class preparation, presentation, and testing. Accessible through Cengage.com/login with your faculty account, you will find the following available for download: book-specific Microsoft® PowerPoint® presentations; a Test Bank in both Microsoft® Word® and Cognero® formats; an Instructor Manual; Microsoft® PowerPoint® Image Slides; and a JPEG Image Library.

The Test Bank, offered in Microsoft® Word® and Cognero® formats, contains multiple-choice and essay questions for each chapter. Cognero® is a flexible, online system that allows you to author, edit, and manage test bank content for Hauss, *Comparative Politics*, 9th Edition. Create multiple test versions instantly and deliver through your LMS from your classroom, or wherever you may be, with no special installs or downloads required.

The Instructor's Manual contains the following for each chapter: an outline and summary; critical thinking questions; in-class activities; lecture launching suggestions; a list of key terms with definitions; and suggested readings and Web resources.

The Microsoft® PowerPoint® presentations are ready-to-use, visual outlines of each chapter. These presentations are easily customized for your lectures, offered along with chapter-specific Microsoft® PowerPoint® Image Slides and JPEG Image Libraries. Access your Online PowerLecture at www.cengage.com/login.

Free Companion Web Site

ISBN-10: 1285834852 | ISBN-13: 9781285834856

This free companion website for *Comparative Politics*, accessible through cengagebrain.com, allows access to chapter-specific interactive learning tools including flash-cards, quizzes, glossaries, and more. Instructors also have access to the instructor's manual, PowerPoint presentations, and a test bank.

CourseReader 0-30: Comparative Politics

PAC ISBN: 9781111477608
IAC ISBN: 9781111477622

CourseReader: Comparative Politics allows you to create your reader, your way, in just minutes. This affordable, fully customizable online reader provides access to thousands of permissions-cleared readings, articles, primary sources, and audio and video selections from the regularly-updated Gale research library database. This easy-to-use solution allows you to search for and select just the material you want for your courses. Each selection opens with a descriptive introduction to provide context and concludes with critical-thinking and multiple-choice questions to reinforce key points.

CourseReader is loaded with convenient tools like highlighting, printing, note-taking, and downloadable PDFs and MP3 audio files for each reading. CourseReader is the perfect complement to any Political Science course. It can be bundled with your current textbook, sold alone, or integrated into your learning management system. CourseReader 0-30 allows access to up to 30 selections in the reader. Please contact your Cengage sales representative for details.

Acknowledgments

No one who writes a book this long—let alone one that has been through nine editions—works wholly on his own. Over the years, I have amassed hundreds of intellectual and personal debts that fall into six main categories.

First are the three generations of comparativists I have shared my career with. The oldest include my own professors and other scholars from my youth who shaped my career. John Lewis, Roy Pierce, Chuck Tilly, and others helped make me who I am. Of the few who are still alive and professionally active, I owe a lot to Bob Putnam, Bill Gamson, and Ron Suny. Second are the people I have taught and written with over the years, including David Rayside, Ken Wedding, Lee Wilson, Philip Giddings, Guilain Denoeux, Sharon Wolchick, Val Bunce, and, most of all, Melissa Haussman, who was co-author of the eighth edition and chose not to continue with the ninth. Third are the handful of students who have gone on to build their own careers in political science, starting with Melissa and also including Alan Carlson and Robin Bye, not to mention the thousands of others who had the common sense to find other careers.

Second are my colleagues in the peacebuilding field, especially those at the Alliance for Peacebuilding—Melanie Greenberg, Melanie Kawano-Chiu, Roxanne Knapp, Emily Malozzi, Bob Berg, Rob Ricigliano, Peter Woodrow, Joel Peters, Guy and Heidi Burgess, and more.

Third, much of what I am I owe to Oberlin College. Not only did I get turned on to comparative politics there when I took time off from organizing anti-war demonstrations, I made lasting friends among my teachers and my fellow students, many of whom remain close friends to this day. Most of the royalties I earn from *Comparative Politics* goes to endow the Oberlin Social Capital Fund that helps current and future students defray the cost of doing summer internships at organizations that promote social change.

Fourth, the Cengage team, as always, made the book possible and the less creative parts of finishing it tolerable. Carolyn Merrill and Josh Allen shepherded it through the production process after nagging me to make the book better, shorter, and cheaper. Michael Kopf, Sandhya Gola, and Joanne Johnson put up with my sloppiness in turning the manuscript into a finished product. Most of all, I owe more than I will ever be able to repay to Clark Baxter who originally signed me to write *Comparative Politics* before moving on to (for him) more interesting subjects at Cengage and then went on to become one of my best friends and the father of one of my best interns. In addition to the folks at Cengage, I want to thank the colleagues who reviewed this and earlier editions. I am always amazed at how insightful and helpful those anonymous critiques are.

The Cengage team and I would like to thank the following reviewers for their perspectives and feedback. For this edition, we would like to thank Christopher Muste, University of Montana, and Mark Croatti, George Washington University.

The following reviewed earlier editions:

Alex Avila, Mesa Community College; Valentine Belfiglio, Texas Woman's University; Clifford Bob, Duquesne University; Huiyun Feng, Utah State University; James Hedtke, Cabrini College; Sarah Henderson, Oregon State University; Edward Kwon, Northern Kentucky University; Shannan Mattiace, Allegheny College; John Mercurio, San Diego State University; Kevin Navratil, Moraine Valley Community College; Amy Risley, Rhodes College; Anca Turcu, Iowa State University; Walt Vanderbush, Miami University; Phillip Warf, Mendocino College; Wendy Whitman Cobb, Santa Fe College; Bruce Wilson, University of Central Florida; Nozar Alaolmolki, Hiram College; Leslie Anderson, University of Florida; Yan Bai, Grand Rapids Community College; Steve D. Bollard, Western Kentucky; Alan D. Buckley, Santa Monica College; John M. Buckley, Orange Coast College; William E. Caroll, Sam Houston State University; Kristine K. Cline, Riverside Community College; Richard Deeng, Temple University; Jana Eaton, Unionville High School, Kennett Square, Pennsylvania; Larry Elowitz, Georgia College;

Stacey Epifane, Saint John's University; Edward Epstein, University of Utah; Leslie Fadiga-Stewart, Delta State University; Joshua B. Forrest, University of Vermont; E. Gene Frankland, Ball State University; Susan Giaimo, Marquette University; Kristina Gilbert, Riverside Community College; Michael Gold-Biss, St. Cloud State University; Kerstin Hamann, University of Central Florida; Phil Huxtable, University of Kansas; Donna Johnson, Pace University; Ersin Kalaycioglu, Sabanci University; Amal Kawar, Utah State University; Michael Kenney, University of Florida; Stuart Krusell, Bentley University; Frank P. La Veness, St. John's University; J. Edward Lee, Winthrop University; Paul Lenze, Washington State University; David A. Lynch, St. Mary's University of Minnesota; Clinton W. Maffett, University of Memphis; Margaret Martin, University of St. Thomas; Hazel M. McFerson, George Mason University; Marian A. L. Miller, University of Akron; Richard M. Mills, Fordham University; Andrei Muntean, Drexel University; David J. Myers, Pennsylvania State University; Jeffrey R. Orenstein, Kent State University; William J. Parente, Sr., University of Scranton; Colin Ramsay, Lemon Bay High School, Englewood, FL; Steven Roach, University of South Florida; Bradley Scharf, Seattle University; Richard Stahler-Sholk, Eastern Michigan University; Pak W. Tang, Chaffey College; Hubert Tworzecki, Emory University; and Carrie Rosefsky Wickham, Emory University.

Fifth, I have to give special thanks to Dick O'Neill. Dick and I have known each other since we were in nursery school. While I became a 1960s leftist activist, Dick spent thirty years in the U.S. Navy and retired to create the Highlands Group, a think tank to help the Pentagon think outside the clichéd box. Dick introduced me to working with the military as a peacebuilder. We have had so much fun working together that our next project is to write a book together that builds on the themes of Chapter 16 and that we hope to use to catalyze a movement of audacious and creative thinkers who just might be able to end the paralytic nature of American politics.

Finally, I also have to thank my family—by no means as an afterthought. The first eight editions of this book were dedicated to my wife, Gretchen Sandles, and her daughter, Evonne Fei. Gretchen is a top-notch political scientist in her own right and has spent her career helping U.S. government analysts write briefings for policy makers that are rarely more than two pages long—yes, the length of this book makes her cringe. Evonne was in high school when I started writing this book. Now, she is a clinical psychologist who works with soldiers. She convinced me to change who the book was dedicated to when one of her patients mentioned seeing her name in the last edition.…She and her husband, Igor Petrovski, keep me on my political toes.

This edition is dedicated to their son—my grandson—Kiril Petrovski—whose very gene pool shows why comparative politics is important. His mother is half Chinese-American. His father was born and raised in Macedonia, and Kiril will be merely bilingual until I teach him French. He is also going to be a child of his times. Before he was two, he was already better at using an iPad than I am. He skypes his Macedonian grandparents several times a week. But most of all, he demonstrates why "doing" comparative politics is important every day by reminding me of the words on the coffee cup his mother gave me twenty years ago that I still use to end the book. It shows a picture of a cat holding up the world. It has the caption, "Fragile, Handle with Care."

Contact Me

I enjoy hearing feedback from readers. You can reach me at:

chiphauss@gmail.com

To Kiril Petorvski

Grandson extraordinaire and living proof that comparative politics matters.

Introduction

PART 1

CHAPTER 1
Seeing with New Eyes

AP Photo/Nader Daoud

© Cengage Learning

CHAPTER OUTLINE

1

Seeing with New Eyes

The voyage of discovery consists not in seeking new lands but in seeing with new eyes.

MARCEL PROUST

Comparative politics is one of the most exciting and challenging parts of political science. Those of us who study comparative politics for a living find it exciting because it constantly exposes us to new countries, concepts, ideas, ideals, people, values, and choices. The very things that make comparative politics exciting also make it challenging. It is a field full of tough questions, which can't be answered in a single course or a single book. In fact, it isn't clear that many of the questions we will be raising can be answered at all, in part because they are so complicated and in part because we disagree about what should be done in response to them.

For that reason, this is also going to be an unusual textbook for an unusual course. I will cover the material one typically finds in a textbook: Concepts. Names. Places. Events.

However, if you are going to get as much as possible out of either the book or the course, you will have to stretch yourself. In addition to the nuts and bolts of our part of political science, *Comparative Politics* will lead you to think about the "big ticket" questions that have altered and raised the stakes of political life during the course of my lifetime, not to mention yours.

It is hard to single out any one thing you absolutely have to do in order to understand the material covered in this book. However, if my years of teaching and writing about comparative politics are any indication, the statement by Marcel Proust that begins this chapter is a good place to start.

Proust was a novelist who never heard of comparative politics. But he got one thing about it right. Comparative politics is not about visiting places you've never been before, as interesting and enlightening as that can be. Rather, if he is right, we learn the most about new places, people, ideas, and events by looking at them differently—by "seeing with new eyes."

Five Big Questions

Most people are drawn to comparative politics by tough questions with implications that resonate around the world, which makes them a good jumping-off point for a book like this one. Unfortunately, because political scientists disagree about almost everything, there is no definitive list of such questions. I have chosen to focus on five of them because they meet three criteria:

- They show how uncertain and changeable our world is.

- In recent years, political scientists and others have made significant strides in understanding each of them.

- Despite what we have learned, political leaders and average citizens alike are still far from finding definitive answers to any of them.

And they are all presented as questions, because that is exactly what they are. And, whatever list we could agree on, political scientists are a contentious enough lot that we would disagree profoundly about the answers to them.

Change Is the Only Constant in a 2.0 World?

Nearly 3,000 years ago, the philosopher Heraclitus claimed that "change is the only constant." We will never know if his statement made sense for the Greece he lived in, but it certainly does today.

To get a first glimpse at that, take a step back from political science and consider some broader historical themes about change in general. More than forty years ago, Alvin Toffler wrote *Future Shock*, which argued that change of all sorts was occurring at an ever-accelerating rate.[1] Between the start of the industrial revolution and the end of World War II, people invented more things than they had in all of history until that time. Between the mid-1940s and the time Toffler wrote in 1970, the number of inventions doubled again twice, and he accurately predicted that the number of inventions would continue to skyrocket.

In 1965, there were no PCs, no color televisions, and no push button telephones. Cell phones existed only on the original version of *Star Trek*. News spread at what now feels like a snail's pace. Vietnam had just become the first war in which television viewers could see what had happened within 24 hours on the next evening's nightly news. Today, breaking news reaches us all but instantaneously in a 24/7 news cycle.

Figure 1.1 is a simplified way of thinking about the pace of change as he saw it. By his calculations, we were then living in humanity's 800th lifetime and are now in our 803rd. If Toffler was right, ours is a world of ever-accelerating change whose upward slope may actually be steeper than the figure suggests.

In at least one important way, Heraclitus and Toffler were both wrong. Political life is not all about change. In every chapter that follows, we will find ample evidence of continuity, including policies and institutions that have outlived their utility no matter what your point of view.

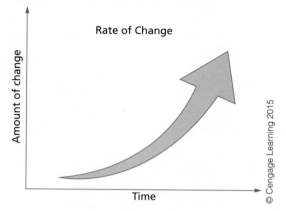

FIGURE 1.1 New Innovations over Time

© Cengage Learning 2015

You can get a first glimpse of the staying power of the status quo in this extract from *The Economist*'s editorial "commemorating" the death of Leonid Brezhnev in 1982.

> **In life, he stood for the status quo—as firmly as a man can stand when he is in fact moving slowly backward on a conveyor belt that is moving slowly forward beneath his feet.[2]**

We will return to Brezhnev and this surprisingly funny obituary in Chapter 8. For now, it is enough to note that *The Economist* only got one thing wrong. The conveyor belt was moving anything but slowly, which would turn the Communist Party's resistance to change into political

Another Look at Continuity and Resistance to Change

To see this point about the way continuity can often be a powerful yet destructive force, take that quotation from *The Economist* and substitute the name of any of today's political leaders you are interested in for Brezhnev's, and ask yourself if the statement is a fair description of that person as well.

suicide by the time the decade was out.

The change depicted in Figure 1.1 can only partially be described using quantitative indicators like the number of inventions. Political life around the world is changing *qualitatively* as well.

To see that, consider the case of Wael Ghonim. In 2010, he was a young and unknown Egyptian marketing executive at Google's offices in Dubai. That year, forces loyal to

---

[1] Alvin Toffler, *Future Shock* (New York: Random House, 1970). As a sign of the times, Toffler did not list his wife as a coauthor even though she was. They changed that "omission" in their later books. Their conclusions have been echoed with an even longer historical time frame in Ian Morris, *Why the West Rules—For Now* (New York: Farrar, Straus and Giroux, 2010).

[2] "Brezhnev's Legacy." *The Economist*, November 13, 1982, 7.

AP Photo/Maya Alleruzzo

Egyptian woman at a Silent Stand.

President Hosni Mubarak killed Khaled Said, whom they claimed had swallowed a fatal dose of marijuana while being taken into custody. Ghonim created the Facebook page, "We Are All Khaled Said" to protest the government's blatantly illegal and unjust actions.[3]

Ghonim insisted that the page's administrators remain anonymous to protect them from the secret police, who seemed willing to go to any length to protect Mubarak's regime. Nonetheless, thousands of people flocked to the page. In late 2010, Ghanim took the movement beyond the Internet and organized a series of "silent stands" in which protesters gathered and said nothing in order to demonstrate their opposition to the Mubarak regime.

After the stands grew beyond his wildest expectations, Ghonim decided to organize even more assertive demonstrations. At that point, the authorities discovered that he ran the site and had him arrested. When he was released, the revolution he helped spark brought the regime to the brink of collapse. Fifteen days after their first demonstration, Mubarak became the second long-lasting Middle Eastern leader to resign. He would not be the last.

Ghonim and his Facebook friends did not act alone. Reformist movements seemed to appear out of nowhere.

What came to be known as the **Arab Spring**[4] toppled entrenched authoritarian regimes in Tunisia, Yemen, Libya, and (or so one hopes as I write), Syria.

The title Ghonim chose for the book about what he and his friends did may be as important as their accomplishments themselves: Revolution 2.0. As they saw it, their movement was different from anything that had come before it because it relied heavily on social media and was leaderless, with individual members organizing themselves and deciding what to do on their own.

Ghonim was not the first to call something "2.0." Internet developers followed the lead of Tim O'Reilly, who started talking about Web 2.0 as early as 2004, the same year Facebook went live. They believed that social media were the start of something big that would soon allow us to share almost anything online and unleash tremendous creative potential in the process.

I was fortunate enough to attend one of the first conferences O'Reilly organized on Web 2.0 in which the people in the auditorium and countless others watching the event online sent Tweets that scrolled across a giant screen behind the speakers on the podium. I had a hard time seeing how my political friends and I could use the new media in our own work.

Then, the two Obama campaigns, the uprising by Iranian students in 2009, and Ghonim's Facebook friends convinced me I was wrong. In fact, I suspect that the term I now like to use, "Everything 2.0," just scratches the surface. Researchers in fields as different as organizational management and spirituality are exploring issues he either raises or alludes to, such

---

[3] Wael Ghonim, *Revolution 2.0: The Power of the People Is Greater Than the People in Power: A Memoir.* (New York: Houghton Mifflin Harcourt, 2012). www.youtube.com/watch?v=tPMU4rzE9i4. This video is in Arabic, but it doesn't matter because video often doesn't need words. The English titles, in fact, are often grammatically incorrect. It was made by a thirteen year old.

---

[4] Terms in bold are included in the lists of key terms at the end of each chapter and defined in the glossary at the end of the book.

as crowd sourcing, self-organizing phenomena, emerging patterns, and virtual organizations, as part of systems theory, which we will turn to later in this chapter.

Not everyone uses the 2.0 label to describe the profound social and economic changes they seek. That kind of terminology may have been a bit too trendy for the Tea Party and Occupy Movement activists in the United States.

In short, we know that change is under way. That is about all we can say with any certainty, however. In fact, the events changing our world are coming so quickly that pundits have a hard time even naming them, as the widespread use of labels such as "2.0," "post-," and "neo-" suggest.[5]

Democratization?

Ghonim and his fellow activists did not simply want to throw out the likes of Mubarak. They wanted to replace their hated **regimes** with **democracies**.

In Part 2, we will see that almost all of the longest-lasting and most firmly established democracies emerged as the unintended byproducts of other historical processes. Today, by contrast, conscious efforts to democratize other kinds of regimes are central features on the political agenda in just about all of them.

For activists like Ghonim, democratization is a goal worth struggling and even dying for. However, as the aftermath of the Arab Spring has so tragically shown us, budding democracies all too often lapse back into **authoritarian** regimes—or worse.

There have been several so-called waves of **democratization** since the middle of the nineteenth century (see Table 1.1). The first covers the establishment of democratic regimes in parts of Europe and North America, the second covers its spread and solidification in more of Europe, and the third its continued expansion into the rest of Europe and the Global South, to the point that as many as two-thirds of the countries at least had competitive elections. The final one *may* be happening today with trends such as the Arab Spring and the **colored revolutions** that have arisen there, in Eastern Europe, and in Central Asia.

There is little doubt that **democracy** is popular. However, as we will see in Part 2, no country lives up to any version of the democratic ideal. And creating democratic regimes—whether by design or by historical accident—has always been difficult and given rise to intense conflict, including war. In Parts 3 and 4, we will see that political scientists have learned a good bit about how democratization has taken place so far. Unfortunately, policymakers have had a hard time turning that academic understanding into viable, practical public policy.

---

[5]I have a lot of books with 2.0 in the title. On the day I finished this chapter, Amazon sent *Capitalism 3.0* to my Kindle. The spectacular growth of Amazon, e-readers, and information technology (not to mention my first 3.0 book) reinforces the pace and uncertainty of the trends being discussed here.

TABLE 1.1 Three (or Four?) Waves of Democratization

WAVE OF DEMOCRATIZATION	BEGINNING IN	KEY FEATURE
First	Nineteenth century	First democracies in Europe and North America
Second	1945	Creation of democracies in newly independent countries and solidification of older ones in Europe
Third	Mid-1970s	Spread to the Global South and Eastern Europe, accelerated by the End of the cold war
Fourth (?)	Twenty-first century	Arab Spring and "Colored Revolutions"

© Cengage Learning 2015

Identity?

There are only a handful of countries that are homogeneous enough to avoid **identity politics**. In country after country, differences over race, religion, language, ethnicity, and region give rise to intractable conflicts that seem to defy solution (www.beyondintractability.org).

Comparative Emphasis: A Box about Boxes

Like any textbook published today, *Comparative Politics* has its share of boxes to help focus the reader's attention. Most of them highlight a single theme in the text itself.

This one, however, is about boxes themselves—of the mental rather than the printed variety.

One of today's most widely used clichés urges us to think "outside the box" and come up with creative new ideas. For good or ill, the opposite is likely to happen whenever a politician or pundit in Washington (where I live and work) uses the phrase.

Comparative Politics actually requires you to think both inside *and* outside the box. In my nonacademic work, I try to get people to think very far outside any conventional political "box." To the degree that my colleagues and I succeed, it is largely because we also anchor our work in conventional political life, which can be a constraining box if there ever was one. ■

That is easiest to see quickly using religion as an example. Many of my European colleagues are perplexed by the political role religion plays in the rest of the world. Religion was once one of the most contentious issues there, touching off countless revolutions and civil wars. Today, religious practice in Europe is at an all-time low, and disputes about religious issues no longer divide people in politically significant ways.

In much of the rest of the world, religion remains as much of a political lightning rod as it ever has been.

That begins with the United States, where opposition to gay rights, a woman's freedom to choose, and even presidential candidate Mitt Romney's Mormon faith all have deep religious roots. Often, issues that do not seem to be primarily religious have faith-related overtones as in the "birther" claim that Barack Obama was not born in the United States and therefore is not eligible to hold the presidency.

Religious differences have far more devastating consequences along the tenth parallel to the north of the Equator, which the journalist Eliza Griswold calls the fault line between Christianity and Islam.[6] From Nigeria in the west to the Philippines in the east, disputes anchored in religion spill over into every other potentially disruptive issue and threaten to tear society after society apart.

In that sense, religion and other identity-based issues can be an analytical stepping-stone to help us understand political conflict in general. Researchers in a number of fields see religion as a key ingredient of people's identities and the way they answer such basic questions as "who am I?" Put simply, it is far easier to find common ground even on tough issues such as cutting budgets where the parties to a dispute can compromise by splitting the differences between them than it is when their very self-definition is at stake.

Because religious differences so often ignite irreconcilable conflicts, they keep us from seeing the more constructive role that religion can play in political life. At times, religious leaders have played a major role in bringing adversaries together to help resolve identity-based conflicts. Some are world famous, including Dr. Martin Luther King, Jr., in the United States or Archbishop Desmond Tutu in South Africa. Other less well-known figures will be discussed in some of the chapters to come, such as Pastor James Wuye and Imam Muhammad Ashafa, who have been among the few people to have had any impact in stemming the violence between Christians and Muslims along the tenth parallel in northern Nigeria.[7]

Human Security, Sustainability, and Resilience?

The changes discussed so far also cast doubt on many of the core assumptions about political life that date back at least to the creation of the modern nation-state more than three centuries ago. As we explore those assumptions, we will also journey the farthest from the traditional domains of academic political science, which, toward the end of this chapter and again in the conclusion to the book as a whole, I will argue we have to do.

Again, a single issue helps to get the discussion started—security. Until the end of the **cold war**, most international relations experts focused on national security, which they defined in terms of conventional definitions of power that include at least the threat of force. Today, the environment and other global issues have led more and more of us to focus on **human security**, which rests on the notion that we have to do more than just safeguard our vital geopolitical interests but meet basic social, economic, and environmental needs as well.

At first, it was mostly people in **nongovernmental organizations (NGOs)** like the one I work for who talked about human security. Now, such ideas are commonly discussed (although rarely by political scientists) in ways that help us glimpse what Everything 2.0 could be like.

Perhaps because my NGO works on peace building, I find an approach to human security written for the then Chair of the Joint Chiefs of Staff particularly compelling. In 2011, Admiral Michael Mullen asked Marine Colonel Mark Mykleby and Navy Captain Wayne Porter to draft a new approach to security for the post–cold war and post-9/11 world. In what is known as the Y Report, they wove together five themes that seemed surprising when I first saw them, especially given who the authors are.[8]

- National security requires global security. No country can be truly secure unless everyone else is. And "security" includes not just the geopolitics of traditional international relations but environmental, economic, and gender security as well.

- All systems are open and subject to constant change in ways that no state or any other actor can hope to control on its own.

- We need to adopt policies that build sustainability by stressing the ways that all pressing social problems overlap.

---

[6]Eliza Griswold, *The Tenth Parallel* (New York: Farrar, Straus and Giroux, 2010).

[7]See www.youtube.com/watch?v=xy1DfcyYX7c.

[8]Mark Mykleby and Wayne Porter, "A National Security Narrative" (Washington: Woodrow Wilson Center, 2011). www.wilsoncenter.org/sites/default/files/A%20National%20 Strategic%20Narrative.pdf.

- Instead of traditional national defense, we have to work on all of the world's pressing problems and seek solutions for them in cooperation with people we might initially think of as adversaries.

- To use the jargon of conflict resolution, we have to try to find **positive-sum** or **win-win** solutions to our problems rather than the **zero-sum** or winner-take-all ones envisioned in traditional definitions of power and politics.

Human security also requires governments and other social organizations that are **resilient**, another concept to which political scientists are just beginning to pay attention. Resilience is based on many of the same assumptions Mykleby and Porter make: that systems are interconnected by way of tightly connected, complicated, and unpredictable feedback loops that constantly provide challenges, which are themselves tightly connected, complicated, and unpredictable.

As the subtitle of a recent book puts it, resilience can be thought of as the study of "why things bounce back,"[9] which leads to two more political questions, the first of which political scientists have long worried about. How do individuals and organizations respond after they have faced a major, traumatic challenge? As we will see, many countries have "bounced back" from adversity. We pose the second one far less often. How can politicians and citizens alike learn to anticipate crises and plan ways of reacting to them before they happen? If Mykleby and Porter and others like them are right, that may be the most important question to ask. It also is certainly the most difficult to answer.

Globalization?

Globalization is one of the most important but least understood buzzwords in the social sciences today. Everyone "knows" that the world is shrinking. The word *knows* is in quotation marks in the preceding sentence because we all know that it literally is not true. My office and the room you are reading this book in are as far apart as they were when they were built. What we can say is that the distances and borders that separate us socially, economically, and environmentally don't matter as much as they did a few short decades ago.

Look around the room you are in now. Count all the countries the things in that room came from, including the labels inside your clothes. Without taking anything apart, I counted 27 on the day I wrote this chapter.

The exercise I just asked you to do is itself misleading because it masks even more complexity; many everyday objects are made up of parts that come from a number of places, no matter what their packaging says. My iPad, for example, was put together in China, not at Apple's world headquarters in Cupertino, California. It includes products manufactured in North America and East Asia by ten other companies with headquarters in three countries. The previous editions of this book were printed in Canada and Singapore. Cengage sells this book all over the world from offices in half a dozen countries.

If you believe the optimists, globalization could be one of the most positive features of modern life. More people are better off than ever before. We will see that most clearly in the **BRICS** (Brazil, Russia, India, China, and South Africa) countries, where economic growth is occurring at such a fast and sustained rate that millions of people have been pulled out of poverty in the last couple of generations.

More pessimistic analysts, instead, focus instead on globalization's social and economic shortcomings. Somewhere around two billion people live on less than $2 a day. As Katherine Boo shows in her riveting book on the slums of Mumbai (formerly Bombay), the residents of Annawadi do not have access to safe drinking water, electricity, adequate health care, indoor plumbing, and dozens of other things we in the West take for granted.[10]

Many analysts think of globalization primarily in economic terms. There is more international trade, movement of workers, and even international marriage than ever before.

There are signs, too, that something like a global culture is taking hold, especially among the young. Hip-hop, basketball, and MTV are becoming global phenomena. We are not becoming exactly the same. There may be McDonalds restaurants almost everywhere, but they do not all serve the same food (foodnetworkhumor.com/2009/07/mcdonalds-menu-items-from-around-the-world-40-pics/). Nonetheless, the fact that the Golden Arches™ have become a global phenomenon tends to overshadow the differences in what the national franchises serve.

Similarly, migration is literally changing the face of almost every wealthy society. American, Canadian, and European cities are turning into cultural mosaics. People from a dozen countries live in my neighborhood. Within a mile or two of our house, we can eat at Mexican, Salvadoran, Peruvian, Turkish, Thai, Chinese, Japanese, Vietnamese, Indian, Korean, Greek, French, and Italian restaurants.

[9]Andrew Zolli and Ann Marie Healy, *Resilience: Why Things Bounce Back* (New York: Simon and Shuster, 2012).

[10]Katherine Boo, *Behind the Beautiful Forevers: Life, Death, and Hope in a Mumbai Undercity* (New York: Random House, 2012). www.youtube.com/watch?v=dSK5Jrb6mXA.

Globalization is also undoubtedly changing the college or university you attend. Your school may have opened campuses in other countries. At some schools, study abroad has become the norm; a few have even considered requiring it. Campuses themselves are changing. When I was a student at Oberlin College in the late 1960s, there were no more than a dozen foreign students. Today, they make up 10 percent of the student body. Grinnell College announced that it had 200 Chinese applicants with an 800 score on at least one SAT exam for its class of 2017.

Just as is the case with the economy, migration and other aspects of globalization are a mixed blessing politically. There is no better example of that than the terrorist attacks on 9/11. A small group of men had traveled halfway around the world to carry out the most devastating terrorist attacks the world had ever seen. By the end of that day, it was clear to most of us that our political world had changed forever because the world had shrunk in ways the cartoon on this page so brilliantly and tragically depicts. On September 10, vast oceans separated the continents from each other. By the next day, the *de facto* distance across the oceans had all but disappeared.

According to some observers, the attacks were, at least in part, an angry response to the global spread of Western culture. If so, today's terrorism may only be the tip of the clichéd political iceberg. As the world shrinks, the clash of contrasting cultures often gives rise to conflict albeit rarely of the magnitude we saw in 2001. France, in particular, has seen massive demonstrations protesting policies that prohibit girls who wear the *hijab* and other religious clothing from attending school.

Globalization is also important for students of comparative politics because it shows us that we are less and less masters of our own destinies, however you choose to define the word "us." National governments are losing the capacity to make and implement decisions on a host of issues that matter to their citizens.

Yet, when it comes to responding to global challenges, political leaders tend to look for national solutions first. The French parliament passed the law against wearing religious clothing and jewelry in the belief that it could integrate the Muslims who make up about 10 percent of the population by treating them exactly the same as everyone else. The American government tries to limit imports to "protect" endangered domestic jobs. The Chinese and Iranians are fighting what seems to be a losing battle to keep their citizens from having full access to the Internet.

The discussion so far leads us to this book's subtitle—domestic responses to global challenges—and draws our attention to the challenges facing political scientists as well as political leaders. We political scientists have long drawn a clear distinction between comparative politics and international relations. Comparativists focus on events *within* countries; international relations (IR) specialists concentrate on what happens *between* them.

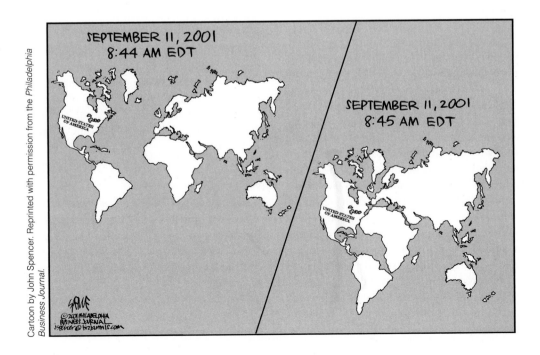

Cartoon by John Spencer. Reprinted with permission from the *Philadelphia Business Journal*.

A few scholars now make the case that such a distinction never made sense. This book is based on the premise that it certainly does not today. National borders are still important but they matter a lot less than they used to both in determining how issues arise (global challenges) and in the ways we react to them (domestic responses).

Most people reading this book live and/or study in an advanced industrialized democracy. In other words, "global challenges" are anything but abstract to you, because you have seen the difficulties government after government have had in trying to pull their countries out of the great recession. As with identity politics, it is easiest to see that abstract point with two concrete examples—the economic **crisis** and climate change.

The causes of the greatest economic downturn since the 1930s are indeed global and may seem quite distant from you, including decisions by bankers in Iceland, real estate bubbles in the United States and Europe, and increased spending on social services, which together sent economic shockwaves around the world. But, if you are like the students I know, the crisis has hit close to home as you worry about finding a job, buying a house at some time in the future, or even paying for college today.

You have also seen that few national governments are rich or strong enough to be able to have slowed the decline on their own. Nonetheless, most people in most countries expect their national leaders to "fix" the crisis by taking action when and where they can, which mostly takes place within national borders. And as dozens of politicians around the world have discovered to their chagrin, incumbents tend to take the blame, whether they were responsible for the downturn or not.

Fifty years ago, no one worried about climate change. Next to nobody recycled. There was no Earth Day. Today, **sustainability** is one of the world's most hotly debated topics. Whatever one thinks about the causes or the extent of climate change, carbon footprints and renewable energy are now part of our everyday vocabulary.

Environmental issues are quintessential global problems. While it is true that some countries contribute more than others to most environmental problems, no one country is responsible for global warming or any of the other major ecological concerns. None of them can be solved by national governments acting on their own. Yet, as with the recession, most of us assume that our leaders have to respond to them as if they were primarily national problems for which international cooperation is the exception rather than the rule.

Before moving on, the book's subtitle itself should probably have a question mark. As I will discuss in more depth in the final chapter, it may well be that there *aren't* any domestic responses that can help us make significant progress in solving any of those global challenges.

Politics, Science, and Comparison

These five questions require the kind of new eyes Proust had in mind. To help you "see" that way, the rest of this chapter discusses the key concepts in comparative politics while setting the agenda for the book as a whole. Before we turn to the specifics of comparative politics, we will start with three concepts you will need in order to make sense of the thousands of names, facts, and figures discussed in the pages that follow—political, scientific, and comparative.

Think of them as the equivalent of the three lenses in a pair of trifocal glasses. Each one gives you a needed and unique perspective on comparative politics that, together, will give you a realistic chance of seeing the whole field with any degree of clarity.

Politics

The online version of the Merriam-Webster's dictionary starts with a conventional definition of **politics** as "the art and science of governing." There is nothing wrong with that definition. Most political scientists, however, prefer a broader one that also includes **power**, which political scientists define as one side's ability to get another to do *what it otherwise would not do*.

The six italicized words in the previous sentence are critical. Whether we like it or not, people with power have to convince or compel others to do things that are against their better judgment in some way. To cite an example anyone reading this book will be familiar with, teachers exert power over students when they take points off their grade if an assignment is turned in late.

That example illustrates one final point. Politics exists in any organization in which power is used. That includes the nation state, which we will concentrate on in this book. However, towns, cities, and other subnational governments all have politics. So, too, do some less obvious examples, including businesses, universities, classrooms, and even families.

Science

We call ourselves *political scientists*, which many people think is a pretentious title. After all, we have little in common with physicists or chemists whose multimillion-dollar grants and fancy labs yield sophisticated and precise results the likes of which political scientists can only dream of.

Yet, in one critical respect, we are scientists. Like physicists or chemists, we are less interested in the facts we uncover than in the broader conclusions they point us to.

In other words, like our colleagues in the "hard" sciences, we try to develop **theories** that help us understand some phenomenon or phenomena. The best of them cover a wide variety of subjects. Thus, explaining voting behavior in all democracies is more useful than doing so for Alabama and Mississippi. We also prefer relatively simple theories that boil cause-and-effect relationships down to a few key factors, such as Einstein's famous equation, $e = mc^2$.

Ultimately, we would like to come up with a theory that covers an entire discipline, which is referred to as a **paradigm**. Given the complexity of human behavior, we are not likely to develop one for comparative politics any time soon. Nonetheless, designing new and better theories is something we can all do, including students in introductory classes.

Developing theory might seem like a complicated task given the misconceptions most of us have about the scientific method. However, at this level, thinking theoretically is no more complicated than moving above and beyond the facts and figures in two ways.

The classical versions of the scientific method are based on deductive research and reasoning. A researcher starts with a theory and tests it with systematically gathered evidence. That, in turn, allows the scholar to take advantage of one of the key features of "doing science" that seems counterintuitive, at least at first.

No body of evidence can ever prove that a theory is true. However compelling the facts might seem, there could be other instances where the theory's predictions and explanations are not confirmed. Instead, the most interesting thing we can do is **falsify** the theory by finding at least one example in which the hypotheses we *deduced* from the theory are wrong. Doing so introduces creativity into scientific research because our next task is to figure out *why* the theory did not work. That usually means stepping back from the computer screen or piles of lab results and thinking outside whatever preconceptions the theory had led us to accept at the outset.

Once again, an example from outside political science is illustrative. Until the English colonized Australia, Europeans "knew" that all swans were white. All of their "research" (watching swans) had confirmed that "fact." Then, when they arrived in Australia, they encountered black swans, thus undermining whatever theory they had about swans. Nassim Nicholas Taleb (the popularizer of the black swan phenomenon) argues that the process of reconciling "black swans" and conventional wisdom makes our theories more powerful and more complete, a point we will return to in Chapter 16.[11]

Although we will encounter the occasional political black swan, deductive theory will not feature prominently in this book, for two reasons. First, few undergraduates are comfortable working with deductive theory. Second, very few of the deductive theories at our disposal are very good to begin with.

Instead, we will work more often inductively, starting with evidence and then climbing "up" what the psychologist Chris Argyris calls the ladder of inference. You can take the evidence on any country or any other political phenomenon and ask this grammatically awkward question: "of what is Germany an instance?" What does the information we uncover about Germany tell us, for instance, about democracies in general? Or countries that became unified after their neighbors? Or countries that are the wealthiest today?

Comparison

The third lens is the easiest, because you already use it even if you are not aware that you are doing so. We have all compared things. Which college to attend? Which car to lease? We may not always make the best decisions. Nonetheless, the judgments that we make invariably involve comparisons.

Think about computers. I have always used Macs. When they were introduced thirty years ago, my decision was easy. Macs were *easier* to use than the first PCs (that, of course, is no longer the case). I still use a desktop because its screen is *larger* than the one on my laptop. When it came time to buy a tablet, I chose an iPad because it did *more* of what I needed than any of its competitors, including running Amazon's software for my burgeoning collection of ebooks.

Note the use of comparative endings in the preceding paragraph. I chose Macs because they seemed superior after I compared them with the competition. Whatever form it takes, we learn more about something if we compare it with something else of the same ilk.

Along those same lines, consider two simple political examples. When then Senator Barack Obama had to choose a running mate in 2008, he compared a number of possible candidates and decided that someone with Joe Biden's vast experience would give his ticket the balance the youthful nominee needed.

In a second example, 66 percent of the registered voters cast ballots in the 2010 British general election. That one fact tells us very little about Britain or its political system. The picture changes dramatically once you add two more pieces of information. That figure was one of the lowest there since the 1930s. By contrast, it is rare that even that many Americans show up at the polls. In fact, turnout in the United States reached a modern record high of 56 percent two years earlier. With those two pieces of comparative data, you can pose far more insightful questions about

---

[11]Nassim Nicholas Taleb, *The Black Swan: The Impact of the Highly Improbable* (New York: Random House, 2007), prologue.

elections in general than you could with the British total for 2010 alone. Why is turnout in British elections normally higher than that in the United States? Why has it been declining in recent elections in both countries? What difference does turnout make?

The Political System

The Big Picture

Comparative Politics will use the **state** as the organizing concept for the rest of the book because it puts the allocation of scarce resources and power on center stage. We will examine the state and politics as a whole through the lens of **systems theory** because it does the best job of helping us see how the state, society, and global environment interact (see Figure 1.2). In this section, we will see how systems theory offers us the equivalent of an accurate snapshot of political life. The next section shows how we will use it to understand tough questions like those we just considered, although we will have to put off seeing why that's the case until the final chapter.

The State

Many people mistakenly use the words **government**, state, nation, and regime interchangeably. Doing so is not a serious problem for a country like the United States where

FIGURE 1.2 The Political System

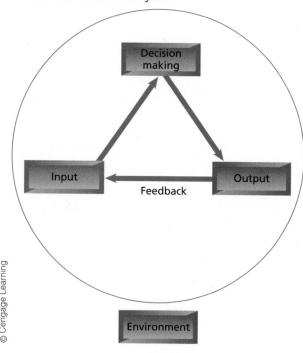

© Cengage Learning

they overlap significantly. When we consider the former Soviet Union or Iraq before the 2003 war, however, treating them as synonyms can be misleading indeed.

Government refers to the institutions that pass laws, issue regulations, control the police, and so on. Often, those powers are outlined in a **constitution**.

The government rarely holds all the power and, in some cases, can even be overshadowed by other actors. Private-sector executives may not hold any formal governmental position, but they routinely have a major say in economic policy making, even in supposedly communist countries like China. In the so-called failed states, which we will consider later in this section, the government lacks the ability to do much of anything.

The **nation**, by contrast, is a psychological rather than an institutional concept and covers the cultural, linguistic, and other identities that can either tie people together or drive them apart. As we will see in several chapters, a lack of national identity often reflects deep-seated ethnic and other divisions that can undermine support for any state, whatever institutional levers it may have at its disposal.

We also have to distinguish between the government of the day and the underlying regime that remains in place from one government (or administration to Americans) to the next. Most industrialized democracies can weather all but the most difficult crises because there is almost total acceptance of the regime that serves to insulate it from such divisive protests as those led by the new left of the 1960s and 1970s. In those countries, most people have drawn an unconscious mental "line" between protesting against a government and its policies, which they accept as part of the democratic process, and questioning the structure and underlying values of their regime, which they are unwilling to do. As we will see in Parts 3 and 4, that is not the case in much of the rest of the world where few regimes enjoy that kind of bedrock popular support, which leaves them vulnerable to the wrenching conflict that can give rise to a new regime at almost any moment in time.

Political scientists have been using the concept of the regime for a half-century or more. The term only entered popular political discourse more recently, most notably with President George W. Bush's insistence on a regime change in Iraq in the months before the 2003 invasion of that country.

Inputs

In the language of systems analysis, the state responds to (and sometimes ignores) **inputs** from the rest of the system. These are easiest to describe in democracies where people have the greatest freedom to exert influence over what the state does. Nonetheless, as we will see in Parts 3 and 4, no state is wholly immune to pressure from below.

All countries have a **political culture** that consists of commonly held values about the nation, state, regime, and more. Political scientists rarely include attitudes toward current leaders or issues in a country's culture. In other words, analyses of the American political culture focus on attitudes about the presidency in general rather than what people think about Barack Obama or any other individual president.

In many ways, a country's culture is a reflection of the impact its history has on popular values today. Thus, Indians' strong attachment to the caste system and the antagonism between Hindus and Muslims both have to be traced back hundreds of years to the way their social structures evolved before and after the arrival of the Mughals a thousand years ago.

A political culture is very much an individual's "second nature." It is so ingrained in our minds and so taken for granted that we rarely have to think about it. We are probably no more consciously aware of most of our cultural values than we are of the rules for tying our shoes when we lace them up each morning.

Cultural norms rarely determine what anyone actually does at any particular time. Instead, they set the political stage by determining some things that are generally considered politically acceptable while ruling others out. Thus, it is certainly legal to support socialism in the United States. However, the individualistic American culture is so pervasive that a socialist candidate has almost no chance of winning an election.

Last but by no means least, no country has a single political culture. Rather, many of the countries we will consider have deeply divided cultures which serves as a breeding ground for the identity-based conflict discussed above.

There are also many ways people can take part in political life. In the established democracies, individuals can act on their own by, for example, voting or writing a letter to the editor. However, most **political participation** is channeled through two types of organizations.

A **political party** tries to combine the interests of a number of groups together in order to win control of the government either on its own or as part of a **coalition**. Not all parties seek to do that through elections, as we will see was the case in the former Soviet Union. However, except for truly minor parties that are so small that few will find their way into this book, these institutions are defined by their desire to directly exercise power.

Interest groups deal with a narrower range of issues and represent a more limited segment of a country's population. Trade unions, business associations, environmental groups, and others organize and "lobby" around specific issues and other concerns. There are so many kinds of interest groups that political scientists often have trouble actually analyzing them as a single category.

Whether participating as individuals or in groups, people can either give **support** to or place **demands** on the state. They engage in the former by paying taxes on time or standing when their country's national anthem is played.

AP Photo/Pewee Flomoku

Women protesting against Charles Taylor's dictatorial regime in Liberia.

In placing demands, people are trying to persuade or force the government to do what they want. Sometimes, they use what are often called "inside the system" tactics by voting for an opposition party, writing a letter to the editor, or marching in a peaceful protest. Sometimes, they organize "outside the system" campaigns that try more aggressively to force the state to change, as the women in the photograph on p. 13 did when their protests helped bring down Charles Taylor, who was the dictator of Liberia from 1997 to 2003. On the other hand, radical protest does not have to threaten or actually use violence, as the example of Wael Ghonim's "stand" for Khaled Said attests.

Outputs

The state's **output** is its **public policy**. Like inputs, there are several kinds of policies.

States can regulate what citizens do by setting speed limits for driving or enforcing a minimum drinking age. These examples make it clear that states do not and cannot always enforce regulatory policy to the full letter of the law.

States also distribute and redistribute resources. The most controversial distributive policies redirect resources from wealthier to poorer people in what are loosely known as welfare programs. I almost certainly pay more income tax than you do. Other distributive policies transfer money and services across generational lines. That will happen more and more in the industrialized democracies as my generation of baby boomers retires and needs ever more expensive medical care. Put simply, your generation will end up paying a lot of the cost for mine, whatever policy options we choose to rein in health care spending.

Finally, policies can be *symbolic*, which is an academic term that covers what journalists mean when they talk about the role of "spin." Symbolic acts may not have the kind of concrete effects of either regulatory or distributive policy. However, there is no doubt that the way political leaders portray themselves has an impact on the way people respond to them, which is one of the reasons political leaders drape themselves in flags or only ride in cars manufactured in their own countries. That impact is, of course, very hard to measure as we will see shortly is also the case for feedback and the media.

Feedback

The fourth concept in systems analysis could well be the most important but is certainly the most difficult to document. Engineers and other natural scientists invented systems analysis, and those roots are still evident in its use of terms like **feedback**. Through feedback, events "today" shape how the components of the system react "tomorrow."

Feedback loops determine how and if a system "learns" from what has happened in the past. In that sense, feedback also makes systems analysis dynamic because it lets us see the interplay of everyone's actions over time. In other words, feedback allows us to turn what might have seemed like a tool that, like my iPhone or iPad, gives us streaming video as well as a snapshot of reality.

Unfortunately, political scientists do not know how to measure feedback with any degree of precision. In this book, we will use media exposure as a very rough indicator for the much larger feedback process. The media are not the only sources of feedback, which also include family, friends, respected opinion leaders, and occasionally even college professors. However, most people get most of their political information from the mass media, whose impact is definitely growing (and became more confusing) with the spread of new electronic media outlets both on- and offline.

The Environment

The **environment** includes everything that lies outside the formal political system. Any system is considered bounded because it has its own internal structure. No system, however, is completely autonomous, because the individuals and institutions inside it invariably have to respond to forces beyond their control. There are three types of forces that can limit their ability to shape their own destinies, each of which has at least been alluded to above and of which we will return to later in this chapter.

- The impact of history on culture and politics in general
- What happens inside their countries, which means that insights from economics, sociology, ecology, anthropology, psychology, and other academic disciplines will find their way into these pages
- Global forces, as reflected in the book's subtitle

System Dynamics

After a flurry of initial interest in the 1960s and 1970s, systems theory fell out of favor in political science because it did not seem to lend itself to the type of research that could lead to the kind of all-encompassing theory mentioned earlier. That is certainly not the case today.

Systems analysis has become the norm in such different disciplines as health care, business management, and engineering precisely because it is an excellent lens through which to see how and why systems evolve over time. Systems theorists today concentrate on three types of outcomes, only the first of which political scientists initially focused on, which partially explains why this approach did not catch on when it was introduced to the field fifty years ago.

Systems approaches were introduced to political science in the early 1960s when my colleagues were primarily interested in preventing the return of totalitarian regimes (see Chapter 6 and Part 3). Although they were worried about system breakdown in ways we will see in the next paragraph, they were more interested in what kept systems stable. Systems theorists often use the image of a thermostat to convey what they have in mind by **equilibrium**. You set the thermostat at a certain temperature. If it gets a bit too cold, the heat kicks on. If it gets a little higher than that predetermined temperature, the heat turns itself off. As a result, the temperature never varies very far from that setting. As we will see throughout the book, that kind of stability almost never occurs in the rough and tumble "real world" of political life.

Systems can also deteriorate in much the same ways that a dysfunctional family does. There is no mechanism to keep it in balance. In the language of systems theory, such a system is characterized by self-reinforcing **vicious cycles**. Once something bad happens, things tend to get worse and the "bouncing back" of resilience becomes all but impossible. In Parts 2 through 4, we will find all too many examples of systems that get locked into such a syndrome.

Finally, in recent years, especially, systems theorists have begun to show more interest in the **virtuous circles** that help systems improve, although we are never likely to agree on what an "improving system" means. As we will also see, these are quite rare at the national level. However, we will see some examples of them, as in the rise of the BRICS, the five countries that have made significant economic and, in some cases, political progress over the past two or three decades.

Those dynamics can become extremely complicated as we will see in the chapters on the individual countries that follow. However, there is one common theme that we will see allows us to see the sharply different impact of vicious cycles and virtuous circles. States that are reasonably effective in meeting their goals tend to build more popular support as a result which, in turn, makes their regimes more secure. However, if the state fails to meet its goals, support declines not just for the men and women in office at a particular moment but for the regime as a whole.

Types of States

No two states are alike. Some, like the United States, are large, rich, stable, and powerful. Others, like Somalia, are so poor, fragile, and weak that it is hard to talk about there being a state at all.

In other words, to make sense of what states do, we have to subdivide them into groups that are small and coherent enough for us to see some patterns that will let us move up the ladder of abstraction. Unfortunately, political scientists have never been able to agree on how to do that.

Before the end of the cold war, most of us divided the world into three types of countries. Events since then have convinced most of us that this division no longer makes as much sense as it did forty years ago. Nonetheless, because no one has suggested a better framework, I have decided to stick with the cold war–era division of the world into:

- Industrialized democracies

- Current and former Communist regimes

- The Global South

There are more differences within the three groups than there were during the cold war. Nonetheless, the states in each of them have enough in common historically in ways that still matter today that no other division of the world's countries works any better, as flawed as this one may be.

The discussion of each type that follows is based in part on Tables 1.2 and 1.3, which I will refer to throughout the book. Somewhat different versions of both of them will also appear at the start of the next fourteen chapters.

They are drawn from different and somewhat incompatible sources. Table 1.2 is based on the World Bank's annual *World Development Report*, which summarizes quantitative measures that most scholars accept as definitive measures. Table 1.3 is based on ratings that leave more room for human judgment and bias. The World Bank's Governance Index includes measures of political stability and the lack of violence, government effectiveness, the rule of law, and corruption control. *The Economist*'s Democratization scale adds measures of the degree to which a country's elections are fair, people can participate in all aspects of political life, the protection of civil liberties, and the openness of its political culture. The United Nation's Human Development Index is a composite measure of social well-being that overlaps with the World Bank data from Table 1.2. The Global Peace Index includes various measures of peacefulness in domestic politics and international relations. Transparency International's Corruption Index is the most subjective of the five because it is based solely on expert assessments, since, for obvious reasons, no reliable nationwide data on corruption are available.

TABLE 1.2 Basic Data

COUNTRY	POPULATION (IN MILLIONS)	POPULATION GROWTH (%)	GROSS DOMESTIC PRODUCT (IN PURCHASING POWER PARITY, PPP $US)	GROWTH IN GDP (%)	LIFE EXPECTANCY (%)	ADULT LITERACY (%)
Brazil	195	1.5	10,900	6.8	90	73
Canada	34	1.0	37,280	0.4	82	99+
China	1,338	0.6	7,570	9.7	81	04
France	65	0.7	34,400	1.0	74	99+
Germany	82	-0.01	38,170	3.9	80	99+
India	1,117	1.4	4,170	8.3	65	63
Iran	74	1.4	11,420	2.0	71	85
Iraq	32	2.3	4,600	10.4	71	78
Japan	127	0	34,790	5.3	83	99+
Mexico	109	1.0	15,000	4.4	76	93
Nigeria	158	2.4	2,100	5.4	49	61
Russia	142	-0.3	19,150	4.1	69	99+
South Africa	50	1.3	10,280	1.5	51	89
United Kingdom	62	0.6	36,580	0.6	80	99+
United States	310	0.8	36,800	0.6	80	99+
Highest income	1,123	.7	36,183	2.3	80	98
Lower middle income	2,467	1.2	6,780	5.7	69	83
Lowest income	817	2.2	1,125	3.8	57	61

Source: World Bank, *World Development Report 2012* (Washington, D.C.: World Bank, 2012). econ.worldbank.org. Accessed: August 24, 2012.

TABLE 1.3 Selected Governance Indicators

COUNTRY	GOVERNANCE (SCORE 0–1)	HUMAN DEVELOPMENT (SCORE 0–1)	DEMOCRACY (RANK)	PEACE (RANK)	CORRUPTION (RANK)
Brazil	.642	.718	45	83	73
Canada	.818	.908	8	5	10
China	.588	.687	141	89	75
France	.778	.884	29	40	25
Germany	.824	.905	14	15	14
India	.543	.547	39	142	95
Iran	.536	.707	159	128	120
Iraq	.402	.573	112	155	175
Japan	.774	.901	21	6	14
Mexico	.656	.770	50	134	100
Nigeria	.489	.459	119	146	143 (tie)
Russia	.577	.755	117	153	143 (tie)
South Africa	.589	.619	28	127	64
United Kingdom	.793	.863	16	29	18
United States	.761	.910	19	88	24

Sources: Governance (http://info.worldbank.org/governance/wgi); human development (undp.hrd.org); democracy (www.eiu.com, available by subscription only); peace (www.visionofhumanity.org); corruption (cpi.transparency.org/cpi2011/results).

The Industrialized Democracies

The **industrialized democracies** have the highest scores on most of the economic and political indicators in the two tables. Because they are the wealthiest, they have the most resources to devote to political and other purposes, which is another way of saying that living conditions in them are higher.

They also rank the highest on the political indicators in Table 1.3. They are the most democratic and least corrupt. If the Governance Index is a good measure of what states can do, the industrialized democracies are in good shape there as well, because they score at least ten percent higher than any of the other countries.

Masked beneath those relatively high scores are some concerns. None of the countries we will be considering, for example, are at the very top of any of these lists. Those positions are held by smaller countries that are less involved in the hurly burly of world politics, most notably including the Scandinavian countries and island states with democratic regimes.

Of particular importance for our purposes will be their shortcomings as democracies. The basic principles that define a democratic state, discussed in the next chapter, may not be violated very often. However, there are drawbacks common to them all that should give readers pause before they make the oft-heard claim that democracies are better than other forms of government.

Poll after poll shows growing dissatisfaction with what people believe is the growing distance between the governed and those who govern. That is easiest to see in the fact that so few incumbent governments have been reelected in recent years.

The industrialized democracies are all characterized by steep, overlapping, and, often, mounting inequalities. Democratic theory does not require absolute equality. Nonetheless, there are worrisome differences in wealth and access to power in all of the countries covered in Part 2. The Occupy Movement in the United States and similar protests elsewhere reminded us of just how biased the distribution of wealth and income is. Those inequalities are also reflected in political life where corporate executives wield far more influence than average citizens. Similarly, there is still considerable inequality along ethnic, racial, and gender lines, which decades of reform efforts have only partially washed away.

Last but by no means least, American readers should notice that the United States does not rank anywhere near the top on any of the noneconomic measures. That the United States does so poorly on the Global Peace Index makes sense given its role in the world. In addition, the inequalities we just mentioned are particularly pronounced in the United States. Its failure to provide basic health care coverage to everyone gets the most publicity. However, recent problems with the budget, immigration, same-sex marriage, and other issues suggest that Americans should think twice before they unquestioningly tout their country as some kind of global role model.

The Current and Former Communist Regimes

It is hard to tease data on this second group of countries from tables such as these because data are no longer collected about them as a group.

Economically, they are less well off than the industrialized democracies, although most of them are wealthier than the poorest countries in the Global South. Russia seems relatively well off on the basis of the statistics used in these tables. However, those figures mask tremendous inequality, persistent poverty, and a dependence on a single commodity, oil. China, by contrast, is more dynamic than its formal statistics suggest, because of its amazingly high growth rates since economic reforms were introduced at the end of the 1970s.

More important for our purposes is the fact that most of them fall short of the industrialized democracies on the political indicators shown in Table 1.3. A handful of them in Eastern Europe (Poland, Hungary, the Czech Republic, Slovenia, and the Baltic states) could possibly be included in the list of industrialized democracies. Most of them have what political scientists call **hybrid regimes** that combine elements of democracy with authoritarianism as suggested by their low scores on both democratization and corruption indexes. Another way of putting it will become clear when we get to Part 3. The stakes of politics are dramatically higher there than in any of the industrialized democracies, however serious their current economic and other difficulties might be.

The Global South

There is even less agreement on how to treat the rest of the world, which starts with the very term used to describe it. I've chosen to call it the **Global South**, which is being used more and more often by NGOs if not by academics. Even the term is misleading, because such countries as Australia and New Zealand are located in the South but share little or nothing with their physical neighbors.

There is even greater variety within the Global South than we find in the other two types. That is hardly surprising because it includes as much as two-thirds of the world's countries and two-thirds of its population, depending on which countries one includes as "Southern."

On balance, they are poorer, more violent, and less effectively governed than either of the first two types of countries.

Two billion people live on less than the equivalent of two dollars a day. The last three rows of Table 1.2 show just how wide the gap is between the industrial democracies and the world's poorest countries on the World Bank's key indicators. Adding more data would only reinforce a stark conclusion. Their governments face a more daunting political agenda than the other two types of states and often have to do so without functioning courts, bureaucracies, and other institutions that people in the industrialized democracies take for granted.

There are exceptions to this otherwise gloomy picture. Most countries in the South are better off than they were thirty years ago. A few have made major strides. In this book, we will pay particular attention to the BRICS that seem to have made substantial progress toward both democracy and development.

Politically, the poorest countries typically have the least effective states. They have the weakest and most corrupt institutions. They are also the least democratic. As we will see most clearly in Part 4, the combination of the load of problems they face and their weak states all too often have led to a vicious cycle of political instability, authoritarian regimes, and unmet human needs. Examples are legion. Nigerian politicians and civil servants are so corrupt that they are known as lootocrats. Mexico's drug cartels have left many parts of that country all but ungovernable. Women in the Global South bear a particularly serious burden of problems that range from the poverty that hits them harder than men to spousal abuse, female circumcision, and honor killings, all of which are far more common in these countries than they are elsewhere in the world.

Templates and the Structure of This Book

When you buy new software, it usually comes with templates that the developer has already designed to help new users perform routine tasks. The company that I use to design websites provides dozens of examples I can choose from.

This book uses five of them, not as options to choose from but as guides to focus your thinking. You have already seen two of them in Figures 1.1 and 1.2. Here we will consider three more.

Four Overlapping Issues

The first template actually combines two ideas, as reflected in Table 1.4. First, politics in any state can be

TABLE 1.4 Factors Affecting the Development of States

	INTERNATIONAL	DOMESTIC
Historical	Imperialism	State building and nation building
Contemporary	Globalization and the end of the cold war	Pressures from people and interest groups

© Cengage Learning

seen as the result of the interplay between historical and contemporary forces that are primarily domestic or international in origin. Second, the degree to which those four forces intersect goes a long way toward determining how calm or how tumultuous that state's affairs are today.

To make it easier to see that point, Table 1.4 lists only the themes in each category that we will concentrate on the most—**imperialism**, state formation, globalization, and the emergence of new issues and the new social movements they spawn.

Start with the cell in the upper-left corner. No state was ever built smoothly. State building left lasting scars, whenever and wherever it occurred. It was particularly difficult when state development spawned antagonisms toward a government that suddenly demanded more of its people or incorporated minority ethnic, linguistic, or religious groups against their will.

Despite the way the table is constructed, imperialism is important in both cells in the top row. Imperialism was one (but by no means the only) of the main causes of the creation of the modern state in Europe. Prior to the 1600s, the European monarchies were weak and decentralized. The decision to expand abroad meant they needed more powerful states that could raise armies and feed, equip, and pay them. When the imperialist powers carved up the Southern Hemisphere, they did so largely for their own reasons, ignored traditional boundaries, and threw historical adversaries together in the same colony. In fact, were it not for the imperialism of the sixteenth through the twentieth centuries, there would almost certainly not be an India, Iraq, Nigeria, or Mexico today.

The bottom row of the table draws our attention to more recent phenomena. Domestically, states of all types face increasing pressures from below on almost every imaginable issue. Not all states are anywhere near failing. However, as social changes such as rapid urbanization, increased levels of education, and the spread of the mass media suggest, new social and political movements create new demands, which are making it harder for governments to do their jobs effectively.

Internationally, globalization and the end of the cold war can both be thought of as capitalist victories. For good or ill, socialist options are no longer "on the table" in most of the world. On the one hand, that may have led to the rapid economic growth of the past thirty—if not the past three—years. On the other hand, globalization has led to dramatic shifts in the quality of life around the world, including climate change and growing inequality, to mention but two examples.

These kinds of factors have not influenced every country in the same ways at all times. In the rest of the book, we will encounter only two countries where the people and policymakers were able to deal with each of them separately and reach some form of closure on one before having to deal with the others. Elsewhere, the problems overlapped more in at least two ways. Not only did they have to be dealt with at the same time, but the effect of international issues inescapably shaped domestic ones, making the "burden of history" all but impossible to escape and raising the political stakes.

Global Challenges and Domestic Responses

The next template integrates one of the oldest issues in comparative politics with the book's subtitle, which, in turn, reflects one of the newest. To see both, start with the right side of Figure 1.3.

At least since Thomas Hobbes wrote in the seventeenth century, most political theorists have pointed out that individuals, and the groups they form, tend to seek ever more freedom and power. The pessimists among them have feared that people motivated by such self-interest would tear society apart if left to their own devices. Thus, like it or

not, we have to create states to maintain order by keeping these centrifugal forces in check.

As a result, most political scientists believe that state and society exist in what they call an inverse relationship. For the power of one to increase, that of the other must be reduced. For example, when the Republicans took control of the House of Representatives in 2010, they were convinced that the way to give average Americans more power was to limit the jurisdiction of what they believed was a far too dominant state. Similarly, the creation of the National Health Service in Great Britain in 1948 left doctors less free to practice medicine as they saw fit and left affluent patients less able to choose their own health care options. Moreover, this inverse relationship seems to hold across all types of political systems. Giving more power to Soviet citizens in the 1980s came at the expense of the state's power and contributed to its collapse.

Figure 1.3 also draws our attention to the way globalization is reshaping political life by reducing the real ability of states to make and implement economic policy. Although international institutions, such as the European Union (EU) and the International Monetary Fund (IMF), play a critical role in this respect, rarely can we pinpoint exactly how such influence is wielded because these pressures are far subtler than those used by the United States and other major powers in fighting the wars that continue to dominate international relations. Nonetheless, they are real and important enough that they may force us to change the ways in which we view global political life, both as academics and as average citizens.

The Political Iceberg

The final template is little more than a verbal rendering of a common cliché. Ninety percent of the mass of an iceberg lies below the surface of the water. In that sense, comparative politics is like a social science iceberg. If you only focus on what you can see on top of the water, you miss a lot. To "understand" the iceberg, you have to "dive" far below the surface.

Doing so will often take us far beyond political science. I have already included references to ideas generated by technologists, journalists, historians, environmentalists, and more. That is unavoidable given the fact that boundaries between academic disciplines seem to be vanishing and insights from political science alone will never be enough to answer any of the questions raised by political scientists. Rest assured, however, that the discussion will also be focused back on the political tip of the iceberg, which is what draws all of us to the subject in the first place.

FIGURE 1.3 The Impact of Global and Domestic Forces on the State

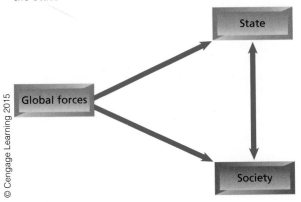

© Cengage Learning 2015

TABLE 1.5 Where the Big Questions Matter

QUESTION	INDUSTRIALIZED DEMOCRACIES	CURRENT AND FORMER COMMUNIST REGIMES	THE GLOBAL SOUTH
Pace of Change	Low	Moderate	High
Globalization	Low	Moderate	Defining
Democratization	Negligible	High	High
Identity	Low	Moderate/High	Defining
Human Security	Negligible	Moderate	Defining

The Big Questions

In ending this section, it is also important to briefly return to the big questions I used to start the book, because they, too, are among the reasons people at least should be interested in comparative politics.

Strangely enough, however, Table 1.5 suggests that they will not play a prominent role in Part 2. I am not leaving them out because they are unimportant. Quite the opposite.

If my own political activities in Washington are any example, we *should* be focusing on them wherever we happen to live. However, they are not central features in political discussions in the industrialized democracies—whether they should be or not.

Once we get to Parts 3 and 4, we will see that they are very much a part of mainstream political discussion everywhere else in the world.

Using This Book

In many respects, you are beginning what will be a typical introductory course with a typical textbook. However, to fully master the material, you will have to go beyond the typical because comparative politics is different from most other subjects you may have already studied.

Almost everything in comparative politics will be new. Almost everything about comparative politics is controversial.

One of the joys of teaching or writing about comparative politics is introducing people to new phenomena. Many will be confusing. Few will not be interesting.

I will also never duck controversial topics. Textbook authors should never try to impose their own interpretations. That is an especially important lesson for an author like me who spends most of his time as an activist. However, big questions like the ones raised at the beginning of this chapter are usually the ones that got us interested in comparative politics in the first place. Instead, I have tried to write the book in a way that gives you the tools to reach whatever conclusions you want.

That's another way of saying that there are no right answers.

To do that, the book actually uses most of the traditional tools one finds in introductory textbooks. Parts 2 through 4 consider each of the three types of states and a sample of countries in each category.

Each chapter starts with an example that lays out the key questions the chapter covers. Each chapter also has a series of boxes that highlight critical themes such as conflict, democratization, identity, globalization, and the status of women. The chapters all have lists of key terms, suggested reading, and useful websites. There could have been critical thinking exercises at the end of each chapter, but because there would not have been much difference in the questions posed in them, there is only one box of critical thinking exercises, which appears on this page. Finally, because they are as important as a framework for the rest of the book, the three figures and three of tables in this chapter are reprinted for your convenience on the inside of the front and back covers.

In short, you will have to do more than memorize the notes you take in class or the key points you highlight throughout these pages. Courses that deal with new, complex, and controversial subjects succeed only when students stretch themselves to consider unsettling ideas,

---

Critical Thinking Exercises

As you finish each chapter, ask yourself the following questions about the material you have just read.

1. Much has changed since this book was finished in 2013. Do the various assertions made in this chapter still make sense? In what ways? Why (not)?

2. Public opinion pollsters routinely ask whether people think the country is heading in the "right" direction or "is on the wrong track." If you were asked such a question about politics in the world as a whole, how would you answer? Why did you reach that conclusion?

3. Take your campus, community, or state, and analyze it using the three templates. What new insights did this exercise lead you to? What, if any, important facts, trends, or institutions were left out of the analysis?

4. Of all the concepts covered in this chapter, which do you think are the most and the least important? Why did you reach this conclusion?

5. You could interpret this chapter as arguing that it is becoming harder for governments to govern effectively. Do you agree? Why (not)?

question their basic assumptions, and sift through evidence to reach their own conclusions.

Over There Matters Over Here

This book is filled with tough and, in some cases, unanswerable questions.

To end this chapter, I want to underscore one thing: Comparative politics should be important to all of us, because as my colleague, Colonel Christopher Holshek puts it, "over there matters over here."[12]

We live in times of momentous change that will involve hundreds of momentous political choices. Some of those decisions will be made by the men and women in charge of governments around the world, not by average citizens like you or me.

But, in one powerful way, Holshek is right. What matters "over there" matters "over here." Those momentous political decisions really do affect us all. And, as we will see time and time again, there will be ample opportunities for you to help to shape the decisions that shape your lives.

Because it is so important, we will return to Colonel Holshek's words to end the book as well.

KEY TERMS

Arab Spring
authoritarian
BRICS
coalition
cold war
colored revolutions
constitution
crisis
demand
democracy
democratization
environment
equilibrium
falsify
feedback
feedback loop
Global South

globalization
government
human security
hybrid regimes
identity politics
imperialism
industrialized democracy
input
interest group
9/11
nation
nongovernmental organization (NGO)
output
paradigm
political culture
political participation
political party

politics
positive-sum
power
public policy
regime
resilient
state
support
sustainability
systems theory
theory
vicious cycle
virtuous circle
win-win
zero-sum

USEFUL WEBSITES

The Internet has become an essential tool for students of comparative politics. There are not many sites dedicated to comparative politics per se. However, the Internet is filled with information on specific countries, individuals, and issues. In particular, because so many newspapers, radio and television networks, and news services have gone online, it is easy to keep up with breaking news and evolving trends around the world.

www.anu.edu.au/polsci/marx/

That said, the Internet is increasingly hard to use because there are so many sites, and even the best search engines can catalogue only a tiny fraction of them. Therefore, I have included links to what I think are the best sites for the issues and countries covered in this book, updates on the countries, sources of statistical and other

---

[12]Christopher Holshek, "Over There Matters Over Here." *Huffington Post.* 22 March 2012. www.huffingtonpost.com/christopher-holshek/us-super-power_b_1362816.html. Truth in advertising. The organization I worked for hired Colonel Holshek, largely on the basis of this article, after he retired from the U.S. Army.

data, and quizzes on each chapter so you can gauge how well you have mastered the material. You can also e-mail me with questions about the book or issues that have arisen in your own course. It is located at:

www.cengage.com/politicalscience/hauss/comparativepolitics9e.

You can email me directly at chiphauss@gmail.com

Each chapter includes a section like this one with Web addresses to portals and other general sites. Specific websites will be inserted in the text the first time an institution or individual is mentioned.

There are other good resources for comparative politics. Here are three general sites that divide the field in different but useful ways; they are from Vanderbilt University and the Universities of Keele and West Virginia, respectively.

diglib.library.vanderbilt.edu/polsci.pl?searchtext=PoComPolitics&
Type=Simple&Resource=DB&Website=POLITICAL

www.psr.keele.ac.uk/area.htm

Globalization 101 is one of the few websites that comes close to living up to its name.

www.globalization101.org

The Internet also has dozens of sources, providing basic data on countries, that take you far beyond what can be covered in a single book and that include material on events occurring after this book was published. The CIA Factbook is a treasure trove of information about the world's countries and is updated quite frequently. The other two sources are the work of international "open source" teams of men and women willing to volunteer their time to provide general information about countries in general and elections in particular. The final one is the best source on election results. Many academics don't like Wikipedia, but this site existed long before wikis were invented and was folded into it because its author believes in open source.

https://www.cia.gov/library/publications/the-world-factbook/

www.adminet.com/world/gov

www.en.wikipedia.org/wiki/User:Electionworld/Electionworld

Finally, it is important to keep up with the news in any course on comparative politics and international relations. At this point, all of the world's major newspapers, news services, and broadcast media put much of their material on the Web. It is impossible to determine which three or four of them are the best. The ones I consult every day are the BBC, Global Post, and Real Clear World.

www.bbc.com/news

www.globalpost.com

www.realclearworld.com

FURTHER READING

Almond, Gabriel, and G. Bingham Powell. *Comparative Politics: System, Policy, and Process*. Boston: Little, Brown, 1978. Dated, but still the best presentation of the classic approach to comparative politics.

Friedman, Tom. *Hot, Flat, and Crowded*. New York: Farrar, Straus & Giroux, 2009. The most influential and controversial book on globalization and its strengths and weaknesses.

Ghani, Ashraf, and Clare Lockhart. *Fixing Failed States*. New York: Oxford University Press, 2008. The best book on rethinking the role of government in places like Afghanistan and Iraq.

Griswold, Eliza. *The Tenth Parallel: Dispatches from the Fault Line between Christianity and Islam*. New York: Farrar, Straus and Giroux, 2010. At first glance, this is a book by a journalist about religious conflict, but Griswold goes much farther to show how religion is at the heart of a host of social and political controversies.

Kaplan, Robert D. *The Revenge of Geography: What the Map Tells Us about Coming Conflicts and the Battle Against the State*. New York: Random House, 2012. Another book by a journalist (and one I do not always agree with) on how borders—changes and otherwise—affect most of the parts of the world this book deals with.

Lim, Timothy. *Doing Comparative Politics*. Boulder, CO: Lynne Reinner, 2006. A rather abstract book aimed more at grad students than undergrads, but it explores three key concepts: rational choice, institutions, and culture.

O'Neill, Patrick. *Essentials of Comparative Politics,* 3rd ed. New York: W. W. Norton, 2009. Unlike Lim's book, it was written for undergraduates but is probably better for upper-level undergrads or grad students.

Pinker, Steven. *The Better Angels of Our Nature: Why Violence Has Declined*. New York: Viking, 2011. A breathtaking book that uses centuries of evolution in the way we govern ourselves to help explain why the world is less violent than it used to be because we have learned how to manage our disputes better than our ancestors did.

Soe, Christian, ed. *Comparative Politics: Annual Editions*. Guilford, CT.: Dushkin/McGraw-Hill, published annually. A collection of recent articles from the press.

Toffler, Alvin. *Future Shock*. New York: Bantam Books, 1970. More than forty years old, this is still a great introduction to accelerating rates of change in all of our lives.

Zolli, Andrew, and Ann Marie Healy. *Resilience: How Things Bounce Back*. New York: Free Press, 2012. Another book written by someone other than a political scientist. A great analysis of how flexible and adaptive organizations work.

Industrialized Democracies

© Cengage Learning

POLITICAL INDICATORS

COUNTRY	GOVERNANCE (score 0-1)	HUMAN DEVELOPMENT (score 0-1)	DEMOCRACY (rank)	PEACE (rank)	CORRUPTION (rank)
Canada	.818	.908	8	5	10
France	.778	.884	29	40	25
Germany	.824	.905	14	15	14
Japan	.774	.901	21	6	14
United Kingdom	.793	.863	16	29	18
United States	.761	.910	19	88	24

CHAPTER OUTLINE

2

The Industrialized Democracies

> Democracy is the worst form of government except all the others that have ever been tried.
>
> WINSTON CHURCHILL

Democracy and the Big Questions

Every other chapter in *Comparative Politics* begins with a story I will use as a springboard to discuss political life in the country or region it covers. Here, however, it makes more sense to start in a more abstract way by reconsidering some of the big questions posed in Chapter 1.

In the rest of this book, the big questions will be scattered throughout the chapter. Here, however, it makes sense to start with them for one simple reason.

Most readers of this book either live or study in an advanced industrialized democracy, which leads many of us to make one or more of the following assumptions, all of which are problematic and should be raised (if not dispelled) at the outset.

First, we tend to take democracy for granted. Second, as the statement by Winston Churchill at the beginning of this chapter suggests, we think democracy is the best type of regime humans can create. Third—and perhaps most dangerous of all—we assume that existing democracies cannot and need not be improved in any significant way.

There is good reason to make these assumptions. The industrialized democracies are the world's richest countries,

---

THE BASICS

The Industrialized Democracies

REGION	DEMOCRACIES	CONTENDERS
Europe	Austria, Belgium, Denmark, Finland, France, Germany, Greece, Iceland, Ireland, Italy, Luxembourg, Malta, the Netherlands, Norway, Portugal, Spain, Sweden, Switzerland, the United Kingdom	Cyprus, Czech Republic, Estonia, Hungary, Latvia, Lithuania, Poland, Slovakia, Turkey
The Americas	Canada, the United States	Argentina, Brazil, Chile, Costa Rica, Mexico, most Caribbean Islands
Asia and the Pacific Islands	Australia, Japan, New Zealand	The Philippines, South Korea, Taiwan
Africa	—	Botswana, Ghana, South Africa

and their citizens enjoy the most comfortable standards of living. They have the most effective and least corrupt governments on almost all of the dimensions tapped in Table 1.3.

Even more important for our purposes is the fact that they all have had stable democracies (to be defined in the next section) for a long time. The last three to establish their current **regimes** (Spain, Portugal, and Greece) have been democratic since the 1970s. Despite the struggles these three countries are having overcoming the current economic crisis, democracy does not appear to be in any jeopardy.

Seen from another perspective, those assumptions can get us in trouble because they keep us from even asking big questions about the industrialized democracies at all, precisely because they have been so successful for such a long period of time. You may end up agreeing with Churchill. However, we will also see that the reluctance of politicians and citizens to ask the big questions is already leading to problems that seem likely to get even more serious as long as we continue to turn a blind eye toward democracy's shortcomings.

Thinking About Democracy

The Bottom Line

Democracy comes from the two ancient Greek words for rule by the people. Literally speaking, there cannot be a democracy in which the people directly govern today's complex societies.

Even the small New England communities that still have town meetings are too big and have to make decisions too often for everyone to take part in them all. Instead, like every other organization that calls itself democratic, they have had to depend on representative institutions in which voters select a small number of men and women to govern in their name.

Beyond that, there is little agreement among political scientists about what democracy means. Some analysts use a fairly "thin" definition that relies on a few basic criteria, such as free speech and competitive elections. Others insist on a "thick" definition that uses more criteria that are harder for countries to meet.

Freedom House (www.freedomhouse.org) has created one of the most widely used indexes of democracy which uses a fairly thin definition. It counts as "free" any country "where there is open political competition, a climate of respect for civil liberties, significant independent civic life, and independent media." By that definition, it classified 45 percent of the world's countries as "free" in 2011 and another 31 percent to be "partly free."

Their list includes more countries than I do in the left-hand column of "The Basics" box at the beginning of this chapter. That's the case because democracy is about more than elections and civil liberties. It is hard to imagine how a country could be democratic without incorporating at least some aspects of them.

As Fareed Zakaria, among others, has argued, before deciding whether a country is democratic, we have to examine the entire relationship between the rulers and the ruled. Plenty of countries hold reasonably free elections but fall short on those other dimensions in ways that lead him to doubt whether we should consider them truly democratic.[1]

Once we do, two conclusions become clear. First, because democracy is more complex than Freedom House's indicators suggest, our analysis will have to be more nuanced. Second, no country is completely democratic. Those covered in the rest of Part 2 come close to meeting most of the criteria laid out here, but each falls short in some significant ways, which also need to have a central place in any analysis of democracy.

I have opted for a middle ground that includes five basic criteria that adds some aspects of the most common thicker definitions (for a short, interesting cartoon version of this, see http://www.youtube.com/watch?v=Arn8Fp1jyok).

Rights

Most definitions of democracy start with the basic freedoms of speech, religion, association, and the press. The reason for doing so is easy to see: how can people effectively participate in making the decisions that shape their lives unless those rights are guaranteed?

Political rights are defined in different ways. Many countries enshrine them in their constitutions. Human rights are affirmed in the first paragraphs of the French Fifth Republic's constitution and in Germany's Basic Law. Even where they are not included in the constitution as in Great Britain, which does not have a written constitution, they are deeply engrained in the culture.

These are not merely paper rights. All countries place some restrictions on people's freedoms, but they are very much on the margins of political life. France has a law that allows the government to ban organizations that try to overthrow the state. Many critics think the USA Patriot Act passed in the aftermath of 9/11 goes too far in limiting freedom of expressions. The Japanese constitution includes a clause that allows the government to place the public welfare ahead of civil liberties

---

[1]Fareed Zakaria. *The Future of Freedom* (New York: W. W. Norton, 2003).

if it believes that national security is threatened. The French and German governments can declare a state of emergency and rule in what amounts to a dictatorial manner for a limited amount of time under certain circumstances. The important point here, however, is that these restrictions are rarely used and have little impact on daily political life.

Competitive Elections

Just as important is the requirement that the government be chosen through regular, free, and fair elections.

Simply holding elections is not enough. Mexico, for example, has held elections for all key offices since the 1920s. However, for seventy years, the opposition had no realistic chance of winning the presidency or more than a handful of seats in the national legislature because of the way the ruling Institutional Revolutionary Party (PRI) rigged election after election. The former Soviet Union and its allies also held elections, but voters did not have a choice—free or otherwise—because only candidates handpicked by the Communist Party appeared on the ballot. Other countries, such as Egypt in this decade, conducted elections only to have the military reject the outcome and seize power.

The United States is unique in having only two major parties. However, minor parties can help determine the outcome of an election, as we last saw with Ralph Nader's campaign in 2000.

Every other industrialized democracy has more parties that matter. In Great Britain and Germany, for example, only two major parties vie for the right to organize the government, but a number of smaller ones play a pivotal role in raising new issues and forming governing coalitions. In Japan, although a single party has dominated electoral politics since the 1950s, it rarely comes close to winning a majority of the popular vote. France and the Scandinavian countries have five or more parties, but they fall into left- and right-wing blocs, one of which almost always wins an election. Israel and the Netherlands have as many as a dozen parties with seats in parliament and often have rapidly shifting government coalitions as a result (see the section on parliamentary systems below).

These differences exist, in part, because of their electoral systems, as the laws that govern the way elections are conducted and votes are counted are known (www.ifes.org). Most important in this regard is the way in which members of the national legislature are selected.

Other things being equal, single-member districts favor large parties. In these first-past-the-post systems, the candidate who gets the most votes wins the seat whether he or she has won a majority of the vote or not. As we will see in

TABLE 2.1 Women in Parliament 2011: Selected Countries, in Percent

COUNTRY	PROPORTIONAL SYSTEM	PERCENTAGE
Sweden	Proportional	5.0
Netherlands	Proportional	9.3
Germany	Half proportional	2.8
United Kingdom	First past the post	2.0
France	Single-member, two ballot	8.9
United States	First past the post	6.0

Note: Sweden and the Netherlands were included in the table, although they are not covered in the book, to illustrate the range of results one finds.

Source: International Parliamentary Union, www.ipu.org. Accessed April 15, 2011.

the next two chapters on the United States and the United Kingdom, the two largest parties normally win a larger share of the legislative seats than of the vote, while small parties are underrepresented.

Under proportional representation, a party's share of the legislative seats is determined by the fraction of the vote it receives. Thus, a party that wins 20 percent of the vote will also get roughly 20 percent of the seats in parliament. As a result, it is much easier for new movements to gain a toehold, and it helps account for why some countries have five, six, or more parties.

Electoral systems also help us understand something that has become important and controversial in recent years—the vastly different number of women holding office from country to country. As Table 2.1 shows, women do not make up the majority in any national legislature. They come closest in countries that use proportional representation, while their numbers lag in those that use any kind of single-member district system. In the latter, local party leaders have the greatest influence over who is nominated to run for office, and they tend to choose candidates whom they think have the best chance of winning. That usually means men. In proportional systems, national party elites determine who runs and who is placed near the top of the lists voters choose from, who are also usually the ones that have the best chance of getting elected. Some countries, like France, even have passed laws that require parties to nominate an equal number of women and men for at least some offices.

The Rule of Law

The last three criteria take us beyond the indicators used in the thinnest definitions of democracy. Related to civil liberties is the reliance on the **rule of law**. Political and other forms of behavior are governed by clear and fair rules rather than by the personal and often arbitrary exercise of power.

What people can and cannot do is specified in the constitution and by ordinary laws. As a result, they can expect to be treated fairly by the government both in their routine dealings with the state (e.g., tax collection) and on those rare occasions when they come up against it (e.g., after being accused of a crime).

In practice, the rule of law is easiest to see in its absence, which will be a common theme in Parts 3 and 4.

Capitalism and Affluence

Most—but by no means all—political scientists assume that democracy can only survive if it is accompanied by an affluent and capitalist economy.

There is no denying that the industrialized democracies are the richest in the world. That wealth allows almost all of their citizens to have access to basic health care, which translates into a low infant mortality rate and a long life expectancy. In fact, it is that wealth that adds the adjective "industrialized" to the phrase used to describe this kind of democracy.

Industrialized democracies are not all equally wealthy of course. Great Britain's **gross national product (GNP)** is only three-fourths that of the United States. Some of the countries not included in this book, such as Spain, Portugal, and Greece, are only about half as well off as the United Kingdom. Nonetheless, only a handful of the countries considered in Parts 3 and 4 enjoy anything like the standard of living found in the poorest industrialized democracy.

Scholars debate how, why, and if either capitalism or affluence must accompany democracy. Although the causal links are murky, there are very few exceptions to the rule that only reasonably affluent societies have been able to sustain a democracy for an extended period of time. The "contender" countries in "The Basics" box that begins this chapter suggest that affluence may not be as critical as some theorists have suggested. Nonetheless, there is *some* connection between the fact that most democratic countries are both industrialized and wealthy.

The *L* Word

American students are often confused by the word "liberal." In the United States, it is used to describe people who support an interventionist government. Everywhere else, however, it means almost exactly the opposite—antagonism to government intervention in the economy and other policy areas in which individuals can make decisions on their own, at least according to neoclassical economic theory. The term will be used in this more widely understood sense in the rest of this book, except in Chapter 3 on the United States.

Civil Society and Civic Culture

In their path-breaking book published half a century ago, Gabriel Almond and Sidney Verba concluded that stable democracies need a **civic culture** in which people not only accept the regime's rules of the game but give the elites considerable leeway in governing them.[2] Other researchers even went so far as to argue that democracies benefited from having what they called "functional apathy" that allowed the governors to govern with a minimum of public interference or oversight.

With the upsurge in protest movements of the 1960s and the more uncertain economic times since then, academic interest in a civic culture and **civil society** waned. The last few decades have certainly seen declining support for politicians and interpersonal trust. With the attempt to spread democratic regimes elsewhere in the world, however, there has been a resurgence of interest in how such factors can psychologically bind people to their states and make it hard for "anti-system" protests to gain **legitimacy**.

That interest has taken us beyond the apathetic aspects of the civic culture to stress the importance of a culture in which average citizens actively support a democratic regime because of what it accomplishes for them and—at times—with them. Along those lines, consider the words of Larry Diamond, who is arguably the most prominent student of democratization in this generation.

> **Developing democracy requires the generation of new norms. As Gandhi put it, "changes of the heart." Democratic structures will be mere facades unless people come to value the essential principles of democracy.[3]**

Diamond also alerts us to a problem in the study of democracy that we will have to defer until Parts 3 and 4. There is an undeniable link between Western cultures and the solidification of industrialized democracies. Throughout his career, Diamond has argued that there is nothing inherently Western about democracy. Unfortunately, we can only explore non-Western approaches to democracy when we consider non-Western countries, which will not happen before Part 3.

---

[2]Gabriel Almond and Sidney Verba. *The Civic Culture* (Princeton: Princeton University Press, 1962).
[3]Larry Diamond, *The Spirit of Democracy: The Struggle to Build Free Societies Throughout the World* (New York: Times Books, 2008), 20.

Comparative Emphasis: Ideal Types

Max Weber introduced the notion of ideal types to social scientists more than a century ago.

Weber did not use the term "ideal" in an ethical sense. Rather, he thought ideal types were definitions of a "pure" form of some concept, in this case democracy. The job of the analyst was to measure and assess how well a given unit did in living up to that definition.

Weber assumed that any real-world example would fall short of any ideal type or norm. The social scientist's job is to understand how and why that is the case. We will do just that in considering almost every important concept raised in this book. ■

Which Countries Are Democratic?

These criteria allow us to identify the twenty-four countries in this chapter's "The Basics" box as unquestionably democratic. All of them have met these five criteria for at least thirty years, which seems to be enough time for them to develop sufficient regime-level support for us to safely say that democracy is no longer in any jeopardy.

Most are in western Europe or in parts of the world Europeans colonized. The one obvious exception is Japan.

Questions about the countries listed as contenders are easier to see. Israel certainly is a democracy for its Jewish citizens, but it excludes both Arabs who are citizens of Israeli and those who live in the Occupied Territories from most aspects of political life. Some former communist states could well be added to this list in the future, but basic freedoms, the rule of law, and fully free elections are still in some doubt. For the same reasons, most observers do not yet classify Argentina, Brazil, Chile, South Korea, Taiwan, or Turkey as full democracies.

As noted earlier in the discussion of the civic culture, the notion that democracy is somehow the province of the affluent North is being called into question today, something we will see most clearly in the discussion of the

BRICS in Parts 3 and 4. However, because their historical experience is so different from that of the established industrialized democracies, I have still opted to place them elsewhere.

Key Questions

The questions we will ask about these countries flow directly from the five criteria:

- Why did democracy first emerge in these countries?
- Why did democracy only become firmly established in many of them during the second half of the twentieth century?
- Why is there so much debate about public policy in the industrialized democracies these days?
- Why has that debate not reached a point where many people question their regimes or democracy itself?

The Origins of the Democratic State

As we explore the development of industrialized democracy, keep three caveats in mind, which will also be important in Parts 3 and 4. First, it took a long time for democracy to take hold. Second, at least until Germany and Japan created reasonably democratic regimes after World War I, national leaders did not consciously set out to build democracies. In fact, it is not too much of an exaggeration to say that these democracies were primarily an unintended byproduct of other social and economic forces that were more important to political actors at the time. Third, leaders elsewhere in the world are trying to condense something that took centuries in Europe, North America, and Japan into a few short years. History suggests that that is a tall order indeed.

The Evolution of Democratic Thought

By most definitions, the first modern democracies only date from the late eighteenth century—if then. There were some partially democratic regimes in the ancient Greek city-states and in medieval Europe, but they are not included here because none had either a large population or extended the full range of civil and political rights to all adult men, let alone women (see Table 2.2).

By the late 1700s, pressures to move toward what we think of today as democracy had been building for two

TABLE 2.2 Key Turning Points in the Development of Industrialized Democracies

CENTURY	TRENDS
Seventeenth	Emergence of the modern state
Eighteenth	First democratic revolutions
	Development of *laissez-faire* theory
Nineteenth	Industrial revolution
	Spread of voting and other democratic institutions
Twentieth	Further expansion of the vote
	Defeat of fascism and solidification of democracy in western Europe

© Cengage Learning

hundred years. Individualism, capitalism, Protestantism, the scientific revolution, and the exploration of the "New World" gave birth to new ways of thinking as different as Newtonian physics and Calvinist theology, all of which left previously powerless people clamoring for a greater impact on the decisions that shaped their lives.

Many of the most innovative thinkers of that era devised ideas that might seem obvious today but which then were revolutionary. Near the top of any such list was the belief that society is composed of independent individuals who pursue their own interests and desires. For many of those new thinkers, the "state of nature" they formed was fraught with danger. Freed from the shackles of feudalism and other social hierarchies, individuals would become more creative and productive.

However, many of these thinkers, most notably **Thomas Hobbes** (1586–1679), also realized that such individuals and the groups they formed would put new demands on the weak monarchies of the late feudal period. Hobbes worried anarchy would follow if people were left to their own devices, which he famously labeled the "war of all against all." Therefore, people had no choice but to give up some of their freedoms to a large and powerful state which he called the Leviathan.

In the century after Hobbes' death, the individualistic side of these new ways of thinking came to the fore. It was, thus, no coincidence that the American Revolution began in the same year that Adam Smith's most famous book extolling economic freedom, *The Wealth of Nations*, was published. At that time, many of the same people started demanding political as well as economic freedom. Their views crystallized as **laissez-faire** capitalism. Derived from a French phrase meaning "allow to do," laissez-faire theory calls for a government that stays out of economic life as much as possible because the "invisible hand" of the market supposedly allocates resources in the most efficient possible manner.

In so doing, the capitalists and their political allies added two new ideas to democratic thought. First, the state should be limited. Second, rather than telling people how to act in all areas of life, the state should serve as a referee that protects society from the arbitrary exercise of power and the excessive demands of average people, who were often referred to as the "mob" or "dangerous classes."

Not even the most enthusiastic supporters of democracy or the free market wanted to get rid of government altogether. They shared Hobbesian fears about the state of nature and **John Locke's** (1632–1704) belief that the most important thing government could do was to protect life, liberty, and property.

During the nineteenth century, industrial capitalism became the driving force behind Britain's unprecedented economic growth, which also led to more insistent demands for political reform. The newly wealthy capitalists resented the fact that their society was still governed by feudal institutions, and they began to insist that the state make room for individuals like themselves.

No country could have been called a democracy at the time using the criteria discussed in the previous section. Although the requirements varied, all future democracies only allowed relatively wealthy, property-owning men to vote well into the nineteenth century. No women and only a handful of African Americans could vote in the newly independent United States. In Britain, barely 5 percent of men had the franchise even after the passage of the Great Reform Act of 1832.

Still, an important precedent had been set. Monarchs could no longer monopolize political power. Instead, important elements of political power were handed over to representatives who could hold rulers accountable and were themselves accountable to voters.

Over the next century, popular pressure forced elites to adopt and, in some cases, strengthen democratic institutions. In the United States, most white men had become eligible to vote by the 1840s. All French men gained it with the creation of the Second Republic in 1848. In Britain, the right of men to vote expanded gradually, culminating in the Reform Act of 1918, which removed all property qualifications and income restrictions.

Women's **suffrage** rights followed more slowly. An Act of Parliament extended the right to vote to all women in 1918. American women gained the vote with the ratification of the Nineteenth Amendment in 1920. French women only got the right to vote after World War II, although there had been women cabinet members before the war. The Swiss were the last industrialized democracy to grant women the vote, in 1971.

Bain Collection/Library of Congress Prints and Photographs Division Washington, D.C. [LC-USZ62-53202]

Suffragettes demanding the right to vote.

Other opportunities for political participation grew as well. Most American states passed laws enabling citizens to place proposed legislation on the ballot in a referendum. In France and Britain, laws limiting citizens' right to form associations were abolished, permitting the growth of trade unions and other **interest groups**.

In much of Europe, popularly elected houses of parliament gained the all-important right to determine who ran the government. By the late 1870s, the French parliament had stripped the presidency of any real power. In Britain, the House of Lords, which represented the hereditary aristocracy, lost the ability to do anything more than delay the final passage of legislation. In country after country, the cabinet became responsible to parliament, which meant that their its members could stay in office only as long as they retained the support of a majority of the members of the lower house.

Comparative Emphasis: A Matter of Scale

In 1955, Quincy Wright estimated that there were about five thousand independent political entities in Europe in the fifteenth century. That number dropped to about five hundred at the time of the Thirty Years War two hundred years later. When Napoléon had himself crowned Emperor, the figure was more like two hundred. In Wright's day, there were only thirty. The number has actually increased a bit since the end of the cold war, but the trend line has long been toward larger and more powerful states. ∎

Four Crises

Nowhere was democracy built quickly or easily. Even where democratization occurred with a minimum of turmoil, it was accompanied by wrenching political fits and starts. In most countries, that included revolutions and periods of authoritarian rule during which democracy seemed a distant and unachievable goal. For the countries covered in Part 2, there were some common challenges, the most important of which were four great transformations that divided each of them in different ways and helped chart their trajectory toward democracy—and often away from it as well:

- Creating the nation and state.
- Defining the role of religion in political life.
- Handling pressures for democracy.
- Managing the industrial revolution.

In places where democracy developed the earliest, such as Great Britain or the United States, those divisions were resolved relatively easily. That happened in part because they were spread out over three centuries or more, which allowed their leaders to reach something approaching closure on each one before the next crisis appeared on the horizon.

The situation was quite different in the countries that had more trouble democratizing. There, these historical crises left lasting divisions in which the crises coincided to the point that leaders had to cope with two or more of them at the same time.

The first one involved the state itself. For a number of reasons too complicated to go into here, the modern state only came into existence during the seventeenth century. National identity developed even more slowly. Nowhere did either happen smoothly. Where the development of state and nation were at odds, the political conflict was particularly difficult (see Table 1.4).

Strangely enough, the second and even more divisive crisis helped forge the modern state. During the sixteenth century, the Protestant reformation divided most of Europe.

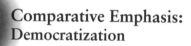

Comparative Emphasis: Democratization

The recent wave of democratization in the rest of the world has led political scientists to reconsider its emergence in Europe and North America and to draw conclusions that are not very encouraging for the new democracies.

There is a tendency among supporters of democracy to see it as the "natural order of things" and therefore the result of consensual and gradual reform. Nothing could be further from the truth. Even the United States and the United Kingdom faced major upheavals, including civil wars and prolonged periods of unrest.

Furthermore, before the creation of the Weimar Republic in Germany after World War I, none of the leaders in these countries intentionally set out to create a democracy. None of them succeeded until after the Second World War.

Leaders in today's new democracies may have learned enough to escape some of the problems that befell all but the most successful of the countries considered in this chapter. History would lead us to assume otherwise. ■

Rulers had to choose between the once dominant Catholic Church and the new Protestant sects. In those days, once a ruler decided which faith to observe, almost everyone followed suit.

The Reformation led to the fiercest wars Europe had ever seen. They pitted Catholics against Protestants and strengthened the emerging states whose rulers had to raise, equip, and feed huge armies in order to fight the wars and finance colonial expansion, which was one of their byproducts. The last of them was the Thirty Years War that ended with the Treaty of Westphalia, which many international relations experts claim was the beginning of the modern state.

The divisions over religion had a lot in common with those over democracy. In most countries, religious authorities sided with the monarchs and resisted extending power to average people. That was especially true in predominantly Catholic countries where the Church enjoyed official recognition and stood to lose much of its wealth and prestige under a democratic regime. Even decades after the establishment of democratic governments, the most important political division in those countries was over the role the Church should play in public life, with **pro-clericals** wanting to maintain its traditional privileges and **anti-clericals** insisting on the all but total separation of Church and state.

An already difficult situation was made worse by the fact that today's Italy and Germany were still split into dozens of often hostile principalities. Nationalist leaders had been trying to unify the two for at least a century before the two came together as states in the early 1870s. Even then, it was difficult for them to fit into the delicate balance of power created at the end of the Napoleonic wars.

In order to have a chance of doing so, the new leadership in Germany and Italy (as well as Japan) came to the conclusion that they had to catch up with Britain and France as rapidly as possible. They were also convinced that they could do so only if their governments took the lead and forced industrial development on a reluctant population, which could only happen if they were denied the rights that were simultaneously being expanded in Britain, France, the United States, and Canada.

At the beginning of the twentieth century, there still were very few democracies. Real political power remained in the hands of the bureaucratic elite in most of Europe as the continent teetered toward World War I, which did little to strengthen support for democratic freedoms whatever the rhetoric of the Allied leaders.

After the war, liberal regimes were established in much of Central and Eastern Europe. Japan adopted a much more democratic constitution. Few of these new democracies, however, survived the early 1930s.

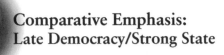

Comparative Emphasis: Late Democracy/Strong State

There is a powerful theme lurking below the surface in this chapter that will take on even more importance later in the book. Because they eschewed democracy in favor of "top down" development, countries like Germany and Japan retained their traditionally strong states into the democratic period after World War II. At that time (though not later), combining a strong state with democracy brought unprecedented economic growth and political stability that lasted until the early 1990s. ■

Extremist parties on the **Left** and **Right** won ever larger shares of the vote. Thousands of disgruntled workers and veterans took to the streets. Effective democratic governance had become all but impossible in much of Europe years before the Great Depression struck in 1929. One after another, the new democracies turned to **fascism** and authoritarian leaders, the most important of whom were Benito Mussolini in Italy and Adolf Hitler in Germany.

It was only after World War II that we can say that democracy was firmly entrenched in the countries covered in Part 2. The rise of fascism and the carnage of the war led many to question whether it would ever be possible to sustain a democracy in Italy or Germany. In fact, concerns about the breakdown of democracy in interwar Europe prompted social scientists to conduct research on political culture and other previously poorly understood forces that could reinforce or undermine democracy.

The start of the cold war led the United States and its allies to take steps to erase those doubts. It took less than a generation for leaders in those countries to use American political and economic help in creating affluent, democratic regimes. Meanwhile, France, Germany, Italy, Japan, and other countries became partners in the struggle to contain what many feared would be global communist aggression.

Now, it is safe to say that democracy is secure in all of these countries. Regime change does not appear to be on the horizon in any of them for the foreseeable future. That does not mean that these are perfect democracies, that they will remain so forever, or that other countries will not enter their ranks.

Political Culture

For understandable reasons, many leading political scientists tried to identify the reasons for the collapse of democracy in Europe and its role in triggering World War II. As noted earlier the key contribution along these lines was Almond and Verba's book, *The Civic Culture.*

They contrasted the United States and Great Britain with Germany, Italy, and Mexico, emphasizing the importance of a culture in which democratic beliefs exist alongside a degree of political passivity. They found that most people in the United States or the United Kingdom had a strong sense of political efficacy and therefore believed that they could do something about political decisions they disagreed with. In practice, however, most of the people they interviewed admitted that they rarely did so because they trusted their leaders to do the right thing.

The protest movements that began shortly after the book was published in 1962 weakened their simplistic conclusions about the link between a civic culture and democracy. Today's political scientists are returning to the impact of political culture in a more nuanced way. Although we are far from reaching a consensus about it, three conclusions from more recent research will reappear throughout Part 2.

First, in successful democracies, most people have a deeply felt sense that their regimes are legitimate and accept the "rules of the game." Critical here is the distinction between the government of the day and the regime. During the 1970s and 1980s, British governments led by both major political parties had to cope with protests that revealed a level of political anger not seen in more than a century. However, there is no evidence that the protesters' ire extended to the constitutional order itself. Much the same is true in countries that had failed to establish strong democratic regimes prior to the war. Thus, massive protests in 1968 in France nearly toppled the government led by resistance hero General Charles de Gaulle. Very few of the protesters I interviewed a few years later even mentioned the possibility of scrapping de Gaulle's Fifth Republic. What's more, that sense of legitimacy has endured despite a dramatic drop in most other indicators of trust in politicians and participation in routine political life.

Second, more recent scholars have dug more deeply than Almond and Verba did into the dimensions of a democratic political culture. Robert Putnam[4], for

---

[4]Robert Putnam, *Bowling Alone* (New York: Simon and Schuster, 2001).

Paul Schutzer/Time Life Pictures/Getty Images

A panoramic view of the hundreds of thousands of nonviolent protesters at the 1963 March on Washington for civil rights.

instance, stresses the role of social capital or the degree to which a society has social networks that build trust and cooperation particularly among people who routinely disagree with each other. Larry Diamond (who is quoted on p. 30) emphasizes the importance of institutions that foster tolerance, because it can put a damper on the passions that could conceivably rip a society apart. My own work to try to get the peace movement and the military to cooperate is based on the assumption that democracies are most likely to thrive in cultures where people who disagree also find ways to work with and learn from each other.

Third, as noted in Chapter 1, political scientists also have come to realize that political culture rarely determines what people actually do. Nonetheless, long-standing attitudes toward democracy, class conflict, the role of religion, and more go a long way toward making some forms of political behavior seem inappropriate if still legal.

Political Participation

Democracies differ from country to country because they give their citizens ways to have a potentially meaningful say in political life. None is more important than voting and, with the exception of a handful of minor races, people who go to the polls make choices among **political parties** that contest elections and form national governments afterward.

There is a bewildering array of political parties in the four countries covered in the rest of Part 2. Most of them do have one thing in common: roots in the divisions left behind by the political crises discussed in the previous section. New parties have emerged since those divisions were established before World War II. Few of them, however, are strong enough—yet—to win elections or take part in governing coalitions.

Left and Right

Most analyses of political parties start with their position on what political scientists call the Left–Right spectrum. The etymological roots of the terms *left* and *right* do not lie in lofty political ideals but in the seating arrangements in the French parliament after the Revolution of 1789. Deputies who favored radical change sat to the left of the Speaker's rostrum, while those who opposed it were placed on his right. Since then, the terms have evolved in the ways summarized in Table 2.3.

On the Left today are the remnants of the communist parties (see Table 2.4). They were formed in the aftermath of the Russian Revolution of 1917, when members of the radical wings of the socialist parties quit and formed new organizations to support the Bolsheviks in Moscow. For most of the time since then, the communist parties have been the most radical critics of and were also loyal supporters of the Soviet Union during the cold war. Of the countries we will be considering, only France still has a significant Communist Party (PCF), and it has been in decline for years.

TABLE 2.3 The Changing Meaning of Left and Right

PERIOD	LEFT	RIGHT
Eighteenth and early nineteenth centuries	Prodemocratic Anticlerical Promarket	Antidemocratic Proclerical Ambivalent on market
Industrial era	Prodemocratic Anticlerical For socialism or welfare state	More prodemocratic Usually proclerical Less positive about welfare state, against socialism
Postindustrial era	Egalitarian but qualms about welfare state and socialism More globalist New social issues	Promarket capitalism Traditional values More nationalistic

© Cengage Learning

TABLE 2.4 Main Types of Political Parties by Country

				TYPE OF PARTY		
COUNTRY	**COMMUNIST**	**SOCIALIST**	**LIBERAL**	**CHRISTIAN DEMOCRATIC**	**CONSERVATIVE**	**OTHER**
Great Britain	—	Labour	Liberal Democrats[a]	—	Conservative	Regional[b]
France	PCF	PS	[c]	[c]	UPM[d]	Greens and National Front
Germany	PDS	SPD	FDP	CDU	—	Greens

[a]Liberal to 1983; Liberal-Social Democratic Alliance 1983–87, Liberal Democrats 1988 on.

[b]Nationalist parties of Scotland, Wales, and Northern Ireland.

[c]The French Radical and Christian Democratic parties have disappeared. See Chapter 5.

[d]Most recent party representing the Gaullist movement.

© Cengage Learning

Next come the **Social Democratic** parties. Social Democrats have been the most important party on the left since 1945 in all of the industrialized democracies other than the United States, Canada, and Japan. Like the Communists, they supported the **nationalization** of industry, extensive social welfare programs, and greater equality in the past. Unlike the Communists, social democrats rejected revolution and were harsh critics of the Soviet Union. During the cold war, most of them shed all but the emptiest rhetorical support for Marxism and nationalization.

In the center are parties commonly known as either **liberal** or **radical** in the European meanings of those terms. They gained their leftist reputation in the nineteenth century when they did stand for what was then fundamental change—the separation of church and state, a market economy, and democracy. With the emergence of socialist and later communist parties, they "lost" their place on the left end of the spectrum.

The Liberals were one of the two major British parties until the 1920s, and the Radicals were France's most influential party under the Third and Fourth Republics (1875–1958). Today, the British Liberal Democrats win votes mostly from the wealthy and had been out of government for decades before joining the Conservative-led coalition government after the 2010 election. The one consistently influential liberal party is the German Free Democratic Party (FDP). Although it has never done well at the polls, it has provided the votes either the socialists or the Christian Democrats needed to form a governing coalition for all but ten years since the creation of the Federal Republic in 1949.

Countries that had large Catholic parties and deep divisions over the relationship between church and state also had Christian Democratic parties. They were by no means a unified political force. Some had qualms about democracy; others advocated social reforms along the same lines as the social democrats. After World War II, most of them drifted rightward to support the Americans in the cold war

and mixed capitalist economies at home. They have been in power far more than they have been in opposition in Germany and dominated all postwar Italian governments until a wave of dissatisfaction destroyed the entire party system there in the 1990s. In France, Christian Democrats never did as well as one might have thought given the size of the Catholic population, and the secular Gaullists now occupy the same ideological space.

With very few Catholics and Christians, respectively, Britain and Japan, not surprisingly, never had an explicitly Catholic party. Instead, secular conservatives have been the dominant right wing force at the polls. The British Conservatives and Japanese LDP (Liberal Democratic Party) are not all that different from the Christian Democrats ideologically other than on the few remaining divisive religious issues such as abortion and same sex marriage.

Catch-All Parties

The favorability ratings of democratic politicians around the world are at an all time low in part because the partisan divides grow out of old issues that are often not the ones most people focus on today.

Today's political parties are also having problems because of the way they go about doing their job. They have become what one political scientist in the 1960s called **catch-all** parties, because they literally try to "catch" voters from the entire political spectrum rather than from the narrower ideological niches of their prewar predecessors.

Catch-all parties emerged because the combination of sustained economic growth, the expansion of the welfare state, and the escalation of the cold war undermined support for radical politics. Voters left the extremes and converged on the center in droves; the parties had no choice but to eventually follow suit.

Religious and secular conservatives led the way. The British Conservatives, French Gaullists, and German CDU

(Christian Democratic Union) made their peace with the Keynesian interventionist state and embraced the idea that government should provide extensive social service programs.

The Left was slower to respond. The British Labour Party and the German Social Democrats (SPD) clung to their socialist rhetoric even though their electoral fortunes plummeted as a result. Gradually, however, a new generation of leaders moved these parties toward the center and began leading them to regular victories beginning in the 1960s.

The moderation was so pronounced during the 1950s and early 1960s that some analysts began writing about the "end of ideology" (see the top half of Figure 2.1). They were convinced that sharp ideological divisions were a thing of the past and that future elections would be contests between similar teams of politicians.

The shift toward catch-all parties was reinforced by dramatic changes in the way election campaigns are conducted. By the 1960s, most people were getting most of their political information from television. Because it is impossible to say anything nuanced in a sixty-second news clip or an even shorter ad, the reliance on television accentuated the trend away from ideological politics. Even in today's more ideologically charged climate, parties build their campaigns around slick politicians who succeed in large part because they know how to "use" television and other electronic media.

As we are about to see, events proved the "end of ideology" thesis incorrect. However, the technological changes since then have intensified pressures for parties to use the media and seek middle-of-the-road voters most of the time. There have been times when values mattered, most recently with the rise of the Tea Party Movement in the 2010 election in the United States. Nonetheless, polls, focus groups, and other forms of market research have led party leaders to run campaigns that "sell" their candidates to undecided voters far more often than not and have no doubt contributed to the cynicism many voters feel toward politicians today.

New Divisions

Although the names of the most important political parties look quite similar to those of forty years ago, the coalitions of voters they attract has changed through what political scientists call **realignment**. Until the 1960s, most people had a strong sense of **party identification**, which led them to vote for the same party from one election to the next.

Strength of party identification has dropped dramatically since the 1960s. As a result, voters are far less loyal to any one party than they used to be, which has made election results a lot more volatile. Among other things, that has led voters in the last few years to vote incumbents out of office whichever side of the political spectrum they are on.

FIGURE 2.1 Political Participation in Flux: Two Versions

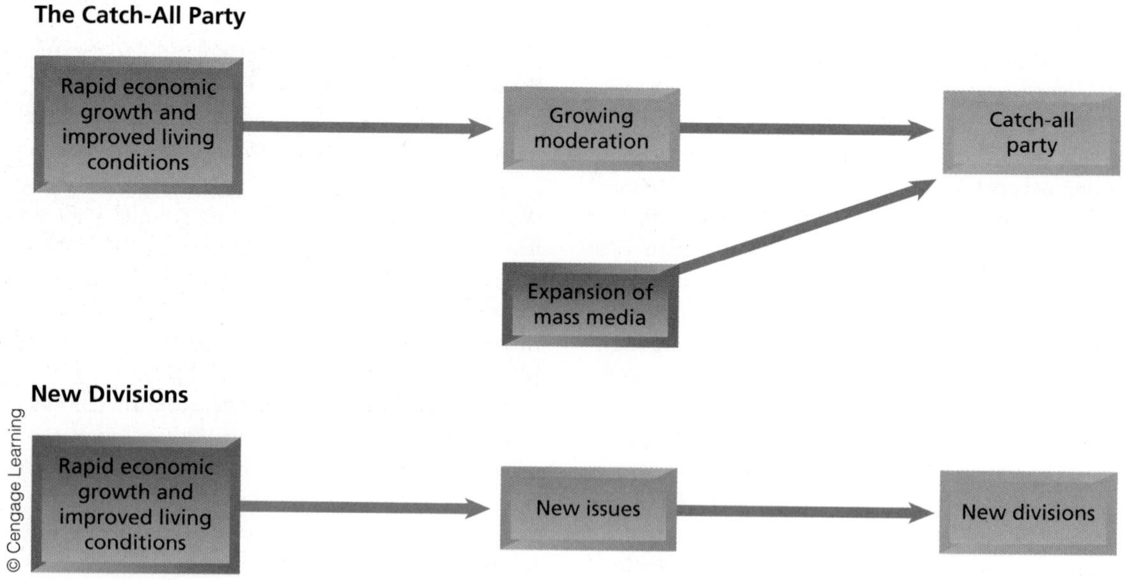

The Catch-All Party

New Divisions

© Cengage Learning

At the same time, the last fifty years have seen a "rebirth" rather than an end of ideology. New issues have spawned new political parties and social movements that have made Table 2.4 somewhat misleading, although none of these new groups is a serious contender for power at the national level.

Nothing reflects the new politics in these countries more than the changing status of women. Until the 1960s, women as a whole were more conservative than men. For example, because they were less likely to work outside the home, women were therefore less exposed to the left-leaning influence of trade unions. They were also more religious and thus more likely to follow their church's line on political issues.

During the 1960s, more women went to work. At almost exactly the same time, the newest version of the feminist movement took off and "liberated" millions of women from traditional social and economic roles. As a result, many women began to question their conservative views, especially those involving reproductive rights and the family.

Many women decided that their interests lay with the more progressive parties. In the United States, this led to the "gender gap" in which as many as 20 percent more women than men vote Democratic. The disparity in the vote is not as pronounced in France, Germany, and Great Britain, but even there left-of-center parties have taken the lead in recruiting more women to run for office and appointing them to key positions at all levels of government.

The gender gap is but the tip of a much larger, but poorly understood, political iceberg. More working class white men whose parents were on the left now tend to vote for conservative parties, especially when gender, environmental, and race-related issues are at the heart of a campaign. Meanwhile, left-of-center parties now attract a disproportionate number of women, minority, "green," and LGBT (Lesbian-Gay-Bisexual-Transgendered) voters.

American readers who stayed up long enough to watch Romney's concession and Obama's victory speech on election night 2012 would have had no trouble seeing this point. The Romney supporters were mostly well-dressed, middle aged whites. The not surprisingly more elated Obama crowd was visibly more diverse in racial, gender, and age terms, with hardly a coat and tie or pair of heels in sight.

For more than forty years, Ronald Inglehart and his colleagues have been studying how the changes giving rise to **postindustrial society** are playing themselves out politically (see the bottom half of Figure 2.1). Their research is among the most controversial in all of political science. Nonetheless, their findings are consistent enough that it is clear that they have tapped into something important.

Inglehart starts with the same social and economic dynamics as the end-of-ideology theorists but then heads in a very different analytical direction. His data suggest that the unprecedented economic growth of the past half-century has given birth to a new type of middle-class voters, whom he calls **postmaterialists**. They are often the third generation to have been raised in affluent circumstances and can realistically expect that they will have productive and rewarding careers and will not have to worry much about their economic security. Therefore, they tend to focus on what he calls "higher order" values, including job and personal satisfaction, self-actualization, and international understanding.

(Top): **Two Tea Party activists.**
(Bottom): **Voters celebrating just before President Obama delivered his victory speech in 2012.**

In the process, postmaterialists have become far less conservative than earlier generations of economically privileged voters. They are not traditional leftists. Most have qualms about the welfare state and reject socialism out of hand. However, they tend to support peace movements, environmentalism, and rights for women and the LGBT community.

Postmaterialists are also the strongest supporters of the **Greens**, the one type of new party that has made any headway in redefining what it means to be on the left. Greens are best known for their strong stands against nuclear weapons and power and for their support of the environment. Their ideology, in fact, goes much farther, to stress "deep ecology." Like some of the versions of systems theory discussed in Chapter 1, Green analysts assume that all of life is interconnected and that no social or political problem can be solved on its own. Green parties have done rather well in Europe, often approaching 10 percent of the vote. They have enjoyed the most success in Germany, where they have been in parliament since 1983 and were in the governing coalition from 1998 until 2005.

On the other end of the political spectrum are people who have not benefited as much from economic growth. Indeed, in a high-tech world in which low-skill jobs are increasingly being automated or outsourced, poorly educated, older people have good reason to be worried.

Inglehart calls this slice of the population materialists who make maintaining their own standard of living and national security their highest priority. Many grew up in left-wing families. Over the last few decades, however, millions of them have voted for politicians and parties that are skeptical about women's rights and other new issues while defending "traditional values" and defending security in all its guises. In the United States, if "soccer moms" epitomize the postmaterialist voter, "NASCAR dads" do the same for the new brand of conservatives.

There is no single equivalent of the Green parties for these new conservatives. Some have found homes among traditional conservatives, which we will see most prominently in Great Britain under Margaret Thatcher and in the United States since the presidency of Ronald Reagan and the recent emergence of Tea Party Republicans. Elsewhere, they have been drawn to new populist right-wing parties, such as France's National Front, which routinely wins between 10 and 20 percent of the vote.

Interest Groups

Interest groups promote just about every possible position on just about every imaginable issue in the industrialized democracies. Because there are so many interest groups, political scientists have tended to concentrate on the ones that have been the most influential over the last few decades, especially labor unions and business groups.

The largest and best organized groups usually have easy and even privileged access to decision makers, something we will see mostly clearly for business and union leaders in what political scientists call **corporatist** states. But they are by no means the only ones we should pay attention to. Unions, in particular, are nowhere near as powerful as they were thirty or fifty years ago.

In addition to the new political parties, we will encounter new interest groups that work on the kinds of issues we just discussed, such as gender, the environment, and the defense of traditional values. Some rely on lobbying, community organizing, and other "inside-the-system" tactics, including Habitat for Humanity and Doctors Without Borders, which operate in most if not all of these countries. Some, on the other hand, are more aggressive, such as the animal rights groups in the United Kingdom that disrupted fox-hunting parties in opposition to what they are convinced is the inhumane slaughter of animals.

Political Protest

Groups that do not enjoy easy access to elite decision-making circles often choose to either turn to the "streets" or drop out of political life altogether because they "know" they can't make a difference. Because they are not active, political scientists have a hard time studying the sullen nonvoters who shun all forms of political activity. Therefore, we will concentrate on organized protest movements instead.

The Occupy Wall Street and Tea Party Movements in the United States have little in common other than their conviction that "they" refuse to listen to "the people." The solutions they seek may be as different politically as night and day. However, a common sense of frustration with business as usual led them, respectively, to set up camp in American cities and bring a new generation of conservatives to the fore in the Republican Party.

The two are uniquely American phenomena. However, movements reflecting similar views exist in almost all industrialized democracies today.

As with interest groups, protest movements come in so many types and have such differing impacts that it is hard to reach more than a single conclusion about them. Although some protesters call for profound changes, and demonstrators sometimes use the word "revolution," virtually no prominent dissidents in the industrialized democracies question the core legitimacy of the regime, as discussed in the section on political culture.

Only rarely do protests from the Left or Right turn violent, and when they do the mental health as well as the political

Antoine Serra/In Visu/Corbis

Antiglobalization protesters marching from Annemasse, France, to Geneva, Switzerland, during the G-8 summit held in Evian, France, in June 2003. The sign reads, "Eight Deadly Sins: Globalization, Speculation, Exclusion, Corruption, Privatization, Manipulation, Lying, Contempt." Protesters clashed frequently with police in normally staid Geneva and caused millions of dollars in damage.

views of the perpetrators are involved. That was certainly the case in the most (in)famous example, Anders Breivik's killing of 77 young people in Norway in 2011 or the terrorist bombing at the finish line of the Boston Marathon in 2013.

The Democratic State

Elections, interest groups, and other forms of political participation give people in the industrialized democracies more clout than their counterparts who live under any other kind of regime. That does not mean that there is anything like a one-to-one correspondence between what the people want and what the state does. Political scientists often claim that the state is autonomous, which is another way of saying it has a life of its own. Put simply, how the state and its institutions are structured and who runs it at any particular moment in time matter.

Presidential and Parliamentary Systems

The most important thing to understand in this respect is that there are two main types of democratic systems—presidential and parliamentary. Both are based on the key democratic principle that free and competitive elections determine who governs. However, their markedly different ways of putting democratic theory into practice lead to equally markedly different kinds of policy outcomes.

It is actually misleading to speak of presidential systems in the plural because there really is only one of them—the United States. Presidents in many other democracies are elected and exercise considerable power on their own. However, only the United States has a marked separation of powers, which Americans often call checks and balances.

As we will see in more detail in the next chapter, the drafters of the U.S. Constitution set out to create a state in which it would be very difficult for rulers to abuse their power or act quickly and decisively. Each branch of government, therefore, has ways to "check" the power of the other two.

Critical in this respect is the way a bill becomes a law—or doesn't as the case may be. The final version of a bill that reaches the president's desk will almost certainly be very different from the one that was originally introduced, because no one—including the president—has much leverage over the legislative process as a whole. A bill has to pass through a number of hurdles, including committee and floor debates in both houses (see Figure 2.2). The bill can be defeated or dramatically altered at each stage. The bills that do pass are invariably the result of compromises worked out by representatives of the White House, Congress, interest groups, and more.

That is what happened to the Affordable Care Act of 2010 even though President Obama's Democratic Party had large majorities in both the House of Representatives and Senate. Later that year, the Republicans won a majority in the House of Representatives, and the U.S. fell into

FIGURE 2.2 The President and Congress

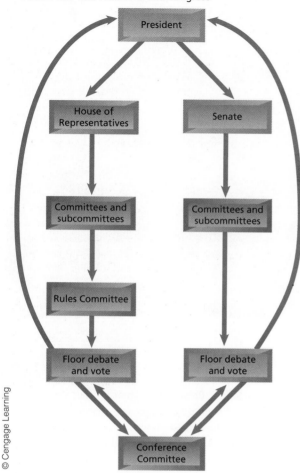

© Cengage Learning

country to country) are also **members of parliament (MPs)** who retain their seats in parliament while they serve in the cabinet and resume their role as normal legislators should they lose their position in the executive. Together, the prime minister and the cabinet members form the government.

The most important feature of a parliamentary system is the doctrine of **cabinet responsibility** to parliament. The government can remain in office until the next scheduled election *only if* all of its major legislative initiatives pass and it wins all formal **votes of confidence** in which the parliament is explicitly asked to affirm its support for the prime minister and cabinet. If the government loses either type of vote, it must resign. At that point, either a new majority forms a government in the existing parliament or the parliament is dissolved, leading to a new election within a matter of weeks.

Parliaments have committees, debates, and votes. Unlike in the United States, however, the prime minister has almost total control over what MPs do, because of the parliamentary system (see Figure 2.3). If the government has a clear majority, the government will almost never lose one of those votes. The bottom line is that there is almost complete party discipline, which means that members of the majority almost always vote the way the prime minister wants, while members of the opposition vote against the government the vast majority of the time. The costs of ousting a sitting prime minister are too high. Voting against a prime minister from one's own party can destroy an ambitious politician's career. The best a defeated government can look forward to is the uncertainty of an early election.

gridlock in which Republican and Democratic leaders rarely found enough common ground to agree on legislative language. Almost nothing got done, including addressing the country's massive debt, which has left the country teetering on the edge of the "fiscal cliff" for most of this decade.

Parliamentary systems are very different. No two are the same, but all share one key feature with the Westminster system in Britain on which they were based. There is little or no separation of power. Instead, legislative and executive authority are fused. Although the president has some independent leeway in hybrid systems that combine the presidential and the parliamentary models, countries other than the United States adhere to some version of the principles and procedures discussed in the rest of this section.

The chief executive is rarely directly elected. In classical parliamentary systems, the majority party in parliament chooses the prime minister, who then appoints the rest of the cabinet. Most cabinet ministers (the proportion varies from

FIGURE 2.3 The Parliamentary System

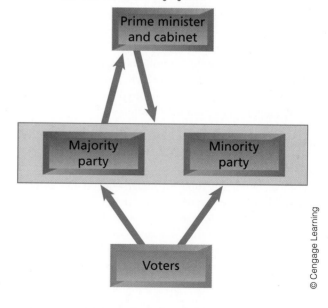

© Cengage Learning

TABLE 2.5 The British General Election of 2005

	LABOUR	CONSERVATIVE	LIBERAL DEMOCRATS	OTHERS
Share of the vote (%)	35.3	32.3	22.1	11.3
Number of seats	356	198	62	30

© Cengage Learning

TABLE 2.6 The French Chamber of Deputies, 1951

PARTY	NUMBER OF SEATS
Communists	101
Socialists	106
Christian Democrats	88
Radicals	76
Independents and Peasants	95
Gaullists	120
Others	40

© Cengage Learning

Consider the example of Great Britain after the 2005 election (see Table 2.5).[5] The Labour Party won 356 out of 646 seats in the all-powerful House of Commons. The prime minister could therefore count on winning every key vote until the parliament's term ended.

Debates in the House are even more heated than in the American Congress, but the rhetoric rarely amounts to much. The House of Commons will only make minor alterations to the bills before it—and then only if the government agrees to them.

Politicians face their fair share of pressure from constituents and interest groups in a parliamentary system. Interest groups can and do have an important role to play in drafting bills. However, once a formal bill is written, it is too late for them to have any hope of significantly reshaping its provisions.

We need to add an important caveat here. Legislation passes this quickly and easily only if a single party or firm coalition has a majority of the seats. If not, a situation akin to gridlock in the United States results.

Here, contrast Britain with France after the 1951 election for the Chamber of Deputies, which only differed in detail from others in the Third (1875–1940) and Fourth (1946–1958) Republics (see Table 2.6). Six main parties plus a smattering of independents won seats. The parties held sharply different views. Many of their leaders also disliked each other personally. Not surprisingly, there was little chance of forming the kind of coalition the British did after the 2010 election, when the Conservatives and Liberal Democrats agreed to govern together for the five-year term of the House of Commons.

Throughout the history of the two republics, France faced a cabinet crisis every nine months or so. A government would either lose a vote of confidence or resign knowing that it was about to do so. For reasons to be discussed in Chapter 5, the premier could not dissolve parliament and force new elections. A new majority had to be cobbled together in the existing Chamber, but that new cabinet, in turn, would usually fall as soon as it had to deal with the

first controversial issue on its agenda after it dealt with the one that had brought it to power in the first place.

Under such circumstances, parliamentary systems yield anything but effective governments. Neither republic could meet the serious challenges the country faced, which culminated in the collapse of the two regimes under pressure from the Germans in World War II and revolts by colonists and French soldiers in Algeria barely a generation later.

In recent years, however, few parliaments have been this hamstrung. More often than not, elections have produced either a single party with a majority of its own or a coalition that pledged to stay together for the life of that parliament, as was the case following the 2005 (single party majority) and 2010 (coalition) elections in Great Britain.

The Rest of the State

All kinds of governments today have to deal with highly technical issues for which few legislators have anywhere near enough expertise. As a result, two groups not included in Figures 2.2 and 2.3 have pivotal roles in any state— senior civil servants in the **bureaucracy** and the interest groups mentioned above.

Max Weber (1864–1920) was the first social scientist to focus our attention to the importance of highly trained civil servants in a modern state. They are supposed to be civil *servants* who work dispassionately for their political masters in the cabinet, whatever party happens to control it for the moment. Recruited and promoted on the basis of merit, bureaucrats are supposed to be objective experts. Their behavior is not driven by ideology or personal whims, but by clearly defined legal rules.

Despite their training and prestige, most senior civil servants do not and cannot live up to the dispassionate and apolitical Weberian ideal. Because their professional technical expertise is almost always needed, they have become policymakers in their own right. Their role in the decision-making process poses problems for democratic theory because they are not elected and it is hard to hold them accountable whatever institutions a particular country uses. This is especially true in countries where the

---

[5]Britain had a more recent election, in 2010. However, as we will see in Chapter 4, the 2005 results were typical of recent elections and therefore a better example to use here.

business, bureaucratic, and partisan elites overlap so much that scholars speak of them as an **iron triangle**.

France and the United States represent the two extremes on this score. Even before the rise of the Tea Party, Americans were wary of any close relationships between interest groups and politicians. For example, former civil servants cannot lobby members of the agency they used to work for until two years after they retire. In addition, the separation of powers doctrine often makes it hard for members of Congress and their staffs to pry information from government agencies.

Cooperation among business executives, politicians, and bureaucrats is the norm in France. Many ambitious young people begin their careers by attending one of the prestigious *grandes écoles*, which prepare them for bureaucratic careers. After ten years or less in the civil service, the most talented and ambitious of them leave the government through a process known as *pantouflage*, which literally means putting on soft, cushy slippers. At that point, they either become politicians or top corporate executives. In other words, current and former civil servants with similar social backgrounds and early career paths head up most key government agencies and private sector businesses.

Countries with the most **integrated elite** were among the most successful economically during the first forty years after World War II. In the last two decades the momentum has shifted to those that rely more on market forces and entrepreneurship. However, as we will see in Chapter 5, France still uses the strong state with the integrated elite at its core to help spur the development of those very entrepreneurs.

The Courts: The Forgotten Link?

American readers, in particular, may be surprised that the policy-making role of the legal system has not received much attention in this chapter. In few other countries do the courts have the sweeping powers they do in the United States, where the Supreme Court regularly rules on the constitutionality of actions undertaken by the legislative and executive branches.

Elsewhere, the role of the courts varies. In Great Britain, they cannot practice constitutional law or engage in judicial review. In other countries, what the courts do falls somewhere in between these two extreme examples. In Germany, for example, the Federal Constitutional Court has made a number of key rulings, including several that limit a woman's right to choose. However, only in the United States do the courts rival the legislative and executive branches in terms of power.

The Democratic State: A Recap

Because the "Political Indicators" table at the start of this chapter only includes the industrialized democracies, it can be misleading. There is *some* variation in the way democratic states are structured. However, they have more in common with each other than they do with any of the other kinds of states covered in this book. That is one of the conclusions from this chapter that you will have to take as a leap of faith until you have read Part 3 and Part 4.

Public Policy

The industrialized democracies do not have the world's most active states, and none of them could ever be called authoritarian or totalitarian. All of them, however, have a history of deep engagement at home and abroad. Indeed, the modern activist state emerged because citizens and leaders alike concluded that government could not stay on the sidelines as the challenges their countries faced mounted from the end of the nineteenth century onward.

That said, there is considerably more variation in their public policy than the numbers in "The Political Indicators" table might suggest, in at least two main ways, and the United States is an outlier in both of them. First, most other democracies are more intentional in using their governments to provide social services and steer the economy. Second, because it is the world's only superpower, the United States has by far the greatest impact on the rest of the world on almost every dimension imaginable.

The Interventionist State

Most mainstream, neoclassical economists believe that the state should keep its hands off the economy. As they see it, a freely functioning market driven by the "laws" of supply and demand provide the maximum possible wealth at the minimum possible cost.

Markets have never worked as well as the theories predict for two reasons that have been at the heart of democratic policy making for the better part of a century. First, even the most passionate advocates of laissez-faire economics realize that markets do not do a particularly good job of providing public goods such as a clean environment, general education, or the national defense. The population of a country may decide it wants or needs them, but it is rarely in any individual's or firm's self-interest to do so. Second, markets work at their best when neither capitalists nor workers control enough wealth to shape markets and undermine the effects of free competition.

CHRISTIAN CHARISIUS/Reuters/Corbis

German parents picking up toys for their children at a government-funded day care center.

To make a long and complicated story short, the industrial revolution made it more and more difficult for a capitalist economy to supply public goods, especially those that involved social equality. Democratic states found that they had little choice but to act in order to overcome what economists call market failures. By the start of the twentieth century, these failures included overcrowded and filthy cities, widespread poverty, and pollution, all of which led people—especially those on the Left—to demand change. In one form or another, that led to the creation of an **interventionist state** throughout the industrialized world.

What they do, who is covered by their programs, and how they do it varies from country to country. Nonetheless, all industrialized democracies provide more than rudimentary services in:

- Health care
- Education
- Income support
- Unemployment compensation
- Pensions and other programs for seniors

Conservatives today find little to like in these programs. Among other things, they think they are inefficient, contribute to the current fiscal crisis, and sap people of individual initiative, which the free market advocates believe offers the only permanent solution to our social and economic problems. Some want to replace national pension programs with publicly funded but privately managed ones that do not guarantee a fixed benefit. There are pressures everywhere to control health care spending as the cost of coverage spirals and the population ages. On balance, however, these programs are very popular and have proven hard to cut, let alone eliminate, and will probably remain so for the foreseeable future.

Conservative critics also frequently equate these programs with socialism, but they are definitely wrong on that score. As we will see in Part 3, the many definitions of socialism all revolve around substantial government ownership and control of the economy. Most of the economy is privately owned in each of the industrialized democracies. All have some industries that are owned and operated by the government, including AMTRAK in the United States, the National Health Service in Britain, and much of the electric grid in France. If anything, however, the recent momentum has been toward less government ownership, not more, given the wave of **privatizations** of state-owned industries since the 1980s.

The United States is an outlier on all of these fronts. It is the only major industrialized country that does not provide comprehensive basic health care to everyone and will not do so even after the Affordable Health Care Act is fully implemented in 2014. Not only does it do less than other democratic governments, many of its programs are not very effective because of everything from its cultural norms to the way its policy-making institutions function. To cite but one example, the United States spends more on health care per capita than any other country despite providing the spottiest coverage.

All industrialized democracies, including the United States, are actively involved in trying to shape the economy as a whole, as well as individual industrial sectors. The ways they have intervened has varied tremendously. During the first thirty years after World War II, France tried to plan much of its economy by determining the likely outcomes of a number of policy options. The Germans often relied on **corporatism**, through which the government and leading interest groups met to set the broad economic parameters for the following year or two. Great Britain and the United States relied more on market mechanisms, and their growth rates lagged, at least until the oil embargo was imposed by the Organization of Petroleum Exporting Countries (OPEC) in 1973 to 1974. The o policy on which almost everyone is agreed these da that government ownership of industry is not a good idea, which we will see most clearly in the privatization programs pursued by the British and French governments over the past thirty years.

During that time, neither active state intervention nor more market-driven approaches to economic policy making have had consistently positive results. That leads to one broader common denominator to their economic policies that will reappear in many guises throughout the rest of the book. Whatever kind of policies they have tried to pursue, none of the interventionist states has fared all that well in this century. One unquestioned impact of globalization is that no state—including the wealthiest and the most powerful—can hope to shape its economic destiny even to the degree that it could during the thirty years of almost unbroken prosperity after World War II.

Foreign Policy

As noted in Chapter 2, foreign policy is included in this book first and foremost to help break down the intellectual firewall between comparative politics and international relations. In addition, we will see that the determinants of foreign policy have their roots in the histories, cultures, and institutional arrangements that come into play domestically.

Here, the United States has by far the most active state. As the world's one remaining superpower, it could hardly be otherwise. Historically, the other industrialized democracies included in this book have been among the world's great powers, but since World War II, their relative standing has been reduced.

The United States was drawn into its dominant international role slowly if not always reluctantly. Today, it is safe to say that there is no foreign policy issue that is beyond Americans' interests, at least as they perceive them. American policy abroad today reflects not only its position as a superpower but also the ideological and structural differences that long antedate the Obama presidency.

The other countries covered in Part 2 are what international relations specialists call mid-level powers. They have significant influence abroad but by no means rival the United States, especially when issues of force are involved. As we will see most clearly in Chapter 7 on the European Union, economic policy undoubtedly matters more to them.

Whatever similarities there are in their domestic policies, there is more variation in what they do internationally, especially since the end of the cold war and the increased importance given to the political economy.

The United Kingdom has typically had the most pro-American foreign policy through what they often call their "special relationship" with the United States. That is also one of the reasons the British have been the most skeptical of the three European countries covered in this book.

France has probably had the most independent—and some would say disruptive—foreign policy. However, at least since the resignation of President Charles de Gaulle in 1969, France has gradually moved back into the European foreign policy mainstream.

Germany still lives in the shadow of its Nazi past nearly seventy years after the end of World War II. Its constitution, for instance, limits what its military can do. What distinguishes Germany today is its economic power, which it displays politically most obviously as the leading force in the EU.

Finally, we will also consider the most innovative aspect of democratic foreign policy in the last half century—the European Union. As we will see in Chapters 7 and 16, it is by far the most successful attempt yet to create governing bodies that transcend the nation-state, and, for the purposes of this book, it will be our first opportunity to explore the "big questions" introduced in Chapter 1 in any depth.

Comparative Emphasis: Globalization

The liberal democracies have the most effective states in the world—especially the larger ones analyzed in Part 2. In this sense, Figure 1.3 could well have been drawn with arrows "out" from them to reflect the way that they can shape global forces, especially on geopolitical or military issues. But these countries are still affected by global forces in at least three ways.

First, their strengths are now mostly a function of their wealth and of the clout wielded by their corporations. Second, despite those strengths, international forces limit their ability to set and implement economic policy. This is especially true for the twenty-seven members of the European Union, which is increasingly responsible for their economic policies. Third, because of their locations and the consumption that accompanies their wealth, they are among the countries that contribute the most to climate change and other global environmental dangers. ■

The Media

Although the term never appears in the classic texts, the media have always been a key component of the real world of democracy. Given their importance, it is surprising to see how little research political scientists have conducted on their role. Nonetheless, it does seem safe to reach two conclusions.

First, for some people, it is getting easier, but also more confusing, to find out about politics at home and abroad. Because of the telecommunications revolution, the world's news is now delivered to us all but instantaneously. Though some argue that the television networks, and even venerable newspapers such as the *New York Times* or the *Times* of London, have "dumbed down" and are nowhere near as informative as they used to be, people who are interested now have access to far more information than they did in the past. Cable news networks are on the air twenty-four hours a day. You can buy the *New York Times* almost any place in the United States. The blogosphere and sites such as YouTube provide huge amounts of information, the accuracy of which is, however, all but impossible to verify.

Comparative Emphasis: What Happened to the Big Questions?

Given Chapter 1, it might seem surprising that the five big questions have not featured in this chapter and frankly will not appear all that often in the rest of Part 2.

That doesn't mean we could or should ignore them. Globalization, democratization, the shift toward Everything 2.0, and the like are all important forces facing these countries.

However, the key point to keep in mind at this point is that most of them are not on the political agenda in these countries. I finished writing this chapter a few weeks after the 2012 presidential election in the United States. I was amazed at how little these issues were discussed during the campaign either by the candidates themselves or in the millions of ads they ran.

I will discuss why that is the case in each of the next four chapters and again in the final one. For now, it is enough to note that, for good or ill, they rarely make it onto either politicians' or pundits' radar screens. ∎

Second, average citizens view the world in their own terms, which may be quite different from those of either the politicians or media moguls. At this point, one of the common denominators among the mass publics in most democracies seems to be disinterest in what happens outside of their own country or region. More and more people are tuning the political world out altogether. To some degree, this reflects what many feel is the cynical coverage by the media themselves, which has turned off millions. It may also, in part, be the result of the fact that, with the cable and satellite revolution, we can now watch reruns of *American Idol*, a soccer game from Spain, or any of the (currently) 53 global MTV stations instead of the news. But, most of all, the declining interest in politics has less to do with the media than with the general cynicism about and skepticism toward politics and politicians.

The Worst Form of Government Except for All the Others

Given what we have seen, it is hard not to agree with the first half of Winston Churchill's statement that begins this chapter. The industrialized democracies have obviously accomplished a lot; just as obviously, they face serious problems, some of which—for the moment—seem to be insurmountable.

The second half of the statement may be true as well, though you will have to take it as a leap of faith until you learn more about the countries covered in Parts 3 and 4. From that perspective, democracy's problems, however serious they may be, pale in comparison with those in the rest of the world.

Before closing, however, consider the last five words of Churchill's statement "that have ever been tried". In previous editions of this book, I have not included those final five words. Now that this edition emphasizes the five big questions, it is definitely worth including them.

Democracies may fare better in most ways that matter to political scientists and their citizens alike. But lurking just below the surface of this chapter is a concern that being the best form of government that has ever been tried may not be enough, because accepting Churchill's statement lends itself to a certain smugness. The industrialized democracies all face major problems, some of which have implications for the very nature of their regimes and perhaps of the nation-state itself.

We will begin to address some of these issues in Chapter 7 on the European Union and again in the conclusion to the book.

For now, it is enough to simply pose a question that political scientists cannot easily answer. Shouldn't we also consider some alternative forms of government that have *never* been tried?

KEY TERMS

Concepts
bureaucracy
cabinet responsibility
civic culture
civil society
coalition
corporatism
democracy
electoral systems
gross national product (GNP)
integrated elite
interest groups
interventionist state
iron triangle

laissez-faire
Left
legitimacy
liberal
members of parliament (MPs)
nationalization
party identification
political party
postindustrial society
postmaterialist
proportional representation
radical
realignment
regimes

Right
rule of law
single-member districts
suffrage
votes of confidence

People
Hobbes, Thomas
Locke, John

Organizations, Places, and Events
catch-all parties
fascism
Greens
Liberal parties
Social Democratic parties

USEFUL WEBSITES

There are not all that many websites that deal with democracy *per se*. That's partly because theorists do not use the Internet as comparativists do. It's also because few comparativists study all democracies as a whole. Nonetheless, there are a few sites that can help sharpen your understanding of the ideas behind and the realities of democracy today.

The U.S. State Department has an excellent site that explores many of the issues raised in this chapter. Political Resources is a wonderful source for material on individual countries, whereas Election World has the most recent election results from every country in the world.

www.democ.uci.edu/resources/guide.php

www.ned.org

www.state.gov/documents/organization/55989.pdf

www.politicalresources.net

www.en.wikipedia.org/wiki/User:Electionworld/Electionworld

FURTHER READING

Almond, Gabriel, and Sidney Verba. *The Civic Culture*. Princeton, NJ: Princeton University Press, 1962; and Almond and Verba, eds. *The Civic Culture Revisited*. Boston: Little, Brown, 1979. The two best books on civic culture. They do, however, probably take the argument about the importance of culture a bit too far.

Barber, Benjamin. *Strong Democracy: Participatory Politics for a New Age*. Berkeley: University of California Press, 1984. A theoretical look at how to enhance participation to enhance democracy.

Diamond, Larry. *The Spirit of Democracy*. New York: Holt, 2008. Covers the meaning of democracy in all types of societies, not just those covered in Part 2.

Keane, John. *The Life and Death of Democracy*. New York: W.W. Norton, 2009. A mammoth book that studies the evolution of democracy from the Greeks to the future.

Macpherson, C. B. *The Life and Times of Liberal Democracy*. New York: Oxford University Press, 1977. A classic analysis of the way democracies work, though written from a more left-wing and democratic perspective.

Putnam, Robert D. *Making Democracy Work*. Princeton, NJ: Princeton University Press, 1993. Ostensibly only about Italy, a controversial book that provides the best recent analysis of the role of "social capital" and political culture in general.

Reid, T. R. *The Healing of America*. New York: Penguin, 2009. A sweeping book on the politics of health care, which may itself become the most sweeping issue facing all of these countries.

Samuels, David, and Matthew Shugart. *Presidents, Parties, and Prime Ministers*. New York: Cambridge University Press, 2010. Uses rational choice theory to explore differences among liberal democratic regimes beyond the simple presidential versus parliamentary models used here.

Tilly, Charles. *Democracy*. New York: Cambridge University Press, 2007. A masterful compendium of almost fifty years of his writing in the field, which stretches back to topics almost one thousand years ago.

Zakaria, Fareed. *The Future of Freedom*. New York: W.W. Norton, 2003. A thoughtful book about liberal, as well as what he calls illiberal, democracies. Worth considering for most of the countries covered in the rest of the book.

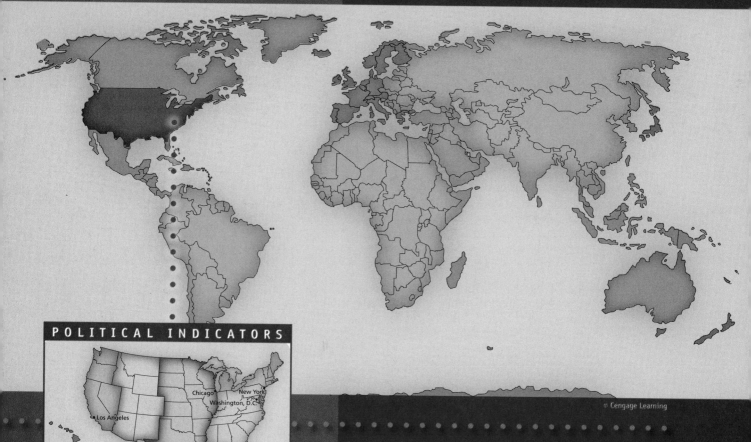

POLITICAL INDICATORS

GOVERNANCE (score 0–1)	HUMAN DEVELOPMENT (score 0–1)	DEMOCRACY (rank)	PEACE (rank)	CORRUPTION (rank)
.761	.910	19	88	24

3

Perhaps the most striking feature of the United States is the stability of its basic institutions despite the stress of associations, wars, racial strife, political scandal, and economic differences.

ALAN ABRAMOWITZ

The United States

THE BASICS

The United States

Size	9,158,960 sq. km
Population	314,000,000
GNP per capita	$48,300
Ethnic composition	77% white, 13% black, 4% Asian, 2% Native American, 4% other[a]
Life Expectancy	78.5
Religion	56% Protestant, 28% Roman Catholic, 2% Jewish, 4% other, 10% none
Capital	Washington, D.C.
President	Barack Obama (2009–)

[a]*The United States Census Bureau does not keep separate statistics on Hispanic Americans. According to its criteria, they can be of any race.*

It's Even Worse than It Looks

The 2012 campaign was by far the most expensive and among the nastiest in history. The candidates hurled accusations at each other and invented new terms to describe America's problems. "Kicking the can down the road." "Throwing bodies under the bus." "The fiscal cliff." It barely touched on the "big questions" discussed in Chapter 1.

To make matters worse, the election settled next to nothing. President **Barack Obama** (1961–) was reelected. Each party retained control of the chamber it controlled before the election—the **Democrats** in the Senate and the **Republicans** in the House of Representatives.

The U.S. still faced the same mammoth problems. Gridlock over what to do about the economic crisis. Health care. Abortion. Immigration. Race relations. Same sex marriage. The wars in Iraq and Afghanistan. The spread of nuclear weapons to North Korea and Iran. Disappearing hope for peaceful outcomes in Egypt and Syria. The list went on and on.

Nothing got better in the weeks after the election. On December 31, 2012, two sets of drastic policy changes were scheduled to go into effect. A series of tax cuts introduced under the George W. Bush and Obama administrations were set to expire. Massive across-the-board budget cuts would begin in a process known as **sequestration** that the president and congressional leaders had adopted after a failed attempt to deal with an earlier financial crisis.

The numbers were huge. The annual federal deficit was well over one trillion dollars a year. The total federal debt was more than fourteen trillion dollars. A last-minute agreement between the White House and the Republicans

President Obama and House Speaker Boehner discussing another failure in their attempt to reach a budget agreement.

in the House of Representatives delayed the encounter with the fiscal cliff for a few months.

Yes, the politicians kicked the clichéd can down the road one more time and still were no closer to reaching an agreement when this book went to press in summer 2013.

A few months before the election, two respected analysts published a book whose title summed up what many Americans felt—it's even worse than it looks.[1] Thomas Mann and Norman Ornstein epitomize insider Washington. Mann is a Democrat; Ornstein works for the Republican-leaning American Enterprise Institute. They have been best friends since they were graduate students. They are convinced that American politics has become self-destructive. Extreme partisanship and personal antagonisms are preventing political leaders from passing legislation that comes anywhere near close to meeting the country's policy needs. For the moment, they lay most of the blame on the Republicans, but if they are right, there is plenty of responsibility to go around.

But even Mann and Ornstein fail to raise two important questions about the American political dilemma that are of particular importance to comparativists.

First, could the root causes of the problem extend to the very roots of the American system rather than its current, ideologically charged climate? Americans tend to revere their system at least in part because it has survived for more than two centuries. Could it be that the constitutional system created in 1787 has outlived its usefulness? However you answer that question, it is hard to avoid the point, which begins the chapter, made by the equally prominent political scientist, Alan Abramowitz. The key to

American politics in comparative terms lies in understanding its stability *despite* these and dozens of other problems. In fact, Professor Abramowitz wrote those words not about America during the Obama presidency but in the late 1970s when the United States was emerging from Vietnam and Watergate and faced pressures that were at least as severe as the ones on its agenda today.

Second and related, why are the big questions raised in Chapter 1 mostly missing from mainstream discussions about politics in the United States? Other than the fiscal crisis, issues of that magnitude played next to no role in the 2012 campaign. We will see that the same was largely the case in recent election campaigns in Britain, France and Germany. In other words, couldn't all of the industrialized democracies be in the midst of a period of political denial in which we could be heading for even more severe problems in the not so distant future precisely because we are *not* asking them those big questions?

It will take at least the rest of Part 2 if not the rest of this book to even begin fully answering these questions. However, as a comparativist, it makes sense to read this chapter both as an analysis of the United States *and* as an introduction to the potential costs of not answering those and other tough questions.

Thinking About the United States

Why a Chapter on the United States?

Twenty years ago, few authors included a chapter on the United States in comparative politics textbooks written mostly for American readers. Now, almost all of them do, for two reasons.

First, the market for our books has changed. They are now sold to English-speaking students around the world. As the most important country in the world, the United States is almost always included in introductory courses taught elsewhere.

Second and more important, most American instructors have realized that the United States has to be included in introductory courses for American students for the simple reason that they will be using it as their main frame of reference. There is nothing wrong with that *as long as* readers keep in mind that the United States is quite different from the other industrialized democracies and understand that using the United States as a norm—let alone as some sort of political ideal—can be extremely misleading.

This chapter is designed to meet the slightly different needs of both sets of readers. For those outside the

---

[1]Thomas Mann and Norman Ornstein, *It's Even Worse than It Looks: How the American Constitutional System Collided with the New Politics of Extremism.* (New York: Basic Books, 2012).

United States, it covers the basics. However, because most readers—American and otherwise—already have some exposure to American politics, this chapter is a bit shorter than those that follow and concentrates primarily on the ways the United States is unusual.

The Wrong Name

This chapter has already misused the word "American" several times. We in the United States use it as a shorthand term to describe our country and ourselves. We should not do so because Canadians, Mexicans, Brazilians, Peruvians, and more are Americans, too.

Alas, our version of English has evolved in such a way that it is the only viable term we have to describe ourselves.

The Bottom Line

Most political scientists do not accept so-called **American exceptionalism** arguments that hold that the United States is somehow unique and therefore superior to other countries. Nonetheless, the United States is different from the other industrialized democracies in at least four ways, which helped shape the rest of this chapter.

First, as the world's only superpower, no other country can come close to matching its geopolitical might. Only the United States has the capacity to intervene anywhere in the world it chooses. Some Americans worry that China or some other country will overtake it. Realistically speaking, that is not likely to happen during the lifetime of anyone reading this book.

Second, its military might is matched by its size and wealth. Only Canada, Russia, and China are physically larger, and only China and India have a larger population. The United States may no longer be self-sufficient in many resource areas, but it is poised to become the world's largest producer of oil and natural gas by the end of this decade.

Over the last two hundred years, the U.S. has used its size, natural resources, and other assets to become by far the world's wealthiest country. Some countries have a higher per capita GNP. A few do better in health care and on some other indicators of human development. Still, examples of American economic clout are hard to miss, from its standard of living to the global influence of corporations based in the United States.

Wealth also has its costs. The distribution of income and wealth *within* the United States is becoming more and more unequal. While there are dozens of statistical indicators I could turn to in illustrating that point, none is more telling than the fact that six Wal-Mart heirs control more of the country's wealth than the poorest 42 percent of its total population.

Third, the United States also casts a huge cultural shadow in a way that is hard to pin down but will probably be even more important in the years to come. Much of what is popular in much of the world is American in origin—the Internet, rock and roll, the NBA, Hollywood, fast food, and the twenty-four-hour news cycle, to name but a few. Not everyone likes the growing American cultural hegemony, which some blame for what the late Samuel Huntington called the clash of civilizations. His thesis is hotly contested, but there is no denying that if such a clash exists in any form, it reflects a reaction against values, norms, and tastes that were "made in America."

Fourth, the United States is one of the world's most socially diverse countries. Most Americans are proud to call themselves a nation of immigrants whatever they think immigration policy should be today. Only a tiny proportion of the population is made up of Native Americans whose ancestors arrived before the Europeans. The rest of us have ancestors who came to the U.S. voluntarily, except, of course, for the millions of Africans who were forced to come to American shores as slaves. If anything, the United States is becoming even more diverse and is set to become a "majority minority" country sometime around the middle of this century, a trend that the Mitt Romney campaign discovered to its chagrin in 2012.

Key Questions

Each of the chapters on an individual country will consider the basic questions built into the diagram of the political system introduced in Chapter 1 and reprinted on the front inside cover. Each will also focus on questions specific to that country's past and present that we will use both as a lens through which to make sense of its political life and as a springboard for comparative analysis. For the United States, those include:

- How is its history reflected in distinctive and enduring political characteristics?

- How has the United States largely escaped the ideological divisions that have defined partisan and electoral life in most other democracies?

- Why does the United States have an unusually weak state, and why do most Americans seem happy with that fact?

- Why, despite more than a hundred years of isolationism, did the United States become the world's superpower?

- Perhaps most important of all, why are almost all Americans reluctant to even consider the possibility of reshaping the constitutional regime despite the severity of the problems the country faces today?

The Evolution of the United States

As we review American history, it should become clear that little in its early history led contemporaries to expect it to become the world's most powerful country (www.americanhistory.about.com). In other words, if there is a case to be made for American exceptionalism, it lies more in its past than its present.

The key point to make in that respect is that the United States has had a *relatively* easy time handling the four transformations discussed in Chapter 2. The civil war aside, national identity and support for a gradually expanding state grew more or less in tandem. Despite periodic flare-ups over the role of religion, including the one Americans are living through today, no other industrialized democracy was able to separate church and state as easily. Class, too, left the United States less divided even than its neighbor to the north. Perhaps most important of all, no other regime enjoyed the wealth, power, and political support that helped make the United States the first superpower after World War II.

Still, as in Great Britain, it is important to stress the term *relatively* because none of the trends or events discussed in the rest of this section came about smoothly. Nonetheless, compared to most countries, the United States was fortunate. From a comparative perspective, Americans were able to reach more of a consensus on all of the issues that would bedevil the European countries we will turn to in the rest of Part 2.

Creating the Constitutional Order

As we will see was also the case in many other new states, independence did not bring with it a stable or legitimate regime. From 1776 until 1787 the United States was governed under the Articles of Confederation, which vested almost all power in the states. That had made sense in 1776, because the thirteen colonies had staked their claim to independence on what they saw as unjust, centralized, and arbitrary English rule (See Table 3.1).

TABLE 3.1 The Making of an American State

YEAR	EVENT
1781	Independence
1787	Constitution
1861	Start of Civil War
1917	World War I
1933	Start of New Deal
1941	World War II
1945	End of World War II; start of cold war
1964	Start of Great Society
1974	Resignation of Richard Nixon
2008	Election of Barack Obama

© Cengage Learning 2015

Quickly, however, the United States faced problems that threatened to tear the new country apart and that could not be solved using the Articles. States imposed tariffs on each other that all but brought interstate trade to a halt. Rural and urban interests—or factions, as they were known—clashed violently in many states.

By 1787, most state legislatures had come to the conclusion that the Articles of Confederation were not working, so they sent delegates to a convention in Philadelphia that summer. Ostensibly, they met to revise the Articles of Confederation, but they rapidly realized that they had to start from scratch and draft an entirely new constitution, the ratification of which is usually considered to be the founding of the American state.

The Constitution was a remarkable document for its day. And the fact that it has lasted for more than two centuries is a testament to both its framers' insights and to the abilities of successive generations to adapt it to the changing realities of American life.

The Constitution did not appear out of political thin air. The Framers did not totally turn their backs on the English values and institutions they had rejected and fought over in the Revolutionary War. In fact, many of their key ideas and ideals had clear European roots, including the rights of man, the **separation of powers**, and the pursuit of life, liberty, and happiness. However, the Constitution did strike important new ground that amounted to one of the first major steps toward American distinctiveness, if not American exceptionalism (www.archives.gov/exhibits/charters/constitution.html).

For our purposes, the Framers' key accomplishment was the way they reconciled two goals that most theorists then thought were incompatible. They realized that they had to centralize government to overcome the squabbling and incompetent state legislatures and to continue to protect against the arbitrary exercise of power. They did so through a momentous series of **compromises** that enabled them to draft the new Constitution.

Because the states had to ratify the draft constitution, which was by no means a foregone conclusion, James Madison, Alexander Hamilton, and John Jay wrote the now-famous *Federalist Papers* (http://avalon.law.yale.edu/subject_menus/fed.asp). For comparativists, their eighty-five essays highlighted two major innovations that helped shape the evolution of American democracy.

First, they drew on the then largely untried beliefs of the French philosopher, Montesquieu, about separating the powers of three branches in a federal government. Although the balance among them has changed dramatically since 1787, one key principle remains the same. No one branch of government can do much without significant oversight and often the explicit approval of the others. What's more, in what became known as the division of powers, the national authorities would have to share power with the states in what was one of the first avowedly federal regimes in the modern era.

Second and even more important, they came up with a new way to, in Madison's terms, "cure the evils of faction." Unlike most of their contemporaries, the Framers assumed that factions were an inescapable part of life in an open society. They only became a problem in small units that a single group could control, leading to what Alexis de Tocqueville would call the "tyranny of the majority" a half-century later. Therefore, in *Federalist* #10, Madison advocated concentrating power in larger jurisdictions such as the federal government. That way, there would be little chance that any one of them could dominate and, therefore, they all would have to compromise to get anything done.

Shortly after the Constitution was ratified, Congress and the states adopted the first ten amendments, known as the Bill of Rights. From a comparative perspective, the most important were the initial sixteen words of the first amendment: "Congress shall make no law respecting an establishment of religion, or prohibiting the free exercise thereof." Prior to independence, most states had official or established churches. Massachusetts and Connecticut were Puritan, Pennsylvania was Quaker, Maryland was Catholic, and most of the South was Episcopalian. No single faith was acceptable to everyone. As a result, the Framers decided to remove religion from formal political life, all the while guaranteeing "the free exercise thereof."

The separation was never complete. Nonetheless, the Framers succeeded in removing conflict over church and state from the list of potential dangers to the regime well over two hundred years ago.

Comparative Emphasis: Democratization

Unlike many of the other countries we will consider, the United States did not consciously set out to build a democracy. Most of the founders, in fact, had serious doubts about the ability of average people to make intelligent political decisions. Democracy was, thus, an outgrowth and unintended consequence of the twists and turns in American political history.

To cite but one example of how difficult it was, the Declaration of Independence included the statement that "all men are created equal." At the time, "all men" did not include African Americans and poor whites. It would be a century and a half before "all men" came to include women and another half-century before the last racial barriers to formal political participation were removed. And, if you listen to some feminist, minority, or gay-lesbian-bisexual-transsexual (GLBT) activists, we still may have a way to go. ■

After the Framers

The debate over the Constitution was ancient history by the second decade of the nineteenth century. Meanwhile, the redesigned United States of America accomplished a lot. It fought the British again in the War of 1812, and it more than doubled its territory on two separate occasions with the Louisiana Purchase and its victory in the Mexican-American War. It so impressed visitors like de Tocqueville that they wrote glowingly about the prospects for democracy, something few influential thinkers had done since Athens' heyday two thousand years earlier.

That did not mean that the new state was secure and legitimate enough to survive the biggest crisis the United States ever faced—slavery and the civil war it led to. After decades of grudging compromise, the Southern states no longer felt they could stay in the Union and seceded. For four years, "brother" killed "brother" in a war that ended with the defeat of the Confederacy and the assassination of President Abraham Lincoln.

But, in a way, the Civil War reminds us of just how successful the United States already was. The Confederacy, for example, had more in common with the Union than it did with any of the European powers.

It is even more important to see how the country rebuilt itself after the war. At first, the North imposed a coercive regime to "reconstruct" the defeated South. Yet, within a decade, the former Confederate states had been readmitted to the Union. Surprisingly, rather than bearing Washington the resentment many expected, white Southerners became the most patriotic and conservative segment of the population.

The Modern American State

The modern American state is a product of a number of twin forces that surfaced in the second half of the nineteenth century but only began having a lasting political impact at the system or regime level in the middle third of the twentieth century. The Industrial Revolution transformed American social and economic life. Millions of immigrants came to the United States seeking political freedom and/or a better standard of living for themselves and their families. They worked in the new factories and slums of urban America, and in the process they turned the United States into a world economic power, although it must be said the benefits of that newfound wealth were mostly enjoyed by a small slice of the population.

Not surprisingly, the Industrial Revolution did lead to class conflict but not the radical socialism we will see in the next three chapters. The Socialist candidate Eugene Victor Debs won almost a million votes in the 1912 and 1920 presidential elections. Communists gained a toehold in some parts of the labor union movement. The mostly anti-socialist unions and other progressives called for an activist or interventionist state.

The American response to these and other demands for change, however, was unusual. Rather than enacting extensive welfare programs or taking over industries, the United States started with a series of antitrust laws designed to break up monopolies and oligopolies. The reformers—then and now—have consistently sought to use government intervention only as a last resort.

The United States did adopt extensive social service and welfare programs during the Great Depression and as part of Lyndon Johnson's Great Society in the 1960s. Whatever we may think of those programs today, they did mark a dramatic expansion of the American state. That should not keep us from seeing that these programs have always been less extensive and less well received by the public than those in the other liberal democracies.

In recent years, industrial issues receded in importance while new social issues took center stage. The 1960s and 1970s saw the birth of the civil rights movement out of which grew the **new Left**, environmentalism, feminism, and demands for equality from the GLBT community.

Although those of us who were swept up by the various strands of the new Left did not realize it, a new kind of conservatism was being born at that time. It—and not the Left—ended up setting the tone of the American political agenda in the twenty-first century.

To be sure, the status of women, minorities, and gays has improved dramatically. And even the most conservative Americans recycle, think about buying hybrid cars, and worry about climate change.

On balance, however, the center of political gravity has shifted rightward since Ronald Reagan's election in 1980. The **new Right** groups are almost mirror images of the ones in the preceding paragraph. The Christian right. The pro-life movement. Opposition to affirmative action. Doubts about the human causes of global warming. Perhaps most of all, the new conservatism is marked by America's renewed embrace of the market and limited government. Whatever the causes of the recent recession, even liberal Democrats acknowledge that the momentum is toward less government, not more.

There is no better indicator of the shift in the ideological balance of power than the Affordable Health Care Act of 2010, now all but universally known as Obamacare. The act drew universal opposition from the Republicans and was upheld by a paper-thin majority in the Supreme Court. What is remarkable here is that the conservative Nixon administration proposed far more sweeping and egalitarian health care reform forty years earlier, only to see it rejected because it did not go far enough toward providing universal coverage.

Unlike the other industrialized democracies other than Canada, the United States never developed a powerful socialist party. As we will see below, the Industrial Revolution did not produce the kind of divisions it did in Europe, most notably because of the way the American political culture evolved, the topic we turn to next.

The bottom line for this section is clear. Despite the many twists and turns of American political life, there is far more cultural continuity than in any other major country, with the possible exception of Great Britain. Were the founders to rise from their graves today, they would be surprised by many things: television, public opinion polls, tight security at federal buildings, and more. Yet the basic institutions and practices they created remain intact and operate in ways they would easily recognize—and endorse.

Comparative Emphasis: Identity

In Parts 3 and 4, we will see how identity issues have the potential to destroy regimes elsewhere in the world. While that is rarely the case in the industrialized democracies, identity issues are increasingly important, and there is no better example of that trend than in the United States in two broad ways.

Identity issues are not as divisive in the United States or in any of the other countries covered in Part 2. They are important, however, in part as a reflection of demographic changes and the divisive issues of postindustrial society (see Figure 2.1 on p. 38).

There is no question that identity issues have made a major contribution to the ideological divisions of the last half century or so. The most obvious examples are in the various "liberation" movements that emerged from the social divisions of the 1960s. Not all should be seen as leading the U.S. toward the left, most notably with the equally significant rise of Evangelical and other Christian denominations that have arisen at least in part in reaction against new progressive demands. ■

The American Political Culture

Until the late 1960s, most observers thought that the United States was one of the countries most conducive to democracy because its people were tolerant of both the regime and of each other. Attitudes have changed about "each other" but apparently not about the regime.

At the time, the United States had what Gabriel Almond and Sidney Verba called a civic culture.[2] Americans were more convinced than their counterparts in Europe or Japan that they could have an impact if the government did something they disagreed with, yet few Americans ever did so.

[2]Gabriel Almond and Sidney Verba, *The Civic Culture: Political Attitudes and Democracy in Five Nations* (Princeton, NJ: Princeton University Press, 1963).

The statistical evidence about American cultural norms through the mid-1960s overwhelmingly supports those kinds of interpretations. So, too, does the popular culture of the time. In recent years, I've discovered that students actually get a better feel for those years by watching reruns of sitcoms and other televisions shows. The United States of *Leave It to Beaver* or *The Dick Van Dyke Show* has little in common with the one we live in today. In their world, all families are intact. Everyone is white. Women do not work outside the home. Young people respect their elders. There are few hints of controversy.

Therefore, any description of the core American political culture has to start with three key trends that emphasize the continuity and reasonably smooth history outlined above. In fact, these themes are so deeply ingrained that they are rarely included in the kinds of public opinion polls that have been at the heart of the study of any country's political culture (see, for example, www.pollingreport.com).

First, no more than a tiny minority of Americans has questioned the regime based on the Constitution, since the Civil War. Second, almost all Americans believe that the state should be as small as possible, including those who would like to see it add extensive new programs. Third, **individualism** remains one of Americans' most cherished values.

Events since the early 1960s have eroded parts of the **civic culture**—but only parts of it. Substantial numbers of people would like to see constitutional amendments passed on a number of issues, including a woman's right to choose, same-sex marriage, and a balanced budget. Such support is a far cry from the wholesale changes in the post–World War II years we will see soon in the chapters on France and Germany.

The United States today is a far more divided country than it was a half-century ago. However, the data on political trust presents a slightly different, although perhaps no less discouraging, picture. The decline in overall trust in politics began long before the Obama administration, the rise of the Tea Party, or the looming of the fiscal cliff (see Table 3.2). There have been some ebbs and flows. Nonetheless, the most significant decline began no later than 1970 and probably had more to do with Watergate and Vietnam than the issues that grab the headlines today.

Last but by no means least, none of this suggests that, however unhappy Americans are, many Americans are even thinking of the kind of constitutional reform that would come close to a regime change the likes of which we will see in the chapters on France and Germany.

TABLE 3.2 Declining Support in the United States: Selected Indicators

YEAR	PERCENT GENERALIZED SUPPORT
1960	45
1964	38
1968	30
1972	27
1976	30
1980	27
1984	38
1988	26
1992	34
1996	36
2004	37
2008	26

Source: American National Election Studies (electionstudies.org). Accessed November 28, 2012.

TABLE 3.3 Recent Presidential Elections in the United States (Percentage of the Popular Vote)

YEAR	DEMOCRAT	REPUBLICAN	MAJOR INDEPENDENTS
1964	61.1	38.5	—
1968	42.7	43.3	13.5
1972	37.3	61.3	1.4
1976	50.1	48.8	1.0
1980	41.0	51.0	7.0
1984	40.8	59.2	—
1988	46.0	54.0	—
1992	43.2	37.7	19.0
1996	49.2	42.8	8.0
2000	48.3	48.1	3.6
2004	48.0	51.0	1.0
2008	52.9	45.7	1.4
2012	50.9	47.3	1.8

© Cengage Learning 2015

Democrats: Johnson 1964, Humphrey 1968, McGovern 1972, Carter 1976 and 1980, Mondale 1984, Dukakis 1988, Clinton 1992 and 1996, Gore 2000, Kerry 2004, Obama 2008 and 2012.

Republicans: Goldwater 1964, Nixon 1968 and 1972, Ford 1976, Reagan 1980 and 1984, G. H. Bush 1988 and 1992, Dole 1996, G. W. Bush 2000 and 2004, McCain 2008, Romney 2012.

Major independents: Wallace 1968, Schmitz 1972, McCarthy 1976, Anderson 1980, Perot 1992 and 1996, Nader 2000 and 2004, Nader and Barr 2008, Goode 2012.

Political Participation

A Two-Party System?

The United States is unusual because it only has two parties with a realistic chance of winning elections. Before we consider them, it is important to note ways in which the party system is more complicated than the simple "two-party" label might suggest.

First, the United States does not literally have a two-party system. Many other "third-party" candidates run for the presidency and other offices. Usually, they are little more than historical footnotes. Occasionally, some do well

enough to have an impact on who ends up winning, as was the case most recently with the Perot and Nader candidacies in 1992 and 2000, respectively (see Table 3.3). Similarly, a few independents win elections, including Angus King and Bernard Sanders, who were elected to the Senate in 2012, but even they caucus and usually vote with the Democrats.

Second, in keeping with the diversity of the population and the state's federal structure, American parties are

STAN HONDA/AFP/Getty Images

Barack Obama and Mitt Romney square off at a presidential debate in the 2012 campaign.

far from monolithic. The Republican Party is not made up exclusively of Tea Partiers. Moderate Republicans, for example, may be a vanishing breed, as we saw when Olympia Snowe (R-Maine) announced her decision to retire from the Senate in 2012. On balance, the Democrats and Republicans are both loose and undisciplined coalitions of politicians representing different regions, interests, and ideological points of view. Indeed, it is difficult to think of the American parties as single organizations because they are archetypical catch-all parties and have to be in order to compete in such a diverse country.

Third, while many political scientists historically thought that the two-party system was one of its strengths, more and more now think that it is a major cause of the enduring problems woven into this chapter and more. Thirty years ago, political scientists were worried that parties "failed" because catch-all organizations have a hard time taking clear and innovative positions on burning issues. Today, if the likes of Mann and Ornstein are to be believed, they are a major cause of gridlock because they are so ideological and take positions such extreme that compromises in Congress are all but impossible to work out.

The Democrats

The Democratic Party (www.democrats.org) dates from the 1830s. For most of its history, it has tried to present itself as the party of the "little man." The Democrats have not always been the more left-wing of the two parties. Most of the Progressives of the late nineteenth and early twentieth centuries were Republicans. At that time, the base of **Democratic** support lay in the largely nonideological and corrupt urban machines that mobilized immigrant voters in the urban North and in the white, segregationist South.

The reforms of the 1930s and 1960s changed all that. Now, Democrats champion their party's record in spearheading passage of most progressive reforms of the last century, including the New Deal, the Great Society, and the civil rights laws passed since the 1960s. Today, it claims to support the middle class (one of the vaguest terms in recent political history), environmental protection, and women's and, to a lesser degree, GLBT rights. Under President Obama, the Democrats have gotten the credit and taken the blame for passing the Affordable Care Act and endorsing a more equitable tax system in which the wealthy would pay a fairer share of their income—at least in Democratic eyes.

Mann and Ornstein are more critical of Republicans today, but they are quick to point out that the Democrats were just as polarizing from the late 1960s into the 1980s. Then, dissatisfied voters pulled the party dramatically to the left and led to disastrous defeats in 1972 and the two contests won by President Ronald Reagan in the 1980s. After that, Bill Clinton and others moved the party so far back to the center that the ideological left has disappeared as a viable contender for power inside the party. In fact, mainstream Democrats are often baffled by the anger Tea Partiers and others have for President Obama, who they believe is by no means either on the left or a socialist.

The Republicans

The Republican Party (www.rnc.org) was created in the late 1850s with the merger of a number of parties and other groups,—all of which opposed slavery. After the Civil War, their reconstruction policies alienated most white southerners and led to the creation of legal segregation by Democrats after they returned to power in the last quarter of the nineteenth century.

The Republicans may have lost the South at that point, but they solidified their base of support among upper- and middle-class Protestants in the North and in most of rural America. Republicans supported business interests. At times, however, they did support "good government" reforms such as antitrust economic policies, the use of primary and recall elections, a merit-based civil service system, and nonpartisan local elections.

The Republicans have unquestionably been the more conservative of the two parties since the Great Depression. Because Herbert Hoover's administration could do little to improve the state of the economy, the Republicans took the blame for the wretched conditions and many of them at least tacitly supported President Roosevelt's New Deal.

Although it is hard to remember today, there were prominent moderates in the Republican leadership well into the 1980s. Some of them had a notable impact on the passage of civil rights legislation during the 1960s and the creation of the Environmental Protection Agency a decade later. During the Reagan presidency (1981–1989), the moderates began to be shunted to the party's sidelines. Since then, it has consistently opposed social service legislation, expanding federal budgets, and steps toward more equality at home while supporting a strong defense defined largely through expanded spending on defense.

Mann and Ornstein are certainly right about one thing. While the Democrats have shed themselves of their left wing from the 1970s, which made compromise hard then, it is the Republican center that has disappeared, which makes finding legislative common ground all but impossible today. It also puts the Republican Party in a perilous position if it cannot find a way to appeal to more minority voters, who will play an ever greater role in determining winners and losers at the polls as the country's demographic composition continues to change.

Comparative Emphasis: Conflict

Examining political conflict in the United States is a good way to reveal the critical distinction between the government of the day and the regime.

The United States has seen major protest movements for civil rights, women, and gays on the Left, and against abortion and excessive government spending on the Right. Although most of those efforts have been nonviolent, the United States is hardly immune from confrontation. Some of the individuals and organizers have turned to violence, including the Weathermen faction of the Students for a Democratic Society in the 1960s and a small number of antiabortion activists who have recently been involved in bombing clinics and killing doctors.

However widespread the confrontational and violent protests may be, the protesters rarely question the legitimacy of the regime created by the founders over two hundred years ago. To be sure, some groups, such as the militias, advocate radical change in the constitutional framework. However, there are few such people, and they have virtually no support in the country as a whole. ■

American Elections

The American electoral process shares three features with most of the industrialized democracies. Americans, however, have taken all three of them farther than the others in ways that have led some to question the health of democratic regimes in general.

Limited Engagement

Like voters elsewhere, most Americans are not deeply involved in political life. Few Americans vote. Turnout reached a recent high of 63 percent in the 2008 presidential election. As is almost always the case in congressional elections, only about four in ten people bothered to vote in 2010, which meant that only about twenty percent of the electorate contributed to the Republican landslide that year.

Public opinion polls provide equally depressing evidence about what Americans know about politics. As we will see in the section on media, fewer and fewer people read a daily newspaper or watch the nightly news. Relatively few people have a solid understanding of what is included in proposed legislation. That is true of activists, not just voters. Research on the Tea Party movement showed that many of them were convinced that President Obama was not born in the United States and that the Affordable Health Care Act had provisions for "death panels." Along those same lines, many "occupy" movement members had at most a fuzzy idea of how rich someone had to be to make it into their hated "one percent." Of these three areas, the decline in civic engagement may be the least distinctively American, although it is impossible to tell because it is hard to measure nationally.

Elections "on Steroids"

Even though a German political scientist was the first to use the term, American politicians probably invented and certainly perfected the catch-all party. They have long been the acknowledged global "leaders" in using polling, focus groups, advertising, slogans, and telegenic candidates.

Even more important are the laws that have always allowed American parties and politicians to spend more on election campaigns than anyone else except, possibly, the Japanese. Whatever meaningful limits there were on campaign spending disappeared with the 2010 Supreme Court decision in *Citizens United v. Federal Election Commission*. The Court ruled that most limits on what candidates and others could spend on behalf of either their positions on issues or candidates were unconstitutional. No one knows how much the first election after Citizens United cost, since many of the so-called Super PACs (political action committees) do not have to declare either their contributors or expenses. The best guess is that total spending for all federal, state, and local races that year topped $6 billion. In my state of Virginia, the two candidates and outside groups spent over $130 million on the Senate race or more than $35 for every voter.

It was hard to escape the ads. It was also hard to miss how negative and how inaccurate many of them were. It is never easy to say anything meaningful in a thirty-second ad. However, the negative tone and the slanted and often misleading messages were among the unpopular campaign's least popular features.

The 2012 election also gave new importance to the electronic media. The role of Facebook, Twitter, and other social media software was a frequent topic in the news coverage. Even more significant was the way Obama's campaign (but not Romney's) was able to use information technology tools to identify likely voters and then get them to the polls in their vaunted "ground game."

Comparative Emphasis: Women in American Politics

The modern feminist movement began as part of the new Left in the 1960s. Since then, American women have been in the forefront of what has become a global effort to take the "men" out of statements like "all men are created equal."

The political accomplishments of American women have been substantial but have fallen far short of what many feminists hope for. For example, twenty of the one hundred senators in 2013 are women, but that is still only twenty percent of the total. Women made up 17 percent of the members of Congress elected in 2010, which left the United States tied for eighty-second in the world, with Morocco and Venezuela.

Few Americans are against having more women in public office. The same is not true of what conservatives often call the "feminist agenda." Indeed, the right to choose (or to life, depending on your perspective), support for affirmative action, and opposition to sexual violence are among the "hot button" issues in American political life and are more controversial than they are in most other democracies.

One offshoot of the women's movement is the one to extend equal rights to the increasingly vocal GLBT community. The issues they champion are even more controversial, although the growing support for same-sex marriage suggests that the tide may be turning on this issue. ■

When most voters have a strong sense of party identification, people tend to vote according to those loyalties, especially in contests that don't draw a lot of public attention. In that sense, party identification is not terribly different than the loyalty you may feel toward your favorite brand of car or to my unwavering preference for Macs over Windows PCs, even though there are almost no differences between them these days.

However, when voters are not in synch with the parties, they tend to dealign and loosen or even abandon the ties that psychologically predispose them to vote for one of the two major parties. When this happens, elections are far more volatile because voters are "freer" to shift from one party to the other.

There have been a number of periods in American history when voters disengaged from their parties until they redefined their positions on key issues, which set off a dramatic realignment of voter affiliations and a new stable distribution of party identification. At those times, parties often change their appeals, and entire blocks of voters change their affiliations, as African Americans did by moving to the Democrats during and after the civil rights movement.

Since then, there has been more dealignment than realignment. The number of independents has grown from 23 percent in 1964 to 40 percent in 2008, the last year for which we have National Election Study data. The growth in the number of independents only tells part of the story since ninety percent of regular voters admit to at least "leaning" toward one party or the other, which is why the 2012 campaign was a contest for the support of a relatively small number of undecided voters.

Below that apparent stability, there have been widespread shifts among certain groups. Table 3.4 lists the groups among whom Obama or Romney won at least

Then, of course, there is the question of whether the campaign "on steroids" made much of a difference in the outcome. All the signs are that it probably did not.

Realignment

American political scientists coined two terms that are central to the study of elections in all industrialized democracies—**party identification** and **realignment**. Party identification measures the strength of a person's long-term attachment to one party or another, if any. Historically, when the parties have been relatively strong, most Americans thought of themselves as Democrats or Republicans. Most voters who claimed to be independents admitted to "leaning" toward one party or the other.

TABLE 3.4 Social Groups in Which President Obama and Former Governor Romney Won At Least 55 Percent of the Vote

OBAMA	ROMNEY
Women	Men
Blacks	White
Hispanics	Over 65 years old
Asians	Income over $100,000
Under 30 years old	Small city or rural
Income under $50,000	Married
Graduate degree	
Big city	
Single	
Gay, lesbian, or bisexual	

Source: Based on The New York Times. http://elections.nytimes.com/2012/results/president/exit-polls. Accessed 30 November 2012.

55 percent of the vote, which are typical of what we have seen at least since the Reagan presidency. Obama did best among women, racial minorities, the poor, and single people. Romney did best among the wealthy (although not the best educated), men, Whites, and Evangelical Christians, who were not included in the study the table was drawn from. Those results are typical of what pollsters have found in every election since before the start of this century.

Despite the importance of catch-all parties, the American electorate is more deeply divided than it has been in decades, which helps explain the gridlock in Washington. The 2000 election was only decided when the Supreme Court decided in *Bush v Gore* to give the state of Florida, and thus the election, to George W. Bush, who actually trailed in the popular vote nationwide. Bush won more easily in 2004, but a swing of 200,000 votes in Ohio would have given the victory to then Senator John Kerry. The two presidential elections since then have not been as close, but the way people voted reveals how ideological and cultural differences leave the two parties with very different regional and social bases.

The polarization is even more pronounced in congressional races, in which the partisan balance is also just about even. In 2012, for example, the Republicans retained control of the House of Representatives even though the Democrats won slightly more votes nationwide. That anomalous result occurred because of the way state legislatures redraw district lines after the census is published every ten years. Because Republicans controlled a majority of the states, they determined most of the new boundaries and often did so in a way that favored their candidates. Even more telling is the fact that lines are also drawn to protect incumbents. As a result, most observers thought that no more than 75 of the 435 congressional races were truly competitive in 2012.

Beyond Voting

American political scientists were almost certainly the first ones to use the term interest group. And the United States has an organized group for almost every interest you can imagine. In fact, I work for one!

Interest groups played a central role in creating the dysfunctional mess Mann and Ornstein and others worry about. Depending on your point of view, the unions, environmentalists, and women's groups "forced" the Democrats into wasteful spending during President Obama's first term. Or big businesses funded the Republican attack ads that made living in a swing state all but unbearable yet did not seem to affect the outcome of many races in 2012.

On one level, it might make sense to provide an overview of them all here, but doing so would not add much to what we have already seen. However, concentrating on four of them will help deepen your understanding of the logjam in American politics.

Comparative Emphasis: Controversy and Bias

The author of a book like this cannot and should not avoid controversial issues. There is no better example of that than the material on the few pages just before and after this box.

How could an author write a textbook including a chapter on America politics today and not include the Tea Party, the Occupy movement, gay rights, racism, the fiscal cliff, climate change, or immigration?

I try to handle the thorny question of authorial bias here and elsewhere by presenting the material in a way that lets you reach your own conclusions. I have clear and strong views on these issues and almost everything else in this book. However, my job is not to convince you that I'm right. Instead, I want to give you the tools to help you make up your own mind on those many occasions when you are likely to disagree with me, your instructor, or your friends. ■

Super PACS

Although it is hard to measure such things, there is no doubt that the wealthy have more influence than the poor in all industrialized democracies. The *Citizens United* decision and other trends have sparked the emergence of Super PACs, most of which support conservative causes.

Their impact became impossible to miss during the 2012 election campaign. Each campaign had at least one supposedly unrelated Super PAC that spent around $100 million.

Perhaps more important for our purposes here are organizations like American Crossroads, which operates as a conventional interest group as well as a source of campaign funds. It is led by George W. Bush's chief strategist, Karl Rove. Some analysts argue that another conservative group, Freedom Works, largely created the Tea Party movement.

The Tea Party

The loosely organized group of Tea Party movements burst onto the political scene during the campaign for the 2010 mid-term congressional elections when candidates they supported won at least seventy-five House seats in the most dramatic Republican victory in a generation. Their brand of conservatism should not have taken us by surprise, however. Over the last thirty to fifty years, a number of once small conservative groups increasingly found common ground with each other out of their common hostility toward the changes in American government and culture since the 1960s. All existed before President Obama's election, but he quickly became a symbol of just about everything they disliked, which galvanized unprecedented unity among conservative voters.

First, and probably least important today, is a longstanding strand in conservative foreign policy that dates at least to the height of the cold war. Some on the right (most recently libertarians close to Rep. Ron Paul or the Cato Institute) have long had isolationist tendencies, which lead them to want to avoid an active international role for the United States. Most conservatives, though, have favored a strong defense, which led them to support arms buildups during the cold war and the maintenance of a strong military ever since. Whether on Israel, Iran, North Korea, or Cuba, most Tea Partiers can trace their ideological roots back to those who worry about the risks of appeasement.

Whatever their views on foreign policy, conservatives have long been hostile to what they think of as "big government" even though the American state actually does less than the ones in the other industrialized democracies. Many Tea Party activists are older and fit the socioeconomic profile of the materialist voters discussed in Chapter 2. Some, but not all, of them oppose abortion, gay marriage, and other issues near and dear to the religious right. A smaller number of them are influenced by libertarian economic thought and by anti-tax groups such as Grover Norquist's Americans for Tax Reform.

Analysts reach two broad conclusions about the Tea Party in ways that reflect the ideological preferences of the observers. Tea Party supporters portray it as a grassroots movement. Critics tend to see it largely as a byproduct of the organized conservative right, including the Super PACs discussed above.

The Tea Party, per se, may prove to be a flash in the pan. The movement has never been well organized. Public support for it has declined in the polls. Candidates associated with it did not do very well in 2012. Tea Party support cost Republicans victory in five or six Senate seats in 2010 and 2012, which, together, would have given the party control over both houses of Congress. Whatever happens to the Tea Party itself, there is no question that it has tapped into widespread frustration on the conservative end of the political spectrum, which is not about to disappear.

Tea Party activist in full regalia.

Jeff Malet Photography/Newscom

The Occupy Movement

The Tea Party may well be the new conservative movement of this century that best fits the image of the materialist voter. The men and women who occupied Wall Street and whose protest spread to most major cities around the country less obviously embody postmaterialist values.

Left-wing voters might not have seemed to be as angry as the Tea Partiers were in 2010. After all, President Obama was widely seen as a liberal Democrat whose party controlled both houses of Congress.

Nonetheless, the recession hit young people particularly hard. Jobs were scarce. Student loans had to be repaid. Then, the Obama administration seemed to many to bend over backward to help the banks and other financial firms get through the crisis while not helping the poor or anyone else.

In early 2011, small groups of veteran leftist activists began organizing demonstrations that culminated in Occupy Wall Street and the takeover of nearby Zuccotti Park.

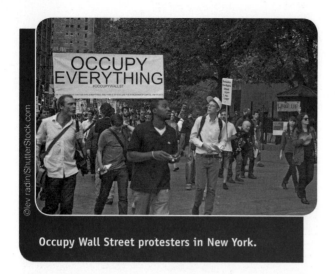

Occupy Wall Street protesters in New York.

The movement spread to dozens of other cities where similar occupations took place. With the exception of Oakland, California, the protesters initiated little or no violence. The Occupiers rarely made crystal clear demands and were best known for their claim to represent the "99 percent," which, as they saw it, included everyone who was hurt by the recession and ignored by Wall Street, corporate heavyweights, and the Obama administration.

Demographically, the Occupy activists had almost nothing in common with the "Tea Party Patriots." Most were young. Most shunned any involvement with organized political groups and did not have the equivalent of the conservative interest groups to turn to had they wanted to.

Like the Tea Party movement, the Occupy movement may become a historical footnote. However, the frustration with an elite that has not apparently done much to meet the needs of young people, who, among other things, fear they will not enjoy the same quality of life that their parents' generation does, is not likely to disappear.

The Interruptors

Guns are an important part of many American social problems. There are nearly 300 million weapons in circulation or more than one for every adult citizen. In 2009, more than 31,000 Americans were shot to death (including 10,000 suicides). More than twice that many survived gunshot wounds. In the week including the Newtown tragedy, 158 people died as a result of shootings in the United States—130 more than were killed on that dreadful morning. The Newtown attack was at least the fiftieth mass shooting incident in this century.

One new approach to teen violence that has shown considerably promise and is engendering political support is championed by Cure Violence (www.cureviolence. org), which began as an attempt to stop teen shootings in particularly dangerous neighborhoods in Chicago and was featured on a PBS *Frontline* episode in 2012 (http://www .pbs.org/wgbh/pages/frontline/interrupters/). Cure Violence confronts teen violence in the same way physicians treat epidemics. It hires a team of local activists to stop crises from turning violent. Most of those "interrupters" are themselves veterans of gang wars; many are former prison inmates. Once the immediate crisis is defused, the interrupters and social service and mental health professionals address the root causes of the violence itself, such as dysfunctional families, poor job prospects, addiction, problems reintegrating released prisoners, and so on. In its original Chicago neighborhood, deadly violence has been cut by two-thirds in the last few years.

Since 2010, the model has been implemented in more than fifteen other American cities. Cure Violence specialists have also worked with the U.S. State Department and other partners in Palestine, Kenya, Iraq, Central America, and Northern Ireland.

The Weak American State

Chapter 2 made the stark claim that the U.S. has a weak state vis-à-vis the other industrialized democracies. Statements like that tend to confuse people who aren't trained political scientists. After all, the United States is the world's only superpower and seems able to exert its influence wherever and whenever it wants.

That does not mean that the United States has a strong state when it comes to the kinds of domestic issues comparativists are most interested in. The American government has taken on fewer social and economic responsibilities, adopted them later when it has chosen to enact them, and proceeded in a less comprehensive and effective manner— even before the gridlock of the last decade set in.

The weak state is no accident. It was built into the system the Framers created. They wanted multiple, overlapping layers of authority so that no one person, group, or party could get everything it wants, which some political scientists call **pluralism**.

The Legislative Process

To begin seeing that, consider the way Richard Neustadt started his path-breaking book on presidential power:

> In the early summer of 1952, before the heat of the campaign, President [Harry S.] Truman used to

contemplate the problems of the general-become-president should Eisenhower win the forthcoming election.

"He'll sit here," Truman would remark (tapping his desk for emphasis), "and he'll say, 'Do this! Do that!' And nothing will happen. Poor Ike—it won't be a bit like the Army. He'll find it very frustrating." Eisenhower evidently found it so.[3]

Presidents before and after Truman have all learned that there are very few things a president can do on his own, because, as Neustadt went on to put it, the president's power is the power to persuade.

The president has the authority to do a number of things on his own, including the right to issue executive orders under certain circumstances. Nonetheless, the American president spends more time persuading than most democratic leaders because he lacks the institutional leverage most leaders in parliamentary systems take for granted. The president is little more than the most important person in a complicated "game" of political give and take with people acting in at least a dozen different bodies whose members often have no compelling reason to do what the president wants.

The president's difficulties start with his own administration. He appoints over four thousand men and women to policy-making positions, about a quarter of whom require Senate confirmation before assuming their office. Simply finding that many qualified people is difficult and time consuming. Many political appointees know less about the policy areas they will be working on than the civil servants who hold comparable positions in Europe.

Coordinating an administration and its policies is made all the more difficult by the fact that lines of authority are not clearly drawn. For example, the Departments of Defense, State, and Energy and the Director of National Intelligence all make policies designed to prevent the proliferation of nuclear weapons. Even more telling, the creation of a single Department of Homeland Security required the merger of dozens of agencies previously housed in several different departments, ranging from Defense to the Treasury.

Over the last century or so, the president has assumed the task of setting the national agenda, even when the opposition party controls at least one house of Congress. Despite highly visible congressional initiatives such as the budget plan initiated by Representative Paul Ryan (R-WI) before he become Mitt Romney's vice-presidential nominee, most major legislative proposals emanate from the White House.

Once a presidential proposal is formally introduced as a bill (officially by a sponsor in each house), it faces its most serious hurdle, Congress itself. Legislating is particularly difficult when one party controls the presidency and the other has a majority in at least one house of Congress. Even when a single party controls both the legislative and executive branches, passing legislation is a messy process (http://thomas.loc.gov).

In order to pass, any bill must be approved at each of the multiple, independent decision-making points outlined in Figure 2.2 on p. 42. When a bill is submitted, it goes through a ceremonial first reading. Then, it "goes to committee" where the hard work is done. Usually—but by no means always—a single committee in each house has jurisdiction on the subject matter contained in a given bill. In the much larger House of Representatives, the bill usually goes to one or more subcommittees before being passed on to one or more full committees.

The first thing the committees have to do is decide whether to consider a bill at all. If it chooses not to, the bill dies on the spot. If the committee does consider a bill, it often does research and holds extensive hearings, some of which are televised on C-SPAN (www.cspan.org). After that, the committee "marks up" the bill. Despite what those words may suggest, this is not merely an editorial task. More often than not, major portions of the proposed legislation are eliminated or replaced with entirely new provisions.

The same thing can happen to the bill when and if it reaches the full House and Senate after favorable committee action. More amendments can usually be offered, and once again, a negative vote or a failure to take up a bill can kill it outright, which has happened with great frequency of late in the Senate, where sixty votes are needed to break a filibuster.

The House and Senate almost never pass identical versions of a bill. Therefore, their two texts are sent to a conference committee where members from both houses attempt to "iron out" the differences. When and if the conference committee does so, the new version of the bill is returned to both houses, which have yet another opportunity to vote on it.

Only then does the bill go to the president for his signature or veto. If he signs a bill, it becomes law. If he refuses to do so, the bill returns to Congress where a two-thirds majority in each house is required to override the veto.

In principle, the same thing can happen in parliamentary systems. All have committees, floor debates, and votes. But because prime ministers can almost always count on keeping their majority intact because of strict party discipline, their legislative initiatives are normally passed quickly and without major changes.

---

[3]Richard Neustadt, *Presidential Power: The Politics of Leadership* (New York: Wiley, 1960), 9.

American members of Congress do not have to toe the party line, no matter how hard the party whips may try to compel them to do so. Five main factors shape the way members vote, and the presidency is only one of them.

He is the first—and usually the most important—one. The White House Congressional Liaison Office regularly lobbies on Capitol Hill. Whenever a bill the president is especially interested in nears a final vote that is likely to be close, the nightly news shows a parade of senators and representatives visiting the White House. But the president's power to persuade in this respect is always limited. He can threaten to oppose legislation members are personally interested in or even try to block their reelection. As the difficulties in securing passage of the Affordable Care Act in 2010 show, even when the Democrats have a comfortable majority in both houses, he has to assume that he will not get everything he wants.

A distant second is the party. Both parties' whips try to convince members to follow their leadership's wishes. Voting the party line can help advance a member's career and can even help win support for a bill he or she is sponsoring. Party discipline was unusually tight during the 113th Congress in 2011 and 2012. Republicans rarely broke ranks to support legislation introduced by President Obama. Similarly, the paper-thin Democratic majority in the Senate usually held. However, the experience of those two years was very much the exception to the rule. In more typical times, a substantial number of representatives and senators break party ranks on most pieces of legislation.

Third are other members of Congress. Senators and representatives cannot stay on top of all pending legislation, especially on matters that neither they nor their own constituents have a particular interest in. Consequently, members often defer to their colleagues who care deeply about the legislative outcome. My member of Congress in Northern Virginia no longer has many farmers in his district. Therefore, if a fellow Democrat favors a piece of legislation that would help debt-ridden small farmers, Congressman Moran will usually go along. One downside of this trend is the billions of dollars that are still being spent on individual members' pet projects through "earmarks" such as the one that authorized building the infamous bridge to nowhere in Alaska.

Fourth, there is an important link between members and their constituents. Voters are not likely to elect someone who does not share their views about important local issues. In addition, members tend to keep the people back home happy both by voting the "right way" and by providing services to their communities and constituents. Their staff members conduct polls, track constituent mail, and follow the press back home to get a sense of where voters stand on the issues. Some critics argue that members can never really know what all of their constituents want and end up paying the most attention to the donors who fund their ever more expensive campaigns. Whoever they end up listening to the most, representatives and senators rarely cast votes that are at odds with what they think their constituents want. That helps explain why the vast majority of House members, in particular, are reelected even though only about 10 percent of the public now says it trusts Congress as a whole.

Less Popular than Congress

In 2012, popular support for Congress reached an all time low.

Therefore, the Public Policy Polling firm decided to find out just how little the American public thought of Congress. They asked a sample of voters to rank Congress on the same scale as other well-known institutions and personalities. At least in that poll, Congress was less popular than root canals, colonoscopies, cockroaches, NFL replacement referees, used car salesmen, Genghis Khan, Donald Trump, and France.

Not all the news was bad. Congress was more popular than the Kardashian twins, North Korea, meth labs, Fidel Castro, and lobbyists.

But, then, at a total support rate of 10 percent, it could not have outpolled them by much.

Finally, there are the members' own views. Americans expect senators and representatives to exercise their judgment at least on matters that are not important locally. There are, however, some examples of members voting their conscience against their constituents' wishes—as, for example, the late Senator William Fulbright (D-Ark.) did in supporting civil rights legislation during the 1960s. In the current senate, for example, Rand Paul (R-KY) is known for supporting libertarian views he shares with his father, Congressman and former presidential candidate Ron Paul (R-TX).

In sum, the American state usually cannot enact legislation quickly or coherently even when the same party controls the White House and Capitol Hill. Instead, policy making tends to be slow and lead to limited changes.

It is hard to see how it could be otherwise. There are simply too many decision-making points, and a group only has to win at one of them to block change.

With but very few exceptions, this is the way the legislative process has always worked on domestic issues (see the section on foreign policy below). On rare occasions, the government has been able to act decisively during times of crisis, as it did most recently with the swift passage of the USA Patriot Act in the aftermath of 9/11. Normally, however, it takes months or years before a bill passes and then it does so in a form that bears little resemblance to the one initially introduced. To cite but one example, it took Congress a decade to pass the Civil Rights Act of 1964 after the Supreme Court decided that segregated schools were inherently unequal in *Brown v Board of Education.*

Some political scientists think that this tradition of slowly reaching compromise that yields only incremental change has served the United States well. It is not easy to make that case today as the government struggles to respond to global recession and the many other problems of the early twenty-first century.

The Rest of the Weak State

The other countries covered in Part 2 have parliamentary systems and have been able to avoid their own version of gridlock in recent years, which helps explain why many political scientists think they have stronger states. However, there is more to any such analysis, which we can see by briefly considering three other factors that weaken the American state.

First is the bureaucracy. Only some of the presidential appointees are experts in their field and step into their jobs ready to go. Even the best-prepared members of his team have to rely on senior civil servants who are subject matter experts and retain their jobs from administration to administration. Members of the Senior Executive Service are as well trained and hardworking as their European counterparts. However, in keeping with the tradition of a weak state, they do not play as important a role in policy making as their European counterparts. By contrast, official policymakers try to maintain a hands-off relationship with civil servants who, in turn, are legally prohibited from taking part in partisan politics while employed by the government and from taking certain policy-related jobs after they retire.

Second, the United States is one of the few countries whose courts have the power of judicial review. The Supreme Court and lower federal and state courts can rule on the constitutionality of government actions to the point that judicial decisions have often served as important turning points in the evolution of American public policy. The most striking examples in recent years have to do with civil rights. It was a Supreme Court decision (*Plessy v Ferguson*) that initially upheld Southern laws segregating blacks and whites in 1896. Another decision almost sixty years later (*Brown v Board of Education*) overturned the doctrine of "separate but equal" and also served as a major catalyst for the modern civil rights movement. Since the 1980s, a more conservative Court has issued a series of decisions that sharply limited affirmative action.

Third, the United States is a federal system, which means that Washington shares power with state and local governments. Most other liberal democracies have unitary states in which the central government legally is sovereign, although it may delegate some of its powers to subnational units by law. In the United States, the Constitution grants state and local governments wide responsibilities which today includes most education policy, the administration of social services, and the management of elections.

Public Policy

American cultural qualms about an active state and the fragmented nature of its institutions have resulted in a government that does less than those in most of the other liberal democracies. There is, of course, one exception. No country comes close to matching American involvement in world affairs. However, even there, we will see plenty of evidence of the weak and fragmented state.

Domestic Issues

In recent years, discussion of American social policy has focused on health care. Most middle-class and wealthy Americans receive top-notch medical treatment because they can afford good insurance and can pay for services the policies do not cover. However, more than 45 million uninsured Americans had to fend for themselves, making it the only industrialized democracy that does not provide at least basic health care coverage for everyone. Although the Affordable Care Act will eventually narrow the gap between the well- and the underinsured, the new programs will still not cover as many people or as many services as the Canadian or any western Europe government's programs.

It would be one thing if it were just health care. Unemployment compensation and pension payments are below the Organisation for Economic Co-operation and Development (OECD) average. So, too, is the minimum wage. Publicly supported mass transit systems are almost never found outside major urban areas, and the passenger rail system is a shadow of its former self.

A slightly different picture emerges when we shift to economic management. American liberals are correct when they point out that the American government does less. Conservatives are also right that the United States has an active government that does try to manage and steer the overall economy—and intervenes far too much from their perspective.

How can we reconcile both points of view? In terms of finding agreement on what should be done, there probably is little common ground. However, liberal and conservative explanations of what the government actually does have their roots in everything we have seen so far in this chapter.

The lack of a strong left-wing party or trade union movement helps explain why the United States has a less extensive and less integrated system of social service programs and is also one of the reasons why the distribution of income and wealth is so skewed in favor of the relatively well to do. Also related to the lack of a strong socialist tradition is the American commitment to individualism and suspicion of an interventionist state. In the language used by many democratic theorists, Americans are more interested in ensuring equality of opportunity than they are in equality of outcomes. Whatever their ideological beliefs, almost all Americans agree with one statement that is at the heart of its political culture: the government that governs least governs best.

Liberals and conservatives alike both find fault with what they believe is the ineffectual way the American government intervenes in overall economic policy making. Other than a few libertarians, both, however, realize that given domestic and global realities, the state has no choice but to act economically.

Critics of pluralism on both the left and right say that the fragmentation built into the system in 1787 has a lot to do with why it cannot act coherently in economic or any other sphere of policy making. Given the number of independent decision-making points discussed earlier, it could hardly be otherwise. Even if a president submits a coherent proposal (whatever we mean by that), the compromises made along the way sap it of much of the logic that held it together.

The Tea Party and Occupy activists also remind us that not all groups have equal access to the give and take of congressional and bureaucratic policy making. Whatever their differences, they are convinced that people like "us" (the 99 percent or the hard-working Americans as the case may be) are frozen out, while the super-rich or power-hungry Washington career politicians get what they want—at "our" expense.

Foreign Policy

At first glance, American foreign policy seems less chaotic, and few people worry about having too strong a state—especially among conservatives. The United States is the only country that acts as if it could and should be involved in any foreign policy issue on the face of the earth. There is a fair amount of arrogance to the American assumption that it can act anywhere and everywhere. However, one of the consequences of being the world's only superpower is captured in my colleague Colonel Christopher Holshek's statement at the end of Chapter 1—that what happens over there does matter over here, and it is no longer possible to completely distinguish between foreign and domestic policy.

But it isn't as simple as that. The Left and Right come close to switching positions when it comes to foreign policy. The Left wants the state to do less, especially by resisting the temptation to intervene in the internal affairs of other countries whenever possible. By contrast, the Right is more inclined to accept a strong military and arguments that equate peace and strength.

Even more important, America's role abroad also reflects the fragmented, pluralistic decision making, discussed in the section on domestic policy, and the disproportionate influence of a few, usually wealthy, actors. Consider the following three brief but controversial examples:

- It has been all but impossible to cut funding for strategic missile defense programs because defense contractors and Congress have made certain that jobs in every district would be threatened if the program were discontinued.

- Despite virtual unanimity among serious scientists, well-funded conservative interest groups have been able to block most attempts to address global warming while expanding efforts to exploit domestic deposits of fossil fuels.

- Even though Jews only make up about four percent of the total population, the so-called Israel lobby has a disproportionate interest on American policy toward the Middle East.

The Media

Of all the countries covered in this book, the United States is the one on which the most research on feedback has been done. The results are mixed but are worrisome whatever one's ideological perspective. Although there has been an explosion in the number and type of media available, there has actually been a sharp decline in the quantity and quality of the political news most Americans pay attention to.

Readership of quality newspapers and magazines is down. Most people rely primarily on television news for their political information, and the consensus among researchers is that network television does a less effective job of covering "serious" political news than it once did. To make matters even worse, fewer and fewer people are watching the news now that cable and direct satellite broadcasters give them dozens of other options during the slots the networks and local stations typically reserve for it.

Last but by no means least, American politicians are the acknowledged world masters at the art of spin doctoring, or packaging their statements and actions in ways they think people will find most attractive, and often hiding the real import of the activity in the process. They do rely heavily on public opinion polls and focus groups, but one has to question how valuable these are for a public that is increasingly disinterested in political life and whose views are shaped by the spin doctors themselves.

As a Frame of Reference

There is a lot missing from this chapter, including the differences between the House of Representatives and the Senate, the Electoral College, and pressures for tax and campaign finance reform, not to mention the five big questions. Adding more material would take most readers—especially those who have had a course in American politics—more deeply into American political dynamics than they need to go. Doing so might also obscure the key point being made here: that the United States has an atypical democracy and readers would be well advised to limit how much they use it as a frame of reference, for reasons we are about to see.

KEY TERMS

American exceptionalism
Obama, Barack
civic culture
compromise
Democratic
individualism

judicial review
new Left
new Right
realignment
party identification
pluralism

Republican
separation of powers
sequestration
unitary state

USEFUL WEBSITES

There are literally thousands of websites on politics in the United States. No one site can hope to link users to everything. One of the best sites is maintained by the British academic Richard Kimber at the University of Keele.

> http://www.politicsresources.net/area/usa.htm

The White House and Thomas (run by the Library of Congress) provide gateways to the executive and legislative branches.

> www.whitehouse.gov

> http://thomas.loc.gov

The Supreme Court also has its own site, but, in my opinion, the one maintained by Cornell University's Law School is better.

> www.law.cornell.edu/supct/index.html

Polling Report is the best online source for public opinion data. Vote Smart provides nonpartisan, unbiased information on pending issues to help voters make up their minds, and it does so in a quirky way that students, at least my students, love. The Public Agenda Foundation does much the same in analyzing policy issues themselves. Five Thirty Eight burst on the scene in 2008 making projections based on statistical techniques its owner developed to model likely baseball outcomes.

> www.pollingreport.com

> www.vote-smart.org

> www.publicagenda.org

> www.fivethirtyeight.com

FURTHER READING

Ambrose, Stephen, with Douglas Brinkley. *The Rise to Globalism*, 8th ed. New York: Penguin Books, 1997. The best short volume outlining global history since World War II.

Gitlin, Todd. *Occupy Nation*. New York: Harper Collins, 2012. An intriguing book by one of the leaders of the 1960s Students for a Democratic Society, who later became a leading academic sociologist.

Hacker, Andrew. *Two Nations: Black and White, Separate, Hostile, Unequal*. New York: Scribner, 1992. A brief but comprehensive book on the sorry state of race relations in the United States.

Kabaservice, Geoffrey. *Rule and Ruin: The Downfall of Moderation and the Destruction of the Republican Party from Eisenhower to the Tea Party*. New York: Oxford University Press, 2012. A persuasive lament about the decline of Republican moderates but written by a scholar/journalist with close ties to the party.

Mann, Thomas, and Norman Ornstein. *It's Even Worse Than It Looks*. New York: Basic Books, 2012. By far the best book on the current crisis in American politics, by two veteran observers, one normally associated with the Left and the other with the Right.

Neustadt, Richard. *Presidential Power: The Politics of Leadership*. New York: Wiley, 1960. The classic book on the presidency. It has been republished in several new editions since 1960.

Putnam, Robert D. *Bowling Alone: The Collapse and Revival of American Community*. New York: Simon & Schuster, 2000. The most thorough and most controversial book on declining civic engagement in the United States.

Reid, T. R. *The Healing of America*. New York: Penguin 2009. The most sweeping book on the politics of health care, which may become the most sweeping issue facing all of the industrialized democracies.

Shipler, David K. *The Working Poor*. New York: Knopf, 2004. The best recent work on poverty in the United States.

Skocpol, Theda, and Vanessa Williamson. *The Tea Party and the Remaking of Republican Conservatism*. New York: Oxford University Press, 2011. By far the best (and most readable) academic work on this new phenomenon in American politics.

Tocqueville, Alexis de. *Democracy in America*. New York: Vintage Books, 1945. The classic account of American life by a French traveler and theorist, written in the 1830s.

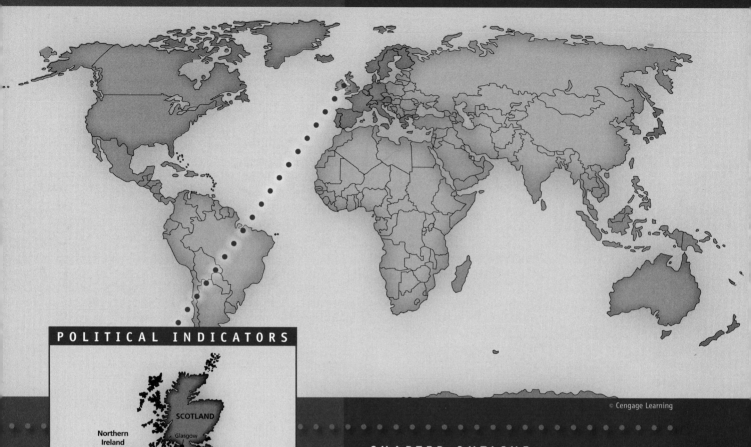

© Cengage Learning

POLITICAL INDICATORS

SCOTLAND

Northern
Ireland

Glasgow

Edinburgh

Belfast

REPUBLIC
OF
IRELAND

Manchester

WALES

Birmingham

ENGLAND

Cardiff

London

GOVERNANCE (score 0–1)	HUMAN DEVELOPMENT (score 0–1)	DEMOCRACY (rank)	PEACE (rank)	CORRUPTION (rank)
.793	.863	16	29	18

4

The United Kingdom

The British happened to the rest of the world. Now the rest of the world happens to Britain.

ANDREW MARR

THE BASICS

The United Kingdom

Size	244,820 sq. km (about the size of California)
Population	63 million
Ethnicity	92% White, 8% other
Religion	72% Christian, 5% other, 23% none
GDP per capita	$36,500
Currency	1£ = US$1.53 (August 3, 2013)
Head of State	Queen Elizabeth II (1953–)
Head of Government	David Cameron (2010–)

Pasty-Gate

Most chapters start with a major story that easily lends itself to discussions of the big issues about that country. Not this one. It begins with a story that is so unimportant that my British colleagues laughed uproariously when I told them I was starting with Pasty-gate. Yet, more than any other issue in the news in 2012 (including the British version of the fiscal cliff), it opens the intellectual door to everything that follows.

In late March 2012, the chancellor of the Exchequer (the equivalent of the American Secretary of the Treasury), George Osborne, set off a furor[1] by announcing that in its next budget the government would include a 20 percent tax on pasties and other take-out food, which was certain to pass given the government's secure majority in the House of Commons.

A pasty (pronounced *pass tea*) is a less than nutritious meat-filled pastry, which many working-class people eat for lunch. There are many kinds of pasties, but the most famous ones were first made in Wales and consist of a folded-up triangle of dough filled with lightly seasoned chopped beef, potato, onion, and rutabaga (which the British call swede). Pasties were a bargain at about $1.50 apiece.

Neither the cost nor the nutritional value of the pasty was at issue. The tax was. Not only would it be a burden on the mostly poor people who eat pasties for lunch, but it would be accompanied by a reduction of the overall income tax rate on the wealthiest citizens from 50 to 45 percent.

The controversy then took on more comic proportions. Osborne backed down a bit. Cold pasties would not

---

[1]To reinforce the fact that British and American English are not the same, they spell the word "furore" and pronounce it "furor—ee."

A Cornish pasty, a fork showing its relative size.

be taxed. Only preheated ones would be. As part of their coverage, journalists flocked to Greggs, the pasty shop closest to Osborne's elegant London home. One electrical technician told *The New York Times*, "We cannot all afford to pay £3 (about $5) a day for a sandwich lunch."[2] Prime Minister **David Cameron** (1966–) said he always ate a pasty when he visited Wales. It turns out that the shop he said he visited closed in 2007. The recently weakened Labour Party tried to turn Pasty-gate into a class issue, which was not hard given the fact that Cameron and Osborne are wealthy products of the country's top private schools and universities.

Pasty-gate was an unusual issue that arose at an unusual time in British politics. When it broke, the Cameron government had been in trouble for the two years since its victory in the 2010 election.

For the first time since the 1920s, the country had a coalition government because no party came close to winning a majority of the seats in the all-powerful House of Commons in 2010. Cameron's Conservatives had been forced to share power with the Liberal Democrats. The two parties had handily defeated Labour, which had been in power for thirteen years. Most voters thought they had run out of new ideas and blamed them for the country's failure to successfully tackle the global recession which was already in place when **Gordon Brown** (1951–) took over the prime ministry from **Tony Blair** (1953–) in 2009. Although coalition governments are decidedly not the norm in Great Britain, the two parties agreed that they

would keep the coalition alive at least until the next election, which had to be held by 2015.

That was important because support for the government was plummeting in large part because it had adopted strict economic austerity policies. As we will see in detail later, both government spending and tax rates for the wealthy were slashed in an attempt to restart the economy and create new jobs. By early 2012, it was clear that Cameron's policies were not working either and that the country was heading back into what economists call a "double dip" recession. Polls conducted even before the humble pasty made the front page of *The New York Times* showed the **Tories** (as the Conservatives are also known) trailing by 10 percent, a gap they have done little to close since then.

The saga of the pasty shows us many differences between the United States and Great Britain. Unlike President Obama, Cameron and the rest of the coalition had had no problem getting their legislative agenda approved. Because the country is far more centralized, almost all key tax rates are determined by the national government in London. And, of course, Cameron's government had started with policies that were as different from those endorsed by the Obama administration as one could imagine. While this chapter will stress those and other differences, we will also highlight three ways in which British and American politics have a lot in common.

First, the great recession dominates political life in both countries today. Like the 2008 and 2012 presidential races in the United States, the British general election of 2010 was largely a referendum on the policies of the outgoing government. Furthermore, the fact that Keynesian policies have had problems in the United States while more market-oriented ones have fared little better in the United Kingdom suggest that both countries are in the midst of a period of economic uncertainty because national political leaders do not seem able to do much about the economy.

Second, despite those problems there is next to no discussion of making fundamental change in the British or American regimes. To be sure, the British have some constitutional issues on their political plate, including their relationship with Europe and the distribution of power among the country's regions. Nonetheless, proposals for profound changes in the Westminster system, which, in many ways, is much older than the American Constitution, are not on the political horizon.

Finally, few of the five big questions raised in Chapter 1 are central to political life there today, although one could easily make the case that they should be. The British do have to deal with aspects of globalization as part of their continuing debate over membership in the European Union. Identity issues are on the table, involving both demands for regional autonomy and the impact of the changing composition of the British population, but have not produced even the degree of soul searching one finds in the United States. The pace of change, human security, resilience, and the reconsideration of democratic practice are for all intents and purposes missing from the national agenda.

Thinking about Great Britain

Fifty years ago, Britain was included in comparative politics textbooks for four related reasons. First, it was the incubator, if not the originator, of liberal democracy. Second, its democracy evolved over a number of centuries in a process political scientists call **gradualism**. Third, Britain was the world's greatest power from the middle of the eighteenth century until well into the twentieth and was still strong enough to warrant a permanent seat on the United Nations Security Council. Fourth, its political system was similar in many ways to those in other English-speaking countries, which makes it an easy country for most readers to grapple with first.

Today, only the first and last reasons keep it in this book. Britain's ranking among the world's powers has been in gradual, but constant, decline for more than a century. In short, if the United Kingdom belongs in a book like this today, it is primarily because of its historical role—in particular for what it can tell us about the ways democracies develop and survive.

The Bottom Line

Barely the size of California, the UK has just over 63 million people, which makes it one of the most crowded countries in the world. The congestion is actually worse than these figures might suggest because more than 70 percent of its people live in urban areas located in a two-hundred-mile-wide band between London in the south and Newcastle in the north. Put in other terms, almost half the country is open pastureland and home to tens of millions of sheep.

What's in a Name?

The country's official name is the United Kingdom of Great Britain and Northern Ireland and is routinely abbreviated as the UK. It has four parts.

England is its historical core where the crown gradually solidified its hold on power centuries ago. Only later did the English conquer the Celtic fringes of their island: Wales and Scotland. The three are commonly referred to as Britain.

The UK also includes the predominantly Protestant counties of Northern Ireland (or Ulster, as it is known to

the Protestants). When the rest of Ireland gained its independence in 1922, Northern Ireland chose to remain in the UK.

Differentiating among the four regions can get confusing. Scotland (but not Northern Ireland) has its own bank notes and legal system. England, Scotland, Wales, and Northern Ireland have their own international soccer teams but play together in cricket and, sometimes, rugby. It takes three years to get an undergraduate degree in England, but four in Scotland.

The regions have not always been important politically, because the United Kingdom is a **unitary** state that constitutionally gives all power to the national government, but this has changed in recent years. Northern Ireland was convulsed by what are known as **"the troubles"** which took more than 3,000 lives before the signing of the **Good Friday Agreement** and its power-sharing deal between Catholics and Protestants in 1998. During those same years, people in Scotland and Wales also grew dissatisfied with their second-class status and began demanding more autonomy if not outright independence. In part as a response to these new centrifugal pressures, the central government created regional parliaments in Northern Ireland, Scotland, and Wales. Tensions today are particularly high in Scotland, where the Scottish National Party won a landslide victory in 2011 and has begun negotiations that could result in the province's independence.

Social Class

Historically, nothing has divided the British more than social class. More than in most countries, you can tell peoples' backgrounds by their clothing, accents, and even the sports they follow. In England, rugby union is a middle- and upper-class sport; soccer and rugby leagues traditionally appealed to the working class. Many in the upper and middle classes carry themselves with a degree of self-assurance that borders on arrogance, which is "bred" by generations of wealth and the education they received at one of Britain's prestigious private schools (to make things confusing for Americans, the best of them are known as public schools).

Until recently, most people voted for the political party that took positions closest to those associated with their class. The working-class left, for example, advocated both more government ownership of key industries and a vastly more equitable distribution of income and wealth. Most members of the middle and upper classes took exactly the opposite position.

Religion

The regional differences overlap with religious ones. About two-thirds of the people belong to the **Church of England**

(Episcopalian to Americans). As an official, or "established," church, it receives funding and other support from the state. Twenty-six of its top leaders serve in the House of Lords.

Other Protestant sects are strongest in the working class and in Scotland, Wales, and Northern Ireland. About 10 percent of the people are Catholic, most of whom either live in Northern Ireland or are descendants of Irish immigrants to "the mainland."

The country has a long history of religious intolerance, only traces of which remain today, including the unwritten rule that the monarch and prime minister must be members of the Church of England. The morning news on the BBC's flagship Radio 4 starts with "Prayer for the Day." Other than in Scotland, the main religious denominations run most schools, especially at the elementary level. Religious education is part of the curriculum, including those operated by the local governments.

With the possible exception of Islamic extremism, religion is not a major issue in political life today. For example, reproductive rights and the other issues that define much of the appeal of conservatism in the United States do not divide a country where abortion on demand has been legal and widely accepted for more than forty years.

Race and Immigration

Far more important politically is the fact that Britain is no longer an all-white country. Close to 10 percent of the population is of African, Asian, or Caribbean origin.

Most members of minority groups were born in the United Kingdom. Although the size of the minority population pales in comparison with that in the United States, curry is the UK's most popular food. Most fish and chips shops are run by Chinese immigrants, and they also carry egg rolls and fried rice, not to mention curry. The success of the film, *Bend it Like Beckham*, which features a racially mixed women's soccer team, is a sign of how much the "new Britain" has permeated mainstream culture. In perhaps the most telling (but wholly apolitical) change, Mohammed was the most popular name given to newborn boys in 2010, replacing Jack, which had led the list for fourteen years.[3]

Anti-immigrant and racist beliefs are impossible to separate. Together, they have been on the rise since the first large wave of West Indians settled in England after World War II. As in the United States, young black men are more likely than their white contemporaries to be pulled over by the police "on sus" (racial profiling to Americans) and to be treated arbitrarily after an arrest. Some Conservative politicians

have called for an end to immigration and, at times, even the repatriation of Britain's nonwhite residents, despite the fact that most members of the minority community were born in the UK and are thus as British as anyone else.

Overt instances of racism have been most common in the grimy industrial cities in the north, where racist candidates won a handful of seats in local elections. However, most racism today is the indirect byproduct of two forces that are not British in origin.

First, the 1972 Maastricht Treaty on European Union made it possible for most members of the European Union to live and work in any of the now 27 member states (see Chapter 7). For good or ill, many people have chosen to blame immigrants (most of the Europeans, of course, are white), for the rise in unemployment, especially since the start of the recession.

Second, minority political issues have become even more controversial since both 9/11 and a succession of terrorist attacks since then. Many immigrants from Africa, the Middle East, and South Asia are Muslims. Although most Muslims have nothing to do with the terrorist networks, anti-Muslim hostility is on the rise and often spills over onto attitudes toward all immigrants and their British-born children.

(Relative) Economic Decline

As Table 4.1 shows, the United Kingdom used to be one of the richest country in the world. Since the 1930s it has lost its position near the top of the world's rankings of wealth and influence to the point that today it is the poorest country covered in Part 2.

Until the start of the current recession, the UK's growth rate was among the highest and its unemployment among the lowest in Europe. Nonetheless, signs of the longer-term decline still exist. Most salaries are no more than two-thirds of what they would be in the United States. In the three years I lived there in the late 1990s, my academic colleagues had fewer clothes, older cars, smaller personal libraries, and slower computers than my counterparts in the United States.

TABLE 4.1 Britain's Decline in International Rank in GNP per Capita

COUNTRY	1939	1960	1974	1995	2000	2006	2009
United States	1	1	3	5	3	1	1
Great Britain	2	6	14	18	14	8	7

Source: Data for 1939, 1960, and 1974 from Walter Dean Burnham, "Great Britain: The Collapse of the Collectivist Consensus," in Louis Maisel and Joseph Cooper, eds., *Political Parties: Development and Decay* (Beverly Hills, California: Sage, 1978), 274; data for 1995 onward from the World Bank's annual *World Development Report*. Other ways of calculating the data lead to slightly different results. Whichever measures you use, the basic trend line is identical www.worldbank.org (accessed December 12, 2011).

---

[3] There were 7,549 of them in 2010. The name was spelled in 14 different ways (see Chapter 13 for an explanation).

That said, few British people are poor by any reasonable definition of the term. As the basic table shows, its GNP per capita is still remarkably high. Most British citizens I know own cars, take annual vacations, and use personal computers and smart phones.

Despite the Conservative government's budget cuts, the welfare state is still strong enough to guarantee basic health care, education, and pensions for everyone. However, other public services, most notably the country's extensive railroad system, cannot raise the money they need to modernize their infrastructures. And, in late 2010, the country faced massive protests by university students who were upset that tuition and fees could rise to the equivalent of about $20,000 a year.

Key Questions

Given what we have already seen, we will be exploring five related questions in the rest of this chapter to help highlight the ways in which Britain is similar to and different from the other democracies covered in Part 2.

- Why is the UK one of the few countries in which terms such as gradualism are even close to being accurate?

- Given that history, why does Britain face more serious problems than most other democracies today?

- Why have all governments since **Margaret Thatcher** took office in 1979 pursued market-oriented policies?

- Will the coalition government elected in 2010 have any more luck than its predecessors did in solving Britain's enduring economic and other woes?

- Given the burden most recent governments have faced, why does the regime seem as secure today as it was in the halcyon days of British politics in the 1950s?

The Evolution of the British State

Largely because Britain handled the four great transformations discussed in Chapter 2 relatively easily, political scientists have long used the term gradualism in describing the evolution of the British state. Before turning to that history, note the importance of the term *relative*. As was the case in the United States, British history has by no means been tranquil. Nevertheless, as will be clearer after reading any of the remaining chapters, its relative calm was a major contributor to the consensus about the rules of the political game that remains in place there to this day.

Most countries in Europe faced two or more of these transformations at the same time, which also meant that they left lasting ideological divisions and political instability in their wake. By contrast, the British were able to deal with the most vexing aspects of each one of them separately. The individual crises were wrenching. However, with the exception of the industrial revolution, the country emerged from them with a rough consensus rather than the lasting divisions that left France and Germany paralyzed at several critical junctures in their histories. One decisive issue was left unresolved—class. Even there, the conflict was never intense enough to pit workers demanding revolution against an upper class desperately holding on to its property and privilege.

British history is all the more remarkable because the country does not have a formal constitution. There is a constitution that almost everyone understands and endorses. However, the United Kingdom is unique in having a constitution that consists simply of acts of Parliament and widely shared traditions.

The Broad Sweep of British History

The roots of today's British state can be traced back at least to 1215, when a band of nobles forced King John to sign the **Magna Carta** (See Table 4.2). It declared that the king was not an absolute monarch. From then on, the Great Council of leading nobles and churchmen—the precursor of the current House of Lords—had to agree before the king could impose new taxes or spend money.

England in the Middle Ages was a far cry from today's parliamentary democracy. The Council met wherever the king happened to be. The king and his ministers sat in the front, the nobility sat on benches facing them, and the commoners knelt in the back. After they heard the king's requests, the latter two groups met separately, which ultimately led to the creation of the two houses of Parliament (http://www.parliament.uk/about/living-heritage/evolutionofparliament/). Nonetheless, the signing of the Magna Carta launched England on a path toward more inclusive political institutions and, eventually, democracy.

TABLE 4.2 Key Events and Trends in British History

YEAR	EVENT
1215	Magna Carta signed
1532–36	Reformation; establishment of the Church of England
1642–60	Civil war and Restoration
1688	Glorious Revolution
1701	Act of Settlement
Early 1700s	Emergence of the prime minister
1832	Great Reform Act
1911	Reform of the House of Lords
1928	Right to vote for all adults

© Cengage Learning

Over the next four centuries, a succession of kings united most of England into a loose and decentralized state. The English people did not have a sense of national identity, and the government in London had relatively fewer powers and even fewer responsibilities. Still, there was an England, which was more than one could say for Italy, Germany, or, to some degree, France.

In short, by the time the Reformation threw political as well as religious life into turmoil, the British already had made major strides toward meeting the first challenge that shaped modern Europe. The fact that the theological split between Catholics and Protestants did not produce as deep or lasting divisions as it did in the rest of Europe further helped state and nation building although it was far from obvious at the time. The fact that Henry VIII wanted to divorce and remarry but did not have profound theological qualms with Catholicism, the Church of England he created did not constitute as sharp a break with the past as Lutheranism or Calvinism proved to be on the continent.

It would be centuries before the British state tolerated other religions, and the division between Anglicans and Puritans would be one of the causes of the English civil war in the 1640s. Nonetheless, Henry's actions began a century-long process that removed religion as a serious bone of contention.

England did suffer through two revolutions in the seventeenth century. They were, however, relatively mild, and the way they were resolved helped pave the way for parliamentary democracy. During the civil war of the 1640s, Oliver Cromwell and his supporters among Parliament members, businessmen, Puritans, and soldiers overthrew the monarchy and beheaded Charles I. In 1660, Charles II was restored to the throne on the condition that he accept parliamentary sovereignty. Charles and his successors tried to reassert royal power and even flirted with Catholicism, which led to the Glorious Revolution of 1688 and the passage of laws that ended any pretense of an absolute monarchy and made the king accountable to Parliament in almost everything he did.

Royal prerogatives continued to disappear. The new king and Parliament agreed to a Bill of Rights, which made it illegal for the monarch to impose taxes or enforce laws without the consent of Parliament. In 1701, the Act of Settlement regularized the succession to the throne and asserted that the king and queen had to obey laws passed by Parliament.

In 1707, Queen Anne failed to give her royal assent to a bill passed by Parliament, the last time any British monarch did so. Shortly thereafter, King George I stopped attending cabinet meetings (in part because he only spoke German), a practice his successors have continued ever since. People began to refer to the man who chaired the cabinet as prime minister, although it would be another two centuries before the title was mentioned in any law.

When the American Revolution broke out, the king had become little more than the head of one parliamentary faction. He still appointed cabinet ministers, but "his" government could only remain in office if it retained the confidence of Parliament. English political institutions were already on a trajectory that would make them the most inclusive in the world over the next century. The suffrage was still limited to the nobility and the wealthiest commoners, but pressures to expand the suffrage already existed by the time of the American and French revolutions.

During the nineteenth century, capitalism changed Britain more than any of the other upheavals discussed in this section. The industrial revolution and the imperialism that fed it made Britain the world's richest and most powerful country.

Few of the men and women who worked in the mills and mines shared in that wealth. Hundreds of thousands left the countryside to work in the unsafe factories and live in the filthy, overcrowded cities Charles Dickens so powerfully described in his novels. Bands of workers and artisans, known as Luddites, broke into the new factories and destroyed their machines. By 1810, the term working class was commonly used—and feared. Friendly societies, new denominations such as Methodism, and the great petition drives of the Chartist movement demonstrated that the working and middle classes had become forces to be reckoned with.

Despite these rumblings from below, not even five percent of adult men were wealthy enough to vote. The ranks of the disenfranchised included most of the new generation of increasingly wealthy and increasingly dissatisfied capitalists.

Rural districts were overrepresented in the House of Commons. Many of them were referred to as "rotten boroughs" because they had so few constituents that a single lord determined who was elected.

Eventually, dissatisfaction grew to the point that members of Parliament (MPs) realized that they had a difficult choice to make. Either they could respond to the new movements by passing the **Great Reform Act** of 1832 or face widespread protests that could easily turn into the kind of revolution France had just suffered through.

Despite its name, the reform was not all that great. Only about three hundred thousand more men could vote, and the aristocracy continued to dominate political life. Nonetheless, by agreeing to the Reform Act, the aristocratic elite showed that it was willing to adapt to changing circumstances by sharing political power with the growing entrepreneurial class who, in turn, moved the country in a very different economic direction.

A second Reform Act in 1867 increased the size of the electorate to nearly three million. In 1870, Parliament introduced the secret ballot. After the Representation of the People Acts of 1884 and 1885, working-class men constituted the majority of the electorate. By the early twentieth century, all men could vote. Most women won the suffrage in 1918, and the vote was extended to all women ten years later.

Parliamentary leaders who now needed to win the support of the newly enfranchised voters to stay in office formed the first modern political parties. The Conservative National Union did surprisingly well among the working class as well as the aristocracy, while the National Liberal Federation did particularly well among the middle-class voters and in Ireland. MPs were now dependent on well-organized party machines whose leaders in Parliament began to determine who would run for office and serve in cabinets. Strict party discipline was imposed. In 1911, the House of Lords was stripped of its remaining power, marking the final step in the evolution of British parliamentary democracy.

A brief comparison with France should show just how far Britain had come since the Glorious Revolution. Its parliamentary system was getting ever stronger, while French democracy remained shaky at best. France had just suffered through the Dreyfus affair in which trumped up treason accusations against a Jewish army officer unleashed such passionate protests that the Third Republic nearly collapsed. Significant divisions over the role of religion and the nature of the state spawned anti-regime parties that typically won a third of the seats in Parliament.

Only one of the four challenges had a divisive political impact that endures to this day: class divisions growing out of the industrial revolution. But, even the impact of social

Comparative Emphasis: Democratization

Comparatively speaking, both Britain and the United States have had peaceful histories. When crises did occur, they were usually resolved before the next major transformation took hold. Some were quite wrenching, most notably each country's civil wars. However, they were less divisive than conflicts on the European continent and, more importantly for our purposes, were largely resolved once almost everyone accepted the outcome. ■

class in Britain paled in comparison with the insurrectionary mood on the continent.

To cite but one example, in 1926, the **Trades Union Congress (TUC)** called for a general strike. Workers walked off the job en masse. In France or Germany, such a strike would have been accompanied by violent clashes between police and strikers. In Britain, instead of fighting, many of the policemen and strikers played soccer together to pass the time.

During the 1926 general strike, workers who walked off the job did not confront the police. Instead, the policemen and strikers played football (soccer) together.

Topical Press Agency/Stringer/Hulton Archive/Getty Images

The factory owners rarely met workers' demands. However, most of their frustrations were channeled through the moderate TUC and the Labour Party. By the 1920s, Labour had outpolled the Liberals and become the main opposition to the Conservatives.

The Great Depression that began in 1929 hit Britain harder than any European country other than Germany. For most of the next decade, no party had a clear majority in Parliament, and a succession of weak governments failed to ease the country's economic woes or meet the mounting threat from an ever more aggressive Nazi Germany. Few social service programs that could have blunted the effects of the depression on the poor were introduced before World War II put all hopes for domestic economic and political reform on hold for the duration of the war.

The Collectivist Consensus

The period from 1945 until the mid-1970s is often portrayed as the golden era of British politics (See Table 4.3). The wartime experience transformed both parties. Afterward, both Labour and the Conservatives ended up supporting interventionist policies that sought to guarantee full employment and economic growth while expanding social services to ensure at least subsistence-level living conditions for all. Together, they produced what political scientists call the **collectivist consensus**.

Although the Liberal-Labour coalition government of 1906–11 had introduced limited unemployment and health insurance programs, the most important roots of the modern British welfare state lie in World War II. The war started disastrously for the United Kingdom and its allies. Country after country fell to the Nazis. British troops were

TABLE 4.3 The Collectivist Years and Beyond

YEAR	EVENT
1942	Beveridge Report published
1945	Labour elected
1948	National Health Service created
1951	Conservatives return to power
1964	Labour returns to power
1972	Heath government forced into U-turn
1974	Labour wins two elections without a working majority
1979	Thatcher elected
1990	Thatcher resigns, replaced by John Major
1997	Blair elected
2007	Brown replaces Blair as prime minister
2008	Onset of the economic crisis
2010	Coalition government elected

© Cengage Learning

forced to withdraw from Europe. German planes by the thousands bombed London and other major British cities. Many feared a German invasion, which would have been the first time hostile foreign troops had set foot on the island since 1066.

With defeat staring the UK in the face, Sir Winston Churchill replaced the ineffectual Neville Chamberlain as prime minister. Although his Conservative Party had a majority in the Commons, Churchill chose to head an all-party coalition. The opposition parties agreed to suspend elections and the rest of normal politics for the duration of the war. As a quid pro quo, Churchill and his Tory colleagues established a commission headed by the civil servant William Beveridge to plan for the overhaul of the social service system after the Allies won. The 1942 Beveridge Report called for health care, unemployment insurance, pensions, and other benefits including free tuition at the country's universities.

The 1945 election centered on the Beveridge Report. Both major parties endorsed its main goals, although Labour was committed to going further and faster in enacting its recommendations and to nationalizing key industries, a goal the Tories did not share.

Labour won a resounding victory, taking office for the first time with a parliamentary majority of its own. Prime Minister Clement Attlee's government (see Table 4.4) proceeded to turn the party program into legislation, which the House of Commons passed with only slight modification.

By 1949, the surge of reform had come to an end. Throughout Europe, the cold war sapped socialist parties of their momentum. Furthermore, with recovery well under way, Labour decided to end its efforts to plan the entire economy. Labour's popularity began to wane. It barely won a majority in the 1950 elections, and when Attlee dissolved Parliament again the following year, the Conservatives won.

To the surprise of many, they did not repeal most of Labour's new programs. The steel industry was privatized, and people had to pay a nominal fee for prescription medicines and eyeglasses. Otherwise, the Conservatives retained the welfare state Labour had created.

In retrospect, the Conservatives' actions should not have come as much of a surprise. The 1945 campaign had been fought over the pace and extent at which the reforms should be enacted, not whether they should be adopted at all. In his first speech as leader of the opposition, Churchill stated:

> It is evident that not only are we two parties in the house agreed on the main essentials of foreign policy and in our moral outlook on world affairs, but we also have an immense program, prepared by our joint

TABLE 4.4 British Prime Ministers Since 1945

NAME	PARTY	YEARS IN OFFICE
Clement Attlee	Labour	1945–51
Winston Churchill	Conservative	1951–55
Anthony Eden	Conservative	1955–56
Harold Macmillan	Conservative	1956–63
Alec Douglas Home	Conservative	1963–64
Harold Wilson	Labour	1964–70
Edward Heath	Conservative	1970–74
Harold Wilson	Labour	1974–76
James Callaghan	Labour	1976–79
Margaret Thatcher	Conservative	1979–90
John Major	Conservative	1990–97
Tony Blair	Labour	1997–2007
Gordon Brown	Labour	2007–2010
David Cameron	Conservative	2010–

© Cengage Learning

exertions during the coalition, which requires to be brought into law and made an inherent part of the life of the people. Here and there, there may be differences of emphasis and view but, in the main no Parliament has ever assembled with such a mass of agreed legislation as lies before us this afternoon.[4]

For thirty years, government spending grew steadily no matter which party was in government. The size of the national budget grew at almost exactly the same rate year in and year out. Elections were fought by catch-all parties using slogans such as the Conservatives' "You Never Had It So Good" in 1959 or over Labour's claim that it would bring more modern management practices to government in 1964.

The two main parties routinely won over 90 percent of the vote and an even larger share of the seats in the House of Commons. The electorate was divided along class lines. Normally, about 70 percent of the working class voted Labour, and an even larger proportion of the middle class voted Conservative. But on balance, the class divide was not very divisive, since almost everyone accepted the broad contours of the welfare state and the political system that had created it.

Many political scientists saw the collectivist years as the natural culmination of British political history. The few protest movements were tiny, such as the annual march in opposition to nuclear weapons which descended on the home of the British bomb at Aldermaston.

[4]Quoted in Allen Sked and Chris Clark, *Post-War Britain: A Political History*, 3rd ed. (London: Penguin Books, 1990), 24.

Thatcher, Blair, and Their Legacies

By the late 1960s, two new issues undermined the collectivist consensus revealing more dissatisfaction than the country had seen for nearly a century. Though the overwhelming majority of the population stayed on the sidelines, popular participation took on a decidedly confrontational tone and left many worried that Britain was becoming ungovernable.

The first was identity politics. Northern Ireland had been relatively quiet in the years after the rest of the island gained its independence after World War I. That changed with the birth of a movement for Catholic civil rights and the reinvigoration of the **Irish Republican Army (IRA)**. The British had sent troops to Northern Ireland in 1969 in response to a series of violent protests and equally violent reactions from the Protestant-dominated provincial government. Their presence eventually led to "Bloody Sunday" in January 1972, when twenty-six Catholics were killed by British troops. For the next quarter century, the IRA and various Protestant paramilitaries carried out attacks, including one that nearly killed Margaret Thatcher (1925–2013) and the rest of the Conservative leadership at the party's annual conference in 1984.

Britain also had to come to grips with racism for the first time. The Conservative and, later, Ulster Unionist (Protestant) politician Enoch Powell built a career exploiting the fear and antagonism many felt toward Asians, Africans, and Afro-Caribbeans. The National Front, whose racism was at best thinly veiled, did well in local elections in working-class white neighborhoods. White toughs repeatedly attacked blacks and Asians in London, Liverpool, Birmingham, and smaller cities.

Second, economic issues became controversial for the first time since the Depression. The economic growth that gave rise to the collectivist consensus disappeared. Instead of prosperity, the British faced rates of inflation and unemployment they hadn't seen since the 1930s. By the mid-1980s, unemployment had topped three million, six times what it had been during the 1950s and 1960s. Workers who still had jobs saw their standard of living eroded by inflation that regularly outpaced their annual raises.

Some union members, in particular, began to doubt how much the welfare state had truly helped them and began to move further to the left. Strikes were larger and lasted longer. Violence at the factory gates and the mine pits was an all but daily occurrence. After losing the 1979 election, the Labour Party began to radicalize, giving rise to what critics called the "loony left."

In response, many conservatives started to question their own commitment to collectivism. They turned instead to the pro-market economic strategies that had

PROFILES   Margaret Thatcher

Margaret Thatcher's legacy is still the key to British politics today, even after her death in 2013.

Margaret Roberts was born in 1925 in Grantham, which has often been described as the most boring town in Britain. Her father owned a small corner grocery store and was a member of the town council. He instilled traditional Tory values in his daughter—self-reliance, self-discipline, and acceptance of traditional values—which were reinforced by a youth spent during the Great Depression and World War II.

Roberts went on to study chemistry at Oxford, but she soon realized she was more interested in politics than science and so became a lawyer active in Conservative politics. Marriage to the wealthy banker Denis Thatcher allowed her to turn to politics full time, and she was first elected to a safe Tory seat in suburban London in 1959.

In 1970 she was named minister of education. She gained the nickname "Margaret Thatcher, milk snatcher" for eliminating free milk from school lunches in one of her least popular acts as minister.

After the Conservatives lost in 1974, she and a number of her colleagues abandoned their commitment to the collectivist consensus. She was named leader of the Conservative Party two years later and became prime minister when it won the 1979 election. She served for eleven years at Ten Downing Street, making her the longest-serving prime minister in more than a hundred years. Her successor, John Major, elevated her to the House of Lords in 1993, where she will almost certainly be

© David Fowler / Shutterstock.com.

Prime Minister Margaret Thatcher speaking in London on July 1, 1991.

the last member to be named to a hereditary peerage that can pass to her descendants. Thatcher died in 2013 just as this book went to press. ◼

been discredited forty years earlier, which culminated in the selection of Margaret Thatcher as party leader in 1974.

Thatcher led the Tories ever further to the right. During the eighteen years she and her protégé John Major governed, they privatized dozens of industries and tried to dismantle much of the welfare state, including the highly respected National Health Service. But she will probably be best remembered for ending trade union militancy.

Both Thatcher and the unions held firmly to their beliefs, which put them on a collision course. The government provided the pretext for the confrontation everyone expected by passing the 1984 Industrial Relations Act that forced union leaders to use a secret ballot to get their members' approval ballot before calling a strike. The miners' union refused to comply with the law and declared a nationwide strike, which lasted for almost a year and cost the British economy about £3 billion. Finally, the miners admitted defeat and in March 1985 reluctantly returned to work.

The strikes and other protests were extremely unpopular even among traditional Labour voters. Finally, after four consecutive defeats at the polls, Labour shed its radical leanings under the youthful leadership of Tony Blair and his long-time deputy Gordon Brown. They breezed to victory in 1997 and went on to win the next two elections. First under Blair and then under Brown, "new Labour" made its peace with many of Thatcher's reforms, including the wholesale privatizations. Instead of traditional socialist approaches, they sought public-private partnerships and used an extended period of growth to redistribute some income and wealth from the rich to the poor. They were so successful in appealing to the young and the middle class that the country was often referred to as "cool Britannia." However, twelve years in power and the unpopular war in Iraq took their toll. Blair gave way to Brown in 2007. When he finally faced the voters in 2010, Labour seemed to have run out of ideas and lost to Cameron's Conservative/Liberal Democratic coalition.

In short, thirty years after the confrontation between Thatcher and the unions, the "iron lady's" impact can still be felt. British politics is more manageable. It is also more conservative. The traditional, socialist left has all but disappeared. Class still matters, but the UK is a country in which the industrial working class is disappearing. Perhaps most important of all, it is a country struggling to find policy solutions after both Thatcherite conservatism and Blair's third way have been found wanting.

British Political Culture

At the height of the collectivist period, Gabriel Almond and Sidney Verba conducted a survey of voters in the United Kingdom and four other countries.[5] Although we do not have enough comparative data to fully support any such statement, no other country's people seem to have been as satisfied with their government or regime at the time. Except for a tiny handful of Communists and fascists, there was virtually unanimous agreement that the political system was legitimate.

The British were also remarkably tolerant of each other and of the people who led them. Poll after poll revealed a British public that trusted its politicians and institutions. Most adults felt they could influence the political process, which social scientists at the time called a sense of political efficacy. However, few people actually placed demands on decision makers other than by voting,

leading observers like Almond and Verba to conclude that democracies actually need a relatively inactive and uninvolved electorate.

The British also thought of themselves as patriotic. Waving the flag and singing the national anthem were—and still are—almost as widespread as in the United States. But even this patriotism was muted and did not lead to anything approaching jingoistic involvement abroad as can be seen most easily in the ease with which most people accepted the end of the British Empire.

Public opinion data gathered since Almond and Verba did their research have led most political scientists to conclude that the British political culture was not as supportive as they thought. There were, for instance, hints that many young people chafed at the norms and laws that limited what they could do socially if not politically. Nonetheless, the political snapshots they and other analysts took of Britain in the collectivist years go a long way toward explaining why the British regime and democracy were not put in jeopardy during the crisis years of the 1970s and 1980s.

The Civic Culture Survives—Sort Of

The protests from the 1960s through the 1980s were intense enough to produce a long-term decline in support for politicians and their policies. However, on balance, the British culture "held."

Contemporary fears that Britain was becoming ungovernable were overstated. Despite what the far left may have wanted, revolution was never on the horizon. The British public was too committed to established parliamentary institutions.

That said, Thatcher tried to dispel what fears there were by meeting the unions' challenges head on. Unlike previous prime ministers of both parties, Thatcher was able to take advantage of dissatisfaction with union demands to bring the miners to their knees at the time and limit the TUC's influence to this day.

The important point here is not whether Thatcher was right or wrong. What matters is that her strong stance helped reduce the political tensions that some observers thought could imperil traditional British institutions and practices.

That does not mean that the British are as placid as they were in the 1950s and early 1960s, in at least two respects. The first mirrors changes we saw in the United States; the second is peculiarly British.

Declining Trust and Confidence

Despite the all but total disappearance of the radical left, there is plenty of dissatisfaction, at least some of which

---

[5]Gabriel Almond and Sidney Verba, *The Civic Culture* (Princeton, NJ: Princeton University Press, 1962).

Darren Staples/Reuters/Landov

Racist, right-wing protest.

can be seen in the streets. As in the United States, a growing but unknown number of British citizens have come to the conclusion that their politicians are too distant, selfish, incompetent, and even corrupt. The fury of students who protest against tuition hikes, environmentalists who try to block highway construction, or the seemingly apolitical violence of what have been mistakenly called race riots in recent years have no equivalents from the days of the collectivist consensus.

Like all of the other countries covered in Part 2, the British have to deal with the unintended political consequences of the country's changing demographic. The "face" of the new Britain is easiest to see in its athletic teams, but its political ramifications leap to the fore in the small number of terrorist attacks and the public reaction to them.

The UK has not had a single terrorist incident as devastating as the attacks on New York and Washington on 9/11. A handful of Muslims have conducted a number of bombings, the most serious of which disrupted much of the London subway system and killed 56 people in 2005. In perhaps the most appalling act which may or may not deserve be called political, two men of Nigerian origin killed a British soldier in broad daylight on a London street corner in 2013. The people who carried out these

and other attacks had spent all or most of their lives in the UK.

Will There Always Be a Britain?

The second area in which the rock-solid support of the civic culture days is eroding has no parallels in the other countries discussed in Part 2—the remote possibility that the United Kingdom as we know it today might not survive. We will see that identity politics is far more important in much of the rest of the world in Part 4. However, fewer and fewer people in Northern Ireland, Scotland, and Wales think of themselves as British, and at least some mainstream politicians in all three regions are talking about dramatic decentralization and even outright independence.

Northern Ireland has received the most attention because of the Troubles. But the British government and representatives of the Protestant and Catholic communities have reached a series of agreements since 1998, which have brought a power-sharing government and unexpected stability to the province. The IRA still says it wants a united Ireland but it has disarmed, and there is next to no chance that the conditions for a reunification of the island that were spelled out in the Good Friday Agreement will be met in the foreseeable future.

The real challenge today comes from Scotland. One 2000 poll asked people about the levels of government they most identified with. Eighteen percent of Scots said Britain, and 72 percent mentioned Scotland. The comparable figures for Wales were 27 percent for Britain and 81 percent for Wales. The English were split down the middle, with 43 percent mentioning Britain and 41 percent England.

As we will see in the next section, these changing identities have been reflected in growing support for regional parties in Scotland and Wales (the national parties do not run candidates in Northern Ireland). In 2011, the Scottish National Party won an unprecedented victory in elections to the Scottish Assembly. The new Chief Minister, Alex Salmond, began discussions that could lead to a referendum on independence. As I write in early 2013, it is not clear how those events will play themselves out. In fact, it is not even clear who has jurisdiction to hold such a vote! The polls suggest that any referendum would be defeated. However, the fact that one is even on the agenda is a sign of how much the non-English parts of the British population have changed since the 1950s.

Britain's "Britishness" will also probably be challenged if the UK stays in the EU. Its role in an integrating Europe has been controversial since European integration was first proposed after World War II. As we will see later here and in Chapter 7, the UK was not one of the original EU members and many on the left and right still have qualms about membership and its implications. Long before the crisis over the euro began, Conservatives, in particular, began to express doubts about what they see as the gradual erosion of British sovereignty as the powers of the EU grow, which seems likely to come to a head if a referendum on British membership is held sometime after the 2015 election.

Very few British citizens think of themselves as European, although the percentage of self-identified "Europeans" is higher in Scotland, Wales, and Northern Ireland. Nonetheless, the fact that so many British citizens live and work on the continent and so many other Europeans now do the same throughout the UK seems bound to have an impact on the way people think of themselves.

Political Participation

As in all of the democracies, any discussion of political participation in Britain has to start with elections, because voting is the only way most people take part in political life.

As is the case in the United States, British elections revolve around two main political parties. Either Labour or the Conservatives has won every election since 1918. Since 1945, one or the other of them has won a majority of

the seats in the House of Commons in all but two elections, which helps make any Westminster-style system function in ways discussed in Chapter 2.

Until the late 1960s, a single issue—social class—was the driving force in the competition between the two parties. Like everything else, voters and the parties began to change in the 1970s. Both Labour and the Conservatives became deeply divided internally as more radical activists moved away from the center and rediscovered their traditional ideological roots in socialism and capitalism, respectively.

The ideological passions of the 1970s and 1980s have subsided. Labour, in particular, has shed almost all of its radical baggage, and the Tories have shown signs of doing the same, although—as in the United States—its more extreme faction still holds considerable sway on social, economic, and European issues.

Whatever their ideological views, Labour and the Conservatives are undeniably catch-all parties whose primary goal is winning elections. However important their ideological positions are to their grassroots activists, both parties' leaders have shown a willingness to sacrifice ideological purity for likely electoral gains, at least since Mrs. Thatcher retired. Like their American counterparts, the three major parties are increasingly under the sway of spin doctors who sometimes seem more like advertising executives than committed partisans.

The Conservatives

We start with the Conservatives, not only because they are in power today but because they are often referred to as the "natural party of government" (www.conservatives.com). While that may be an overstatement, it is true that the Tories controlled most governments before World War II and were in office for thirty-nine of the first fifty-eight years afterward.

Historical Roots

In many ways, the Tories epitomize the gradualism of British politics. Their roots lie in the aristocracy. Most politicians who formed the modern Conservative Party had deep doubts about democracy, socialism, and anything else they feared might change the traditional order of life. More often than not, Conservative leaders were pragmatic enough to change their positions as circumstances warranted.

The Conservatives have never been unquestioning supporters of a market economy. Until Thatcher's rise to prominence, most Tories were willing to use the state to set economic goals and drew on the feudal tradition of noblesse oblige to justify their support for the social and economic services created after the Beveridge Report. In fact, during the nineteenth century, the first generation of industrial capitalists felt more at home in the more laissez-faire-oriented Liberal Party.

It was only in the Thatcher years that their pragmatic bent coincided with strident calls for less economic intervention and a smaller state. Thatcher, too, helped create a party that was no longer dominated by a traditional elite, many of whom could trace their families' influence back for generations.

Thatcherism

Thatcherism served the Tories extremely well during the 1980s. In large part because of its own difficulties to be discussed in the next section, Labour dumped the 1979 election in Thatcher's lap. At first, she was obliged to include most of the senior party leaders in her cabinet, including many who did not share her objections to collectivist politics. Over the next few years, however, she replaced most of the moderates with ideological conservatives who also were personally beholden to her. Even when she had to share power with what were disparagingly called the Tory "wets," her government easily enacted the sweeping social and economic changes we will see in the section on public policy.

When Thatcher's popularity slipped and she was forced to resign in 1990, the challenge came not from the moderates, but from her erstwhile supporters who had come to see her as an electoral liability. They then chose **John Major** (1943–), a lackluster leader who neither enjoyed much popular support nor coped with the party's deepening divisions over Europe. Major resigned as party leader the day after the 1997 election and was replaced by a series of even more ineffectual leaders. Finally, after its third consecutive defeat in 2005, the party made a bold move that few expected of it.

It turned to David Cameron.

Cameron's Conservatives

Cameron was only forty when he became leader of the Conservative party, making him one of the youngest politicians to occupy that high a position in the Western world. He was first elected to Parliament in 2001. In a country in which people typically spend more than a decade on the backbenches before joining the top leadership, Cameron became party leader less than five years later.

Under Cameron, the party has tried to distance itself from the more intransigent rhetoric of the Thatcher years. Nonetheless, his is still very definitely a conservative party in a country where the entire political center of gravity has shifted to the right. In that sense, today's Conservatives are more like the American Republicans on everything but

social issues than any of the others covered in this book in these main ways.

- Capitalism. Cameron has made it clear that he is a "liberal conservative" even if he does not rely on language reminiscent of such free market stalwarts as Milton Friedman or Friedrich Hayek. He is conservative in that he is pro-business and liberal because he wants to free the economy of "unnecessary" regulations in order to give more space for entrepreneurship and job creation.

- Spending cuts. Cameron has actually gone farther than Thatcher did in making the national debt a top priority. As we will see below, his government has enacted sweeping spending cuts of as much as twenty-five percent in some ministries.

- Euroskepticism. Cameron's Conservatives have not stressed opposition to European integration as much as their predecessors did for one simple reason. They haven't had to. Almost everyone agrees with the Tories now that the UK will not consider adopting the euro anytime in the near future and will not allow further expansion of the EU's powers without a referendum. Cameron has even suggested that he would call a referendum on the UK's membership in the EU that almost certainly would be held after the next election, if it is held at all.

- Social issues. Although the Tories have normally lagged behind Labour and the Liberals in supporting minority rights, almost all Tories are in favor of keeping abortions legal and paid for by the National Health Service. Cameron has also been especially vocal in his support for gay rights, including the granting of full legal rights to same-sex couples.

Last but by no means least, the Tories face even more serious organizational difficulties than the other two major parties. Like them, it has seen its number of active members plummet over the last forty years. It has also struggled to become a more open party in which grassroots activists share decision-making responsibilities with the London-based elites who have historically dominated it. The Tories are also an old party. As many as a third of its dues-paying members are over sixty-five, which might make it hard for the Tories to appeal to younger voters despite the youth of its leadership.

Cameron had an easy road to 10 Downing Street. Even before the crisis began, the Conservatives were ahead in the polls. Their lead later slipped enough that the party fell short of a parliamentary majority, forcing Cameron into the UK's first peacetime coalition government in eighty years, the details of which we will put off discussing until the sections on the state and public policy later in the chapter.

PROFILES David Cameron

David Cameron became leader of the Conservative Party on December 5, 2005, and was widely hailed as a breath of fresh air both because he was so young and because he seemed to be more moderate than his predecessors.

There was little in his past to indicate that he would become an unconventional politician. He was raised about sixty miles from London where his father ran the family financial empire. His paternal grandfather was a baronet. He is also a direct descendent of King William V and one of his mistresses, which also makes him a fifth cousin of Queen Elizabeth.

Cameron had a typical education for someone of his class. When he was seven years old, he was sent to boarding school around the corner from Windsor Castle. He then went to England's most prestigious public (that is, private) school, Eton, which overlooks Windsor Castle from the other side of the River Thames. He was a brilliant student, but he did have a run in with the authorities after he was caught smoking marijuana; his punishment was to copy five hundred lines of Latin prose.

He then attended Oxford where he studied under Vernon Bogdanor, arguably this generation's best constitutional scholar. Cameron graduated with a "first," roughly the equivalent of summa cum laude in the United States.

After working for a few years as a Tory researcher and then for a television production company, he was elected to Parliament from an overwhelmingly Conservative constituency near his family home. Four years later he was his party's leader.

Although his ideological positions are not as consistently conservative as those of his predecessors, he is enough of a Thatcherite to champion the austerity policies his government introduced immediately after taking office. Cameron also has

David Cameron.

deep qualms about European integration. However, he did vote for the Civil Partnership Act in 2004, which gave gay and lesbian couples the same benefits as heterosexual ones, and has signaled support for same-sex marriage.

Cameron and his wife have four children. The oldest was born with cerebral palsy and epilepsy. The fourth was born during the family's first summer vacation after he was elected prime minister. He is one of the rare British politicians who is willing to talk about his family life in public. ■

Labour

Labour may not be the natural party of government, but that does not make it the natural party of opposition either. In two of its three periods of government, it did as much to change Britain as the Tories ever have.

Historical Roots

According to its own history, the Labour Party was created in 1900 as "a new party for a new century" (www. labour.org.uk). At that point, it was a tiny alliance of trade unions, independent socialist movements, and cooperative societies. It began to make inroads at the polls during the latter part of that decade and first became head of a coalition government in 1925.

The impact of its three constituent groups has ebbed and flowed over the years. More often than not, the TUC dominated the party in part because union members were automatically enrolled in the party, thereby providing most of its members and funds.

Even at the height of the depression, it could never have been confused with socialist parties on the continent (see the next two chapters) which at least spoke bravely about revolution. Clause 4 of the original party program did call for the nationalization of the "commanding heights" of British industry. However, because the unions were more interested in improving the lives of their members than doctrinal purity, Marxists never had much of an impact on a party that accepted the parliamentary system and the democratic rules of the game from the very beginning.

Labour did not win an election on its own until 1945. The Attlee government used its overwhelming majority and demand for reform that had built up during fifteen years of depression and war to implement the provisions of the Beveridge report, nationalize dozens of key industries, and organize planning boards with business and TUC leaders to steer postwar reconstruction.

The party lurched leftward during the turbulent 1970s and early 1980s after Labour governments led by Harold Wilson and James Callaghan proved unable to deal with the country's first major postwar recession between 1974 and 1979. After Labour lost to the Conservatives in 1979, its leaders kept moving further to the left, which made it easy prey for the Tories, who won easy victories again in 1983, 1987, and 1992.

By the time Labour lost for the third consecutive time in 1992, almost everyone had grown convinced that its leftist stands amounted to a death wish for a party whose whole raison d'être was to win a parliamentary majority. Over the next five years, Labour began to moderate. It rebuilt much of its popular support but still managed to lose the 1992 election, which many pundits expected it to win. This time, defeat did not splinter the party. Neil Kinnock, the incumbent leader, immediately stepped down and was replaced by the even more pragmatic John Smith (1938–94), who accelerated its move back toward the center before his sudden death.

New Labour

Radical control of the party ended after Tony Blair and Gordon Brown took over after Smith's death. Both were too young to have risen to the top of a party under normal circumstances. Labour, however, was so short of innovative leaders and ideas that it had no choice but to skip to the next generation, much as the Tories were to do with Cameron.

Both men were ambitious and coveted the top job. They were also allies in the reformist wing of the party. At a now-famous dinner at a now-defunct restaurant, they agreed that Blair would lead Labour and eventually give way to Brown. The fact that they never specified a date helped turn them into rivals a decade later.

At first, they were a remarkable team. Blair was a telegenic and charismatic leader, which is one of the main reasons they decided to give him the top job first. Brown was more of a policy wonk who effectively managed its economic policy as Shadow Chancellor and then as Chancellor of the Exchequer for the entire time Blair was prime minister.

The Blair government's actions will be discussed in depth in the section on public policy. Here, it is enough to see his impact on the party. Blair deservedly gets most of the credit for creating new Labour and making it victorious. He was part of a generation of left-of-center leaders in many of the industrialized democracies who helped formulate what was called the third way and helped the party shed the vestiges of the old Left. Within a year, Clause 4 was gone. The party announced that it would not reverse the changes introduced by Thatcher and Major. Blair even acknowledged that he respected Thatcher's style, if not her policies. The weight of the unions in the party leadership was reduced, and most of the leftists were shunted aside.

The third way meant more than just shedding long-standing commitments to policies Labour used to appeal to a working-class electorate. Basing the party's campaigns on that single base of support had turned into a recipe for disaster for the simple reason that there were no longer enough manual workers to provide Labour the votes it would need to win an election.

At first, Blair seemed almost as popular as a rock star. However, as invariably happens with leaders who remain in power for more than a decade, Blair's luster began to fade even though he led the party to three consecutive electoral victories, the first time a Labour leader had done so.

As with his rise, there was no single factor that destroyed his career. His support for the American-led war in Iraq cost him tremendously among party activists and came close to bringing his government down. A number of Labour politicians were implicated in scandals.

But the biggest issue was his rivalry with Brown, which eclipsed their friendship after the start of the twenty-first century. Brown grew more and more impatient the longer Blair put off his retirement.

Shortly after its victory in 2005, Blair announced that he would not lead the party in a fourth election campaign. Over the next two years, pressures on him to resign continued to mount—especially from Brown's supporters. Ultimately, he gave in and handed power to his former friend turned bitter rival in 2007.

Brown did not turn out to be an effective leader, at least when compared with Blair, which, of course, was the electorate's frame of reference. Moreover, he moved into 10 Downing Street just as the recession hit. He also proved to be a lackluster campaigner. All in all, few observers were surprised when he lost the 2010 election and resigned as head of the Labour Party immediately thereafter.

Not So New Labour

Brown's resignation sparked one of the most unusual leadership contests in the history of the democratic world. Everyone realized that Labour needed new leadership that could take the party beyond what now seemed to be the failed promise of new Labour.

The only real surprise is that the party ended up choosing between two brothers, Ed and David Miliband. David probably had more support among party members. He had been close to Blair and served in a number of cabinet positions, including Foreign Minister. Younger brother Ed was less well known and was more closely linked to Brown, neither of which suggested he would prevail. In the end, Ed won, with 50.65 percent of the vote, largely because he had more support from the unions. The two brothers are close, so David graciously admitted defeat and announced he was retiring from active politics.

Ed Miliband has not turned his back on new Labour. But, he has also made it clear that the Blairite era is over. As befits someone who has strong roots in the unions and whose father was a leading socialist intellectual, Miliband has stressed some more traditional leftist themes. However, there is little chance that he will lead Labour dramatically back to the left as some of his critics first feared.

After nearly three years in charge, it still is not clear where Miliband will lead the party. At this point, Labour is far ahead in the polls, but that is less an endorsement of Miliband's leadership than it is a rejection of Cameron's policies so far. In short, Miliband's version of new Labour is still a work in progress and probably will remain so until the months before the next election.

The Liberal Democrats

Historical Origins

The Liberals were the main alternative to the Conservatives until Labour shoved them into third place in the 1920s. The Liberals were politically irrelevant until they began a resurgence in the 1970s which culminated in their joining

PROFILES Ed Miliband

Ed Miliband (1969–) became Labour's new leader on September 25, 2010, replacing Gordon Brown after the party lost the election that spring.

Miliband continues the recent trend of major parties picking young leaders—he is actually younger than either Cameron or Clegg. He, too, has had a meteoric rise up the partisan ranks by British standards. Miliband comes from an intellectual family (his father was a renowned socialist scholar) and graduated from Oxford and the London School of Economics before becoming a researcher for Labour. There Miliband became close with Brown, who helped him get elected from a working-class district in 2005 and then named him to a series of cabinet posts after Blair's resignation.

Many think Miliband will take the party back to the left. Although he wants to shed the "new Labour" label, he has also cautioned the party that it has to adopt a center-left stance. The most curious thing about his selection as party leader is that he ran against and barely beat his more popular and older brother in the electoral college that chooses new leaders. Had all party members been eligible to vote, it is likely that the better-known David Miliband would have won.

Ed Miliband is also the first party leader of Jewish origins since Benjamin Disraeli launched his career in the early nineteenth century. Unlike Disraeli, Miliband did not have to convert to Christianity before starting a serious political career. ■

Cameron's government. Despite their prominence today, it is safe to say that the Lib Dems' (as they are widely known) success is still fragile and probably had more to do with the major parties' weaknesses than their own strengths (www.libdems.org.uk).

The old Liberals were liberal in the way Europeans use the term, as noted in Chapter 2. Like the Conservatives, they were staunchly pro-capitalist, but they saw unregulated markets as the best vehicles for promoting free enterprise.

The Liberals traditionally did best in Ireland, Scotland, and Wales because their vision of democracy included a strong commitment to minority rights. By the 1960s, that support in the Celtic fringe was just about all the Liberals had left.

Vainly, Liberal leaders tried to define a place for themselves between the increasingly ideological Labour and Conservative parties so that the party could become a haven for the growing number of dissatisfied voters. They made little progress until Labour began to fragment during the 1970s. In 1981, four prominent leaders (known as the gang of four) quit Labour to form the **Social Democratic Party (SDP)**. They assumed that millions of voters would follow them. When that didn't happen, Liberal and Social Democratic leaders decided to form the **Alliance**. The two parties kept their own identities and organizations, but agreed to run a single candidate in each district in 1983. The Alliance did well in the popular vote, trailing Labour by only two percentage points. However, the Alliance fell victim to Britain's first-past-the-post, or winner take all, electoral system and won only twenty-three seats, or 3.5 percent of the total.

The Alliance itself fell apart after a similar result four years later. The two parties' leaders decided to merge and create the Liberal Democrats. The new party and its leader, Paddy Ashdown, embarked on the 1992 election campaign with high hopes. Unfortunately for them, it did even worse than the Alliance.

To the surprise of many, the party turned its fortunes around. The LibDems capitalized on dissatisfaction with the Conservatives to build a strong base in local government. In the run-up to the 1997 parliamentary election, it cast itself to Labour's left on a number of issues by supporting stricter environmental protection and an income tax hike to fund better health care and education. The Liberal Democratic vote did not increase, but its number of MPs nearly tripled because many traditional Labour voters chose a Lib Dem candidate in districts that their own standard bearer had little chance of winning.

However, the party went through a wrenching change after the 2005 election when Charles Kennedy, its leader at the time, was forced to resign. After an interim leader stepped down, the party turned to **Nick Clegg** (1967–).

The party gained slightly less than one percent of the total vote but actually lost a handful of seats in 2010. Nonetheless, the Conservatives' failure to win a majority made the coalition government necessary.

Clegg and most of his fellow leaders do not come from the reformist wing of the party. Clegg himself is the son of an investment banker who spent the first years of his career working in Brussels, including a stint at the European Union, which left him predisposed to return to the party's traditional support for pro-market economic policies.

PROFILES   Nick Clegg

There was little in Nick Clegg's early life to suggest that he was destined to become one of the most dynamic politicians of his generation.

His father's mother fled the Bolshevik revolution in Russia before finally settling in the Netherlands. His mother's Dutch family left the Netherlands under a political storm and ended up being interned by the Japanese in Indonesia during World War II. Nick's father and grandfathers were intellectuals with a flair for finance—not politics.

His childhood was at least as privileged as David Cameron's, but he did show more reformist instincts early on—for example, appearing in a play on HIV/AIDS while an undergraduate. It is also not surprising that he began his professional career in Brussels, not London.

He was lucky to return to the UK at a time when the Liberal Democrats were struggling to find a leader. He was first elected to the European Parliament in 2004 and to Parliament in London a year later. In 2007, he was chosen party leader.

He has been the most successful Lib Dem leader in living memory. The party's vote grew by more than one percent in 2010, although the UK's unusual electoral system also cost it six seats from its 2005 total. Because the Tories fell short of winning a parliamentary majority on its own, the Lib Dems' votes were needed to form a government. Clegg was named Deputy Prime Minister in Cameron's cabinet. ■

JOHN GILES/PA Photos/Landov.

An Encounter with Clegg

On the Saturday before the British 2010 general election, I got on a surprisingly crowded train and finally found a seat. A few minutes out of Reading Station, a black lab emerged from under a seat and, knowing a dog fanatic when he saw one, he immediately came across the aisle and started licking me, at which point I said to the dog's "mother" that the pup would be the star of the train. She said, "No, Nick Clegg is at the front of the car."

I started talking with the lab's "parents" who were reading *The Guardian*, which had supported Labour for decades but had come out for Clegg in that very morning's edition. I, too, had read and agreed with the editorial and found myself supporting a party other than Labour for the first time since the 1960s. We talked politics to pass the time.

Then, the lab's ten-year-old "sister" went to get a snack. Passing Clegg's seat she was surprised to discover that he was speaking a foreign language and rushed back to tell her family. I told her that Clegg's wife is Spanish and that he is actually fluent in five languages. The girl encouraged me to go meet Clegg.

At the front of the car, I started talking to a fairly young guy who wasn't wearing a tie. We discussed the election and why I was supporting the Lib Dems despite the fact that I couldn't vote and my opinion wouldn't make any difference anyway. I then asked what this savvy guy did for the Clegg campaign. He replied "I *am* Clegg." After some mortified blushing on my part, the journalists pounced. My understanding of British politics and my gaffe made it into three of the better newspapers the next day (mercifully only at the end of long articles).

My brief moment of fame should drive home one important lesson.

Textbook writers are definitely not infallible.

As successful as Clegg has been, the Liberal Democrats have not been able to escape the dilemma they have faced since their heyday more than a century ago. Their vote is distributed more or less evenly around the country, leaving them with only a handful of safe seats. Like the Tories, they have also seen their support in the polls decline because of public dissatisfaction with the government's austerity policies. If current trends hold, the Lib Dems will almost certainly again be out of power after 2015.

Minor Partiems

Many people mistakenly refer to the British as a two-party system because only Labour and the Conservatives have a realistic chance of winning a national election. However, in addition to Liberal Democrats, the country has a wide variety of minor parties, the most successful of which only contest elections in one of the Celtic regions.

The two major parties combined routinely won well over 80 percent of the vote in every election from 1945 through 1970 (see Table 4.5). Since then, their share has dropped to barely two-thirds. However, like the Liberal Democrats, none of the other parties is poised to score a breakthrough at the polls, and we can therefore dispense with them quickly.

Local parties dominate in Northern Ireland, because the three leading "mainland" organizations never run candidates there. None of them, however, has ever made a difference in national politics.

Nationalist movements—including political parties—are nothing new in Scotland and Wales. The **Scottish National Party (SNP)** and **Plaid Cymru** (it now refers to itself just as Plaid) gained a new lease on life with the resurgence of regional identification. In the 1970s, Plaid Cymru and the SNP each won seats in the House of Commons. In 1974, the SNP leapt ahead of the Tories into second place in Scotland.

The regional parties' fortunes have ebbed and flowed since then. In recent parliamentary elections, they have often come in second in their regions. They were strong enough to shut the Conservatives out completely in Scotland and Wales in 1997 and to have limited them to a single seat in Scotland in 2001. However, the two parties combined won only nine and ten seats in the last four national elections, respectively.

They have done better in elections for their regional parliaments. The SNP scored a major breakthrough in 2011, which will almost certainly lead to a referendum that could begin a move toward Scottish independence as early as 2014.

There are three other minor parties that operate more or less nationally that also deserve at least a passing mention, even though they have never won more than a handful of votes. Of the three, the Greens probably have the least promising future even though they won a seat in Parliament for the first time in 2010. The British National Party has won a few local council seats in poor, racially divided cities. The United Kingdom Independence Party (UKIP) was enjoying a surprising rise in the polls as I wrote these lines, but it is hard to see a group basing its appeals solely on the alleged costs of membership in the EU challenging either Labour or the Conservatives.

TABLE 4.5 British General Election Results Since 1970

YEAR	CONSERVATIVES		LABOUR		LIBERAL DEMOCRATS		OTHER	
	VOTES (%)	SEATS	VOTES (%)	SEATS	VOTES (%)	SEATS	VOTES (%)	SEATS
1970	46.4	330	43.0	288	7.5	6	3.1	6
1974 (Feb)	37.8	297	37.1	301	19.3	14	5.8	23
1974 (Oct)	35.8	277	39.2	319	18.3	13	6.7	26
1979	43.9	339	37.0	269	13.8	11	5.3	16
1983	42.4	397	27.6	209	25.4	23	4.6	21
1987	42.3	376	30.8	229	22.6	22	4.3	23
1992	41.8	336	34.4	271	17.8	20	6.0	24
1997	30.6	165	43.2	419	16.7	45	9.7	30
2001	31.7	166	40.7	413	18.3	52	8.5	28
2005	32.3	198	35.3	356	22.1	62	10.3	30
2010	37.0	306	29.7	258	23.6	57	7.5	29

© Cengage Learning 2015

Note: Others consist almost exclusively of regional parties in Scotland, Wales, and Northern Ireland. Liberals includes Liberals up to 1983, the Liberal–Social Democratic Alliance in 1983–87, and Liberal Democrats in 1992. The total number of seats varies from election to election.

The British Electorate

During the collectivist years, the British electorate was among the easiest to understand. A single issue—social class—shaped the way most voters viewed the political world (see Table 4.6). Most people had a strong sense of party identification that tied them to one party election after election. Far more often than not, people identified with that party primarily because they believed it best represented the interests of their social class. Both mattered

TABLE 4.6 The Changing Role of Class and Gender in British Politics (Percentage Voting Labour)

YEAR	WORKING CLASS (%)	WOMEN (%)
1974 (Oct)	57	38
1979	50	35
1983	38	26
1987	42	32
1992	45	34
1997	58	49
2001	59	42
2005	48	38
2010	35	31

Sources: Based on Dennis Kavanaugh, Thatcherism and British Politics: The End of Consensus, 2nd ed. (New York: Oxford University Press, 1990), 168; Philip Norton, The British Polity, 3rd ed. (New York: Longman, 1994), 91–92; and David Sanders, "The New Electoral Background," in Anthony King et al., ed., New Labour Triumphs: Britain at the Polls (Chatham, NJ: Chatham House, 1997), 220. Data for 2001, 2005, and 2010 adapted from www.ipsos-mori.com, accessed August 20, 2010.

more than the issues of the day when people decided how to vote.

So did the fact that most voters were not all that engaged in political life. At most, 2 or 3 percent of the electorate had clearly defined and consistent belief systems. No more than 25 percent had anything approaching a firm understanding of such central political concepts as the difference between Left and Right. In fact, people changed their opinions on such issues as British membership in the Common Market so frequently that pollsters wondered if they really had opinions on anything but the most visible and controversial matters.

One railroad worker graphically revealed what such a less than insightful understanding of political dynamics was like in 1963:

> Well, when I was in the army you had to put your right foot forward, but in fighting you lead with your left. So I always think that the Tories are the right party for me and that the Labour party are fighters. I know that this isn't right really, but I can't explain it properly, and it does for me.[6]

The close ties between class and partisanship had begun to unravel by 1979. At first, observers interpreted Thatcher's victory as a vote against the radicalism of the Labour government rather than as a first step toward a

---

[6]David Butler and Donald Stokes, *Political Change in Britain*, 2nd ed. (New York: St. Martin's Press, 1976), 232.

lasting realignment. Over the course of the next decade, however, it became clear that a substantial number of workers and lower middle class voters had become consistent Tory voters.

Labour did regain some of its working-class support in 1997 and 2001. That proved to be temporary, since the two main parties did just about as well among workers in 2010.

Whatever the parties did, the political importance of class was bound to decline because of the social and economic changes discussed in Chapter 2. The continued growth of the new service economy meant that there are not as many workers as there were fifty years ago, and Labour can no longer hope to win if it appeals primarily to them.

Overall, party identification is also weaker. In 1964, 45 percent of those polled said they identified very strongly with one of the parties. Another 39 percent did so fairly strongly. By 2010, the number of strong identifiers was down to 11 percent. Fewer than 20 percent of voters said that they would trust a government led by any party or agreed that politicians live up to their promises.

In general, British voters are a lot like their counterparts in most democracies. They are as inclined to vote *against* the party in power as they are to cast an enthusiastic vote *for* the opposition and its program. That certainly was the case in 2010, which turned into a referendum on thirteen years of Labour government and its hesitant initial response to the recession. All the polls suggest that the next election will be a vote for or against what Cameron's team has done.

Interest Groups

Britain has hundreds of interest groups, ranging from the highly politicized unions to the world's best organized backyard gardeners. For our purposes, the most important thing to see is that most of them act very differently from their American counterparts.

Because the results of most votes in the House of Commons are a foregone conclusion, there is little of the kind of lobbying one finds in the United States. Groups try to maintain good relationships with the parties. However, most focus their attention on the people who draft a bill, not on how it is dealt with on the floor of the House. Governments have to consult with interest groups for information and expertise when they draft legislation. They also often need interest group cooperation in implementing new laws, something the Heath government learned to its regret when the TUC refused to comply with the Industrial Relations Act of 1971. They also provide

parties with more and more of the funds they need to run election campaigns.

Despite the declining importance of class issues, the two most important groups in British politics have their roots in the divisions growing out of the industrial revolution.

First, at the height of the collectivist era, many observers felt that Labour and the TUC were one and the same (www.tuc.org.uk). The TUC represents more than 300 individual unions that enroll about one-fourth of the workforce. Though still a powerful force, that membership rate has dipped to less than half of what it was in the 1960s. Then, part of union members' dues automatically went to Labour unless they opted out of the payment. Some Labour MPs had their then meager salaries supplemented by the unions. In recent years, parliamentary rules have tightened and TUC power has eroded, thereby weakening the toes between the unions and the party.

Second are business associations, which have always been close to the Tories. As in the United States, there are trade associations for most industries. The **Confederation of British Industries (CBI)** is the most important one (www.cbi.org.uk). Although more than 250,000 companies and trade associations are members, most of its income comes from the large firms with over a thousand employees which dominate it.

During the collectivist years, the government openly consulted the TUC and CBI in what were known as tripartite or **corporatist** arrangements. Today, their influence is harder to pin down, although the recent scandals involving Rupert Murdoch's NewsCorp shows that big business has a significant influence on both major parties. Similarly, Ed Miliband's defeat of his brother in the contest for the Labour Party leadership shows that the TUC is still a force to be reckoned with.

The British State: Enduring Myths and Changing Realities

In 1867, Walter Bagehot (1826–77) published *The English Constitution*. Much like Alexis de Tocqueville's *Democracy in America*, Bagehot's book is still read both as a classic historical document and because its insights about politics are still useful today.

His continued impact begins with the very fact that he wrote about the constitution at all. That may not seem important to people from other liberal democracies, but it is in this case, because Britain does not have a written constitution. Bagehot was one of the first people to point out that the UK does indeed have one, but it is unusual in that

TABLE 4.7 The British and American States

FEATURE	UNITED KINGDOM	UNITED STATES
Basic constitutional arrangements	Unwritten Unitary Fusion of powers Relatively strong	Written Federal Separation of powers Relatively weak
Executive	Dominant Recruited from Parliament	Power to persuade Recruited everywhere
Legislature	Mostly debating Party voting	Making laws Coalition-based voting

© Cengage Learning

it is unwritten and consists of acts of Parliament, understandings, and traditional practices that were accepted by just about everyone.

Just as importantly, Bagehot drew a distinction between what he called the "dignified" and the "real" parts of government. The dignified side included the monarchy and other institutions that no longer had much impact on day-to-day political life. Instead, he argued, the real power in the English constitutional system lay with the House of Commons (see Table 4.7).

The Monarchy and the Lords: Still Dignified?

It has been hard to miss the dignified part of the British state in the last few years. However, neither the scandals of the last thirty years nor the royal family's renewed popularity growing out of Queen Elizabeth's diamond jubilee and Prince William's marriage should obscure the main point of this section: The monarchy and the House of Lords have no real impact on what the government does.

On paper, the monarch still rules "in Parliament." Queen Elizabeth II officially names the new prime minister and the rest of the cabinet, who kneel in front of her when taking the oath of office. She opens each session of Parliament by reading a speech from the throne outlining what "her" government plans to do during the upcoming term. A bill only becomes law once she gives it her royal assent (www.royal.gov.uk).

In practice, the monarch has no such powers. She does not determine who forms the government nor does she approve legislation. The prime minister writes the queen's speech from the throne. Although Queen Elizabeth II did play a minor role in the negotiations that led to the creation of the coalition government in 2010, it is safe to say, however, that the serious work was done by the Tory and Lib Dem leadership.

The same is true of the other dignified part of the British state—the House of Lords (http://www.parliament.uk/lords/). As we saw in the section on British history, the Lords

ANWAR HUSSEIN COLLECTION/SIPA/Newscom

Queen Elizabeth II at one of the celebrations marking her sixty years on the throne.

were once the more powerful chamber and essentially had the same legislative powers as the House of Commons until the early twentieth century. Today, the Lords technically have to approve all legislation, but, in practice, all it can do is delay passage of important legislation, especially items included in the Queen's Speech from the throne.

Before 1958, they all were hereditary peers whose members (or their ancestors) were made lords because of their service to the crown—meritorious or otherwise. Sons inherited those seats from their fathers. Daughters were not eligible. Senior members of the clergy and judiciary were also members of the Lords.

Since 1958, the monarch (but, in practice, the prime minister) has been able to name Lords for exemplary service in politics, business, or other walks of life. Their peerages end with their death and are not inherited by their children. Those "life peers" make up the vast majority of members of the House of Lords today. In 1999, Parliament (including the Lords themselves) passed a law that eliminated the right to vote in the House of all but ninety-two of the hereditary peers.

The second Blair government outlined plans for a reformed second house that would be partially elected and partially appointed. Neither Blair nor Brown ever introduced legislation that would have restructured the Lords. Further reform is not a high priority item, at least for the Conservative side of the coalition government. Nonetheless, almost everyone agrees that the House of Lords is an anachronism. The problem is that no one can agree on what should replace it.

The House of Lords does serve one useful purpose. By tradition, cabinet members must be members of Parliament. In order to appoint people to the cabinet who are not in the Commons, the prime minister can name them to a life peerage.

Parliamentary Sovereignty—Sort Of

The **House of Commons** (www.parliament.uk) was the heart of what Bagehot thought of as the real British state, because it alone determined who governed and which laws were passed. In that sense, Parliament was and still is sovereign.

However, the Commons has not been the real day-to-day decision-making body for more than a century. Its impact is more subtle and indirect and rests on what political scientists call the parliamentary arithmetic or the distribution of seats among the parties. In other words, the power of the Parliament lies in the composition of its majority.

Party Government

When there is a majority party, its leader becomes prime minister and can almost always count on the support of the other MPs from his or her party. If no single party wins a majority, the monarch asks the leader of the party that came in first to form a government. If he or she cannot, things would get complicated, but the monarch has not had to go beyond his or her first choice for the better part of a century.

The prime minister then chooses the rest of the government, all of whom must be MPs. As we saw in Chapter 2, they keep their seats in the Commons or the Lords while they serve in government.

The head of the largest minority party becomes leader of the opposition and appoints the shadow cabinet, whose members monitor and criticize the actions of their counterparts in the government. And, because of the way Westminster systems operate, the team that wins at the polls can see most of its campaign pledges turned into public policy in an arrangement that is often referred to as party government.

The majority and minority leaders are senior politicians who enjoy the ideological and personal support of the other MPs in their party. As such, they are quite different from most recent American presidential candidates, who won their party's nomination because of their personal bases of support often built during careers spent outside of Washington. In Britain, there is only one road to the top—the parliamentary party—and, it usually takes decades for a politician to build that kind of support, as we can see in the ways that Margaret Thatcher and Gordon Brown rose to power.

Thatcher was elected to Parliament for the first time in 1959 when she was thirty-three years old. She spent the next decade on the **backbenches**, as the seats reserved for MPs who are not in the leadership are known. Only then was she appointed to her first cabinet post. Six years later, her fellow Conservative MPs chose her as the party leader. Three years after that she became prime minister.

Brown was thirty-two when he was first elected. Because Labour was in disarray, young politicians like Brown rose through the ranks more quickly than Thatcher did. Still, Brown had spent eleven years in the House before he became one of the party's leaders and had twenty-four years' experience in the House of Commons, including ten as Chancellor, before moving into 10 Downing Street.

Cameron, Clegg, and Miliband were able to reach the top of their parties far more quickly largely because all three parties had leadership vacuums after the 2005 or 2010 elections. In all likelihood, they will turn out to be exceptions to the rule. Future party leaders will probably have career paths more like Thatcher's or Brown's.

The British system is also often called cabinet government because it is the body in which all the important policy decisions are formally made. The cabinet is also a powerful body in the United States. Other than that, the two have little in common.

Britain's unwritten constitution allows the prime minister to redefine the structure of government by combining, breaking up, or creating ministries and determining who sits in the cabinet. At the end of 2012, twenty-two people were ministers or secretaries of state; six others routinely attend cabinet meetings (www.number-10.gov.uk).

Each minister is responsible for a department, such as foreign affairs, the Exchequer (economics), or defense. Men and women are appointed to cabinet positions that roughly correspond to their positions in the party's power structure, which do not necessarily correspond to their interests or talents. Consequently, they are less likely to be experts in the areas they are responsible for than their American counterparts.

Unlike the United States, ministers only have a small staff of political advisors, all of whom are MPs. Thus, on June 8, 2012, Defense Secretary Philip Hammond had four MPs and one Lord serving under him. By contrast, then

U.S. Secretary of Defense Leon Panetta had more than forty offices and countless sub-offices, most of which were led by political appointees, almost none of whom had ever been members of either the House or Senate.

Also unlike the United States, the cabinet operates under what is known as **collective responsibility**. Individual ministers must publicly support all cabinet decisions, including those they disagree with. If not, they are expected to resign, as Clare Short and the late Robin Cook did over Iraq. Collective responsibility has not been applied as rigidly by the coalition government, with Lib Dem leaders occasionally voicing their disagreements with Tory policy, although the two parties have never come close to a parting of the ways on anything that could be construed as a vote of confidence.

The House of Commons

As a result, the House of Commons rarely has much of an impact on the legislative process. In fact, Parliament often appears to be little more than a rubber stamp giving formal assent to bills drafted at the cabinet level or higher.

That does not mean that it is unimportant. Elections to the Commons determine who forms the government.

The House of Commons currently has 650 MPs. Like members of the House of Representatives in the United States, MPs represent single-member districts and are chosen through a **first-past-the-post** electoral system, but there the similarities between the two systems end.

MPs are not expected to represent constituent interests in the ways members of Congress do. They do not even have to live in their districts. The national party organization will frequently "parachute" leading politicians into safe seats, all but guaranteeing that they will be reelected time and time again. For example, in the late 1990s, I lived near Henley-on-Thames, the site of the world-famous regatta. Our MP was Michael Heseltine, a prominent Tory who served as deputy prime minister during the last two years of the Thatcher government. Few of my neighbors knew that Heseltine did not live in the district. Even fewer of them cared because they understood that MPs are not primarily elected to reflect the views and preferences of the "folks back home."

Debate in the House of Commons is among the most acrimonious in the world, as reflected in the very architecture of its chamber in the Palace of Westminster. Most legislatures are laid out in a semicircle with the speaker's podium in the center. In the UK, the government and opposition face each other on benches that, tradition has it, are separated by the distance of two drawn swords. Members hurl political charges and personal insults at each other. They often shout so loudly that the person who has the floor cannot be heard, while the Speaker pounds the gavel and screams "order, order" to no avail. Sessions are especially heated when an important bill is being debated or the prime minister takes the floor on Wednesday afternoons to answer whatever questions MPs want to ask. In fact, no introduction to British politics would be complete today without watching Prime Minister's Questions which are readily available on the Internet on the Parliament's own site, C-SPAN (which televises them on Sundays in the United States), and YouTube.

However intense it may be, that debate almost never makes a difference. As long as one party or coalition has a majority in Parliament, it is virtually assured of getting its bills passed. The government introduces all important legislation. Much of it is included in the party's manifesto, which it ran on in its election campaign and is used as the basis for the Queen's Speech from the Throne, which opens each session of Parliament.

A vote on any such piece of legislation is considered a vote of confidence in which the Commons not only votes on the legislation but also affirms its support for the government. MPs know that a vote of confidence is being held if they receive a **three line whip**, which informs them that a vote is scheduled and includes a note such as "your attendance is absolutely essential," which is underlined three times. When it is time for a division (the MPs literally divide and go into separate rooms for those in favor of a bill and the other for those opposed), the prime minister invariably gets enough votes to win passage of the bill— and survive in office.

Violating a three line whip is considered a serious breach of party discipline and rarely goes unpunished. MPs routinely follow party discipline because failure to do so could bring their party's (or coalition's) government down, although that has not happened in eighty years. The few who repeatedly ignore them will see their prospects for promotion end or even be expelled from the party.

During a typical parliamentary term, well over 90 percent of the legislation proposed by the majority party is passed. Backbench pressure can sometimes force the government to modify or even withdraw a bill, but that almost never happens on what it considers to be major legislation.

"Rebellions" that do not threaten the survival of a government are now more common than they used to be. Dozens of Labour MPs voted against the war in Iraq and increases in university tuition fees while Blair was prime minister. Similarly, eighty-one Tories voted against the Cameron government's ratification of the Treaty of Lille, which strengthened some of the EU's powers. However, the life of the government was never in serious jeopardy on any of those occasions.

MPs can make a difference on some kinds of minor legislation, the most important of which are "free votes"

PA PHOTOS /LANDOV.

David Cameron at Prime Minister's Question Time.

in which the party lets members vote however they want. These occur in a number of ways and for a number of reasons. All involve issues that are not included in the party's manifesto, are initiated by backbenchers, or deeply divide the party. They are never issues that the government needs to stake its confidence on. For instance, in 2006, the Labour government allowed a free vote on a bill that would ban smoking in most pubs and restaurants, because it feared that so many Labour members would defect that the bill would be defeated.

Backbenchers' influence is limited, too, by the way the House of Commons is organized. It does not have the kind of committee system in which members and their extensive staffs develop expertise in a given policy area. Members of the Commons have one or two full-time staffers, compared with an average of eighteen for members of the House of Representatives in the United States. Their office budgets are barely a fourth of that of an American representative.

Limits on Party Government

Even though they have so much power, British governments rarely act rashly or irresponsibly. Sweeping new legislation is usually introduced only after an extended period of study and debate. The discussions that culminated in the creation of the National Health Service in 1948 began in the mid-1930s, when major flaws in the old insurance system became inescapable. Another decade passed before the government white paper on the subject was published in 1944. Four more years went by before the bill was passed.

Furthermore, when governments do blunder, there are ways, however imperfect, for disgruntled MPs to respond.

For example, when British and French troops occupied the Suez Canal in 1956 after it had been taken over by the Egyptian government, Conservative MPs continued to support Anthony Eden's government, which easily survived a vote of confidence. It was clear, however, that Eden's actions had cost him the confidence of his own party. Sensing that, he resigned the following year, citing his declining health. In fact, he did not resign because of his health—he lived until 1977. Eden quit because enough Conservative MPs had exerted behind-the-scenes pressure that he realized he had to leave.

Far more often than not, the government does get what it wants. As Andrew Marr put it:

> Government backbenchers can, at rare moments, exercise some leverage on the general drift of the executive policy which can, from time to time, help change the world beyond Westminster. But most of the time, frankly, it's more like children shouting at passing aircraft.[7]

In the end, even the idea of party or cabinet government may understate just how closed the process is. Even though British cabinet meetings are not open to the press let alone political scientists, we know a lot about what goes on at them. When it suits their purposes, ministers leak what the cabinet has discussed to the press.

---

[7] Andrew Marr, *Ruling Britannia: The Failure and Future of British Democracy* (London: Michael Joesph, 1995), 115.

Many ministers, like the late Richard Crossman, write memoirs after they retire. Crossman was one of the Labour party's leading intellectuals in the early 1960s and hoped to head one of the major ministries. However, because of his relatively low position in the party hierarchy, he had to settle for Housing, a position he was neither particularly interested in nor qualified to hold. Nonetheless, Crossman came to office committed to fulfilling the goal for his ministry as it had been laid out in the party's manifesto: constructing five hundred thousand new houses and apartments during his term in office.

He assumed, too, that he would simply tell his civil servants what the cabinet wanted, and they would say, "Yes, minister," and get busy making it happen. But, as the sitcom of the same name shows (www.yes-minister.com), "yes, minister" often means exactly the opposite, which is how each episode ends. Officially, the civil servants are there to do what their title suggests—serve their minister. In reality, they have spent so many years in government service and have so many influential contacts within the bureaucracy that they can delay or undermine their political master's goal without ever having to come out and say, "no, minister." In this case, they kept finding technical obstacles to convince Crossman that they could not conceivably build that many homes that fast.

More important for Crossman, instead of the excitement and power of making the "big decisions" about his country's future, he found himself preoccupied with seemingly never-ending public relations functions and paperwork. Meanwhile, Prime Minister Harold Wilson and the handful of ministers closest to him made the important decisions and then presented them to the cabinet as a whole as faits accomplis. Ministers outside of that inner circle, like Crossman, only had a say on issues that affected their own ministries rather than the central issues of national policy that had drawn them into public service in the first place.

That trend was magnified to such an extent under Blair that observers today talk about the "presidentialization" of the cabinet in which the prime minister exerts the kind of personal influence and patronage that are common in the United States. Blair relied heavily on personal advisers, many of whom were not in the cabinet. He assumed all but total control of the Labour Party, exiled ideological rivals from the cabinet, and used his personal popularity to build support for his policy agenda. Little seems to have changed under Cameron, which, at times, has led to tensions with his Lib Dem coalition partners. All in all, there is next to no chance that Britain will return to the time when the prime minister was literally the *prime* minister or the first among equals.

Comparative Emphasis: Women

The last two governments have done a lot to improve the political impact not only of women but of minorities and people with disabilities as well.

Women traditionally voted for Conservatives more than for Labour until the women's movement led many to move leftward. Today, women and men usually vote the same way, meaning that there is nothing like the "gender gap" in the United States.

Under Blair, Labour did take steps to give more women a real chance of winning by insisting that they be included on short lists for the party nomination in all open seats. That led to the election of more than one hundred women in each of the three elections in which he led Labour to victory. With a large number of women with young children in the Commons, the government ended the practice of holding debates and votes as late as 10:00 P.M. so that MPs (men and women alike) could get home to their families.

The Equality Act was one of the last laws enacted under Labour. It bans and provides compensation for almost all forms of discrimination that touch on women's lives. Some of its funding was cut as part of the austerity policies discussed later in the chapter. But Theresa May, the Home Secretary and Minister for Women and Equalities under Cameron, has made it clear that the law will not be gutted. ■

The Rest of the State

The other parts of the British state are nowhere near as important. Nonetheless, three of them are worth mentioning in passing.

First, the British bureaucracy is weaker than its equivalents on the European continent and in Japan. There, top civil servants believe that it is part of their job to help coordinate economic policy making. In the UK, most senior bureaucrats think of themselves as neutral experts and administrators whose job is limited to fleshing out the details of proposed legislation and keeping politicians from making major mistakes.

Until recently, the top ranks of the civil service were mostly staffed by white male "mandarins," who were recruited and promoted on the basis of their general intellectual ability rather than their technical expertise. Since the 1990s, there have been a number of changes, including the creation of a Senior Civil Service. It consists of about four thousand people and is about half the size of the American Senior Executive Service. About a third of its members are technical experts, not generalists. In 2011, 35 percent were women and 5 percent were members of racial minorities.

Second, Thatcher and Major diluted cabinet and parliamentary sovereignty by giving two types of nonelected bodies more authority. First are regulatory agencies, which supposedly oversee the newly privatized companies, most of whose names begin with "Of." Thus, Oftel deals with telecommunications, Ofwat with water, and Ofsted with standards in education.

In addition, there are about eight thousand quasi-autonomous nongovernmental organizations (QUANGOs), which are roughly equivalent to independent American entities such as the Environmental Protection Agency. During the 1960s and 1970s, Conservative and Labour governments alike decided to "hive off" many regulatory, commercial, and cultural functions to these organizations. QUANGOs were set up, for example, to coordinate the development of new towns, to regulate health and safety at the workplace, and to improve human resources. Some of them, like the Consultative Panel on Badgers and Tuberculosis or the Welsh Office Place Names Advisory Board, rarely raise political eyebrows. Yet, some, like the University Grants Committee, which funds universities, have some of the most controversial assignments in British politics.

Third, the courts have not had a major policy-making role since the end of the Glorious Revolution of 1688 forbade judges from ruling on the constitutionality of an act of Parliament. In the last generation or so, however, a new generation of more activist judges has stretched that centuries-old policy to its limits. In 1991, a judge overturned the law that did not allow men to be tried for raping their wives. Two years later, another ruled that doctors do not have to keep brain-dead patients alive if their condition is irreversible. In addition, in 1995 the country's most powerful judge publicly criticized Home Secretary Michael Howard's plans to require stiffer sentences for repeat offenders.

Constitutional Reform

Under Blair, Britain adopted a number of constitutional reforms that did not alter the distribution of power at the national level but did decentralize and marginally democratize decision making.

The new regional assemblies in Wales, Scotland, and Northern Ireland have considerable leverage over education and social policy, although most decisions that matter are still made in London. As we have already seen, Labour dramatically altered the composition of the House of Lords without reducing its negligible role in policy making any further.

The Liberals, not surprisingly, have long supported electoral reform that would give smaller parties representation in the Commons that was more in keeping with their share of the vote. A referendum that would have led to the adoption of one such system failed in 2011 which almost certainly killed hopes for reform for years to come. The government may introduce legislation to reduce the size of the House by about fifty, but that will do even less than the reform of the Lords to redistribute power.

The one constitutional issue on the horizon would be any new treaty or other agreement that would cede more power to the EU. As we will see later in this chapter and in Chapter 7, the major parties agree that any such initiative would have to be voted on in a referendum and would certainly fail given the current climate of opinion.

Public Policy: Foreign and Economic Policy

Recent British public policy can be subdivided into two parts. Domestically, the British have been innovators. Internationally, government after government has followed the broad contours of American foreign policy.

The Thatcher and Blair (and Major and Brown) Revolutions

Their supporters often call Margaret Thatcher's and Tony Blair's public policies revolutions. By the standards we will see in later chapters, that is certainly an overstatement.

Whatever we decide to call them, the reforms they undertook echo three of the themes introduced in Chapter 2 that appear in the rest of Part 2.

- The socialist left has suffered serious and perhaps fatal political blows, and social and economic policy goals are now based more on the private sector and the market.

- Rarely have the public policies led to the kind of sweeping and positive outcomes that their advocates anticipated or addressed most of the big questions raised at the beginning of Chapter 1.

- These policies have enjoyed only limited success largely because states everywhere are less and less masters of their social and economic destinies.

In the UK, a single question has dominated domestic policy making ever since Margaret Thatcher became leader of the Conservative Party. As support for collectivism has declined, what should British governments do instead?

Before then, Clause 4 of the Labour Party policy program set the frame of reference for most issues in the public policy debate. The party adopted Clause 4 in 1919 and thereby committed itself to state ownership of the "commanding heights" and central management of the rest of the economy. Labour leaders assumed that nationalization and planning would stimulate unprecedented growth, the benefits of which could be passed on to the working class, creating a more just and equal society in the process. The Conservatives certainly did not share that commitment to democratic socialism, but even they anchored their alternative policy positions on the assumption that the state could and should play a major role in steering the economy.

By the early 1970s, most of the industries nationalized after World War II were losing money, the remnants of the planning apparatus was not producing anything approaching rapid growth, and the welfare state was proving increasingly expensive, especially health service. Overall government spending had grown to over 40 percent of GNP.

Even before the union-led protests of the early 1970s, a group of Tories had crystallized around Thatcher, rejected the collectivist consensus, and wanted to sharply reduce the role of the state as much as possible. During the eighteen years she and Major held the prime ministry, most public utilities, telecommunications, the airlines, and even parts of the National Health Service (NHS) and the BBC were privatized. Thatcher also allowed most council (public) housing tenants to purchase their homes.

Privatization was extremely popular at first. Home ownership reached 60 percent of the total population during Thatcher's first term. Though institutional investors purchased most of the stock in the privatized firms, 2.2 million citizens bought shares in British Telecom and 4 million did the same with British Gas. Government subsidies to industry were cut. Firms were encouraged to modernize and to reduce "redundant" labor, even though that meant the number of unemployed rose to over three million. Taxes that hit the wealthy the hardest were slashed to generate more money for investment. In their place, taxes were raised on cigarettes, alcohol, and gasoline, which disproportionately affected the poor.

The Tories did not have as much success with the other half of their economic policy—rolling back the welfare state. As the Thatcherites saw it, the collectivist policies that previous Tory governments had supported were wasteful because they handed out money without giving recipients the ability to permanently pull themselves out of poverty. Unlike the nationalized industries, however, the social services programs were still highly popular, and attempts to reduce them met with stiff resistance. Still, the government cut funds for programs that helped single parents, university students, and the unemployed.

More than thirty years have passed since Thatcher left office, but her policies and her legacy remain controversial. To her supporters, she saved the British economy by bringing both inflation and unemployment under control and by creating a more dynamic private sector. To her detractors, she created new problems and exacerbated existing ones by widening the gap between rich and poor and by allowing the quality of public services to deteriorate.

Blair and Brown never planned to roll back Thatcher's and Major's reforms. Indeed, in some ways, they out-Thatchered Thatcher. In one of its first acts, Blair's administration gave the Bank of England the power to set interest rates without consulting the government. His government privatized some more services, including failing local education authorities, parts of the London Underground, and more of the NHS. The first Blair government kept its promise not to raise taxes for the life of its Parliament or to increase spending above the levels in the budgets they inherited from the Conservatives for two years.

It also took steps to redesign the welfare state. Instead of simply giving grants, Blair and his colleagues experimented with public-private partnerships that would help recipients gain skills that would allow them to take more control of their lives. For example, they introduced a "new deal" that required unemployed young people to enroll in training programs partially run by employers that held out the hope of real opportunities for long-term jobs. Of the 250,000 chronically unemployed young people, three-quarters found and kept jobs for at least three months after they finished training.

Despite its pro-market rhetoric, the first Blair government was able to redirect quite a bit of money to the poor and to the public services. After the self-imposed spending limit ended, the government was able to devote significantly more money to education and the NHS. The poorest retirees saw their incomes grow by at least 3 percent per year. The income of the poorest two-fifths of the population rose by 8 percent. During Blair's second term, the government added ten thousand teachers, twenty thousand nurses, and ten thousand doctors. The minimum wage rose to £4.85, or nearly $8 an hour.

Blair's innovations went beyond the traditional welfare state. For instance, Blair and his colleagues worked with the new city government to address the fact that London was one of the most congested and polluted cities in the world. Drivers entering the city center are now assessed a toll of approximately $15. The scheme has already reduced traffic congestion dramatically and is now paying for itself. Within ten years it is expected to generate over $2 billion, which will be used for investment in the country's dilapidated mass transit network (www.cfit.gov.uk/congestion-charging/factsheets/london/index.htm). Similar plans are under consideration in cities like Reading, where I could walk the three miles from my wife's office to my own faster than I could drive it during rush hour.

Not everything Blair and Brown did was either progressive or popular. To cite a single example, theirs was the first government to charge fees for university tuition, which had been free until then. Prior to the late 1990s, higher education was free other than room, board, books, and incidental expenses. In 2013, a year's tuition at most major universities costs £9,000 or about $15,000.

Long before Blair stepped down, Labour had run out of innovative ideas, and the economic crisis denied Brown any hope of moving the UK in a more egalitarian direction. In other words, the Blair revolution was over long before its namesake returned to private life.

Cameron and the Coalition Government

Thatcher and Blair reshaped much of British politics. David Cameron, by contrast, came to office with seemingly more limited ambitions. Given the depth of the economic crisis and the constraints that are part and parcel of a coalition government, most observers thought that they would likely be able only to pursue incremental reforms. However, because the coalition partners agreed on economic policy and the crisis was even more severe than people realized at the time of the election, they may end up having more of a lasting policy legacy than either of their far flashier predecessors.

As Cameron and Clegg both saw it (rightly or wrongly), big government was the source of most of Britain's problems. In ways that echo what we will see in the next three chapters, their response can be summed up in a single word, *austerity*. On that front, at least, their impact may turn out to be more sweeping than Thatcher's.

One of their first and most dramatic initiatives was the passage of sweeping budget cuts. Almost every cabinet department has been hit hard. The business and innovation, local government, and the environment and rural affairs budgets were reduced by more than 7 percent a year between 2011 and 2014. Some ministries—including defense and international development—were cut far less. However, they can expect no increase in spending during the life of the government.

As I write in early 2013, Britain is poised to enter its second recession in the last five years. Economists refer to it as a double dip recession in large part because they failed to adequately address the causes of the first one despite a brief period of temporary recovery early in this decade.

Foreign Policy

As is the case in most countries today, its domestic and foreign policies are increasingly and inextricably intertwined. That is easiest to see in the UK's tangled, troubled relationship with the rest of Europe and, less directly, in its so-called **special relationship** with the United States.

Europe

At the moment, the British are as divided as any European society about their relationship with their increasingly interdependent—if not unified—continent. Britain's ambiguity about Europe is reflected in its geography. It is little more than twenty miles from Dover in Kent to Calais in France, a distance that high-speed trains cover in ten minutes. However, for many in the UK, the English Channel is the psychological equivalent of an ocean.

The debate over its role in Europe is not new. The Conservative Macmillan government decided not to join the Common Market when it was established in 1957 (see Chapter 7). When it tried to join in the 1960s, France's President Charles de Gaulle twice vetoed its application. De Gaulle's successor, Georges Pompidou, was less hostile toward the British, and the UK was allowed to become a member in 1972.

Its membership has always been controversial. At first, many on the left opposed joining the European Community, as it was known then. That led the Wilson government to hold the country's first-ever referendum in 1975. After it passed, virtually all politicians came to accept membership in one form or another. However, that was all they accepted.

Thatcher's wing of the Conservative Party consistently opposed further expansion of either the size or the powers of the European Community. Her government negotiated compromises that enabled the UK to opt out of some of the provisions of the Single European Act (1986) and Maastricht Treaty (1991), including membership in the Eurozone. By the time Major became prime minister, almost all Tories had become **euroskeptics** who objected to anything they feared would infringe on British sovereignty. Think here of two examples from the late 1990s that were more important symbolically than substantively. First, the EU ruled that the British violated the human rights of IRA terrorists killed in Gibraltar. Shortly thereafter, it banned the worldwide export of British beef because of "mad cow disease."

During this century, the euro has been the ideological flashpoint in European policy. The Tories rejected adopting

Comparative Emphasis: Globalization

Britain probably provides the best illustration in this book of the impact of globalization on an industrialized democracy. In many ways, the quote from Andrew Marr that begins this chapter tells it all. The country, which once "ruled the waves," finds itself increasingly buffeted by forces that have their origins beyond its shores.

Perhaps most important—although hardest to pin down—is the role economic forces in other countries play in Britain. Thus, 99 percent of the automobiles assembled in the UK are made by companies that do not have their headquarters there. Twenty percent of the shares in one of the few remaining automobile manufacturers that make the famous London black taxis (not all of which are black any more) were sold to a Chinese company in January 2013. In turn, the United Kingdom is a major site for direct foreign investment, in large part because its industrial workers are relatively poorly paid by European standards. ■

the new currency from the beginning, while some in the Labour party favored doing so. However, given both the state of public opinion and the British economy, neither the Blair nor the Brown government came close to formally proposing British adoption of the euro and made it clear that if the UK government ever chose to do so, its decision would have to be approved in a referendum. If one were held today, it would almost certainly fail.

In the long term, however, opposition to further European integration may turn out to be a rear-guard effort assuming the EU weathers its current crisis, which is by no means certain. Even though the UK does not use the euro, most of its companies conduct business in it. Citizens can be paid in euros and do their banking in them as well. And, it's more than just the currency or the constitution. When I taught at the University of Reading in the late 1990s, fully 20 percent of its students came from other European countries. Today, almost a third of the faculty comes from outside of the UK. In the village where I lived, there was at least one family from each of the EU member states other than Luxembourg.

Iraq and Afghanistan

Despite its glorious past, Britain today is one of a handful of "second tier" states whose influence pales in comparison with that of the United States or even the BRICS (Brazil, Russia, India, China, and South Africa) discussed in Parts 3 and 4. In the changed international environment since the end of World War II, the UK has seen its empire disappear, while government after government has had no choice but to reduce its global footprint.

There is no question that Britain today is a junior party in the Western coalition of nations dominated by the United States. British politicians of all stripes claim that they have a special relationship with Washington which gives the UK more influence than other middle-level states, but the reality is that Britain carries roughly the same weight as France, Germany, or Japan internationally. Many people outside of the political establishment may not like it, but the fact is that Britain almost always ends up following the policy lead set in Washington.

Nothing illustrates that better than Iraq and Afghanistan.

Blair may have built his reputation on his domestic record, but foreign affairs proved to be his downfall. Blair took his country to war more often than any prime minister in recent British history. More than anything else, it was his decision to support the American-led invasions of Iraq and Afghanistan that drove him from office.

It was hardly surprising that Blair supported the United States in invading Afghanistan after the terrorist attacks of 9/11. The attacks shocked the world, especially people who lived in a country that had known its share of terrorism in recent years. Blair also had little choice in the matter, because the NATO treaty obliged Britain to defend any member that is attacked by another state that is not part of the alliance.

The British decision to send the second largest contingent of troops in support of the American invasion and occupation of Iraq in 2003 is nowhere near as easy to understand. Blair and President George W. Bush had almost nothing in common. Nonetheless, Blair supported Bush from the beginning and never wavered in his support for the United States as the plans to go to war progressed. The two leaders took all but identical positions, including on the claim that Iraq had weapons of mass destruction, which proved to be grossly inaccurate. Blair made it clear that Britain would send troops to join the so-called coalition of the willing even after Bush gave him a convenient way to drop out without losing face.

About fifteen thousand British troops were deployed to Iraq at the time of the 2003 invasion. After the Baath regime fell, Britain was given primary responsibility for security and reconstruction near the southern city of Basra until it withdrew its last troops in July 2009.

AP Photo/Charles Dharapak.

Cameron and Obama at their 2011 summit. Being in England, of course it was raining.

From the outset, much of the public opposed the war, including the overwhelming majority of Labour voters. Blair was never in danger of losing a vote of confidence over the war because the Tories supported the British role in it. Nonetheless, support for his policies continued to plummet. One former leader of the Liberal Democrats referred to him as "Bush's poodle." The derogatory label stuck.

If Blair had allowed a free vote for Labour MPs on Iraq, far fewer than half of them would have supported him. Anger and frustration about Iraq, and Blair's leadership style in general, helped convince him to announce before the 2005 election that he would not run for a fourth term as Labour leader and sped up his decision to leave office two years into his third term.

British involvement in Afghanistan has not been as controversial, although it has been no more popular. In fact, British troops faced some of the toughest combat of all the allied forces, most notably in Helmand province. By mid-2012, the UK had lost over four hundred soldiers.

The Media

As in all the industrialized democracies, most people get most of their political news from the mass media. British television and radio networks and printed media, however, are quite different from those in the United States. To begin with, they are far more centralized, with most political information coming from national newspapers and television and radio stations.

American readers would be surprised by British television news. To begin with, there is very little local news on television. In most regions, the local news is only on for half an hour a day. Conversely, the five main "terrestrial" networks carry their national news programs at different times, so you can watch the news at 6:00, 7:00, 8:00, 9:00, 10:00, and 10:30 P.M. every evening.

BBC Radio 4's news programs are also widely listened to and have a greater impact than their equivalents on National Public Radio in the United States. Although British networks tend to be impartial, that is not necessarily true of individual journalists. Interviewers are known for the way they grill politicians, especially those thought to be arrogant or to be withholding information. Some interviewers, including John Snow, the most popular anchor, openly display their personal views from time to time.

England has eleven main daily newspapers, all of which are edited in London and distributed nationally. Scotland, Wales, and Northern Ireland have their own papers, but the London dailies are available there as well. Five are "quality" newspapers known as broadsheets. The *Guardian* and *Independent* usually support Labour (though neither did in 2010), the *Times* and *Telegraph* almost always endorse the Tories, and the *Financial Times* is aimed at the business community. Each has the kind of high-quality and in-depth coverage American readers find in the *Washington Post* or *The New York Times*. Together, the broadsheets sell about two million copies a day.

The rest are tabloids whose political coverage is much more superficial and whose tone is often scandalous and even racist. The *Mirror* normally supports Labour but opposed the war in Iraq, including publishing a fake picture supposedly showing the abuse of prisoners by British soldiers. The others are strongly Conservative. In all, the tabloids sell about ten million copies a day.

There are also local daily papers. They do not, however, cover much national news, and their political influence is largely limited to local issues.

In 2012, the UK's most powerful media mogul and his empire became the subject of intense controversy. Australian-born Rupert Murdoch is by far the most powerful media magnate in the world. In addition to a majority of the Australian press, he owns controlling interests in the *Wall Street Journal,* the *New York Post,* and the various Fox networks in the United States and the *Times, Sun,* and B-Sky-B, by far Britain's most-watched satellite and cable provider.

Murdoch has long been known for his conservative political views which are reflected in the coverage of Fox News in the United States. In Britain, Murdoch had supported Blair early on and enjoyed a close personal and—some feared—political relationship with new Labour.

By the time Cameron took office, the Murdoch empire was clearly back in the Conservative camp. Soon, however, scandals involving allegedly improper ties between his News Corporation and the Tory leadership surfaced. Murdoch was forced to close the Sunday version of the *Sun, The News of the World.* In December 2012, an inquiry led by Lord Leveson led to the creation of a new independent press watchdog, whose impact obviously remains to be seen.

Conclusion: The Stakes of 2015

Many analysts thought the election of 2010 was a watershed event. It was the first coalition government in decades. The revitalization of the Liberal Democratic Party made the end of nearly a century of domination by Labour and the Conservatives seem at least possible.

Two and a half years into the coalition, the possibility of dramatic change that could shake British politics to its constitutional core no longer appears to be on the agenda. All the signs are that the United Kingdom will follow the familiar dynamic of most other industrialized democracies in recent years. Like other leaders in office during difficult economic times, Cameron already seems to be taking the blame for the UK's economic woes. Were an election to be called in 2013 rather than in 2015 when it almost certainly will be held, Cameron would almost certainly lose and be replaced by Ed Miliband's Labour with a majority government.

That leaves us with more questions than answers. Would that government be appreciably different? Would it be more willing to address the big questions raised in Chapter 1?

KEY TERMS

Concepts	People	Organizations, Places, and Events
backbenchers	Blair, Tony	Alliance
collective responsibility	Brown, Gordon	Beveridge Report
collectivist consensus	Cameron, David	Church of England
corporatist	Churchill, Winston	Confederation of British Industries (CBI)
euroskeptic	Clegg, Nick	Good Friday Agreement
first-past-the-post	Major, John	Great Reform Act
gradualism	Thatcher, Margaret	House of Commons
Magna Carta		House of Lords
Party government		Irish Republican Army
special relationship	**Acronyms**	Plaid Cymru
three line whip	CBI	Scottish National Party
troubles	SDP	Social Democratic Party (SDP)
unitary	MPs	Trades Union Congress (TUC)
	TUC	Unionist

USEFUL WEBSITES

There are dozens of good Internet gateways on aspects of British politics. The following is the best and is hosted by the British Politics Group, which brings together American and British scholars.

www.britishpoliticsgroup.org

The most complete public opinion data are found on the site of the UK's biggest polling firm, MORI.

www.ipsos-mori.com

All of the quality British newspapers are online. However, most useful for readers of this book is the BBC's site, which has every story it has run since it went online.

news.bbc.co.uk

Direct.gov is a well-designed entry point for people seeking services and jobs from the government. From C-SPAN's website you can also watch the weekly debate when the prime minister goes to the House of Commons for Question Time. You will have to navigate a bit around the C-SPAN site because its layout changes frequently.

www.gov.uk/government/organisations/prime-ministers-office-10-downing-street

www.direct.gov.uk

www.cspan.org

FURTHER READING

Allen, Nicholas, and John Bartle, eds. *Britain at the Polls 2010*. London: Sage, 2011. A solid collection of essays on the election put in a very broad context.

Beer, Samuel. *British Politics in the Collectivist Age and Britain against Itself: The Political Contradictions of Collectivism*. New York: Norton, 1982. An examination of the origins and workings of politics during the collectivist era and the reasons it came under pressure during the crisis.

Blair, Tony. *A Journey: My Life in Politics*. New York: Knopf, 2010. A very self-reflective view of his entire career. Readers might find the analytic book by Andrew Rawnsley (see below) more useful.

C-SPAN. *Commons Sense: A Viewer's Guide to the British House of Commons*. Washington, D.C.: C-SPAN, 1991. A short booklet to help viewers understand the parliamentary debate that C-SPAN has regularly televised since 1990. Probably the best short source on the House of Commons.

Heffernan, Richard, Philip Crowley, and Colin Hay. *Developments in British Politics*, vol. 9. New York: Palgrave/Macmillan, 2011. The most recent in a series of edited volumes on British politics with a focus on the broader implications of the 2010 election.

Hennessy, Peter. *The Prime Minister*. New York: Palgrave/St. Martin's, 2000. An encyclopedic but readable account of all postwar prime ministers and what made some more effective than others.

Lee, Simon, and Matt Beech, eds. *The Cameron-Clegg Government: Coalition Politics in an Age of Austerity*. New York: Palgrave/Macmillan, 2011. A very early look at the causes of their victory with implications for what they would do in office.

Norton, Bruce. *The Politics of Britain*. Washington: CQ Press, 2007. The best full-length text on British politics.

Rawnsley, Andrew. *The End of the Party*. New York: Penguin, 2010. The most comprehensive book on why Labour lost, written shortly before the 2010 election.

Toynbee, Polly, and David Walker. *Did Things Get Better? An Audit of Labour's Successes and Failures*. London: Penguin Books, 2001. A comprehensive and in some ways surprising assessment of the first Blair government's public policies, by two left-of-center journalists.

POLITICAL INDICATORS

FRANCE

Paris

Lyons

Bordeaux

Marseilles

GOVERNANCE (score 0–1)	HUMAN DEVELOPMENT (score 0–1)	DEMOCRACY (rank)	PEACE (rank)	CORRUPTION (rank)
.778	.884	29	40	25

CHAPTER OUTLINE

France

President Hollande and the Future of the Left?

On May 6, 2012, France elected François Hollande (1954–) as the seventh president of the Fifth Republic. The unpopular incumbent, Nicolas Sarkozy (1955–) had long been expected to lose, but the election turned out to be closer than expected, with Hollande winning just under 52 percent of the vote in the second and decisive round of voting.

Sarkozy started his term as the most popular president in the history of the Fifth Republic. Four years later, his unfavorable ratings topped 80 percent.

Almost everything he did backfired. He was not part of the traditional French political and economic elite. Unlike his predecessors who were all part of that elite, Sarkozy was brash and flashy. Instead of fine wine, he drank cola. Most importantly, he took the blame for France's poor economic performance in recovering from the great recession. Most notably, at a time when unemployment was soaring, Sarkozy and his German counterpart, Angela Merkel, strongly supported economic policies based on austerity that seemed to make the economic difficulties worse, especially in response to the sovereign debt crisis, which will be covered in more detail in the next two chapters.

THE BASICS

France

Size	547,030 sq. km (more than two times the size of the United Kingdom)
Population	65.6 million
GNP per capita	$35,100
Currency	€1.33 = US$1 (August 1, 2013).
Ethnic composition	Over 90 percent white, but with substantial minorities of African, Middle Eastern, Asian, and Caribbean origin
Religion	83–88 percent Catholic, with small minorities of Protestants, Jews, Muslims, and atheists
Capital	Paris
Head of state	President François Hollande (2012–)
Head of Government	Prime Minister Jean-Marc Ayrault (2012–)

When Sarkozy was elected in 2007, few people even knew who Hollande was; if they did, it was because he was the recently spurned partner of that year's Socialist candidate, Ségolène Royal (1953–), not because he was head of the **Socialist Party (PS)**. As the 2012 election neared, Hollande was not on most people's lists of serious socialist candidates, which included Royal and the initial front runner, **Dominique Strauss-Kahn** (DSK as he is known), who was then the president of the International Monetary Fund.

Then disaster struck DSK's campaign. He was accused of being involved in a sexual incident with a worker in a New York hotel. Although criminal charges against him were eventually dropped, his presidential campaign was ruined. Hollande entered the race and easily defeated a number of socialist rivals, including his former partner.

Given Sarkozy's mediocre track record, it is surprising that Hollande did not win in a cakewalk. But he was anything but an ideal candidate himself. His strongest selling point was the fact that he was as unlike Sarkozy as a candidate could possibly be. He is steady, consistent, and reliable, but is he neither charismatic nor telegenic. One French journalist even labeled him an "anti-hero."

The Socialists went on to win a substantial majority in the subsequent parliamentary election. The Left now controls the levers of power in what has been one of the most effective states in Europe for the last fifty years. However, the global recession and the crisis that has shaken the Eurozone to its core have made it difficult for any French leader to solve the significant policy problems he or she has to deal with, starting with a history of uneven economic growth that has defied solution for forty years.

After a year in office, Hollande and his government are struggling. Like Cameron in the UK, Hollande was expected to spark a rapid turnaround in French and European economic performance. He has tried to do so using policies inspired by the Left, but so far has had no more success than his conservative counterpart across the Channel.

There is one more parallel between the two countries and two leaders who seemingly have very little in common. The big questions raised in Chapter 1 are not on France's daily political agenda even though their impact is harder to miss in the themes raised in the rest of this chapter, especially its place in a globalizing world.

Although no one has yet used the term "France 2.0", someone should. French (and German) politics reflect how two once troubled countries met the big challenges they faced two or three generations ago. As we explore why the French succeeded then, and why they do not seem poised to do so today, we will be able to push the comparative analysis forward in at least two ways, by:

- Introducing another type of democratic system that is dramatically different from either the United States or the United Kingdom.
- Providing the first significant insights into the book's subtitle—domestic responses to global challenges.

Thinking about France

Every other chapter in this book begins with a statement by some kind of political expert. The one in this chapter comes from the father of one of my students' roommates thirty years ago. When her father was in college in the 1950s, his statement made a lot of sense. It does not now. Since then, the center of gravity in French politics is a strong state that has had a lot to do with the fact that the country is once again one of the wealthiest and most powerful countries in the world.

The Fifth Republic (1958–) should be thought of as akin to France 2.0 because it marked the first time that the country has had a democratic regime that is effective and legitimate at the same time. As we will see, establishing and consolidating the Fifth Republic was no mean feat. Nevertheless, the regime has been so successful that it suffers from the same shortcomings as the United States and Great Britain—the absence of any fundamental criticism of the basic rules and procedures that shape political life.

The Bottom Line

France is a big country by European standards. It has more than 65 million people, just about the same number as Britain. But it is almost two-and-a-half times the size of the UK, which means that France has more open space and less-congested cities.

Diversity

France was a relatively homogeneous country in the 1950s. Almost everyone spoke French. There were still noticeable local accents, and some older people only spoke Breton, Occitan, or a regional dialect. The spread of radio and television, however, had already made standard French as widely used and understood as English is in Great Britain.

Almost 90 percent of the population is at least nominally Catholic, although not more than 5 percent of the population attend church regularly. Roughly 2 percent of the population are Protestants and 1 percent is Jewish. Somewhere around 8 percent of the population—mostly postwar immigrants from former French colonies and their children—are Muslim. A slightly larger proportion of the population is neither White nor ethnically French, however you choose to define that term.

As many conservatives see it, France really isn't French any more.

More than half of the players on the team that won the 1998 World Cup were either born in or were first-generation immigrants from Armenia, Algeria, Guadeloupe, New Caledonia, Argentina, Ghana, Senegal, Italy, French Guyana, Portugal, Spain, Martinique, and the Basque Country. The team competing for the 2014 cup is even more diverse.

On December 31, 2012, the top nine songs on the French hit parade were by singers who weren't French. Number 10 was by a French singer, but Matt Pakora's father was born of Polish parents. The only artist on the list with a name my student's roommate's father would have recognized as French was Canadian—Céline Dion. Among first names for boys, François was in 313th place in 2010, trailing Matheo, Mohamed, Amine, Diego, and Ibrahim, among others.

If anything, diversity is an even more vexing political issue in France than in Great Britain. Members of minority groups are less well integrated into French society despite the best efforts of governments on the left and right. In France, concerns about diversity are now seen more in religious than racial or ethnic terms given the ban the government has imposed on wearing everything from burkas to yarmulkes.

Comparative Emphasis: Identity

Of all the countries considered in Part 2, identity politics has the most visible impact in France today. It is the only country we will consider that has a political party whose electoral appeals are all but openly racist in tone and that has had the most significant and uncontrollable violence based on racial, religious, and cultural issues.

But it is also the European country that has most integrated foreign cultural values and tastes into its mainstream. Recent immigrants are to be found in all the major political parties other than the National Front. Although it is almost impossible to define or measure, France has the highest mixed marriage rate (defined as a native-born French person marrying someone born outside the country) among the larger European countries. Most importantly for our purposes, France has the most active political movements consciously trying to reduce the role of racism and other forms of intolerance. ■

Centralization

France is also more **centralized** than the United Kingdom. Although it is hard to measure such things, no other capital city dominates its country the way Paris does. Depending on exactly where one draws the boundaries, the Paris region has between a quarter and a third of France's total population.

Paris dominates the rest of the country culturally, politically, and economically. Almost all big businesses and government agencies are headquartered there. Road and rail systems were built with Paris as their hub. Paris has long been a thriving metropolis, whereas the major provincial cities were dull and drab, leading one observer to call them the "French desert" in the 1960s. Even now, plenty of "turboprofs" teach at provincial universities but refuse to move from Paris, even though they have to commute as much as eight hours each way on France's high-speed trains.

Throughout this chapter, we will encounter examples of that centralization. Here, it is enough to consider two remarkable examples that have since gone by the political wayside given the diversity of the new France.

France is one of the few countries with an official agency that determines which new words can be added to its language. In recent years, it has struggled to keep foreign—mostly English—words out. People may well want to refer to le one-man show, disc jockey, or hit parade, but the High Commission for the French Language insists on *spectacle solo*, *animateur*, and *palmares*. Not that long ago, the commission fined American Airlines for issuing English-language boarding passes at Charles de Gaulle Airport and hauled a furniture store owner into court for advertising his showroom rather than his *salle d'exposition*.

Until the early 1990s, the government insisted that children be given the name of a saint or a figure from classical history in order to qualify for the extensive benefits it offers families. Breton, Occitan, and German names were forbidden. Richard Bernstein tells of a friend whose first and middle names were Mignon Florence, which was double trouble. Not only was Mignon not on the list of approved names, but the registry office staff was convinced that, as a girl, she should have been Mignonne. Later, her teachers insisted that she spell her name that way. Officially, she had to be Florence, which she remained until the rules were relaxed when she was an adult.[1]

A Modern Economy

France was an economic backwater in the 1950s. That is no longer the case.

[1]Richard Bernstein, *Fragile Glory: A Portrait of France and the French* (New York: Penguin Books, 1990), 110ff.

France is one of the world's richest countries. Most families enjoy a standard of living roughly equivalent to that in the United States. American salaries are a bit higher, but the French make up for that with guaranteed health care, university tuition that still costs between $300 and $700 a year, and a day-care system integrated into the public schools and open to all children over the age of two that is provided at no cost to most parents.

There are more French than German firms among the world's top businesses. The French make the world's fastest trains, the TGV *(trains à grandes vitesses)*, which can travel comfortably at more than two hundred miles an hour. The French play a leading role in Airbus, which makes state-of-the-art jumbo jets, and Arianespace, which now surpasses the American NASA in commercial space ventures.

Not everyone has benefited equally from what the late John Ardagh called the "new French revolution." Three relatively disadvantaged groups, in particular, stand out. First are older people who cannot afford to move out of their isolated villages or dingy urban apartments. Second are women, who have yet to make as much political or professional progress as their counterparts in the United States. Third are members of minority groups, most of whom still work in jobs whites are not willing to take and who are often discriminated against in ways reminiscent of the American South before the civil rights movement.

Key Questions

In 1958, France adopted the constitution for its Fifth Republic under the leadership of **Charles de Gaulle** (1890–1970). For the first time, France had a democratic government that could govern effectively. The country has had its ups and downs since then, but next to no one doubts that France deserves its position near the top of any list of the world's most influential democracies.

This chapter focuses on that transition and other changes that came produced in its wake:

- Why did it take so long for a stable democratic regime to take hold in France?

- How did de Gaulle's changes to the country's institutions and social, political, and economic processes contribute to the creation of an effective democratic state that seems all but certain to endure whatever problems it might face in the foreseeable future?

- Why is the bureaucratic elite, of which Hollande is a member, at the heart of its political system?

- Why, despite the rapid growth during the first quarter-century of the Fifth Republic's life, has the French economy proven more resistant to reform over the past twenty years?

- How and why have international forces arising in the European Union and elsewhere constrained what Fifth Republic governments have been able to accomplish in the early years of the twenty-first century?

The Evolution of the French State

Comparativists usually cite Great Britain as the model of a democratic state that evolved relatively smoothly over the centuries. They turn to France to illustrate a more difficult, but far more common, trend in which state building is a long and wrenching process. Nowhere is that easier to see than in the fact that France has had eleven regimes since the revolution that began in 1789. The United States and Great Britain have had one each (see Table 5.1).

Transformations and Divisions

To see why state building was so arduous in France, it makes sense to ask the same question we did for Britain. How did the four transformations discussed in Chapter 2 help shape French history and, in turn, the nature of its state today? Unlike the UK, those conflicts were largely left unresolved, leaving deep scars that continue to affect French politics today (http://europeanhistory.about.com).

The first transformation led to the formation of France itself. Although centralization did not leave the country politically divided, it is arguably the tradition that defines France the most to this day.

As early as 1500, there was an entity a modern-day observer could identify as France. Its government was

TABLE 5.1 French Regimes since 1789

YEAR	REGIME
Until 1792	Bourbon Monarchy
1792–1804	First Republic
1804–15	First Empire
1815–30	Bourbon Restoration
1830–48	July Monarchy
1848–51	Second Republic
1851–70	Second Empire
1875–1940	Third Republic
1940–44	Vichy Regime
1944–46	Liberation Government
1946–58	Fourth Republic
1958–	Fifth Republic

© Cengage Learning

headed by a king, but his power was limited, especially the farther one travelled from Paris. Because France was not as isolated as the British Isles, it was unable to avoid the wars of religion and national expansion that ravaged Europe for much of the next two centuries. In order to fight them, France created one of the first strong states in Europe, which most historians date from the reign of Louis XIV (1643–1715).

The revolution of 1789 further centralized power in Paris and made France by far the most uniformly administered country in Europe. Some revolutionary groups did want to drastically scale back state power. By 1792, they had lost out to the Jacobins, who were, if anything, more supportive of centralization than the Bourbon monarchs they overthrew and beheaded. For instance, they divided the country into departments that were controlled from Paris rather than by local officials.

However, centralization also led many to view the state as a distant and arbitrary political stone wall that frustrated them everywhere they turned. In that sense, centralization at least contributed to the intensification of the other three transformations, which did leave deep and lasting divisions.

For a century and a half, French politics was shaken by the third and fourth transformations. One of them was by no means new, while the other hit the country in earnest with the revolution. During that time, France used a number of regimes, all of which remained divided over the role the church should play in public life and democratization. To make matters more difficult, the two fed off and reinforced each other.

The church had been the monarchy's strongest ally. Many of the best-known leaders of the *ancien régime*, including Armand Jean du Plessis Richelieu, Jules Mazarin, and Jean-Baptiste Colbert, were cardinals as well as ministers to the king. The revolution of 1789, therefore, not only overturned the monarchy but also reinforced controversies surrounding the Church's political might.

More often than not, the most intense confrontations pitted an **anticlerical** Left against a **proclerical** Right. The liberals and radicals claimed that the France could not democratize without total separation of church and state. On the other side, royalists and other conservatives believed the clergy should play a leading role in a restored monarchy or other conservative regime. The decision to separate church and state and thus undermine ecclesiastical wealth and power provoked such resistance from proclerical groups that the **Third Republic** (1875–1940) nearly collapsed.

Those clashes occurred despite the fact that France has one of the world's oldest and strongest democratic traditions. It was the first country to formally endorse human rights with the adoption of the declaration of the rights of man in 1789. France was also the first country to extend the right to vote to all men after the revolution of 1848.

Nonetheless, France could not democratize gradually the way the British did where, among other things, traditional elites grudgingly acquiesced to their loss of power. Instead, the transition toward democracy in France came in lurches, many of which did not last.

Finally, the industrial revolution divided France in more complex ways than it did in Britain. Many workers were social democrats who believed that fundamental change in social and economic life could be achieved by working through the parliamentary system, much as Labour did in Great Britain. Others insisted that meaningful change could only be achieved by revolution. In 1920, their differences led to their division into two parties, the reformist *SFIO* and the **Communist Party (PCF)**, which was inspired by the Bolshevik revolution in Russia. Yet others were practicing Catholics who opposed both wings of the socialist Left.

Also unlike Britain, the capitalists were divided, too. Most small shopkeepers, merchants, and farmers had qualms about the industrial revolution. They used free-market rhetoric to help prop up the traditional economy under which they prospered. Because they supported the political parties that resisted social and economic change which were often in power, capitalists who wanted to modernize and industrialize argued that concerted state action was needed to overcome the market's biases toward stability. The growth-oriented industrialists got some of what they wanted when de Gaulle briefly returned to power at the end of World War II, but they lost most of their political access under the **Fourth Republic** (1846–1958),

Traditional Republican Politics: A Vicious Circle

The sad history of the Third and Fourth Republics is complicated and depressing. On average, governments lasted nine months. Prime ministers rarely lost a vote of confidence because they usually resigned once they realized they were about to lose one. We could go through those events in chronological order. However, because governments came and went at such dizzying speed, it makes more sense to focus on what I call the traditional republican syndrome. I chose the word *syndrome* intentionally, because physicians use it to refer to a pattern of symptoms that occur together and often have disastrous consequences.

At its heart were the ideological divisions left by the four transformations, which spawned six major "political families" of roughly equal size as can be seen in the results of the 1951 election (see Table 5.2).

TABLE 5.2 Seats in the French Chamber of Deputies, 1951

PARTY	SEATS
Communists	101
Socialists	106
Christian Democrats	88
Radicals	76
Minor parties	40
Independents and Peasants	95
Gaullists	120

© Cengage Learning

As we just saw, the Socialists and Communists represented the two halves of the socialist tradition and had been bitter rivals ever since their political divorce in 1920. Much like the Socialists, the Catholic Popular Republican Movement (MRP) supported the welfare state and European integration, but the two had a hard time working together because of their sharp disagreement over church-related issues.

The **Radicals** got their name in the nineteenth century, when support for liberal democracy, anticlericalism, and free-market capitalism squarely placed people on the left. The Independents and Peasants shared many of the Radicals' economic beliefs but were staunchly proclerical.

Finally, the **Gaullists** were the most recent in a long line of groups that demanded strong leadership, and they had deep roots in monarchism and Bonapartism. The Gaullists claimed to be solid republicans. They simply wanted to replace the Fourth Republic with a stronger one!

The existence of so many antagonistic parties made the second component of the vicious circle—a deadlocked parliament—all but inevitable. As in most parliamentary systems, the president was little more than a figurehead. Real power was shared by the parliament and cabinet and supposedly exercised by the prime minister or *premier ministre*.[2]

Because no party ever came close to winning a majority, members of parliament (MPs) had little choice but to form coalition governments that included members of three or four parties who had little or nothing in common. Often, tiny parties held the balance of power. Members of the coalition routinely found themselves on both sides of most important issues. As a result, almost every government rapidly saw its majority evaporate and resigned before a vote of confidence was held that would have thrown it out. The ensuing cabinet crisis would last until the parties were able to reach a compromise on the

issues that brought the old government down and form a new one. That cabinet, in turn, would survive only until it had to confront the next tough question. Not surprisingly, most of France's pressing and enduring problems went unsolved.

There was one tool that many prime ministers in other states have at their disposal that French leaders could not use—dissolving parliament in order to hold new elections. Marshal Macmahon, the first president of the Third Republic, had done just that in 1877 in the hope they would result in the election of a monarchist majority. Instead, the republican parties won a resounding victory. They immediately forced Macmahon to resign. From then on, there was an unwritten rule that neither the president nor the prime minister could dissolve parliament before the end of its term.

The Macmahon fiasco was the first of many episodes that convinced politicians that ambitious colleagues were dangerous. Reform-minded leaders were routinely passed over whenever a new cabinet had to be formed. The king makers preferred politicians whom they could count on, which meant those who were happy with the deadlocked system.

Matters were made even worse by the fact that politicians were willing to sacrifice just about everything else to advance their own careers. Most political scientists at the time believed that their ideological rhetoric was little more than a veneer to hide their self-serving goals. Many were willing to sabotage cabinets and to destroy other politicians' reputations to enhance their prestige and power.

Last, but by no means least, there was a "negative" consensus on what the state should do, which Stanley Hoffmann called a republican synthesis that sustained a stalemate society. The dominant centrist politicians represented the peasantry and the petite bourgeoisie of the small towns, who were particularly resistant to social and economic change. Although these politicians could rarely agree on what to do about the "big issues," they had little trouble seeing eye to eye on what France should *not* do, which was just about everything.

In the absence of effective parliamentary government, what power there was devolved onto the third part of the syndrome: the bureaucracy. Extreme centralization and bureaucratic inflexibility rippled throughout society. All schools, for example, followed the same curriculum to prepare students for national examinations that determined whether they passed or not.

Centralization also contributed to the final component of the vicious circle—an alienated political culture. Political scientists did not gather systematic evidence on French values until the 1960s. Nonetheless, the French

---

[2]Readers who speak French will realize that the two terms are literally interchangeable, since *premier minister* literally means first or prime minister. English speakers often simply use the term "premier" interchangeably with prime minister.

were almost certainly as frustrated and ideologically divided as any mass public in the industrialized world. Unlike the British, they frequently questioned the regime's basic structures and practices. Many were defensive individualists, convinced that there was little they could do to protect themselves from government officials and all other outsiders, who, they "knew," were out to do them in.

Consequently, the French suppressed their anger until something triggered an explosion. This was not merely a feature of national politics. What Michel Crozier called the "bureaucratic phenomenon" was the defining characteristic of an entire society that was built upon centralized, unresponsive institutions. Students, for instance, hated the rigid rules of the national education system, but they grudgingly accepted a classroom experience they disliked as long as they felt that the teacher was doing a good job preparing them for the exams that determined their academic future. If, however, the students felt that a teacher was not doing a good job, it was a different story. Then the students might suddenly break out into a wild demonstration or *chahut* (from the words for *screaming cat*), which William Schonfeld graphically described:

> Students might constantly talk with one another, get up and walk around the room whenever they feel like it, and if the teacher should call on them to respond to a question, they would answer disrespectfully— e.g., Teacher: "When you mix two atoms of hydrogen with one atom of oxygen, what do you get?" Pupil: "It rains," or "*merde.*" Or the students might jeer at the teacher in unison, call him nasty names and run around the classroom. In certain classes, wet wads of paper will be thrown across the room, landing and then sticking on the wall behind the teacher's desk. Or there might be a fistfight, with the winner ejecting the loser from the room, while the other pupils stand around cheering for one or the other of the pugilists. With some teachers, the students might bring small glass sulfur bombs into class, which would be simultaneously broken, creating such a stench that the teacher is usually driven into the hall while the pupils stay in class, happily suffering the odor. Finally, students might bring a tent, camping equipment, and food into their class and, during the lesson, set up the tent, prepare lunch for each other, and then eat it—the teacher being powerless to help.[3]

In the terms of systems analysis, that alienation fed back into the party and parliamentary morass to complete

[3]William Schonfeld, *Obedience and Revolt* (Beverly Hills, CA: Sage, 1976), 30–31.

Comparative Emphasis: Democratization

France's difficulties in building any kind of legitimate state, let alone a democratic one, illustrate just how fortunate the United States and Great Britain were.

By 1900, both the American and British states had broadly based support. The basic contours of democracy were established as well, although it would be a generation before women in either country could vote and sixty years before most African Americans could do so.

Meanwhile, the Third Republic was teetering on the brink of collapse. Though it somehow managed to weather a long string of crises, it survived only because, as one-time president and prime minister Georges Clémenceau put it, it was the form of government that divided the French the least. The Third Republic accomplished very little other than surviving, which is one of the reasons that France developed the reputation epitomized by the statement that begins this chapter. ■

the vicious circle. Nathan Leites titled one of his books about parliament *The House Without Windows*. The main section of the Parliament building actually is windowless, but he did not choose the title because of the Hôtel Matignon's peculiar architecture. If he was right, its political windowlessness went in both directions. There is little evidence that the elected officials cared a lot about what their voters wanted so they didn't look "out" much. The French people did not try to look "in" all that often either. Even though they complained about the irresponsible politicians and their ideological squabbles, they consistently reelected the MPs who enacted pork barrel legislation but could not get the bureaucracy or anyone else to move on an individual's or a community's problems.

De Gaulle's Republic

The Third and Fourth Republics were not abject failures. The church-state issue receded from center stage. There was more ministerial stability than one might expect because most of the same parties and politicians appeared in government after government.

But none of this should obscure the basic point. The two republics failed to meet France's pressing problems.

After its liberation from German occupation in 1944, France did have one brief flirtation with effective government. The old political guard had been discredited by the depression, defeat, and collaboration with the Nazis. Few people wanted to go back to the *status quo ante*. The provisional government headed by de Gaulle nationalized major industrial and financial firms and established a planning commission to supervise economic recovery. Even the bureaucracy changed with the establishment of the Ecole Nationale d'Administration (ENA) to train civil servants who would be committed to democracy and modernization.

Unfortunately, the flirtation *was* brief. When the politicians finally agreed on a constitution for the Fourth Republic, it was essentially a carbon copy of the one in use before the war. De Gaulle resigned in protest.

The history of the Fourth Republic was a sorry one indeed. The mismatch between an unchanging, ineffective government and a society facing unsolved problems was more serious than ever. At home, successive governments failed to build the social infrastructure a rapidly urbanizing population needed. Abroad, French colonies were beginning to demand their freedom, which put even more pressure on the beleaguered state.

Support for politicians was at an all-time low. Young people were so turned off that they did not even bother to learn who their leaders were. One public opinion poll showed that 95 percent of the men drafted into the army in 1956 knew who had won the Tour de France that year, but only 17 percent could name the prime minister.

Although domestic issues were the undoing of most governments, it was a foreign policy crisis that brought the Fourth Republic's short life to an end. In 1954, a revolution broke out in Algeria, where the majority Arab population demanded independence. By 1958, many of the European settlers were in revolt as well, blaming Paris for failing to put down the insurgency.

In spring 1958, the Fourth Republic's seventeenth prime minister resigned. It soon became clear that the little-known Pierre Pflimlin would be the next man to hold the job, and he was expected to begin negotiations with the Algerian Arabs.

That proved to be the last straw for the army and the white colonists. On the night of May 12–13, soldiers seized Algiers. Rumors quickly spread that the military was getting ready to invade the mainland. Finally, on June 1, the politicians turned to de Gaulle, who agreed to become prime minister again on the condition that they grant him extraordinary powers not only to deal with the rebellion but also to revise the constitution (see Table 5.3).

TABLE 5.3 Key Events in French Politics since 1958

YEAR	EVENT
1958	Creation of the Fifth Republic
1961	End of Algerian War
1962	Referendum on direct election of president First parliamentary majority elected
1965	De Gaulle reelected
1968	Events of May and June
1969	De Gaulle's resignation
1970	De Gaulle's death
1973–74	OPEC oil embargo
1981	Mitterrand and Socialists elected
1986	First period of cohabitation
1993	Second period of cohabitation
1995	Chirac elected
1997	Socialists' return to power
2012	Election of Hollande

© Cengage Learning 2015

Nonetheless, most politicians expected de Gaulle to be a typical heroic leader. On several earlier occasions, the parliament had turned to exceptional men to deal with crises and then had gotten rid of them as soon as the immediate danger passed. They had every reason to expect the same would happen with de Gaulle. He was already sixty-eight years old. Even after the 1958 elections, he had, at most, the reluctant support from the politicians in Parliament, the majority of whom were waiting for him to leave so they could return to business as usual.

De Gaulle proved them wrong.

In his decade as president, he and his colleagues ended the war in Algeria, introduced the direct election of the president, created a majority party, and survived the 1968 upheaval. When he lost a referendum on two seemingly trivial constitutional reforms and resigned, the Fifth Republic was securely in place.

Routinized Charisma: The Fifth Republic since de Gaulle

As we will see in the chapters on China, India, and Iran, charismatic leaders have a hard time making extraordinary leadership ordinary in ways that "normal" politicians can in more routine times and in more routine ways. The Fifth Republic is very much an exception to that rule. No president since de Gaulle could be called charismatic. However, each of them—with the possible exception of Nicolas Sarkozy—has helped make the presidency the most powerful chief executive in any of the industrialized democracies.

As we will see in the rest of this chapter, there were many reasons why this happened. For now, it is enough to spend a paragraph on each of the men who held the presidency between de Gaulle and Sarkozy to see that the Fifth Republic has achieved the same kind of bedrock stability we saw in the United States and the United Kingdom.

Georges Pompidou (1911–1974) won the election held after de Gaulle resigned. Because he was rather bland and colorless, Pompidou had no choice but to govern as a "normal" leader. His most enduring legacy was the creation of a well-oiled Gaullist party machine. He died of cancer five years into his term.

Valéry Giscard d'Estaing (1926–) was never an orthodox Gaullist. He served as the General's popular Minister of Finance and convinced a small group of Independents to join him as part of the Gaullist coalition. Though by no means charismatic, he used all the tools the constitution gave the presidency. He also had the misfortune of governing during the first post-war recession following the 1973–74 OPEC oil embargo which, some argue, France has yet to fully recover from.

He was followed by the Fifth Republic's first president from outside the Gaullist camp, François Mitterrand (1916–1996). In order to get elected president, Mitterrand had had to rebuild the Socialist Party from the top down. His rather imperious manner also reinforced the fact that the president would dominate the Fifth Republic, whoever was in power. Mitterrand's first government tried—and failed—to move France dramatically leftward. From 1983 until the end of the term, global economic conditions ruled out radical economic initiatives. His election marked the first time the Fifth Republic had a true alternation in power, which is an important turning point in the history of any democratic regime. In addition, Mitterrand had to share power with a National Assembly with a Gaullist majority and prime minister after the 1986 legislative election, which the French refer (and perhaps only the French) to as cohabitation. The sense that the political stakes were no longer all that high was reinforced after the 1993 and 1997 elections, when Left and Right had to cohabit again and again did so with surprising ease.

Two Gaullists who followed Mitterrand: Chirac and Sarkozy could not have had less in common with each other. Jacques Chirac (1932–) epitomized the Gaullist machine. He began his career as a bureaucrat before embarking on a political career. Before being elected president, he held a succession of positions, including cabinet minister, head of the Gaullist party, prime minister, and mayor of Paris. Chirac reflected the nearly larger than life nature of the French presidency despite his rather bland personality. He used the levers of power from the "distance" that by then had come to be the norm for French presidents who tried to stand above the hurly burly of everyday political life.

Sarkozy is anything but laid back. He was not part of the intellectual-bureaucratic elite. He was flamboyant and, in the eyes of many, too earthy. While running for president, he separated from his wife without telling the voters, and before he was inaugurated, he married an Italian pop star who also did not fit the stereotype of French first ladies, who had all rarely been seen or heard. However different he was from Pompidou, Giscard, Mitterrand, and Chirac, there was no doubt that Sarkozy presided over a presidential republic in which the chief executive had more power than his equivalent in any other country that could have been included in Part 2.

Political Culture

Stereotypes about French culture abound. The French are arrogant and rude. They love to argue. Their erratic and deadly driving habits are a sign of their reluctance to follow any rules, values that somehow led to the protests that have occurred on and off throughout French history.

Stereotypes aside, there is no question that the French were more divided and less civic-minded than the British or Americans until the 1970s. The past forty years, however, have brought a dramatic easing of ideological tensions. Widespread protests still occur, but, on balance, it is safe to say that the success French governments have enjoyed since 1958 is now mirrored in popular attitudes and beliefs. Virtually no one now talks about moving on to a Sixth Republic, let alone returning to a monarchy or empire.

Taming Political Protest

Return for a moment to the distinction between the government of the day and the regime as a whole. Public opinion polls in the United States and Great Britain suggest that, however intense opposition might be to a David Cameron or Barack Obama, it stops at opposition to individual leaders and does not extend to the regime or the constitutional order. The same is true in France today.

The turning point occurred no later than May 1968, when a wave of strikes and demonstrations paralyzed the country. The movement started innocently enough. Facilities at the suburban branch of the University of Paris in Nanterre were not very good. Students chafed under strict rules regarding dormitory life at what had been billed as France's first American-style campus. To protest what they believed were intolerable conditions on these and other fronts, a small group of student organized a demonstration that had next to no impact beyond the campus.

When the university authorities decided to discipline some of the student leaders, the hearing was held at the Sorbonne in the Latin Quarter, because it was the home of the sprawling University of Paris, of which Nanterre was a part. While they were interrogating the students, a small group of their supporters staged a demonstration in solidarity with the hitherto unknown group from Nanterre. The police responded by entering the Sorbonne, the first time that this had happened in centuries, which sparked another demonstration in the surrounding neighborhood.

During the night of May 10–11, the demonstrators erected barricades reminiscent of those used in previous revolutions. The authorities sent in antiriot troops. The police intervened with such force that many middle-class onlookers were outraged by what they felt was the government's overreaction. By the next morning, leaders of the major trade unions and other left-leaning interest groups had come to realize that they had the same adversary as the students—the Gaullist state.

After a joint rally two days later, students seized the Sorbonne and other buildings in the Latin Quarter. Without the authorization of union leaders, workers followed suit and began occupying factories around the country. Within days, eight million people were on strike, and more than two million had taken part in a demonstration.

Many of them were particularly upset by the centralization of power under the Gaullists. Along with personal attacks on de Gaulle (*Dix ans, ça suffit!*—Ten years, that's enough!) came demands for increased participation, freedom of speech, decentralization, labor reform, an improved quality of life, and **autogestion**, a participatory, decentralized form of self-managed socialism.

The government and the regime held, however. At the end of May, de Gaulle used one of the new presidential powers and dissolved the National Assembly. The Gaullists played on the growing fear of disorder to win the legislative elections by a landslide and put an end to the crisis.

The most diverse coalition of the 1960s, new Left came together because the strikers and demonstrators could see that they had a common adversary in the state. The spontaneity and size of the protests reflected the breadth and depth of dissatisfaction that was anything but trivial or traditional.

Many observers (myself included) believed that the events of May suggested that this new kind of alienation could bring about the end of both capitalism and the Gaullist regime. We were wrong.

Virtually no one questioned the legitimacy of the Fifth Republic. Even the most outspoken veterans of the "events

TABLE 5.4 Support for the Fifth Republic

YEAR	FUNCTIONED WELL (%)	NOT FUNCTIONED WELL (%)
1978	56	27
1983	57	25
1992	61	32
2000	71	21

Source: Adapted from Olivier Duhamel, "Confiance institutionnelle et défiance politique: la démocratie française," in *L'état de l'opinion* 2001, Olivier Duhamel and Philippe Méchet (eds.) (Paris: Editions du Seuil, 2001), 75.

of May" I interviewed four years later were convinced that their goals could be reached without altering its institutional arrangements in any appreciable way. The next year, Mitterrand took over the Socialist Party and, among other things, brought the ideas raised in 1968 into the political mainstream, channeling the conflicts growing out of the protests into conventional political life.

Public opinion polls since then have consistently shown a public that is satisfied with French political institutions. Depending on the year, between 55 and 71 percent of the voters stated the institutions of the Fifth Republic "functioned well" during the last quarter of the twentieth century (see Table 5.4). Other polls typically find that two-thirds of the population express confidence in the president's judgment, and a similar number believe that elections make politicians pay attention to what average citizens think.

We cannot attribute all of the changes in French political culture to the aftermath of 1968. Whatever uncertainty there may be on the reasons the change occurred, one conclusion is clear. If there is such a thing as a civic culture, France has one. There is perhaps no better evidence of this than the fact that most pollsters have stopped asking questions about support for the regime.

New Divisions

Although the survival of the Fifth Republic is no longer in jeopardy, France is divided in two ways that reflect the new issues in postindustrial society discussed in Chapter 2: race and Europe.

Until the economic downturn of the 1970s, few people objected to the presence of a growing number of immigrants. That is not the case today.

It is hard to tell how prejudiced many French men and women have become. No matter how one measures it, there are significant pockets of racism, nationalism, and/or xenophobia, primarily among poorly educated, underemployed men. There is no denying the resentment against non-whites who hold jobs while the unemployment rate among "French" people is at near-record levels. We will see the new racially tinged conservatism more clearly in the discussion of the all but openly racist National Front (FN) which has routinely won between 10 and 20 percent of the vote since the 1980s.

We also should not make too much of the new French racism. There are probably as many people who oppose racism and who embrace the more multicultural and diverse France.

European integration became controversial with the referendum on the Maastricht Treaty on European Union in 1992. It reappeared when French voters became the first to reject the proposed European constitution in 2005. For our purposes here, it is more important to see that anti-immigrant and anti-European attitudes overlap, because the fault lines cut across traditional left-right divisions in three ways.

First, when I did my first research in France forty years ago, few observers would have expected that public opinion would move so sharply to the right. For good or ill, the Left in industrialized democracies has had a hard time coming up with creative new ideas, at least since the heyday of Tony Blair and Bill Clinton. If anyone has the initiative today, it is the Right, especially when it can combine support for free-market capitalism with this kind of nationalist, if not racist, appeal.

Second, these values are not limited to France. As we saw in the previous two chapters, they have given rise to the American Tea Party, British euroskepticism, and more. However, because of the way political life is structured in France, they have had a longer and stronger impact on political life there.

Third, no matter how much one may oppose the emergence of these attitudes, there is little or no sign that they will prove to be precursors to the emergence of a neofascist or other type of authoritarian regime.

Political Participation

A textbook has to be organized in a linear manner, with Point A leading to Point B leading to Point C and so on. As the logic of systems theory suggests, however, reality is often far more complicated than that because of the feedback loops that keep those points interconnected over time. In this case, there is little doubt that changes in cultural norms helped produce shifts in the way French citizens participate in politics and vice versa.

Renewing the Party System

Any analysis of political participation in French political life has to begin with its political parties. They were one of the main reasons the Third and Fourth Republics were so dysfunctional. And, as we have already seen in the preceding three chapters, catch-all parties get much of the blame for the broader difficulties most industrialized democracies are going through today.

For at least the first twenty years of the Fifth Republic, French political parties defied both their own historical legacy and broader global trends. Although they have relied on media-based campaigns and telegenic leaders like the other catch-all parties, that has not kept them from presenting clear alternatives for voters to choose from or emphasizing strong leadership when they have been in office.

In the words of one American political scientist writing in the 1980s, they refused to fail. Instead of the fragmentation reflected in Table 5.2, the party system now revolves around reasonably coherent coalitions on the Left and Right. From 1962 on, one or the other of them has won the presidency as well as a majority of seats in the National Assembly (see Tables 5.5 and 5.6).

The Majority

The Gaullists are one of the main reasons why the French party system has done so well, at least in comparative terms. Although they have never won a majority of the legislative vote, they like to refer to themselves as the majority, because they were in power for thirty-eight of the first fifty-four years of the Fifth Republic.

I will be using the generic term *Gaullist* here because the party keeps changing its name. The one common denominator is that it has never called itself a political party! Under de Gaulle and Pompidou, the name always included the terms *union* and *republic*. After Chirac took over in 1974, it became the **Rally for the Republic (RPR)**. In 2002, it became the Union for a Presidential Majority. Afterward, it renamed itself the **Union for a Popular Movement (UMP)**, www.u-m-p.org.

No Gaullist party existed in 1958. The General disliked parties and disbanded the one he created after it failed to win in 1951. Seven years later it was hard to tell what being a Gaullist meant because a wide variety of candidates ran under a number of labels all claiming to be his loyal supporters.

By the mid-1960s, the Gaullists had created the first disciplined conservative party in French history. Since then, the Gaullists have regularly won at least a quarter of the vote, which has been distributed fairly evenly across all segments of French society.

TABLE 5.5 Parliamentary Elections, 1958–2012: Major Parties Only

YEAR	PCF		PS[a]		CENTER[b]		GAULLISTS[c] AND ALLIES		FN	
	VOTES[d] (%)	SEATS	VOTES (%)	SEATS	VOTES (%)	SEATS	VOTES (%)	SEATS	VOTES (%)	SEATS
1958	19.1	10	15.5	47	41.0	215	17.6%	212	—	—
1962	21.8	41	12.5	66	26.5	84	36.4	269	—	—
1967	22.5	73	19.0	121	12.6	41	37.7	242	—	—
1968	20.0	34	16.5	49	10.3	33	43.7	354	—	—
1973	21.2	73	20.4	101	12.4	31	34.5	261	—	—
1978	20.5	86	24.7	117	—	—	43.9	274	—	—
1981	16.2	44	37.6	281	—	—	40.0	150	—	—
1986	9.7	35	31.85	210	—	—	42.0	274	9.9	35
1988	11.3	27	35.9	276	—	—	37.7	258	9.8	1
1993	9.2	23	20.3	70	—	—	39.5	460	12.4	0
1997	9.9	37	28.6	282	—	—	39.5	257	15.1	1
2002	4.8	21	24.1	140	—	—	38.5	386	11.3	0
2007	4.3	15	33.6	212	—	—	45.6	345	4.3	0
2012	6.9	10	29.4	306	—	—	27.1	229	13.6	2

FN, National Front; PCF, Communist Party; PS, Socialist Party.

[a]SFIO before 1971. Includes parties allied with the Socialists, usually the left wing of the radicals.

[b]Includes MRP, Moderates, Radicals not allied with the SFIO, and other centrists not part of the Gaullist coalition.

[c]Includes both the Gaullist Party and, after the 1962 election, Giscard's Party, both of which kept changing their name from election to election.

[d]Left Front in 2012.

© Cengage Learning 2015

The Gaullists have always insisted that they are above ideology. Rhetoric aside, however, they have consistently stood for two things:

- An unwavering commitment to General de Gaulle's legacy, which has led them to focus all incarnations of their party around a single leader.

- A resolutely procapitalist stance, although not one that makes a free market its top priority.

Even under de Gaulle, the party was a loose coalition based on two parts of the political elite. First were local conservative politicians who shared the general's ideological goals and wanted to change France accordingly.

TABLE 5.6 French Presidential Elections, 2007 and 2012: Major Candidates Only

PARTY	2007 FIRST BALLOT (%)	2007 SECOND BALLOT (%)	2012 FIRST BALLOT (%)	2012 SECOND BALLOT (%)
Gaullist	31.2	53.1	27.2	48.4
Socialist	25.9	46.9	28.6	51.6
Democratic Movement	9.1	—	18.3	—
National Front	10.4	—	17.9	—
Communist/ Far Left	1.9	—	11.1	—

© Cengage Learning 2015

Second, and more prominent, are members of the bureaucratic elite who graduated from ENA and other elite schools and will be discussed in more detail later in the chapter.

The balance between the two has ebbed and flowed ever since. Other than under Sarkozy, the majority had a patrician public face based on the leader's roots in the bureaucratic elite. Everything from their family backgrounds to their educations to their careers before they entered politics predisposed them to support a version of capitalism in which the state and its allies in the biggest companies (many of which are state owned or controlled) dominated. At the same time, the party's electoral machine was able to tap public support for a strong state at home and abroad. The Majority rarely needed to use the populist appeals that worked so well for conservatives in the United States and Great Britain, although it certainly was willing to draw on popular concerns about the pace and cost of social and economic change when they felt they had to, as in the 1968 election.

That balance changed a bit under Sarkozy. His brash, populist style undoubtedly won him support just before and after the 2007 election. It is also clear that it cost him votes—along with his failure to forge a French response to the global recession—five years later.

As I write in early 2013, it is not clear where the UMP is heading. Like many defeated leaders, Sarkozy announced his withdrawal from political life immediately after the 2012 election. The party then literally split down the middle when it had to choose his successor. Outgoing Prime Minister François Fillon represented the traditional, elite wing of the party. Jean-François Copé, who is stylistically and ideologically far more like Sarkozy, won the party primary by 96 votes. Fillon demanded a recount arguing that if ballots from France's overseas territories were counted, he would have had a plurality of 23 votes. Eventually, the two men agreed to share power within the party, but it is fairly clear that the situation will have to be resolved before the next national elections in 2017.

Note that the Majority has never been exclusively Gaullist. Even at their peak, they had to depend on allies to end up with enough seats to form a legislative majority and, usually, to win enough votes to win the second or run-off round of presidential elections.

The second component of the conservative coalition got its start when Giscard broke ranks with most moderate politicians and supported the 1962 referendum on the direct election of the president. Giscard then formed his own small party, the Independent Republicans (RI), which did well enough to provide the Gaullists with their first stable parliamentary majority in the legislative elections that fall. After his defeat in 1981, the RI merged with a number of other moderate parties to form an even looser coalition which then joined the UMP in the 2002 election to help defeat Le Pen's second ballot candidacy (see the section on the National Front).

A small group continued the effort to retain a non-Gaullist conservative force under the leadership of François Bayrou (1951–), who formed a new party, the Democratic Movement (http://www.mouvementdemocrate.fr/) in 2007. The new MoDem, as it is known, is the closest equivalent of a liberal party in either the British or German senses of the term. Bayrou just about doubled his vote in the 2012 election and came in a respectable third. Many of his votes came from moderates who were not willing to support Sarkozy again but also could not bring themselves to choose Hollande. In short, MoDem's future is very much up in the air.

The Left

The Left offers even clearer evidence of the ways the party system has changed. The social democratic SFIO was in its death throes in the early years of the Fifth Republic, while the new PS has been one of the two parties competing for control of the national government since 1973. Meanwhile, the Communists have all but disappeared along with the rest of the far left, which had seemed so promising in the late 1960s.

The old SFIO went into a prolonged decline after World War II, which left it with barely 5 percent of the vote in 1969. When Mitterrand took over and renamed it the PS

(www.parti-socialiste.fr) two years later, he took the party in two seemingly contradictory directions. Nonetheless, within a decade it was in power.

First, Mitterrand succeeded in large part because he broke with socialist tradition and formed an electoral alliance with the PCF that helped the PS dominate a reasonably unified Left for the last forty years. Second, after a brief period in the 1980s when it tried to start a "rupture with capitalism," Mitterrand and his successors left little doubt that the PS is a party of the center left.

After two failed attempts, Mitterrand finally won the presidency in 1981, but mostly because Giscard took the blame for the post-OPEC recession. He immediately dissolved the National Assembly, and the PS also won an overwhelming parliamentary majority in the elections that followed. The government adopted policies that authorized new social service programs, altered the tax code in favor of the poor, and nationalized key banks and other large, privately owned companies. Unfortunately for the PS, they had to abandon further reform because they took power at the height of another recession during which its left-leaning policies had all but catastrophic economic consequences. Ever since, the PS has dropped all talk of policies that would radically redistribute income or nationalize more industries.

Mitterrand stepped down at the end of his second seven-year term in 1995, and the party's fortunes foundered until Hollande's victory. It reached its most recent low point in 2002 when it came in third in the first round of the presidential election which allowed the National Front's Jean-Marie Le Pen to face off against incumbent Jacques Chirac in that year's runoff.

As we have already seen, the party's fortunes recovered in 2012. However, as was the case in most recent elections in the advanced industrialized democracies, the PS won less because of the alternatives it offered than because a majority of the voters cast their votes against the incumbent and his party.

The rest of the Left is in disarray, beginning with the Communists (www.pcf.fr). The Party was born on Christmas night 1920, when socialists who supported the Bolshevik revolution in Russia split from the SFIO. From the end of World War II until the late 1970s, the PCF normally won between 20 and 25 percent of the vote. However, few of its voters were committed Marxists. Rather, the PCF thrived because it gained a disproportionate share of the country's large protest vote and had a well-organized subculture within the working class.

The PCF was already in trouble when the end of the cold war removed socialism as a politically viable alternative to capitalism. Support for the PCF had steadily declined from the 1960s onward. The increasingly well-off working class was no longer drawn to a party whose most widely touted goal was a total break with capitalism. Moreover, the size of the working class itself continued to shrink, which further diminished the appeal of a party that claimed to speak on its behalf. By the early 2000s, winning even 10 percent of the presidential or legislative vote would have been considered a remarkable achievement.

The party had deteriorated so much that it did not even run a presidential candidate in 2012. Instead, it supported Jean-Luc Mélenchon, who quit the PS to form the Left Front in 2009. He did significantly better than the PCF's candidate in 2007, but the Left Front as a whole only elected eleven deputies to the National Assembly. The PCF did provide the new Union with the bulk of its organizational and financial support and is generally given credit for its limited success. In short, while the Union may have kept the PCF from completely disappearing, there is no reason to believe that the party or any alliance it forms will be able to reverse a now decades-long decline anytime soon.

The National Front

The final party to have done well enough for long enough to warrant attention here and the only far right organization covered in Part 2 is the National Front (www.front-national.com). France has long had organizations that actively opposed democracy, including, most recently, the neo-Nazis and others who collaborated with the Germans during World War II. Although the FN is able to draw on some of those traditions, it is very much a new party in the sense that it reflects the issues and divisions of postindustrial society more clearly than any group covered in this book, including the American Tea Party.

The FN was founded in the 1970s and was led by Jean-Marie Le Pen (1928–) until he retired and turned the leadership over to his daughter Marine (1968–). The FN struggled until it scored a breakthrough in 1983 and won control of Dreux, a city about sixty miles west of Paris with a large immigrant population. The next year, the FN won 11 percent of the vote in balloting for the European Parliament and has done that well or better in most elections since then. In other words, it had done well enough that its total vote in 2002 did not come as a surprise—only the fact that Le Pen came in second did.

The elder le Pen is a colorful character, known to make outrageous statements, including one questioning challenging whether the Holocaust ever occurred. However, on balance, his party did a good job of presenting its racist ideas with a more acceptable pro-family and patriotic veneer. As a result, it has been able to make inroads in most socioeconomic groups, especially those whose security is most threatened by the changes sweeping the Western world.

PROFILES　Marine Le Pen

Marine le Pen was born in the posh Parisian suburb of Neuilly-sur-Seine in 1968, four years before her father cofounded the FN. Like her father, she is a lawyer.

She joined the party at age 18 shortly after it had made its first breakthrough in municipal elections in Dreux. Since then, she has been part of the Front's inner circle and has generally been seen as more sophisticated and nuanced than her often cantankerous father. That said, she has not shied away from statements that many have seen as racist, including one in which she likened the closing of a Parisian street on Fridays to ease access to a mosque to a form of foreign occupation.

She succeeded her father as head of the National Front in 2011 and ran in the presidential election the following year, when she won almost 18 percent of the vote. ∎

GRANIER-DEFERRE/SIPA/Newscom

The transition away from a charismatic leader is as difficult for political parties as it is for countries as a whole, especially when one leader passes the "baton" to one of his children. Despite her lack of leadership experience, the Front did exceptionally well, coming in a strong third in the presidential race and winning almost as many votes and two seats in the National Assembly.

The FN's prospects seem promising for now. Its positions on the issues are as popular as they have ever been. For the moment, it is also attracting support from the divided UMP and could well continue to do so if the erstwhile majority returns to more centrist leadership.

However, for reasons that will become clear in the next section on the electoral system, the FN is unlikely to mount a viable, long-term challenge for one of the two top spots at the ballot box.

Minor Parties and the Newly Fluid Party System

France also has an ever-changing array of small parties of little political significance. For instance, it has two main groups of Greens and three small parties to the left of the Communists, all of which compete for about 5 percent of the vote. There are also "flash" parties that burst onto the scene for an election or two before disappearing. Some can be intriguing, such as the oddly named Extreme Center Party that ran four candidates in 1967 or Hunting, Fishing, Nature, Traditions, which has contested most elections in this century. Exploring these groups in any detail would not add much to any understanding of French politics. In 2012, minor party and independent candidates combined only won 11 percent of the first ballot vote and three seats.

Why Change Happened: The French Electoral System

There are many reasons why the French party system changed so dramatically in the 1960s. In all likelihood, the electoral system adopted in 1958 and used in every National Assembly election since then, other than in 1986, was the most important.

The Fourth Republic used a form of **proportional representation** that gave each party the same share of seats in parliament that it won at the polls. As a result, it was easy for small parties to gain a toehold in the Chamber of Deputies, thereby reinforcing fragmentation and ideological division.

The Fifth Republic uses a **single-member district, two-ballot system** *(scrutin uninominal à deux tours)*. France is divided into districts, as are Britain and the United States. Anyone who gets a minimal number of signatures can run at a first ballot. If one of them wins a majority, he or she wins the seat. First ballot victories are rare; there were only 36 of them in 2012. If no one gets a majority at that point, a second ballot is held one week later. Any candidate winning at least 12.5 percent of the vote at the first ballot can stay on the ballot for the runoff. A candidate who has the right to continue, however, may decide to withdraw and support someone else who has a better chance of winning.

Therein lies the electoral system's significance. In 1958, a single pro-Gaullist candidate contested the second ballot in most districts. Because Communist and Socialist candidates often both remained in the race, the

Gaullists won a much higher percentage of the seats than their share of first ballot votes alone might have suggested. In 1962, the Communists, Socialists, and other left-wing parties realized that they were actually helping the Gaullists by competing with each other in the second round. As a result, between 1962 and 1967, they negotiated deals in which only the left-wing candidate with the best chance of winning ran at the second ballot, which they have renewed for each election using the single-member district system ever since. In other words, almost every decisive ballot in almost every district now pits a single candidate from the left against a single one from the right.

The electoral system also froze out the centrist parties that had dominated the Fourth Republic. Their voters realized that they would have to choose between Left and Right on the second ballot, and so, as early as 1962, began voting for one or the other coalition in the first round. The centrist parties vainly tried to stem the tide, but by 1974 they had disappeared as a viable political force.

Today, the same system hurts the FN and any other party without some kind of deal to form a coalition for the second ballot. The electoral system has not reduced the number of first-ballot candidates. However, only candidates who are affiliated with the two broad coalitions have a reasonable chance of winning a seat unless they can command a majority of the vote on their own, as was the case for the two victorious FN deputies in 2012.

The shift toward two coalitions has been reinforced by the system used in presidential races although in a slightly different way. Anyone who obtains the signatures of a few hundred local officials can run on the first ballot. If a candidate wins a majority at that point, the election is over. However, no candidate has ever come close to doing so. Therefore, there has always been a second ballot. Unlike legislative elections, only two candidates can stay in the race, thereby magnifying the trend toward a more bipolar and consolidated party system.

Parity: A Victory for Feminism?

France does not have a good track record when it comes to including women in politics. The first country to grant the vote to all men (1848) was one of the last to give it to any women (1944). In the 1993 National Assembly election, fewer women were elected than in 1946. France did better in later elections. Still, not quite 19 percent of National Assembly members are women, which leaves France in fifty-ninth place worldwide, between Tajikistan and Mauritius.

The visibility of women in politics began to increase in 1995 when the new Prime Minister, Alain Juppé, appointed twelve women to his cabinet. But, in a sign of lingering sexism, they were immediately dubbed the *juppettes* (French for *miniskirt*). Then, in an attempt to solidify his right-wing support, Juppé dismissed half of them (referring to them as "old biddies"), in so doing inadvertently launching support for a more equitable role for women in political life which culminated in passage of the parity law.

In 1997, activists issued the Manifesto of 577 with one signee for each National Assembly member. Of the total, 289 were women, and 288 men. The Manifesto called for a constitutional amendment that would require parties to run slates of candidates with equal numbers of men and women candidates in all elections conducted using proportional representation. Support for parity built slowly and only received significant public attention in 1997 when the PS surprisingly won the legislative elections and introduced a constitutional amendment on parity that passed parliament and went into effect two years later.

For some, passage of the constitutional amendment was a major victory for women. For others, it was a sign of their weakness, because, without it, women would never have gained any meaningful political impact. And perhaps most important of all, the law does not cover legislative or presidential elections, but its provisions do cover local, regional, and European elections.

Interest Groups

It is hard to reach firm conclusions about French interest groups. The limited data available to us suggest that the French are not joiners. Only about 10 percent of the population belongs to an environmental group, and an even smaller percentage belongs to the antinuclear or the peace movement. France's organized women's movement is among the weakest in Europe. Racial minorities are also poorly represented in the interest group arena.

Political scientists have paid the most attention to the trade unions, perhaps because of their role in fomenting protests since the first ones were formed in the nineteenth century. The unions claim that about 25 percent of all nonagricultural workers belong to one or another of them, but most observers think that the real figure is closer to 10 percent. Moreover, there is no equivalent to the British Trades Union Congress (TUC), which brings together most individual unions in a single peak association.

Instead, French unions are fragmented, with three main ones competing for members in most factories and offices. The **Confédération Générale du Travail (CGT)** was the largest one for most of the twentieth century and is affiliated with the Communist Party. During the1960s, however, it faced a challenge from the **Confédération Française Démocratique du Travail** (CFDT). The CFDT began as a Catholic union but dropped its links to the church and moved dramatically to the left in the aftermath of 1968. It now has close ties to the PS. **Force ouvrière** (Workers' Force) broke away from the CGT at the beginning of the cold war. It was then the most moderate of the three, but it has become more aggressive in recent years. It, too, has a working relationship with the PS.

There are separate unions for teachers and most professional groups, including business managers. Even students have unions.

Until the 1980s, the unions epitomized the radicalism that filled so many stereotypes about French political life. In the 1960s, for instance, the CGT demanded the

Comparative Emphasis: Women

France has long been a laggard when it comes to the role of women in politics. It was one of the last countries to give the first woman served as a cabinet member (1944), but women served as cabinet members a decade earlier. It was also one of the last to legalize abortion in the early 1970s.

A succession of French governments have done as much as any democratic government in enacting laws about families, although they have not done much to advance the role of women *per se*. Yet, it is also one of the few countries in which women have been serious candidates for national leadership positions. The current head of the PS, Martine Aubry, is a woman, but many analysts think of the position as a consolation prize for someone who would have preferred being president.

France is also a country known for its political humor, although it has been sorely lacking in feminist politics until 2008, when *La Barbe* was formed. The name is a pun because it means both "beard" and, in slang, "enough is enough." The women of La Barbe have a history of showing up at male-dominated events while, of course, wearing fake beards. In 2012, Barbe activists disrupted the Cannes Film festival, which had no women nominees for its prestigious *Palme d'or*, and a public lecture at the all-male lodge of the Parisian masonic order. Their home page has a delightful video in French, but you don't need to be bilingual to get a feel for what they do (www.labarbelabarbe.org). ∎

nationalization of all major industrial firms, a ban on lay-offs that did not also fund the retraining of the affected workers, and a reduction in the work week without a pay cut. In the early 1970s, the CFDT added support for auto-gestion to its list of demands.

The unions also practiced what they preached. From 1963 through 1973 (even without counting 1968), an average of 2.5 to 3 million work days were lost to strikes each year. After the economic downturn of the mid-1970s, union membership and militancy both declined and have not recovered. The CGT has dropped its demands for more nationalization and mandatory retraining. For the CFDT, autogestion has become a slogan with little or no meaning.

The unions have enjoyed something of a renaissance since 1995, when a massive wave of strikes and demonstrations forced the government to roll back some of its plans to cut social services and raise taxes. In 1997, unions occupied employment offices to protest the Socialist government's failure to move fast enough in creating jobs for the eighth of the workforce that was unemployed. Truck drivers engaged in wildcat strikes that brought parts of the country's commercial life to a halt for as long as a week or two. In 2010, the unions led a doomed effort to block passage of the law that raised the age at which retirees could collect a full pension.

On balance, the unions are struggling to protect the gains they made over the years and are, at most, a disruptive, rather than a potentially revolutionary, force. In fact, France now loses fewer days to work stoppages each year than Spain, Italy, or Great Britain, and the unions have largely been ineffective in opposing austerity policies imposed by the EU and the last two Gaullist governments in Paris.

There is one exception to this picture of divided and weakening interest groups: big business. As we will see in the next section, corporate executives have had such easy access to the upper levels of the civil service and to elected officials that it has often been hard to tell where one ended and the other began. Big business does not wield its influence primarily through its main association, the **Movement of French Enterprises** (MEDEF, www.medef. fr), but through informal ties that link them to politicians and civil servants, which we will be exploring in the discussion of the state.

The French State

Louis XIV was one of the inventors of the modern state. His creation fell on hard times between the revolution of 1789 and de Gaulle's return to power when he combined a strong state with the institutions and practices of a liberal democracy.

The contemporary French state is a hybrid. Unlike most parliamentary systems based on the Westminster model, it has a directly elected president. At the same time, the prime minister and cabinet have to retain the confidence of the National Assembly in order to stay in office, which means the state also has important parliamentary features.

But make no mistake. The Fifth Republic has always been dominated by the president. No president has been as charismatic as de Gaulle, but none has had to be. De Gaulle succeeded in doing something few other charismatic leaders have done by "routinizing" his authority so that more conventional leaders could govern effectively using the institutions he created.

Toward a Presidential Republic

Any understanding of the strong French state has to combine the institutions created by the Fifth Republic's constitution and the way de Gaulle and his successors made it a decidedly presidential regime. In that sense, the French state underscores one of the most important points in all of comparative politics. Institutions as laid out in constitutions and other organic laws are important building blocks that go a long way toward determining what a state will be like. However, they are *only* building blocks, whose day-to-day functioning emerges as a result of what political leaders and average citizens do in the years after the constitution goes into effect.

The Constitution

Recall that the twin uprisings in Algeria left the Fourth Republic's political leaders with a choice between two bad alternatives as they saw it. They could either succumb to a likely military coup or bring de Gaulle back. They chose the latter.

The General insisted that the parliamentary leaders give him emergency powers for six months. During that time, he would be free to govern without any meaningful oversight and appoint a commission to revise the constitution, which was led by the prominent but little-known lawyer **Michel Debré** (1912–1996). The two of them quickly decided that the current constitution was beyond repair and that they had to start from scratch and create a Fifth Republic.

Debré had long been an admirer of British party government. Because he assumed the country was too divided to ever elect a disciplined majority, the constitution gave the executive comparable powers that it could use even if it did not have a loyal (and docile) majority. Those provisions were designed to simultaneously strengthen the president and prime minister while weakening the parliament (www.elysee.fr).

The president would be much stronger than the figure-heads who held that office during the Third and Fourth Republics. The constitution listed the powers of the president ahead of those of the cabinet and parliament, thereby sending a signal that the office was to take on new importance and could even exercise the most draconian of all measures—dissolving parliament and calling new elections. He (so far, all have been men) was granted emergency powers to rule as a de facto dictator for up to six months (Article 16) and to call a referendum (Article 11) on matters related to the "organization of governmental authority."

A new electoral system was also expected to strengthen the presidency. Until the Third and Fourth Republics, the two houses of parliament met together to choose the president. After his election, he could not be removed through a vote of confidence and was almost completely beyond the reach of parliament. The parliament got around any possibility that a president might have threatened their prerogatives by routinely choosing elderly, incompetent, or unambitious men to hold what turned into little more than a ceremonial position.

The Fifth Republic's president was to be chosen by an electoral college of more than eighty thousand voters that would give him a far broader mandate and, with it, far more legitimacy. It did include the members of both houses of parliament. The other electors, who made up 98 percent of the college and were chosen by local and departmental councils, however, dwarfed their potential impact.

The Constitution also strengthened the cabinet and weakened the lower house, now called the **National Assembly**. It retained the principle of cabinet responsibility to parliament. However, in order to reduce the odds that France could return to the days of revolving-door prime ministers, the constitution included a number of provisions that strengthened the government's hand in legislative–executive relations (www.assemblee-nationale.fr/english/index.asp).

For example, a new cabinet no longer had to win a vote of investiture as soon as the president appointed it. Similarly, it could not be defeated in a vote of confidence unless the opposition won an absolute majority of the deputies, not a simple majority of those present and voting, as had been the case under the Third and Fourth Republics. These may seem like minor differences, but under the Fourth Republic several cabinets lost those initial investiture votes, and almost half were defeated by relative, not absolute, majorities.

The **incompatibility clause** (Article 23) required members of parliament to give up their seats in the legislature as soon as they are appointed to a cabinet. No longer could ministers undermine a government they served in, knowing they had a legislative seat to return to.

The National Assembly was not allowed to either raise the expenditure levels or lower the tax rates proposed in the government's budget. The government also could demand a **bloc vote** in which the National Assembly had to vote up or down on a bill without even proposing any amendments

President Holland and Prime Minister Ayrau

to it. Much of economic and foreign policy making was placed in a "domain of regulation," which meant that the government could rule by decree, without parliamentary approval. The government could even determine when the parliament met and what would be on its agenda.

The Presidential Republic

Although the constitution shifted the balance of power toward the executive, it did not spell everything out, including whether the president or prime minister would dominate. It did not take long before it became clear that only the president was going to count.

The signs of that were obvious from the moment Debré became the new republic's first prime minister (see Table 5.7). Debré was neither a popular politician nor a member of the elite that had led the country for three-quarters of a century. He was always de Gaulle's lieutenant who did what the president wanted, which has been the case for every prime minister since then other than the three who served during periods of cohabitation.

De Gaulle used all the new powers the constitution gave the presidency and more. He held two referenda on Algerian independence in order to bypass the National Assembly on measures it would never have approved. He

TABLE 5.7 French Presidents and Prime Ministers since 1958

START OF PRESIDENTIAL TERM	PRESIDENT	PRIME MINISTER
1959	Charles de Gaulle	Michel Debré
		Georges Pompidou
		Maurice Couve de Murville
1969	Georges Pompidou	Jacques Chaban-Delmas
		Pierre Messmer
1974	Valéry Giscard d'Estaing	Jacques Chirac
		Raymond Barre
1981	François Mitterrand	Pierre Mauroy
		Laurent Fabius
		*Jacques Chirac
		Michel Rocard
		Edith Cresson
		Pierre Bérégovoy
		*Edouard Balladur
1995	Jacques Chirac	Alain Juppé
		Lionel Jospin
		Jean-Pierre Raffarin
		Dominique de Villepin
2007	Nicolas Sarkozy	François Fillon
2012	François Hollande	Jean-Marc Ayrault

* Cohabitation period.

invoked emergency powers so the government could act decisively against a rebellion by white settlers and soldiers from Algeria. Most importantly, after a failed assassination attempt by one of those groups in 1962, he initiated a referendum that authorized the direct election of the president, which has been in use ever since.

De Gaulle also clarified the unequal relationship between the president and prime minister. At the height of the political uncertainty in 1962, he asked for and received Debré's resignation and replaced him with Georges Pompidou (1911–1974), who was even more of a lightning rod for the political establishment since he had never even run for political office before.

He also began a tradition that all presidents and prime ministers have followed ever since. He and his prime ministers issued decrees that effectively bypassed Parliament. Technically, they can only do so on minor matters that are not normally under parliamentary control. Nonetheless, the presidents have interpreted these constitutional provisions liberally and used decrees to introduce some of the most sweeping reforms with minimal legislative oversight.

Similarly, the constitution mentioned a "reserved domain" in which the president would dominate, but it did not specify what it covered. Within the first few years, de Gaulle made it clear that it included anything he thought was important in domestic as well as foreign policy making.

Thus, the decision to build the first atomic bombs was made without parliamentary approval. More recently one of Hollande's first actions was to issue a decree rolling back provisions of one of Sarkozy's least popular laws that raised the retirement age for most workers.

The president can also draw on a much larger team of personal advisors than the British prime minister. Currently, the Elysée staff numbers over seven hundred and includes the president's closest advisers, many of whom are drawn from France's remarkable civil service.

At first, many thought this combination of the two kinds of democratic systems would become the Fifth Republic's Achilles heel if and when the president was controlled by one coalition and the parliament by its opposition, and the two coalitions would have to share power. That happened after the 1986, 1993, and 1997 legislative elections.

None of those earlier concerns materialized, however, when the French had to cohabit. To be sure, the president and prime minister had to share power more than under "normal" circumstances. Nonetheless, even under cohabitation, the Fifth Republic has remained a regime in which the president is the dominant official. The modus vivendi under cohabitation made the president the key leader in foreign policy, while the prime minister took the lead domestically. Typically, too, periods of cohabitation are not ones in which the government embarks on bold new initiatives unless a consensus bringing the Left and Right together has emerged. A constitutional amendment shortened the president's term to five years for the 2007 election, which means that contests for both offices normally occur within a few weeks of each other thus reducing the likely need to return to cohabitation at least for now.

The Parliament

The National Assembly is the more important of the two houses of parliament. Its 577 members are directly elected from single-member districts.[4] The districts are supposed to be of roughly the same size, but significant disparities occurred in the early part of this century because district boundaries were not redrawn between 1982 and 2009.

Only the National Assembly can cast a vote of no confidence against a sitting government. It only did so once during the controversy surrounding Debré's resignation, Pompidou's appointment, and the referendum on the direct election of the president. Ever since, either the Left or the Right has had a firm majority, and no vote of confidence has come close to passing.

When key initiatives have come before the National Assembly, the majority now swings into line in much the same way and for many of the same reasons it does in the British House of Commons. Backbench revolts have occasionally delayed passage of legislation, but such incidents are rare, and the president and prime minister almost always prevail. Indeed, the best book on economic planning through the 1970s devotes only a two-page chapter to parliament's role because it had so little influence over one of the most important policy-making arenas during the Fifth Republic's early years.

The Senate is slightly more influential than the British House of Lords, although that is not saying much. The Senate has 348 members who serve six-year terms, half of whom are elected every three years. Twenty-six of the senators represent either France's remaining overseas departments and territories or French citizens currently living abroad.

The senators from "mainland" France represent 326 *cantons*, which are otherwise unimportant subdivisions of its ninety-six departments. They are indirectly elected by about 150,000 "grand electors," 90 percent of whom are local, departmental, or regional councilors. Given the way the district boundaries are drawn, the Senate had a strong conservative majority until 2011 when the PS won control of it for the first time.

---

[4]Seven districts are reserved for the overseas departments and territories. In 2012, one of those on the island of Réunion was won by Corinne Nassiguin, who is a long-time resident of New York City. She and her handful of New York–based supporters watched the returns at an Irish-Mexican pub in Manhattan.

The Senate has the right to initiate legislation. However, because the government controls the agenda of both the Assembly and the Senate, its bills take priority and routinely are first passed by the lower house. If the two houses do not pass the same version of a bill, a complicated process known as "the shuttle" begins which the government controls. If the Assembly and Senate remain deadlocked, the Assembly's version prevails.

The Integrated Elite

There is an obvious question to ask given what we have seen so far. If its legislative–executive mechanisms work in much the same way as Britain's, how can the French state be stronger?

The answer lies in the distinction between the government and the state, introduced in Chapter 1, in which the latter includes more than constitutional provisions or elected officials.

For France, that means extending our analysis to the bureaucracy, which has been the linchpin of the strong state since 1958. Not only are civil servants themselves powerful, but former bureaucrats dominate the political parties and big business and serve as the glue holding a remarkably integrated elite together.

As part of their attempt to limit the power of the traditional political elite, De Gaulle and Debré appointed a number of bureaucrats to the first cabinet. On average, about a third of all subsequent cabinet members started their careers in the civil service.

Some of them are chosen for their expertise. Pompidou for instance, became prime minister after a career as an investment banker. Similarly, Bernard Kouchner joined one of the later Mitterrand governments after building a worldwide reputation as head of Doctors without Borders (*Médecins sans frontières*), a group of physicians that provides humanitarian aid in war-torn areas. In one of the more unusual twists in the history of the Fifth Republic, the conservative Sarkozy later named the Socialist Kouchner his first foreign minister.

Former President Chirac's case is typical. He began his career as a civil servant and worked on a number of ministerial staffs in the early 1960s before being appointed agriculture minister in one of Pompidou's first governments. Only later, in 1967, did he run for electoral office.

The fact that so many key leaders are not career politicians is just the tip of the iceberg. Current and former civil servants have made a major contribution to the French state's dynamism because of the close and informal ties between them and other key decision makers. Some observers call this either an **integrated elite** or an **iron triangle**.

The fact that the elite is so tightly integrated is probably the most important reason why France scores a bit below the average for industrialized democracies on both the governance and corruption indices. There may not be many more instances of clearly illegal activity on the part of government officials than there are in the U.S. or the UK. However, the concentration of power makes it relatively easy for office holders to ignore the wishes of the people they disagree with, as we are about to see.

It is an integrated elite because so many powerful people in all walks of social, political, and economic life share a common background and worldview. Many are sons (and now increasingly daughters) of the Parisian elite. Many of those who aren't Parisian born and bred spent their high school years at one of the city's prestigious *lycées*.

Almost all of them went on to ENA (www.ena.fr/en/accueil.php). It is one of the prestigious **grandes écoles,** the specialized and highly selective institutions of higher education that were created to train high-level civil servants. ENA stands head and shoulders above the others as a stepping stone to a political career. In fact, there is no other school in the world quite like ENA. It is a small institution that admits about a hundred students each year and has fewer than five thousand living graduates. Founded after World War II, ENA was designed to train civil servants committed both to democracy and the use of the state to spur economic growth.

For the first half century of its life, it was located in the heart of Paris in a building directly behind the equally influential *Institut d'études politiques* (Sciences Po) which many of its students attended while they prepared to take the entrance exam for ENA. In 2005 it merged with other schools and moved most of its operations to Strasbourg.

Its first generation of graduates reached the peaks of their careers at about the time de Gaulle returned to power, and their views on economic modernization meshed with his on restoring France's international prestige. As we will see in the section on public policy, the civil servants and the politicians had an easy time finding common ground in using the state to stimulate what had long been a moribund economy.

The influence of the ENArques (as its graduates are known) extends far beyond the advice civil servants give their political bosses. Grandes écoles graduates only owe the state ten years of service and in some cases can buy their way out sooner. Then they can resign and move into big business or politics. Most of them have done just that in a process known as **pantouflage**—literally putting on soft, comfortable slippers.

Some become politicians. The leadership of both the UMP and the PS is filled with ENArques. They first gained prominence with Chirac's generation that dominated the center-right from the 1960s onward. Former President Giscard d'Estaing was a double member of this elite group, having graduated from both ENA and the equally prestigious *Ecole polytechnique*. The Socialists, too, have attracted more than their share of ENArques, including President Hollande. Only a handful of the leading politicians in the last few decades were not ENA graduates, most notably Mitterrand, who was too old to have gone there, and Sarkozy, who failed the admissions exam.

Four of the 2012 presidential candidates were ENA graduates. Two of them (Hollande and former Prime Minister Dominique de Villepin) were from the same eighty-member Promotion Voltaire that entered in 1980. So, too, were Ségolène Royale, Hollande's ex-partner and the defeated PS candidate from 2007, the head of France's financial regulation agency, several other former ministers and ambassadors, and Hollande's chief of staff. The ENA in general and that class in particular had such an impact that one of the cable television networks made a loosely fictionalized series about it, *l'Ecole du pouvoir—The Power School.*

ENArques are at least as prominent a force in French business. One recent study found that 46 percent of the chief executives of the biggest French companies graduated from ENA or one of the other two top *grandes écoles.*

Because so many of them share the same background, training, and values, elite integration has facilitated coherent policy making for most of the last half century. This tightly knit elite had a lot to do with the sweeping changes during the first quarter century after 1958, which will be discussed in the public policy section. Paris, for example, was transformed. Real estate speculators bought up old buildings that housed workers, small shopkeepers, and artisans and replaced them with expensive office and apartment complexes. Businesses and families were displaced by the thousands and forced into dreary, working-class suburbs that one urban activist I interviewed referred to as "people silos." New neighborhoods with tens of thousands of inhabitants had few cafés or other public places where people could gather.

In interviews with Ezra Suleiman, bureaucrat after bureaucrat tried to put their newfound power in the best possible light. Most claimed that they did not have this kind of relationship with any interest groups. As three of them put it:

> **The contact with groups is mostly to inform them, to explain to them. It's true that they can't influence policy.**

> —*Ministry of Industry*

We always consult. It doesn't mean we listen, but we consult. We don't always reveal our intentions. We reveal only as much as we think it is necessary to reveal.

—Ministry of Education

First, we make out a report or draw up a text, then we pass it around discreetly within the administration. Once everyone concerned within the administration is agreed on the final version, then we pass this version around outside the administration. Of course, by then it's a fait accompli *and pressure cannot have any effect.* [emphasis added]

—Ministry of Industry[5]

Their comments then—and they would not be terribly different today—were somewhat misleading because they most definitely did not ignore people they considered "serious," including representatives of big business and other groups who shared their aspirations for France's future. They simply did not think of them as interest groups. As a result, a narrow elite made the most important decisions about the allocation of economic resources. And it has not mattered much whether the Left or the Right was in office. Perhaps most importantly of all, this decision making has remained the norm even though it has been decidedly less effective in the past two or three decades, which we will also see in more detail below.

People outside the integrated elite do not have any such privileged access to policy-making circles. Under the Gaullists, workers had a hard time getting decision makers to take their views on ending France's chronic youth unemployment seriously. Immigrants were not able to do much about either the racism or the horrible living and working conditions they endured, leading to the frustrations that have erupted repeatedly in suburban streets.

New admissions procedures have made it easier for underprivileged youths to get into the grandes écoles. In the current business climate that stresses the importance of small business and entrepreneurial skills, schools like ENA have lost some of their luster. Still, it will take a generation before these new leaders reach the top. And even then, their attitudes and behavior may not change. After all, many frontline leaders of the 1968 movement ended up as "members" of the integrated elite.

Whatever your ideological preferences, the integrated elite has to be seen as a mixed blessing. There is little

doubt that it has helped spark France's dramatic social and economic turnaround since 1958. At the same time, the criticisms often made of the iron triangle of interest group lobbyists, bureaucrats, and members of Congress in the United States hold even more for France. The closed nature of the elite does lead to policy making that favors some groups over others. There is no denying, too, that it keeps France from living up to any of the "thicker" definitions of democracy discussed in Chapter 2.

The Rest of the State

Local Government

France was arguably the most centralized country in Europe before the socialist victory in 1981. Until then, the closest the French came to American governors were the **prefects**, who were civil servants appointed to their jobs by the minister of the interior. In addition to not being elected officials, prefects never came from the department they managed and were transferred to a new one every two or three years so they would not get too close to the local population. Prefects also could use the **tutelle**, which gave them de facto veto power over almost all local and departmental decisions, down to naming schools or streets and approving all major local expenditures in advance.

By the 1970s, this degree of centralization had become a burden on local and national leaders alike. Departments, cities, and towns simply had too many responsibilities for the central bureaucracy to manage them all. Moreover, even if they could not formally make many final decisions, their administrative duties and local connections gave the mayors considerable leverage over the prefect. The mayor's power was reinforced by the fact that most big city mayors were also members of parliament and some were even cabinet ministers under a peculiar tradition that allows French citizens to hold several elected positions at once.

Socialist mayors, who chafed under the tutelle, convinced the PS to make decentralization a major plank in the party's program. When the Socialists finally won in 1981, decentralization was the first major piece of legislation they passed. The tutelle was abolished, though it was later restored for the smallest towns, which actually benefit from the services the prefectural offices provide. The authority of the central government was cut significantly. Cities and towns (*communes*) gained control of urban planning, the departments assumed jurisdiction over most social service programs, and the regions got responsibility for economic planning. The central government now issues block grants to fund long-term investment programs and gives local authorities the revenue from the annual automobile registration fees. Communes also have the freedom

---

[5]Ezra Suleiman, *Politics, Power, and Bureaucracy in France* (Princeton, NJ: Princeton University Press, 1974), 335–36.

to set real estate and other local tax rates. The heads of the elected departmental and regional councils are at least as important as the prefects were.

The Courts

The Fifth Republic has a large and strong judiciary. The *Cour des comptes*, which is the country's chief financial investigator, and the *Conseil d'état*, which has jurisdiction over the state and its actions, have long been prestigious bodies and now attract more than their share of grandes écoles graduates.

As in Britain, the Third and Fourth Republics' tradition of parliamentary sovereignty meant that the courts did not have the power of judicial review and therefore could not rule on the constitutionality of laws or other governmental acts. The Fifth Republic constitution created the **Constitutional Council** (http://www.conseil-constitutionnel. fr/conseil-constitutionnel/english/homepage.14.html) with the power to rule on the constitutionality of bills passed by the National Assembly sometimes even before they formally become law. Its nine judges serve staggered nine-year terms. The president and the leaders of the two houses of parliament each appoint three of them. Former presidents are also members of the council, but they rarely take part in its deliberations.

Under de Gaulle, the council was little more than a political joke. The one time it tried to assert its power by ruling his decision to hold a referendum on the direct election of the president unconstitutional, de Gaulle simply ignored its judgment.

In the 1980s, however, it became more assertive. For the first few years of the Mitterrand presidency, the council was still dominated by judges appointed by the Gaullists, and it forced the Socialists to modify a number of their reforms—among other things, dramatically increasing the compensation to the former owners of nationalized firms. After 1986, the new conservative government faced a court with a Socialist majority, which overturned four of the fourteen laws that would have sold off much of the state sector. The Council's most recent major decision came on December 29, 2012, when it ruled that portions of the Hollande government's new tax on the wealthiest citizens was unconstitutional because it was based on individual rather than total household earnings. As I write, the government was making plans to resubmit the tax in a form that the Council would accept.

One should not, however, draw too many parallels between the French and the American or even the German courts, which will be covered in the next chapter. The French judiciary's powers are far more limited both by the constitution and by tradition.

Public Policy: The Pursuit of Grandeur

So far, it would be tempting to read this chapter as saying that the Fifth Republic created a strong, dynamic, and democratic state that is capable of reaching its goals. That interpretation largely held true for the twenty years after 1958. It has been less and less accurate since then, because of the implications of this book's subtitle. Whatever levers it has at its disposal, no state can come close to shaping its own destiny in the early twenty-first century because of social, economic, technological, cultural, and political forces that are beyond its control, as we will see in each of the three following policy arenas.

Economic Policy

In the eighteenth century, the French coined a word to describe state management of a capitalist economy: **dirigisme**. Between 1789 and 1958, however, republican governments rarely used the policy levers available to them. That began to change under the provisional government after the end of World War II. However, given the paralysis of most Fourth Republic governments, it was another twelve years before the state could truly help lead the transformation of the country that rendered the statement that begins this chapter obsolete.

Les Trentes Glorieuses

From the end of World War II until the recession after the OPEC oil embargo of 1973–74, France enjoyed a period of unprecedented economic growth, which one historian called *les trentes glorieuses* (the thirty glorious years). Economists do not know how much each causal factor contributed to this unexpected prosperity. However, the policies pursued by the Gaullists during their years in power after both World War II and 1958 have to be near the top of any such list.

The provisional government nationalized a number of firms, including the Renault automobile company and the three largest savings banks. De Gaulle also created the General Planning Commission to speed the recovery by bringing business leaders and civil servants together to rebuild key industries, including electricity generation, cement production, and the railroads. Meanwhile, a number of business leaders realized that they had to modernize, which they decided could best be done by cooperating with the planning commission and the government in general.

Growth continued under the Fourth Republic. Little of it could be attributed to concerted state action, because most political leaders were opposed to dirigisme, and its supporters were too far removed from power to have an impact on domestic policy.

That changed when de Gaulle came back to office. From 1958 until 1973, the economy, on average, grew faster each year than it did during the entire interwar period. Its growth rate also outstripped that of its main competitors other than Japan. Growth was concentrated in the large firms that produced automobiles, machinery, electronics, chemicals, and other durable goods.

In the late 1950s, none of the world's most profitable hundred firms were French. By 1972, France had sixteen of them, whereas West Germany had only five. That was not an accident. The government encouraged firms to merge, creating larger companies that would be more competitive in the increasingly important European and global markets. During the 1950s, companies responsible for an average of 85 million francs a year in revenues merged. By 1965, that figure had topped one billion, and by 1970 it reached five billion. Typical of that growth was the consolidation of five relatively weak automobile manufacturers into two then highly profitable giants: Renault and Citroën-Peugeot.

Economic growth also had a human side. The improved standard of living was easy to see in the new houses, larger cars, and even the changed diets that produced a generation of taller, thinner people. The *hypermarché* (a combination supermarket and department store that was a common feature in France a quarter century before Wal-Mart) all but wiped out the quaint but inefficient corner shops in most urban neighborhoods.

This economic growth did not appear out of thin air. It was in large part a product of the new Gaullist state. It relied primarily on discretionary tax rates, investment credits, subsidies, and other state programs that encouraged the formation of larger and more competitive firms. Five giant corporations received about half of the subsidies granted in the mid-1970s, a figure that reached 80 percent by the end of the decade. In all, an average of 2.7 percent of the gross national product went to support industry. Under President Giscard d'Estaing, the government's explicit goal became the creation of one or two large firms in each industrial sector to produce what he called "national champions" that could lead in world markets.

I am not claiming that there was a one-to-one correspondence between elite integration and economic success, only that there was a strong connection between them. Other advanced industrialized countries also did well after the end of World War II. Of them, only Japan had anything like this kind of integrated elite. However, all stressed some version of close cooperation between the state and the private sector, whereas the countries that relied most heavily on market forces—including Great Britain and the United States—did not fare as well for most of that period.

Stagnation

The French economy went into a tailspin after the OPEC oil embargo from which it has never fully recovered (see Table 5.8). The economy has never come close to collapsing. Nonetheless, it has never recovered the sustained growth or dynamism of les trentes glorieuses, which has been translated into sluggish growth and high unemployment, especially among younger workers.

When the Left came to power in 1981, the effects of the second of the 1970s oil shocks were wearing off. The Mitterrand government immediately nationalized nine major industrial and financial conglomerates, redistributed more of the income toward the poorest groups in French society, and expanded social services. The new nationalization, in particular, put the government in control of about 60 percent of France's industry and even more of its investment capital, which the PS and its ENArques assumed would enhance their ability to steer the way the entire economy evolved.

That is not what happened.

The Socialists soon had to abandon their most ambitious goals because, to make a long story short, they wanted to expand the economy during a steep and sudden recession. Within a year, the Mitterrand team faced growing unemployment and inflation rates. The budget deficit skyrocketed in large part because many of the newly nationalized firms lost money. In 1983, the Socialists did a U-turn, adopting a policy of economic austerity and abandoning all talk of further radical reform.

The first cohabitation government controlled by the Gaullists returned fourteen of those companies to private ownership. Another ten followed in the 1990s. The Gaullists

TABLE 5.8 The French Economy in Decline

YEAR	UNEMPLOYMENT (%)	GROWTH IN GDP (%)
1979	5.9	3.2
1981	7.4	1.2
1983	8.3	1.7
1986	10.4	2.5
1988	10.0	4.5
1993	11.7	2.9
1995	11.7	2.0
1998	11.5	0.3
2001	12.2	0.3
2006	9.5	2.2
2008	7.4	0.2
2011	9.2	1.7

Source: Adapted from David Cameron, "Economic Policy in the Era of the EMS," in *Remaking the Hexagon*, Gregory Flynn (ed.). (Boulder, CO: Westview Press, 1995), 145; and *The Economist*, February 10, 1999, 134. For 2001–2008, various online sources.

have **privatized** state assets more quickly and more often than the Socialists, although the PS did preside over the partial privatization of such high-visibility companies as Air France and France Telecom.

By 1988, a rough consensus had emerged on both the Left and Right that took a dramatic expansion or reduction of the state's economic role off the political agenda. Recent Gaullist governments have wanted to move sharply toward a greater reliance on the market, but they were largely prevented from doing so by international economic forces that drastically reduced their maneuvering room.

Since then, average industrial growth has hovered around 1 percent per year, while unemployment has rarely dipped much below 10 percent. During the 1990s, France lost an average of 150,000 industrial jobs each year as corporate failures increasingly replaced the success stories. The shipbuilding sector all but collapsed. The steel industry was in so much trouble that the government had to restructure it in the late 1970s and was forced to take it over altogether in the 1980s. French automobile companies saw their share of the European market cut by a third while the number of imported cars grew by more than half.

We should not confuse French privatization with what happened in Great Britain under Prime Ministers Thatcher and Major or with any broader adoption of market principles. Despite this wave of privatizations, the government still employed more than a quarter of the workforce as recently as 2007. Because they provide a public service and are what economists call natural monopolies, the government still owns most public utilities. Thus, the generation and distribution of electricity and natural gas, the railroads, and the postal service remain publicly owned. Some utilities have been privatized, most notably the telephone system and airlines, but these had already come under intense international competition, which meant that they had to be run like private corporations no matter who owned them.

Gaullist rhetoric has emphasized a shift toward a freer market especially under Sarkozy. In practice, their behavior in government reflects the continued importance of dirigiste ideas in both the public and private sectors.

Few of the newly privatized firms are truly private. The Gaullists left the government and its political allies with de facto control of many of them through what is called a *noyau dur* (hard core) of stock. Sometimes, the government itself retains a significant ownership stake. Thus, the United States did not allow France Telecom to bid for the cell phone contract in postwar Iraq because the state still held more than a 5 percent stake in it. Sometimes the state made sure that "friends" in the business community gained a controlling interest. Sometimes it refused to allow

foreigners to buy any stock in a privatized company, claiming doing so would jeopardize national security.

Lionel Jospin's Socialist government used its significant financial influence to try to convince three banks to merge and create one firm that could compete with British, German, and American financial giants. In 2004, the government bailed out the industrial giant Alsthom (which, among other things, builds the high speed trains) to prevent its takeover by Siemens.

It was clear even before the election that Hollande's economic policies would not be like Sarkozy's. The Socialist agenda of thirty years ago—especially nationalizing industry—is long gone. Nonetheless, the new president wasted little time in demonstrating that his government's policies would help the poor more than those formulated under his predecessor. Salaries of cabinet members and the heads of public corporations were cut so that they would not be more than about thirty times that of the organization's lowest paid workers. Senior officials gave up their most luxurious cars, private jet travel, and (shockingly at least in France) champagne at public receptions. These were symbolic steps that, by themselves, would do little to redistribute income or ease the budget deficit. Everyone assumed, however, that these would be the first of many more egalitarian initiatives.

Nonetheless, the European fiscal crisis and France's own budgetary woes have limited what government could hope to accomplish. Whatever egalitarian hopes the Socialists or the voters may have had, budgetary realities meant that it would have to *expand* some of the austerity measures begun under Sarkozy. For example, the budgets of most cabinet-level agencies will be cut by 7 percent in 2013 and another 4 percent in each of the following two years.

In short, the new consensus to reinforce the private sector and use the market more fell far short of the one that emerged in Britain. Thus, Harvey Feigenbaum, Jeffrey Henig, and Chris Hamnett have labeled British privatization systematic because the Thatcher and Major governments truly believed in it and sold off every nationalized firm they could. By contrast, they consider French privatization to be pragmatic, conducted less out of principle than because policy makers realized that selling off state assets would either help an individual firm or bring in needed funds to the state's coffers.

Social Services

France's generous social service system gives us a slightly different glimpse at the political and economic dilemmas all industrialized democracies will face for years to come. As is the case throughout western Europe, French social services cover most French citizens from cradle to grave.

PROFILES François Hollande

François Hollande is the Fifth Republic's seventh president and is very much cut from the mold of most contemporary French politicians. He was born in 1954 to an upper middle class family which moved to Neuily-sur-Seine, the same exclusive Parisian suburb where Marine Le Pen lives and Nicolas Sarkozy once served as mayor.

He attended a prestigious Parisian lycée, Sciences Po, and another grande école before entering ENA, at which point he was already a longtime member of the PS. After graduation, he joined the Cour des Comptes, the government's leading auditor.

While at ENA, he became a protégé of Jacques Attali, one of Mitterrand's leading advisors, who convinced him to run in the 1981 legislative elections against Jacques Chirac. Of course, he lost.

Hollande gradually rose through the ranks of the PS until he became its president when his then partner Ségolène Royal ran for president in 2007. After Dominique Strauss-Kahn was forced to drop out, he became the PS standard bearer in 2012.

Hollande and Royal separated during the 2007 campaign. His current partner, Valérie Trierweiler, is a prominent journalist at the weekly Paris Match and is no stranger to the public limelight. ■

The national health care system covers almost all normal medical expenses. The government also offers extensive pensions, unemployment benefits, and subsidized housing and public transportation.

There are some distinctively French features to its social service system. In the 1930s, France introduced family allocations to help parents meet the cost of raising children and boost the overall population to meet the looming threat from Germany. The German threat is long gone, but the payment scheme remains on the books. France also has one of the world's most extensive government-run preschool programs, which guarantees almost every child a spot in a program staffed by trained teachers. Finally, France is one of the few governments that still cover virtually all tuition costs for higher education in addition to funding the grandes écoles which actually pay their students, because they officially become government employees when they enroll.

French social service programs are also so popular that they have proved very hard to change despite financial pressures to do so. For instance, massive protests came close to blocking President Sarkozy's proposal to raise the retirement age in a country in which some public employees could retire before they were sixty. Although the protests could not block enactment of the legislation at the time, one of Hollande's first initiatives was to return the retirement age for most government employees to sixty.

The social services are costly and have operated at a loss for many years. Shortly after taking office, Hollande announced that taxes on the wealthy would be raised and some programs cut in order to balance the budget during his first term. Nonetheless, the pressures to cut back popular programs will only increase as the population ages and, most notably, health care costs continue to soar.

The Politics of Headscarves

Like its neighbors, France has become a country of immigrants. For the last several centuries, it welcomed both political refugees and people simply looking to improve the quality of their lives. As we saw above, immigration has become one of the most divisive issues in French politics. It is relevant as a public policy issue as a reflection of French centralization that has served to make the treatment of minority members even more controversial than it is in the United States or Great Britain, especially during the Chirac and Sarkozy years, Of particular importance are Arabs from Morocco, Algeria, and Tunisia and many of the others from sub-Saharan Africa and Turkey who are also Muslims.

Disputes about immigration also inevitably blend into those over race and other aspects of identity, which therefore means they can turn toxic. In the French case, two overlapping issues came to the fore early in this century. First, many immigrants and their children have refused to learn French or adopt mainstream French values. Second, many conservatives began to object to the fact that more and more Muslim women were wearing headscarves, burkas, and other items of clothing that they believe are required by their faith.

The government's response has been ambiguous. On the one hand, in keeping with French tradition, every government has insisted that immigrants enjoy the same rights and privileges as native-born French men and women once they become citizens. Blatant acts of racism have been dealt with sternly.

On the other hand, governments on the Left and Right alike have refrained from introducing policies that would address some of the specific problems faced by non-whites

Charles Platiau/Reuters/Landov

A Muslim high school student protesting the ban on wearing headscarves.

because politicians believe they have to treat everyone in exactly the same way.

That coincides with French policies about the separation of church and state that date from 1906. Unlike the case then, the separation of church and state has been one of the most widely agreed on principles in French politics for decades. However, the French approach to such issues is not to ban most forms of religious expression in public spaces altogether in yet another attempt to treat everyone the same.

In this case, it first led some school administrators to prohibit girls from wearing headscarves, arguing that it introduced religion into the schools. A number of girls were expelled and enrolled in private Muslim academies, which are not recognized by the government. Many Muslims were, not surprisingly, incensed because no such effort was made to keep Christians from wearing crosses.

The issue came to a head in 2004 when President Chirac announced a plan to introduce legislation to ban "conspicuous" religious symbols from the schools. Small crosses or stars of David would be allowed, but not yarmulkes or headscarves. Public opinion polls found that almost 60 percent of the public supported the ban and a similar one that already existed for civil servants. Three days after Chirac's declaration, massive protests were held across the country in which, among other things, girls marched wearing red, white, and blue headscarves.

The bill on the schools easily passed the National Assembly early the next year, with 494 votes for it, 36 against, and 31 abstentions. The law by no means settled the issue. In fact, it only reinforced the anger many Muslims feel toward a society they believe treats them as second-class citizens.

The issue did not go away under Sarkozy, who argued that immigrants have to conform to French cultural norms just as his family did. His government passed a law forbidding women to wear the burka or any other clothing that covered their face in public. Ostensibly, this was passed for security reasons; presumably police officers could not identify anyone whose face was hidden. Many Muslims reacted to this law as yet another example of racism and discrimination.

Finally, although the politics of headscarves has often been portrayed as a right-wing issue by the English language press, that is not the case. During the 2012 campaign, Hollande announced that he would not challenge the law, and his government did not take any steps in that direction during the first nine months it was in office.

Foreign Policy

French social and economic policy is controversial, especially for British and American students who tend to think in terms of (relatively) free markets and limited states. If anything, its international role is even more controversial. Many American observers, in particular, have been critical of what they see as an irrational and unacceptable streak of independence in its international relations, from de Gaulle's flamboyant search for **grandeur** to its refusal to support the United States in its invasion of Iraq in 2003.

This section will make the very different case that French foreign policy should not be seen as irrational if one takes de Gaulle's notion of grandeur and his broader political strategy as the analytical starting point. Rather, French presidents from de Gaulle to Sarkozy tried to pursue what they saw as their national interest in ways that the Fifth Republic now allows them to do, whether one agrees with their actions or not.

The Gaullist Years

Before World War I, France was one of the world's great powers. It had the largest and best-equipped army in Europe. Its empire was second only to that of Great Britain.

France's world standing deteriorated badly over the next thirty years. It emerged from the second world war with its economy in tatters, its leaders discredited, its empire threatened, and its fate largely in American hands.

De Gaulle succeeded in stemming that decline. That is why he got involved in politics in the first place and made restoring France to its "proper" place among the world's major powers his primary mission. The general believed that all countries have an inherent national interest akin to what Jean-Jacques Rousseau called the general will in the eighteenth century. In de Gaulle's terms, that meant grandeur or the restoration of the country to its traditional position among the world's great powers.

De Gaulle is frequently accused of having acted in excessively nationalistic, bombastic, and even dangerous ways. However, he was neither a romantic nor a utopian. De Gaulle combined his own charisma with the institutional levers at his disposal in the unbending but normally pragmatic pursuit of grandeur. His form of pragmatism was unusual, because everything he did was undertaken to produce symbolic as well as substantive prestige even if doing so seemed at odds with the way the superpower rivalry defined international relations during the decade he was in office.

De Gaulle ended the Fourth Republic's policy of all but blindly following America's lead. He rejected proposals by Presidents Dwight Eisenhower and John Kennedy to integrate French forces more fully into the **North Atlantic Treaty Organization (NATO)** because this would have meant surrendering part of French sovereignty. In 1964 and 1965, he responded favorably to Soviet proposals for improving Franco-Soviet relations. The next year, de Gaulle withdrew French forces from NATO control.

Much the same can be said of France's nuclear weapons program. De Gaulle had no illusions that the bomb would make France the equal of either superpower. He only hoped that having even a small nuclear arsenal would give the country a more important role in international affairs. It was also clear that he thought of the bomb as a symbol of France's geopolitical renaissance that would instill a sense of national pride that would spill over into other policy areas.

That same desire to maximize French power and prestige lay behind his position on European integration. De Gaulle agreed that the countries of western Europe had to cooperate to meet the challenges posed by American economic and political might. Therefore, de Gaulle firmly supported the elimination of tariff barriers and the provisions of the Common Market that unquestionably worked in France's interest.

There were limits, however, to how much cooperation he would tolerate. French grandeur was incompatible with a multinational, integrated, homogeneous Europe. He preferred a loose community of sovereign states that cooperated in ways that were beneficial to France. Consequently, he opposed British membership in the Common Market because the UK did not share his values and might challenge France's influence in the still-young European institutions.

To the degree that de Gaulle was seen as a visionary nationalist, Pompidou is portrayed as a moderate pragmatic practitioner of realpolitik. In fact, Pompidou continued the quest for grandeur, though he did it in more conventional ways. He was not as brash or as flamboyant as de Gaulle. Because he had firmer parliamentary support than de Gaulle did in the early 1960s and because France's position in the world had improved substantially, he did not have to.

Pompidou did not question the central tenets of Gaullist grandeur. He never considered integrating French forces into NATO. Getting rid of nuclear weapons or submitting them to international control were never options. France continued trying to play its self-defined role as an intermediary between East and West, most notably doing what it could to settle disputes in Indochina and the Middle East.

After OPEC

President Pompidou died during the OPEC oil embargo of 1973–74 and therefore did not have to deal with the worldwide recession it helped spark. For the rest of the century, French foreign policy was noticeably less successful as the forces, reflected in the arrows of Figure 1.3, intensified.

On occasion, French leaders reverted to the independent and anti-American tone of the Gaullist years. All of them accepted that France would hold on to its nuclear arsenal. Gaullist and Socialist officials were critical of what they saw as American cultural hegemony and led efforts to limit American imports, including curved bananas on the pretext that straight ones (grown in former French colonies) are better. But overall, France began to move toward a foreign policy that is more in line with those of the other major Western powers especially regarding the end of the cold war and the EU.

As we will see in Chapters 6, 8, and 9, the end of the cold war took almost everyone by surprise, including the French. France was only a minor player in the negotiations that led to the reunification of Germany in 1990. As one of the four powers that occupied Germany after World War II, France was a participant in the "four-plus-two" negotiations that officially ratified the merger of the two countries. The two superpowers and the two Germanys, however, made all the decisions that really counted.

Since then, French leaders of the Left and Right have vainly tried to find a way to pursue grandeur in a suddenly uncertain world. France has played an active role in most of the international crises since the 1990s, most notably the first Gulf War, the efforts to stop the fighting in the former Yugoslavia, and the campaign to combat terrorism following the attacks on 9/11. But France has not been able to play the kind of role it did at the height of the cold war when it wielded an influence greater than one might expect from a country with its geopolitical resources.

Almost all politicians have stopped talking about grandeur. France has turned into a loyal NATO ally. The differences between Washington and Paris seemed to have moved to the margins at the dawn of the twenty-first century.

Iraq

The one exception was Iraq. Many Americans thought that France went back to its old ways when it refused to support the American-led war in Iraq in 2003.

France was by no means the only country to oppose what it saw as a rush to war by the George W. Bush administration. Russia and China also used their veto power on the United Nations Security Council in refusing to authorize the use of force in Iraq.

France alone became the object of American fury. Sales of French wine and cheese plummeted. Some of New York's most famous French restaurants had to close because diners boycotted them.

On closer inspection, the French position does not seem all that irrational or all that critical of American policy. As late as his New Year's Eve address to the French people in 2002, Chirac advised that their sons and daughters could be heading into war.

Chirac and the other critics insisted that United Nations inspectors should be allowed to finish their work and determine once and for all if Iraq had weapons of mass destruction. Of course, there were other issues involved. France had closer commercial and diplomatic ties to Iraq than did the other major Western powers. Many in France also felt insulted when Defense Secretary Donald Rumsfeld made statements that seemed to belittle France, its power, and its priorities.

From the beginning, France made it clear that it welcomed a regime change in Iraq. What it objected to was the way the United States managed the planning of the war.

It is not clear if Chirac would ever have endorsed an invasion. In retrospect, it seems that his government understood more clearly than the Bush administration did that Iraq's weapons of mass destruction program had been shut down and that the invasion would launch a long and bloody insurgency.

The point is not to question whether either the war in Iraq or France's response to it was appropriate. Rather, the key here is that the French reacted out of what they perceived to be their national interest, something they have done consistently since 1958.

French Fries and French Toast

One of the most bizarre American reactions to French opposition to the war in Iraq was the boycott of french fries and French toast that many Republicans endorsed. It turns out that the French do not call them french fries. They refer to them as *frites* and they were most likely invented in Belgium. Likewise, what Americans know as French toast is *pain perdu* in French and is almost unknown there except as a dessert at Christmas dinner. Instead, rumor has it that Americans call it French toast because the dish was first introduced at French's Tavern near Albany, New York, at the time of the American Revolution.

This was not the first time Americans modified their language for political purposes. During World War I, hamburgers and frankfurters become Salisbury steak and hot dogs. The Danish do not eat Danish pastry. Russians "play" pistol roulette, not Russian roulette. The list goes on and on.

The EU: The Merger of Domestic and Foreign Policy?

European integration is now the lightning rod for the dissatisfaction that has been brewing in French politics in the twenty-first century (see Chapter 7). Even though most mainstream politicians continue to support European integration, it has been controversial among voters for a generation.

After de Gaulle stepped down, France joined Germany as the strongest champions of a more united Europe. As with so much in the Fifth Republic, the growing consensus on Europe was confirmed under the Socialists, especially when President Mitterrand nominated his former finance minister, Jacques Delors, to be president of the European Commission in 1984. Delors was the chief architect of the expansion of what is now the EU to then fifteen members and the leading force behind the Single European Act and the Maastricht Treaty.

In other words, even before the end of the cold war, Europe had become one of the defining issues in French foreign policy. France had become the strongest proponent of the efforts to deepen and broaden European institutions. It parlayed its presence in Europe into expanded markets for its goods and as a vehicle to help strengthen its currency. In the first post–cold war years, many French politicians also saw Europe as a way of diluting unified Germany's power.

The consensus on European policy began to unravel after the Maastricht Treaty was signed in late 1991. It strengthened existing European institutions, renamed them the EU, and paved the way for the euro. When the treaty was signed, all leading French politicians supported it, and it was assumed it would pass easily even after the Constitutional Council ruled that it had to be put to the people in a referendum. As the campaign unfolded, it turned out that the treaty divided the three largest parties, while the PCF and the FN—unusual political bedfellows, to say the least—both opposed it. Despite the growing opposition, most observers assumed that the treaty would be passed overwhelmingly. When the vote was held, the French came within a whisker of turning it down.

Part of the opposition to the EU has roots in French nationalism and concerns about its increasingly diverse population that have little directly to do with European integration. However, there is now ample evidence that adoption of the euro and other steps to strengthen the EU have failed to breathe new life into France's still-stagnant economy.

All of this has taken place at a time when international trade and globalization in general are an inescapable fact of political life. The raw statistics in Table 5.9 have real meaning for people's lives. The fact that imports and exports account for more than a quarter of French consumption and production means that more people eat at McDonald's, drive Nissans, and, shockingly, drink Italian or German wine. By the same token, France's prosperity

Comparative Emphasis: Globalization

Recent French governments have taken relatively ambiguous positions on globalization. For example, they have tried to promote international rules that would restrict the number of foreign television programs and movies that could be shown in the country. But they have also been among the most resolute supporters of the European Union. In particular, they recognize that France's economic success is inextricably intertwined with that of the EU and have thus firmly supported the single currency and other attempts to deepen integration. Conversely, public opposition to the EU and other "foreign" influences has risen noticeably since the mid-1990s. ■

is ever more dependent on its ability to sell Renaults, Airbus jets, and gastronomical treasures abroad. It also means that people who lack the education or skills to shift from the dying heavy industries to more high-tech ones are losing out and, not surprisingly, becoming increasingly dissatisfied.

Frankly, European issues will matter more for the daily lives of French citizens than what their government did about Iraq or how it responds to almost any future global hotspot. As such, European policy is a sign of how

TABLE 5.9 France and the Global Economy

YEAR	EXPORTS AS PERCENT OF GDP	IMPORTS AS PERCENT OF GDP
1962	12	11
1974	20	22
1980	22	23
1992	23	22
1999	26	24
2002	27	25
2004	26	26
2008	22	24
2012	26	28

Source: Data from 1962–1992 from David Cameron, "Economic Policy in the Era for the EMS," in *Remaking the Hexagon*, Gregory Flynn (ed.). (Boulder, CO: Westview Press, 1995), 121; data for 1999 from the World Bank (www.worldbank.org, accessed July 20, 2001); data for 2002 and 2004 from the United Nations Development Programme (www.undp.org, accessed November 15, 2004); and for 2008 from the World Bank (accessed January 20, 2013).

important the global forces sketched in Figure 1.3 are in the politics of almost every country today, a phenomenon we will return to time and time again in the rest of this book. It will also not be the last time we see the domestic political implications of the retired colonel's statement introduced at the end of Chapter 1. What happens "out there" truly influences what happens "back here," often by shaking up domestic political life and the coalitions that have dominated events for decades if not longer.

The Media

In most respects, the French media resemble the British. The print press is dominated by Parisian-based dailies, which are sold throughout the country. Each of them has a distinctive political slant. Some are very good, especially *Le Monde*, which is widely considered to be one of the world's four or five best newspapers. Television news, too, is based primarily on national channels rather than on networks of locally owned and controlled stations. Yet, there are also some important differences.

The tabloid press has a much smaller circulation and more limited influence than that in Britain. France has three high-quality weekly news magazines, each of which takes a different political line. Finally, until the early 1980s, the government routinely influenced the content and tone of television news. That changed once Giscard's government began privatizing television and radio stations and Mitterrand's administration decided to adopt a more hands-off policy. As in most countries, with the spread of cable and satellite television systems, France has seen the launch of dozens of niche program providers. A recent example is Pink TV. It is not the first gay-oriented station in the world, but it's the first one projected to turn a profit.

France 24 (www.france24.com/france24Public/en/news/world.html) is a largely online service that streams text and video. It also has an English version.

One of the quirks of French political life is that pollsters are not allowed to publish their findings in the week before an election. They can and do carry out surveys for parties and candidates. However, the law prevents them from making the money and getting the exposure they would otherwise obtain through contracts with the print or audiovisual media. Pollsters have always found ways to partially get around the law by publishing their results abroad; in 1997, they also began posting their findings on the Internet using foreign-based websites.

Where Are the Big Questions?

As with Chapter 4 on the UK, the big questions raised in Chapter 1 are largely missing from this discussion of France. There are many reasons why that's the case, two of which top most lists. First, political careers are based on candidates, and parties respond to immediate issues more than overarching and long-term ones such as the pace of change or globalization. Second and more importantly, like the British and Americans, the French have a certain smugness about their political system. Many people think that things may not be going all that well today, but few of them are willing (yet) to take the next step and ask if France should consider embarking on social and political change of a more profound nature.

These questions are important. However, because they are not really on the agenda in France, we will defer dealing with them until Chapter 16 at the conclusion of this book.

KEY TERMS

Concepts
anticlerical
autogestion
bloc vote
centralization
cohabitation
dirigisme
grandeur
incompatibility clause
integrated elite
iron triangle
pantouflage

parity law
prefect
privatization
proclerical
proportional representation
single-member district
sovereign debt
tutelle
two-ballot system

People
Chirac, Jacques
de Gaulle, Charles

Debré, Michel
Giscard d'Estaing, Valéry
Hollande, François
Le Pen, Jean-Marie
Louis XIV
l Marine
Mitterrand, François
Pompidou, Georges
Royal, Ségolène
Sarkozy, Nicolas
Strauss-Kahn, Dominique

Acronyms	Organizations, Places, and Events	grandes écoles
CFDT	Communist Party (PCF)	Movement of French Enterprises (MEDEF)
CGT	Confédération Française Démocratique du Travail (CFDT)	National Assembly
ENA	Confédération Générale du Travail (CGT)	National Front (FN)
FN	Constitutional Council	North Atlantic Treaty Organization (NATO)
MEDEF	École Nationale d'Administration (ENA)	Radicals
NATO	events of May	Senate
PCF	Fifth Republic	Socialist Party (SP)
PS	Force ouvrière	Third Republic
UDF	Fourth Republic	Union for French Democracy (UDF)
UMP	Gaullists	Union for a Popular Movement (UMP)

USEFUL WEBSITES

There are fewer English websites on France than there are on Britain or the United States. Gradually, however, French organizations are adding English versions of their French ones. In the body of the chapter's text, I have included a few French-only sites. Those listed here are all in English.

There are two American-based sources for links to political topics in France. The first is a project run by a consortium of librarians. The second is an offshoot of H-France, a listserv for scholars working on things French.

> wess.lib.byu.edu/index.php/French_Studies_Web
>
> www.h-france.net

There are surprisingly few ways of getting news on France in English. The best source now is:

> www.france24.com

The best, though still limited, English-language source on public opinion polls is run by the firm CSA.

> www.csa-tmo.fr/accueil.asp?lang=en

The president's office site is a good entry point for websites from most government offices and agencies.

> www.elysee.fr

FURTHER READING

Allwood, Gill, and Khursheed Wadia. *Women and Politics in France: 1958–2000*. London: Routledge, 2000. A fine overview of the role women play (and do not play) in French politics.

Badiou, Alain. *The Meaning of Sarkozy*. London: Verso, 2008. An unusual book by a French Marxist. The only book on Sarkozy in English.

Elgie, Robert, ed. *The Changing French Political System*. London: Frank Cass, 2000. An excellent anthology by some of the best French, British, and American academic analysts of French politics.

Fenby, John. *The General: Charles de Gaulle and the France He Saved*. New York: Skyhorse Publishers, 2012. The newest and one of the best biographies that focuses on his political impact.

Gaffney, John. *Political Leadership in France: From Charles de Gaulle to Nicolas Sarkozy*. London: Palgrave/Macmillan, 2012. A good overview of presidential leadership styles.

Hauss, Charles. *Politics in France*. Washington: CQ Press, 2008. The newest full-length text on French politics. I will not claim that it is the best.

Robb, Graham. *The Discovery of France*. New York: W. W. Norton, 2007. Not the most popular book among academics, but probably the best overview of the country covering the last two hundred years. Written in the form of a travelogue by someone who toured the country on his bicycle.

Sa'adah, Anne. *Contemporary France*. Boulder, CO: Rowman and Littlefield, 2003. The best available overview of French history by a political scientist.

Timmerman, Kenneth R. *The French Betrayal of America*. New York: Crown, 2004. An important but, to my mind, wrong-headed view of how France has systematically undermined American interests over the years.

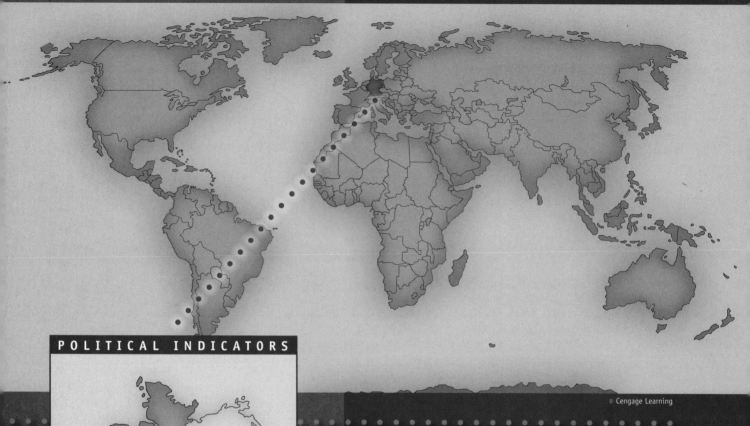

© Cengage Learning

POLITICAL INDICATORS

GERMANY

- Berlin
- Dresden
- Bonn
- Frankfurt
- Munich

GOVERNANCE (score 0-1)	HUMAN DEVELOPMENT (score 0-1)	DEMOCRACY (rank)	PEACE (rank)	CORRUPTION (rank)
.824	.905	14	15	14

CHAPTER OUTLINE

Germany

Germany's resurgence as a world power has been driven by no one and no cult but by many Germans pulling together in an elaborate democracy and market economy.

NICO COLCHESTER

THE BASICS

Germany

Size	356,910 sq. km (about two-thirds the size of France)
Population	82 million
GNP per capita	$38,100
Currency	1.33€ = US$1 (August 3, 2013).
Ethnic composition	91.5% German; of the largest remaining groups, 2.4% Turkish
Religion	34% Protestant, 34% Catholic, 3.4% Muslim, remainder unaffiliated or undeclared
Capital	Berlin
Form of government	Federal republic
Head of state	Joachim Gauck (2012–)
Head of government	Angela Merkel (2005–)

Austerity and the Sovereign Debt Crisis

Political scientists have long drawn a sharp distinction between comparative politics and international relations. One of the most important reasons why we have done so is the fact that, historically, political life for most people has largely revolved around domestic issues other than during times of war. In what may prove to be a sign of things to come elsewhere in the world, the most important issue in German politics in early 2013 is international but has nothing to do with war. The resolution of the sovereign debt crisis in the European Union will go a long way toward defining the future of German politics, including whether the government led by Christian Democratic (CDU) Prime Minister Angela Merkel (1954–) is returned to power in an election to be held shortly after this book goes to press.

We will put off discussing the specifics of the sovereign debt crisis until the next chapter on the EU itself. For now, it is enough to note that the Federal Republic of Germany (FRG) had little to do with creating the crisis, but it would have the biggest say in ending it—however that finally happens.

The stakes are high. The introduction of the euro as the common currency in the seventeen members of the eurozone tied their economies more closely together than ever before. As a result, they suffered together through the recession that began in 2007.

They did not, however, all suffer equally. For reasons that will become clear later on, Germany has long made controlling inflation its most important economic priority. The other countries in the eurozone have not always followed suit. Portugal, Italy, Ireland, Greece, and Spain had all accumulated massive national debts before the recession . Then, they spent more money (that they did not have) to introduce new public works programs to minimize the impact of the downturn.

Their policies did not work. Greece was hit especially hard. Almost one in four Greeks was unemployed. The government and many Greek banks teetered on the brink of bankruptcy.

Europe faced a choice. It could let Greece default on its loans and probably take the euro with it. Or, it could bail out the Greek government and banks.

For all intents and purposes, the euro's–and perhaps the EU's — fate rested largely in German hands, because no other member state had anywhere near enough resources to make much of a difference. It is the EU's largest and wealthiest member. Until François Hollande's election in 2012, France usually followed Germany's lead on fiscal matters. Because Britain had chosen not to adopt the euro, it stayed on the political sidelines.

Merkel and the German electorate both understood they were in a bind. They did not want the euro to collapse, but they wanted to strengthen it in ways that made economic sense, at least as they saw it.

Given Germany's traditional opposition to inflation, its own financial difficulties, and her own personal preferences, Merkel wanted to force Greece and the other debt-laden governments to adopt **austerity**, including sharp budget cuts that would have led to more unemployment, reduced wages, and eroded living conditions. At the same time, they were reluctant to have the German government (and hence the German people) pay the price. During 2011

and 2012, the EU lurched from crisis to crisis, with Merkel always capitulating at the last minute to guarantee new loans to the banks and governments.

The deadlock continued until Hollande made it clear that Germany would have to find some kind of common ground with France. Still, the crisis was far from over and remained up in the air when this book went to press.

The stakes are also high for Merkel, for Germany, for the euro, and for the EU. Germany's economic health depends significantly on trade with the rest of the EU which, in turn, will certainly suffer if the value of the euro and the status of the regional economies in general remain in flux.

But, compared to what we will see in Parts 3 and 4, the stakes are not all that high. Nothing in the crisis is likely to put Germany's standing as the largest and richest country in Europe in jeopardy. No one in Germany wants to risk what it has accomplished since the end of World War II. And make no mistake. It has accomplished a lot.

Its regime is as stable as any of the others covered in Part 2. It has had its share of protest movements, but they have been so rare and so mild over the last half century that we tend to take particular notice of them when they do occur. Germany is ahead of most other countries in many fields. For example, it leads the world in requiring cars, appliances, and other goods to be made with materials that will be recycled once the equipment is no longer in use.

In other words, this chapter is about a success story on at least two levels.

Sean Gallup/Getty Images

German Chancellor Merkel and French President Hollande holding their first summit in the afternoon of his inauguration day in 2012.

First, viewed solely through the lens of its own political history, Germany's success has been nothing short of a miracle. Not even half a century ago, most observers assumed that what we will call the **German question** would be a permanent disruptive force in international relations. Today, Germany is Europe's unquestioned leader, and Germans have every reason to be proud of building their economy, solidifying their democratic regime, and integrating what used to be the **German Democratic Republic (DDR)**.

Second, for comparativists today, Germany is the one country covered in Part 2 in which political leaders have addressed some aspects of the four big questions introduced at the start of Chapter 1. Although those issues are not always near the top of the political agenda on a daily basis, it is hard for Germans to avoid thinking about how quickly their society has changed, how globalization has affected their lives, and how resilient their democracy has become.

Thinking About Germany

Until recently, few introductory courses in comparative politics included Germany. It is hard to leave it out today.

Germany is, after all, one of the world's leading political and economic powers largely because it has been able to combine a functioning liberal democracy with a strong state that has emphasized reconciliation, consensus, and transformation more than any other industrialized democracy. Germany today bears little resemblance to the country that went to war in 1939. The country has had to successfully rebuild its political bridges twice since 1945, first with its former adversaries in World War II and then among its own people after the unification of East and West Germany in 1990. It has done that and much, much more, primarily by forging broad agreements that transcend partisan and other ideological divisions in ways that no other industrialized democracy has matched.

The Bottom Line

Wealth

Germany is the second largest country in Europe, trailing only Russia. Its GNP per capita of roughly $38,000 a year also makes Germany one of the world's richest. Less fortunate Germans are covered by an extensive social service system that protects them from poverty, homelessness, or treatable ill health.

Germany's prosperity is all the more remarkable because the country was in ruins after World War II. The Federal Republic turned the economy around so fast that its growth was referred to as the **economic miracle**. Two decades later,

Social Democratic politicians dubbed their policies *Modell Deutschland* (the German Model), with its not very subtle hint that its consensus-driven, balanced, and sustained growth was a formula other countries could emulate.

The country has its share of problems, beginning with the fact that the five *länder* (states) inherited from East Germany remain far poorer than the rest of the country. Nonetheless, only a country with Germany's assets could have incorporated sixteen million people with such a lower standard of living and different political history virtually overnight and with minimal political or social disruption.

Diversity

Like Britain and France, Germany is no longer homogeneous. Roughly ten percent of its population are either immigrants themselves or children of immigrants. Those appearances aside, immigration to Germany has been different in three critical respects.

First, the immigrants did not come from former German colonies. It never had as many as France or Britain to begin with and then lost them all at the end of World War I. As a result, most immigrants came from such countries as Turkey and the former Yugoslavia and had no cultural or linguistic ties to their new home. In the last 20 years or so, the pace of immigration has slowed and the patterns have changed to include more people from Eastern Europe, the Middle East, and Africa.

Second, officials never wanted Germany to become a country of immigrants. Most were officially known as *gastarbeiter*, literally guest workers, who came on short-term contracts and left their families at home. They were recruited by the West German government to help fill a severe labor shortage in a country that had more than five million of its citizens killed or wounded during the war. The government stopped officially importing workers in 1973. By that time, many of them had found a way to stay permanently and have their families join them.

Third, in part as a result, Germany had Europe's most restrictive citizenship laws until the SPD-Green government changed them in 1999. Even today, it is relatively difficult for people who are not of German ancestry to become naturalized, and only children who have at least one parent who is a legal resident automatically become citizens at birth. Difficulties in integrating the immigrants and their German-born children is reflected in everything from a reluctance to embrace bilingual education to the fact that the citizenship laws leave it with one of the least diverse national soccer teams in western Europe.

Aging

Germany shares one more demographic concern with the rest of Europe—an aging population. Although its population is

Reuters/CORBIS

A right-wing rioter tossing a firebomb at a hostel for asylum seekers in Rostock, Germany.

not as old as Japan's, 21 percent of all Germans were over 65 years old in 2012. So few German women are having babies that the population is shrinking at the rate of 0.2 percent per year. Some projections suggest that the total population of Germany will decline by as many as ten million people over the next forty years.

The aging population is likely to have two significant political implications. First, because most people will live longer, health and pension costs are almost certain to keep going up. As in most industrialized democracies, the young and the relatively healthy will end up paying for the pensions and health care of the elderly. Second, Germany may not be able to continue limiting immigration, because its offices and factories are likely to suffer from a massive labor shortage. In other words, whether the "native" population likes it or not, Germany will have to become a more welcoming, multicultural society.

Decentralization

Unlike Britain and France, Germany has a federal government. As we will see in more detail in the section on the state, the sixteen **länder** have many powers they can exercise on their own and are directly represented in the national government.

Federalism is a byproduct of German history. As we will also see, modern Germany was built on the basis of dozens of once independent and vastly different jurisdictions, which made anything approaching a centralized government all but impossible. Then, when the Federal Republic

was created in the late 1940s, devolving power to the states was seen as one of many ways to prevent a German return to the horrors of Nazism.

There is one other aspect of federalism worth noting. There is no German equivalent of London or Paris that dominates political, economic, and cultural life. Until the end of World War II, Berlin came close to playing that role. However, because West Berlin was surrounded by East Germany, the capital of the Federal Republic was located in Bonn. The capital moved back to Berlin after unification, but it is by no means the center of economic life.

Key Questions

In 1945, no serious observer would have predicted that Germany would become so rich, so stable, and so democratic so quickly. The country had been defeated and dismembered. Most people outside the country treated it as a pariah.

Yet, that is not what Germany is like today. As a result, the main goal of this chapter is to show how Germany's dramatic and tragic history paved the way for its equally dramatic and unexpected postwar turnaround.

Germany still has some right-wing extremists who direct their hatred at immigrants, asylum seekers, and other foreigners. However, their influence is limited, and despite an occasional breakthrough at the state level, no extremist party has come close to breaking the 5 percent barrier parties need to gain representation in parliament.

Democracy is as strongly established in Germany as it is anywhere. To refer again to that key distinction made in Chapter 1, its regime is as secure as any in an industrialized democracy, whatever voters think of the government of the day.

Germany's often traumatic past and remarkable present situation lead us to ask five questions about this country and its transition.

- Why did it take Germany so long to unite and have trouble building a viable state?

- Why did Germany's first attempt at democracy disintegrate and make possible the rise of **Adolf Hitler** (1889–1945) and his **Nazi** regime?

- Why did the division and trauma of the Third Reich give way to reconciliation, consensus, and transformation?

- Why did unification occur and how did the regime handle the new challenges posed by adding the five eastern states?

- Why has Europe been so important for at least the last twenty years, and why is it the most pressing issue facing Germany today?

The Evolution of the German State

Scholars have been preoccupied with the German question since the end of World War II. In fact, it is a series of related questions all of which lead to answers that begin to help us understand how that troubled past can coexist with the comparatively placid present.

Unification and the Kaiser's Reich

In Chapters 4 and 5, we saw that the state and nation developed roughly in tandem in Great Britain and in France. That was not the case in Germany.

During the early Middle Ages, Germany had one of the most advanced political systems in Europe. It was more united than most "countries" under the Holy Roman Empire, which some Germans call the First Reich. More than most, too, Germans were unified around a common culture and spoke closely related dialects if not a single language. It would take, however, centuries for a politically unified Germany to come into existence.

By the middle of the thirteenth century, any semblance of unity had disappeared once the German components of the Holy Roman Empire splintered into hundreds of principalities. The Reformation made the fragmentation

worse as local rulers lined up on both sides of the split between Catholics and Protestants. The Thirty Years' War (1618–48) brought the wars of religion to an end but failed to unify the country. As a result, Germany remained a patchwork of tiny states, some Catholic, some Protestant, almost all of them authoritarian.

The first tentative steps toward unification were taken when the eastern province of Brandenburg became the Kingdom of Prussia in 1701. Under Frederick I (ruled 1640–88), Frederick Wilhelm I (ruled 1688–1740), and Frederick the Great (ruled 1740–86), Prussia gradually gained control of more and more territory. By the end of the eighteenth century, it was one of Europe's great powers and also one of its most conservative. Prussia was poor and had few natural resources of its own. Therefore, its rulers had to rely on discipline, thus strengthening authoritarian values that were already under pressure to the west (see Table 6.1).

The end of the Napoleonic Wars had had the unintended consequence of uniting many of the smaller states. The Congress of Vienna in 1815 continued that trend, leaving thirty-eight German states, of which only two, Prussia and Austria-Hungary, were big and strong enough to unite Germany (See Table 6.2).

Under the skilled, if often ruthless, leadership of Chancellor **Otto von Bismarck** (1815–98), Prussia defeated Denmark, Austria, and France between 1864 and 1870. At that point, Bismarck had brought all the German states under Prussian control other than Austria. In 1871, they "asked" the Prussian king, Wilhelm I, to become emperor, or Kaiser, of a new Reich.

Bismarck and his colleagues extended the Prussian constitution to the entire country, giving it a strong, authoritarian regime. That could not hide the fact that Germany was deeply divided. The religious disputes of the preceding three centuries had left a country split not only between clericals and anticlericals but also between Catholics and Protestants. Germany's democrats were sharply at odds with the dominant Prussian elite. For its first twenty years, Bismarck dominated the Second Reich. He stepped down in 1890 but the Kaiser and the nobility (mostly the Prussian **Junkers**) continued to dominate politically, socially, and economically.

TABLE 6.1 German Regimes Since 1871

YEAR	REGIME
1871–1918	Second Reich
1919–33	Weimar Republic
1933–45	Third Reich
1949–90	German Democratic Republic
1949–	Federal Republic

© Cengage Learning

TABLE 6.2 Key Events in German History 1870–1945

YEAR	EVENT
1871	Establishment of the German Reich
1914	Start of World War I
1919	Creation of Weimar Republic
1933	Nazi Victory
1939	Start of World War II
1945	End of World War II

© Cengage Learning 2015

All men were granted the right to vote in 1867, but Germany was still far from democratic. The **Social Democratic Party (SPD)** was the largest faction in the Reichsstag but had no real influence because the new parliament could neither vote on the budget nor hold the cabinet accountable through a vote of confidence.

Unified Germany lagged behind Britain and France, where the impetus for the industrial revolution had come "from below" and capitalist entrepreneurs operated on their own, largely independent of the state. Both countries also took substantial, if less than complete, steps to incorporate the working class and other underprivileged groups into the political process. Perhaps most important, both strengthened their parliaments, thereby curbing the arbitrary power of unelected elites.

That is not what happened in Germany. Instead, the Prussian-based elite clung to power. The leadership realized that it could not afford the time it would take to modernize if they relied on market forces. Instead, they used the state to steer the development of an industrialized capitalist economy, sometimes called a "revolution from above."

By the end of the century, a modern army and navy had turned Germany into a global power that rivaled Britain and France. The new industrial centers made not only weapons but also railroads, chemicals, and telephone and telegraph equipment. To cite but one example, the production of both iron and steel grew by more than 700 percent between 1870 and 1910.

Germany found itself isolated from most of the rest of Europe. There was no easy way to fit a newly powerful and ambitious German state into the elaborate and fragile international system created at the Congress of Vienna in 1815. Germany's imperial aspirations were mostly thwarted. It did take over a few colonies, but its empire was far smaller than those of the Netherlands, Belgium, and Portugal, let alone Great Britain and France.

Germany had become what scholars call a **faulted society** beset by both domestic and international fault lines. Just like their geological namesakes, geopolitical fault lines ultimately produce human earthquakes.

Millions of workers and others became frustrated by changes they neither controlled nor benefited from, which led many to fear the outbreak of civil war. The government did introduce social insurance programs to try to gain the support of the working class. Yet, it also passed a series of antisocialist laws and repressed the growing trade union movement, which left an unusually alienated and potentially revolutionary working class.

To the surprise of many, the international fault lines "gave way" first. The European balance of power finally crumbled early in the twentieth century. The major powers had agreed to a series of public treaties and secret pacts that ended up pitting Germany and the Austro-Hungarian and Ottoman empires against Britain, France, and Russia.

In 1914, a Bosnian Serb nationalist assassinated the heir apparent to the Austro-Hungarian throne. That isolated act by a single individual culminated in the outbreak of World War I, a war no one wanted, but no one could prevent.

At first the war went well for Germany. Hopes for victory in a matter of weeks, however, soon disappeared and the war turned into a bloody stalemate. By the time the fighting ended, more than eight million people were dead, more than half of them civilians.

The German military took control of the government in early November 1918. Three days later the Kaiser was forced into exile, and the monarchy was replaced by a hastily organized group of politicians who declared Germany a republic. On November 11, Germany surrendered.

Weimar and the Rise of Hitler

In August 1919, the **Weimar Republic** was created in the city that gave it its name. It never had a chance.

Overnight, Germany went from being one of Europe's most authoritarian countries to being one of its most democratic. The political and bureaucratic elites who had taken Germany to war were stripped of almost all their power. A reformed Reichstag gained the authority to cast votes of no confidence in the cabinet. But, as we have already seen in France, constitutional provisions alone are never enough to ensure any democracy's survival, let alone its success.

In 1919, the three parties that most strongly supported the new republic—the SPD, the Catholic Zentrum (Center), and the mostly Protestant and liberal People's Party (DDP)—won over three-quarters of the vote. In the next two elections, their share of the vote began to slip to the benefit of the Communists on the Left and the Nazis and German National People's Party (DNVP) on the antidemocratic Right.

The Treaty of Versailles that formally ended the war only made life more difficult for the new republic. American President Woodrow Wilson had called for a "just and lasting peace" preserved by a powerful League of Nations. The British and French, however, were far more vindictive. Their conditions included strict limits on the size of the German military and steep **reparations** that forced Germany to repay the allies for the costs of the war, which worsened an already serious economic crisis. Inflation skyrocketed, unemployment tripled, and the purchasing power of those who kept their jobs was reduced by as much as two-thirds. Especially hard hit were the veterans who had survived four years of hell at the front only to return to a social, political, and economic hell at home.

By the middle of the 1920s, few politicians outside the SPD were giving Weimar their wholehearted support. Radical leftists, however, wanted nothing to do with it and attempted revolutions in 1919 and 1920. Although they were quickly put down, the uprisings drove a deep wedge between the increasingly moderate socialists and the new Communist Party (KPD) that was, for all intents and purposes, run by the new Soviet Union.

The challenge that eventually did the Weimar Republic in came from the Right, not the Left. Millions of Germans refused to come to grips with the fact that weak leadership was the main reason it lost the war. Instead, dozens of small, antidemocratic nationalist groups sought scapegoats among Jews, socialists, and the Weimar politicians. It also didn't help that the Weimar leaders had adopted **proportional representation**, which made it easy for extremist parties to get their foot in the parliamentary door and left Weimar with a far more fragmented and polarized party system than France's Third Republic.

Weimar faced its first serious crisis in 1923, when the little-known Adolf Hitler and his equally little-known party, the Nazis or **National Socialist Democratic Workers Party (NSDAP)**, tried to overthrow the republic. They failed miserably. Many Nazi leaders were arrested, including Hitler, who spent nine months in prison, where he wrote his infamous Mein Kampf.

Conditions seemed to improve in the middle of the decade. The economy recovered somewhat, which cost the extremists much of their short-term support. Better news came from abroad, too, when the Allies agreed to a reduction in reparation payments.

The calm was not to last. In 1929, the bottom fell out of the economy after the New York stock market crash. Unemployment leapt from 6 percent to 30 percent in less than three years. No family was spared.

The Great Depression struck at a time when it would have taken a political miracle to form an effective government. The three main Weimar parties saw their share of the vote drop below 50 percent. In other words, as the crisis deepened, German governments were even more paralyzed than those we saw in Third Republic France.

A succession of right-wing governments pursued orthodox economic policies that emphasized fiscal responsibility and deflation. As President Herbert Hoover discovered in the United States, those policies only worsened the depression.

PROFILES Adolf Hitler

Adolph Hitler was born in Austria in 1889. Prior to 1914, he was a ne'er-do-well who had dreams of becoming an artist, although his biographers say he had little or no talent. He joined the German army in World War I, experienced the horrors of trench warfare, and eventually was wounded.

Hitler came back to a weakened and dispirited Germany. Like so many of his generation, he could only make sense of the defeat by viewing it as the result of a conspiracy on the part of Jews, the Left, and others he despised.

He was imprisoned after the failed 1923 putsch. After he got out of jail later that year, he wove together an appeal that focused on nationalism and widespread hatred of the republic, Jews, and the Left.

Over the next ten years, Hitler used his impressive oratorical and organizational skills to build the Nazi Party. After it came to power, he began systematically wiping out all opposition, creating a totalitarian state, and taking the aggressive steps that would ultimately lead to World War II and the Holocaust.

Hitler died in his bunker during the final days of the war. ■

Adolf Hitler, reviewing Nazi forces.

AP Photo

Turmoil in the streets only heightened the tension. The Communists, the SPD, and the Nazis all had massive militias, which fought against each other and against the police, who could do little or nothing to stop the violence.

The big winners were the Nazis. After the failed putsch in 1923, Hitler realized it would be far easier to come to power by winning elections. For the next decade, he dedicated his demagogic skills and the party's organization to that effort.

Their electoral fortunes had sagged during the relative calm of the mid-1920s, but when the depression hit, they were ready. Their popularity took off, especially among small-town and lower-middle-class Protestants.

Support for the regime continued to evaporate. The anti-system parties won over 40 percent of the vote. By 1932, the NSDAP had become Germany's largest party. Even more important, the party's influence in the streets had grown to the point that its *Sturmabteilung* (SA) was the largest and most feared partisan paramilitary.

The increasingly isolated political leaders invoked the emergency powers provisions of the constitution, but they could not stop either the depression or disorder in the streets. The balance of political power shifted from the moderates to the extremists on both Left and Right. Finally, the politicians had to make a choice, and on January 30, 1933, they invited Hitler to form a government on the assumption that they would be able to control him once he became chancellor or that they would be able to get rid of him after the immediate crisis had passed. However, Hitler used his coalition with the mainstream right-wing parties to piece together an unbeatable majority in the Reichstag, which he used to pass legislation that created one of the most repressive and reprehensible regimes in history.

The Third Reich

Hitler started dismantling the Weimar Republic within weeks of taking office. The Reichstag building burned down on February 7. Hitler blamed the Communists, even though the Nazis themselves had started the fire. The Nazi-controlled police started arresting Communists the next day. New parliamentary elections were held less than a week later. Even though the NSDAP fell short of an absolute majority, it won enough seats to pass the infamous Enabling Act, which became the legal statutory basis for the creation of the Third Reich.

By year's end, the Nazis had outlawed the trade unions and all of the other political parties. In 1934, Hitler declared himself *führer* as well as chancellor and abolished most of the remaining Weimar institutions. Universal military service was reinstated. The infamous Nuremberg laws were enacted, which barred Jews from all positions of responsibility. It began the officially sanctioned anti-Semitism that

would only end with the appalling "final solution" and the death of over six million Jews.

Nazi organizations blanketed the country. Hitler and his henchmen used the new media of radio and film to reach, seduce, and mobilize millions of Germans. The 1936 Olympics were organized to show off the new Germany.

To undo the "damage" of 1918 and 1919 and restore Germany to its "rightful" place among the world's powers, the Nazis looked beyond Germany's borders. Hitler's notion of Aryan superiority meant that all other nationalities were inferior to and therefore should be ruled by Germans. Moreover, as the world's superior race, the Germans needed to expand and take over the new "living room" (*lebensraum*).

Germany withdrew from the League of Nations. After rearming, it set its sights on neighboring countries with a substantial German population. In 1936, Hitler remilitarized the Rhineland along the French border in violation of the Treaty of Versailles. Two years later Germany annexed Austria and intervened in the Spanish civil war on the side of Generalissimo Francisco Franco's neo-fascist forces. Later in the year, it laid claim to the Sudetenland, a region in the new country of Czechoslovakia that was predominantly German.

Germany's actions caught Britain and France unprepared. At the 1938 Munich conference, Prime Ministers Neville Chamberlain and Edouard Daladier acceded to Hitler's demands in what has come to be called appeasement. Despite Hitler's success at Munich, German ambitions were not satisfied. In March 1939, its forces occupied the rest of Czechoslovakia. In August 1939, it signed a nonaggression pact with the Soviet Union in which the two countries pledged not to attack each other and secretly planned to dismantle Poland, Lithuania, Latvia, and Estonia.

Germany's aggression finally encountered resistance when it invaded Poland on September 1, 1939. Two days later France and Britain declared war on Germany. World War II had begun, barely twenty years after the first one ended.

Poland and the rest of Eastern Europe were quickly overrun. The German blitzkrieg shifted to the west, defeating Belgium, the Netherlands, and France in a matter of weeks. Despite the nonaggression pact, Germany attacked the Soviet Union in 1941, laid siege to Leningrad, reached the outskirts of Moscow, and penetrated 1,500 miles into Soviet territory. Britain was the only major European power to avoid being invaded, and then, only barely.

At the time, it seemed that Hitler might have been right in calling the Germans the master race. The Nazi regime might well turn into what he called a Thousand Year Reich.

After the Soviet Union and the United States entered the war on the Allied side, German fortunes began to sag. The Soviet army finally halted the German advance at the battle of Stalingrad in the winter of 1942–43 and then launched a counterattack that would continue until the end of the war. At about the same time, Allied troops invaded Sicily and began a slow, steady campaign up the Italian peninsula. Their planes began an air assault on the German homeland that would leave the country in ruins. The final straw came with the Allied D-Day invasion of the beaches of Normandy in France on June 6, 1944.

On April 30, 1945, Hitler committed suicide. Eight days later, the German general's staff surrendered unconditionally.

The Thousand Year Reich was over, twelve years after it began.

Occupation and the Two Germanys

Although the circumstances of the defeat and subsequent occupation varied from country to country, the Allies were committed to avoiding the "mistakes" of Versailles. Given what we have seen so far, that must have seemed a daunting, if not impossible, challenge (see Table 6.3).

France, Great Britain, the United States, and the Soviet Union divided the defeated Germany into four zones, each occupying one of them. The Western powers would have liked to transform Germany into a strong democratic regime right away, but they were convinced that authoritarian values were too deeply engrained. Therefore, they removed Nazis from leadership positions, and the most nefarious of them were tried and executed.

Even though the cold war did not begin in earnest as soon as World War II ended, the eastern and western zones of occupation evolved in very different ways from the beginning. In the long run, the most important thing the Western powers did in their zones grew out of their decision to rebuild rather than exact revenge on Germany. Most important was the aid provided by the United States through the Marshall Plan. Between 1948 and 1951, Germany received about $1.5 billion, which it used to buy food and equipment from the United States and rebuild the core of its economy. By the early 1950s, the economic miracle, which we will return to regularly throughout the rest of this chapter, was well under way.

TABLE 6.3 Key Events in German History Since 1945

YEAR	EVENT
1949	Creation of Federal Republic and DDR
1966	First Grand Coalition
1969	First SPD government
1982	Helmut Kohl becomes chancellor
1990	Unification
2005	Angela Merkel becomes chancellor

© Cengage Learning 2015

The educational system was redesigned so that the schools could help forge more support for democratic values. Tentative steps were taken to reestablish the German government as well. Leaders who had not been part of the Nazi regime were identified and allowed to organize new parties. Limited authority over education, welfare, and other policy areas was given to the three Western zones.

Many Germans and residents of the other Axis powers turned inward as they tried to come to grips with the values that had brought the fascists to power. In so doing, some key politicians were able to draw on the less than successful, but still significant, experiments with democracy the defeated countries had had before the fascists came to power.

In 1947, the Soviets began systematically imposing Stalinist governments on the countries in their sphere of influence. Because Germany straddled the informal border between east and west, it quickly became the focal point of the cold war. Among other things, the United States and the other Western allies quickly decided that it was in their interests to create an economically strong Germany, which, in fact, was one of the main justifications given for the Marshall Plan.

The intensification of the cold war led the allies to shift their emphasis to policies that would quickly lead to a strong western Germany rather than longer term, democratic goals. For example, they ended the purge of former Nazis. Some former party members whose involvement in the old regime was limited were allowed to hold bureaucratic and teaching positions.

Most importantly, the Western powers sped up the political integration of their three zones. In 1948, they introduced a currency reform that would bring the three economies closer together. The momentum to create a Western state increased after the Soviets imposed a land blockade on West Berlin, which was deep inside their zone of occupation. A Western airlift the likes of which the world had never seen kept the besieged city supplied until May 1949.

While the airlift was under way, a Constituent Assembly met to draft a constitution, which was completed three days after the blockade was lifted. Because they assumed it would only be in place until Germany was reunited, the drafters called it the **Basic Law** instead of a constitution.

On August 14, the first postwar elections were held. The Christian Democratic Union (CDU), the successor to the prewar Zentrum, and its leader, the anti-fascist mayor of Cologne, **Konrad Adenauer** (1876–1967), won a slim plurality of the votes (see Table 6.4). Chancellor Adenauer then put together a coalition consisting of his CDU, the liberal **Free Democratic Party (FDP)**, and a number of regional parties, which became the Federal Republic's first government.

TABLE 6.4 German Chancellors Since 1948

YEAR	CHANCELLOR	POLITICAL PARTY
1948–63	Konrad Adenauer	CDU
1963–66	Ludwig Erhard	CDU
1966–69	Kurt Georg Kiesinger	CDU
1969–74	Willy Brandt	SPD
1974–82	Helmut Schmidt	SPD
1982–98	Helmut Kohl	CDU
1998–2005	Gerhard Schröder	SPD
2005–	Angela Merkel	CDU

© Cengage Learning

There was no guarantee that the economic recovery would continue indefinitely or that the Federal Republic would be any more successful than Weimar. The new West Germany had to assimilate more than ten million refugees from countries that had come under communist rule. Everyone acknowledged, too, that not enough time had passed for there to have been much change in basic German values.

But that is precisely what happened.

Building a Democratic Germany

Adenauer and the CDU provided Germany with effective leadership, which they used to give life to the new political institutions. Moreover, the CDU and its FDP allies forged links with the business, industrial, bureaucratic, and trade union communities through which they presided over the longest period of growth the country had ever seen.

Adenauer made it all possible. He had been a leader of the Catholic Zentrum Party during the Weimar Republic and had impeccable anti-Nazi credentials. That made him an obvious choice for the Allies to turn to when they began the transition that led to the creation of the Federal Republic.

Like his contemporary in France, Charles de Gaulle, Adenauer used his personal reputation to build broad-based support for the new regime. He led the CDU to four election wins in a row, including the one and only time a single party has won an outright majority in the **Bundestag**.

Like most politicians of his day, he was skeptical about how quickly Germany could turn into a democracy. Therefore, he centralized power in his office, forging a system now known as **chancellor democracy**.

When Adenauer was finally urged into retirement at age eighty-six, he left the same kind of legacy as de Gaulle—stability that made domestic and foreign policy success possible. He was succeeded by Ludwig Erhard (1897–1977), who is usually given credit for masterminding the economic miracle. Erhard, however, was not an effective chancellor and took the blame for the first postwar recession, which began in 1966. In the midst of the downturn, the neo-Nazi **National Democratic Party (NPD)** began to make major gains and threatened to

cross the 5 percent barrier, raising concerns about continued German susceptibility to right-wing extremism.

Erhard resigned in 1966 and was replaced by another Christian Democrat, Kurt Georg Kiesinger. Kiesinger decided not to form a government with the FDP but turned instead to a **grand coalition** with the SPD that would be better able to take steps to end the recession and, with it, the NPD threat. With passage of the 1967 **Law for Promoting Stability and Growth in the Economy**, the two parties committed themselves to policies designed to sustain balanced growth and consensus building that has characterized German politics ever since.

After the 1969 elections, a coalition government between the SPD and FDP was formed, removing the CDU from office for the first time. Under the leadership of **Willy Brandt** (1913–1992) and then **Helmut Schmidt** (1918–), the SPD-led governments passed modest social reforms and opened up relations with the communist world. Far more importantly, the two socialists demonstrated their commitment to working within the policy consensus established during the grand coalition years.

In the early 1980s, however, support for the Schmidt government disintegrated. The SPD's left wing pulled it in one direction and the increasingly conservative FDP pushed it in the other. Finally, in 1982, the FDP decided to quit the center-left coalition and ally once again with the CDU. On October 1, the Schmidt government lost a vote of confidence. Because of the rules on **constructive vote of no confidence** (see the section on the state), the Bundestag immediately selected **Helmut Kohl** (1930–) as chancellor. Because the Bundestag was not dissolved when the FDP switched camps, no new elections were held. Kohl agreed to early elections the next year, which the CDU-FDP team won easily, the first of its four consecutive victories.

Kohl and the New Germany

Kohl was chancellor for sixteen years. During that time, he helped lead his country out of years of economic malaise and the shock of absorbing the DDR overnight. Although some still doubted Germany's commitment to democracy when he took office, everyone had come to take it for granted when he left.

He did not follow Ronald Reagan's and Margaret Thatcher's lead and try to move Germany toward a more market-oriented economic policy. Rather, he did little more than tinker with the social market economy and never came close to undermining the consensus on balanced growth. Unlike his American and British contemporaries, Kohl's government increased the already generous social benefits the working class enjoyed and encouraged the trade unions and corporate executives to cooperate with each other.

Kohl did not overreact to the cultural and political shock waves following the election of Green Party members to the Bundestag in 1983. Instead, Germany became an environmental leader. Tough laws made the recycling of 80 percent of all cardboard and plastics and 90 percent of all aluminum, glass, and tin mandatory. Germany also agreed to reduce its greenhouse gases more than it was later required to do under the provisions of the Kyoto Treaty on climate change.

Even though he came to office without any experience in international relations, Kohl had an even greater impact on foreign policy. He skillfully guided Germany through a difficult decade that began with renewed superpower tensions but concluded with the unexpected end of the cold war. Germany remained one of the strongest advocates of European integration and became one of the chief architects of the Single European Act, the Maastricht Treaty, and the euro. Most important of all, Kohl skillfully engineered the later stages of the reunification of Germany in the months after the collapse of the Berlin Wall and then the DDR.

We could go on and consider the details of what happened after Kohl left office. But that would add little to what should be a clear picture by now. While there have been policy differences dividing political leaders and economic problems at home and abroad, the most striking theme we will see is the continuity hinted at in the statement by Nico Colchester that begins this chapter.

Creating a Democratic Political Culture

At the end of the war, most analysts were convinced that the values that had given rise to the Third Reich were deeply ingrained in German society. As they saw it, Weimar had been a "republic without republicans." Even the most sympathetic observers believed that the overwhelming majority of Germans had openly supported the worst aspects of Nazism, silently accepting Hitler's Reich, or did nothing about its excesses when opportunities to do so arose. No one put those sentiments more eloquently than Pastor Martin Niemöller, writing while in a concentration camp in 1944:

> First they came for the Socialists, but I didn't do anything, because I wasn't a Socialist.
>
> Then they came for the Jews, but I didn't do anything, because I wasn't a Jew.
>
> Then they came for the trade unionists, but I didn't do anything, because I wasn't a trade unionist.
>
> Then they came for the Catholics, but I didn't do anything, because I wasn't a Catholic.
>
> Finally, they came for me, and there wasn't anyone left to do anything.[1]

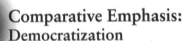

Comparative Emphasis: Democratization

The Federal Republic of Germany was the first country whose leaders consciously tried to create a democracy. In fact, they did so twice following the end of World War II and unification. They succeeded both times.

Historians still debate why democracy gained a permanent foothold so much later in Germany than in the United States, Great Britain, or France. Most of them agree that there was little in German history before 1945 to suggest that it could democratize quickly or easily.

After World War II, however, a combination of international and domestic forces made effective democracy possible. The three occupying countries in the west avoided the mistakes they made after World War I, helping to rebuild rather than cripple their former enemy. More important, many Germans themselves "turned inward" and sought their own path toward avoiding the forces that had led to the creation of the Third Reich.

Just as remarkable was the smooth political integration of the DDR into the Federal Republic after 1990. Despite forty more years of authoritarian rule, it was fairly easy for *ossis* to adapt to most West German values. After all, people in the east had long listened to its radio and watched its television and, of course, also benefited from the remarkable wealth the Federal Republic could offer to ease the transition.

In other words, the German experience is probably not a model that other countries can follow. None of these other countries has either the luxury of extensive outside support or the time to rethink national priorities that so aided Germany from 1949 onward. ∎

[1]There are several versions of this poem, since Niemöller apparently never wrote it down. This one is from the United States Holocaust Memorial Museum (www.ushmm.org/wlc/en/article.php?ModuleId=10007392). All of the versions are identical in tone and meaning.

There is no question that many Germans still held anti-democratic and authoritarian beliefs. Public opinion polls indicated that many people preferred authoritarian governments. New anti-Semitic and militaristic organizations were formed that were the same as the Nazis in everything but name.

The first elections confirmed those fears. Turnout was low, especially among the young *ohne mich*, or "count me out," generation, which wanted nothing to do with politics in any form.

Creative artists explored the German soul, trying to discover how the nation that had produced Beethoven and Hegel had also given rise to Hitler and Goebbels. In his novel *Dog Years*, for instance, Günter Grass gives 1950s German teenagers special eyeglasses that allow them to see what their parents had done during the war, which led many of them to suffer nervous breakdowns or commit suicide.

Even after the Federal Republic began to take hold, skepticism remained. Observers worried that support for the system was contingent on continued economic growth and that hard times could strengthen the antidemocratic movements. As we will see, most notably in the chapter on India, such fears are far from atypical. People rarely decide to endorse democracy as an abstract set of ideals. Rather, they do so because their support for its concrete, successful actions is gradually transformed into support for the system as a whole.

Those concerns were emphasized in the late 1950s when pioneer political scientists Gabriel Almond and Sidney Verba found substantial differences between German and British or American values, which they thought did not augur well for German democracy.[2] Very few Germans took pride in their political institutions. They were less trusting of authority figures and felt less able to influence decision making than their British or American counterparts. In trying to explain why Germans held these views, Almond and Verba pointed to German history and to the continued authoritarian structure of their schools and families.

Their snapshot of German culture may have already been outdated when their book was published in the early 1960s. By the time they gathered a group of scholars to reevaluate their conclusions twenty years later, it definitely was. By then, the Germans had the kind of civic culture they argued democracy needed but that they assumed would long be beyond Germany's grasp.

There are still hints of the "old Germany" that some foreigners find annoying. Germans cannot, for instance, mow their lawn after 8:00 pm or at any time on Sunday in order to avoid disturbing their neighbors. Most stores have to close in the early evening and are not allowed to open on Sundays. There was even a protracted struggle between workers and a major bank during the 1990s on how long workers could take for their *pinkelpause*, or bathroom break. The workers insisted that the legally allowed two minutes and seventeen seconds were not enough. Laws once even prescribed what Germans could include in the outgoing messages on their answering machines.

One should not make too much of such rules, however quaint and irksome they can be for visitors from more informal societies. As far as political values are concerned, Germans have more in common with their counterparts in other industrialized societies than these laws might lead one to believe.

Although it is hard to draw conclusions across national lines on the basis of spotty comparative research, the conclusions about Germany itself are striking (see Table 6.5). Germans are as supportive of democratic practices as citizens anywhere. According to a typical poll conducted in 1977, only 7 percent of the public could imagine voting for a new Nazi party. Well over 90 percent routinely agreed that Germany had to have a democratic government with a multiparty system.

That said, there are some residual concerns about the German political culture. There have also been occasional outbursts of racist, anti-Semitic, and neo-Nazi activity since unification, especially in the east. Thus, in late 2011, law enforcement authorities and the intelligence services sought three right-wing extremists who were accused of killing nine immigrants and a police officer over the

---

[2] Gabriel Almond and Sidney Verba, *The Civic Culture: Political Attitudes and Democracy in Five Countries* (Princeton, NJ: Princeton University Press, 1962) and their edited volume, *The Civic Country Revisited* (Boston: Little, Brown, 1979).

Double Standards

For understandable historical reasons, observers have been reluctant to label Germany or Japan democratic and have been quick to voice concerns about incidents involving the far Right in both countries. Although there are plenty of reasons to worry about such events, we should also be careful not to use a double standard and hold these countries to higher criteria than we apply to others with fewer historical blemishes. All democracies have imperfections—including Germany. But Germany's are no more (or less) worrisome than those we find in the United States or Great Britain, countries that are usually portrayed as paragons of democratic virtue.

TABLE 6.5 Germans and Democracy

	1980 (%)	1983 (%)	1989 (%)
The present national government protects our basic liberties	89.5	81.6	79.0
The political system as a whole is just and fair	87.6	86.8	77.0

Source: Adapted from Dieter Fuchs, "Trends of Political Support in the Federal Republic of Germany," in *Political Culture in Germany*, ed. Dirk Berg-Schlosser and Ralf Rytlewski (London: Macmillan, 1993), 249.

preceding three years and were associated with the then legal, right-wing National Democratic Party. There were rumors that at least some members of the intelligence services had known about the so-called Zwickau group and done little or nothing to stop it.

Obviously, any such behavior is reprehensible, but we should not overstate its importance. When viewed from a comparative perspective, there is far more of this kind of racist and antidemocratic behavior in both France and Great Britain.

In 2010, the intelligence services reported that there were 25,000 right-wing extremists and fewer than 6,000 neo-Nazis. Seventy percent of the people arrested for participation in racist attacks over the last three decades are men with little education who seem angrier about their personal prospects than by their commitment to right-wing extremism.

One human rights group estimates that there had been 180 politically motivated murders committed by right-wing activists and sympathizers in the last twenty years. However, more than that many people are killed *each day* in American cities. Given its racist and violent past, academic and journalistic observers react faster and more critically to any sign of support for the far Right even though people who think and act that way are more marginalized there than in the other major democracies.

If anything, worries about the vestiges of Germany's past have kept most of us from seeing the fact that its people support the new kind of progressive initiatives that are an outgrowth of the postmaterial values discussed in Chapter 2. Polls have consistently shown that fully a third of the electorate could be classified as postmaterialists, which is far more than the European average and three times the figure for Germany in 1970.

Those views are most evident in support for environmental causes, which have had their most significant impact in Germany. Well over 80 percent of all postmaterialists vote for the SPD or the **Greens**, the first party in the world to gain widespread support on the basis of "new politics." Along similar lines, thousands

Comparative Emphasis: Identity

Historically, the region that became Germany faced more identity-related issues than other leading Western European powers. It had to deal with Catholics and Protestants as well as anti-clericalism. Regional loyalties were unusually strong because dozens of principalities and city states survived into the nineteenth century. Last, but by no means least, intense nationalism was one of the main contributors to Hitler's rise to power.

Most of those identity issues have disappeared. If they have any importance at all it is on the margins and no more disruptive than the tendency for regular church attenders in France or Great Britain to vote for the Right.

The politics of identity in the twenty-first century revolves around immigration. Even here, Germany has had fewer protests and violent outbursts aimed at immigrants and long-term residents who are not of German origin than most European countries.

As the discussion of double standards suggests, Germany's track record on this front is not much better or worse than that of other European democracies. The one difference is that criticisms of and protests against diversity draw more attention there. ■

of locally based, issue-oriented groups have sprung up in recent years to oppose the storage of nuclear waste, expand kindergarten space, support recycling programs, improve the conditions of immigrant workers, and more.

There is one final area in which the German political culture has changed. The overwhelming majority of Germans have come to accept their geopolitical status. Most are profoundly antimilitarist and endorse the government's leading role in the European Union, North Atlantic Treaty Organization, and other international organizations. Many scholars are convinced that Germany's new peaceful (if not pacifist) culture is one of the reasons it has not sought to assert its newfound power militarily even though it has participated in peace-keeping and peace-building operations in Kosovo and Afghanistan.

Political scientists have pointed to three broad reasons why the political culture has changed so dramatically in little more than fifty years.

The first and most obvious is that the Federal Republic has worked. As was the case with the Fifth Republic in France, one of the "virtuous circles" in German politics lies in the way the Federal Republic's success has contributed to growing support for it and vice versa.

Second, there has been considerable change in two of the major "agents" of political socialization. Under Allied pressure, the states began teaching civics during the occupation years and have included it in their curricula ever since. The right-wing bias of the prewar teacher corps disappeared. Similarly, the impact of the "authoritarian father" declined. Child-rearing patterns have been liberalized, and, as in all industrialized democracies, the family is less important in most people's lives in general.

Finally, and perhaps most important, we are now three generations removed from the Nazi era. Far fewer than 10 percent of those in the current electorate reached adulthood during either the Weimar or the Nazi periods, and even the current generation of political leaders experienced Nazism and World War II as teenagers if they did at all.

Political Participation

Perhaps the easiest way to see how much Germans have changed is by examining their political participation.

Parties and the Electoral Process

A century ago, Germany was home to the first "mass" parties that had hundreds of thousands of activists, which also formed the nucleus of the partisan militias that had so much to do with the fall of Weimar. Many observers expected that something like those fragmented and polarized parties would reappear in the Federal Republic.

By the mid-1950s, however, Germany had developed what political scientists call a two-and-a-half-party system. Although it might more accurately be called a two-and-three-half-party system today, its basic contours have not changed appreciably in sixty years.

Germany has the most centrist and consensus-driven party system of all the countries covered in *Comparative Politics*. The parties have distinct ideological backgrounds and priorities. However, there has been little of the acrimony that has shaken British or American politics during the last few decades.

The sustained economic growth of the 1950s undermined support for left-wing radicalism, while the very success of the regime did the same for neo-Nazis and

others on the Right. Divisive ideological issues disappeared as voters flocked toward the center. To maintain their share of the vote, first the CDU and then the SPD had to follow suit. Each became a **catch-all party** because they had to water down their ideologies to appeal to the increasingly moderate voters. The number of ideologically motivated activists diminished, forcing the parties to rely more on leaders who were effective campaigners. Because the now vitally important television news stories rarely last more than a couple of minutes, parties had to sacrifice the complexities of a sophisticated belief system for slogans that would fit into sound-bite journalism.

The CDU and SPD have always come in first and second, and one or the other of them has led the government. Between them, they always won in excess of sixty percent of the total vote until the most recent election in 2009 (see Table 6.6).

Since 1961, the winner has always needed a coalition partner to form a parliamentary majority. After the 1965 and 2005 elections, the SPD and CDU governed together as part of a grand coalition.

More often than not, whichever party had come in first turned to the FDP, which has won between 5.1 percent and 12.8 percent of the vote over the years, thus earning the half-party designation. The Greens were the first party to overcome the 5 percent barrier nationwide and win seats in the Bundestag on a consistent basis. The Greens joined the SPD government between 2002 and 2005.

Another organization has recently joined the Greens to make them the second and third "half parties." The **Left Party** was created when the Party of Democratic Socialism (successor to the East German communists) merged with activists who had broken from the SPD.

The Basic Law gives political parties a more prominent legal role than most constitutions. The major parties have a say in the nomination of judges, university professors, television and radio station managers, and directors of firms ranging from the big banks to local public transit authorities. Public funds provide about 30 percent of the $100 million or more each major party spends during a national election campaign. The government also helps

TABLE 6.6 German Elections Since 1983 (percent of votes)

PARTY	1983	1987	1990	1994	1998	2002	2005	2009
CDU/CSU	48.8	44.3	43.8	41.5	35.2	38.5	35.2	33.8
FDP	7.0	9.1	11.0	6.9	6.2	7.4	9.8	14.6
SPD	38.2	37.0	33.5	36.4	40.9	38.5	34.2	23.0
Greens	5.6	8.3	3.9	7.3	6.7	8.6	8.1	10.7
PDS-Left	—	—	4.4	2.4	5.1	4.7	8.7	11.9

This table only includes votes cast in the proportional half of Bundestag elections.

© Cengage Learning 2015

fund the charitable foundations each party runs that provide assistance to the developing world and help find peace initiatives between Israelis and Palestinians.

Article 21 of the Basic Law also established what was then a unique electoral system, but which has since been copied many times (see Chapter 9 on Russia). Its dual system for electing Bundestag members was designed to minimize the number of new and small parties.

Half the seats are elected in 299 single-member districts. Any number of candidates can run, and whoever wins the most votes takes the seat as in the United States or United Kingdom. This makes it easy for the SPD and CDU to convince people that casting a ballot for a new, small, or extremist party amounts to wasting their vote. Indeed, they rarely lose any single-member districts.

Winners of the second half of the seats are determined at a second ballot in which voters choose from lists of candidates who are nominated by the party organizations. Seats are allocated proportionally to all parties that win over five percent of the national vote. The second ballot results are also used to ensure that all parties that cross that threshold get the number of seats that corresponds to its share of the overall votes cast in the proportional ballot. Thus, because the FDP won 14.6 percent of the vote in 2009, it ended up with a total of 93 Bundestag seats even though it did not win a single district. In order to make certain each party gets the proper overall proportion of the seats, the authorities are allowed to add a few seats to the total. In 2009, that meant that 24 additional members of the Bundestag were elected from the second ballot lists. In practice, it makes little or no difference which ballot Bundestag members are elected from.

The Christian Democrats

The CDU has been by far the most powerful party in the Federal Republic (www.cdu.de/en/3440.htm).[3] Officially, the CDU is a partnership between two distinct parties. The CDU runs in every state other than Bavaria, where it cooperates with a local partner, the Christian Social Union (CSU). During the 1970s and early 1980s, the CSU was noticeably more conservative than its larger partner. After the death of its leader, Franz Joseph Strauss, in 1988, however, the ideological differences largely disappeared, and we can easily treat them as a single organization.

After World War II, Adenauer and other surviving Zentrum leaders chose not to re-create a Catholic party whose appeal would be limited to about half of the population. Instead, they decided to form a more broadly based organization that drew on all basic Christian principles and applied them to political life.

The new CDU drew on its Catholic roots in making a clear commitment to social justice. Its 1947 Ahlen Program called for egalitarian social reforms and the nationalization of critical industries. The CDU also promoted the codetermination law in 1951 (see the public policy section), which gave union representatives seats on the boards of directors of large firms.

Soon, however the party's progressive leanings gave way to pressures that pulled it to the Right. Domestically, the party had to appeal to an increasingly conservative electorate to win elections. Then, as Germany came to be the flash point in the cold war, the CDU's support for conservatism at home was easy to reconcile with a pro-American foreign policy.

The CDU slumped for the first time after Adenauer retired. In order to combat the recession and stave off the feared rise of the NPD, the party ended its partnership with the FDP and formed the first grand coalition with the SPD. Then, in 1969, it lost to the Socialists. For much of the next thirteen years, it floundered. It had never developed either a large mass membership or a strong central organization. As a result, state party organizations and their leaders dominated its internal politics. Following the CDU's defeat at the polls in 1972 and 1976, the party's drift was compounded by a deep ideological struggle between its right wing, headed by Strauss, and the moderates, increasingly dominated by the young Helmut Kohl, minister president of the state of Rhineland-Palatinate.

In 1980, the party suffered its third straight defeat with Strauss as its candidate for chancellor. Power inside the party quickly swung back toward Kohl and the moderates.

Kohl did not follow Thatcher and Reagan and lead his party sharply to the Right. He didn't have to. His first decade in office was marked by a dramatic economic upturn that allowed the government to maintain popular support without questioning the social and economic status quo in place since the first grand coalition.

From 1990 on, Kohl's popularity grew even further because of his successful handling of German unification. To the surprise of many, Kohl proved an effective negotiator with both the DDR and the World War II Allies who had to approve any agreement changing the status of either Germany.

By the middle of the 1990s, however, the costs of unification had become clearer and the CDU saw its support drop. It only won in 1994 because the SPD ran a lackluster campaign. Finally, the CDU's and Kohl's string of successes ended in 1998.

---

[3] For the moment, at least, the CDU is the only German party with an English language website. I have not added those for the other parties, because the automatic translation programs on most web browsers are not very good—yet. If you speak German, they are easy enough to find.

PROFILES   Helmut Kohl

Helmut Kohl (1930–) is the longest-serving chancellor in the history of the Federal Republic. He was also the first to have come of age after World War II and the Third Reich. Otherwise, his early career was fairly typical. After graduating from university, he began his political career in his home state, Rhineland-Palatinate. Following the party's loss to the SPD in 1972, Kohl was chosen national party leader. At the time, few expected much of a man known for his pragmatism, especially after the CDU's defeat under his leadership in 1976.

But, as so often happens in politics, events transformed Kohl and his career. The collapse of the SPD-FDP coalition brought him to power in 1982. At the end of the decade, he skillfully guided the Federal Republic through unification and then was a major player in the strengthening of the EU.

Kohl is a remarkably unpretentious man, known to prefer vacationing at home, watching television while wearing his Birkenstocks. He is also an extremely large man who, with his wife, has published a cookbook of traditional (and fatty) German dishes. ■

Kohl did not leave an entirely positive legacy. In 1999, he was implicated in a financial scandal. The CDU had accepted millions of dollars in illegal contributions, and Kohl personally acknowledged taking at least $1 million, though he refused to name the donor. The CDU had to pay over $1 million in fines and forgo at least $20 million in federal campaign funds. To make matters worse, Kohl's designated successor, Wolfgang Schäuble, was forced to resign as party leader when he was also implicated in the scandal.

Angela Merkel then became party leader after she became one of the first CDU leaders to break with Kohl once news about the illegal contributions broke. Initial reaction to her was positive, but serious concerns were soon aired about her lack of experience in economic policy making. And in April 2001, she, too, had to admit involvement in obtaining questionable funds. Therefore, in January 2002, she decided not to try for the nomination to head the ticket that year (unlike Great Britain, the party

leader does not automatically become its candidate for chancellor). Perhaps because the CDU lost yet again, the lack of any serious western or male candidate left the field open for her in 2005.

The election that year led to the second grand coalition. Given the parliamentary arithmetic, Merkel knew she had to form a government with the SPD but was willing to do so only if it parted ways with most of its key leaders. Despite the recession, Merkel did not have much trouble winning in 2009. This time, she had enough support to abandon the SPD and form a government more to her liking.

Since then, she and the CDU have devoted almost all of their attention to finding a solution to the EU-wide economic crisis. Despite their lack of success on that front, Merkel and the CDU seem certain to win reelection in a contest that will take place shortly after this book goes to press.

The Social Democrats

The SPD has come in second in most elections. Although the SPD has controlled the government for two extended periods (1969–82 and 1998–2005), it has only outpolled the CDU twice. The SPD has lagged behind the Christian Democrats in large part because it did not become a catch-all party as quickly.

Its early leaders all survived the Third Reich as prisoners, exiles, or members of the small underground resistance. Most continued to support the prewar party's commitments, including the enactment of legislation that nationalized major industrial firms.

The SPD's string of losses in the 1940s and 1950s touched off a heated internal debate over what it should stand for, much like the one over Clause 4 in Britain's Labour Party. At the 1959 Bad Godesberg conference, moderates finally won and the party dropped all references to Marxism and nationalized industry from its program. At about the same time, a new generation of younger and more pragmatic politicians reached the top of the party hierarchy, the most important of whom was the mayor of West Berlin, Willy Brandt (1913–1992).

The party made significant progress in 1961 and 1965. Its fortunes continued to improve when the CDU brought it into the grand coalition. Socialist ministers performed well, and the party demonstrated its acceptance of capitalism with its ringing endorsement of the 1967 law on balanced growth.

The SPD finally got control of the government when the FDP decided to form a coalition with it rather than the CDU after the 1969 election even though the socialists, again, had come in second. Rather than embarking on a bold program of social reform, Brandt stressed "continuity and renewal." In fact, his greatest accomplishment came not in expanding socialism but in improving relations with the Soviet bloc, for which he won the Nobel Peace Prize in 1971.

Brandt was forced to resign in 1974 after one of his key advisors was exposed as an East German spy. He was succeeded by the even more moderate Helmut Schmidt. Most proposals for social reform ground to a halt as Germany struggled to cope with the turbulent economic conditions after the OPEC oil embargo. Schmidt's moderation earned the respect of leaders around the world but opened deep divisions within his own party. The economic problems and the ideological infighting cost the SPD four percent of the vote in 1980, but it won enough seats to form another government with the FDP. Two years later, the FDP put the Schmidt government out of its misery in a no-confidence vote, the one and only time that has happened in the Federal Republic's history.

The sixteen years spent in opposition were difficult for the SPD. The party was slow to endorse unification, and some of its leading intellectuals actually opposed it until the last moment. The party then contested the 1994 election under the rather lackluster Rudolph Scharping, who became chancellor candidate only after a scandal forced his predecessor to withdraw.

Then, in 1997, **Gerhard Schröder** (1944–) burst onto the political scene. Dubbing himself Germany's Tony Blair or Bill Clinton, he openly wooed the middle class and the business community, which gave him massive media exposure and popular support. That said, his seven years in office did not leave as sweeping an impact as his other "third way" colleagues did on the left elsewhere. Traditional Social Democrats still have a strong influence in the SPD, and the country's social service and social market economic policies are popular and more effective than those in Britain or the United States. Last, but by no means least, whatever Schröder may have wanted, the SPD had to keep the support of its coalition partners, the environmentally oriented Greens, who will be discussed shortly.

What little enthusiasm Schröder engendered disappeared, leading to the 2005 defeat that brought Merkel to power. She made Schröder's departure a requirement for forming the second grand coalition that year, which was the only possible government given the election results. The SPD went into formal opposition after the 2009 election when Merkel was able to form a government with the FDP which had always been their preference.

With the 2013 election looming on the horizon as I write, the SPD is in trouble. Despite the European crisis, Merkel herself remains amazingly popular. During 2012, its own candidate, Peer Steinbrück (1947–), committed gaffe after gaffe prompting one major newspaper to quip that he was running a perfect campaign—for his opponent.

Whatever happens in 2013, the SPD is widely seen as bereft of innovative ideas. It is more favorable to policies that might stimulate economic growth and more hostile to austerity than the CDU. However, polls conducted since the recession began suggest that the public does not have much confidence in the SPD's ability to do a significantly better job in steering the country and the EU through the current crisis.

The Free Democrats

The FDP has always come in a distant third behind the CDU and SPD. Although it normally only wins between five and ten percent of the vote, the FDP has a disproportionate impact because it has been needed to form all but four governments since 1949.

Like the CDU and SPD, the FDP had its predecessors in Weimar, when there were a number of predominantly middle-class, Protestant parties that called themselves liberal. But these parties were marked by an economic more than a political liberalism, which was one of the reasons why they did not stand in the way of Hitler's rise to power.

The postwar FDP has been more consistently liberal on political issues, endorsing personal responsibility, individual freedom, and respect for the rights of others over what it sees as the collectivist tendencies of the SPD and CDU. Mostly, though, the FDP carved a niche for itself as the party its two larger rivals needed to form a government. In that role, the FDP has provided the Federal Republic with a number of important leaders, most notably Hans-Dietrich Genscher (1927–), who was foreign minister from 1974 until 1992.

The FDP struggled after Genscher's retirement. Its vote recovered somewhat after its poorest showings in 1994 and 1998, but mostly because disgruntled CDU supporters chose it as a protest vote, not because they supported the FDP *per se*. In an attempt to make a comeback, the party named Guido Westerwelle (1961–) its leader, making him the first openly gay person to lead a major party in German history. Although the luster has worn off his leadership, there are few signs that any leader could turn the FDP into a viable contender for power. However, with a consistent 8 to 10 percent of the vote, it is also not likely to disappear.

The Greens

In 1983, the Green Party became the first new party to enter the Bundestag. The Greens are Germany's most intriguing and least understood party. At first, many people considered them to be weird and, perhaps, even dangerous. Its first group of deputies insisted on wearing jeans and sporting shaggy beards. At the time, the party's rules called on its elected officials to resign and be replaced by colleagues halfway through their terms so that they could never let power go to their heads.

Their offbeat image, however, misses the most important lesson to be learned about the Greens. The success they have enjoyed in Germany and in several other

European countries is no fluke. No one else on the left has done a better and more consistent job of raising the big issues discussed at the beginning of Chapter 1. Their ideology is based on deep ecology or the belief that all aspects of life, and thus all of our problems, are interconnected. Pollution, militarism, sexism, homophobia, poverty, and the like are part of a single general crisis that can only be addressed through an equally general and radical shift to a worldview that puts the good of the planet and humanity first, points we will return to in Chapter 16.

The Greens scored major breakthroughs in the 1983 and 1987 elections, but the party was already split, with the more radical *fundis* gaining influence at the expense of the more pragmatic *realos*. It then slipped below the 5 percent barrier in 1990 in large part because of both factions' qualms about unification.

By 1994, the pragmatists had gained the upper hand. Ever since their surprising success in 1983, realo leaders, such as Joska Fischer (1947–), had grown frustrated by what felt to them like a permanent and uncomfortable position on the political fringes and had begun to question their own (and the party's) more radical past. Therefore, the Greens reached an agreement that year with the SPD to form a "Red-Green" coalition, which was already in place in several state governments. It lasted for the life of the Schröder government, in which Fischer served as foreign minister.

If anything, the Greens have continued to moderate. In particular, like many individuals and organizations with roots in the new Left of the 1960s, they reluctantly abandoned their pacifism and supported Allied intervention in the former Yugoslavia following ethnic cleansing in Kosovo in 1999 and in Afghanistan following the attack on the World Trade Center and the Pentagon two years later.

The Party of Democratic Socialism/Left Party

The Greens are no longer the only new party to have made it into the Bundestag. The **Party of Democratic Socialism (PDS)** was created out of the ashes of the East German Socialist Unity Party (SED). From 1949 until 1989, it controlled everything in the DDR (see Chapter 8). After the DDR collapsed, the SED tried to reform itself, among other things changing its name to the PDS. It also chose a new leader, Gregor Gysi, who was well known for defending dissidents under communist rule and is now a Bundestag member. He is also the most prominent German politician of Jewish origin.

In 1990, the PDS benefited from a one-time modification of the electoral law that allocated proportional representation seats separately in the east and west. Germany returned to its normal system in 1994, and the PDS survived only because it won a handful of single-member seats. Most observers doubted the PDS could win seats again, but it confounded the pundits by getting nearly 20 percent of the vote in the old DDR, thus topping 6 percent nationwide in 1998. It fell short of the 5 percent barrier in 2002 and only won two single-member seats.

Before the 2005 election, the PDS merged with a breakaway faction of the SPD, led by its former leader, Oskar Lafontaine, to form the Left Party. That gave it new support in the west and led to an almost 9 percent share of the vote that year. It did a bit better in 2009, winning almost 12 percent of the vote. It is hard to tell how much influence the Left can have because there is little or no chance that the SPD will form a coalition with its erstwhile colleagues and Communist rivals.

The Far Right

Throughout its history, the Federal Republic has had to deal with right-wing parties that drew on some of the same traditions as the Nazis. As we saw earlier in this chapter, the NPD came close to breaking the 5 percent barrier in 1966.

Since unification, there has been another flurry of support for far Right parties, given the pressures of integrating the former DDR and immigration. A number of them have done reasonably well in state and local elections. However, the far Right has never come close to the 5 percent barrier in national elections, reinforcing the belief that it is not going to be a serious force in German politics. Or, put in comparative terms, even combined into a single organization, the far Right normally only wins about one-sixth to one-fifth of the National Front's share of the vote in France.

The most prominent of them, the NPD, did have seats in two state legislatures in 2012. However, given its alleged

Comparative Emphasis: Conflict

Given Germany's history, readers are often surprised to learn that Germany has less overt and violent conflict than any of the other industrialized democracies included in this book. That is true in almost all areas, but it is especially true of identity-based conflict. As noted in the text, the few incidents that do occur draw plenty of press attention, largely because of that history. In all likelihood, Germany is relatively peaceful because of the support the success of its state has engendered over the last sixty years. ■

role in the hate crimes discussed earlier, the governors of all sixteen states launched an attempt to have the party declared illegal just before this book went to press.

The Stakes of 2013

As I write just before the 2013 election, Chancellor Merkel remains remarkably popular given the severity of the sovereign debt crisis and the uncertainty about her government's response to it among right-of-center German voters. Polls suggested that the CDU would do significantly better than it did four years earlier, with the Left and the FDP as the biggest losers. Moreover, Merkel herself was preferred by almost two to one over any of the other candidates for chancellor. There is more uncertainty about the parties that would be in the coalition government after the election. There is little doubt that it will be led by the CDU, but just about as many voters favor a grand coalition with the SPD as a continuation of the one with the FDP.

Interest Groups

As we will see in the discussion of corporatism, German interest groups have a more important impact on policy making than similar organizations do in Britain and the United States.

Unlike France, Germany has a large and unified labor movement. About two-thirds of industrial workers and 40 percent of the total workforce are unionized. As in most countries, the number of unionized workers has been shrinking for some time as employment moves out of manufacturing.

The overwhelming majority of workers belong to the **Federation of German Labor (DGB)**. The DGB is an umbrella association representing seventeen unions, each of which organizes a single industrial sector. Its two largest groups (IG Metall and Ver.di) have over two million members each, in the manufacturing and service sectors, respectively.

The business side is more complicated. The Federal Association of German Employers (BDA) and the Federation of German Industry (BDI) represent associations of business groups organized on geographical and industrial lines. Although it is harder to determine membership rates for business associations than for trade unions, most businesses belong to one or the other of them. In addition to the BDA and BDI, quasi-official chambers of commerce and industry (DIHT) promote business and provide job training and certification services for the government.

However, these organizations are not the routes through which German businesses have exerted their influence the most often or the most effectively. Traditionally, the economy has not been dominated by large, impersonal companies that dominate these associations but by the middle-sized *Mittelstand*, many of which are family owned and have been in business for at least a century. Despite the global reach of companies like Volkswagen or Siemens, these middle-sized companies have been at the heart of postwar German economic success.

Furthermore, German companies have not traditionally raised capital through the stock market but from banks with which they have long-standing privileged relationships. In fact, at the height of the corporatist period thirty or forty years ago, three massive banks controlled the shares of most major Germany corporations.

Both business and labor have close connections with the political parties. Union officials hold important positions in the SPD. Agricultural and business interests have a similar relationship with the CDU. Church groups also have a significant impact on the CDU and some parts of the SPD, helping to explain why Germany has one of the most restrictive abortion laws in Europe.

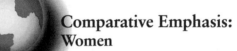

Comparative Emphasis: Women

Despite Merkel's prominence, women in Germany have less of an impact both on who serves in governments and the policies they puruse than in any of the countries discussed in Part 2.

In early 2013, almost a third of the Bundestag members were women, as were six of the fifteen cabinet ministers. Despite those numbers, little has been done to raise women's issues, per se, as, for example, Hillary Clinton did in her years as Secretary of State.

The problem is even more pronounced in corporate governance. In 2011, there were only four women among the 180 board members of the largest corporations. In the United States the number is more like 15 percent of the total. Merkel and her minister for Labor and Social Affairs (also a woman) argued that things do have to change in corporate boardrooms. However, Merkel has rejected a proposal from the relevant cabinet ministers that would require 30 percent of corporate board members to be women.

That said, Germany does have an active feminist movement. Most recently, Alice Schwarzer and others have helped create a movement that is autonomous or independent of other political parties and interest groups. ■

As we will see repeatedly throughout the rest of this chapter, organized labor and business have both been known for their restraint and willingness to work with each other since long before the Law on Balanced Growth was enacted. Unions, for instance, have been willing to forego demands for large wage increases in exchange for assurances of job security.

Interest groups in other areas are nowhere near as strong or as well connected politically. One exception to that rule is locally based citizens' initiatives were important building blocks for the early Greens. Among the most interesting today are locally owned and managed cooperatives that generate electricity but do not try to have much of a political impact at the national level.

The German State: A Smoothly Functioning Democracy

In some social sciences (but not political science), there is growing interest in consensus policy making. Those of us who work in that field do not always agree on what the term means. However, most of my colleagues in dispute resolution agree with this basic description of what happens in a consensus process:

> **The parties reached a meeting of the minds sufficient to make a decision and carry it out. No one who could block or obstruct the decision or its implementation will exercise that power. Everyone needed to support the decision and put it into effect will do so (www. policyconsensus.org/tools/practicalguide/docs/ PracGuideAbbreviated.pdf).**

Most policy making in Germany falls short of fully meeting those criteria. However, of all the countries included in Part 2, the German state comes closest.

The architects of the Federal Republic designed the new republic with the goal of minimizing the likelihood that the country would return to authoritarian rule. Nonetheless, their efforts had the unintended byproduct of creating institutions and informal policy-making procedures that include more incentives for elite cooperation than can be found in the other industrialized democracies covered in Part 2. Before moving on, it is important to stress a point that will become clearer at the end of this section. Germans are not able to routinely enact public policy cooperatively primarily as a result of what the constitution calls for but through procedures that rarely have found their way into the statute book.

Chancellor Democracy

We start with the core institutions of a parliamentary system that have little or nothing to do with cooperative decision making, most notably the chancellor. As in other parliamentary systems, the chancellor started out literally as the "prime" minister, the first among what were supposed to be equally powerful members of the cabinet. During the twentieth century, however, the powers of prime ministers everywhere grew to such an extent that all notions of their being first among equals disappeared (www.bundesregierung.de/Webs/Breg/EN/Federal-Government/federal-government.html).

Weimar had many flaws. Among the most damaging of them was the overlap between the powers of the chancellor and the president. Therefore, the drafters of the Basic Law decided to clarify their responsibilities from the beginning. They believed that having a dual executive was a good idea as long as the largely ceremonial functions of a head of state (president) and the actual control of the government (chancellor) are in separate hands. Therefore, as in most parliamentary systems, the president has little influence on day-to-day politics, while almost all real power is given to the chancellor and the rest of the government.

As in all parliamentary systems, executive and legislative power is fused. The chancellor and most members of the cabinet also sit in the Bundestag and remain in office as long as they have the confidence of the parliamentary majority or their four-year term ends. Because of the powerful link between cabinet responsibility and party discipline, German chancellors have been able to see most of their policy proposals enacted without major modifications imposed by the Bundestag (but see the section on the Bundesrat).

The German chancellor is more influential than most prime ministers. Article 65, for example, states that the chancellor is responsible for determining the government's "course of action," resolving differences within the cabinet, and proposing virtually all major legislation.

Another innovation in the Basic Law is its provision for a constructive vote of no confidence. The opposition can throw a chancellor out *only* if it simultaneously agrees on someone to take his or her place. As a result, the chancellor is far less vulnerable than prime ministers in most parliamentary systems. In fact, one of the reasons most of the Greens who opposed German involvement in the war on terrorism did not vote no confidence in Schröder's government in November 2001 was that there was no viable alternative majority that could have been stitched together from the sitting Bundestag members.

The chancellor has a staff of over five hundred advisors. A team that large gives the chancellor the opportunity to coordinate the entire executive. Indeed, each Monday, the chancellor's chief of staff (who holds cabinet rank) meets with the top civil servants in every department to do just that.

With only fifteen members, German governments are more streamlined than most. Most departments only have the minister and one other political appointee. In all, only about 8 percent of all Bundestag members (as opposed to 17 percent in Britain's House of Commons) serve in the government, thereby giving the chancellor considerably more flexibility in choosing a leadership team.

Cabinet ministers tend to serve unusually long terms in a single department and can thus develop more expertise than their British or French counterparts. Erhard, for instance, was economics minister from 1949 until he became chancellor in 1963. Similarly, Genscher was foreign minister for nearly twenty years.

The cabinet plays a slightly different role as well. Much of the administrative work done by cabinet ministers in

The old Reichstag building in Berlin, which became the new Bundestag building when the German capital was moved there from Bonn in 1999. The new illuminated dome, designed by a British architect, is a sign of how much more "European" Germany has become.

PROFILES Angela Merkel

Angela Merkel could not have dreamed of becoming the first woman chancellor of the Federal Republic during the first thirty-five years of her life, because she was born and raised in East Germany. As the daughter of a pastor and a practicing Christian herself, she had no chance of rising to the top in an officially atheist country. Her father got along well with the SED, but a political career was closed off to his daughter. Merkel received a doctorate in physics in 1978 and served as a research scientist for the next decade—it may well be the case that her distance from the SED made it impossible for her to obtain a professorship.

In 1989, she joined the movement that toppled the communist regime the following year by which time she had joined the short-lived eastern branch of the CDU. Merkel was elected to the Bundestag in 2000. Chancellor Kohl named her Minister of the Environment and Nuclear Safety four years later, making her the youngest member of the government at the time. The next year, she outmaneuvered more experienced CDU politicians and became the party's chancellor candidate. She became chancellor following the 2005 election and has held that post ever since. ■

France or Britain is the responsibility either of the states or of independent agencies. Cabinet ministers are thus free to spend most of their time crafting rather than implementing public policy.

The chancellor, however, is not as powerful as the French president. The chancellor cannot, for instance, go to the public with a referendum, and the emergency powers available to the government are harder to invoke. There is no German equivalent of the domain of regulation that allows the French government to rule by decree in many policy areas.

The chancellor's power is also less personalized. As in Britain, there is little room for an outsider to make it to the top on the basis of his or her personal popularity. Despite Merkel's meteoric rise after unification, chancellor candidates normally progress through their party's ranks, much like British prime ministers. Negotiation and coalition-building skills are often key to climbing up the parliamentary ladder.

The Bundestag

Like most lower houses in parliamentary systems, the Bundestag has to pass all legislation and has sole responsibility for holding the prime minister accountable (www.bundestag.de/htdocs_e/parliament/index.html). As is also the case in most countries, real power lies elsewhere. Because the chancellor is responsible to the Bundestag, he or she can expect the majority to hold on any crucial vote, thereby all but eliminating the actual impact any member can have on any major business that comes before the chamber.

The Bundestag is not powerless, however. Although the comparative evidence is sketchy, the Bundestag is a bit more powerful than the lower houses in Britain or France. For one thing, the Bundestag plays a pivotal role in determining who becomes chancellor when an election does not yield an obvious choice.

That was the case in 1972. Paradoxically, the Brandt government did not think it had enough popular support to pursue its reform agenda. At the same time, polls showed the coalition's support would increase substantially if he called a snap election. The Basic Law, however, only allows the chancellor to dissolve the Bundestag if he or she loses its confidence and no alternative majority exists to replace it. Brandt engineered that outcome by retaining the support of almost every SPD and FDP deputy, but having seventeen of the eighteen cabinet members abstain, leaving the government one vote shy of a majority.

It could also prove to be the case after the 2013 election if the FDP does not get at least the 5 percent of the vote it needs to win seats. If that happens, the CDU will almost certainly not be able to form a majority on its own. It could then try to form a third grand coalition with the SPD, or the socialists could try to assemble a majority with the Greens.

Bundestag committees have a bigger impact on legislation than those in either the British House of Commons or the French National Assembly. Each of the twenty-one standing committees has several specialized subcommittees that consider the details of pending legislation. A surprising number of committee amendments to government bills are accepted. Because the votes cast by individual committee members are not made public, party discipline is not as strict in the committees as it is on the floor. That said, they are considerably less powerful than American committees, because it is virtually impossible for them to kill a piece of legislation.

In addition, the way the Bundestag is organized gives it a bit more leverage than other national legislatures. As in France and Britain, the Bundestag elects a speaker (president) and a broader leadership group, the Council of Elders, which is responsible for organizing its schedule. In the Bundestag, the party groups (*fraktionen*) also have some

autonomy. Individual members have larger staffs, which allows them to develop something like the experience and expertise of many American senators and representatives.

The Bundesrat

The **Bundesrat** has little in common with any other upper national legislature (www.bundesrat.de/EN). Most countries' upper houses have lost any real power to affect the content of legislation. The Bundesrat has not, because it was created to give the now sixteen states a say on the passage of laws that would directly affect them. The authors of the Basic Law had an even more important goal in mind. They wanted it to be one of the new institutions that could reduce the possibility of any future Nazi-like regime emerging by limiting the independent power any national government could wield.

The Bundesrat has sixty-nine members, who are chosen by their respective state governments. Officially, they are chosen from its cabinet members. In practice, the demands of running a state are so time consuming that they normally send senior civil servants instead. States cast their votes as a bloc. If a state government represents a coalition other than the national government or opposition, it normally abstains in votes on pending legislation (see Table 6.7).

The Bundesrat does not have a role in cabinet formation. Similarly, it can only delay enactment of laws that do not have a direct impact on the states. However, the Bundesrat must approve all "consent" bills that affect the länder, which accounts for more than half of legislation. When the two houses disagree, the Bundesrat convenes a Mediation Committee composed of members of both houses, which tries to iron out the differences.

The Bundesrat has vigorously defended state interests without being an exceptionally partisan or disruptive force. For most of the Federal Republic's history, the two houses have been dominated by the same coalition of parties, so there have been few ideological disputes.

Even when the Bundestag and Bundesrat majorities have been at odds, it has not been a disruptive force on major legislation. Instead, the federal government has sought to reach agreements with individual states that allow bills to pass, thus creating another institution that

TABLE 6.7 Bundesrat Delegations: February 2013

PARTY/COALITION	STATES CONTROLLED	BUNDESRAT SEATS
CDU/FDP	4	21
CDU/SPD	5	18
SPD	1	3
SPD/Left	1	4
SPD/Green	5	23

leads politicians to seek compromise. This informal role has led some observers to think that the Bundesrat has enough clout to give Germany what amounts to a permanent grand coalition government.

Federalism

Most other parliamentary systems, including Britain and France, are unitary states in which virtually all power is legally lodged in the central government. The Basic Law, by contrast, divides responsibility between the national and state governments.

The national government has sole responsibility for matters that transcend state boundaries, including foreign policy, defense, citizenship, the economy, transportation, communication, and property rights. Everything else is left to the states, including civil and criminal law, the organization of associations, broadcasting, welfare, mining, industry, banking, labor, education, highways, and health. The states also have considerable leeway in determining how to administer most federal law.

But, as in other federal systems, the balance of power has long been tilting toward the national government. Most of the important policy issues, including those we will focus on in the next section, are predominantly federal in nature. And even for many of those that are not, the federal government has imposed more uniform rules and procedures on the states than is the case in the United States.

Over the years, the most important role of state politics has been as a source of national-level leaders. Kohl, Strauss, Brandt, Schröder, and Merkel all rose to prominence at the state level first. That is quite different from the situation in France or Britain, where leaders spend almost their entire political careers in Paris and London. The state governments are also important because they provide opportunities to try out different types of coalitions that would not be possible at the federal level at the current time, but could prove to be so in the future.

The Civil Service

Like MPs in all industrialized democracies, most Bundestag members are ill equipped to deal with the technical issues facing most governments today. As a result, bureaucrats are playing an increasingly influential role in policy making, as well as implementation.

High-ranking civil servants have long been an important force in German politics, although they have not always been a constructive one. At the beginning of the Second Reich, only the chancellor was a political official. The other cabinet members were civil servants. Under Weimar, the bureaucracy was still extremely conservative; many were active Nazis.

De-Nazifying and democratizing the bureaucracy was one of the Allies' highest priorities after the war. About 53,000 civil servants lost their jobs. The purges, however, came to an end once the British, French, and American authorities realized they needed a strong administrative service if the new republic they were creating was to get off the ground and Germany was to become an effective Western ally in the cold war. In the end, there was surprisingly little change in the civil service, with one important exception. The Federal Republic's bureaucracy is decentralized, with only about 10 percent of the top civil servants, or Beamten, working directly for it.

Federal bureaucrats do relatively little administrative work, most of which is handled at the state level. Instead, federal civil servants spend most of their time drafting legislation and regulations for their partisan bosses.

Most civil servants accept their political role far more readily than do their British or American counterparts. Many, in fact, are open party members or sympathizers. Some move on to political careers.

Civil servants may not be politically neutral. However, they have largely been spared ideological interference other than on two occasions. In the aftermath of student protests and terrorist attacks in the late 1960s and early 1970s, the SPD government severely restricted the hiring of alleged radicals, especially as teachers and social workers. After unification, many communist officials were purged in the east, most notably in the education and foreign ministries.

The Federal Constitutional Court

Before 1945, judges were civil servants. Like their nonjudicial colleagues, most of them were conservatives who at least sympathized with the Third Reich. In yet another attempt to minimize the possibility of a Nazi revival, American advisers insisted on introducing a revamped judiciary that would be more politically neutral but that could also buttress the new democracy.

The **Federal Constitutional Court** (FCC) has more sweeping authority than similar courts in any democracy other than the United States (www.bundesverfassungsgericht.de/en/index.html). Its two chambers, or "senates," each have eight judges who serve nonrenewable twelve-year terms. Half are chosen by the Bundestag and half by the Bundesrat. In each house, a two-thirds vote is required, which means that any judge has to be acceptable to members of both major parties.

The court has wide-ranging powers. It can hear cases involving the constitutionality of state and federal law. Through the process of abstract review, an issue can go directly from the parliament to the court without any prior legal action. The court has had a hand in almost all important policy areas involving all aspects of the Basic Law.

Over the years, it has ruled that:

- The Communist Party and the neo-Nazi Reichs Party were illegal under the provisions of the Basic Law concerning political parties.

- The Adenauer government could not establish a second, nationally directed television network because the Basic Law gives states responsibility for the media.

- The treaty with the DDR that opened relations with the Soviet bloc was constitutional.

- The codetermination law that gives workers nearly half the seats on the boards of directors of large firms was legal.

- The first elections in the newly unified Germany could be conducted with separate allocation of seats in the west and east.

- A woman's right to have an abortion could be strictly limited.

- The federal government had to ensure more equitable revenue sharing with state governments.

- German troops could legally be deployed in Afghanistan.

- The government could fund the European Central Bank's bailout of other EU economies.

Corporatism

The most unusual feature of the German state is informal and therefore hard to describe. **Corporatism** is not mentioned in the Basic Law and only rarely appears in legislation. Nonetheless, it has been an important part of economic policy making in Germany in ways that roughly parallel the role of the iron triangle in France.

Corporatism is one of the most controversial concepts in modern political science. Its origins lie in nineteenth-century Catholic thought. Later, fascists throughout Europe used it to describe the sham legislatures they created that supposedly represented major interests or "corporations." In other words, when scholars first began using corporatism to describe close relationships between the state and interest groups, their very choice of words underscored their deep doubts about it.

Corporatist negotiations take place behind closed doors. Neither political parties nor backbenchers have much of a role in them. Rather, cabinet members and high-level civil servants help interest groups reach agreements, which are then accepted by all of the participants.

Germany has used corporatist procedures more than any of the other countries covered in Part 2. That said, they only came "on the books" when the SPD was first in office and helped orchestrate Concerted Action meetings involving business, government, and labor together between 1966 and 1977. They were introduced by the first grand coalition as part of its efforts to end West Germany's first recession. Over the next three years, the groups met annually to hammer out agreements on wage and price increases, broad macroeconomic and social policy issues, and the landmark 1967 law on balanced growth. Once the CDU went into opposition and the post-OPEC economic slump hit, the discussions became more acrimonious and less productive and were discontinued in 1977.

Since then, corporatist decision making has continued in a more informal—but no less important—way. For example, the Economics Ministry sees itself as the *Anwalt*, or attorney-spokesman, for industry. Most ministries' planning staffs cooperate with business and labor in trying to determine what their goals could and should be for the next five years or more.

Those informal arrangements have been an integral part of the common ground business and labor have found on basic economic priorities. Here, labor has been the key. The unions initially shared the SPD's commitment to socialism. However, as the economic miracle unfolded, they too, made their peace with capitalism and began concentrating on reforms that would give their members a larger share of the expanding economy. For the last half century, German unions have usually been willing to sacrifice short-term wage gains for job security and long-term corporate growth. Similarly, wage increases have usually been limited to the inflation rate plus a suppplement that reflects overall growth in workplace efficiency. The annual national wage and price agreement reached by big business, the DGB, and the government now only covers about half of the work force. Nonetheless, they still go a long way toward keeping everything from worker demands to the overall inflation rate in check.

One union official summed these arrangements up this way more than twenty years ago. His words still ring true today:

> It is true that relations have become a little more conflictual nowadays, owing to lower growth and higher unemployment. But basically, we still believe that it is by cooperating with management, rather than fighting it, that we stand the best chance of securing better pay and working conditions—and the results prove it. What is more, as we see it, our obligation is not just to our own members or to other workers but to German society as a whole, where we must play an active role in

upholding democracy and the rule of law. We're part of the establishment and proud of it. We're certainly not revolutionaries; we do not want to overthrow capitalism but to reform it from inside, in a more "social" direction, within the social market economy.[4]

At least as important today is Germany's unique system of **codetermination**, which gives unions half of the seats on the boards of directors of all companies with more than two thousand employees. All firms have work councils that bring employees and management together to discuss job-related issues. The workers' representatives are not quite as powerful as those named by the ownership, because the law reserves one of the union seats for someone representing management employees and automatically gives the chair of the board to stockholders.

Until its most important functions were taken over by the European Central Bank in 1998, the **Bundesbank** was Germany's most powerful economic institution. The bank has always been officially nonpartisan. However, it worked closely with the cabinet for the fifty years following its formation in 1948. In particular, it single-mindedly sought to use interest rates and other financial levers to keep inflation down and thereby help the country avoid one of the main problems that led to the collapse of the Weimar Republic. As we will see in the chapter on the European Union, the new European Central Bank was patterned on the Bundesbank and plays a similar—and not always popular—role for the EU as a whole. The two banks have their main offices within a few blocks of each other in Frankfurt-am-Main.

The final piece of the informal corporatist system is the interwoven ownership of German banks and nonfinancial firms. Until the shakeup of the global financial system in the years before the current crisis, three private banks—Deutsche, Dresdner, and Commerz—owned about 10 percent of all the stock in Germany's biggest firms. In addition, most individual depositors give one of them proxies for their shares, leaving the banks with *de facto* control of almost all major enterprises. Thus, a relatively small number of bank officials could work with a similarly small number of colleagues in the public sector to coordinate much of economic policy. The banks are no longer as powerful; in fact, Commerz bought Dresdner in 2009. Nonetheless, many firms in the mittelstand are still largely family owned, and it is common for a single shareholder to own at least 20 percent of the shares in publicly owned companies.

---

[4] Cited in John Ardagh, *Germany and the Germans: After Unification* (New York: Penguin Books, 1991), 125.

When all is said and done, corporatism is a mixed blessing. Corporatist systems underrepresent labor. Compared with what we saw in France or Britain, labor has fared rather well in Germany. Even so, it has only approached being an equal partner with business during the first few years the SPD was in power in the early 1970s.

Labor is not the only group to get short shrift. The consensus and the neo-corporatist arrangements are used almost exclusively for economic policy making. Groups concerned with issues such as women's rights, immigrant workers, and the growing elderly population have far less access to top decision makers.

Corporatism also poses problems for any of the versions of democratic theory outlined in Chapter 2. Much of policy making takes place behind closed doors and involves bureaucrats, not the elected officials over whom the voting public has some degree of control. That does not mean that Germany and other relatively corporatized countries are not democratic given the way most political scientists define the term. However, the realities of corporatism reveal one of the most important trade-offs in German politics today. There is little question that these cooperative arrangements have helped Germany become one of the world's leading economic and political powers, which we will see in more detail in the rest of the chapter. Yet that success has come at the cost of widespread popular participation in the setting of economic priorities.

Public Policy: *Modell Deutschland*

The most important theme underlying this chapter can be found in the statement that begins it. The Federal Republic has succeeded in large part because it has rarely tried to do anything rash or dramatic. Instead, its leaders have preferred to take incremental steps that were anchored in a broad national consensus whenever possible. We can see this by turning to three policy areas. The first two reflect the success the regime has enjoyed since the late 1940s. The last one focuses on today's European crisis, which will also be featured in the next chapter.

The Social Market Economy

Germany has not always been one of the world's richest countries. In 1951, GNP per capita stood at five hundred dollars or about a fourth of what it was in the United States. By the end of the 1980s, it had drawn even with the United States on most major economic indicators. Only Japan's economy grew at a faster pace over the last sixty years.

Stable Growth

As was the case with the Gaullists in France, the state is not solely responsible for this remarkable track record. Germany's recovery got a needed boost from the Marshall Plan and the influx of fourteen million refugees from the east who helped keep labor costs down.

Still, we cannot ignore the important role the state played first in Germany's turnaround and later in its remarkable prosperity. Since the 1950s, the government has followed remarkably consistent and successful economic policies, which were formalized in the 1967 law that committed the government to maintaining stable prices, full employment, adequate growth, and a positive balance of trade. SPD and CDU governments have largely agreed that Germany needed a strong private sector in order to sustain that growth. But they also agreed that it needed to maintain and, when possible, even expand its already extensive welfare state.

Of those many goals, two have figured most prominently in the nearly half-century-old consensus.

First, given the Weimar Republic's sorry history, all parties and interest groups have made keeping the inflation rate as low as possible their top economic priority. Governments on the left and right alike have been unwilling to run large budget deficits, endorse wage increases, or pursue other policies that might imperil postwar Germany's long-standing price stability.

Second, they all have been committed to expanding German companies' market share at home and, especially, abroad. They have done so even when it came at the cost of their short-term profit margins. German firms are also known for their quality workmanship, which, in turn, grows out of the loyalty of workers who enjoy stable, if not lifelong, employment.

By the time Kohl took office, those patterns were already in place. Unlike other leaders at the time, his government's policies were characterized more by continuity than change as it tried to recover from years of sluggish and intermittent growth. Rather than embarking on a radical Thatcheresque economic restructuring, Kohl advocated minor reductions in government spending in order to make more funds available for private investment which had had so much to do with creating the economic miracle in the first place.

Kohl's strategy seemed to work. By 1986 the budget deficit had been cut by two-thirds and inflation had been all but eliminated. Industrial production increased by an average of 15 percent per year. As we will see in the next section, unification sent the economy into an extended tailspin. Even then, economic policy making was characterized by remarkable continuity.

As one would expect, Schröder's Red-Green government tilted the policy balance somewhat to the left, but only somewhat. In fact, it even cut unemployment benefits, made it slightly easier for firms to fire long-standing employees, and reduced some social service programs. To compensate, the few people who lost their jobs were placed in government-funded part-time positions which ended up saving as many as 200,000 jobs that might have been lost if the SPD had moved dramatically leftward.

Had the Left stayed in power after 2005, it is doubtful that its policies would have been dramatically different given the depth of the German commitment to economic stability. Merkel has had to deal with two overlapping crises that have not shaken Germany's commitment to stability and consensus, including adopting austerity budgets in order to weather the domestic and European economic crises. Domestically, the CDU-FDP government shied away from either major stimulus or budget cutting policies followed by the Obama and Cameron governments, respectively, which helped it weather the crisis more easily than any other major democracy.

Economic Success

That Germany has done well is best seen in the standard of living its citizens enjoy. The average industrial worker makes about fifty dollars per hour in wages and nearly as much again in fringe benefits and social services. Most workers also earn the equivalent of another month's wages in annual Christmas bonuses. Until France passed its thirty-five-hour work week, the Germans worked the shortest hours and enjoyed the most vacation time (forty-two working days a year) in Europe. Most Germans are able to afford large cars, which they drive as fast as they want on the country's superhighways that for all intents and purposes do not have any speed limits.

Germany has the most rapid and consistent growth rate in Europe. Its unemployment and inflation rates remain consistently low. Earlier concerns that past success left German firms too rigid and reluctant to innovate have largely gone by the wayside because dozens of existing companies have proved their agility in adapting to global markets, and a new wave of startups have found profitable niches in everything from industrial production to software development.

The success of *Modell Deutschland* is by no means assured. Again, as we will see near the end of this section, much depends on the future of the euro.

Unification

Unlike most public policy issues covered in *Comparative Politics*, unification in Germany can largely be discussed in the past tense. Although unification occurred unexpectedly and caused profound changes the likes of which postwar Germany had not seen before and has not seen since, the merger of the two countries reflects the importance of cautious and consensual steps throughout the history of the Federal Republic.

For forty years, leading politicians in the west (but not in the DDR) called for unification, but no one realistically expected it to happen until the remarkable events of 1989 unfolded. As we will see in more detail in Chapter 8, reform movements swept through Poland and Hungary that spring, culminating in the Hungarian decision to dismantle the iron curtain along its border with Austria. An average of five thousand East German "vacationers" headed west each day—permanently. The DDR closed its border with Hungary, but East Germans who wanted to found other ways out.

In September, the focus shifted to Germany itself. Weekly rallies in the East German city of Leipzig gradually raised the ante from reform to regime change. Soviet President Mikhail Gorbachev attended the DDR's fortieth anniversary the next month. While he was in Germany, it became increasingly clear that the East German regime was in deep trouble because of its resistance to the pressure to change that was coming from Moscow as well as its own citizens.

Shortly after Gorbachev returned home, the Communist Party's elite forced the aging and intransigent Erich Honecker to resign and replaced him with the younger, but still hardline, Egon Krenz. His leadership team was unable to stop either the protests or the flood of DDR citizens fleeing to the west. On November 9, he gave up. All travel restrictions were lifted. That evening, people began tearing down the Berlin Wall. Krenz resigned, and his successor, Hans Modrow, began planning free elections for the spring. The Federal Republic's parties moved into the east, and their candidates dominated the campaign.

Kohl, who had said little publicly until then, apparently first raised the possibility of rapid unification in a telephone call to Krenz two days after the wall came down. From then on, Kohl did everything in his power to incorporate the DDR into the Federal Republic as five new states under Article 2 of the Basic Law rather than through Article 146, which would have required adopting a new constitution. He also proposed that the all-but-worthless East German marks be exchanged for deutsche marks on a one-for-one basis. Finally, he insisted that newly united Germany remain in NATO and the European Community (EC), as today's EU was then known.

During the next few months, Kohl and the Western Allies overcame staunch Soviet opposition to his preconditions for unification. In March 1990, Kohl's supporters won an overwhelming victory in the east's one and only free election, which served to speed up negotiations with the west. With the strong encouragement from the George H. W. Bush administration, the Soviet government agreed to join "four plus two" talks between the four former occupying powers and the two Germanys.

They decided to merge on July 1. In September, the Soviets agreed to German membership in NATO after the German government formally accepted the boundaries drawn after World War II and committed itself to spending

AP Photo/Finck

Crowds scaling the Berlin Wall following the DDR announcement that it would no longer restrict travel to the west.

$8 billion to repatriate the 340,000 Soviet troops stationed in East Germany, build needed housing units, and retrain them for civilian jobs. On October 4, the two Germanys were united.

It is important to underscore one critical point here. West Germany was not the major force behind unification. The major steps that made it possible were taken elsewhere. However, to the degree that Federal Republic leaders did make a difference, they took bold steps only after building a consensus that included most major social and political groups.

Unification itself posed new challenges that could not be met using the incremental policy making that German governments had relied on since the 1960s. Almost everything in the east was substandard—workforce training; environmental conditions; the highway, rail, and telecommunications infrastructure; factory equipment; and housing. Only 7 percent of DDR households had a telephone, and there were only a few hundred lines that could handle international calls, even ones to the Federal Republic. Per capita income in the east was a quarter of that in the west. Economists estimated that it would take up to $100 billion to modernize the rail system alone and determined that no more than 20 percent of eastern enterprises could survive in a competitive economy.

In response, the Federal Republic decided to go through the transition as quickly as possible, even if doing so would lead to hardships in the short run. A new agency, the *Treuhandanstalt*—or **Treuhand** for short—was created to manage the privatization of East German firms. Until they could be sold, the state-owned industries were subjected to the same market forces operating in the west, which meant that workers could be laid off and the firms could go bankrupt. Once privatization was completed, the Treuhand was disbanded.

At first, the results were painful indeed. A year after unification, industrial production in the east had declined by 70 percent. Unemployment had risen to 3.5 million in a workforce of 8.5 million. The Treuhand discovered that it could not easily sell off antiquated industries even though the federal government offered a 40 percent tax credit for firms that invested in the east. Even when buyers could be found, the terms and conditions were difficult. BASF, for instance, bought a reasonably modern chemical firm in the east only to discover major environmental problems, a 74,000-person workforce that would have to be cut in half and a management filled with former Communist Party loyalists. To make matters worse, there was no market for the factory's goods because its primary outlet had been the former Soviet Union, which could no longer pay for the chemicals it produced.

During the 1990s, the federal government devoted an average of over $100 billion a year in aid and subsidies to the east, which was the equivalent of 40 percent of the

Comparative Emphasis: Globalization

So far, globalization has affected Germany less than the other European democracies. Despite the costs of unification, its companies and its currency (until the launch of the euro) remained the strongest in Europe.

That said, Germany is by no means immune from global pressures. In particular, its high labor costs make its goods expensive in most foreign markets. And some of its legal restrictions have forced its companies to do some cutting-edge work abroad. For example, constitutional court decisions have made embryonic stem cell research illegal. This does not mean that German firms do not conduct it; they simply do it in Britain or France, where there are no such restrictions. ■

former DDR's GNP. This spending also had a noticeable and negative impact on the lifestyles of those in the west, because the government imposed a 7.5 percent increase in the income tax and what amounted to a supplemental $0.55 per liter tax on gasoline.

Eventually, economic conditions in the east began to improve. By 2000 unemployment had dropped to 17 percent, only 10 percent more than in the FRG. Per capita income had topped $16,000 a year, almost twice what it was at the time of unification. Today, household income in the eastern states has reached 80 percent of the western average.

Integrating the east was not simply an economic challenge. Although most DDR citizens had been able to watch television shows and listen to radio broadcasts from the west for many years, they were largely isolated from the political and, even more so, cultural trends that remade the Federal Republic after 1945. Most had never lived in a market economy or a democracy, and many have had a hard time adapting to both.

Perhaps the most important long-term obstacle to effective unification is what many Germans call the "wall in the mind." Other terms used to describe the difficulties in combining the ossis and wessis (easterners and westerners, respectively) include "united but not together" and "sharing a bathroom with a stranger." Most observers are surprised by how different the two societies had grown despite having been separated for only forty-five years. There are clear signs that the cultural gap continues to narrow. Having Merkel in office has undoubtedly helped.

There is perhaps no better sign of the smoothness and success of the transition than the fact that the building that used to be the secret policy headquarters is now a museum.

Europe

Chapter 7 will cover the current European crisis itself. Here, we will use it to briefly stress one last time the consensual nature of German politics.

In 2011 and 2012, press coverage of the threats to the future of the euro often revolved around the demands for policies based on austerity that came from the German government. Many commentators worried that German intransigence on that score could well keep European institutions from taking steps that might stimulate the weakened economies of a number of member states, which could lead to the end of the single currency and the EU itself.

As I write in early 2013, all the signs are that Germany will rediscover its pragmatic tradition. Already the German-dominated European Central Bank has made it clear that it will do all in its power to preserve the euro.

The Media

Just like the British and the French, Germans have access to a wide variety of sources of information about politics. Also like their counterparts, few take much advantage of them.

Germany's newspapers have surprisingly small circulations. The five main "quality" dailies sold only 157,000 to 405,000 copies a day at the end of 1997, a number that has declined since then. As in Britain and France, they each have clear, traditional political leanings. However, as the 1998 election neared, the *Frankfurter Allgemeine Zeitung* was unusually critical of the Kohl government it had long supported. The CDU has also been able to count on support from the Axel Springer media empire, with its high-quality daily *Die Welt* and Germany's main tabloid, *Bild*. In short, the printed press has probably become less partisan than it was before unification.

Germans have more locally produced television stations than people in Britain or France in part because the Basic Law gives states primary responsibility for the audiovisual media. Subscribers to the many satellite systems (cable is much less developed in Europe) can receive more than thirty German-language stations with a "basic package." The most popular private station (SAT 1) has been more supportive of the CDU than the state-owned ones (ARD, ZDF), and it is widely believed that it played a major role in the CDU's reelection in 1994. There is an all-news channel and another channel that resembles C-SPAN, but they are not very popular. The one event that usually draws a large audience is the so-called elephant round table, or debate among the party leaders, which occurs in the last few days before a Bundestag election.

Conclusion: The Big Questions

The big questions raised in Chapter 1 have not gotten a lot of attention since then. At least so far. That has been the case because most people—politicians and average citizens alike—have not thought the questions needed attention.

Whether one agrees that people elsewhere made the right decision in not asking the big questions the fact of the matter is that Germans have had to address them more explicitly than Americans, the French, or the British for two main reasons:

■ The upheavals and traumas of German history have all but forced people to ask them in unprecedented ways as recently as unification barely a generation ago.

■ Because German politics is more clearly intertwined with European and even global networks, its politicians have done more to think through the implications of life in a globalizing, interdependent, changing, and "2.0" world than their counterparts.

As we will see beginning in the next chapter, those big issues matter far more for the other kinds of political units that will be focused on in the rest of the book. It may well be that people in the other industrialized democracies should be posing those questions more seriously and rigorously, but reaching a conclusion either supporting or opposing such a statement takes us far beyond the domain of an introductory textbook!

KEY TERMS		
Concepts	corporatism	German question
austerity	economic miracle	grand coalition
Basic Law	euro	*Junkers*
chancellor democracy	faulted society	*länder*
codetermination	federalism	*Modell Deutschland*
constructive vote of no confidence	führer	proportional representation

reparations

sovereign debt crisis

People

Adenauer, Konrad

Bismarck, Otto von

Brandt, Willy

Hitler, Adolf

Kohl, Helmut

Merkel, Angela

Schmidt, Helmut

Schröder, Gerhard

Acronyms

CDU

DDR

DGB

FCC

FDP

FRG

NPD

NSDAP

PDS

SPD

Organizations, Places, and Events

Bundesbank

Bundesrat

Bundestag

Christian Democratic Union (CDU)

Federal Constitutional Court (FCC)

Federal Republic of Germany (FRG)

Federation of German Labor (DGB)

Free Democratic Party (FDP)

German Democratic Republic (DDR)

Greens

Law for Promoting Stability and
  Growth in the Economy

Left Party

National Democratic Party (NPD)

National Socialist Democratic Workers
  Party (NSDAP)

Nazi

Party of Democratic Socialism (PDS)

Social Democratic Party (SPD)

Treuhand

Weimar Republic

USEFUL WEBSITES

There are three good entry points to German politics on the Internet, though none of them are as good as the portals for most of the other countries covered in this book. WESS has an excellent site on German studies in general. The editors of H-Net, a collection of list-servs for scholars, maintain a set of links on German issues, including politics. Finally, Professor Russell Dalton of the University of California-Irvine has an excellent but brief set of links he has chosen for his own students, including quite a few rare historical YouTube clips.

> wessweb.info/index.php/German_Studies_Web

> www.h-net.org/~german/

> www.socsci.uci.edu/~rdalton/germany/other/weblinks.htm

The German government provides a gateway to the chancellor's office and government agencies, most of which have material in English, as well as in German.

> www.bundesregierung.de/Webs/Breg/EN/Homepage/home.html

There are two good sources of news about Germany. The first is from the English-language feed of Deutsche Welle, one of the country's leading radio and television broadcasters. The other is provided by the German Embassy in Washington.

> www.dw-world.de/dw/0,1595,266,00.html

> www.germany.info/

FURTHER READINGS

Almond, Gabriel, and Sidney Verba. *The Civic Culture: Political Attitudes and Democracy in Five Nations.* Princeton, NJ: Princeton University Press, 1963. The classic study of political culture, including significant doubts about German commitment to democracy.

————, eds. *The Civic Culture Revisited.* Boston: Little, Brown, 1979. A volume that includes substantial data on the way German culture changed during the 1960s and 1970s and became more "civic."

Ardagh, John. *Germany and the Germans: After Unification*, rev. ed. New York: Penguin Books, 1991. An encyclopedic look at modern Germany, with an emphasis on culture and economics rather than on politics.

Ash, Timothy Garton. *The Magic Lantern: The Revolution of '89 Witnessed in Warsaw, Budapest, Berlin, and Prague.* New York: Random House, 1990. One of the best journalistic accounts of the events that swept through Eastern Europe in 1989.

Berghahn, V. R. *Modern Germany: Society, Economy, and Politics in the Twentieth Century*, 2nd ed. New York: Cambridge University Press, 1987. A historical overview that provides the best link among political, social, and economic trends.

Bracher, Karl Dietrich. *The German Dictatorship*. New York: Praeger, 1970. Still perhaps the best and most accessible analytical study of the Hitler years.

Chin, Rita. *The Guest Worker Question in Postwar Germany*. New York: Cambridge University Press, 2007. One of the few books in English on the new multicultural Germany. Unfortunately, it ends with unification.

Fisher, Marc. *After the Wall: Germany, the Germans, and the Burden of History*. New York: Simon & Schuster, 1995. An analysis of contemporary Germany by the *Washington Post*'s correspondent; especially good on ethnic issues.

Goldhagen, Donald. *Hitler's Willing Executioners*. New York: Random House, 1997. An extremely controversial book that argues that most Germans cooperated willingly with the Third Reich.

Green, Simon, Dan Hough, Alister Miskimmon, and Graham Timmins. *The Politics of the New Germany*. New York: Routledge, 2008. Not quite as exhaustive as the work by Hancock and Krisch (see below), but covers social and institutional issues better.

Hancock, M. Donald, and Henry Krisch. *Politics in Germany*. Washington, D.C.: CQ Press, 2008. The one up-to-date, full-length textbook on Germany.

Vanberg, Georg. *The Politics of Constitutional Review in Germany*. Cambridge: Cambridge University Press, 2005. The one English-language book on judicial review in Germany. It may go too far in stressing what the court can and cannot do.

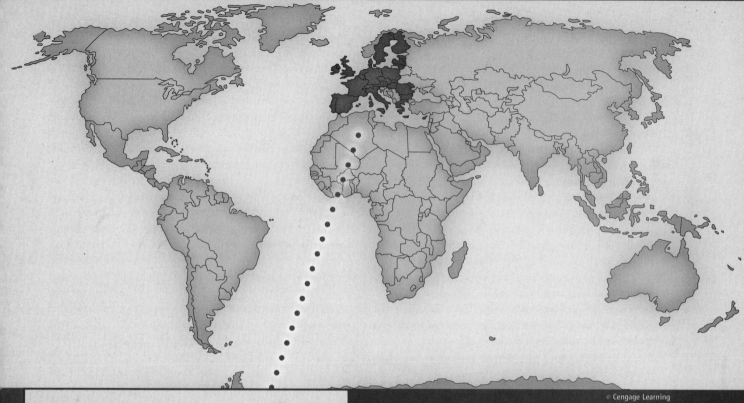

© Cengage Learning

7

The European Union

> *The stabilizing part played by the European Union has helped to transform a once torn Europe from a continent of war to a continent of peace.*
>
> THORBJØRN JAGLAND

THE BASICS

Size	4,324,782 sq. km, not quite half the size of the United States
Population	583 million
GNP per capita	$34,100
Currency	1€ = US$1.33
Capital	Brussels, Luxembourg, Strasbourg
Commission President	Jose Manuel Barroso (2004–)
EU President	Herman van Rompuy (2009–)

Europe's Present/Europe's Future

The European Union (EU) was in the news for two reasons in 2012. The first kept it in the headlines all year—the crisis shaking the eurozone, the term used to denote the seventeen countries that have adopted the euro (€). Then, in the midst of the crisis, the Norwegian Nobel Prize Committee surprised the world by awarding the EU its annual peace prize. Given the attention given the crisis, many observers thought the prize was some kind of bizarre joke. However, the two events together illustrate why the EU needs to be included in introductory comparative politics courses even though it is not a national government.

The Crisis

The euro was introduced in 2002 to tremendous enthusiasm (ec.europa.eu). Since then, it has become the only currency used in seventeen of the twenty-eight EU member states.

It is also in serious trouble. Uncontrolled spending by national governments, ill-conceived economic decisions, the global recession, and bursting economic "bubbles" left many of its member states on the brink of financial collapse. The slump took a particularly heavy toll on Greece, Spain, Portugal, Italy, and Ireland, which were among the poorest countries to have adopted the euro. None of them was able to solve any of the interrelated economic problems they faced, most notably massive unemployment and a growing national debt. They all teetered on the brink of default, which is the governmental equivalent of bankruptcy. Many feared that the default of even a single government might destroy the euro and take the whole EU with it (see Table 7.1).

The five countries needed hefty loans and other infusions of cash to meet their social obligations, which would in turn

AP Photo /Heiko Junge, NTB Scanpix, POOL

European leaders at the ceremony awarding it the 2012 Nobel Peace Prize.

add to their debt and deepen the recession. All eyes turned to the **European Central Bank (ECB)** and the International Monetary Fund of which the ECB was the more important politically. Following the lead of the German government, it insisted that the troubled governments institute budget-tightening policies, labeled **austerity**, that many felt would only make bad social conditions worse.

Greece got the most publicity, perhaps because its economic and political conditions were the most perilous. By the end of 2011, the Greek government had amassed a debt of nearly half a trillion dollars—in a country of only eleven million

people. The Greek Left, the trade unions, the unemployed, young people who had little hope of finding a job, and others rejected the ECB's insistence on austerity. The government fell, and it took two elections before any semblance of political stability was restored. Even then, the economic crisis continued despite a series of loans aimed at slowing the growth of the government's debt and the private sector's impending collapse.

In 2011 and 2012, it seemed as if one false step could bring a half-century of European integration to an end. Despite the loans from the ECB and assurances from Germany and the International Monetary Fund, Greece came close to defaulting. The other countries were heading toward the same economic precipice.

Most mainstream economists thought that the economic steps needed to solve the crisis were not all that complicated. The EU as a whole could take responsibility for the debt by "federalizing" it and spreading the cost across all member states as the EU leaders proposed late in 2012. If the EU decided to guarantee loans owed by all member states, the financial situation would stabilize, and the EU could create new institutions that could better manage future economic crises.

This is not an economics book, and I am not qualified to make a case for or against federalizing the debt. However, like so many of the issues covered in *Comparative Politics*, the difficulties the EU is facing are largely economic in origin but have important political ramifications as well that are central to a book like this one.

TABLE 7.1 Key Events in the Eurozone Crisis

YEAR	EVENT
2002	Introduction of euro bills and coins
2007–08	Start of global recession
2009	Greek debt reaches €800 billion
2010	EU austerity plan provokes strikes and riots in Greece
	Irish bailout
2011	European Stability Mechanism created
	More bailouts
	European Central Bank unveils emergency plan for banks
2012	Standard and Poor's downgrades credit ranking of nine currencies
	Greek government agrees to austerity
	European Banking Union plan introduced

© Cengage Learning 2015

Blanchin-lebleavec/Sagaphoto.com/Alamy

Demonstrators gather in the smoke-filled streets of Athens, Greece, in 2011, protesting new labor reforms amid persisting austerity.

In this case, the crisis itself had many political causes. The EU created the eurozone without either anticipating the problems that were bound to occur when countries with such different economies adopted the same currency or defining an "escape hatch" which countries could use to leave it. More importantly, despite the institutions that will be discussed in the rest of this chapter, its decision-making bodies lacked the kind of authority national governments use to respond to domestic crises—economic or otherwise.

PIIGS and BRICS

In Parts 3 and 4, we will spend a lot of time looking at the BRICS countries. The term was coined by analysts at Goldman-Sachs to describe four rapidly growing, developing economies—Brazil, Russia, India, and China. The S was added later when some started including South Africa in the group.

At about the same time, other investment bankers began using the much less flattering term, PIIGS, to describe the five European countries—Portugal, Italy, Iceland, Greece, and Spain—with the most troubled economies.[a] Needless to say, many political and economic leaders in those countries took offense.

---

[a]The word could just as easily be PIGS. Iceland is not a member of the EU. It is a sovereign state but under the Danish crown. Denmark is a member of the EU but does not use the euro.

The crisis also produced a backlash in the countries that were not in danger of default but would have to pay most of the costs of whatever solution the EU ultimately adopted. The reaction was particularly intense in Germany, which would have to take on that economic burden and where, as we saw in Chapter 6, the crisis was seen as a sign of wastefulness by their fellow Europeans. At the height of one of its episodes, a leading German tabloid wrote, "Sell your islands, you bankrupt Greeks—and the Acropolis too!" Poll after poll showed that German public opinion was almost two-to-one in opposition to the bailout.

As I write in mid-2013, it seems as if the EU and the euro will survive. The planned European Banking Union will probably be implemented. No country is likely to default.

That does not mean that the EU is out of trouble. The economic difficulties—including the gap between rich and poor—will continue. So, too, will a host of political problems, including Germany's dominant position and the alienation growing out of what is often referred to as its **democratic deficit**. There is even a chance that Britain might leave if the right-wing faction of Prime Minister David Cameron's Conservative Party has its way.

The Peace Prize

At the height of the euro crisis, the Nobel Prize Committee announced that the EU had won its 2012 peace prize. Questions were immediately raised about its timing, with critics arguing that the Norwegian officials who make the decision had intentionally weighed in to prop up the euro.

We will never know why the committee chose the EU at that time. One possible reason is clear, however. If one took a step back from the EU's fiscal cliff, the EU's track record since the **European Coal and Steel Community (ECSC)** was formed in 1951 was impressive. At the award ceremony, the committee's chair, Thorbjørn Jagland, listed many of its accomplishments—helping bring peace to Europe, rebuilding war-torn economies, protecting human rights, and expanding democracy in Eastern Europe. But he went on to suggest that the Committee had chosen the EU as much because of its future promise as for its past accomplishments.

> In the light of the financial crisis that is affecting so many innocent people, we can see that the political framework in which the EU is rooted is more important now than ever. We must stand together. We have collective responsibility. Without this European cooperation, the result might easily have been new protectionism, new nationalism, with the risk that the ground gained would be lost (www.nobelprize.org/nobel_prizes/peace/laureates/2012/presentation-speech.html).

In other words, despite the EU's troubled present, the five Norwegians (whose country is not even a member) who chose it seem to have understood the comment by political scientist David Cameron (not related to the British prime minister) I used to begin this chapter in previous editions of *Comparative Politics*. "Over the long term, the institutions and powers of the (Union) will continue to expand and certain policy making powers will be delegated or transferred to, or pooled and shared with, (Union) institutions. As a result, the sovereignty of the member states will increasingly and inevitably be eroded."[1]

Thinking About the European Union

The Bottom Line

Twenty years ago, few instructors included the EU in introductory courses on comparative politics, because most of my colleagues saw it as part of international relations instead. Now it is hard to ignore for the simple reason that it has a huge and growing impact on the domestic politics of its member states, especially on their economic policies. More importantly for comparativists, the EU already has some of the features comparativists typically include in their definitions of a national state giving yet another reason to those introduced in Chapter 1 for including more than national states in our work.

The EU is the most prominent institution showing us that we also have to move "up" and consider bodies that include more than a single country. Although we will focus on more in the final chapter rather than here, there are signs that **multilevel governance**, in which states share power and sovereignty with **supranational** bodies, may become a more common way to address political problems that transcend national boundaries.

At the very least, the growth of the EU so far underscores the importance of two themes that will be on intellectual center stage throughout the rest of *Comparative Politics*.

- How global forces shape what states can accomplish.

- How national sovereignty is being questioned by at least some prominent political leaders.

In other words, we will go far beyond the current crisis and ask questions like these that do not have obvious answers. That said, we can already reach one conclusion you should keep in mind.

Despite its state-like attributes, the EU is far from being a state. If nothing else, it lacks the monopoly over the legitimate use of force that most political scientists argue makes a state a state. More generally speaking, whether the EU or any other international organization will gain enough power to rival that of the nation-state is very much an open question. Even if it does, it is unlikely to do so during the lifetime of any reader of this book.

What Is the EU?

Before we get to the big issues that eddy around the EU, we have to start by clarifying the people and places this chapter covers. The institutions that make up the EU have gone by four different names:

- The **European Economic Community (EEC)** was established by the Treaty of Rome in 1957.

- The **Common Market** is an informal term used to describe the bodies created by the Treaty and is still informally used today.

---

[1]David R. Cameron, "The 1992 Initiative: Causes and Consequences." In Alberta Sbragia, ed, *Euro-Politics: Institutions and Policymaking in the "New" European Community* (Washington: Brookings Institution, 1992), 64.

- The European Community (EC) was created in 1965 in recognition of the fact that the EEC's functions had expanded beyond economics.

- The European Union was the product of the 1992 Maastricht Treaty on European Union.

Who's In? Who's Out?

Just as I was finishing this book, the EU added its twenty-eighth member, Croatia (see Table 7.2). France, Germany, Italy, Belgium, the Netherlands, and Luxembourg were charter members of the EEC. Britain, Ireland, and Denmark entered on New Year's Day 1973. Greece joined in 1981 and Spain and Portugal followed five years later. Finland, Austria, and Sweden became members in 1995. Cyprus, the Czech Republic, Estonia, Hungary, Latvia, Lithuania, Malta, Poland, Slovakia, and Slovenia were admitted in 2004. Bulgaria and Romania joined in 2007. Applications from several more states are pending. Of the major European countries, only Norway and Switzerland have shown little or no interest in "acceding" to the EU.

The EU has slightly more than 500 million residents, or roughly 200 million more than the United States. Its combined gross domestic product in 2011 was about the same as that of the United States, though Europeans had only about two-thirds of the average American's disposable income. Still, the EU is an economic powerhouse, generating about 30 percent of all international trade (see Table 7.3).

The EU also has many of the trappings of a state. Its flag of fifteen yellow stars on a blue background flies from official buildings. This is also a common logo in advertisements, and you can get it emblazoned on T-shirts and umbrellas (I have one of each). The EU even has three capital cities—Brussels, Luxembourg, and Strasbourg. And

TABLE 7.2 Members of the European Union

COUNTRY	YEAR JOINED
Belgium, France, Germany, Italy, Luxembourg, Netherlands	1957
Denmark, Great Britain, Ireland	1972/73
Greece	1981
Portugal, Spain	1986
Austria, Finland, Sweden	1995
Cyprus, Czech Republic, Estonia, Hungary, Latvia, Lithuania, Malta, Poland, Slovakia, Slovenia	2004
Romania, Bulgaria	2007
Croatia	2013

© Cengage Learning 2015

TABLE 7.3 The European Union and the United States, 2011

	EUROPEAN UNION	UNITED STATES
Population (in millions)	504	314
GDP (in trillions of US$)	17.1	14.8
Imports (in trillions of dollars)	1.8	1.5
Exports (in trillions of dollars)	2.0	1.2

Sources: *CIA World Factbook* (www.cia.gov). Accessed January 14, 2013.

now, the EU has one of the most important attributes of a state, other than an army and police force: its own currency, the euro.

Three Pillars

As the confusion over its name suggests, many people mistakenly think of the EU as an economic organization. Although it began as a trading bloc whose authority was limited to a few economic sectors, its founders always intended it to be much more than that. Since its creation, the EU has expanded to embrace other powers that are together known as its three pillars, denoting its spheres of activity in which states cooperate and "pool" national sovereignty to some considerable extent:

- Trade and other economic matters.
- Justice and home affairs.
- A Common Foreign and Security Policy (CFSP).

Key Questions

This chapter provides a first concrete look at the trends that might be leading us into a new historical period in which the five big questions outlined in Chapter 1 are at the heart of day-to-day political life and the nation-state is no longer the only, or even the primary, unit comparativists should focus on. If that is our future, we are still a long way from getting there, which will be the focus of Chapter 16.

Here, we will concentrate on less grandiose possibilities by considering the current state of the EU, which can mostly be addressed by asking the same kinds of questions used throughout this book:

- How and why did the EU emerge?
- What is its political culture, and how does it affect the way people participate in political life?
- What are its main decision-making bodies?
- What are its critical public policy initiatives?
- How did the European people learn about and react to that policy?

The Evolution of the European Union

Unlike the United States, Great Britain, France, and Germany, it did not take centuries or require lots of conflict to create the EU. European integration is a recent phenomenon. Also unlike the national democracies, its development has been almost exclusively the handiwork of political, technical, and economic elites. They have not always agreed with each other. However, their disputes have never led them to consider the use of violence, which, of course, is one of the EU's most important accomplishments given the continent's bloody history.

The EU has expanded in two main ways:

- By adding new member states, known as broadening.
- By adding new powers, known as deepening.

Progress on either front has rarely come smoothly. As we will see, the EU has developed as a result of a number of fits and starts and is currently in the midst of one its more troubling "fits."

Not Such a New Idea

Political leaders have dreamed of a unified Europe since the Roman Empire, if not before. When European leaders tried to turn those dreams into reality in the past, they relied on military might in their attempts to do so. Despite some initial battlefield successes, they all failed sooner rather than later (www.hum.leiden.edu/history/eu-history).

Attempts to unite Europe through peaceful means began after the creation of the League of Nations in 1919. Many countries went on to sign the Kellogg-Briand Pact, which formally outlawed war, although it was obviously honored in the breach.

The outbreak of World War II brought their efforts to an abrupt end. In the end, the wartime experience only strengthened the Europeanists' resolve. People who had few ties to the discredited prewar regimes led Resistance movements against the Nazis. After the war, they also wanted to create new European institutions because they realized that Europeans simply could not afford to keep fighting each other (see Table 7.4).

A small group of them met in neutral Switzerland during the middle of the war and called for a supranational government that would be directly elected by the European people. Its military, which would replace national armies, and an international court would settle disputes that arose

among them. The early Europeanists, like Jean Monnet (1889–1979) in France and Paul-Henri Spaak (1899–1972) in Belgium, were idealists and visionaries who wanted nothing less than a permanent end to the continent's history of warfare.

From the beginning, the Europeanists fell into two strategic camps. Federalists wanted to move directly and quickly toward some sort of Europe-wide government, while functionalists felt the new Europe would have to be created in a piecemeal manner by integrating decision making one policy area at a time, while building momentum for further integration along the way.

As it turned out, neither side got its way. The first important steps toward a united Europe were a byproduct of the early cold war, which turned security into the paramount concern on both sides of the iron curtain. The tensions between east and west convinced the western Allies of the need to reconstruct the war-ravaged economies and strengthen the new regimes in Germany, France, and Italy. The United States decided not to give Marshall Plan aid to individual governments. Instead, it chose to distribute the money through the predecessor of today's Organisation for Economic Cooperation and Development (OECD).

For the rest of the 1940s, most of the movement toward integration came as a result of the cold war rather than the economy. The widely held belief in the need for Western military cooperation led to the creation of the

TABLE 7.4 Key Events in the Evolution of the European Union

YEAR	EVENT
1951	Creation of ECSC
1957	Treaty of Rome signed
1967	Creation of EC
1972	First expansion
1981	Admission of Greece
1985	Single European Act passed
1986	Portugal and Spain admitted
1991	Treaty of Maastricht signed
1995	Austria, Finland, and Sweden admitted
1997	Treaty of Amsterdam signed
1998	Twelve countries agree to join the European Monetary Union (EMU)
2001	Treaty of Nice signed
2002	Euro launched
2004	Ten new members added
2007	Bulgaria and Romania admitted
2009	Treaty of Lisbon goes into effect, first president and foreign minister appointed

© Cengage Learning

North Atlantic Treaty Organization (NATO) in 1949. To the degree that anyone paid attention to integration other than in security affairs, the assumption was that key leadership would have to come from Britain, which was still Europe's leading power. In what would prove to be decisive later on, that leadership never materialized.

The supporters of a politically integrated Europe did not give up. In 1949, they created the Council of Europe. It had little power because each state could veto anything the Council proposed. Nonetheless, it did give a venue for national leaders to meet and laid the groundwork for the intergovernmental component of what became the EU.

The following year, Foreign Minister Robert Schuman of France issued a plan (actually written by Monnet) for a supranational authority that would manage coal and steel production. The two sectors were chosen because they are at the heart of any industrial economy, had been damaged heavily in the war, and were an obvious place to start cooperative endeavors. Other than Italy, the five countries that formed the ECSC also bordered the Rhine River valley where much of their coal and iron production was located. Negotiations were able to proceed quickly in part because Britain was not involved and because Christian Democratic and other pro-European politicians ran most of the governments of the six founding countries.

The ECSC established a single market for the two products through the gradual elimination of tariffs and other barriers to trade. The treaty also created four institutions that remain at the core of the EU today albeit with different names and powers:

- A High Authority of representatives named by the national governments who served as its administrative body at the supranational level.

- A Special Council of Ministers composed of cabinet members from the individual governments that was responsible for policy making.

- A Court of Justice to resolve disputes involving the ECSC, national governments, and private companies.

- A Common Assembly of delegates chosen by the national parliaments.

It is important to emphasize two points here. First, however small and tentative these steps may have been, the creation of the ECSC did transfer some elements of national sovereignty to a supranational body. Second, the ECSC was funded directly from fees paid by companies doing business in the two industries. Having an independent and autonomous source of funds from the very beginning put the new European institutions on a firmer footing than other international organizations, including the United Nations.

PROFILES   Jean Monnet

Jean Monnet was a remarkable man. In his long career, he was everything from a brandy salesman to the primary architect of both the French economic planning system and European integration. In a professional life that spanned two world wars (which, perhaps not coincidentally, he could not fight in because of ill health), he came to see the need to replace the carnage produced by trench warfare and the blitzkrieg with a new kind of transnational economic cooperation.

After World War II, he dedicated his energies to reconstruction and peace through planning and integration, which he believed were inseparable. Among the few official positions he held was president of the European Coal and Steel Community (ECSC) from its founding until 1955. He spent the next twenty years trying to create a fully United States of Europe. Monnet died at age ninety (so much for ill health) without seeing his broader dream realized but having left an indelible mark on his continent and the world. ■

Jean Monnet giving a radio address on European union.

The ECSC was not an overnight success. The governments began squabbling almost immediately. Some of the issues seem minor in retrospect, such as the language it should use and where its offices should be located. Still, the ECSC lived up to the functionalists' most important expectation. Support for the ECSC spread to other sectors.

By the middle of the decade, plans were under way to move on to agriculture, the military, and transportation.

Meanwhile, the High Authority discovered that eliminating tariffs and quotas alone would not be enough to create a truly common market. In 1955, the foreign ministers of the six member countries named Spaak to head a committee to explore further options. Its report called for a common market and an integrated approach to the new industry of nuclear power. Spaak's group then drafted the Treaty of Rome, which was endorsed by the same six governments in 1957. The treaty established two bodies—the EEC and the European Atomic Energy Commission (Euratom) that would oversee the elimination of all internal tariffs and the adoption of common external ones within fifteen years.

The EEC kept the ECSC's main institutions. The High Authority was renamed the **Commission** and was given responsibility for representing supranational interests as well as administering the EEC. Though the Treaty gave it few formal powers, it was assumed that the Commission would also be the major initiator of new policies.

The **Council of Ministers** gave national governments a direct role in governing the EEC because it had to approve all policy initiatives. In those days, if a state decided that an issue before the Council directly affected its national interests, it could veto any proposed community initiative. In other words, the six members had to reach unanimity before the EEC could take any major new step. Only a few relatively minor kinds of proposals could be passed through a system of qualified majority voting, which is now used for almost everything the EU does.

The treaty increased the size of the renamed **European Parliament** and gave it the right to review decisions made by the Commission and Council. Nonetheless, it remained the weakest of the four main European institutions.

The **European Court of Justice (ECJ)** had seven members. Each government chose one justice, and the six of them together chose the seventh one. The court was given jurisdiction over cases in which the EEC itself, the member governments, or companies conducting business in them were accused of violating the provisions of the Treaty of Rome. Like members of the Commission, the justices ceased being employees of their home governments and supposedly had no contact with politicians back home during their deliberations.

Creating the Common Market

The EEC actually finished revising the tariff laws ahead of schedule. Along the way, it also decided to streamline its institutions by merging the EEC and Euratom into the single EC in 1967.

European Union flags fly outside the European Commission headquarters in Brussels, Belgium.

Despite that success, the early EEC had no choice but to take on an issue that has been a stumbling block in the way of further European integration ever since. How much power should be assigned to the supranational institutions, and how much should remain in national hands through the Council?

National differences on that front first surfaced in 1963 when France vetoed membership applications by Denmark and the United Kingdom. At a press conference announcing the decision, President Charles de Gaulle declared that he was for a *Europe des patries*—a Europe based on nation-states—and that Britain was not sufficiently European to join. Then in the "empty chairs" crisis of 1965–66, the French government boycotted all Council meetings, thereby paralyzing the organization because the unanimity rule required that all countries agree on all policy decisions. De Gaulle's successor, Georges Pompidou, was a far more committed European. He did not block applications from Britain, Ireland, Denmark, and Norway,[2] which were approved in January 1972.

The EC (as it now became known) grew in ways functionalists would have predicted. In 1966, the **Common Agricultural Policy (CAP)** was created. The **European Monetary System (EMS)** established a "snake," or band, in which member currencies floated against each other. Members of the European Parliament were chosen in direct elections beginning in 1979. The workings of the Council were made more routine with the establishment of the **Committee of Permanent Representatives (COREPER)** from the member states.

Even during this period of growth, the EEC encountered problems. The generation of visionary, functionalist leaders either died or retired. Their replacements were far less committed to further European integration. The EC bore the brunt of the criticism when European economies failed to recover after the OPEC oil embargo of 1973–74, prompting pundits to talk about "eurosclerosis" rather than further integration.

Meanwhile, a growing number of business leaders came to the conclusion that a sustained recovery could only be achieved if the political leaders acted together. That realization brought two further obstacles to light. First, eliminating internal tariffs was not going to be enough to create a single, common market. The free movement of goods and services was impeded, for example, by national standards for the licensing of goods and services and other policies that required state agencies to make purchases from domestic sources whenever possible. Second, the EEC's founders' assumption that success in producing a limited common market would be translated into new support for deepening European powers failed to materialize.

The first step toward the **Single European Act (SEA)** and the Maastricht Treaty was a report prepared under the direction of Belgian Prime Minister Leo Tindemans in 1976. It called for a monetary and economic union, a common defense and foreign policy, and a joint industrial development program. The Tindemans Report did not lead directly to any policy changes. It did, however, set the European political agenda for the next fifteen years.

The pace picked up when the appointment of **Jacques Delors (1925–)** as president of the Commission in 1985 breathed new life into European integration. Delors had been France's minister of finance and one of President François Mitterrand's closest advisers.

All those efforts culminated in the passage of the SEA in 1985, which strengthened the EC by:

- Completing what came to be called the internal market. As noted earlier, the abolition of internal tariffs and quotas did not remove all barriers to trade. It took seven years to draft and ratify more than three hundred regulations before truly free trade of goods and services across the borders of the member states became the norm.

- Changing the way the EC is governed. That started with a reduction in the use of the **unanimity principle**. Complete agreement by all the member states would now only be required to admit new members, adopt a budget, or embark on wholly new policy initiatives. Otherwise, the EC would use the less demanding qualified majority procedure.

- Formalizing the semiannual summit meetings of the national leaders and the links between the Council, Commission, and European Parliament.

- Recommending more cooperation in foreign and national security policy, though it did little to specify exactly how that would occur.

The SEA by no means unified Europe. It remained primarily an economic union that had little or no authority over social, environmental, and political issues. In most ways, national sovereignty had not been challenged. Even in the economic arena, the all-important issue of monetary and financial integration had barely been addressed.

Momentum for further deepening was built even as the bureaucrats were fleshing out the details of the SEA. The end of the cold war made a strong Europe all the more desirable, because Eastern Europe was going to need billions of dollars to ease the transition from communism to capitalism. Furthermore, the departure of Margaret Thatcher in 1990 removed the leader who was most skeptical of any expansion of the EC's power, which she had labeled "eurononsense."

That momentum carried over into the negotiations for the Maastricht Treaty, which authorized the first steps toward the creation of a single currency and a central bank. The treaty also gave what was now officially called the European Union authority to act in new areas, including monetary policy, foreign affairs, national security, fisheries, transportation, the environment, health, justice, education, consumer protection, and tourism. The Treaty gave the three pillars legal grounding. The treaty defined EU citizenship through which people carry European passports, can work in any member country (with the exception of some in Eastern Europe), and can vote in European parliamentary and local elections wherever they live. All EU nations other

---

[2]The Norwegian voters rejected membership in a referendum in 1972. They did so again in 1994.

PROFILES Jacques Delors

Jacques Delors is generally considered the second most prominent architect of the EU after Jean Monnet.

Born in 1925 in a working-class neighborhood of Paris, Delors was unable to attend university because his father insisted that he go to work at age sixteen. He thus started his career as a clerical worker in a Parisian bank and came to politics through his involvement in the Catholic trade union movement.

In the 1950s and 1960s, he was an active member of small groups that tried to redefine what it meant to be on the Left. At times this led him to work with groups to the Left of the Communists, and at others to serve as an adviser to Gaullist ministers.

President François Mitterrand appointed him minister of finance, from which position he was largely responsible for the U-turn of 1983 that ended the Socialists' radical reforms. Two years later, he went to Brussels as president of the Commission.

He retired after two terms amid rumors that he would become the Socialist candidate for president of France, which he squelched. In retirement, he continues to support European initiatives. His daughter, Martine Aubry, has been leader of the French Socialist Party since 2008. ∎

be approved without difficulty. However, the Danish voters rejected it in a referendum, and parliamentary debates dragged on in Britain and Germany. Despite the support of all mainstream politicians, a referendum on the treaty barely squeaked through in France. Great Britain and Denmark eventually did ratify it but only after provisions were approved that would allow them to opt out of the social chapter and single currency.

The EU also had trouble finding someone to succeed Delors in 1995. After a long process that included a British veto of everyone else's first choice, the members chose the little-known former prime minister of Luxembourg, Jacques Santer. Although a committed European, Santer lacked Delors' charisma and clout, and his selection was widely seen as a sign that few major initiatives would be forthcoming under his leadership.

Doubts about the leadership mounted with the 1999 publication of the European Parliament's inquiry into allegations of mismanagement and corruption by Commission members. Noone was accused of wrongdoing. Nonetheless, all twenty Commissioners decided to resign, provoking what many thought would be a setback the EU might not recover from.

The crisis turned out to be nothing of the sort. Within days, an agreement was reached. The outgoing Commission remained in office in a caretaker capacity much as a cabinet that lost a vote of confidence would in any of the member states. A week later, the national governments agreed on a successor to Santer, former Italian prime minister Romano Prodi, who would take over with a full complement of new members when the outgoing Commission's term expired the following January.

Since then, the EU has adopted three new treaties, whose impact we will explore in more detail in the sections on governance and public policy. The 1997 **Treaty of Amsterdam** extended the **Schengen Agreement**, which eliminated most border controls inside the EU and gave it more responsibility over some legal matters, including issuing residence permits to immigrants, determining asylum procedures, and promulgating directives on judicial and police cooperation. The Amsterdam accord also declared that the EU would defer to NATO as the dominant security organization in Europe, while reinforcing its desire to chart its own foreign policy in other areas, including the creation of a rapid deployment force for use in humanitarian and other emergencies.

In 2001, the leaders of the member states agreed to the Treaty of Nice, which opened the door to the membership expansions of 2004 and 2007. It adjusted the way key positions were filled to smooth expansion to twenty-five and, later, twenty-eight member countries. The 2007 Treaty of Lisbon made other relatively minor adjustments

thank Britain agreed to harmonize their labor relations and social service policies. In an attempt to meet the concerns of many national politicians, the treaty also endorsed the principle of **subsidiarity**, which empowers the EU to act if and only if it can do so more effectively than national or regional governments.

The rest of the 1990s were not easy for the EU. Europe experienced a serious recession, which reinforced qualms about the EU and put talk of further deepening on hold. The costs of German unification, the EU's inability to end the fighting in the former Yugoslavia, internal divisions over most major issues, and uncertainties about the euro renewed fears of eurosclerosis.

The troubles began with the ratification of the Maastricht Treaty itself. At first, everyone assumed it would to EU governance possible—and necessary—because the states had failed to ratify the proposed constitution two years earlier.

Since then, the EU has largely been paralyzed by in its failed attempt to recover from the recession and solve the euro crisis. As a result, neither further broadening nor deepening is even remotely possible today. If anything, it is more likely that Britain will leave the EU, something Prime Minister Cameron has vowed the British public will vote on in a referendum if his government is elected for a second term in 2015.

Political Culture and Participation in the European Union

The chapters on individual countries have long sections on political culture and participation. This one does not, simply because they are not (yet) very important in the EU.

In fact, it is hard to even speak of a European political culture. The few scholars who have worked on European identity cite evidence that people know that the EU plays an increasingly important role in their lives. Most, too, see at least indirect signs that people are able to think of themselves as both Europeans and citizens of a country.

Nonetheless, there are still very few people for whom the statement "I am a European" is anywhere near as important as "I am French" (or German, or whatever). Younger, well-educated people who have traveled extensively are the most European, but even they tend to put their national identity ahead of any transnational one. One political scientist calls these people the "Erasmus generation" after the EU program that allows students to attend universities in any member state for the equivalent of in-state tuition in the United States.

The lack of a European identity can be attributed to many things. Nothing is more obvious than the language gap. All official documents are published in twenty-three languages. Many Europeans are bi- or even trilingual, but there is no common language that more than 20 percent of them are comfortable using. Furthermore, if there were a common language, it would be English, and there is strong opposition in France and elsewhere to adopting it or any other single tongue.

There is also a backlash against the EU which we first saw in the comment from a German tabloid included near the beginning of this chapter. The pro-European side has lost support in most recent national referenda and would fail were one to be held today on almost anything involving the

Comparative Emphasis: Women

As in most areas of political life, women play a more important role than they used to in the EU. A third of the members of the European Parliament (MEPs) elected in 2009 are women, which is almost twice the total in the first directly elected body in 1979. A number of women have held important positions in the EU hierarchy, including the Luxembourgeoise Viviane Reding, who became Commissioner for Justice, Fundamental Rights, and Citizenship in 2010. She is well known for her demands that more women serve in top positions in EU agencies and European corporate boards.

Otherwise, the status of women is not as clearly on the upswing, for the same basic reason that most social movements have failed to find much traction at the European level. Political life is still largely defined domestically.

Typical is the European Feminist Forum, which served as a vehicle for women of all political persuasions to share their experiences. It thrived from 2005 to 2008 as an online organization, but disappeared after it failed to secure funding for a face-to-face meeting in 2009. ■

EU in Great Britain. Yet, as Table 7.5 suggests, the dropoff has not been as dramatic as some critics have expected (or wanted). In fact, support for the EU in general and the euro in particular both grew significantly between 2006 and 2012 during which time the great recession was at its peak.

The average citizen is also not deeply engaged in European affairs because the key EU institutions have not sunk very deep roots. People tend to think of Europe as

TABLE 7.5 Attitudes About European Integration

	2006 (%)	2012 (%)
Respondent has a positive image of the EU	50	39
Respondent supports the euro	59	52

Source: Based on Eurobarometre Standard Poll 77. http://ec.europa.eu/public_opinion/archives/eb/eb77/eb77_first_en.pdfs. Accessed 15 August 2012.

Comparative Emphasis: Democratization

In comparison with the countries covered in Part 2, we can treat democratization in the EU quickly.

Thus far, the EU has been constructed by and remains of importance primarily to elites. As a result, it kindles surprisingly little interest among its citizens. There has been more and more grumbling about the EU's lack of democracy, but so far, it has not erupted into anything approaching massive, organized protest movements. There were anti-EU protests in Greece and Spain during 2011 and 2012, but they have not come close to touching off Europe-wide demands for more democracy.

This situation may change as the EU becomes an even more inescapable part of everyone's life. Furthermore, any further deepening of the EU's powers likely will require greater involvement and more active support from rank-and-file voters. As the EU's powers expand, as it has to cope with the political and economic differences between its old members and the new ones, and as it tries to figure out how to create a multispeed Europe, more intense conflict between citizens and elites could emerge. ■

contributes to the resentment toward "Brussels" that so many Europeans feel.

The European State?

The title of this section ends with a question mark because many political scientists have trouble thinking of the EU as a state. In particular, it does not have either an army or a police force, which most political scientists think all states need, because they give it a monopoly on the legitimate use of force. That said, the EU has many state-like features, including the ability to enact laws and issue decrees that are binding on member states and their citizens.

The degree to which it is like a state varies from time to time and from issue to issue. Most notably, the EU is most like a state in exercising sovereign power in the economic pillar. By contrast, the states wield the most power when it comes to major new initiatives and other policy areas in which unanimity is still required.

Toward a Constitution?

In order to become more like a state, the EU has made two attempts to draft a constitution since 2000. In 2004, after two years of difficult negotiations, its heads of state reached an agreement on a draft constitution (european-convention.eu.int) that would have replaced the treaties and other interstate agreements. The more than five-hundred-page document would not have dramatically altered how the EU went about its work. What mattered is that the leaders were using the term *constitution* rather than *treaty* to describe it.

The member countries all had to ratify the draft. That was no problem in countries such as Germany, where the parliament cast the decisive vote. In France and the Netherlands, the governments decided they had to hold a referendum, and the draft constitution was defeated, which effectively killed it.

Instead of a constitution, the members agreed to the Treaty of Lisbon in 2007. It retained most provisions from the 2004 draft but was easier to sell to parliaments and voters precisely because it was not called a constitution. Like the constitution, it struck a delicate balance between big and small states and old and new members. Even so, it ran into roadblocks, most notably when Poland insisted on having roughly the same number of votes in the Council as Germany, which has almost twice as many inhabitants. It also created an EU president and foreign minister and changed the way qualified majority voting works. But like the constitution, the treaty only changed day-to-day politics on the margins.

something that affects them more than as a set of political institutions they themselves can influence.

Turnout in European elections is lower than in national ones. Only 43 percent of the eligible voters went to the polls to choose the European Parliament in 2009.

People tend to make up their minds about how to vote in European elections on the basis of national issues and partisan loyalties. Political parties in the European Parliament are organized along transnational lines (e.g., the socialists from all twenty-seven states form a single group and sit together). Other than that, partisan life remains almost exclusively national. Most interest groups, too, are still organized nationally, even those that maintain lobbying operations in Brussels.

The lack of public involvement in the EU has given rise to what critics call its democratic deficit. Its citizens have at most an indirect role in determining who sits on its most important decision-making bodies, which

The Institutions

The Commission

The most European institution is the Commission, because it has consistently led the way in defining and, at times, expanding the EU's authority. The responsibility for actually making the most important decisions lies elsewhere, but the Commission initiates most new programs and is responsible for implementing them once they are enacted.

Until 2004, the Commission had twenty members who served renewable five-year terms. Britain, France, Germany, Italy, and Spain each had two commissioners. Traditionally, one of them was named by the governing party or coalition, and the other by the opposition. The other ten countries had one commissioner each.

After the expansions of 2004 and 2007, the Commission was redesigned to have one member from each country. Once the Lisbon Treaty goes fully into effect, the Commission will be reduced back to 20 members, with states nominating members on a rotating basis (see Table 7.6).

Commissioners are nominated by their home governments and are approved by the Council using the qualified majority vote system to be discussed shortly. Most commissioners are prominent politicians in their home countries, and their independence from leaders there is often questioned. For example, the current commissioner responsible for the internal market, Michel Barnier, joined the Commission after a long and distinguished career in the Gaullist party in France.

After they are appointed, Commission members swear an oath of allegiance to the EU and are not supposed to take instructions from their national government. Given their prior careers, however, it is not always clear how rigorously such a rule could be enforced. In some ways, the Commission looks like a national cabinet, but we should not push that analogy too far. Most obviously, because its members are chosen by twenty-eight different governments, there is far more diversity and disagreement than we would expect in a national executive.

The Commission inevitably reflects the personality, style, and preferences of its president. Under Delors, the Commission assembled a staff of dynamic young civil servants who helped him turn his agenda into policy, often against the wishes of some of his reluctant fellow commissioners and the national governments.

In reaction to Delors' impact, the governments of the member states (especially Great Britain) were reluctant to choose a successor who would be anywhere near as prominent or dynamic. None of his successors, Santer, Prodi, and the current incumbent, **Jose Manuel Barroso** (1956–), have had that kind of dramatic impact.

Along with the new president and foreign minister, the Commission is the EU's permanent executive. It supervises the work of the twenty-two directorates general and eight services, which roughly correspond to the departments run by members of a national cabinet.

The Commission also supervises 2,500 high-ranking civil servants and another twenty thousand staff members. Some of these men and women are on loan from their national governments, but the overwhelming majority are permanent EU employees on career tracks reminiscent of the French ENArques and the German *Beamten*.

The Commission's most important job is to propose new laws, which the EU refers to as directives. The Treaty of Rome and later agreements gave it the exclusive right to put new policy proposals on the EU's agenda. Although agenda setting is by no means the same as the ability to pass legislation, the Commission has used this power to become the driving force behind most of the initiatives that ended up strengthening the EU as a whole.

On a day-to-day basis, the Commission's primary job is to write detailed rules. Commission drafts immediately have the force of law in some minor and technical policy areas. Otherwise, its drafts have to be approved by the Council and the Parliament.

The Council of Ministers

If the Commission represents the supranational side of the EU, the Council of Ministers shows us the continued power of the national governments. The Council actually meets in several guises, whose specific structures—if not their powers—vary considerably.

In the beginning, the Council met when needed. National governments would send the cabinet member concerned with the issue under consideration. Over the years, the Council has become more formally organized in two distinct ways.

TABLE 7.6 Presidents of the European Commission

START OF TERM	NAME
1958	Walter Hallstein
1967	Jean Rey
1970	Franco-Maria Malfatti
1972	Sicco Mansholt
1973	Francois-Xavier Ortoli
1977	Roy Jenkins
1981	Gaston Thorn
1985	Jacques Delors
1995	Jacques Santer
2000	Romano Prodi
2004	Jose Manuel Barroso

© Cengage Learning

SERGIO BARRENECHEA/EPA/Newscom

EU leaders and their hosts at a press conference following a summit on the EU and the Americas.

First, national governments still send their relevant ministers to make policy decisions and consult on specific issues. The foreign ministers meet monthly as the General Affairs Council, as do the finance ministers in the Economic and Financial Council (ECOFIN).

Second, the heads of state now meet at least three times a year in summits, which are known as the European Council. Most major decisions are made and/or announced at these events, although the meetings themselves normally ratify agreements already completed by the national governments and the Secretariat.

Until 2009, the presidency of the Council as a whole and leadership summits rotated from country to country every six months. That country's chief executive chaired each Council meeting, represented the EU at diplomatic functions, and issued its public declarations. The Treaty of Lisbon turned the presidency into a troika (from the Russian word for three) of countries serving eighteen months each, with one leaving every six months.

Since then, the Council has elected a full-time president and foreign minister. The first two people to hold those positions, Herman van Rompuy (1947–) and Baroness Catherine Ashton (1956–), were not major European leaders at the time they were appointed, and it remains to be seen how these new institutions will evolve.

Both versions of the Council operate in more or less the same way. In order for most Commission initiatives to become law, they have to be approved by the Council. Since the passage of the SEA, the Council has had to share

most of its decision-making power with the Parliament and Commission and can override parliamentary objections only if it acts unanimously.

As we also saw earlier, the unanimity principle that often paralyzed the EEC early in its history has been eliminated except for the most dramatic new initiatives, including the admission of new members. Otherwise, the Council uses qualified majority voting. Each country is assigned a number of votes in rough proportion to its share of the EU population, which it casts as a bloc (see Table 7.7).

The formula used to allocate those votes is due to change after the next European parliament is elected in 2014, although members can decide to continue using the old one for three additional years. Whenever the change occurs, there will be a total of 345 votes, with the number each country casts determined by its population. Thus, Germany, France, Britain, and Italy will have 29 votes, while Malta will have 3 and Latvia, Estonia, Cyprus, Slovenia, and Luxembourg will have 4 each.

To pass, a Commission proposal must win Council votes representing more than half of the countries that together have at least 55 percent of their population. If the Council votes on something other than a Commission initiative, it will need votes representing 72 percent of the population to pass. To simplify things a bit, 255 votes will be needed to pass most directives, and 91 votes will be enough to block anything. The system tends to over-represent small countries since all four of the largest ones would have to vote

TABLE 7.7 Size and Voting Power in the European Union: Prior to Treaty of Lisbon

COUNTRY	POPULATION IN MILLIONS	SEATS IN EUROPEAN PARLIAMENT	VOTES IN QUALIFIED MAJORITY VOTING
Germany	82.0	99	29
United Kingdom	59.4	78	29
France	59.1	78	29
Italy	57.7	7	29
Spain	39.4	54	27
Poland	38.6	54	27
Romania	21.7	35	14
Netherlands	15.8	27	13
Greece	10.6	24	12
Czech Republic	10.3	24	12
Belgium	10.2	22	12
Hungary	10.0	22	12
Portugal	9.9	22	12
Sweden	8.9	19	10
Austria	8.1	18	10
Bulgaria	7.7	18	10
Slovakia	5.4	14	7
Denmark	5.4	14	7
Finland	5.2	14	7
Ireland	3.7	13	7
Lithuania	3.7	13	7
Latvia	2.4	9	4
Slovenia	2.0	7	4
Estonia	1.4	7	4
Cyprus	0.8	6	4
Luxembourg	0.4	6	4
Malta	0.4	5	3

© Cengage Learning

together in order to block a draft directive. Yet, it will be difficult to form a qualifying majority without the support of two or three of the big countries.

In practice, these technical details are not likely to have much of an impact. The full European Council rarely votes, because it reaches most of its decisions by consensus instead.

The European Parliament

Scholars and politicians worry about the democratic deficit in part because the European Parliament has always been by far the EU's weakest institution. Until 1979, members of Parliament, or MEPs, were chosen by national governments. Thus, they tended to act as emissaries of their political parties at home and docilely voted the way their leaders wanted them to on matters over which they didn't have much leverage to begin with (www.europarl.europa.eu).

Since then, MEPs have been directly elected, and the powers of the Parliament have grown. The SEA gave the Parliament more influence by instituting a cooperation procedure for most legislation now known as codecision. The Council and Commission have to submit new directives to the Parliament for approval. If the Parliament and the Council agree, the proposed directive is adopted. If not, the Parliament has to be consulted again, at which point one of three things can occur:

- 1 If the Parliament agrees or takes no action within three months, the Council's bill is adopted.
- 2 If the Parliament proposes amendments, they must be considered by the Commission within a month.
- 3 If the Parliament rejects the Council's position altogether, the Council can only adopt the initiative if it votes to do so unanimously.

The Parliament now has the right to approve all nominees to the Commission and can remove the entire Commission if a vote of censure passes by a two-thirds margin. The Parliament also has to approve the budget.

The last two treaties altered the size of the Parliament, which will reach its "permanent" number of 751 members after the 2014 election. The fact that the parliament is so large contributes to the psychological distance many Europeans feel from the EU and thus is a major contributor to the democratic deficit.

The European Court of Justice

The European Court of Justice (ECJ) is more powerful than the highest courts in almost all of its member states (curia.europa.eu/jcms/jcms/Jo2_7024/). Each government appoints one member to the ECJ. It also has nine advocates-general who aid it in its work. The court rarely meets as a whole. Instead, it sits in smaller "chambers" for all but the most important cases. No votes or dissenting opinions are published.

In a typical year, the ECJ hears more than four hundred cases that reach it through a number of routes. The Council, Commission, and Parliament can challenge each other's actions. Member states can contest EU laws and regulations. Individuals and firms can sue the EU. However, states can bring cases against each other only if the claimant can show it had been directly harmed. Over the years, the court has overturned actions by the other EU institutions, all member states, and hundreds of private companies and individuals.

Shortly after it was created, the ECJ asserted that the states had relinquished some of their sovereignty by ratifying the Treaty of Rome and subsequent accords. In other words, it ruled that it practiced American-style constitutional law because it had the right of judicial review, which few national supreme courts enjoy. It has routinely ruled that European laws and regulations take precedence over national law.

Among the most important of the ECJ's decisions was the seemingly innocuous 1979 Cassis de Dijon case. Cassis is a liqueur that, when combined with white wine, makes the smooth, sweet, and potent drink known as *kir royal*. The tricky part politically is that "true" cassis is only produced from black currants grown near Dijon, France. A German firm wanted to import cassis, but the national government banned it ostensibly because it was not alcoholic enough to qualify as a liqueur but contained too much alcohol to be considered a wine under German law. The court held that the Bundesmonopolverwaltung für Branntwein (the Federal Monopoly Agency for Spirits) was really trying to protect German producers of ersatz cassis. The justices therefore ruled in favor of the importer, arguing that if cassis met French standards for a liqueur it should qualify under Germany's as well.

The decision introduced the notion of mutual recognition, which holds that member states must recognize standards adopted by other countries except under the most unusual of circumstances. That, in turn, meant that the Commission could avoid the cumbersome task of harmonizing rules and regulations across national lines and simply assert that if one national government decided that a good or service met its standards, it had to be accepted by all of them.

Another ruling with broad—and even fewer political—ramifications came in 1995. Jean-Marc Bosman was a mediocre Belgian soccer player whose contract was expiring. Bosman wanted to sign with a new team in France, much like a free agent in American sports. However, his old team and the Belgian football authorities would not let him do so. Bosman took his case to the ECJ, arguing that what the Europeans call transfer restrictions violated the provisions of the Maastricht Treaty regarding the free movement of labor within the EU.

The court ruled in Bosman's favor and simultaneously threw out not only the rules restricting the freedom of players to move but others limiting the number of foreigners who could play for a team at any one time. The wealthiest teams in England, Spain, Italy, and Germany immediately went on spending sprees, signing players from around the EU and beyond. The impact of the decision was almost immediate. In the 2001 final of the European Champions League, London's Chelsea faced Rome's Atalanta. Not a single player on Chelsea's starting team was born or raised in the United Kingdom; in fact, Chelsea had more Italian players than did Atalanta!

The European Central Bank

The Maastricht Treaty created the European Central Bank to provide the fiscal and monetary management that had previously been the responsibility of its national equivalents. It was modeled heavily on the German *Bundesbank* and located in the same city, Frankfurt-am-Main, which gives the EU a *de facto* fourth capital city (www.ecb.int/ecb/html/index.en.html).

The headquarters of the European Central Bank on the Main River in Frankfurt, Germany.

Like its German namesake, the ECB has made controlling inflation its highest priority. According to its website, "The ECB's main task is to maintain the euro's purchasing power and thus price stability in the euro area." It does that by setting interest rates, coordinating policies with the EU's remaining national banks, maintaining stable currency values, and issuing euros. It is run by a six-member governing board which can draw on the assistance of representatives from the now largely powerless national banks. Like the Commission, its board members are not allowed to accept instructions or advice from their national governments.

The ECB has become the most important institution in charting the EU's response to the eurozone's fiscal crisis. We will focus on that in the policy section below. For now, it is enough to note that the EU's newest major institution is currently its most important and is likely to remain so as long as economic issues remain on center stage.

The European Union and National Sovereignty

The most important question to ask about the EU in a comparative politics course is whether it could supplant the state as the most important actor in European governance. As is the case in much of this chapter, the answer is ambiguous.

It is tempting to follow the lead of most international relations experts and argue that the nation-state is not about to go the way of the medieval European principalities. This certainly is true if we focus on questions of national security and identity.

However, if we focus instead on economic or social policy, the EU seems a lot more powerful. In those areas, its powers certainly limit the freedom of member states to make and enforce their own policies whether or not analysts explicitly mention the declining sovereignty of the twenty-seven member states.

The two issues that follow may not be earth shattering, but in some ways that is the point. On a day-to-day basis, the EU has taken on many of the powers that have been the province of nation-states for the last several hundred years—at least outside of the traditional domain of international relations scholars.

The first involves chocolate. As we have already seen, the EU devised common standards for thousands of goods and services as part of its goal of creating a single market. In 1973 it issued Directive 73-241 on the "harmonization" of chocolate recipes. As one British observer put it:

> This directive was drawn up in the early, heady days of European integration, when European leaders believed that all products must be harmonized in every member state if the single market was to operate properly. All food had to be made to the same

specification. Drawing up a European chocolate recipe meant agreeing on rules on such ingredients as vegetable and cocoa fat. Directive 73-241 declared that chocolate shall be: "the product obtained from cocoa nib, cocoa mass, cocoa powder and sucrose, with or without added cocoa butter, having, without prejudice to the definition of chocolate vermicelli, gianduja nut chocolate and converture chocolate, a minimum total dry cocoa solids content of 35 percent—at least 34 percent of nonfat cocoa solids and 18 percent of cocoa butter—these weights to be calculated after the weight of the additions provided for in paragraph five and six have been deducted.[3]

Chocolate became a problem because candy manufacturers in Britain and a few other countries did not meet those standards. British consumers apparently liked their chocolate with less cocoa nib. After a brief tiff, the European bureaucrats allowed the British to "opt out" of these requirements, and there was something of a two-tiered chocolate market for the next twenty years.

In the mid-1990s, the chocolate controversy reared its ugly head once again. French and Belgian chocolatiers claimed that inferior and cheaper British candy was undermining their markets. They threatened to go to the ECJ and demand a ruling forcing the British companies to use the term vegolate instead. The court put an end to the litigation by invoking the mutual recognition principle to allow the British to continue selling their products as chocolate.

Second, in one of its most controversial moves, the EU banned the export of British beef in 1996. Over the previous decade, thousands of British cattle had come down with BSE, known to most people by its nickname—mad cow disease. In March 1996, the British government published research findings that linked BSE with Creutzfeld-Jakob Disease (CJD), which is fatal to humans. The announcement touched off a furor on both sides of the English Channel. Within days the Council voted to ban the sale of British beef in the EU, which also amounted to a ban on exports to the entire world. The British government was furious because no more than fifteen people had actually come down with CJD. British agriculture minister Quentin Hogg (the pundits had great fun with his name) floated a plan that would only have required the UK to slaughter a million cows in an attempt to eradicate the disease. That was not enough for the EU, which insisted on a total "cull" of the herd before allowing British beef back on the market.

---

[3]Sarah Helm, "The Woman from Mars," *Prospect (UK)*, March 1996, 21.

Negotiations dragged on into 1999, even though there was virtually no chance that anyone could actually contract CJD. Nonetheless, politicians on the European continent, leery of public opinion at home, kept the ban in place. Finally, when the cull of the herds progressed to the point that no cow born before 1996 could have entered the food chain, the Commission lifted the ban.

The Complexity of European Union Decision Making

Decision making in the EU is more complex—and confusing—than in any of the countries we have considered so far, for two main reasons.

First, the EU has more interests to balance. As the term multilevel governance suggests, it adds a new tier of decision makers to the already complex mix we saw in Chapters 3 through 6.

Second, the complexity is also a reflection of the fact that the EU is new and still being built, which makes it quite different from the states covered in the rest of Part 2. In some areas (e.g., trade), European institutions and practices are well developed; in others (e.g., defense), they are not.

When all is said and done, however, it does seem safe to reach at least one tentative conclusion about the EU's "state." It is most successful in those policy arenas where the interests of the major national governments and its own institutions coincide as they did in the months leading up to the signing of the Maastricht Treaty. When those interests diverge—as has often been the case since Maastricht—it becomes more difficult for further European integration to proceed.

Next Steps?

The EU is not likely to either broaden or deepen in the next few years.

Turkey is the most important country with a membership application pending. However, there is little or no likelihood that it will be admitted soon. Most objections center on Turkey's human rights record, especially regarding its Kurdish minority. Although few people mention it publicly, the fact that Turkey is a predominantly Muslim country currently governed by a pro-Islamic party has not helped its case. Other countries in Eastern Europe seem even further away from being voted in as members.

Further deepening is even more problematic given the recent constitutional difficulties and the economic crisis. There undoubtedly will be some tinkering with the existing institutions. There is even talk of yet another treaty. But whatever happens, the changes will almost certainly be on the margins.

However, the next truly important step in building what could potentially be a "United States of Europe" would be the commitment to a common foreign and security policy—the third pillar of the post-Maastricht EU. As noted at the beginning of the chapter, the EU is committed to that on paper. However, establishing it has not been easy, to say the least.

Some progress has been made. The EU has created a rapid deployment force that will be able to respond to humanitarian disasters as well as the kinds of conflicts that devastated the former Yugoslavia in the 1990s. It has also made great strides in determining how it can coordinate its activities with NATO, the Organization for Security and Co-Operation in Europe (OSCE), and other bodies whose membership overlaps with, but is not the same as, its own.

However, as the debates within Europe over the war in Iraq showed, the European states do sometimes still view their national interests differently. Most notably, France and Germany opposed the U.S. declaration of war on Iraq. The United Kingdom, Italy, and Spain supported the George W. Bush administration, though Spain pulled out after a socialist victory at the polls following the March 11, 2004, terrorist attack there. In other words, foreign policy is one of those areas where deepening has not progressed as far as it has with the economy. As a result, national governments and their perceived national interests are likely to trump communitywide ones unless and until the consensus on arenas for cooperation expands.

Public Policy in the European Union

The EU will spend about $1.5 trillion between 2014 and 2020 in dozens of policy areas. Some are big ticket items, such as the $30 billion it will spend on reversing climate change. Some of it is below most people's radar screens, including such activities as sponsoring research on high technology and coordinating student exchanges. Here, we will focus on the two that illustrate what the EU has done on issues that are frankly far more important than chocolate or beef: the creation of a single market and the CAP.

The Internal Market

Economic integration has always been the EU's most important policy goal. Indeed, despite the uncertainties surrounding the euro, its most significant direct accomplishment has been the creation of what is, for all intents and purposes, a single internal market.

Goods and Services

As we saw earlier, that began with the gradual abolition of tariffs and other barriers to trade. By the time the SEA was up for consideration, most of the major legal barriers had been overcome. Those that remained were technical in nature but were also very easy for the average consumer to see. Truckers, for example, could spend hours filling out paperwork or having their cargoes inspected before they were allowed to cross national borders. Although it may be hard to believe, such rules and regulations added as much as 10 percent to the cost of transporting goods from one country to another. One study estimated that if you took a dollar and exchanged it for the national currency in a member state and continued to do so in the then fourteen other countries, you would have under $.50 left when you reached the last one's ATM machines.

As we saw with the Crème de Cassis case, each country had its own standards for determining the goods that could legally be sold in its market, which it used to keep imports from other EU countries out. The same held for professional licenses, which meant that doctors, lawyers, beauticians, and so on could only work in the country in which they were trained. National governments were required to buy from domestic firms whenever possible, which accounted for nearly 10 percent of the EU's total production of goods and services in the 1980s.

Most of those barriers disappeared when the SEA's rules and regulations were put fully in place in 1992. Goods that meet the standards of one country are assumed to meet the standards of all as was the case in the chocolate/vegolate dispute. The same is now true for most professional licenses—though not for lawyers, reflecting the continued differences among national legal systems. Finally, financial institutions are free to invest and loan money throughout the EU. Gone, too, are most border checks when travelers travel from one EU member to another, although Britain and Ireland were allowed to opt out of the so-called Schengen Agreement.

The reasons for moving to a fully open internal market were laid out in a report the economist Paolo Cecchini prepared for the Commission in 1988. He predicted that removing the remaining barriers to trade would lead to increased private investment, higher productivity, lower costs, and reduced prices. European industry, in turn, would become more profitable, stimulating more growth, jobs, and government revenue.

In the short run, Europe fell short of those expectations. The recession of the early 1990s slowed growth everywhere. Cecchini could not have anticipated the political changes that would sweep Europe and divert billions of dollars from the EU and its member states eastward. Still, there seems to be little question that the removal of these barriers has had the kind of impact the framers of the SEA had in mind in the long term.

Regular visitors to Europe cannot help but notice the explosion of transnational enterprises facilitated by the easing of these restrictions. The EU is not always a major actor in these endeavors, but the opening of the market has made the ones described here, and dozens of others, much easier to create or expand. For example, Airbus, which makes commercial jet airplanes, is a joint effort on the part of French, German, Spanish, and British companies and is now Boeing's only serious competitor. In the automobile industry, Fiat forged close links with Peugeot, and in 1999 Ford bought Volvo. In the last few years Daimler-Benz bought and abandoned Chrysler, only to have the rejuvenated Fiat assume its stake in the then-troubled American automaker. In 1985 the Commission established Eureka, a joint research and development program to help Europeans compete with Japanese and American computer, telecommunication, and other high-tech firms.

The internationalization of European businesses through the EU seems to have led them to be more aggressive globally as well. The most notable example is the tremendous increase in European investment in the United States. To cite but a few prominent examples, Renault bought Mack Trucks in 1990 and then sold it to Volvo in 2001, yet another European firm now owned by Ford. Michelin acquired Uniroyal Goodrich, making it the largest tire manufacturer in the world. Britain's Martin Sorrell purchased two of the largest advertising agencies in the United States, the Ogilvy Group and J. Walter Thompson, and public relations giant Hill and Knowlton.

For our purposes, though, the important thing to understand is that the single market has had a tremendous impact on both European governments and their citizens. States now have far less control over what is made and sold inside their borders. Of course, policy differences remain from country to country. Britain, for example, still imposes higher taxes on liquor than France and has strict rules regarding the import of pets into the country. Such examples aside, governments have ceded much of their control over microeconomic policy.

The single market has expanded the options available to consumers. German supermarket shoppers can now purchase French wine, Italian pasta, and Spanish oranges more cheaply than before the trade barriers came down. French consumers find that Rovers, Fiats, or Volkswagens are now as affordable as Renaults, Citroëns, or Peugeots.

The single market has not benefited all Europeans. Increased competitive pressures have forced hundreds of inefficient firms into bankruptcy, leading to at least temporary unemployment for their workers.

Nonetheless, there is little doubt that the EU has made a considerable contribution to economic growth since 1957. Among other things, a 1999 Commission report suggested that the single market was responsible for creating as many as nine hundred thousand jobs, adding as much as 1.5 percent to per capita income, reducing inflation by a similar amount, and increasing trade in goods and direct foreign investment in the EU by about 15 percent each. Its contribution may be even more important in some less visible policy arenas, as we saw in the discussion of the Bosman ruling.

The true impact of the EU goes beyond the statistical indicators. I was fortunate to live and teach in England from 1995 to 1998. Because of the EU, I could have any major European newspaper delivered to my door the next morning. According to the owner of the corner store that delivered the papers, citizens of fourteen of the then fifteen member states were living in that village of less than three thousand residents. Because EU students pay the equivalent of in-state tuition anywhere in the EU, I had students from France, Greece, Spain, Finland, Denmark, Germany, Portugal, Ireland, Italy, and Belgium, as well as the United Kingdom, which made teaching highly enjoyable.

Monetary Union

As the discussion of the fiscal crisis in the eurozone suggests, monetary union has not led to a fully integrated economy. It was, however, a logical next step following the creation of a single internal market.

From the Treaty of Rome on, the most visionary European leaders believed that monetary union was the biggest step toward fully integrating Europe. To see why, think about what the United States would be like if the states had their own currencies. It would be all but impossible for the federal government to coordinate economic policy, and it would be costly and complicated for companies to do business across state lines.

Monetary union, however, was a long time coming. The first significant steps were taken in 1979 with the creation of the European Monetary System (EMS), which had two broad features. First, it created the European Currency Unit (ECU), which was used in international business transactions. The ECU existed purely for accounting purposes and enabled companies to avoid paying commissions when they converted funds from one currency to another. Second, it also established the Exchange Rate Mechanism (ERM), whereby all the currencies floated together in global markets. No currency was allowed to move more than 5 percent above or below the ERM average. If one of them came close, the national central banks would intervene in financial markets to bring it back into line.

The reforms were small steps toward deeper economic integration. The ECU simplified business dealings and reduced the substantial costs that accompany frequent currency conversions. The ERM gave a degree of predictability to European financial markets so that, for example, Fiat in Italy could be reasonably certain how many francs or pesetas, as well as how many lire, it could get for its cars.

It took another twenty years to create the euro. The very fact that it exists is one of the reasons why the EU is the world's most successful international organization to date.

As should also already be clear, the euro is no panacea. Only seventeen of the twenty-eight member states use it. Not all of the new members met the conditions that allowed them to join. Denmark, Sweden, and the United Kingdom decided not to join the zone. And, of course, the EU is experiencing the growing pains from using the same currency in very different economies without strong institutions to manage other financial transactions.

There is more involved than "simply" having a single currency. Previously, governments determined their own fiscal and monetary policies, in particular, setting basic interest rates for lenders and savers. Now that power has been transferred almost entirely to the European Central Bank, which sets a common interest rate for countries with economies as diverse as Germany's and Greece's.

Obviously, not everything about the euro is working as well as its founders had hoped. National economic differences were exacerbated by the great recession that began in 2008. As we saw at the start of the chapter, the richer countries have had to bail out the poorer ones in what many fear will turn into a never-ending transfer of funds. Consequently, anti-European sentiment grew in Germany and other creditor countries, as did resentment toward the EU in countries that received much of the aid and saw their ability to control their own economic future evaporate.

This is one of the many reasons why the euro is controversial and is seen by some observers as a "make it or break it" issue for the EU. Even before the crisis, many political leaders, especially in Britain, saw their local currency as an important symbol of national pride, and abandoning it is seen as an unacceptable loss of national sovereignty. But just as important, now that the euro is in place, there may be no going back. Nothing in political life is irreversible, but it is hard to imagine the seventeen members abandoning the euro and reintroducing their own currencies.

So far, debate on the European Monetary Union (EMU) has focused largely on whether it makes sense economically—an issue that is far beyond the scope of this chapter. Here, it is enough to see that it will have a tremendous impact on the balance of political power in at least two ways. First, it can strengthen the EU as a whole because the euro is already one of the world's three leading currencies along

Comparative Emphasis: Globalization

The EU is one of the best vehicles we have for illustrating the impact of globalization. Critics have properly pointed out that European economies and cultures would have opened up to a considerable degree without the EU. There can be little doubt, however, that it has sped up the flow of people, information, goods, and money within its borders and has generally been a major advocate for liberalizing trade as well. It also demonstrates that even the strongest powers are vulnerable to global pressures. ∎

with the dollar and the yen. Second, it provides yet another area in which national governments are ceding some of their sovereignty to a supranational body over which they have relatively little day-to-day control—whatever the legal statutes and treaty provisions might formally say.

But the fact is that the EU is the one and only international organization to have its own currency, which is a major symbol of national (or international) sovereignty.

The Common Agricultural Policy

Not everything the EU has done has been successful. The Common Agricultural Policy (CAP), in particular, has virtually no supporters. *The Economist* went so far as to call it the "single most idiotic system of economic mismanagement that the rich western countries have ever devised."[4]

The CAP reflects two important political dynamics. First, it demonstrates how pressure on member states can lead to policies that impede progress toward a more united Europe. Second, some recent reforms to the CAP have been forced on the EU by other international bodies, thereby demonstrating that it is also affected by aspects of globalization itself.

But that does not mean that the CAP never made any sense. In the 1950s, there were about 15 million farmers in the original EEC countries combined. Although their numbers were declining rapidly, farmers were still a major political force, especially in France, where they lobbied

persuasively to keep small, inefficient family farms alive. Meanwhile, countries with fewer working farms needed to import food and wanted to keep prices as low as possible. Thus, agriculture was a divisive issue from the beginning and almost destroyed the EEC in the early 1960s. The members finally reached a compromise in 1966 and created the CAP. First, it took steps to modernize inefficient farms so that they could be more competitive in the European market. Second, to ease the fears of farmers whose livelihood was threatened, the EC established the European Agricultural Guidance and Guarantee Fund (EAGGF), which gave them subsidies and guaranteed the purchase of surplus goods at artificially high prices.

Over the years, the modernizing side of the CAP fell by the wayside. Payments to farmers consumed more than half of the EC budget. By the early 1970s, food prices in Europe were two to four times higher than they would have been had they been determined by market forces. In 1991 alone, the EC purchased 25 million tons of surplus cereal grains, eight hundred thousand tons of butter, and seven hundred thousand tons of other dairy products. Pundits joked about its butter mountains and wine lakes.

The CAP was also a major stumbling block in the Uruguay round of the GATT (General Agreement on Tariffs and Trade) negotiations, which led to the creation of the WTO (World Trade Organization). American objections to the EAGGF payments almost led to a trade war between the United States and Europe in 1992 even though the United States still heavily subsidized its own farmers. In the end, the EU and the other parties reached a compromise in which the EU agreed to scale back subsidies and guaranteed payments by about a third. Nonetheless, the continued political clout of agricultural interest groups kept the CAP alive, leaving Europe with extremely inefficient farms and burdening the EU's budget in the process, about 45 percent of which goes to the CAP.

As always, the CAP remains controversial. The Commission opened a debate in 2010 about its future but is not likely to reach a conclusion for a few years. It may well end subsidies to individual farmers, who get $500 million a year and, thus, oppose any change. Other reformers revise the CAP as part of a broader plan to make EU policy in general more "green."

The Media

The media in the EU illustrate the importance of things that do not happen in political life. Put simply, there is very little feedback because of the way the EU is structured and the way people participate (or do not participate, as the case may be) in it.

---

[4]Cited in Helen Wallace and William Wallace, eds., *Policy Making in the European Union*, 4th ed. (Oxford: Oxford University Press, 2000), 182.

How can that be for something that is this important to almost every European? It's simple. Coverage of the EU in the press is spotty and, as in most areas of political life, concentrates on its problems, not its accomplishments. There is, for instance, a mere handful of English-language newspapers that concentrate on the EU. The largest and best of them is the *European Voice,* which has about 18,000 subscribers, half of whom work for the EU. It struggles to survive. Coverage in national newspapers and television takes second place to almost everything else, such as in the British tabloid press.

When people are drawn to events in the EU, they tend to focus on the often demagogic claims about "faceless bureaucrats" in Brussels stealing their power. By contrast, as also noted previously, very few people think of themselves primarily as Europeans, even though the number of people living, working, and even marrying across national borders is growing rapidly.

This lack of media attention overlaps with the notion of the democratic deficit. Critics properly point out that the size of the EU as well as the fact that the European Parliament has relatively few—and weak—mechanisms for enforcing accountability make it difficult for average people to have much of an impact on decision making within it. In other words, the perceived lack of political clout magnifies the sense of distance and disinterest evident in most polls.

The lack of Europeanness is also indirectly reflected in the mass media, through which people learn about political life at the national and supranational levels. Attempts have been made to create everything from Europe-wide soap operas to political newspapers. The only real success story is Eurosport, a satellite TV provider that sends out a single video feed of mostly second-tier events with audio channels in all the major languages. There are two different television systems—PAL (used in Britain, Germany, and the Netherlands, among others) and SECAM (most notably used in France and Spain). Viewers with televisions that use one cannot watch programs on the other. Although people can get all the major European newspapers wherever they live, the fact remains that these papers are all nationally based.

KEY TERMS

Concepts
austerity
broadening
codecision
deepening
democratic deficit
euro
multilevel governance
qualified majority voting
subsidiarity
supranational
three pillars
unanimity principle

People
Barroso, Jose Manuel
Delors, Jacques
Monnet, Jean
Spaak, Paul-Henri

Acronyms
CAP

CFSP
COREPER
EC
ECB
ECJ
ECSC
EEC
EMS
EMU
EU
SEA

Organizations, Places, and Events
Commission
Committee of Permanent
   Representatives (COREPER)
Common Agricultural Policy (CAP)
Common Foreign and Security Policy
   (CFSP)
Common Market
Council of Ministers

European Central Bank (ECB)
European Coal and Steel Community
   (ECSC)
European Community (EC)
European Court of Justice (ECJ)
European Economic Community
   (EEC)
European Monetary System (EMS)
European Monetary Union (EMU)
European Parliament
European Union (EU)
eurozone
Maastricht Treaty
Marshall Plan
Schengen Agreement
Single European Act (SEA)
Treaty of Amsterdam
Treaty of Lisbon
Treaty of Nice
Treaty of Rome

USEFUL WEBSITES

The EU's website is an excellent portal to everything the Union does, and the information is available in more than twenty languages.

www.europa.eu

Many of the academic centers that focus on the EU have websites with good collections of links to other online EU material. Among the best are the European Union Studies Association and the libraries at the University of California-Berkeley, the University of Pittsburgh, and the New York University Law School.

www.eustudies.org

www.lib.berkeley.edu

www.library.pitt.edu

www.law.nyu.edu/library

european-convention.eu.int

European Voice is the only weekly newspaper on the EU and is published by *The Economist*. Its website provides the most comprehensive, up-to-date information about things European.

www.european-voice.com

There are many "euroskeptic" websites that are highly critical of the deepening and broadening of the EU. The website mentioned below has links to many such websites.

www.euro-sceptic.org

FURTHER READING

Bellamy, Richard, and Alex Warleigh. *Citizenship and Governance in the European Union.* New York: Continuum, 2002. A theorist and EU specialist look at the overlap (or lack thereof) between the way the EU is run and how average citizens respond to it.

Checkel, Jeffrey, and Peter Katzenstein, eds. *European Identity.* New York: Cambridge University Press, 2009. A bit of a tough read for undergrads, but it explores why there has been both an expansion and a contraction in support for the EU.

Dinan, Desmond. *An Ever Closer Union: An Introduction to the European Community*, 2nd ed. Boulder, CO: Lynne Rienner, 1999. The most comprehensive survey of European integration and its impact up to and beyond Maastricht.

Moravschik, Andrew. *The Choice for Europe.* Ithaca, NY: Cornell University Press, 1999. The best overview of EU history through Maastricht.

Reid, T. R. *The United States of Europe.* New York: Penguin, 2005. An extensive overview of post-Maastricht events by a very thoughtful—and very funny—former journalist at the *Washington Post.*

Rosamond, Ben. *Theories of European Integration.* Basingstoke, UK: Palgrave, 2000. A look at the EU through the lens of various theories of integration and international relations.

Ross, George. *Jacques Delors and European Integration.* New York: Oxford University Press, 1995. An insider-like account of the workings of the Commission by one of the leading American experts on French politics, to whom Delors gave unprecedented access late in his presidency. Not the easiest read, but probably the most insightful book on the EU ever written.

Sbragia, Alberta M., ed. *Euro-Politics: Institutions and Policymaking in the "New" European Community.* Washington, D.C.: Brookings Institution, 1992. An anthology that includes articles on most of the critical issues facing the EU; especially strong on the causes and consequences of the Single European Act.

Schmitter, Philippe. *How to Democratize the European Union . . . and Why Bother?* Boulder, CO: Rowman & Littlefield, 2000. A fairly abstract but powerful argument by one of the leading political scientists working on democratization.

© Carlos Caetano/Shutterstock.com

© Cengage Learning

POLITICAL INDICATORS

COUNTRY	GOVERNANCE (score 0–1)	HUMAN DEVELOPMENT (score 0–1)	DEMOCRACY (rank)	PEACE (rank)	CORRUPTION (rank)
China	.588	.687	141	89	75
Russia	.577	.755	117	153	143 (tie)
United Kingdom	.793	.863	16	29	18
United States	.761	.910	19	88	24

8

Socialism cannot exist, no matter where, contrary to the will of the people.

GEORGI ARBATOV

Current and Former Communist Regimes

THE BASICS

REASONABLY DEMOCRATIC	HYBRID	AUTHORITARIAN	MARXIST-LENINIST
Czech Republic	Albania	Azerbaijan	China
	Armenia	Bosnia-Herzegovina	Cuba
Estonia	Belarus	Kazakhstan	People's Republic of Korea
Hungary	Bulgaria	Kirgizstan	Laos
Latvia	Cambodia	Tajikistan	Vietnam
Lithuania	Croatia	Turkmenistan	
Poland	Georgia	Uzbekistan	
Slovenia	Macedonia		
	Moldova		
	Mongolia		
	Montenegro		
	Romania		
	Russia		
	Serbia		
	Slovakia		
	Ukraine		

Crisis? Which Crisis?

Germans are not normally known for their comedy films, and certainly not ones about politics. *Good Bye, Lenin!* is an exception.

The film begins during the peaceful uprising that brought down the Berlin Wall and took East Germany's communist regime with it in 1989. A young man, Alex, joins one of the protests. He did not leave home that day planning to join one of the marches. He sympathized with the demonstrators' demands, but his main reason for joining the protests was to meet a young woman who becomes the love of his life and his mother's nurse and caretaker.

Alex gets arrested almost by happenstance. To make matters worse, his staunchly communist mother, Christine, just happens to wander by the demonstration and watches as he is taken into custody. Shocked by what her son is doing, she suffers a heart attack and slips into a coma. When she regains consciousness months later, the German Democratic Republic (DDR) has disappeared and has been united with the West as part of the Federal Republic of Germany (West Germany).

The plot takes another implausible twist when Christine's doctor tells Alex that any serious shock could kill her, including any inkling that East Germany is gone. Alex understandably does everything he can to convince his house-bound mother that East Germany still exists. He has friends make fake television and radio broadcasts, including one that seems to show disgruntled residents of West Berlin crossing the wall to move to the east. He madly shops for her beloved brand of pickles, which are no longer available because the company that made them has gone bankrupt. He comes up with ingenious explanations for why his mother can hear what she thinks are illegal Western broadcasts through her poorly soundproofed walls. Christine eventually wanders out of the house and sees ads for BMW and Coke. Alex convinces her that Coca-Cola is a communist invention and that the BMW ads target the many Westerners who have fled to the east to avoid crime and inequality.

More than twenty years have passed since the time of *Goodbye, Lenin!* Most of this book's readers were not even born in 1989. You should therefore ask the same question I do every time I revise Part 3 of *Comparative Politics*. Does this book still need an entire section devoted to a form of government that no long exists—at least in the form Alex's mother had grown to love but most of the rest of us were glad to see disappear? Each time, I start by planning to drop it, and each time I change my mind.

Alex and his family may have said good bye to Lenin, but Lenin's remains are still powerful enough a quarter century after the wall came down to keep Part 3. Many of the visible signs of the Communist past are gone. If you go to any of the websites about my son-in-law's home town, Bitola, Macedonia, you will not find any traces of the half century the League of Yugoslavian Communists ruled the country. But his family lives in an austere apartment complex built in the 1960s. It sits across the street from a mostly abandoned military base. His high school is still named for **Josip Broz Tito**, Yugoslavia's idiosyncratic Communist leader who was in power for more than thirty years.

For our purposes, it is important to see that the lingering impact of communism runs far deeper than buildings in Bitola or the memories of a movie character.

There aren't many people like Christine who miss the old days of Marxist-Leninist rule. If my in-laws are any indication, few people have any desire to give up their open economy, Internet access, free press, cable television, or malls that stock Western goods and return to the life they led before the wall came down.

Yet, that does not mean that the countries covered in Part 3 have completely shed their communist past. A few—like the former East Germany—have taken important steps toward democracy and capitalism. Even there, however, the transition away from communism is by no means over. As I was writing these lines, the Hungarian government announced plans to arbitrarily revise the constitution to suit its own interests. In other words, even the most promising of them needs a qualifying modifier like the "reasonably" I used in the table "The Basics" on the previous page.

Almost half of the rest have what political scientists have begun calling **hybrid regimes** because they combine aspects of democracy and authoritarianism. More often than we would like to admit, the authoritarian side outweighs the democratic one, as we will see in the next chapter on Russia. Almost a third of them have either kept Marxism-Leninism or replaced their old regimes with new ones that are almost as authoritarian as the one in place before 1989.

In Marxism-Leninism, these countries also have a common historical past that goes a long way toward explaining their political life today, whatever political trajectory they have followed since the Berlin Wall came down. This point is important enough to be worth underscoring before we continue. These countries *are* moving in very different directions today. However, their communist past continues to weigh heavily on them and will undoubtedly do so for years to come.

Many of them (but not Macedonia or the former East Germany) are still led by former communists whose governing styles have not changed all that much. Everywhere, former communists do well at the polls and win their share of elections, sometimes fairly, sometimes not. State ownership and control of the means of production have disappeared almost everywhere except for North Korea and Cuba, but, more often than not, the communist rulers have been replaced by a new economic elite whose members are drawn disproportionately from veterans of the old regime.

Bloody wars have been fought in what used to be Yugoslavia as well as the former Soviet Union. The Central Asian republics remain mired in poverty, and governments there are almost as authoritarian as the communist states they ostensibly replaced.

Thinking About Current and Former Communist Regimes

The cold war ended more than twenty years ago. For someone like me who was born just as it started, photographs like the one on the next page are etched forever in our minds, because we "knew" that the rivalry between the superpowers would be a permanent part of our political lives. Barely two years earlier, then President Ronald Reagan had stood in front of it and uttered these

One of the many people who took a turn at knocking down the Berlin Wall.

famous words, "Mr. Gorbachev, tear down this wall." Those of us who were active in the peace movement at the time were convinced Reagan's speech was simply empty rhetoric and would amount to nothing. We had no idea that so much could change so quickly (www.youtube.com/watch?v=YtYdjbpBk6A). We also had no idea about how uncertain the future would be.

The Bottom Line

Writing about communism in the early twenty-first century is like trying to shoot at a rapidly moving and even more rapidly shrinking target. In 1984, Reagan had used American fears of communism as a major campaign theme in his landslide victory over Walter Mondale. Seven years later, his "focus of evil in the world" was gone.

Who to Include?

When Reagan spoke, it was easy to define what it meant to be a communist country. Unlike what we saw in Part 2 and will see in Part 4, there was almost no ambiguity about the countries to include. The countries highlighted in the

map at the beginning of this chapter were all part of one of the then sixteen states that employed a Marxist-Leninist regime.

The most important of them, by far, was the **Union of Soviet Socialist Republics (USSR)** or **Soviet Union**. The world's first communist regime came to power there as a result of the October revolution in 1917. Only in Mongolia was another successful communist regime created between the two world wars. After World War II, the Soviet Union imposed regimes that were all but carbon copies of its own in Poland, Czechoslovakia, Romania, Bulgaria, Hungary, and the eastern part of Germany. In the West, these countries became known as Soviet satellites. Communist regimes came to power on their own in Yugoslavia and Albania. None is communist today.

Most of the remaining Marxist-Leninist regimes were in Asia. The Chinese Communist Party won its civil war against the Nationalists in 1949, thus bringing the world's most populous country into the communist camp. Meanwhile, the end of World War II left Korea divided. The northern half became the communist-run Democratic People's Republic of Korea. At the same time, a communist insurgency broke out in the French colony of Indochina. After the French were defeated in 1954, it was divided into four independent countries: Laos, Cambodia, and North and South Vietnam. Of the four, only North Vietnam was communist at the time. After two decades of fighting, Marxists seized power in Laos, Cambodia, and a united Vietnam. Laos and Vietnam still have communist regimes.

The last country on the list is Cuba. It officially became an independent country after the Spanish-American War in 1898. For the next sixty years, however, the United States for all intents and purposes ran the country from behind the scenes, while a series of weak and corrupt dictators officially held power. Revolutionaries led by **Fidel Castro** (1926–) overthrew the last of them in 1959. Relations with the United States quickly deteriorated. Cuba became a Soviet ally and adopted Marxism-Leninism in 1961.

Several other countries are occasionally included in lists of communist regimes, such as Nicaragua under the Sandinistas, North Yemen, Angola, and Mozambique. At one point or another, all of them had decidedly left-wing governments. However, they are not included here because they never fully adopted Marxist-Leninist principles.

The Leninist State

Their most important common denominator was a form of leadership devised by **Vladimir Lenin** (1870–1924) for the prerevolutionary **Bolshevik** faction of the Social Democratic Party in Russia. We will explore its characteristics in detail later on in this chapter and the two that follow. Here, it is enough to note two things.

First, the communist party called all the shots—not just in politics. The party controlled the government, media, economy, educational system, and most social and leisure-time activities. Ruling communist parties relied on **democratic centralism**, which meant that they were democratic in name only. Instead, they were led by a tiny group of self-selected and self-perpetuating officials who sat atop a vast hierarchy that critical analysts labeled **totalitarian**.

Second, the Soviet Union dominated the global communist movement until the late 1950s. Other communist regimes adopted Marxism-Leninism and blindly obeyed virtually every command from Moscow. That unity did begin to unravel even while the cold war was at its peak, and most communist countries went through periods when dissidents openly expressed their opposition to the status quo. Nonetheless, most communist regimes were all but clones of the Soviet Union until the very end.

Command Economies

Until the late 1980s, the communist countries had command economies in which the government owned almost everything. Only in Poland and Yugoslavia, for example, did a significant private sector survive in agriculture (see Table 8.1). The economies were managed by a party-dominated state planning committee (*Gosplan* in the Soviet Union). It devised detailed blueprints for what was to be produced, exported, and sold, typically for a five-year period. Managers were appointed by the party to run individual enterprises by carrying out instructions about what to produce issued by the central party leadership.

During the early years of communist rule, central planning led to rapid economic growth. By the 1950s, communist countries were among the world's leaders in the

TABLE 8.1 The Collectively Owned Portion of the Economy in 1967

COUNTRY	AGRICULTURAL LAND (%)	INDUSTRIAL PRODUCTION (%)	RETAIL SALES (%)	NATIONAL INCOME (%)
Bulgaria	99	99	100	95
Hungary	94	99	99	96
Poland	15	100	99	76
East Germany	95	88	79	94
Romania	91	100	100	95
Czechoslovakia	90	100	100	95
Soviet Union	98	100	100	96
Yugoslavia	16	98	NA	77
Weighted average	92	99	98	95

Source: Adapted from Bernard Chavance, *The Transformation of Communist Systems: Economic Reform Since the 1950s*, trans. Charles Hauss (Boulder, CO: Westview Press, 1994), 28.

production of steel, ships, and other heavy industrial goods. The average person's standard of living improved. Homelessness was eliminated in Eastern Europe, and starvation was done away with in China.

By the late 1970s, however, the benefits of centralized planning had vanished, and all of these countries found themselves in economic trouble. On the one hand, an authoritarian state could force people to act in ways that led to rapid economic growth in the early stages of industrialization. On the other hand, coercion was of little use in laying the groundwork for the high-tech industries that are the heart of a more modern economy. Even though most people were far better off than their parents or grandparents had been, slowing economic growth translated into living conditions that lagged far behind those in the West. Everything from housing to health care was mediocre at best—a fact that was driven home to the millions of people who were able to watch Western television shows and movies long before *Good Bye, Lenin!* was made.

Transitions

In other words, by the 1980s, the communist regimes were neither as strong nor as ruthless as the alarmists had claimed since the start of the cold war. Most of the Eastern European countries had been rocked by massive protest movements. Factional disputes had divided the Chinese Communist Party on several occasions. Even the Soviet Union had lowered some of the barriers that had kept its citizens from exposure to Western popular culture. Nonetheless, virtually everyone assumed that the communist regimes would remain in power and that the cold war would continue indefinitely.

Then, the impossible happened.

The communist world began to unravel shortly after Mikhail Gorbachev became general secretary of the Communist Party of the Soviet Union (CPSU) in 1985. Terms like *perestroika* and *glasnost,* became almost as familiar to Americans as baseball and apple pie. Pieces of the Berlin Wall and shoddy Soviet consumer goods were sold as trendy fads in high-end New York department stores.

"Gorbymania" was not to last, however. The reforms he introduced opened a political Pandora's box. By the end of 1989, every communist regime in Eastern Europe had unraveled. Then, less than barely a year after being named *Time's* man of the decade, Gorbachev and his Soviet Union were gone.

The transition from communist rule has been anything but smooth. Each of the Eastern European and the former Soviet republics declared itself a democracy. Unfortunately, they found that creating a regime that bore more than a fleeting resemblance to those covered in Part 2 was harder than bringing down communism. They not only had to restructure a totalitarian regime but build a capitalist economy at the same time. No one had ever done that before.

The uniformity provided by Marxism-Leninism is gone in all but the countries in the right-hand column of the table that starts this chapter. There is even more variation among the rest of them than we saw in the four countries included in Part 2.

Only a handful of others have made enough progress to be granted membership in NATO and the EU. Even fewer of them have met a key criterion political scientists use in tracking any transition to democracy—experiencing a shift in political power from one governing party or coalition to its opposition and back again. For lack of a better term, political scientists have begun calling them hybrid regimes that combine elements of democracy and authoritarianism, with the latter often more important than the former.

The transition to a market economy has rarely been an unmixed blessing either. Many postcommunist economies went through at least a decade-long slump before bottoming out. Soon thereafter, many were hit hard by the recession of the last few years. Few have developed anything like a competitive market-based economy. Most, instead, have economies in which a handful of economic strongmen (there are very few women) dominate a private sector in which wealth and political power are just about as concentrated as they were before the wall came down.

China, North Korea, Cuba, Laos, and Vietnam remain nominally communist. Their communist parties remain securely in control, but their societies seemingly have little in common with the socialism Karl Marx and Friedrich Engels predicted a century and a half ago. China, Laos, and Vietnam have adopted sweeping economic reforms that outstripped anything Gorbachev proposed in the late 1980s. There are signs that even North Korea and Cuba might change as part of the transition from one generation of political leaders to the next. Even if their regimes survive, they almost certainly will face growing pressure from below.

Raised Stakes/Big Questions

As we consider this second set of countries, we will be raising three issues that were largely "off the table" in Part 2 and, in so doing, bring us back to the big questions I posed in the very first pages of this book.

- Unlike the industrialized democracies, the nature of the regime and the policies of today's leaders are both the subject of open and heated debate.

- As the Political Indicators table at the beginning of this chapter suggests, these states are less democratic and less effective than those in Part 2, however you choose to define either democracy or effectiveness.

- The big questions of democratization, globalization, human security, and resilience are very much on the table in all of them.

Key Questions

In other words, the Eurasian countries are in the midst of an unprecedented social, political, and economic transition. Meanwhile, the leaders of the remaining communist countries are trying to cling to a governing system that seems to have outlived whatever utility it may once have had. In both cases, the political stakes are higher than those in any other countries covered in Part 2.

Studying those countries and their varied transitions does force us to shift intellectual gears somewhat. In addition to the kinds of questions we posed in the last six chapters, we will have to add six new ones that allow us to focus on the issues facing these countries where so much is in flux:

- How could regimes that seemed so strong collapse so quickly?

- Why have some communist systems survived?

- What are the political implications of economic reform in the countries that have kept communism and in those that have abandoned it?

- How can we account for the different ways these countries have evolved over the last quarter century?

- Why are they all facing much more serious domestic and global challenges than any of the countries covered in Part 2?

- Do Marxism and socialism in general have anything even vaguely resembling a viable future?

Socialism, Marxism, and Leninism

Unlike the countries covered in the rest of this book, the current and former communist regimes shared a single ideological starting point. As the communist regimes aged, socialism in general, and Marxism-Leninism in particular, mattered less and less to their leaders and people alike. Nonetheless, if we are going to understand them, we have to start with a basic overview of those underlying theories even though they have little or nothing to do with politics today.

Socialism

The origins of socialism can be traced at least as far back as the Levelers of the seventeenth-century English Civil War and their demand to "level" social, political, and economic

PROFILES Karl Marx

Karl Marx was born in 1818 in Trier, Germany. While a university student, Marx was exposed to the revolutionary ideas sweeping Europe at the time. In the early 1840s, Marx moved to Paris, where he worked for fledgling radical journals. He started reading British capitalist economic texts as well as the philosophy that had so captivated him as a student. He then met **Friedrich Engels** (1820–1895), the son of a rich industrialist and author of one of the first detailed accounts of factory life.

As revolutions swept Europe in 1848, Marx and Engels began writing about a new version of socialism that was later called Marxism or **communism**. Their ideas were first set out in a tract, *The Communist Manifesto*, which they published that winter. Over the next forty years, they wrote dozens of volumes, the most important of which was Marx's three-volume historical and theoretical study of capitalism, almost always referred to by its German title, *Das Kapital*. ◼

A statue of Karl Marx (foreground) and Friedrich Engels overlooks the Marx-Engels Forum in Berlin, Germany.

© Uwe Bumann/ Shutterstock.com.

inequalities. As you would expect with an idea that old, there are too many interpretations of what socialism means to cover in a book like this. For our purposes, it is enough to focus on four characteristics found in almost all of those definitions.

First, socialists believe that capitalism and the private ownership of the means of production have built-in flaws, because they lead to unacceptable amounts of inequality. Not all socialists are convinced that the central government has to control the entire economy. Nonetheless, they agree that representatives of the people as a whole rather than a small group of capitalists should determine how the economy is run.

Second, while most liberals are satisfied if a society guarantees equality of opportunity, socialists go further and insist on substantial equality of outcome as well. They believe that, to be truly "free to" do the things that capitalist and liberal democratic societies offer, people must also be "free from" hunger, disease, and poverty.

Third, they are convinced that liberal democracy is not democratic enough. The social democrats covered in Part 2 believe that personal freedoms and competitive elections are vital. However, Marxists insist on extending democracy to include popular control over all decisions that shape people's lives, most notably at work.

Finally, socialists claim that public ownership and a substantially more egalitarian society will improve human relations in general because they are convinced that capitalism keeps most of us from reaching our potential. In other words, if we could remove the fetters of capitalism, we would all be better off.

Marxism

Despite these common points of departure, socialists have been divided into two antagonistic camps since the late nineteenth century. First are the social democrats, who believe that change can and must be achieved through a democratic, representative system. Part 3 concentrates on the second camp, whose supporters doubt or even reject the possibility that any meaningful transformation can be achieved by working "inside the system." The most influential members of this second group of socialists drew their inspiration from the principles developed by Karl Marx.

As with socialism in general, there is no universally accepted definition of Marxism. What follows is a brief overview that stresses its key principles, most of which ended up being honored in the breach by rulers who claimed to rule in Marx's name.

Like most intellectuals of his generation, Marx believed that societies passed through stages, evolving from primitive groups of hunters and gatherers into the industrial society he lived in. What set Marx apart from most socialists of his time was his belief that industrial capitalism is an irreversible step along the path toward socialism. Marx also agreed with the German philosopher Georg Hegel, who believed that societies shift from one stage to another in a wrenching process they called the dialectic. Incremental reform does not and cannot produce fundamental change. Rather, major shifts occur only when a society's basic values and principles are replaced by new ones.

Hegel thought societies changed when they adopted new guiding principles. Marx, on the other hand, based his theory on historical materialism. As he saw it, power in any society is determined by the relationship between social classes, which defines the economic base of any society (see Figure 8.1). The dominant class controls the means of production and has no choice but to exploit the rest of the population.

However, any society based on private ownership has built-in contradictions because people will not tolerate being exploited forever. Eventually, they will rebel. To keep pressure from below in check, the owners create a superstructure of other institutions, such as the state or religion. The bureaucracy, the police, and the army are used to maintain law and order and protect the power and wealth of the ruling class. Religion exists not to save souls but to spread false hopes about a better afterlife. It is from Marx's discussion of the superstructure that we get two of his most commonly cited statements: "Religion is the opiate of the masses," and "The executive of the modern state is but a committee for managing the common affairs of the whole bourgeoisie."

From Marx's perspective, capitalism was definitely a step forward because it replaced feudalism with an economy that had capital at its core. Under feudalism, the wealthy primarily use money to buy commodities—the C and M of Figure 8.2.

FIGURE 8.2 The Role of Money in Feudalism and Capitalism

In feudalism:
$$C–M–C$$
In capitalism:
$$M–C–M'$$
$$M' = M + \text{profit}$$
But Marxist theory also holds:
$M' =$ total value of the labor that went into making the commodity
$M' =$ wages paid + profit
Or, wages = labor value − profit = exploitation
Legend:
$C =$ commodity, $M =$ money

© Cengage Learning

In capitalism, the pursuit of money itself becomes the main motivating force behind social change. Capitalists are less interested in the goods and services they produce or purchase than in the money they can make from a transaction (M'), which placed the profit motive at the heart of the economy.

The pressure to turn a profit makes capitalists exploit their employees. Here Marx drew on one of his most controversial assumptions, the labor theory of value. The real worth of any good, as well as the price capitalists could sell it for, was equal to the value of the labor that went into making it (also M in Figure 8.2). The problem was that the price capitalists set for their commodities had to include both the wages they paid their workers and their own profit. This meant that capitalists had to pay workers less than they deserved in order to make money.

The need to constantly make a profit also led capitalists to forever be on the lookout for new markets. The resulting unbridled, uncontrolled growth would, in turn, lead to alternating periods of booms and busts (see Figure 8.3).

FIGURE 8.3 Expansion and Collapse of Capitalism

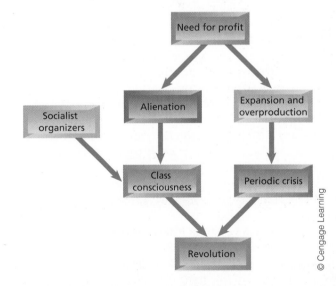

© Cengage Learning

FIGURE 8.1 Base, Superstructure, and Contradictions, According to Marx

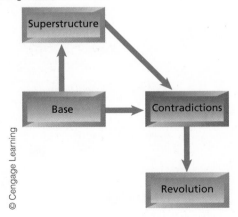

© Cengage Learning

More and more businesses would fail as weaker capitalists proved unable to deal with the heightened competitive pressures. Once that happened, the bourgeoisie, or capitalist class, would shrink, while the working class, or proletariat, would swell until it included the vast majority of the population. Those workers would come to resent their exploitation and take steps to end it. Their alienation and class consciousness would be enhanced by two of capitalism's innovations: the spread of mass education and the political freedoms of liberal democracy.

Marx assumed that those contradictions would lead to massive strikes and demonstrations that turned into a working class revolution that quickly and easily overthrew the bourgeoisie worldwide without the need for much violence. It would be followed by a short transitional period that he unfortunately chose to call the "dictatorship of the proletariat." Once the means of production had been taken over and run collectively, the cultural vestiges of capitalism would be destroyed, resources would be redistributed in an egalitarian manner, and the state would "wither away." People would work voluntarily and efficiently in a society organized by Marx's famous dictum "from each according to his abilities, to each according to his needs."

Marxism-Leninism

As noted earlier, Marx was an evolutionary thinker, which meant that he assumed that socialist revolutions would occur first in the most advanced industrialized and democratic countries. Unfortunately for the future of Marxism, that is not what happened. Rather, the first socialist revolution took place in Russia, which was anything but industrialized or democratic when its revolution occurred. Its working class was small. The tsarist government was strong enough to prevent activists from creating a broadly based socialist movement.

Not surprisingly, orthodox Russian Marxists urged patience because they "knew" that no Marxist revolution was possible in such a society. Others, led by Lenin, were unwilling to wait for history to take its "natural" course.

To come to power in these circumstances, they adopted a strategy that was very different from the one Marx had had in mind. In order to speed things up, Lenin argued socialists had to base their efforts around a highly centralized and disciplined party whose organization was based on what he called democratic centralism.

In fact, the party he built was democratic in name only. Lenin's leadership tolerated no dissent. Rather, party members were expected to enforce decisions made by the top leadership and be part of a disciplined machine.

At the time Lenin convinced the social democratic party to adopt his ideas, they had virtually no impact because he

and most of his Bolshevik colleagues were living in exile and had little popular support in Russia. Yet, within fifteen years, the Bolsheviks had seized power, and Lenin was convinced that they had done so because they had used democratic centralism. Every other communist party that came to power afterward took democratic centralism for granted, no matter how they had actually taken control over their country.

Most historians now argue that Russia's use of Lenin's hierarchical approach to running everything made reaching Marxist goals of human liberation and democracy all but impossible. Too much power was concentrated in too few hands.

Stalinism

After seizing power in the renamed Soviet Union, the Bolsheviks established a regime that they expected would establish Marx's dictatorship of the proletariat and guide the transition from capitalism to socialism. However, something very different—and very tragic—occurred instead (see Table 8.2).

Bolshevism turned authoritarian or, in the eyes of many, totalitarian. To some degree, that was an outgrowth of Lenin's democratic centralism. However, most political scientists argue that Joseph Stalin's (1879–1953) total control over the world communist movement from the mid-1920s until his death in 1953 ended any chance that the countries ruled in Marx's names could reach his ideals. It was during this period that Soviet leaders and then their fellow communist elites in other countries patterned on the Bolshevik model used the party, the mass media, and campaigns of terror to subjugate the population and mobilize the people in pursuit of the leadership's goals.

TABLE 8.2 Key Events in the Evolution of Communist Regimes

YEAR	EVENT
1917	Bolshevik revolution in Russia
1924	Death of Lenin
1924	Stalin begins consolidation of power
1945–47	Start of Cold War Communists seize power in Eastern Europe
1949	Chinese communists come to power
1950	Start of Korean War
1953	Death of Stalin
1956	Secret speech and de-Stalinization
1956	Revolt in Hungary
1959	Castro comes to power in Cuba
1975	End of Vietnam War, solidification of communist rule in Indochina

© Cengage Learning

We could go on and present statistical and other "hard" evidence about those regimes. However, as is often the case with emotionally charged material, it is easier to illustrate this point by turning to a piece of fiction, George Orwell's *Animal Farm*.

Orwell was part of a generation of young European intellectuals who were drawn to Marxism in the 1920s and 1930s. However, he soon became disillusioned with Stalin's dictatorial and opportunistic policies, which he criticized in his writing for the rest of his life.

In *Animal Farm*, the animals (working class) rise up and throw off the yoke (literally and figuratively) of human oppression. They are inspired by an ideology that reads a lot like Marxism and is embodied in the anthem *Beasts of England*, which Orwell tells us was sung to a tune somewhere between *La Cucaracha* and *My Darling Clementine*.[1]

Soon, however, things turn sour. Just like Lenin, the old revolutionary leader dies shortly after the animals seize power. The pigs, the animal Orwell not coincidentally chose to represent the Communist Party, assume more and more power over the other animals. Then a struggle for power breaks out between the two leading pigs. Snowball (based on Leon Trotsky) is the more orthodox "Marxist" who believes that the revolution must spread to all the farms and beasts of England. In the end, he loses out to the dictatorial Comrade Napoleon, who, like both his namesake and Stalin (on whom he is based), is more interested in power for power's sake than in any lofty goals. The subtle complexities of Marxist ideology give way first to the Seven Commandments and then to the simplistic slogan "Four legs good, two legs bad." *Beasts of England* is replaced by a new anthem, *Comrade Napoleon*, which adulates the leader. The pigs lord their power over the other animals and become more and more like their prerevolutionary oppressors. They violate the Seven Commandments by sleeping in beds and drinking alcohol. Orwell ends the novel with a scene in which the pigs are in a house drinking and playing cards with a group of men, their supposed "class" enemy. The other animals look in on the game from outside:

> As the animals outside gazed at the scene, it seemed to them that some strange thing was happening. What was it that had altered in the faces of the pigs? Clover's old dim eyes flitted from one face to another. Some of them had five chins, some had four, some had three. But what was it that seemed to be melting and

changing? Then, the applause having come to an end, the company took up their cards and continued the game that had been interrupted, and the animals crept silently away.

> But they had not gone twenty yards when they stopped short. An uproar of voices was coming from the farmhouse. They rushed back and looked through the window again. Yes, a violent quarrel was in progress. There were shoutings, bangings on the table, sharp suspicious glances, furious denials.

> The source of the trouble appeared to be that Napoleon and Mr. Pilkington had each played an ace of spades simultaneously.

> Twelve voices were shouting in anger, and they were all alike. No question, now, what had happened to the faces of the pigs. The creatures outside looked from pig to man, and from man to pig, and from pig to man again; but already it was impossible to say which was which.[2]

Expansion

Because Marx expected that revolution would spread, two Workingmen's International groups were created in his lifetime to coordinate the actions of the world's socialist movements. During World War I, the second of them failed to keep most socialists from joining the war effort and made no contribution to the Russian Revolution of 1917.

Lenin therefore insisted that the Bolsheviks had won the right to lead the world toward a Marxist-style revolution. Within months of seizing power, they created a Third International, or Comintern, to spread their kind of revolution. Most socialist parties split, with the more radical wing supporting the Bolsheviks.

The revolution did not spread globally in the way either Marx or Lenin had expected. The few attempts to establish Bolshevik regimes in postwar Europe were quickly put down. By the time Stalin had solidified power, there was little or no chance that a successful Marxist revolution would occur in the near future. If anything, the new Soviet state felt threatened by the hostile countries surrounding it.

In response, Stalin responded with a new strategy he called "socialism in one country." The other communist parties were to help the world's one Marxist regime survive, even if that meant slowing the prospects for revolution in their own country.

---

[1]I once asked a group of students to sing it with half the group singing one tune and the rest of the class using the other. It didn't work. In fact, it produced the only moment of humor in the section of the course on Stalinism.

---

[2]George Orwell, *Animal Farm* (New York: Harcourt Brace, 1946), 128.

Following the end of World War II, the number of countries with communist regimes did expand, though again not in the way Marx had anticipated. As the war drew to a close, armed resistance groups dominated by communists drove the Germans and their collaborators out of Albania and Yugoslavia and replaced them with Marxist-Leninist regimes. Between 1945 and 1947, the Soviets imposed communist regimes on the rest of Eastern Europe. In China, North Korea, Indochina, and Cuba, communist regimes came to power through domestically inspired revolutions. Despite these differences, the communist regimes were little more than carbon copies of the Soviet party state.

De-Stalinization

Stalin died in March 1953. The Soviet communist party was reluctant to allow any single individual to amass that much power again. It therefore replaced him with what was known as a collective leadership composed of men who had been his colleagues and henchmen. Surprisingly, they ushered in a period of reform now known as de-Stalinization.

Any idea that the Soviet and related regimes were strictly totalitarian unraveled soon thereafter. Nikita Khrushchev's (1894–1971) 1956 secret speech to the Twentieth Congress of the CPSU documented in gory detail many of the atrocities committed under Stalin. Political controls in some areas of intellectual life were loosened. Works critical of Stalin were published and widely discussed. Universities became politically and intellectually exciting places where a generation of students including Gorbachev and Boris Yeltsin started on the road to becoming reformers.

The authorities did not allow the open discussion of all political points of view. Stalin was the only leader people were allowed to attack. The current leadership, Lenin, and the party's monopoly on power remained strictly off limits.

The Soviets also cracked down whenever they felt that events were getting out of hand. In 1956, reformist communists came to power in Hungary and announced plans to create a multiparty system and leave the Soviet-imposed **Warsaw Pact**. Thousands of people demonstrated in the streets of Budapest in support of their new leadership. Finally, Soviet troops intervened, overthrowing the government and replacing it with new leaders whom Moscow could control.

In 1962, the Soviets suffered a humiliating defeat in the Cuban Missile Crisis that brought this brief period of reform to an end. The United States discovered that the USSR was in the process of installing nuclear missiles on the island. The Kennedy administration imposed a naval blockade on Cuba. In time, a diplomatic agreement was reached, the ships containing missiles and components turned back, and the project had to be abandoned.

Two years later, Khrushchev's more conservative and risk-averse colleagues forced him out of office. He was replaced by another collective leadership team headed by **Leonid Brezhnev** (1906–1982), whose hostility toward change would characterize his seventeen years in power and contribute heavily to the demise of Soviet-style communism.

Less than half a century after the Bolshevik revolution, the Soviet Union and most other communist regimes had been taken over by a generation of aging leaders more committed to stability than to change. Although it was difficult to see at the time, Brezhnev and his colleagues had come to power at a moment when their countries needed to change dramatically. As we will see, that was not something they were prepared to consider.

The Marxist-Leninist State

By that time, Marxist goals were being honored in the breach—at best. Power was concentrated in the hands of a few party leaders. Constitutions gave the party the leading role in government and society, which meant that it, and not the government, held a monopoly on decision-making power.

The Party State

These were **party states** in which the former was far more powerful than the latter. The party's critical institutions were the **Secretariat** and **Politburo**, although the exact titles varied from country to country and from time to time. The most important individuals were the general secretary and the members of the Politburo, who functioned as the equivalent of the prime minister and cabinet in a parliamentary system. The Secretariat managed the party's internal affairs and controlled appointments to all leadership positions that mattered in all walks of life. In most countries, the top leaders belonged to both.

Orthodox communists never abandoned democratic centralism. Leaders at one level continued to coopt those who served under them. Appointments to key positions, included in a list known as the *nomenklatura*, had to be approved by the Central Committee staff. Only people on a separate *nomenklatura* list were eligible to fill those positions. Real internal debate within the parties was forbidden, and rank-and-file members had no choice but to carry out decisions made by their superiors.

The party ran everything that mattered. Anyone who wanted to succeed professionally had to be a member. Almost every child joined the party-dominated Young Pioneers, the equivalent of the Boy Scouts and Girl Scouts in the United States. Teenagers with any ambition at all joined the Communist Youth League, from whose ranks adult party members were recruited. The party determined where young men and women were sent to work. It controlled trade unions, women's groups, and even stamp collecting societies. Most important of all, the Communist Party was in charge of the command economy, determining which goods and services would be produced, where they would be sold, and how much they would cost.

Officially, there was a government, but senior party leaders filled most major offices. It was always their party "hat" that prevailed. In other words, the parliament, cabinet, and other governmental institutions did little more than rubber stamp decisions already made by the party.

Most of the time, the party leader (usually referred to as the general secretary) called the shots. Ironically, Marx had tried to downplay the role that individuals played in shaping history, stressing instead the impact of broad historical and economic forces. Lenin resisted attempts by his colleagues to portray him as a hero. Yet, shortly after he died, Stalin and his supporters transformed him into a symbol that some observers believe was equivalent to a god. Then, as Orwell pointedly shows in *Animal Farm*, Stalin became the center of an even greater **cult of personality**. After Stalin, Marxist leaders maintained various forms of collective leadership in which a number of people shared power. Nonetheless, the prominence of a Castro, **Mao Zedong** (1893–1976), or even Gorbachev suggest that general secretaries continued to wield enormous power well into the twilight of communism.

There was some variation from country to country. In Eastern Europe, Communist control was never quite as absolute as it was in the Soviet Union. There were also some economic reforms in Eastern Europe, most notably, experiments with market mechanisms in Hungary and self-management in Yugoslavia.

China followed yet another path. Unlike the parties in the Soviet bloc, the Chinese Communist Party (CCP) had always been able to maintain a good deal of autonomy, largely because it spent the 1930s and 1940s fighting a guerrilla war which often left it beyond Moscow's reach. After coming to power, the CCP followed the Soviet line until 1956. However, because Mao and the other top Chinese leaders objected to de-Stalinization and the other Soviet reforms, they began adopting their own, more revolutionary policies. The CCP was also divided into factions, although it was no more democratic than any of the other ruling communist parties. Those struggles came to an end after the chaotic and violent **Cultural Revolution**, which lasted from the mid-1960s until Mao's death in 1976. After a brief power struggle, moderates, led by **Deng Xiaoping** (1904–1997), took control and began a program of dramatic economic reforms that we will explore in detail in Chapter 10. At no time, however, have the Chinese elites tolerated any changes that threatened the party's stranglehold on political power.

Comparative Emphasis:
Half the Sky? The Role of Women in Late Communist Regimes

During the Long March (see Chapter 10), Chairman Mao celebrated the role women played in the revolution by saying "they hold up half the sky." Under communist rule, the real figure turned out to be far less than half.

Almost no women have reached the top of the CCP, and most of those who have were either the wives or daughters of male leaders. The same was true in the Soviet Union. Indeed, women were so unimportant that a book—*The Kremlin Wives*—was published about their lack of political ambition.

The one possible exception was Elena Ceausescu, who ran Romania with an iron fist along with her husband. She was virtually illiterate but gave herself an honorary Ph.D. She and her husband were both killed by a firing squad the day after Christmas in 1989. ■

The Graying of Communism

It is impossible to overstate how much Marxist-Leninists changed in the half-century following the Bolshevik revolution. Revolutionary leaders gave way to the likes of Brezhnev with his love of cowboy movies and luxury cars. Purges were replaced by what the Soviets called "trust in cadres" that all but ensured party officials could keep their jobs as long as they did not make too many political waves. They were "machine" politicians intent on maintaining their own power and the perks of office. At best, the communist leaders of the 1970s and 1980s were old men like Brezhnev, clinging to power as the times continued to pass them by. At worst, they were venal and corrupt, like the members of the Ceausescu family, who oppressed the impoverished Romanian people to get castles, personal armies, and Swiss bank accounts for themselves. Somehow, these leaders managed to justify their every action in the name of Marx.

The problem is that their resistance to change was just about the last thing their societies needed. In the early stages of industrialization, a country needs cement, railroad tracks, electric wire, and other relatively low-tech commodities, which can be manufactured by relatively unskilled workers, even ones who are compelled to do their jobs.

Most historians now doubt that forced industrialization was the best way to bring the Soviet Union into the twentieth century. Nonetheless, there is no denying that Stalinist repression got the job done, however brutally.

A more modern, technologically sophisticated economy cannot be built using force alone, because workmanship, quality control, and individual motivations are extremely important. Take, for example, a television. Unlike a tub of cement, a 1980s Soviet television had many complicated parts including everything from the remote control to the picture tube to the electronic circuitry inside the box. If the frequency emitted by the remote control or the circuitry wiring is just a little bit off, the television will not work. For good or ill, the quality of Soviet workmanship was so bad that the most common cause of fires in Moscow in the 1980s was spontaneously exploding televisions!

In other words, Marxism-Leninism became an increasingly ineffective way to run a country. Allowing room for individual initiative and innovation would undoubtedly have meant loosening political as well as economic control and abandoning the two defining elements of communist societies: the party state and the command economy. Yet, even if they had wanted to, it is doubtful that they would have considered modifying either of them.

Instead, the party remained the "leading and guiding force of Soviet society" as proclaimed in Article 6 of the USSR constitution. The secret police and other repressive agencies were always well staffed and equipped.

As a result, the party state increasingly showed its age. Growth rates dropped precipitously. The economic woes were most serious in sectors where individual incentives and entrepreneurship were most needed—research and development, consumer goods production, and the service sector. The downturn was reflected in a poor standard of living that lagged further and further behind that in the West. Most Soviet families, for instance, still lived in tiny, shoddily built apartments, often sharing kitchens and bathrooms with other families. People throughout the communist world had managed to save a good bit of money, but there were not enough goods to satisfy pent-up demand. The waiting list for cars was so long that used cars cost more than new ones simply because they were available.

The military was the most efficient sector of the Soviet economy, but even it failed to keep pace. Soviet submarines were noisier, and therefore easier to detect, than American ones. The United States developed reliable solid fuels for its missiles in the 1960s; it is not clear whether the Soviets ever did. Soviet nuclear weapons were larger than American ones because they had to be. Their missiles were a lot less accurate, so larger warheads were needed to get a "kill" were the missile to land considerably off target.

The Crisis of Communism: Suicide by Public Policy

When Brezhnev died in 1982, the Soviet bloc was in trouble. Very few observers realized it at the time, most notably the conservative Western leaders who had been swept into office in no small measure because of their anticommunist rhetoric and the newly reheated cold war. Many people, especially the young, were chafing under continued repressive rule. The Brezhnevite leaders in all these countries had a harder and harder time controlling their societies even with their continued repression and control over the mass media. People were better educated, and this led them to seek more control over the decisions that shaped their lives. Open opposition to communism began quite early but occurred sporadically throughout the cold war. Demonstrations against the regime broke out in East Germany in 1953. Major protest movements were put down in Poland and Hungary in 1956, but they reappeared with the reform movement in and subsequent Soviet invasion of Czechoslovakia in 1968. After that, the focus turned to Poland, where a series of protest movements culminated in the rise of the independent trade union **Solidarity** in 1980–81, the first time a communist regime officially acknowledged the existence of an independent political organization. After the Soviets and their Polish allies imposed martial law in 1981, very few observers—or even the protesters themselves—thought that the end of communism was right around the historical corner.

Reform: Too Little, Too Late

In retrospect, it is clear that communist leaders at the time could not or would not read the political "handwriting on the wall." The Soviets, in particular, kept recruiting leaders from the same old generation, picking Yuri Andropov to succeed Brezhnev and then Konstantin Chernenko when Andropov died fifteen months later. With the exception of Poland, the Eastern European countries all had general secretaries who had taken office in the 1960s.

European communism's final act began in 1985, however (see Table 8.3). When Chernenko died, the Soviet Central Committee had no choice but to turn to a younger leader and so selected Gorbachev to be general secretary. Gorbachev was by no means responsible for everything that happened in the communist world afterward. Nonetheless, he set in motion the political reforms that, in the end, not even he could control.

Even before assuming office, Gorbachev was known as a reformer, but no one expected him to go anywhere near as far as he did. After all, he had risen through the ranks

TABLE 8.3 Key Events in the Crisis of Communism

YEAR	EVENT
1956	Hungarian uprising
1968	Prague Spring in Czechoslovakia
1980–81	Emergence of Solidarity in Poland and imposition of martial law
1985	Gorbachev chosen general secretary of Communist Party of the Soviet Union
1988	Opening of iron curtain in Hungary
1989	Collapse of communism in Eastern Europe; Democracy movement in China
1990	German unification
1991	Disintegration of Soviet Union

© Cengage Learning

of the Soviet Communist Party and had won because he had gained the support of the old-guard. Quickly, however, Gorbachev began promoting younger men and women with relatively few ties to the CPSU elite. Together, they introduced four types of reforms that they hoped would revitalize communism, not kill it:

- *Glasnost'* to introduce openness into the political system.
- Democratization to add a degree of competition to the way the Communist Party was run.
- *Perestroika* to restructure the economy, including introducing a degree of private ownership.
- New thinking in foreign policy to improve relations with the West.

Gorbachev did not introduce these reforms in order to destroy communism. In fact, it was only when they began to take hold and have unanticipated consequences in Eastern Europe that we began to realize that they could end up killing communism as we knew it. Elderly party leaders throughout the Warsaw Pact there resisted implementing *glasnost'*, *perestroika*, and democratization. East Germany's Honecker, for example, went so far as stopping the press from carrying stories about the changes taking place in the Soviet Union.

But Honecker and his colleagues would not be able to preserve the Brezhnevite status quo. Pressures for change mounted both at home and from abroad. The most important and surprising of them were the reforms in the Soviet Union itself. Gorbachev and his supporters decided that they no longer had to keep an iron grip on Eastern Europe. The security value of the buffer states had declined in a world in which nuclear missiles could fly over Eastern Europe and strike the Soviet Union in a matter of minutes. Eastern Europe had also become such a financial burden on the Soviet Union that, at the height of the popularity of the *Star Wars* films, an American political scientist titled an

article on Soviet–Eastern European relations "The Empire Strikes Back." By 1988, the Soviet Union was prodding the region's recalcitrant leaders to loosen their political control and adopt some version of their own reforms.

Eastern Europe was suffering from the same economic problems as the Soviet Union. But they were also more open to contact with the West, including looser travel restrictions and easier access to the media. And, as would soon become apparent, none of the Eastern European regimes (except, perhaps, Albania) had ever succeeded in completely suppressing dissent or in achieving even the limited degree of legitimacy found in Brezhnev's Soviet Union.

1989: The Year That Changed the World

To no one's surprise, the revolutions started in Poland. In 1988, Solidarity reappeared far stronger than it had been when martial law was imposed in 1981. Protesters quickly forced President Jaruzelski's government into "round table" negotiations. The two sides agreed to hold elections in which some seats would be reserved for the Communist Party while others were freely contested. Solidarity won a resounding victory in the competitive half of the election, and in August 1989 the Communists agreed to give up power—the first time that had ever happened anywhere in the communist world. Jaruzelski stayed on temporarily as president, but the Catholic intellectual Tadeusz Mazowiecki held the more powerful post of prime minister in a Solidarity-run government that started dismantling the command economy within months.

The next to fall was Hungary, where the first liberal economic reforms had been introduced in the mid-1960s. By the late 1980s, reformists within the Communist Party had grown strong enough to replace Janos Kadar, whom the Soviets had forced on the country in 1956. The new leaders took down the iron curtain along the Austrian border. They also roundly criticized the 1956 Soviet invasion and the Hungarians who had cooperated with the invaders. They even stopped calling themselves communists. Finally, the leadership agreed to free elections in April 1990, in which anticommunists won an overwhelming majority.

Meanwhile, protest broke out in East Germany and quickly grew in size until the unthinkable happened. On November 9, 1989, jubilant Germans smashed open the Berlin Wall, and people from both sides celebrated together. The pace of change kept accelerating. The East German government agreed to free elections in spring 1990, which Christian Democrats, who had strong ties to their colleagues in West Germany, won handily. By that time, German unification as a part of NATO, which had seemed impossible a year before, was inevitable.

Comparative Emphasis:
Conflict and Democratization

In Part 2 we saw that democracies have taken firm root—albeit often after centuries of turmoil—and that conflict is viewed as a normal part of political life. In the countries covered in Part 3, however, almost all forms of conflict were suppressed throughout the communist period. All had dissident movements, but their support rarely extended beyond a tiny group of dissidents and never threatened the regime. The collapse of communism in Eurasia and the changes in what remains of the communist world have brought much of the conflict that lurked just below the surface into the open. Indeed, in the first decade and a half of the twenty-first century, many of these countries have experienced more conflict than they can effectively handle and still built a democracy or market economy. That is especially true of countries with deep ethnic divisions, some of which broke into their constituent parts, many of which have ethnic difficulties of their own.

Thus, if there are parallels to the Western democracies, it is to France or Germany of the early 1900s, when their regimes were anything but stable and legitimate in large part because of protests coming from literally dozens of groups. ■

Czechoslovakia fell the fastest. Its government was led by Gustav Husak, whom the Soviets had installed in power in 1968 after their forces put down the Prague Spring. Anti-Soviet demonstrations broke out again in 1988. Hundreds of thousands jammed Wenceslaus Square in Prague on a daily basis. Finally, the previously powerless legislature responded to public pressure and chose Vaclav Havel as the new president. Havel had been in jail less than a year before. Even more remarkably, parliament chose Alexander Dubcek, the leader of the 1968 Prague Spring, as its head. When elections were finally held in June 1990, the Communists came in a distant third.

Only in Romania did the revolution turn violent. The country had been little more than a personal fiefdom of the Ceausescus since the mid-1960s. The Romanian people were among the poorest in Eastern Europe, while the Ceausescus used the money they extracted from average citizens to build monuments to themselves and pay off the country's massive international debt. The Ceausescus were able to do all that because they controlled the *Securitate*, the largest and most ruthless secret police in Eastern Europe.

When protests broke out in the provincial city of Timisoara on December 17, 1989, *Securitate* forces fired into the crowd, killing hundreds. A civil war broke out, pitting the *Securitate* and other forces loyal to the Ceausescus against much of the army and armed citizens. Within a week, the government had been overthrown, and the Ceausescus were executed on Christmas day. By the end of the month, *Securitate* opposition was crushed, and a regime headed by the reform communist Ion Iliescu was in power.

The revolutions in Eastern Europe were not the only earthquakes to shake the communist world in 1989. Economic reforms in China were beginning to show some promising results. Political reform, however, was not forthcoming. In April 1989, prodemocracy protests broke out after a group led by students occupied Beijing's **Tiananmen Square**, the symbolic heart of Chinese politics.

The next month, Gorbachev became the first Soviet leader to visit Beijing in a quarter century. Once again, Gorbachev served as a lightning rod for reformers. Massive, adoring crowds greeted him wherever he went, lending more and more credibility to the prodemocracy movement. The crowds kept growing. As they did, hopes for a negotiated end to the protests evaporated. The government began massing troops around Beijing. On the night of June 3, they stormed the square, killing several thousand people. After martial law was imposed, China was widely criticized for having the most repressive communist regime.

Peaceful regime change was no longer on the dissidents' political agenda. Instead, the CCP expanded economic reform to the point that a quarter century after the occupation of Tiananmen Square, a largely capitalist economy exists alongside a Marxist-Leninist political system.

In 1990, attention shifted back to the Soviet Union, where centrifugal forces were tearing the country apart. The Communist Party had already given up its legal monopoly on power. New organizations were cropping up at every imaginable point along the political spectrum. The new Congress of People's Deputies and Supreme Soviet were turning into real legislative bodies. Groups demanding sovereignty, and, in some cases, total independence, emerged in each of the fourteen non-Russian republics.

At the party congress in the summer of 1990, **Boris Yeltsin (1931–2007)** led fellow radical reformers out of the Communist Party. Meanwhile, Gorbachev increasingly turned to conservative leaders within the military and security apparatus to keep himself in power even though advisers such as former foreign minister Eduard Shevardnadze kept warning of a right-wing coup. By April 1991, the Baltic republics (Lithuania, Latvia, and Estonia) were clamoring for independence. The economy was on the brink of collapse.

Finally, the most improbable of improbable events occurred. On August 19, 1991, military and security service leaders attempted a coup against Gorbachev as he was ending his summer vacation in the Crimea. For nearly four days, Gorbachev was held hostage. His wife was psychologically abused by men whom he himself had put in power. In Moscow, Yeltsin—Gorbachev's most vocal critic—led street protests that broke the back of the coup. On August 22, Gorbachev returned to Moscow declaring that he was ready to continue the reform effort as if nothing had happened.

In fact, the botched coup was the last straw. The Baltic republics were granted their independence in September. The remaining Soviet republics declared themselves sovereign. Finally, in December, the leaders of nine of the republics agreed to form the Commonwealth of Independent States. Gorbachev was not even invited to the founding meeting. On December 31, he resigned the presidency of a country that no longer existed.

The Remnants of the Communist World

In 2013, there are only five communist countries left—China, North Korea, Vietnam, Laos, and Cuba. As we will see in Chapter 10 on China, there is good reason to believe that even in its current attenuated forms, Marxism-Leninism will have a hard time surviving in any of them.

None of these regimes resembles either the totalitarianism of Stalin's era or the complacency of Brezhnev's. In Laos and Vietnam, the communist parties still monopolize political power, but they have allowed a kind of capitalism to take even firmer root than it has in China. Cuba seems almost certain to undergo dramatic changes once Fidel and Raul Castro finally leave the political scene and the country emerges from a half century of social, political, and economic isolation. North Korea remains nominally communist and certainly still has a repressive state. However, its political system is now a reflection of the dynasty created by three generations of the Kim family rather than one that has much of a Marxist or Leninist legacy.

Marxist-Leninist regimes survive in these countries as a result of the interplay among four related forces. First, unlike their counterparts in the former Soviet bloc, each of their parties has been willing to use force. Second, these countries are poorer than the former European communist

states, which means that they did not give rise to a frustrated middle class that was at the heart of the protest movements we just discussed. Third, all five were less susceptible to outside influences. Finally—and ironically—their communist regimes may have survived because they had been outside the Soviet Union's orbit for quite some time before 1989. As each of these factors recedes in importance, so does the likelihood that communism will survive in any of them.

Transitions

Until this point, this chapter has been reasonably straightforward. Of course, political scientists and historians disagree about the importance we should assign to the causes of the events we have seen. However, there is little disagreement about what the key issues are.

That is not the case once we turn our attention to the last twenty years. The seeming uniformity of the communist world has given way to a bewildering variety of new regimes and, in many cases, entirely new countries.

Before turning to what has happened, it is important to underscore one common denominator in the variety and uncertainty to come in the rest of this chapter.

No other countries have undergone such dramatic change in such a brief period of time. In one fell swoop, they all abandoned both some of the most highly centralized political regimes and some of the most highly concentrated and centrally controlled economies in human history. As a result, we should hardly be surprised that the transitions away from communist rule have been far from smooth.

Economic Collapse

The transition did not produce the economic boom that the optimistic (and perhaps naïve) observers had predicted. Given the demonstration of "people power" in 1989, many thought it would be relatively easy for these countries to make the transition to a market economy and democratic government.

That is not what happened. The economic problems began almost immediately. With very few exceptions, their economies hit rock bottom in the early 1990s (see Table 8.4).

Groups 1 and 2 include the countries that had the easiest time for reasons that will become clear toward the end of this section. Even in these fifteen countries, the economy shrank and inflation soared. Perhaps because they were better off to begin with, they were able to find buyers for formerly state-owned industries, attract foreign investors, and create Western markets for their goods and services.

TABLE 8.4 Economic Change in Former Communist Countries, 1989–95

COUNTRY OR TYPE	AVERAGE GROSS DOMESTIC PRODUCT GROWTH	AVERAGE INFLATION (%)	LIBERALIZATION INDEX	CHANGE IN LIFE EXPECTANCY (YEARS)
Group 1	−1.6	106.0	6.9	0.7
Group 2	−4.2	49.2	4.7	−0.2
Group 3	−9.6	466.4	3.4	−4.4
Group 4	−6.7	809.6	2.0	−1.6
Countries affected by regional tensions	−11.7	929.7	3.9	0.5

Notes: Chinese data are for the entire reform period (1979–95) and include Vietnam for the liberalization index.

Group 1: Poland, Slovenia, Hungary, Croatia*, Macedonia*, Czech Republic, Slovakia.

Group 2: Estonia, Lithuania, Bulgaria, Latvia, Albania, Romania, Mongolia.

Group 3: Kyrgyz Republic, Russia, Moldova, Armenia*, Georgia*, Kazakhstan.

Group 4: Uzbekistan, Ukraine, Belarus, Azerbaijan*, Tajikistan*, Turkmenistan.

Countries with an asterisk (*) are among those severely affected by regional tensions. The table does not have data on Bosnia, Serbia, and Montenegro because of the continuing wars there.

Source: Adapted from World Bank, *From Plan to Market: World Development Report 1996* (Washington, D.C.: World Bank, 1996), 18, 33.

The remaining Soviet republics are in Groups 3 and 4. Their economies declined by as much as 10 percent per year, which meant that in 1995 some of them produced only half the goods and services they had before the collapse of the USSR. Inflation rates were typically in the 500 percent range, which meant that prices went up fivefold each year. Even more remarkable than the economic statistics are those on life expectancy. In Russia, it shrank by 10 years due to the failing social welfare, health care, and economic systems. Their liberalization scores are low for the simple reason that few investors at home or abroad were willing to buy firms that could not hope to find a competitive niche in any market.

Most of their economic conditions have improved considerably since then. However, not even the most successful Eastern European economies have come close to catching up with the ones covered in Part 2. Many that have done well depend heavily on a single commodity, most notably oil in the case of Russia. Far too typical are the Central Asian republics, which could easily be included in Part 4 given their economic and political conditions.

The National Library in Sarjevo, Bosnia, just before it was bombed 100 years after it was built.

Ethnic Conflict

President George H. W. Bush used to enjoy noting that the forty-five years between the end of World War II and the collapse of communism marked the longest period in recorded history without a war in Europe. Unfortunately, that period only lasted forty-five years.

Even before the USSR collapsed, sporadic fighting had broken out in a number of the former Soviet republics. It began when Armenia and Azerbaijan went to war over the predominantly Armenian enclave of Nagorno-Karabakh inside of Azerbaijan. As Table 8.4 also suggests, these were the countries that suffered from severe economic setbacks as well while the fighting was at its peak. Few countries have gone untouched. For our purposes, two of the conflicts stand out.

The former Yugoslavia has been through five wars since 1991. Only the first one, over the independence of Slovenia, resulted in few casualties and caused little damage. By contrast, upward of two hundred fifty thousand people were killed and millions more were turned into refugees during the struggle in Bosnia-Herzegovina, which also introduced the notion of ethnic cleansing into the world's political vocabulary.

The wars between Russia and rebels in Chechnya have been even more devastating. Antagonism toward Russians in the tiny, mostly Muslim region has existed since it was incorporated into Russia in the early nineteenth century. Bloody fighting erupted when Russia put down a first bid for independence in 1994–96. After two years of fighting, tens of thousands had been killed and the city of Grozny

had been leveled. The war broke out again shortly after Vladimir Putin (1952–) became Russia's prime minister in 1999. This time the Russians were able to defeat the rebels more handily, but only after thousands of civilians and rebels had been killed. Sporadic fighting continues almost a decade after the war supposedly ended, including the world's deadliest terrorist attack since 9/11.

Hybrid Regimes

It is hardly surprising that the table at the beginning of this chapter leads to less than hopeful conclusions. According to *The Economist* Intelligence Unit's rankings for 2010, only the Czech Republic can be considered a reasonably successful democracy. It considers the other six countries in the first column to be flawed democracies. Thus, the current Hungarian leadership adopted a new constitution in late 2011 that gave the ruling power unprecedented power, limited the independence of the judiciary, gerrymandered the country's parliamentary districts, stacked the membership of key administrative bodies, cut back the rights of women, and listed the crimes of the communist era in the constitution.

Political scientists classify most of them as hybrid regimes that combine elements of democracy and authoritarianism. Some may be heading in a democratic direction, but all also have undemocratic features. Thus, Macedonia has had reasonably free and fair elections since it declared independence twenty years ago. However, tensions between the majority Macedonians and minority Albanians are never far below the surface. There was little or no violence in its most recent election, and international observers stated that the voting was free and fair. Ominously, however, the outgoing prime minister had the police raid the offices of the most widely watched television station that supported the opposition, and a leading opposition politician was arrested. Worrisome, too, was the fact that virtually all Albanians voted for one of the two parties that tried to appeal only to their community. Because Albanians and Macedonians cannot work with each other, the country remains governed by a party that did not win even two-fifths of the vote.

If countries like Macedonia may be turning toward democracy, more of them are heading in the opposite direction as we will see in the next chapter on Russia. Almost all the hopes for democracy voiced just before and after the USSR fell have disappeared. Civil liberties have been curtailed. Elections are routinely manipulated. A tiny elite dominates an amazingly corrupt economy. The mass media are directly or indirectly under government control. The security services arguably have more influence than anyone else on what the government does. Russia has by no means reverted to the totalitarianism of the Stalinist era, but there

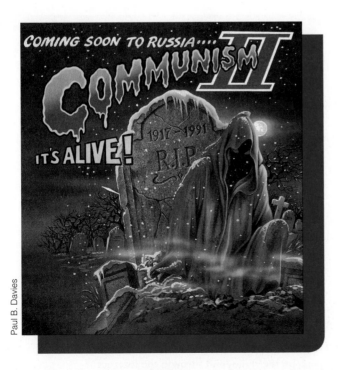

Paul B. Davies

are hints of it in the political air. If anything, the situation is worse in the countries in the third column of the table at the beginning of the chapter that make next to no pretenses at democratization.

Domestic and International Causes

Placing countries in categories such as those in "The Basics" at the beginning of the chapter always involves a judgment call. Even more uncertain are the factors that have led to these very different trajectories. Luckily for us, a growing body of research has identified two whose importance is clear even if their precise impact is not.

First, some of the countries have developed vibrant civil societies that have helped strengthen democracy. In Poland and the Czech Republic, these movements and political parties can be traced back to the informal coalitions that brought the communist regimes down. Perhaps more importantly, other countries in the hybrid category have seen the birth of new dissident movements that have helped defeat postcommunist dictators and deepen the groundwork for democracy. The most intriguing of those was Otpor and the rest of the youth-based movement that overthrew Slobodan Milosevic's authoritarian regime in Serbia in 2000. More than anyone else, Milosevic had been responsible for the wars in the former Yugoslavia. He had stolen the 2000 presidential election, after which a previously unknown group of young protesters forged a massive, nonviolent protest movement that not only toppled what was left of Yugoslav communism but made major strides toward democracy that have continued in Serbia ever since.

Second, unlike Part 2, it is easy to see how global forces directly contributed to the transitions especially in the countries that have enjoyed the most success since 1989. The outside world had a major impact on the countries in the first column of the table of basic information at the beginning of this chapter. All had somewhat open relations with the rest of the world even before 1989 through their diaspora communities, travel, and the availability of Western media. Afterward, the West used the lure of membership in the EU and NATO, foreign investment, and technical assistance to help propel these countries toward democracy.

The other once communist countries were not as open to outside influence. Either they were too big (Russia) or too far away (Central Asia) for Western capitalists, governments, or democratic activists to have had much of an impact.

The Media

When political scientists write about the totalitarian nature of communist regimes, they focus on the media far more than they do in analyzing industrialized democracies, for

Comparative Emphasis:
Globalization

Prior to the 1980s, global trends did not affect communist countries as much as they did the democracies covered in Part 2. However, globalization did have a bearing on them then and has an even more powerful impact today in two broad ways.

First, global forces were at least indirectly responsible for the crisis of communism. The communist countries certainly had their internal problems. However, they might well have survived had they not faced increased economic pressures and a renewed arms race with the West.

Second, international influences have weakened their states today, economically and otherwise. As we will see with the Russian economy in the next chapter, the triumph of capitalism has given Western bankers, industrialists, and politicians unprecedented influence over the internal affairs of most of these countries. In addition, that impact is not merely economic, as the popularity of Western cultural icons from CNN to Coca-Cola to Barbie dolls attests. To cite but one admittedly trivial example, you can buy *matroshka* dolls (nesting dolls within dolls) in Moscow's open-air markets with likenesses of the Clinton family (including Monica Lewinsky), the Simpsons, and the New York Yankees. ■

one simple reason. The party controlled them hook, line, and sinker. Party censors approved the content of what was published in every newspaper, magazine, and book as well as what appeared on television and radio broadcasts. At the same time, the authorities jammed Western broadcasts and did not allow foreign print media into the country.

That started to change in the 1980s. Advances in communication technology made it more difficult to keep Western influences out. Then, during the Gorbachev years, there was a noticeable loosening of controls in the Soviet Union and Eastern Europe.

Since then, the printed press in Eastern Europe has been just as open as in the West and, given the nature of political and economic life, even more contentious. Even in Russia, where the state still dominates the main national television channels, viewers have little trouble finding criticism of the status quo in a dwindling number of independent newspapers, on the radio, and through the Internet.

There are also cracks in the party's protective armor in the countries that have kept their communist regimes. The protesters in Tiananmen Square were able to coordinate their activities in part because of faxes they received from Chinese students abroad, and the CCP is now struggling to limit access to satellite television and the Internet, which has become all the more difficult now that protesters are using social media, as we will see most clearly in Chapter 13 on Iran. Similarly, Cuba's isolation is less than complete, something American sports fans discovered when they learned that 1998 World Series star Orlando Hernandez (El Duque) of the New York Yankees had watched his half-brother Livan's exploits for the Florida Marlins on television beamed from the United States before deciding to make his own escape from the island.

Conclusion: The Big Questions

Those of us who are old enough to have lived through the height of the cold war "knew" that the Soviet Union and its allies would be competitors with and adversaries of the West for the rest of our lives.

But the cold war is gone now. None of us miss it. What is not clear is what happens next.

As already noted a few times in this chapter, the postcommunist transitions are unprecedented and bring large number of crises in their wake. As a result, they will also allow us to truly see the importance of the big questions raised in Chapter 1 for all kinds of countries for the first time. In particular, the next two chapters will all but force us to ask:

- How is rapid social and economic change posing new challenges for everything from cultural norms to forms of governance?

- How can countries with a Marxist-Leninist tradition create their "Everything 2.0" in the light of that history, whether they abandon its institutional arrangements or not?

- Can they develop stable and resilient democratic regimes?

- Will the disruptive potential of identity politics limit what they can do in the future?

- Similarly, will they be able to address the social and economic inequalities that all seem to have widened since the end of the cold war?

- How will globalization magnify the impact of all of these other changes?

KEY TERMS

Concepts
base
bourgeoisie
command economies
communism
contradictions
cult of personality
democratic centralism
dialectic
glasnost'
historical materialism
hybrid regimes
Marxist-Leninist
means of production
nomenklatura
party states
perestroika
proletariat
satellites

socialism
superstructure
totalitarian

People
Brezhnev, Leonid
Castro, Fidel
Deng Xiaoping
Engels, Friedrich
Gorbachev, Mikhail
Khrushchev, Nikita
Lenin, Vladimir
Mao Zedong
Marx, Karl
Stalin, Joseph
Tito, Josip Broz
Yeltsin, Boris

Organizations, Places, and Events
Bolshevik

Comintern
Communist Party of the Soviet Union (CPSU)
Cultural Revolution
de-Stalinization
Federal Republic of Germany
general secretary
German Democratic Republic (DDR)
Politburo
Secretariat
Solidarity
Soviet Union
Third International
Tiananmen Square
Union of Soviet Socialist Republics (USSR)
Warsaw Pact

USEFUL WEBSITES

Communism in Eurasia collapsed just as the Internet was becoming even a minor factor in our lives, therefore there are not as many good sites on it as one would like. Both Marxists.org and the Australian National University maintain archives with many of the basic documents in Marxist history.

www.anu.edu.au/polsci/marx/

Bryan Caplan of George Mason University's Department of Economics runs a highly critical "Museum of Communism" website.

www.gmu.edu/depts/economics/bcaplan/museum/marframe.htm

Transitions Online and Radio Free Europe/Radio Liberty both provide regular news feeds on postcommunist countries.

www.rferl.org

The National Council for Eurasian and Eastern European Research still maintains a limited list of links to sites focusing on this part of the former communist world.

www.nceeer.org/links.html

Communist and Post-Communist Studies is the leading academic journal on the subject to publish its articles free online.

www.sciencedirect.com/science/journal/0967067X

FURTHER READING

Ash, Timothy Garton. *The Magic Lantern*. New York: Random House, 1990. The best general account of what happened in Eastern Europe in 1989 by someone who witnessed most of it firsthand.

Bunce, Valerie, and Sharon Wolchik. *Defeating Authoritarian Leaders in Post-Communist Countries*. New York: Cambridge University Press, 2011. More narrowly focused on the electoral defeats of leaders in hybrid regimes than the Levitsky and Way volume (see below), but goes into their cases in more detail.

Chavance, Bernard. *The Transformation of Communist Systems: Economic Reform since the 1950s*. Trans. by Charles Hauss. Boulder, CO: Westview Press, 1994. The only brief overview of communist political economy and efforts at reform that carries into the early 1990s.

Diamond, Larry, and Marc F. Plattner, eds. *Democracy after Communism*. Baltimore: Johns Hopkins University Press, 2002. A generally excellent collection of articles drawn from the *Journal of Democracy*, which means they were written for a general more than a scholarly audience.

Levistky, Steven, and Lucan Way. *Comparative Authoritarianism: Hybrid Regimes after the Cold War*. New York: Cambridge University Press, 2010. The best overview of the murky world of postcommunist regimes with an emphasis on international as well as domestic actors.

Mason, David S. *Revolution in East Central Europe: The Rise and Fall of Communism and the Cold War*, 2nd ed. Boulder, CO: Westview Press, 1997. An outstanding overview of why communism came to power in Eastern Europe, why it collapsed, and why the countries in that region have had such trouble since then.

Nolan, Peter. *China's Rise/Russia's Fall*. London: Cassell/ Pinter, 1997. The only good book contrasting the reforms in the two countries; makes an unusual, left-of-center argument.

Tucker, Robert C., ed. *The Marx and Engels Reader*, 2nd ed. New York: Norton, 1984. Among the best of the many collections of Marx's and Engels' basic works.

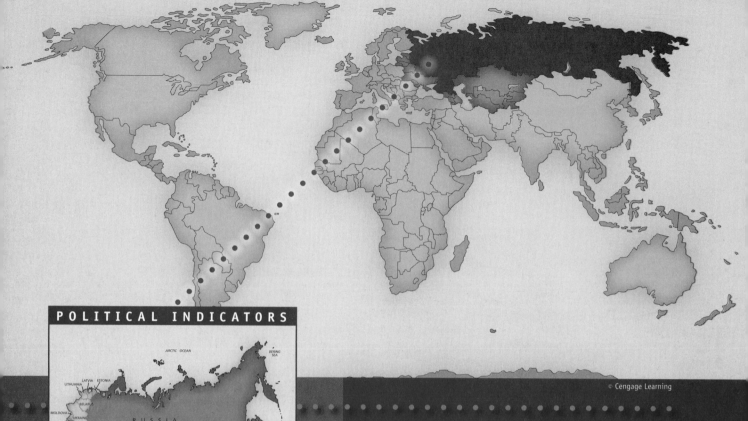

© Cengage Learning

POLITICAL INDICATORS

GOVERNANCE *(score 0-1)*	HUMAN DEVELOPMENT *(score 0-1)*	DEMOCRACY *(rank)*	PEACE *(rank)*	CORRUPTION *(rank)*
.577	.155	117	153	143 (tie)

CHAPTER

Russia

Autocratic leadership existed in Russia for many centuries, changing only its ideological colors and methods of legitimation.

LILIA SHEVTSOVA

THE BASICS

Official Name	Russian Federation
Size	17,075,200 sq. km (roughly 1.75 times the size of the United States)
Climate	Subarctic in much of the country
Population	139 million
Currency	32 rubles = US$1
GNP per capita	$15,100
Ethnic composition	79.8% Russian, 3.8% Tatar, 2% Ukrainian, 14.4% other
Life Expectancy	Men 60, women 73
Capital	Moscow
President	Vladimir Putin (2012–)
Prime Minister	Dmitri Medvedev (2012–)

Déjà Vu All Over Again?

Yogi Berra was one of the greatest baseball players of all time, but he is better known today as a source of one liners that make little sense after you think about them for a second—a skill that got him a late-in-life career promoting AFLAC insurance on television. One of his best quips was

that a game was "déjà vu all over again," which literally means a repeat of the past repeating the past.

Although Yogi will never be thought of as one of the world's greatest political scientists, his statement makes a lot of sense when writing about Russia 2013. A little more than five years earlier, President Vladimir Putin (1952–) had to step down because he had served the two terms the constitution permitted. He was replaced by his hand-picked successor, Dmitri Medvedev (1965–) who won the 2008 presidential election with a mere 71 percent of the vote and then named Putin prime minister, a position from which he continued to run the country, whatever his formal job description might have suggested. As his four years in what was supposed to be the weaker of the two offices was nearing an end, Putin announced to no one's surprise that he would be a candidate for president again and, if he won, Medvedev would go back to being prime minister. Putin then won what was almost certainly the most rigged election covered so far in *Comparative Politics*, with 63.3 percent of the vote.

Déjà vu all over again? Maybe. Putin was back in power, but he returned to the presidency as a leader whose international reputation had all but completely collapsed.

Shortly after the two men assumed office, President George W. Bush declared after his first meeting with Putin, "I looked the man in the eye. I was able to get a sense of his soul."

Incoming President Putin with outgoing President Medvedev at Putin's third inauguration.

When Putin won in 2012, Western reaction was far more muted. In the words of the *New York Times*:

> In the highly coded language of diplomacy, the Obama administration's statement was hardly a valentine. It pointedly congratulated "the Russian people on the completion of the presidential elections," but not Mr. Putin himself. It endorsed the report by European election observers and urged the Russian government "to conduct an independent, credible investigation of all reported electoral violations.[1]

Whether or not Bush was right in 2001, there is ample reason for concern about the state of Russian politics today, because many observers fear that Putin and his colleagues are taking the country dangerously close to its Soviet and totalitarian past, as the statement by Lilia Shevtsova that begins this chapter attests.

The 2012 presidential election may not have been completely rigged, but the legislative race the year before almost certainly was. New laws made it harder for opposition parties to even get listed on the ballot. All television stations, the leading radio networks, and most newspapers are under the Kremlin's control. The ability of interest groups and international NGOs (nongovernmental organizations) to organize has been sharply cut back.

Even members of the oddly named (in Russian at least) performance art group, "Pussy Riot," were in jail on charges of hooliganism as of this writing because they had performed allegedly blasphemous songs inside a cathedral.

Not every indicator of life in Russia is heading in a worrisome direction. Whatever Putin's shortcomings, Russia under his rule is not the laughing stock it was in danger of becoming under his predecessor **Boris Yeltsin** (1931–2007). Its economy is markedly improved from its low point in the mid-1990s (see Table 9.5). Although highly dependent on petroleum products, Russia is one of the five **BRICS** or emerging economies that will figure prominently in the rest of this book. Despite losing its superpower status with the breakup of the Soviet Union, Russia is still one of the world's leading powers.

In other words, this is a chapter about a country that is firmly in the command of a single leader and his close colleagues. It is also a chapter about a country that has at least stopped a period of steep decline. But finally, it is also a chapter about a country with more intractable problems than any we have seen so far.

Thinking About Russia

Russia offers us a very powerful first look at one of the most important themes in the second half of this book. Once we leave the industrialized democracies, the stakes of politics are a lot higher.

---

[1]David Herzenhorn and Steven Lee Myers, "Despite Kremlin's Signals, U.S. Ties Remain Strained after Russian Election." *New York Times*. March 7, 2012: A1.

Most political scientists consider Russia to be one of the hybrid regimes discussed in Chapter 8. That is increasingly a difficult argument to make, because its democratic side is now little more than a veneer. Power is highly personalized in the hands of the president (or, during Medvedev's term, the prime minister). As we will see time and time again, institutions and the rule of law matter far less than in any of the countries covered in Part 2. Furthermore, Russia may be one of the BRICS, but it is highly dependent on the fickle market for petroleum. Last but by no means least, on most indicators of democratization, economic growth, or environmental stability, the trend lines for Russia are not encouraging.

The Bottom Line

Before we turn to politics, we'll see that life is more difficult in Russia with a brief consideration of some key geographic, social, and economic themes.

Geography

The Russian Federation is the world's largest country, stretching across eleven time zones. Although Russia lost about half of its population when the Soviet Union collapsed, it is still the sixth most populous country in the world, trailing only China, India, the United States, Indonesia, and Brazil.

Russia is also blessed with an abundance of oil, natural gas, and precious minerals, though many of these resources lie under permafrost, because Russia is also one of the coldest countries on earth. Almost all its territory lies above the forty-eighth parallel, which separates the United States from Canada. St. Petersburg has six hours of dim sunlight in January. Kotlas, in the northern region of Arkhangelsk, has a growing season of about forty-five days, which makes even raising radishes difficult. If you spend time in Russia in January, the weather forecast becomes boringly monotonous—*sneg ne bolshoi*—snow, but not much.

Diversity

Russia's population is more diverse than any we saw in Part 2, although it is more homogeneous than the former Soviet Union was (see Table 9.1). Before 1991, there were significant minority populations in every republic. Russia, itself, is actually one of the most homogeneous of the fifteen successor countries, with ethnic Russians today accounting for almost 80 percent of the total population.

Most of the minority groups were forcibly annexed by Russia long before the Bolshevik revolution in 1917. That said, the country has never been a melting pot,

TABLE 9.1 Ethnic Composition of the Former Soviet Republics: 1989 Census

COUNTRY	POPULATION (IN MILLIONS)	TITULAR NATIONALITY (%)	MAIN MINORITIES (%)
Russia	147.0	82	Tatars 4
Ukraine	51.5	73	Russians 22
Uzbekistan	19.8	71	Russians 8
Kazakhstan	16.5	40	Russians 38
			Ukrainians 5
Belarus	10.2	78	Russians 13
Azerbaijan	7.0	83	Russians 6
			Armenians 6
Georgia	5.4	70	Armenians 8
			Russians 6
			Azeris 6
Tajikistan	5.1	62	Uzbeks 23
			Russians 7
Moldova	4.3	65	Ukrainians 14
			Russians 13
Kyrgyzstan	4.3	52	Russians 22
			Uzbeks 12
Lithuania Lithuania	3.7	80	Russians 9
			Poles 7
Turkmenistan	3.5	72	Russians 9
			Uzbeks 9
Armenia	3.3	93	Azeris 2
Latvia	2.7	52	Russians 35
Estonia	1.6	62	Russians 30

© Cengage Learning

whoever controlled the national government. The dominant Russians did their best to suppress ethnic and linguistic differences, but most minority peoples resisted them. Few ever became fully assimilated Russians, and their alienation from Russian rule suddenly surfaced in the last years of Soviet rule. Russian nationalism has by no means disappeared, something we will see below in continued demands that Moscow regain what they call the **near abroad**.

Poverty

Russia is also much poorer than the countries covered so far. Fourteen percent of the population made less than $210 a month in 2011, which the government estimated as the minimum needed for an acceptable standard of living. The gap between rich and poor is among the highest in the industrialized world, leaving Russia with a small elite that enjoys a booming luxury goods sector and millions of people whose basic nutritional and health care needs go unmet.

A typical urban family lives in a three-room apartment, does not own an automobile, and may not even have a telephone. Living conditions in the countryside are worse. In 2009, only a third of Russians between the ages of 20 and 40 owned their own home. Half lived with parents or other extended family members. It is not uncommon for three generations to share a two-room, poorly built apartment left over from communist days when it was normal for several families in a *komunalka* to share a bathroom and kitchen. Household tasks take at least twice as long as in the West because stores are poorly organized and few families have washing machines, microwaves, and other labor-saving devices that are standard in Western homes.

Aging

Like most of the countries covered in Part 2, Russia has a population problem. The country is getting older and smaller.

The newly independent Russian Federation had almost 149 million inhabitants in 1991. That number has shrunk by almost six million in the twenty years since then.

As in other industrialized countries, women are having fewer children. That is not, however, the only reason for this precipitous decline. Russia also has seen significant emigration, especially among professionals and members of ethnic minorities, especially Jews. Unlike the countries covered in Part 2, there has been next to no immigration to Russia, except for ethnic Russians who felt less than welcome in other former Soviet states.

Furthermore, the population problem is skewed by gender. On balance, men live almost ten years less than women, largely as a consequence of alcoholism and poor nutrition.

In short, demographic changes are more likely to turn into a political time bomb in Russia than in any of the countries we have considered in Part 2. Not only are the trends themselves more pronounced, they are reshaping a country whose public and private sectors lack the resources to address them.

The Environment

Russia is an environmental nightmare. The 1986 disaster at Chernobyl was the worst accident ever at a nuclear power plant prior to the 2011 Fukushima Daiichi disaster in Japan. It devastated hundreds of square miles of farmland. Scientists predict that upward of thirty thousand people will die over the next three generations as a result of cancer and other diseases caused by radiation released by the damaged plant.

Chernobyl was only the most glaring environmental catastrophe. The Soviet and Russian governments dumped dozens of spent, leaking, and dangerous nuclear reactors from submarines into the ocean. More than seventy million people in the former Soviet Union live in cities where it is unhealthy to breathe the air.

Three-quarters of the surface water is polluted. A water diversion project shrunk the Aral Sea by dozens of miles, and the salt left behind when the water evaporated destroyed the newly exposed surface soil.

The city of Kemerova is all too typical. Its air and water are so dirty that they can never be cleaned up. Its residents have three times the average incidence of chronic bronchitis, kidney failure, and diseases of the endocrine system. In one particularly filthy neighborhood, 7 percent of the children born in 1989 were mentally impaired, more than three times the national average.

Key Questions

Any list of the key questions to ask about Russia begins with the ones covered in previous chapters. Given what we have already seen, however, we will also focus on five others that have not been particularly important until now but have a lot in common with those that will be on center stage for the rest of this book.

- Why did the Soviet Union collapse? What does that tell us about weak states in the rest of the world?

- How has the way the collapse occurred affected Russian politics ever since?

- What have post-Soviet leaders done to strengthen and stabilize the Russian state? Why has that come at the cost of democratization?

- Is rapid and uncontrolled privatization the best response to globalization?

- How will Russia adapt to its new international role as a second-tier power that has little leverage over the increasingly powerful global economic and cultural forces?

The Stakes of Russian Politics: A Lighter View

When the Soviet Union was falling apart in late 1991, the *Economist* ran a tongue-in-cheek contest, asking its readers to suggest names for the new country that would take its place. Here are some of the more revealing entries:

RELICS—Republics Left in Total Chaos

PITS—Post-Imperial Total Shambles

COMA—Confederation of Mutual Antagonism (its people would be called Commies)

UFFR—Union of Fewer and Fewer Republics

The Evolution of the Russian State

Because Russia is a new state, it is tempting to begin this section with the events that led up to its creation. However, it would be a mistake to do so because the Soviet Union's history weighs heavily on the Russian present in ways discussed in Chapter 8. Therefore, not only do we have to examine the basic trends before 1991, we have to dig more deeply into the dynamics of the once-powerful state that collapsed so unexpectedly (www.bucknell.edu/×17601.×ml).

The Broad Sweep of Russian History

Most accounts of Russian history begin with the ninth-century Kievan Rus, which was located in today's Ukraine. The Kievans were but one of many Slavic tribes that occupied a wide arc stretching from the former Yugoslavia (which literally means "land of the southern Slavs") northward and eastward to Siberia, which the Kievans and their Russian successors gradually took over.

This was not simply a history of Russian expansion. Time and time again, Russia itself was invaded and overrun. However, by the early nineteenth century, it had gained control of most of the lands that would become part of the Soviet Union and had become one of Europe's major powers.

Nonetheless, Russia consistently lagged behind the West, because it missed out on most of the transformations that reshaped western Europe from the 1500s onward. The tsars (derived from the same word as Caesar) remained absolute monarchs. There was no Reformation, leaving religious authority in the hands of an Orthodox Church with strong ties to the autocracy. Individualism, the scientific revolution, and the other intellectual trends that played such a key role in the West had next to no impact on Russia.

There were periods of reform. Peter the Great (ruled 1682–1725) imported Western ideas and technologies. From then on, Russia always had Westernizers, who looked elsewhere for ways to modernize their country. Just as important, though, were Slavophiles, who were convinced of the superiority of Russian traditions and did all they could to keep foreign influences out.

As is so often the case, the stark realities Russia faced were inescapably driven home by a relatively minor event. In 1855, Russia was defeated by Britain and France in the Crimean War that set in motion political forces which would culminate in the revolution of 1917 (see Table 9.2).

TABLE 9.2 Key Events in the Origins of the Soviet State

YEAR	EVENT
1854	Start of the Crimean War
1881	Assassination of Tsar Alexander II
1904–05	Russo-Japanese War
1905	First revolution
1914	Outbreak of World War I
1917	February and October revolutions
1921	End of civil war, formal creation of Soviet Union
1924	Death of Lenin

© Cengage Learning

Prelude to Revolution

As we saw in Chapter 8, Marx expected the first socialist revolution to occur in one of the industrialized capitalist countries. Instead, it took place in a Russia that had little in common with the more advanced societies Marx had in mind, in three overlapping ways that go a long way toward explaining why the Bolshevik revolution occurred, and then why the USSR turned out as it did.

Backwardness

The term *backwardness* is value-laden and pejorative. However, it does describe Russia in the second half of the nineteenth century.

As late as the 1860s, most Russians were serfs who were, for all intents and purposes, slaves of their feudal lords. Even at the end of the century, over 90 percent of the population still lived in the countryside.

Russia only had a tenth of the railroad lines of Germany or France. It had just begun to industrialize. Because the modern sectors of the economy were owned either by the government or by foreigners, it did not develop the class of independent capitalists Marx assumed would industrialize society and lay the groundwork for an eventual socialist revolution. Most urban workers were illiterate and lacked the organization and sophistication Marx expected of a mature proletariat.

Failed Reform

Russian rulers snuffed out all attempts to reform the autocracy from "inside the system." As a result, groups advocating individual rights or limits on autocratic power only had one option: become revolutionaries.

After the defeat in Crimea, the new tsar, Alexander II (ruled 1855–81), Russia introduced a series of belated yet far too limited reforms. Serfs were liberated. Some censorship rules were relaxed. Universities and the civil service were opened to commoners.

Alexander was on the verge of introducing a constitution that would give about 5 percent of the male population the right to vote when he was assassinated in 1881. His son and successor was an old-school authoritarian and brought reform to a halt at the same time that the power of kings and lords was disappearing in the West.

A Weak State

This does not mean that Russia had a strong state. In fact, during the reign of the last tsar, Nicholas II (ruled 1894–1917), the state weakened in every respect other than its ability to infiltrate revolutionary movements.

Nowhere was that more evident than in its international relations. The elite continued to think of their country as a great power. The disastrous Russo-Japanese War of 1904–05 drove home the fact that it was not. Russia attacked Japan in part to quell dissent at home, assuming they would win the war easily. In fact, Japan trounced Russia instead, which among other things gave rise to the failed 1905 revolution. Any remaining pretense to great power status was shattered in World War I, when the Germans and their allies mowed down Russian troops on horseback.

Lenin and the (Wrong?) Revolution

Not surprisingly, a growing number of Russians came to the conclusion that their political and economic situation was intolerable. Because the state continued to ban all reformist groups, the ranks of revolutionaries swelled with dissidents of all stripes, many of whom were forced into exile. By the 1890s, they included a small group of Marxists.

They were actually among the least revolutionary because, as orthodox Marxists, they assumed that Russia would have to pass through capitalism before a socialist revolution was possible. Early in the 1900s, however, one of them, V. I. Lenin (1870–1924), reached a conclusion that was to structure political life throughout the Soviet period.

As he saw it, the situation in Russia had deteriorated so far that the country could not wait until the conditions for a Marxist revolution were ripe. In the pamphlet *What Is to Be Done?* (www.marxists.org/archive/lenin/works/1901/witbd/), Lenin claimed that Russia needed a new type of revolutionary organization. He argued that only a small, secretive, hierarchical party of professional revolutionaries could hope to succeed. To circumvent the secret police, the party would have to be based on what he called democratic centralism. Discussion and debate would be allowed before the party decided to act. However, once a decision was made, everyone had to obey. Leaders at the top would coopt officials to run lower-level units, which, in turn, would not be allowed to communicate with each other. Party members would all use pseudonyms.

His ideas touched off a spirited debate at the 1903 congress of the Social Democratic Party, which led to the famous split between the **Mensheviks** and **Bolsheviks**. The Mensheviks called for a more orthodox Marxist approach, but narrowly lost the key vote to Lenin's supporters, who came to be called Bolsheviks—a term that simply meant they were the larger faction.

The partisan infighting had little practical impact because most socialist leaders were living in exile and had minimal support at home. Nonetheless, the Bolsheviks' prospects improved dramatically over the next fifteen years, not so much because of anything they did but because the tsarist regime continued to weaken.

The autocracy collapsed in 1917 as Russia staggered toward defeat in World War I. The tsar was replaced by a provisional government that found itself unable to beat back a counterrevolution by tsarist forces without the help of the Bolsheviks. Finally, in the fall, Lenin decided that the time had come. On the night of November 7, 1917, Bolshevik troops overthrew the provisional government. Marxists had succeeded in taking over a government for the first time anywhere.

But the revolution was far from over. The Bolsheviks quickly gained control of most cities, but they had little support in the countryside. Civil war broke out in 1918. Poorly organized forces loyal to the tsar and the provisional government joined with anti-Bolshevik revolutionary factions in an attempt to topple the new Bolshevik regime. The Bolsheviks responded by reinforcing democratic centralism, laying the groundwork for the totalitarian **Communist Party of the Soviet Union** (CPSU) that came later. They created the **Cheka**, their first secret police, to enforce discipline within the party. At the same time, the Bolsheviks had to bring back members of the old elite to run the factories and the new Red Army. Because the Bolsheviks did not trust them, they assigned loyal political commissars to supervise what the officers and bureaucrats did.

Meanwhile, the Bolsheviks accepted the Brest-Litovsk Treaty with Germany, which cost revolutionary Russia 32 percent of its arable land, 26 percent of its railroads, 33 percent of its factories, and 75 percent of its coal mines. Industrial production dropped to a third of its 1913 level. Thousands of workers fled the cities. No one knows how many people froze or starved to death.

In 1921, the Bolsheviks extended their control to the entire country and formally established the USSR. They kept the overlapping party and state hierarchies and democratic centralism from the civil war days. In addition, the new CPSU was assigned the leading role in policy making.

In the early 1920s, the Soviet Union was not yet a totalitarian dictatorship. There were still open debates within the party. There were also lively cultural and artistic

PROFILES   V. I. Lenin

Lenin was the chief architect of the Bolshevik revolution and the Soviet Union's first leader.

He was born Vladimir Ulyanov in 1870. His father was a successful bureaucrat, and young Vladimir seemed destined for a prominent career himself until his brother was executed for his involvement in a plot to assassinate the tsar. Vladimir entered university shortly thereafter but was expelled and sent into internal exile for his own political activities. He spent those years near the Lena River, from which he derived his pseudonym. While there, he became a Marxist. He finished his studies independently and was admitted to the bar in 1891. Lenin spent the rest of the 1890s organizing dissidents in St. Petersburg and was in and out of jail until he was expelled from Russia in 1900.

V. I. Lenin addressing communist activists and soldiers in Red Square, 1919.

Lenin returned to Russia after the tsar was overthrown and led the Bolsheviks' seizure of power. But he never fully recovered from an assassination attempt that left him with a bullet in his shoulder and another in his lung. He suffered three strokes between 1922 and 1923 and died in 1924. ∎

communities in which dissenting views were openly discussed. Stringent wartime economic measures were relaxed under the New Economic Policy (NEP), which allowed some private businesses to form.

Terror and the Modernization of the Soviet Union

Lenin wrote a political "testament" before he died in 1924, in which he criticized the Bolshevik leadership. In particular, he warned that neither Leon Trotsky (1879–1940) nor Joseph Stalin (1879–1953) should be allowed to take over the party. To make a long and complicated story short, the CPSU did not heed Lenin's wishes. And Stalin won an intense factional fight for control of the party—and, hence, the country (see Table 9.3).

No one expected him to replace Lenin. He was not one of the exiled intellectuals who led the Bolsheviks before the revolution and had not made much of a name for himself inside the party at home. After the revolution, Stalin was put in charge of the party organization, a job few of his colleagues were interested in. From that position, he was able to outmaneuver his more visible rivals because he controlled appointments to senior positions in a party in which all leaders were coopted.

Stalin is typically—and accurately—portrayed as one of the most vicious men in human history. In what is often called the second revolution, as many as twenty million Soviet citizens lost their lives—far too often for little or no reason.

Forced Industrialization

There was, however, a degree of macabre rationality to some of what he did. The Soviet Union was in trouble. Hopes of global revolution had given way to a resurgence of right-wing governments in the countries that bordered the USSR, something that Stalin called "capitalist encirclement."

TABLE 9.3 Key Events in the Evolution of the Soviet State

YEAR	EVENT
1927	Solidification of power by Stalin
	Socialism in one-country speech
1929	Beginning of collectivization campaign
1934	First major purges and show trials
1939	Nonaggression pact with Germany
1941	German invasion of Soviet Union
1945	End of World War II; Beginning of cold war
1953	Death of Stalin
1956	Twentieth Party Congress and Khrushchev's secret speech
1964	Ouster of Khrushchev
1982	Death of Brezhnev

Whoever was in charge, the world's first socialist state had to respond decisively. As Stalin put it:

> To slacken the tempo would mean falling behind. And those who fall behind get beaten. But we do not want to be beaten. No, we refuse to be beaten. One feature of the history of old Russia was the continual beatings she suffered because of her backwardness. She was beaten by the Mongol Khans. She was beaten by the Swedish feudal rulers. She was beaten by the Polish and Lithuanian gentry. She was beaten by British and French capitalists. She was beaten by Japanese barons. All beat her because of her backwardness. We are fifty or a hundred years behind the advanced countries. We must make good this distance in ten years. Either we do it or we shall go under.[2]

Before documenting Stalin's atrocities, note that no country has ever been able to painlessly create a modern industrial economy. This is especially true of states that industrialized late and wanted to close the gap between themselves and their competitors as quickly as possible. Adopting a *laissez-faire* approach seems to condemn them to decades of catching up. Therefore, they often conclude that their only option is to compel their society to industrialize as quickly as possible (also Chapter 6 on Germany).

Stalin therefore forced his beleaguered country to industrialize, which led to some of the worst excesses of his rule. That said, a plausible case can be made that if Stalin had *not* pursued something like the policies described here, the Soviet Union would not have survived.

Because the Soviet Union only had one real resource—human labor—and it was concentrated in one place—the countryside—Stalin felt he had no choice but to restructure rural life. Farmers were herded onto gigantic, supposedly more efficient, farms. The peasants who were no longer needed for farming were forcibly relocated to the cities to work in the factories that were being built at breakneck speed.

The government carried out the **collectivization** of agriculture with violence the likes of which this country with a long history of violence had never seen. In a matter of months, more than nine million peasants were forced to move to the cities. At least that many more resisted collectivization and were sent to forced labor camps, where most of them perished. An unknown number were killed on the spot.

To further speed up industrialization, the party introduced an ambitious **five-year plan** that called for at least doubling the production of coal, oil, pig iron, steel, electricity, and

cloth between 1928 and 1932. The Central State Planning Commission (*Gosplan*) set goals for the entire economy, which the individual ministries turned into specific quotas for each factory and farm to fulfill. As in the rural areas, people who resisted the state's plans were treated brutally. Although the plan fell short of its most ambitious goals, the Soviet Union industrialized as rapidly as any country in history, though at a tremendous human cost.

Foreign Policy

Stalin's so-called second revolution extended to foreign policy as well. Lenin had created the **Third International**, or **Comintern**, to spearhead what he expected to be a worldwide, Soviet-style revolution. However, because the revolutionary tides had ebbed by the time Stalin solidified power, he reversed the course of Soviet foreign policy and called for "socialism in one country," something no orthodox Marxist would have dreamed possible.

Over the next twenty-five years, he led the Soviet Union and the global communist movement through what must seem like a contradictory series of shifts. At first, Stalin prohibited communist parties elsewhere from participating in antifascist coalitions that might, for instance, have kept the Nazis from taking power in Germany. But once he realized how serious the fascist threat was, Stalin switched sides in 1934, endorsing popular or united fronts in which communists cooperated with just about anyone who opposed fascism. In 1939, the Soviets reversed course once again, signing the infamous nonaggression pact with Nazi Germany. It was to last less than two years. In 1941, the Germans invaded the Soviet Union at which point Moscow joined the British-led Allies, which soon included the United States after the attack on Pearl Harbor. Even before the war ended, however, tensions between the Soviet Union and the West escalated into what became the cold war, prompting yet another U-turn in Soviet policy.

The Purges

Stalin's economic and foreign policies made some kind of tragic sense. Obviously, millions of people suffered because of them, but the Soviet Union did industrialize, and it did survive.

There was no such logic to the **purges**. They actually began in a limited way, in the 1920s, when the party threw out opportunists who had joined it in the aftermath of the revolution. Stalin later forced Trotsky and most of his other rivals out of the party.

After that, the purges took on a life of their own that could not be rationalized on the basis of economic necessity. In 1933, the party held what Stalin called the "Congress of Victors" to celebrate the completion of the collectivization campaign. Sergei Kirov, the young party

---

[2]J. V. Stalin, *Problems of Leninism* (Moscow: International Publishers, 1953), 454.

PROFILES   Joseph Stalin

Josif Dzhugashvili was born in the Georgian town of Gori in 1879. Unlike Lenin, he was of humble origins. His mother was a maid and his father a shoemaker who was also an abusive alcoholic. As an adolescent, he entered a seminary, but dropped out in 1899 to become a full-time revolutionary.

Stalin followed Lenin into the Bolshevik wing of the Social Democratic Party, but unlike most of his influential colleagues, he spent the years before 1917 in Russia, organizing the party underground. During those years he took the pseudonym Stalin, which meant "man of steel."

During the revolution and civil war, Stalin was given more and more responsibility for the "nationality question" and for party organization. Despite alienating Lenin because of his "rude" behavior, Stalin was able to outmaneuver his competitors and seize all but complete control of the country by 1927.

Most historians are convinced that Stalin suffered from a series of psychological problems that contributed to making his regime one of the most brutal in history. He died in 1953. ■

Joseph Stalin in 1929, shortly after he consolidated power and began the brutal collectivization campaign.

Hulton Archive/Getty Images

leader in Leningrad, actually won more votes than Stalin in balloting for the new Central Committee. In 1934, Kirov was assassinated on Stalin's orders. Nonetheless, Stalin ordered the arrest of anyone "involved" in Kirov's assassination. That began a wave of torture, show trials, and executions that touched the lives of millions of innocent Soviet citizens.

By the end of the decade, five of the nine Politburo members, 98 of 139 Central Committee members, 1,108 of the 1,966 delegates to the 1933 party congress, and half the army officer corps had been killed. At dozens of show trials, most of the old Bolshevik leaders confessed to crimes they had not committed and then were summarily executed.

In the larger prisons, the authorities executed an average of seventy people per day. Millions of innocent people were sent to the gulag, as the network of concentration camps was known. Many were given eight-year sentences merely for having a "socially dangerous" relative. Very few survived that long.

The purges drained the party of many of its enthusiastic members and qualified leaders. They even decimated the secret police, many of whose own leaders found themselves on trial for their lives after they had themselves consigned hundreds of their fellow citizens to death.

In this nightmarish environment, the only way people could express their feelings was through humor. Consider, here, one "report" of a conversation between two prisoners that sums up just how absurd and horrible the purges were:

Prisoner One: What's your sentence?

Prisoner Two: Twenty-five years.

Prisoner One: What for?

Prisoner Two: Nothing.

Prisoner One: Don't lie. You only get five years for nothing in our country.

Khrushchev, Brezhnev, and the Politics of Decline

Stalin died suddenly in 1953. Like Lenin, he had failed to designate a successor, and a number of men jockeyed to replace him. This time the dozen or so top party leaders agreed that no one should be allowed to amass the kind of power Stalin had and that the Soviet Union should be led by a team of leaders.

Within two years, Nikita Khrushchev (1894–1971) emerged as the most influential of them. He was a typical communist of his generation. Drawn to the party by the revolution, Khrushchev had risen to the top during Stalin's rule and took part in some of the regime's most brutal campaigns.

The basic institutions of the party state remained intact. Nonetheless, Khrushchev proved to be a reformer both at home and abroad.

The first sign that politics was changing came in February 1956, when Khrushchev called the delegates to the CPSU's Twentieth Party Congress back for a special session. For three hours, he held his audience spellbound with his now famous secret speech in which he detailed many of Stalin's many crimes. The speech did not stay secret for long and led to a series of reforms. Censorship was loosened. More open political debate made university campuses exciting places and left an indelible mark on a generation of students that included Gorbachev and Yeltsin. Khrushchev also sought to decentralize economic decision making and to revitalize the flagging agricultural sector. The Soviet Union remained hostile toward the West but also sought to relax tensions through a policy he called peaceful coexistence.

His more cautious colleagues always had doubts about Khrushchev and what they would later call his "harebrained schemes," few of which worked. As social and economic problems mounted, so did opposition to his rule.

He barely survived an attempt to oust him in 1957. The Cuban missile crisis of 1962 proved to be the last straw. That August, American reconnaissance planes discovered that the Soviets were preparing to deploy nuclear missiles in Cuba, a country ninety miles south of Florida that had passed into the Soviet camp a year earlier. Two months later, President John F. Kennedy imposed a naval blockade to prevent the ships carrying the missiles from reaching Cuba. World War III was a real possibility. Eventually, the ships turned around, and the Soviets dismantled their bases.

For Khrushchev's critics, Cuba was a humiliating defeat. Two years later, they succeeded in removing him from office and replaced him with another collective leadership, many of whose members had been his protégés. The most important of them turned out to be Leonid Brezhnev (1906–82), who served as general secretary of the Communist Party until his death. Khrushchev's reforms were quickly brought to a halt, and the leadership took as few risks as possible in either domestic or foreign affairs.

The new leaders could not stem the Soviet Union's decline, which was already under way even though few Western observers noticed it at the time. By the early 1980s, economic growth slipped to 3 percent per year or barely 60 percent of the goal laid out in the Tenth Five-Year Plan (1976–80). In some sectors, the figures were worse. Only a fifth of planned growth targets were reached in coal and chemicals, barely a third in steel and consumer goods, and only half in agriculture.

Economic progress stagnated because further growth would force the Soviet Union to change in ways that would have threatened the two central tenets of Bolshevik rule that dated back to Lenin's time: the party's monopoly on political power and the centrally controlled economy. The Brezhnev generation was not willing to do either.

Instead, it clung to power. By the beginning of the 1980s, the average age of Politburo members was about seventy. When Brezhnev died in 1982, he was replaced by other members of the old guard—Yuri Andropov and Konstantin Chernenko—both of whom died within months of taking office.

Economic conditions continued to deteriorate. People had more disposable income, but there were not enough consumer goods to meet pent-up demand, and those goods that were available were shoddily made. To cite one example, the few people fortunate enough to own cars took their windshield wipers with them when they parked. Otherwise, they would be stolen.

The *Economist* summed up this period brilliantly in its rather snide obituary about Brezhnev:

> The death of Leonid Brezhnev was the only major innovation he ever introduced into Soviet political history. In life, he stood for the status quo—as firmly as a man can stand when he is in fact walking slowly backward on a conveyor belt that is moving slowly forward beneath his feet. Brezhnev, a solid machine man, was put in to reassure the frightened hierarchs that the experimenting would stop. In this he was remarkably successful. He did not just stop the clocks, but turned some of them back. Defying Marx, he virtually halted the evolution of Soviet society in its tracks. But the country, which was intended to be ruled by the Brezhnev men after Brezhnev's death, presumably with the aim of immortalizing his immobilism, had been changing under them despite all their efforts; and the world in which it must live has been changing too. His legacy in foreign as in domestic policy is a set of concepts which were old when his reign began eighteen years ago. In Brezhnev's Russia, only one thing was kept entirely up to date: its military hardware. The most appropriate monument for him would be a multiwarhead nuclear missile linked to a stopped clock.[3]

When Chernenko died in March 1985, there was no one left from the Brezhnev generation to take his place. Someone younger had to take over, and Gorbachev was the obvious choice.

There were signs that he was not cut from the same political cloth as the Brezhnev–Andropov–Chernenko generation. No one, however, expected change to come as quickly as it did.

---

[3] "Brezhnev's Legacy." *The Economist*. November 13, 1982, 7–8.

In December 1984, Serge Schmeman of the *New York Times* wrote about an incident that hinted at that uncertainty. Gorbachev had been sent on a mission to London. He was already in line to replace Chernenko, who was obviously in failing health. Observers like Schmeman hoped that the trip would provide some insight into the next leader of the Soviet Union.

He began his report with Gorbachev's departure from Moscow. Gorbachev, dressed in a somber gray suit, shook the hands of his equally somberly dressed colleagues who had come to see him off. Out of public view, his wife, Raisa, walked up the back ramp onto the plane. When they arrived in London, however, they emerged from the airplane together, wearing colorful Western-style clothes, and enthusiastically greeted the crowd.

Which, Schmeman wondered, was the real Gorbachev?

The Collapse of the Soviet State: The Gorbachev Years

It did not take long to get an answer to Schmeman's question. **Mikhail Gorbachev** (1931–) proved to be a dedicated reformer and one of the twentieth century's most influential leaders. In the end, however, he failed in large part because he was either unwilling or unable to challenge the party state.

Because his reforms went a lot further than Khrushchev's, he provoked fierce opposition within the party hierarchy. However, his reforms probably could never have led to the revitalization of the Soviet society and economy because they did not go far enough in challenging the party's stranglehold on power (see Table 9.4).

The Party State

Gorbachev inherited a country in which the CPSU was for all intents and purposes the same as the state. Senior party leaders made all important decisions. The party as a whole supervised what every individual and institution did.

TABLE 9.4 Key Events in the Gorbachev Years

YEAR	EVENT
1985	Gorbachev becomes general secretary of CPSU
1986	Chernobyl; first summit with President Ronald Reagan
1987	Intermediate nuclear forces agreement; Boris Yeltsin removed from office
1988	Special party conference; Reagan visits Moscow
1989	First somewhat competitive elections; collapse of communism in Eastern Europe
1990	Final CPSU congress; Yeltsin resigns from party
1991	Failed coup attempt; collapse of USSR

© Cengage Learning

The national party organs were at its top. In principle, the most important of them was the party congress, which was normally held every four years. In practice, it was all but powerless. Until the final one in 1990, party congresses did little more than rubber stamp decisions made by the party elite. Much the same could be said of the Central Committee.

Power was concentrated in two small self-perpetuating bodies that were officially appointed by the Central Committee. The Politburo (normally twelve to fifteen members, with another five to six nonvoting, candidate members) acted much like a cabinet in a parliamentary system. The Secretariat (usually about twenty-five members with a staff of 1,500) oversaw the work of the party apparatus. Many of the same people served in the Politburo and the Secretariat. The General Secretary chaired them both.

Because the party continued to use democratic centralism, leaders at one level determined who filled positions one level below them. That allowed the elite to perpetuate itself by choosing people it could count on for all important subordinate positions. That control was exercised through the nomenklatura, lists of important positions and people qualified to fill them, both of which were maintained by the Secretariat.

For all but those at the very top, the party was a massive bureaucratic machine whose primary mission was to ensure that the policies made by the elite were carried out. Most leading journalists, military officers, factory managers, teachers, and even athletes had to join the party, whose members numbered about 10 percent of the adult population. Few of them, however, joined out of a sense of commitment to Marxist ideals. Rather, most entered one of the four hundred thousand or so primary party organizations for a far more pragmatic reason. The CPSU was the only route to success in almost every sector of Soviet society.

Reform

Gorbachev and his colleagues understood that the Soviet Union had to change. Economic growth had all but ground to a halt, and the country was falling behind the West in almost every way imaginable. Therefore, they introduced four sets of reforms designed to reinvigorate Soviet society.

Glasnost'

The first of the reforms, glasnost', turned out to be the most counterproductive. The term is derived from the Russian word for voice and is best translated as openness. It had been used by earlier Soviet leaders but only made it onto political center stage after the 1986 Chernobyl nuclear power plant disaster. After a few days of typical Soviet secrecy, the government began making information about the accident public and allowed foreign experts in to care for people who had been exposed to radiation.

From then on, the system opened up dramatically. The old Soviet aphorism—"Everything that isn't explicitly permitted is forbidden"—was turned on its head. Censors stopped reviewing most works before they were printed. The heavy-handed control of the mass media was lifted. Some conservative newspapers and magazines were still published, but the press and airwaves became filled with material that was critical not only of past but also of current leaders.

Glasnost' did not, however, create the kind of tolerant, Western-style political culture Gorbachev hoped for. Instead, people used their new freedom to vent seventy years' worth of frustrations. Rather than produce a more energized and enthusiastic population, the Soviet Union faced ever larger and more radical protests on a number of fronts. Workers struck against low pay and poor working conditions. Women and environmentalists joined the political debate. An independent peace movement urged the party to move even faster in its rapprochement with the United States and to end its crippling invasion of Afghanistan. Most important of all, separatist movements challenged the legitimacy of the Soviet state itself.

Democratization

The reformers also realized that *glasnost'* had to be accompanied by a degree of democracy. They never planned to turn the Soviet Union into a Western-style liberal democracy. This is hardly surprising, since even the most radical reformers were products of the system and thought of themselves as dedicated Marxists. Therefore, movement on democratization came more slowly.

The reformers did remove Article 6 from the Soviet constitution, which had defined the party as "the leading and guiding force of Soviet society and the nucleus of its political system, of all state organizations and political organizations." A special party conference in 1988 announced the creation of a stronger presidency, a position Gorbachev assumed that September.

Gorbachev also introduced a new parliament, the Congress of People's Deputies, whose members were chosen through partially free elections. During its first and only election campaign, many of the liberal reformers received a lot of publicity, but people who were worried that Gorbachev was moving too fast won more seats. As with so many of his reform efforts, these limited democratic initiatives mostly served to intensify the apprehension and opposition of conservative party members.

Perestroika

When Gorbachev took office, the economy was in serious trouble. Soviet factories were archaic. The country's labor force neither worked very hard nor cared about the quality

Mikhail Gorbachev was born in 1931 near Stavropol in the Crimea. His father was a tractor driver, and Gorbachev himself worked on a collective farm as a teenager. At eighteen, he was already a committed and respected member of the Komsomol, the Communist Youth League, when he enrolled at Moscow State University to study law. Like many of his generation, he was deeply affected by de-Stalinization, which, some say, convinced him as early as the 1950s of the need for reform.

Gorbachev returned to the Stavropol region, where he quickly moved up the party ranks. He was no radical. But like many of his colleagues in out-of-the-way parts of the country, he experimented with some innovative reforms—in his case in agricultural administration—that earned him national attention and a seat on the Politburo in 1980.

Gorbachev was never willing or able to fully break with the party state, which ultimately led to his and his country's undoing. Since 1991, he has headed the Gorbachev Institute, which works for human rights and world peace along the lines of the "new thinking" he championed while in office. He made an attempt at a political comeback in the 1996 presidential election but won less than 1 percent of the vote (www.gorby.ru/en). ■

Presidents Gorbachev and Reagan at their Reykjavik summit.

RIA Novosti / Alamy

of the goods it produced. The service industries were woefully inadequate, and people who could afford to do so turned to the black market to get their cars repaired or to buy decent food. The massive state and collective farms were so poorly run that a third of the harvest spoiled or simply disappeared before getting to market. Last but not least, the peculiar nature of the Soviet currency and the country's arcane laws restricting foreign trade largely kept the USSR from participating in the increasingly important international economy.

At first, there were few signs that Gorbachev was considering radical economic reform. He did try to make improvements within the party state system by increasing the discipline of Soviet workers—for instance clamping down on the sale of alcohol.

As the crisis deepened and his incremental reforms failed to bear fruit, Gorbachev and his advisers decided that nothing short of **perestroika**, or a total restructuring of the economy, would restore the Soviet Union to world prominence or improve the living conditions of its citizens. They realized that such a restructuring would require relinquishing much of the party state's economic power to the market and promoting private ownership, individual initiative, and decentralized decision making.

Perestroika was still a work in progress when the Soviet Union collapsed. Nonetheless, the party had already taken steps to authorize some small, cooperatively owned businesses, ease restrictions on foreign ownership and investment, introduce some competition among state-owned enterprises and farms, and reform the currency so that market forces rather than bureaucratic edicts would determine wages and prices. Like democratization, perestroika faced resistance from much of the party hierarchy, whose power they threatened.

Foreign Policy

Gorbachev will be remembered most positively for his role in ending the cold war. One of his first acts as leader was to declare a unilateral moratorium on nuclear testing, which was followed by even more dramatic initiatives. There was a strong dose of self-interest behind those proposals from a leader who understood that his country was overburdened by defense expenditures that consumed at least a quarter of its GNP.

Gorbachev was the most visionary international leader of his time. Thus, in his remarkable speech to the United Nations General Assembly in December 1988, he talked hopefully about interdependence and a new world order of countries able to solve their differences peacefully. This is not the place to review those actions in any detail because they fall more in the domain of international relations. It is enough to note that they, too, provoked considerable opposition at home from people who feared that they would undermine the Soviet Union's position as one of the world's superpowers.

Crisis and Collapse

All the reforms actually did, however, was polarize the elite and the country as a whole (see Figure 9.1). They dramatically expanded both the number of people who wanted to have a say in the making of public policy and the number of people who had the means to do so. As the 1980s wore on, Gorbachev found himself trying to govern from an ever-shrinking center. That would have been a challenge under the best of circumstances, but Gorbachev also turned out to be quite tentative, especially once it became clear that the party itself was the major roadblock standing in the way of effective, sweeping reform.

FIGURE 9.1 The Changing Soviet Political Landscape

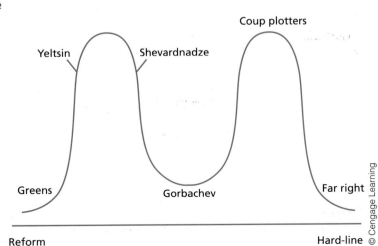

AP Photo

Boris Yeltsin, standing on an armored personnel carrier and rallying the crowd opposing the coup against Mikhail Gorbachev in 1991.

The Soviet Union was already a political tinderbox by the time communism collapsed in Eastern Europe. Rumors of an impending coup were rife. In response, Gorbachev strengthened presidential powers and elevated hard-liners to prominent posts in the military and security apparatus. Both moves backfired.

On June 12, 1991, Yeltsin was elected president of the Russian Republic, which led to the claim that he had a broader mandate than Gorbachev. Five days later, the head of the KGB issued an ominous warning against carrying out liberal reforms "dreamed up across the ocean." The next month, Gorbachev reached an agreement with the presidents of ten of the fifteen republics on a Union Treaty that would have given them sovereignty over most domestic policy issues. The treaty was due to be signed on August 20, the day after Gorbachev returned from his summer vacation.

The morning before his planned return, the Soviet press agency announced that Gorbachev had fallen ill and had been replaced by a group of his hardline colleagues. Gorbachev and his family were taken into custody. Troops occupied critical locations in Moscow and other cities.

Most politicians were slow to respond. Yeltsin, however, opposed the coup from the outset. Overnight, he galvanized the opposition. Within forty-eight hours, it had

become clear that the revolt was a poorly planned act of desperation by leaders who knew that the Union Treaty would mean the end of the Soviet Union as they knew it. The coup collapsed, and Gorbachev returned to Moscow, claiming that nothing had changed.

In fact, *everything* had changed. By September, the Baltic republics were independent states. In December, the leaders of eleven of the remaining twelve republics agreed to form the Commonwealth of Independent States. They did not even invite Gorbachev to the meeting at which they created it. By the end of the month, Gorbachev had resigned his position as president of a country that no longer existed.

Between Dictatorship and Democracy

One of the best books on the first years of post-Communist Russia is entitled, *Between Dictatorship and Democracy*.[4] Although now nearly a decade old, it paints

---

[4]Michael McFaul and Elina Treyger, "Civil Society," in McFaul, Petrov, and Ryabov, eds., *Between Dictatorship and Democracy*, Washington: Carnegie Endowment for International Peace, 2004, 135–36.

a picture of a country that started with high hopes for democracy and prosperity and was already headed toward dictatorship when now Ambassador Michael McFaul and his colleagues edited that book. As we will see in the rest of this chapter, the authoritarian trends they warned about have only been magnified since then.

Birth Pangs

Like most of the post-Soviet republics, Russia got off to a shaky start.

Economic conditions continued to worsen and reached a level no one could have imagined under the communists. Some estimates suggest that the downturn was at least twice as severe as the Great Depression that hit the West after 1929.

There are many ways to document how bad things got, but Table 9.5 offers an excellent—and depressing—glimpse of the crisis, because its indicators reflect changes in the way people actually lived. The table does not show the most dramatic change. The average life expectancy of men declined by about ten years at a time when men elsewhere were living longer. Put simply, Russian health care got worse, which meant that alcohol-related diseases took an ever greater toll.

Production fell by at least a half for almost everything Russia manufactured. The decline was particularly steep for shoes, meat, and clocks. The reader may not think much about coats, refrigerators, and vacuum cleaners. But, remember that Russia is a very cold country which makes coat production anything but a luxury.

TABLE 9.5 Economic Decline in Russia, 1990–97*

PRODUCT	1990	1997
Meat	6.6	1.4
Butter	0.8	0.3
Canned goods (billions of cans)	8.2	2.2
Salt	4.2	2.1
Bread	16.2	8.9
Pasta	1.0	0.5
Footwear (millions of pairs)	385.0	32.0
Silk (millions of square yards)	1,051.0	134.0
Coats (millions)	17.2	2.3
Cement	83.0	26.6
Beer (millions of gallons)	874.0	655.0
Watches and clocks (millions of units)	60.1	5.0
Refrigerators (millions of units)	3.8	0.1
Vacuum cleaners (millions of units)	4.5	0.6

*All figures in millions of tons unless otherwise noted.

Source: Adapted from the *Washington Post*, November 14, 1998, A16.

And, the absence of such things as refrigerators and vacuum cleaners had a particularly hard impact on women who already did most of the family's housework.

The ethnic conflict that had had so much to do with the collapse of the USSR did not disappear after the predominantly non-Russian republics all gained their independence—and inherited ethnic problems of their own. Russia itself was only eighty percent Russian (see Table 9.1). Even though no minority group makes up more than four percent of the population, the new Russian Federation faced breakaway movements, the most important of which came in Chechnya, which we will discuss later on. Not only did Russian troops twice invade that region, but Chechen rebels often bombed buildings and took hostages well inside Russia, including in Moscow.

Russians also had to deal with the humiliating reality that they were no longer a superpower. Even worse, many patriotic Russians were furious that their country had been stripped of territories and peoples, some of which they had controlled for centuries. Even more humiliating and contentious for some was the fact that the Russian government seemed to have to beg for economic aid from the same Western governments that so recently had feared Soviet military power.

Yeltsin

The 1990s proved to be a tumultuous decade. Much of the optimism about a more democratic and more capitalist Russia faded and set the tone for the Putin era in which some observers argue that those hopes have all but completely disappeared (see Table 9.6).

In retrospect, it is easy to see that these political problems stemmed in part from the failure of the new Russian regime to make a fresh start with a new constitution. Instead, the Russian Federation used Soviet-era institutions and was led by politicians who had built their careers

TABLE 9.6 Key Events in Russian Politics

YEAR	EVENT
1991	Collapse of USSR
1993	Referendum supports most reforms, coup attempt, first parliamentary elections, new constitution
1994	Outbreak of war in Chechnya
1995	Yeltsin's second heart attack, second parliamentary election
1996	Yeltsin reelected
2000	Vladimir Putin assumes presidency
2008	End of first Putin presidency
2012	Putin returns to the presidency

© Cengage Learning

as communists which meant that Yeltsin had to govern with a parliament that had been elected in 1989 and was dominated by men and women who had been loyal CPSU members until the bitter end.

Yeltsin also proved to be an erratic leader—at best. He had serious health problems whose effects were almost certainly magnified by his alcohol consumption, which was enormous even by Russian standards. The bold and decisive leader of the last years of communism found it hard to make strong and tough decisions. He surrounded himself with trusted allies who, for good or ill, were drawn from the ranks of the wealthy new **oligarchs**, the security services that replaced the KGB, and what came to be known as his "family" of personal advisors, which was led by his own daughter.

Within two years, Yeltsin seemed to be almost as embattled as Gorbachev had been just a few years earlier. The most radical reformers clamored for **shock therapy** or radical change in the economy through the overnight **privatization** of state-owned industries and strict fiscal policies that could bring the rampant inflation under control. Hardline holdovers from the CPSU became the new regime's conservatives in the sense that they resisted reform, preferring instead to reestablish the stability and social safety net of the Soviet era and, in some cases, to reintegrate the lost republics of the near abroad.

In some respects, the political landscape eerily resembled the one depicted in Figure 9.1 but, this time, with Yeltsin trying to govern from an increasingly shrinking center. Unlike Gorbachev, however, Yeltsin at first acted decisively, albeit in ways that were not conducive to democracy or market capitalism.

Throughout 1993, tensions continued to mount. By summer, Yeltsin's team apparently realized that it had made a mistake in trying to implement meaningful economic and political reforms under a communist-era political system. Therefore, it proposed a new constitution, which met stiff resistance from many parliamentary and regional leaders. In September, Yeltsin issued a decree that dissolved the Congress of People's Deputies and announced new legislative elections for December.

His opponents took the decree as "proof" that the president was trying to create a personal dictatorship. For the next two weeks, hundreds of people, including many parliamentary leaders, occupied the White House, as the then headquarters of the Russian government is known.

In sharp contrast to what he had done in 1991, Yeltsin countered by sending troops to surround the building and cut off its heat, water, and electricity. Once it became clear

PROFILES Boris Yeltsin

Boris Yeltsin was born in Siberia in 1931. Like most Soviet leaders of his generation, he was well educated. After beginning his career as a civil engineer, he soon turned to full-time party work and rose through the ranks in the city of Sverdlovsk, which has since returned to its precommunist name of Ekaterinburg.

Yeltsin was brought to Moscow in 1985 to lead the city's party organization and become a member of the Politburo. He soon became one of the country's most outspoken and radical reformers. For instance, he openly criticized party leaders for their lavish lifestyles. In 1988, Gorbachev felt he had gone too far and Yeltsin was stripped of all his major party and state posts. In 1990, Yeltsin quit the Communist Party at what turned out to be its final congress. The next year, he was elected president of the Russian Republic, which had previously been a minor position of next to no political significance. But with his personal popularity and the position he took in opposition to the August 1991 coup, Yeltsin soon became the most powerful politician in the USSR, as it collapsed, and in the new Russian Federation.

He was less successful as president. His years in office were marred by economic difficulties, ethnic unrest, corruption, and questions about his own health and sobriety.

Yeltsin died in 2007. ■

that the siege was not going to work, he ordered the troops to attack the White House. The occupiers proved no match for the soldiers and soon surrendered, but not before at least a hundred people were killed, the White House was heavily damaged, and the coup leaders were arrested.

At that point, Yeltsin added a new draft constitution to the December ballot. The constitution was approved, but to his embarrassment conservative parties won the most seats in the State Duma, the lower house of the new parliament.

These disruptive events did little to end the political stalemate. The president and parliament were still at loggerheads. If anything, the conservatives grew stronger and forced the president to drop more and more of his reformist goals and advisers. Meanwhile, Yeltsin's declining personal popularity and deteriorating health eroded his influence to the point that he seemed likely to lose his bid for reelection. Then, intense fighting broke out between the central government and separatists in the southern republic of Chechnya.

The elections settled nothing. Yeltsin now had to deal with a Duma that was even more firmly under opposition control. The president had to bring former general Alexander Lebed and other conservatives into his coalition. He also had to draw on support from many of the oligarchs, which led to a concentration of economic as well as political power. As a result, he grew ever more dependent on his political "family" which itself relied more and more on the intelligence services, now including Putin, who became part of Yeltsin's inner circle.

Conditions deteriorated for the rest of Yeltsin's abbreviated second term. As we will see in more detail later, the bottom fell out of the economy in 1998. The president's health was clearly deteriorating as he neared the end of his second and final term. Still, it came as a surprise when he resigned on New Year's Eve 1999, which had the effect of making Putin acting president.

Putin and Stability: At What Cost?

When Yeltsin named him prime minister that August, Putin was a virtual unknown. He had spent the bulk of his career in the KGB and had then served in the mayor's office in St. Petersburg after the collapse of the Soviet Union.

Putin's personal popularity soared that fall because of his successful prosecution of the second war in Chechnya. Some observers thought that the creation of fifteen new countries would ease ethnic tensions. However, because none of the new republics is anywhere near homogeneous, most have faced serious internal difficulties. The situation was by far the worst in Chechnya.

Chechens have long suffered under Russian rule. They were forcibly incorporated into the Russian empire at the beginning of the nineteenth century. They did not fare any better under the Soviets. Fearful that they might collaborate with the Germans, Stalin (and in this case he may have been right) ordered all Chechens deported and resettled more than one thousand miles away. They were only permitted to return as part of the reforms of the Khrushchev era.

Chechen separatists twice started insurrectionary wars, from 1994 to 1997 and then from 1999 until 2009. Together, they cost well over one hundred thousand lives, took a terrible toll on the government's legitimacy at home and abroad, and gave rise to periodic waves of terrorism

MAXIM MARMUR/AFP/Getty Images

Mourners following the 2004 attack by Chechen rebels on a school in Beslan, which killed hundreds of children.

that continue to this day. Nonetheless, the 2000 "victory" made it possible for Putin to consolidate his hold on power.

Putin also proved to be an effective politician, steering the newly found Unity Party to a victory in the 1999 parliamentary elections and then winning the presidency the following March without even having to go through a runoff election.

Putin has had a much greater impact on Russian politics than anyone expected. The turmoil many expected after the erratic Yeltsin retired did not materialize. Instead, Putin drew on colleagues from the security services and Yeltsin's inner circle to solidify his own power and stabilize the regime as a whole.

Putin's reputation, however, soon lost its luster. He clamped down on civil liberties, made it harder for opposition political parties to have a reasonable chance of winning elections, and forced a number of the oligarchs who had been close to Yeltsin into either prison or exile. As we will see in more detail in the rest of this chapter, his four years as prime minister before returning as president in early 2012 only reinforced two worrisome trends in Russian politics that will also reappear in most of the rest of this book.

First is the erosion of democracy. On almost any conventional political science indicator, Russia is less democratic than it was in 1991. Civil liberties are in greater danger. Elections are less free. Power in all forms is more concentrated, and office holders are less accountable.

Second and related is the fact that power is more personalized than anything we saw in Part 2. Both Yeltsin and Putin had touted their humble origins early in their political careers. Within years of taking office, not only had they amassed amazing personal wealth but their persona transcended almost everyone and everything else in ways in ways that would be unimaginable in the United States, Britain, France, or Germany. Put in other terms, institutions—including the rule of law—matter less than in any country we have covered so far.

Political Culture and Participation

It is hard to reach firm conclusions about Russian political culture for three reasons. First, open and voluntary political participation is new, which often makes it difficult to even know what to make of what average citizens do. Second, public opinion polling is still in its infancy, and given the Soviet past, there is every reason to believe that the polls are far from accurate. Third, there is little

doubt that elections are routinely rigged and participation manipulated in ways that also makes it hard to read much into civic engagement.

Nonetheless, we can reach a pair of somewhat paradoxical conclusions. On the one hand, there is reason to believe that most Russians want a democratic regime. On the other, their voting behavior suggests that they are not happy with the regime they have and are expressing that dissatisfaction in ways that seems to be leading the country farther and farther away from democracy.

Political Culture

In Part 2, we saw that most people believe that democracies in Western Europe and North America are legitimate. This is not the case in Russia, where the culture is characterized by widespread frustration and hostility.

It could hardly be otherwise. Russians have never been governed by a regime they considered legitimate. When people were finally given the opportunity to openly express their views in the late 1980s, they did so mostly by venting the anger built up over centuries of imperial rule and seventy years of Soviet control.

The shift to the new regime did not mean that the underlying culture changed. There is no question that most Russian voters think that their system is better than the one it replaced, as suggested in Table 9.7. Note, however, that these polls were conducted before Putin's crackdowns began in earnest, and answers today would probably be somewhat lower had pollsters continued to ask these questions.

There is also less systematically gathered evidence that some values that are not particularly conducive to democracy have carried over from the Soviet—and in some cases the tsarist—past. For instance, there is widespread suspicion of those in positions of authority. Most Russians, especially those who did relatively well under the old system, still seem to want the state to provide critical services, hand down directives, and take the initiative in important social, political, and economic domains.

TABLE 9.7 Percentage of Population Citing Improvement: 1993–2004

QUESTION	1993	1998	2000	2004
Compared to the political system before perestroika.	62	72	73	65
Our present system of governing.	36	70	72	63
The system of government we will have in five years.	52	49	64	88

Sources: Levada Center, www.russiavotes.org, accessed July 28, 2007.

About 65 percent of the respondents in a 2010 poll had a hard time defining democracy. About a quarter of them said that their country had never been a democracy, although a third believed that Russia was a democracy at the time. More than 90 percent of them thought they had no control over the government; almost as many felt little or no responsibility for what happened in the country. Three in five believed the government was above the law. Almost the same number thought that the judiciary should be controlled by state. Only 4 percent felt that private property was secure.

In 2012, 64 percent of one sample thought democracy as a "good fit" for Russia. At the same time, 56 percent also thought that a strong leader who does not have to bother with parliament and elections also made sense. Another poll found that three quarters of the population thought that order was more important than democracy.

Far less hopeful is a trend not seen in public opinion polls and which is even harder to pin down empirically. Many core traditions and values remain from the Soviet era, if not before. There are signs, for example, of anti-Western values that echo those of the tsarist-era Slavophiles.

Demographic trends do suggest that Russian culture may become more democratic over time. Young, urban, and well-educated people support liberal values far more than their older, rural, and poorly educated fellow citizens. But if such a shift occurs, it will take place over the course of the next generation or two, not the next year or two.

Political Parties and Elections

The concentration of power under Putin has led to a vicious circle in which forces loyal to him have made it all but impossible for the opposition to succeed by using tactics that fly in the face of most definitions of legitimate democratic practice. As a result, many potential opposition supporters are demoralized, while those who are involved are convinced they have no choice but to try to do an end run around what is known as the **vertical of power** (see the section on the Russian state). In other words, the electoral process will show us once again why the stakes of politics are so much higher in Russia and, similarly, how the big questions discussed in Chapter 1 are an inescapable part of political life.

The Party System

For the first decade and a half of its history, Russia had what scholars who conduct the New Russia Barometre (NRB) polls call a "floating" party system (www.cspp.strath.ac.uk/). Parties came and went. Few sank deep social roots. Few even offered clear policy options.

The array of parties that voters had to choose from had little in common with the ones covered in Part 2, where

Comparative Emphasis: Women

Few women forged prominent political careers in communist countries. For good or ill, the same is true in postcommunist Russia. Only 13.6 percent of the members of the State Duma elected in 2011 are women, which places Russia 94th out of the 188 countries covered in the International Parliamentary Union's data base. As one journalist put it almost a decade ago, women are "breadwinners at home, outcasts in politics."

Most Russian women have a hard time avoiding "gender inequality." Most have no choice but to work, perform almost all the household chores, and hand over their paychecks to their husbands. One sign of women's second-class status is reproductive politics. Abortion has been legal since 1920. However, it was also used as an alternative to birth control during the Soviet era, and Russia still has the highest abortion rate in the world. In 2001, the number of abortions exceeded that of live births by over a million.

There is a small women's movement. For instance, a small but unknown number of Russian women participated in a demonstration protesting violence against women in November 2010, an event that is held annually as part of a United Nations campaign.

A number of prominent dissident women have been assassinated, almost certainly with the complicity of the authorities. The most prominent of them was Anna Politkovskaya. She was a crusading investigative journalist for one of the few newspapers that didn't fall under Kremlin control. On October 7, 2006, she was shot while taking the elevator to her apartment. It was only five years later that someone was arrested for her murder. ■

voters choose among essentially the same organizations from election to election. And because the parties do not change their positions all that much from one ballot to the next, most voters regularly vote for the same one most of the time. That enduring identification with political parties links people's preferences to what politicians do as policy makers.

TABLE 9.8 State Duma Elections (2003–2011)

PARTY	2003 VOTE (%)	2003 SEATS	2007 VOTE (%)	2007 SEATS	2011 VOTE (%)	2011 SEATS	SEATS
United Russia	37.6	223	64.3	315	49.3	238	238
Communists	12.6	52	11.6	57	13.2	92	92
Liberal Democrats	11.5	36	8.1	40	11.7	64	56
Yabloko, Just Russia and predecessors	17.3	49	8.3	38	20.8	56	64
Independents	21.0	86	7.7	0	3.8	0	---

© Cengage Learning 2015

That is not what Russia is like today. Through the mechanisms hinted at earlier, a single party, **United Russia,** has developed a stranglehold on power that seems likely to last as long as its architect, President Putin, remains in charge.[5] Otherwise, the party system is in disarray. If anyone is going to pose a credible challenge to Putin and his colleagues, it will almost certainly come from outside the electoral process, as we will see toward the end of this section.

United Russia is not like any of the political parties considered in Part 2 in that it has never been defined by its stance on divisive issues. Rather, it is what observers of Russian politics call a **party of power,** created not so much to defend policy proposals or ideological positions as to promote the interests of the current leadership.

It is not the first party of power. In 1995, then-Prime Minister Viktor Chernomyrdin created **Our Home Is Russia.** It, too, was short on ideology and existed largely to support Chernomyrdin and his entourage. When he was forced to resign in 1998, the party's fortunes collapsed and disappeared altogether in 2000.

United Russia was formed for the 1999 Duma election, when it was known as Unity. Its specific origins are shrouded in secrecy, but all signs indicate that the oligarch Boris Berezovsky and other members of the Yeltsin "family" created it. It had little support in the public opinion polls until Putin's popularity began to soar because of his forceful prosecution of the war in Chechnya. Three months after its creation, Unity came within a single percentage point of the Communists. It later merged with Fatherland-All Russia and took on its new name.

Putin publicly kept his distance from the party at first. By the time of the 2003 and 2004 campaigns, there was no longer any pretense of his staying above the political fray. In fact, the most critical observers thought he always intended to restructure the entire party system from the top so that the middle-of-the-road United Russia could dominate, which it has done ever since (see Table 9.8). Later in the chapter, we will consider why these numbers are almost certainly inaccurate, which will also be another sign of democracy's weakness in Putin's Russia.

The most consistent opposition has come from the Communist Party, which reinvented itself as the **Communist Party of the Russian Federation (CPRF)** and won the most votes until it was eclipsed by United Russia. It was the only party that had a nationwide organization, which allowed it to do such things as conduct door-to-door campaigns throughout the country. More important, its support steadily increased until it earned nearly a quarter of the vote in 1999. Its leader and presidential candidate, **Gennady Zyuganov (1944–),** has consistently come in second in presidential elections (see Table 9.9).

Like the reformed communist parties in Eastern Europe, the CPRF is not a carbon copy of the old Stalinist machine. The new party has few prominent Soviet-era communists in its leadership. Zyuganov presents himself as a senior statesman whose party tries to protect the interests of the poor and dispossessed in ways that are not terribly different from those of the social democratic parties discussed in Part 2.

TABLE 9.9 Presidential Elections: 2000–12

CANDIDATE/PARTY	2000	2004	2008	2012
Putin (United Russia)[a]	52.3	71.9	71.3	63.6
Zyuganov (CPRF)[b]	29.2	13.8	18.0	17.2
Zhirinovsky (Liberal Democrat)[c]	2.7	2.0	9.5	6.2
Others	13.9	8.0	1.3	11.8

© Cengage Learning 2015

Note: Figures do not add to 100 percent because "against all" (through 2004) and spoiled ballots have been removed.

a. Dmitri Medvedev in 2008.

b. Nikolai Chartonov in 2004.

c. Oleg Malyshkin in 2004.

---

[5]No major Russian political party has an English language website, and few of them last longer than a single election. Therefore, no links have been included in the text.

That said, the party is far less reformist than its Eastern European counterparts. Zyuganov was a staunch opponent of the Gorbachev-era reforms. He also headed a shady "national salvation front" that seemed to want to re-create the Soviet Union. He also was quoted as saying that the army should combat "the destructive might of rootless democracy," and he served on the editorial board of a conservative and often anti-Semitic newspaper. Like many former communists, Zyuganov and his colleagues have adopted nationalistic positions that sometimes include thinly veiled references to expanding the Russian Federation's border into the near abroad.

The Communists are still the best-organized party in Russia, because they can draw on the thousands of mid- and lower-level party officials from the old CPSU. One asset it does not have, however, is the property the CPSU used to own, which was all transferred to the state.

The CPRF's influence peaked in 1995 when it and other antireform factions held enough seats to block many of Yeltsin's legislative measures. All of those groups began what looks like a permanent decline in 1999 and now seem to have settled in at between 10 and 20 percent of the vote.

Most of the rest of the opposition is in serious trouble—at best.

The one party born after 1991 that has a reasonable chance of surviving is **Just Russia.** It is a social democratic party that would like to fill the same space similar parties occupy in Western Europe. It scored a temporary breakthrough 2011 when it won sixty-four seats, but its presidential candidate, Sergei Mironov, did not even get 4 percent of the presidential vote the next year. In short, its future is very much in doubt.

Yabloko is the last surviving reformist party left from a group of organizations that together once won a quarter of the vote. Yabloko (Russian for *apple*) is an acronym for its three founding leaders, Grigori Yavlinsky, Yuri Boldyrev, and Vladimir Lukin. Only Yavlinsky and Lukin, are still with the party. Of the reformist parties, it has taken the strongest stand not only in support of democracy but also for the retention of some form of welfare state, which makes it most like the European social democratic parties. It also does reasonably well among intellectuals who were prominent supporters of Gorbachev's reforms. Yabloko's vote dropped consistently under both Yeltsin and Putin as Russians grew weary of what most of them saw as an unmet and unmeetable reformist agenda. The party may have received its death knell in 2012 when Yavlinsky was denied the right to run on the claim that a quarter of the signatures on his nominating petition were invalid.

Finally, Russia has one significant party that is clearly antidemocratic—the **Liberal Democrats,** headed by the enigmatic **Vladimir Zhirinovsky** (1946–). Almost everything about him is murky. Despite his anti-Semitic ravings, he is of Jewish origin. Some think he was once a KGB agent who was paid to infiltrate Jewish and dissident organizations during the 1970s and 1980s.

AP Photo/Misha Japaridze

An angry woman confronting Liberal Democratic Party leader Vladimir Zhirinovsky during a Duma debate on Russia's relationship with the North Atlantic Treaty Organization (NATO) in September 1995.

There is no debating one thing. Zhirinovsky is a loose cannon whose often-frightening rhetoric struck a chord with a significant proportion of Russia's most alienated voters. Since he burst onto the scene in 1993, he has:

- Hinted that he would use nuclear weapons on Japan.

- Advocated expanding the Russian border all the way to the Indian Ocean.

- Blamed Western governments and businessmen (in his case, it is always men) for the collapse of the Soviet Union.

- Attacked just about every reformist politician in Russia (for instance, alleging that Yeltsin was in power only because of the Central Intelligence Agency).

The party's fortunes are in decline. Russians have grown tired of Zhirinovsky's positions and antics. The party was technically ruled unconstitutional for the 1999 election and had to rebrand itself as the Zhirinovsky Bloc. It only won 6 percent of the vote in 1999, and then Zhirinovsky did not win even half that in 2000. He rebounded to nearly 12 percent four years later. His party won forty seats in 2007, but it lost most of its autonomy because it came to be widely seen as the right wing of the Putin–Medvedev coalition. It rebounded a bit in 2011 but fell below 10 percent in the presidential election the next year, which is what most observers expect will be its normal total as long as Zhirinovsky heads the party.

Elections

At first Russia had reasonably free and fair elections, the first it had ever had. That is far from the case today when the country is often cited as an example of the way seemingly competitive elections can be used as a veneer for far more authoritarian practices.

Russians' first opportunity to vote in a reasonably free election came in the 1993 referendum (www.russiavotes.org). Yeltsin won a less than ringing endorsement of only some of his plans, revealing some of the dissatisfaction that would culminate in the coup attempt later that year.

Since then, Russians have voted in eleven national elections—six for the Duma (1993, 1995, 1999, 2003, 2007, and 2011) and five for the presidency (1996, 2000, 2004, 2008, and 2012). Each of these elections was less fair and competitive than the one before it. At this point, their results are so obviously rigged that few analysts even bother trying to explain the vote through an examination of why individuals or groups of voters acted voted as they did.

Until 2007, Duma deputies were elected using a system that looked a lot like Germany's. Winners of the 450 seats

Another Look on the Light Side

Russian elections are not (yet) the slick affairs we've become used to in the West. To see why, consider the following descriptions of television ads that aired during the 1995 Duma campaign.

Only Our Home Is Russia had slick, Western-style commercials with rapidly changing and reassuring images backed by synthesized music. All the others ranged from unprofessional to incompetent. Some simply showed "talking heads," and even they were unable to keep within their assigned time limits.

Some of the less-than-serious parties, of course, had less-than-serious ads. The Beer Lovers' Party (0.62 percent of the vote) started theirs with two old women looking disapprovingly at a drunken man staggering along a muddy path, a bottle of vodka sticking out of his pocket. One woman said to the other: "This is not an acceptable way to drink." Immediately the scene shifted to three men at a picnic on a sunny day, drinking beer. One of the women said to the others: "This is an acceptable way to drink." The Ivan Rybkin Bloc (Rybkin was the outgoing speaker of the Duma, although his party only won 1.11 percent of the vote) ran an ad showing a conversation between two cows in which one cow (apparently Rybkin) tried to explain justice to the other by asking if (s)he had ever seen or eaten butter. It ended with the first cow eating a slice of bread covered with butter and saying that they would all have butter with their bread if Rybkin was reelected. The Communists ran a simplistic piece in which they showed horror scenes from the Russian past and asked: "Who will stop this?" The answer was obvious. Yabloko had one of Isaac Newton (though the ad said it was Lord Byron) getting hit by an apple falling from a tree.

The two strangest ads were made by the Liberal Democrats. The first showed a couple watching television in bed. Former Soviet leader Brezhnev came on; they said he was boring. Then came Gorbachev; they said they had seen all that before. Finally it was Zhirinovsky's turn, and this time they said that this was more interesting even as their body language made it clear that watching more television was not on their agenda for the rest of the evening. The second ad took place in an upscale nightclub. After the singer finished her act, she was lured back onstage for an encore that was a much more upbeat song with the refrain, "Without you, this would be boring; Vladimir Wolfovich [as Zhirinovsky is commonly known], you turn me on."

The quality of television ads has improved noticeably since then. However, the state's all but complete control of the mass media has made campaign ads practically irrelevant, whether they are competently made or not.

were chosen on separate ballots. Half were elected by proportional representation, and the rest from single-member districts. In the proportional half of the ballot, seats only went to parties that won at least 5 percent of the vote nationwide. In the single-member district half, whoever got the most votes in a district won.

The dual system for choosing Duma members has led to very different outcomes from those we saw in Germany. There, in every election in the past fifty years, the major parties have won just about all of the single-member districts, and the proportional side of the ballot is used mainly to make minor adjustments so that the parliamentary delegations accurately reflect the parties' overall support.

In Russia, anywhere from 60 to 110 independents were elected from the single-member districts before 2003 when the single-member districts were eliminated. They were a thorn in Yeltsin and Putin's political side because most independent Duma members were beyond the control of national party leaders. Beginning with the 2007 election, all 450 seats are chosen on a proportional basis and allotted only to parties winning 7 percent of the vote. In 2011, only four parties broke that barrier. That allowed United Russia to turn 49 percent of the vote into a commanding 55 percent majority of Duma seats.

Presidential elections follow the French model. Anyone who gets a required number of signatures can run on a first ballot. If no one wins a majority in that first round of voting, the top two candidates compete in a runoff two weeks later. Unlike France, however, the second ballot has only been needed once. In every election since 1996, the winner has won a majority at the first ballot, although there have been questions about the honesty of each of them.

Any pretense of electoral fairness disappeared under Putin. He has reshaped the party system so that it can be more easily manipulated, if not controlled outright, from the center. There has been widespread fraud of almost every imaginable form in each election during this century. In fact, it is probably charitable to call elections in Russia semicompetitive since nothing about them is free or democratic in any meaningful sense of those terms.

Since he came to power in 1999, the government has taken effective control of all the television stations, which it has used to assiduously promote Putin and his policies. Before the 2003 legislative election, he forced a law through the Duma which made it impossible for small parties without nationwide support to even get on the ballot. In 2005, he was responsible for another law that eliminated single-member districts, making it harder for regional parties and independents to run, and raised the

minimum threshold a party needs to get Duma seats from 5 to 7 percent of the vote.

Civil Society

Perhaps the most worrying concern about Russia's path toward or away from democracy lies in the weakness of its civil society. As we have seen in other chapters, a strong civil society is important because it helps build legitimacy *and* the belief that people can have an impact on the policy decisions made by elites.

Not surprisingly, given Russia's history, civil society has always been weak, atomized, and apolitical. Russia does have the trade unions, environmental groups, trade associations, and the other kinds of interest groups found in established democracies. However, they are very weak except for the ones the state controls. As with political parties, the Putin regime has made it harder for groups to organize let alone effectively assert their influence.

Laws passed since 2006 have made this situation worse. The Kremlin had been worried about the role nongovernmental organizations (NGOs) had played in nonviolent protests that produced political change in a number of countries in the near abroad. That year, the Duma passed a law requiring all NGOs to register with the state so that their activities could be monitored by it. Particularly vulnerable are NGOs whose funding comes largely from the West, including such respected organizations as Human Rights Watch.

In 2008, the government issued a decree that cut the number of international groups that could fund Russian NGOs on a tax-free basis from 101 to 12, including the International Committee of the Red Cross and the World Wildlife Fund. A 2012 law forced international NGOs to register as foreign agents, which most observers claimed was sheer intimidation. Another 2012 law that made libel and slander felony offenses punishable by long prison terms was used to prosecute the members of Pussy Riot mentioned at the beginning of the chapter.

Dissatisfaction with the government has periodically erupted in outside-the-system protests, most recently after the 2011 Duma election. There is little doubt that the combination of state control of the media, voter intimidation, and open vote buying paved the way for United Russia's landslide victory in an election it probably would have won anyway. Instances of fraud were reported at more than 100,000 polling places where roughly a quarter of all Russians had voted. Opposition newspapers ran photographs of officials running dozens of ballots they had presumably filled in through the scanning machines that tallied the vote. In perhaps the most preposterous example of all, official returns showed that 99 percent of voters in Chechnya (of all places) had voted for United Russia.

The election was the last straw for many Russians, including well-educated, young, middle-class voters, as well as long-time dissidents. Protests broke out almost immediately when the results were announced and continued until Putin was sworn in as president five months later. Demonstrators demanded changes in the electoral law, an end to all restrictions on free speech, and, in some cases, the resignations of Putin and Medvedev. Most of the demonstrations were peaceful, yet the authorities arrested hundreds of people, including prominent opposition figures and a handful of popular media stars.

The demonstrations petered out once it became clear that they were not going to accomplish anything in the short run. Some small organizations are trying to fill the gaping political void. Among the most prominent is the fledgling People's Freedom Party headed by Ilya Yashin who, then 28 years old, once ran Yaboloko's youth wing. Along with former chess champion and dissident, Garry Kasparov, the young activists are trying to create a counter government through what they call the Coordinating Council. So far, the opposition is deeply divided and is hampered by a lack of funds and organizational skills. It called for a March of Millions that drew more like ten thousand.

More often than not, it faces even larger rallies from the ranks of groups like *Nashi,* which is a neo-nationalist movement that is almost certainly funded by the regime. *Nashi* is a GONGO or a Government Organized Nongovernmental Organization, which may seem like a contradiction in terms, since most NGOs are formed in order to compel states to change their policies and practices. GONGOs, by contrast, are created and funded by authoritarian governments to support or defend the state's interests. For the moment at least, Russian GONGOs have far more influence than the genuine NGOs that the state is simultaneously trying to destroy.

As we will also see in Chapter 13 on Iran, some observers saw harbingers of a more democratic future in these protests. However, these kinds of protests alone are not likely to marshal the resources needed to get recalcitrant leaders to enact meaningful and lasting reforms.

On the other hand, we have also seen revolutions and other forms of sweeping change appear from what seemed like out of nowhere as in the recent Arab Spring or Eastern Europe in 1989. Given that history, it may just be that the small protests in 2011 will prove to be the first step toward something much larger.

Comparative Emphasis: Conflict

As is the case in most of the postcommunist countries, Russia has experienced plenty of conflict since Gorbachev opened the political floodgates. Unlike the industrialized democracies, however, much of the protest is aimed not just at individual politicians and their policies but at the regime as well.

Other than in Chechnya, there have been surprisingly few violent protests. However, dozens of politicians, journalists, human rights activists, and business leaders have been assassinated. In the most blatant attack in recent years, Andrei Litvinenko was attacked in London on November 1, 2006, and died three weeks later. Litvinenko had been a KGB agent. He was poisoned with a radioactive chemical in an attack that was widely believed to have been carried out by the state security service in Moscow. ■

The Russian State: The Vertical of Power

Each country examined in the remainder of this book is different from those in Part 2 in many ways. None is more important than the limited impact of constitutions and the rule law. All have constitutions that supposedly specify how offices are structured, bills are passed, rights are ensured, and the like. However, constitutions matter less than they do in any of the industrialized democracies. In a country like Russia, it is just as important to recognize that other institutions, which are not mentioned in the constitution, probably have more political clout than the State Duma, cabinet, or any other legally authorized body (www.constitution.ru/en/10003000-01.htm).

In Russia, power is more fluid. Its parameters are determined as much by who holds which offices and what resources they have at their disposal as by the rules laid out in the constitution and other legal documents. That was obviously the case when Putin was "demoted" to prime minister in 2008 but still held more power than anyone in the country by far.

Most observers think that the regime is authoritarian as summed up in the badly translated Russian term, Vertical

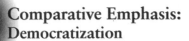

Comparative Emphasis: Democratization

Many terms are used to encapsulate the concentration of power in Russia today.

None is more evocative than Allen Lynch's term "Potemkin Democracy." In 1787, Grigory Potemkin was the member of Catherine the Great's cabinet who was in charge of a military campaign in Crimea. To "convince" the Tsarina that he had been successful, he had a group of "villages" built along the road she traveled while visiting the region. The "buildings" were nothing but façades. To this day, such attempts to mislead Russian rulers or people alike are known as Potemkin Villages.

It is in that sense that Lynch calls Russia today a Potemkin Democracy. ∎

of Power (www.rferl.org/archive/The_Power_Vertical/latest/884/884.html). Like most authoritarian regimes today, Putin's Russia does not aspire to be totalitarian and control all of everyone's life. It almost certainly could not be even if Putin and his colleagues wanted it to, because of the relative openness of our globalizing world. However, his government has done everything in its power to weaken all potential opposition, which has allowed the ruling elite to all but monopolize political and economic power.

The Presidency

Given Russian traditions and the rocky relations between President Yeltsin and what was then still the Supreme Soviet, it came as no surprise that the anchor of Russia's new constitutional order is a strong presidency (www.eng.kremlin.ru). There was every reason to believe that a more conventional parliamentary system would have led to a deadlock that was at least as debilitating as that in Fourth Republic France.

Beginning with the 2012 election, the president is chosen for a six-year term in a two-ballot system. Any candidate who gets a million signatures (which could be bought for a dollar apiece in 2004) can run on the first ballot. If a candidate gets a majority then, he or she wins outright, as has been the case in the last four elections. If, however, no one wins more than half of the votes cast, the first- and second-place candidates meet in a runoff two weeks later.

The president appoints the prime minister and the other cabinet members (see Table 9.10). The Duma can reject the president's choice, but if it does so three times, the president can dissolve the Duma and call for new elections, which almost happened in 1998. Since 2000, United Russia has had a clear majority which has turned the Duma into a rubber stamp. There is also now little or no ambiguity about the relative role of the president and prime minister. After Chernomyrdin was forced to resign in 1998, the prime minister has clearly been number two, much as is the case in France, with the single exception of Medvedev's term when Putin had to give up the presidency and served as prime minister instead. In fact, the switch in positions was little more than a legal fiction, because for all intents and purposes, Putin continued to act as if he were president no matter what his formal title happened to be.

The president can issue decrees that have the force of law in many policy areas. In 2011, President Medvedev issued one to cut the size of the government work force by 20 percent over the next two years. The following year, Putin issued a decree banning Gazprom and other state-owned industries from giving information to or renegotiating contracts with foreign governments.

It should already be clear that presidential power does not rest primarily on the constitution or any other law. Instead, Putin has been able to bypass their provisions to create an extremely centralized administration that seems all but certain to last until he leaves office, which would not be until 2024 if he serves two more full terms.

Since the mid-1990s, authority at the subpresidential level has been concentrated in the **power ministries**—defense; foreign affairs; interior (including the police); the Federal Security Bureau (FSB), which is the successor to the Soviet-era KGB; and the Security Council, sometimes known as the *siloviki*, which is best translated as the "men of force."

TABLE 9.10 Russian Presidents and Prime Ministers

PRESIDENT	PRIME MINISTER
Boris Yeltsin (1991–99)	Boris Yeltsin (1991–92)
	Yegor Gaidar (Acting 1992–93)
	Viktor Chernomyrdin (1993–98)
	Sergei Kiriyenko (1998)
	Yevgeni Primakov (1998–99)
	Sergei Stepashin (1999)
	Vladimir Putin (1999)
Vladimir Putin (2000–)	Mikhail Kasyanov (2000–04)
	Mikhail Fradkov (2004–07)
	Viktor Zubkov (2007–08)
Dmitri Medvedev (2008–12)	Vladimir Putin (2008–12)
Vladimir Putin (2012–)	Dmitri Medvedev (2012–)

Most of them are housed in the **Presidential Administration** which is the rough equivalent to the personal staff of a Western president or prime minister. In this case, however, it consists of upwards of 40,000 individuals whose primary loyalty is to Putin even during his "exile" as prime minister. It coordinates most areas of national policy making and has been the primary mechanism through which Putin's team has controlled the country. Thus, it has been the main force behind the creation of state-led consortia in such industries as energy, aviation, arms sales, and high technology. Critics refer to it as a parallel government that is more important than anything provided for in the constitution.

It is not altogether clear how Putin was able to amass so much power. Part of it has to be the boost in support he got as a result of the forceful prosecution of the second Chechen war right after he was named prime minister. There is little doubt, however, that by 2003, virtually the entire team he had inherited from Yeltsin had been replaced by people almost totally beholden to him. There is little doubt, too, that Putin has been able to use "compromising material" (*kompromat*) to force rivals to either quit or toe his line.

Comparative Emphasis: Constitutions

Constitutions go a long way toward shaping the way political life unfolds in the industrialized democracies, although political scientists probably overestimate their importance.

That is certainly not the case in Russia or the other countries covered in the rest of the book.

It isn't just that Putin and Medvedev have explicitly violated the Russian constitution. Rather, the constitution simply doesn't matter as much as it does in most established democracies, which is part of what political scientists have in mind when they talk about the rule of law—or the absence thereof.

In other words, Putin and his colleagues have been able to do political "end runs" around constitutional and other limitations on their power.

The more limited impact of constitutions and institutions in general in countries like Russia will be a key part of any understanding of the second half of this book. ■

The Oligarchs

That same pattern can be seen in the changing role of the tiny handful of ultra-rich business leaders known generically as the oligarchs. As we will see in the section on economic policy, they owe their existence to the unusual way in which the Soviet economy was privatized. At first, they were powerful in their own right. Without the oligarchs, Yeltsin would almost certainly have lost his reelection in 1996. In retrospect, they probably were even more powerful than he was at the time.

The most influential early oligarch was **Boris Berezovsky** (1946–2013). He grew up in a nominally Jewish family that was part of Moscow's intellectual elite. Berezovsky earned a PhD in mathematics and electronics and then joined the prestigious Academy of Sciences, where he specialized in computerized management systems. He used his contacts to launch his first business during the Gorbachev years. By the time the USSR collapsed, he was already a major trader in the murky market between the state-owned and private sectors of the economy. When the Yeltsin government virtually gave away shares in the nationalized industries, Berezovsky and the oligarchs gained control over thousands of companies.

No one thought it was an outrageous overstatement when Berezovsky declared in 1997 that he and six other businessmen controlled over half of Russia's GNP. Their political power became clear toward the end of Yeltsin's first term in office. Analysts began criticizing what they thought was the undue influence of the family—a small circle of relatives and advisers who had tremendous influence over the president. Berezovsky, himself, was part of that group because of his media empire, which included two of the most respected newspapers and the most widely watched television network, which he used to rescue the floundering Yeltsin presidency. After Yeltsin was reelected, they used their wealth and media power to help United Russia and paved the way for Putin's meteoric rise.

There have always been eyebrows raised about the oligarchs and their lavish lifestyles. Together, they may also have sent more money abroad than foreigners have invested in Russia since 1991. Most, too, have close, if poorly documented, ties to the Russian mafia. All observers agree that the early oligarchs and Yeltsin's biological family made millions of dollars through shady deals, if not outright corruption, which led Putin to grant them all immunity from prosecution in one of his first steps as acting president.

Putin quickly moved to redirect power away from the original oligarchs. Within months of taking power, he held a closed-door (but quickly leaked) meeting with twenty of the leading "businessmen" in which he laid down the law. The oligarchs would be allowed to keep their wealth if—and only if—they made at least semi-reasonable tax payments and stayed out of politics, by which Putin meant that they did not challenge his authority.

He went after everyone else, starting with Vladimir Gusinksy, whose television network, NTV, openly condemned Putin. Gusinsky was arrested for corruption, and control of NTV was handed over to the natural gas monopoly, Gazprom, which the state was simultaneously taking over. After being released on bail, Gusinsky moved abroad. Berezovsky, too, ran afoul of Putin and joined Gusinsky in exile in late 2001 after losing his media empire. After his business empire collapsed, he committed suicide in 2013.

Most of the attention in the last few years has been given to the case of **Mikhail Khodorkovsky** (1963–). He probably was the richest of the oligarchs and apparently thought he could safely remain in Russia even though he contributed money to opposition parties as well as United Russia. Perhaps to his surprise, he was arrested by state security forces on tax evasion charges while his plane was being refueled in Siberia in 2003. Two years later he was sentenced to eight years in prison in Siberia. In 2010, he was tried on other charges and sentenced to another seven-year term. Barring unforeseeable changes in Moscow, Khodorkovsky will spend the rest of his life in prison.

There are still economic oligarchs today. The one difference is that they are almost completely under Putin's control.

Today's oligarchs are as wealthy and even more ostentatious. The top ten are worth about $20 billion each.

Oligarchs head Russia's largest and most visible corporations, such as the petrochemical giants Lukoil and Sibneft. Most maintain residences outside of the country, including Roman Abramovich (1966–), who owns London's Chelsea soccer team. In 2009, he bought a controlling interest in Russia's largest steel manufacturer and was ranked as the fifty-first richest person in the world. Abramovich has largely stayed out of politics other than serving for eight years as provincial governor of Chukhotka, one of the country's poorest regions.

The one possible exception to the rule is Mikhail Prokhorov (1965–), who made his billions in the precious metals business and later bought the Brooklyn Nets of the National Basketball Association (at 6 feet 8 inches, he is the NBA's tallest as well as its only foreign owner). Prokhorov has been critical of Putin and came in a distant third in the 2012 presidential election. It is not clear if he will either lead a full-fledged opposition party or incur Putin's wrath.

The Parliament

A word's history often tells us a lot. I used two terms to describe parliaments in Part 2. *Parliament* itself is derived from the French *parler* which means to speak. The English term *legislature* refers to a body that literally makes laws. *Duma* is based on the Russian word *dumat'* which means to think. Some observers doubt that it does even that.

Mikhail Khodorkovsky in the cage he was kept in during his trial.

TATYANA MAKEYEVA/AFP/Getty Images

Until 1999, the Duma was the main lightning rod in the intense conflicts of the Yeltsin years. That does not mean, however, that the parliament has ever been all that powerful. In fact, the 1993 constitution was written to minimize its impact.

As is the case in most countries, the parliament consists of two houses. The upper house, the **Federation Council,** has two members from each republic and region for a total of 168. Like most upper houses, however, it can do little more than delay the passage of legislation. If anything, its power declined even further when its members became, by all intents and purposes, presidential appointees in 2004.

The lower house, the State Duma, is elected by proportional representation. The Duma itself is a fairly wild place by Western standards. Deputies scream at each other and walkouts are common. So are fistfights. By 1995, eighty-seven candidates had either been convicted of felonies or were under indictment.

More important for our purposes is the fact that the State Duma does not have much real power. It cannot, for example, force the executive to enforce the laws it passes, and it has only limited influence over the budget. The Duma has no effective ability to cast a vote of no confidence and force a prime minister and cabinet out of office. It also can do little to remove a president.

The Communists and other opponents of reform controlled the Duma following the first two elections. They used that base to block many policy proposals requiring legislative approval and to keep reformist nominees from taking or holding onto office. With the emergence of United Russia, however, the Duma has lost the power to obstruct what the president wants. Putin has the kind of disciplined parliamentary majority we find in Britain's House of Commons. What's more, given the loyalty of United Russia Duma members to Putin and the party machine, there is virtually no chance that they will defy leadership wishes on any vote that counts. In short, the Duma now eagerly passes all of their major legislative initiatives, including laws that reduced the power of the republics and regions, restructured the party system, and reduced taxes.

The Bureaucracy

Yeltsin's team wanted to purge the bureaucracy of officials who had been at the heart of the communist system. In areas such as the Foreign Ministry and the various agencies that replaced the KGB, many top officials did lose their jobs. In practice, however, they could not get rid of the entire old guard because the country lacked trained personnel to replace them.

Today, Yeltsin's failures probably no longer matter, because Putin has filled the Presidential Administration and the upper reaches of the bureaucracy in general with his own loyalists. Many of them have backgrounds in the security services, most notably the FSB, the main body that replaced the KGB, which is, of course, where Putin spent his career before moving to Moscow.

Analysts do not worry about their communist background, per se. After all, the Soviet Union collapsed more than twenty years ago, and few of today's leaders played important political roles in it. Rather, they worry more about how they use *kompromat* they have on all leading officials—including Putin—to keep all key decision makers in line.

Also of concern is the corruption that is built into the system. Russian salaries are low. Senior officials rarely make much more than $10,000 a year—officially. Their real income is apparently closer to $1 million. Offices can be bought. Estimates range from $50,000 for a low-level police officer to $1 million for a senior customs official to $10 million for a cabinet ministry.

The Judiciary

The same case can be made for the legal system. Before 1991, the Soviet judiciary was little more than a cog in the party machine.

The new Russian republic has tried to rebuild a judicial system that used to invariably find defendants guilty and historically relied on show trials in high-profile cases. Most notably, it established a Constitutional Court to deal with cases involving legal principle (www.supcourt.ru/catalog.php?c1=English). Similarly, the Supreme Court serves as a final court of appeal in criminal, civil, and administrative cases. Both have been reasonably active. The Constitutional Court, for example, played a major role in determining how the 1993 referendum was conducted.

Today, however, any semblance of judicial independence has disappeared, as one can see in cases ranging from Khodorkovsky's to the prison sentence imposed on the members of Pussy Riot. The president and heads of the two houses (who are themselves controlled by Putin) appoint all senior judges, and they are not about to appoint anyone he cannot count on.

Worries about the legal system go even deeper. Basic civil liberties are by no means guaranteed, especially outside the major cities. At least sixteen journalists have been killed since Putin took office. Although no one has been convicted of any of those murders, the assumption is that the state is responsible for most of them. Of all the postcommunist states, only Turkmenistan and Uzbekistan have lower scores on Freedom House's scale of judicial independence.

The Federation

On paper, the Soviet Union supposedly was a federal system. Its fifteen union republics supposedly joined it voluntarily. The constitutions adopted over the years asserted that republics had a number of rights and could even secede from the USSR. But those were only paper rights. Until the Gorbachev years, party leaders in Moscow determined policy at all levels of government.

The republics' subservience ended when the eruption of decades-old hostilities precipitated the Soviet collapse. In the new Russia, early separatist protests prompted authorities at all levels to agree to a nationwide Federation Treaty and a series of bilateral agreements with eight of the republics, which granted a degree of autonomy when they dealt with local issues and let them keep profits from the sale of locally produced goods.

Tiny Tyva was even given the right to secede, but outright independence has only been a source of major controversy in Chechnya. Most of the larger subnational units are in the heavily populated west and are completely surrounded by Russia. Only Tatarstan and the impoverished Bashkyria have more than three million people; eleven have fewer than one million.

As a result, the Russian Federation is a mixture of twenty-one autonomous republics and sixty-eight other bodies with various titles. All are defined as "subjects of the federation," such as the autonomous *okrug* of Chukotka, mentioned earlier because of its connection with Abramovich. All are represented in the Federation Council. In theory, their governors are chosen by their elected legislatures.

However, as with everything else in Russia, the realities of political life for the republics and regions have little in common with what the constitution calls for. Many local leaders turned their jurisdictions into personal fiefdoms, all but ignoring Moscow's policies and regulations. As a result, in May 2000, Putin created seven new "federal districts" between the national government and the republics and regions, each of which is headed by a presidential appointee. Another law gives the president the power to remove a governor if he or she refuses to make local law conform to national policy. Finally, a 2009 law removes the last figment of democracy from the federal units. Now, the majority party in the legislature (United Russia in all but two regions) nominates candidates for governor, and the president makes the final appointment.

The Military

In studying Russia, we also have to introduce one institution that we could safely ignore in Part 2 but that will feature prominently in the rest of this book, the military. Under the Soviets, the military was not actively involved in politics other than in trying to increase its piece of the budgetary pie.

So far, this has largely been true in postcommunist Russia as well. Yeltsin survived the 1993 coup attempt because the military remained loyal to the regime. They attacked the Russian White House even though one of the leading conspirators, Vice President Alexander Rutskoi, was a former air force general and one of the few heroes of the war in Afghanistan.

However, many commentators are worried that the military might not stay out of politics. Yeltsin needed support from another prominent former general, Alexander Lebed, to win in 1996. There have been rumors of frustration within the military. This is hardly surprising in a country whose past influence was largely a function of its military might, which disappeared virtually overnight. Senior officers are worried, too, because many men and women who serve under them are living in abject poverty.

Still, Russia has the fifth largest military in the world and has several thousand nuclear warheads. Much of its technology is outdated, and few observers think it could be a major fighting force in the near future.

Public Policy

The basic pattern in Russian public policy mirrors what we have just seen about the state. Yeltsin's government pursued an inconsistent set of reforms, support for which mostly fizzled out during his second term. Under Putin, public policy making has been far more consistent and has been part and parcel of the overall consolidation of power under the presidency.

The Economy

By far the most important, and the most problematic, policy area is the economy. To see why, simply recall how deteriorating economic conditions contributed to the collapse of the Soviet Union.

The new Russian leaders faced two related economic challenges they felt they had to address rapidly and thoroughly:

- To shift from a centrally planned economy in which the state owned virtually everything to one based on private ownership and a reasonably free market.

- To ensure that the fruits of these changes would be shared by all Russians.

As they saw things, sweeping economic reform was their only viable option. However, like democratization, actually building a market economy that retained a significant degree of equality was easier said than done.

PROFILES   Vladimir Putin

Vladimir Putin was born in Leningrad (now St. Petersburg) in 1952. His family was poor, but his disabled father almost certainly benefited financially from his party connections. Putin describes himself as having had a troubled youth until he started competing in judo, which has been a passion of his ever since.

In 1975, he graduated from Leningrad State University with a degree in law. He then joined the KGB for which he served in Germany and the Soviet Union until he left to work for the Leningrad city government in 1990.

Putin was brought to Moscow to help run the Kremlin's administrative office in 1996. There, he captured the attention of Yeltsin's "family" or inner circle of politicians, including his powerful daughter, Tatyana Dyachenko. In 1999, Putin effectively was given control of the FSB. That summer, he was named prime minister and automatically became acting president when Yeltsin resigned on New Year's Eve.

He won the next two elections. When his second full term ended, he stepped down from the presidency as required by the constitution and became prime minister. He returned to the presidency in 2012.

His period in power has been marked by a sharp erosion in democratic rights and values. He is apparently driven by both a powerful work ethic and a commitment to restoring as much of Russia's position as a world power as possible. There is also no question that Putin is now an amazingly wealthy and powerful man. ■

Presidents Putin and Obama.

SAUL LOEB/AFP/Getty Images

To begin with, there was no historical precedent they could draw on in planning a rapid transition from socialism to capitalism or from a party state to democracy. Add to that Yeltsin's indecisiveness and his failing health, and the result was a government that was usually unwilling and unable to adopt and then pursue any consistent economic policy. Instead, for the better part of a decade, Russian policy makers oscillated between two approaches, depending on which one had the upper hand at a particular moment.

Most professional economists were staunch reformists who stressed the importance of a rapid and complete shift to a market economy through a policy known as shock therapy. Even its strongest advocates, however, acknowledged that it would have tremendous short-term costs in terms of higher unemployment and a declining standard of living but argued that it was the only path toward sustainable growth.

The conservatives wanted to move more slowly. They stressed the fact that the *laissez-faire* policies have not been all that successful in the West, where all countries have had to turn to a welfare state to help cushion the impact of capitalism's uneven development on the less fortunate.

Given the history of the previous seventy years, most reformist economists were also self-trained and inexperienced. Therefore, they turned to a relatively unrepresentative group of Western neoclassical economists who urged them to move rapidly to a free market economy, whatever the costs.

In 1991 and 1992, deteriorating economic conditions, the popularity of Yeltsin and his administration, and the as-yet untested but theoretically elegant predictions of the economists tilted the balance toward shock therapy. This led the first Yeltsin governments to concentrate on the public sale of state-owned enterprises, which took two forms.

The first burst of privatization bubbled up from below in the almost completely spontaneous creation of small firms, mostly in the service sector. About 95 percent of the restaurants, shoe repair stores, gas stations, barber shops, and other such outlets that existed before 1991 quickly gained private owners, usually the men and women who had managed them under the communists. Other people formed upward of twenty thousand small firms, also mostly in the service sector.

However, that kind of "bottom-up" privatization would not have worked for the free market advocates' second target—the gigantic industrial enterprises that dominated the Soviet economy. Potential investors could not raise the capital needed to buy these firms. And most were of dubious value because they would have had to be gutted and completely restructured before they could turn a profit.

But because the government was committed to ending socialism by privatizing as much of the economy as quickly as possible, it acted in three main ways.

First, it issued vouchers worth ten thousand rubles (then about $25) to all citizens. Recipients could sell their vouchers, use them to buy stock in privatized companies, or invest them in funds that managed shares in those firms. Most chose the latter option, which means that these new bodies, which are roughly equivalent to American mutual funds, became the owners of most of the stock put up for sale through the voucher system.

Second, the firms' managers were offered stock options, which meant that men and women who had been part of the old communist elite were able to enrich themselves and, in the process, strengthen their ties to the new state. Many of them also ended up leading voucher funds.

Finally, shares in most enterprises were offered to foreign investors. At first, there was relatively little interest in them because the companies were inefficient at best and because Russian law limited how much of a stake foreigners could have in companies. After 1993, however, the investment and legal climates improved, and foreigners pumped an average of $100 billion per year into Russia over the next five years and took control of firms such as AO Volga, which produces a third of Russia's newsprint.

We should not, however, equate privatization with success. Selling the state-owned firms did not automatically lead to a competitive market economy. Rather, large conglomerates—most of which are run by oligarchs—came to control an immense share of the economy in which there is no competition to speak of.

As we saw in Table 9.5, the economy went through a steep and rapid decline. Overall production declined by an average of more than 6 percent per year during the 1990s. The downturn was particularly pronounced in heavy industry, which had been the mainstay of the old Soviet economy.

The value of the ruble collapsed. The Soviet government artificially fixed its value at $1.60. When I was there in 1986, people could buy and sell them on the black market at about 20 rubles to a dollar. In mid-1997 it took 5,500 rubles to get a dollar. When these lines were written, it was more than 31,000. (Technically, it was 31 to a dollar, because the Russians introduced a new ruble in 1998 that was worth 1,000 of the old ones.)

The economy hit rock bottom during the 1998 global debt crisis. For a variety of complicated economic reasons, Russia could not pay back its creditors and, for all intents and purposes, defaulted on the massive loans it had taken since 1991. The stock market lost half its value and the ruble fell by two-thirds. Two prime ministers were fired because they could not stem the downturn. Finally, new loans and a stabilization package imposed by Western governments and the International Monetary Fund did the trick.

Since then, indicators of overall economic health have improved considerably. The value of the ruble has stabilized. Growth rates have averaged more than 5 percent per year since 2000 other than 2009. With that growth, Russia has become a BRIC (also Brazil, India, China, and, in some cases, South Africa), as the leading emerging economies are known.

The upturn is most visible among post-Soviet *political* winners. As of 2011, almost 400,000 Russians earned more than $1 million a year. The country ranks third in the world in the number of billionaires, behind only the United States and China. Muscovites buy more Mercedes than residents of any other city, although its national sales are only about a tenth of those in the United States. Moscow's Tepliy Stan Mega Mall is the most visited shopping center in Europe.

But we should not make too much of the upturn, for three reasons.

First, most Russians have not shared this new-found wealth. The average person still makes about $500 a month, which makes buying a Mercedes or shopping at chic malls impossible. After taking the effects of inflation into account, 60 percent of the population makes less than it did in 1991. Fourteen percent of the population lives in poverty. Some Russian think tanks put the figure at closer to 30 percent. Its income distribution is about as skewed as that in Iran.

Second, most of the growth has come from a single industry—petroleum. Because oil prices have skyrocketed since the late 1990s and because Russian supplies are stable and reliable, the petrochemical sector has been enormously profitable. Oil and products derived from it account for about half of the goods and services Russian firms sold abroad. However, any country that relies that heavily on a single commodity has to be considered vulnerable to swings in the global marketplace, especially for one that has as volatile a history as the price of oil.

Third, and most important for our purposes, is the way the state's contribution to the current growth echoes the concentration of power we have seen throughout the second half of this chapter. The companies that have fared the best since 2000 have close ties to the government, which is also true of most of the new millionaires.

Typical in that respect is Gazprom, which has a monopoly on that vital market. The company was created when the Soviet Ministry of Gas was privatized under Yeltsin and is Russia's largest employer and exporter today. Even in the 1990s, the state kept 40 percent of the new company's stock. According to its official website, the state controlled just over half its shares in late 2012 (eng.gazpromquestions.ru/). Over the years, Putin has resisted all attempts to break up the company or dilute the government's control over it.

Overall, some observers estimate that no more than a dozen members of the Presidential Administration own about 40 percent of the stock in all major Russian companies that are nominally privately owned. Statistics on the financial sector are harder to verify, but the president's cronies control an even larger share of the domestic investment capital market.

In other words, a vertical of economic power exists alongside and is very much a product of the political one discussed above. That uneven distribution of economic and political power lends itself to corruption of massive proportion. One report by a leading reformer and former mayor puts the cost of unethical business practices at $300 billion a year or about 20 percent of the GNP. In February 2013, the outgoing president of the Russian central bank alleged that $49 billion had been sent out of the country illegally the year before. If true (of course the number could not be verified), the money spent on narcotics, illegal imports, bribes, and kickbacks amounted to about 2.5 percent of the country's GNP.

All countries have some corruption, and none can realistically hope to get rid of it all. Nonetheless, Russia's is particularly severe, as its low ranking on Transparency International's Index in "Political Indicators" table suggests.

Foreign Policy

There is a similar pattern in Russian foreign policy, which has been far more nationalistic and driven by the pursuit of power under Putin than it was under Yeltsin. There is, however, one significant difference between foreign and domestic policy. For reasons lying largely beyond the Kremlin's control, Putin and his colleagues have faced more impediments in reaching their international goals.

There was no question that Russian foreign policy would have to change. After all, in 1981, the USSR had been at the heart of a renewed cold war and was one of two superpowers. Ten years later, the cold war, the USSR, and its superpower status had all disappeared.

All of a sudden, it became a relatively minor international player and a supplicant for economic aid. To make matters even more complicated, it had to open relations with fourteen newly independent states that had been part of the Soviet Union, which many Russians still felt were rightfully part of their country.

Under Yeltsin, Russia pursued a largely pragmatic foreign policy as it sought to find its place in an all but totally changed international system. His occasional anti-American statements and more frequent diplomatic gaffes worried people who saw him as the West's best hope for stability. And Russia unquestionably was less than vigilant

Comparative Emphasis: Globalization

Visitors to Moscow and St. Petersburg can be forgiven for thinking that globalization has benefited Russia. High-rise office buildings and Western chain stores in gleaming new shopping malls selling luxury goods seem to exist on every street corner.

But such appearances can be deceiving in two ways. First, compared with most countries, there is less foreign investment in Russia as a whole. Thus, in 2010, direct foreign investment was down almost 14 percent to just under $14 billion compared to almost $105 billion in China. Second, few people outside the biggest cities are enjoying the benefits (or enduring the consequences) of globalization.

The BRICS will play an important role in the pages that follow. There is little doubt that China, India, and Brazil have taken major steps toward becoming economic forces in large part as a result of political changes their governments have made in response to globalization.

Given the data presented in this section, it is harder to make that case for Russia. ∎

about the movement of nuclear technology across its borders and the disposal of nuclear waste, which did not allay the concerns of observers.

Otherwise, Yeltsin and his team adapted to their status as a middle-level power, developed reasonable relations with their neighbors, and began putting as much emphasis on economic as on geopolitical issues in their foreign policy.

We can see this if we focus on relations with the United States.

The George H. W. Bush and Clinton administrations took for granted that the United States needed a positive working relationship with the new Russian state. At first, they were genuinely enthusiastic about Yeltsin because of his role in the final days of the USSR.

They were not worried that Russia would pose the same kind of threat to the United States and its allies that the Soviet Union had. Indeed, the United States and Russia agreed to dismantle more than a third of their nuclear arsenals and stop targeting each other. Moreover, the Russian government was so poor, and morale in the army was so low, that it could no longer be thought of as having a fighting force that could be deployed very far beyond its borders.

Rather, the United States and its allies worried that instability in the region and aggression from Russia could exacerbate already difficult situations in Chechnya, Yugoslavia, Georgia, Moldova, and even as far away as the Indian subcontinent. They also had to pay attention to the fears of postcommunist leaders in Eastern Europe, who were not convinced that Russia had given up its designs on them.

As Yeltsin's flaws became more obvious, American and European leaders distanced themselves from him. Most policy makers in the United States and Western Europe understood, however, that however imperfect Yeltsin's leadership was, the alternatives were far riskier.

The new Putin administration started its foreign policy on a seemingly optimistic note. The terrorist attacks of 9/11 occurred three months later, and relations with the West seemed to take an even sharper turn for the better because the Russians realized that they shared concerns about terrorism with the Americans when it emerged that militants affiliated with al-Qaeda had fought in Chechnya and that Chechens had participated alongside the Taliban during the war in Afghanistan. And Washington needed to use bases in several of the former Soviet republics, most notably Uzbekistan, all of which were, in turn, heavily dependent on Moscow for their defense.

In early 2003, however, the Russian–American relationship began to sour and has remained testy every since. Russia took clear steps to distance itself from the West when Putin and his colleagues determined that doing so was in the self-interest of a more nationalist Russia that sought to enhance its global political standing.

Among other things, the Russian government did not share the American view that Iraq and Iran should be seen as targets in the campaign against terrorism. It joined France and China in blocking United Nations Security Council approval for the invasion of Iraq. It should be pointed out, though, that even if Putin was as critical of the George W. Bush administration as French President Jacques Chirac was, Russia never drew the ferocious criticism that the United States leveled at France.

Since then, Putin and his colleagues opposed the so-called "color revolutions" in Eastern Europe and the former Soviet republics if they seemed to threaten Russian influence abroad or had prodemocratic implications at home. More recently, Russia has used its veto power as a Permanent Member of the United Nations Security Council to block U.S.-led initiatives in support of dissidents in Libya and Syria or to deter Iran's alleged program to acquire nuclear weapons.

In early 2012, Putin summed up his policy in an article in the prestigious American journal, *Foreign Policy*:

> **It is no surprise that some are calling for resources of global significance to be freed from the exclusive sovereignty of a single nation. This cannot happen to Russia, not even hypothetically. We should not tempt anyone by allowing ourselves to be weak. We will not be able to strengthen our international position if we are unable to protect Russia. We see ever new regional and local wars breaking out. We see new areas of instability and deliberately managed chaos. There also are attempts to provoke such conflicts even close to Russia's and its allies' borders. The basic principles of international law are being degraded and eroded, especially in terms of international security. Under these circumstances, Russia cannot rely on diplomatic and economic methods alone to resolve conflicts.[6]**

Even though the Russian government has not been able to restore its Soviet-era power or prestige, there is also little that outside forces can do to change its policies and priorities. Unlike the Eastern Europe countries mentioned in Chapter 8, the West has few carrots such as EU and NATO membership to offer Russia and few sticks to use should it want to compel it to follow more democratic or capitalistic policies.

The Media

There is no better example of the vertical of power than the reassertion of state control over the mass media. Before Gorbachev came to power, the communists controlled everything that was legally printed, published, or broadcast. There was a tiny underground, or *samizdat*, press, but its circulation numbered in the tens of thousands at most.

Almost overnight, there was a media revolution. One of the world's most closely controlled media became one of its most contentious. By 1988, almost anything that could be said was available in print and on the airwaves. New newspapers, magazines, and journals were critical of everything and everyone.

After 1991, the major media outlets passed into private hands. Not surprisingly, the most influential (and profitable) of them came under the control of the oligarchs. And in Russia today, it is television that counts because newspaper circulation has plummeted given the rising cost of newsprint, journalists' salaries, and the like. Television's impact became

---

[6]Vladimir Putin, "Being Strong: Why Russia Needs to Rebuild Its Military." *Foreign Policy*. February 2012.

abundantly clear in the 1996 presidential campaign. As we saw earlier, Berezovsky and the other oligarchs orchestrated Yeltsin's reelection campaign largely by manipulating what was (and was not) presented on their channels.

Although there was some criticism of the obviously biased media, television did not become a major issue until the two network-owning oligarchs turned on Putin. He was able to use the power of the Kremlin to force them out of the television industry even before they were forced into exile. Ownership of the networks was transferred to other conglomerates sympathetic to the Putin administration. What that has meant is that the Kremlin has taken de facto control of television news, which is nearly as one-sided as it was before Gorbachev came to power.

The crackdown on independent media continues. On August 16, 2007, the radio regulatory agency informed *Bolshoye Radio* that it would have to drop the BBC World Service or risk being shut down. The authorities told the last network to feature the BBC on the air that it had to produce all of its own content, even if the law officially required that only 82 percent of it to be original. Meanwhile, more print media outlets are now owned by state-dominated companies, including the influential *Izvestia* and *Kommsersant,* which have been acquired by Gazprom. In perhaps the most telling anecdote, a highly critical report on state control of the economy was only available at one Moscow kiosk, because the government controls not only what is published but how it is distributed.

Conclusion: Half Empty or Half Full?

Of all the countries covered in this book, assessments of Russia come closest to reflecting the cliché about whether the glass is half empty or half full. This is the case because, even after more than a generation of transition, it is impossible to predict whether or not Russia will move toward a stable democracy and a prosperous market economy.

On the half-empty side are all the problems laid out in this chapter. Indeed, after analyzing the industrialized democracies in Part 2, it is hard not to be pessimistic given Russia's social, economic, and political difficulties, many of which have worsened since the breakup of the Soviet Union.

But, we should not ignore the "half-full" aspects of Russian life. It has had eleven national elections, a few of which were reasonably fair and competitive. There was a successful transition of power from Yeltsin to Putin. The oligarchs are slightly less powerful than they were in the 1990s. There are signs that the economy has started to make a sustainable recovery.

Nonetheless, there really is only one conclusion we can reach about Russia, one that will apply to many of the other countries we consider in the rest of this book: Transitions to democracy and market capitalism are rarely easy. And, in Russia's case, they may well be off the table until Putin finally leaves the scene.

KEY TERMS

Concepts
autocracy
collectivization
democratic centralism
glasnost'
near abroad
nomenklatura
oligarchs
party of power
perestroika
power ministries
privatization
purges
shock therapy
People
Berezovsky, Boris
Brezhnev, Leonid
Gorbachev, Mikhail
Khodorkovsky, Mikhail
Khrushchev, Nikita

Lenin, V. I.
Medvedev, Dmitri
Putin, Vladimir
Stalin, Joseph
Yeltsin, Boris
Zhirinovsky, Vladimir
Zyuganov, Gennady
Acronyms
BRICS
CPRF
CPSU
KGB
Organizations, Places, and Events
Bolsheviks
Central Committee
Cheka
Comintern
Communist Party of the Russian
　Federation (CPRF)
Communist Party of the Soviet Union

　(CPSU)
Federation Council
five-year plan
Gosplan
Just Russia
Liberal Democrats
Mensheviks
Our Home Is Russia
Politburo
provisional government
Presidential Administration
Russian Federation
secret speech
Secretariat
State Duma
Third International
Twentieth Party Congress
United Russia
Vertical of Power
Yabloko

USEFUL WEBSITES

Due to the shaky state of the Russian economy, many of the promising Internet sites created there a few years ago have fallen by the wayside. The Russian News Online gathers together key articles that have been published in English.

russiannewsonline.com/

There are also a number of public sites that translate some material on their own but mostly mirror what has been on sites housed there. The best of these is Johnson's List.

www.russialist.org/

Some of the best entry points to things Russian are probably those maintained by American-based Russian studies centers, especially those at the universities of Michigan, Pittsburgh, and Washington.

www.ii.umich.edu/crees/resources/relatedunits

www.ucis.pitt.edu/reesweb

www. jsis.washington.edu/ellison/

A number of organizations and NGOs are doing analytical work while helping Russia develop. Among them are:

www.jamestown.org

www.opendemocracy.net/russia

www.theotherrussia.org/

FURTHER READING

Gessen, Masha. *The Man Without a Face*. New York: Penguin/Riverhead, 2012. The best recent book on Putin's rule by an outspoken Russian journalist.

Gorbachev, Mikhail S. *Perestroika*. New York: Harper & Row, 1987. Despite what has happened to his reputation since then, an important and revealing book, especially about the reasons behind *perestroika* and new thinking.

Lynch, Allen C. *Vladimir Putin and Russian Statecraft*. Washington: Potomac Books, 2011. A short biography that focuses as much on analyzing Putin's first eight years in office as on the details of his life.

Mackenzie, David, and Michael W. Curran. *A History of the Soviet Union*. Belmont, CA: Wadsworth, 1991. One of the best of the brief textbooks on the entire Soviet period.

McFaul, Michael, Nikolai Petrov, and Andrei Ryabov. *Between Dictatorship and Democracy: Russian Post-Communist Political Reform*. Washington: Carnegie Endowment for International Peace, 2004. An excellent collection of integrated essays written by McFaul and a number of leading Russian experts.

Nolan, Peter. *China's Rise, Russia's Fall: Politics, Economics, and Planning in the Transition from Stalinism*. Houndsmill, U.K.: Macmillan, 1995 (distributed in the United States by St. Martin's Press). Probably has better coverage on China, but a good exploration of the uncertainties caused by the "stop-start" pattern of Russian reform.

Roxburgh, Angus. *The Strongman: Vladimir Putin and the Struggle for Russia*. London: I.B. Taurus, 2012. Another analytical biography by a respected British journalist who was briefly a key advisor to the president on public relations.

Shevtsova, Lilia. *Putin's Russia*. Washington: Carnegie Endowment for International Peace. 2003. A very good overview of Putin's first term written by one of Russia's leading political scientists.

Shteyngart, Gary. *Absurdistan*. New York: Random House, 2007. A very fun novel about the transition in a fictional central Asian republic as told from the perspective of an American-educated Russian. Caution: contains lots of seemingly gratuitous sex.

Sixsmith, Martin. *Putin's Oil*. London: Continuum, 2010. On the surface a book about the oil industry, but it goes much deeper into Russian politics. By a BBC reporter who has spent much of his career in Moscow.

Von Laue, Theodore. *Why Lenin? Why Stalin?* Philadelphia: Lippincott, 1971. A relatively old book, but still the best short source on why the revolution turned out as it did.

Yurchak, Alexei. *Everything Was Forever, Until It Was No More: The Last Soviet Generation*. Princeton: Princeton University Press, 2005. A remarkable book by an American anthropologist who grew up (and studied physics) in the Soviet Union. Very funny in places.

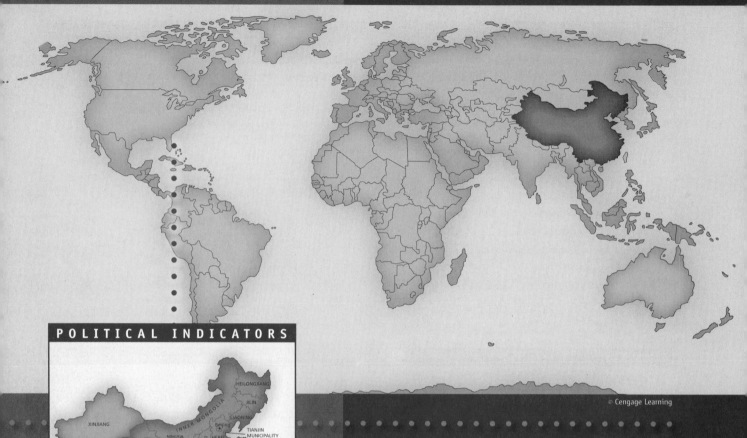

© Cengage Learning

> I don't care if it's a black cat or a white cat. It's a good cat if it catches mice.
>
> DENG XIAOPING

China

THE BASICS
China

Size	9,595,960 sq. km (a bit smaller than the United States)
Arable land	10%, down by one-fifth since 1949
Population	1.33 billion
Population growth rate	0.5%
Economic growth rate	9.1%
GNP per capita	$6,600
Currency	6.13 yuan renminbi = US$1
Life expectancy	75
Ethnic composition	92% Han Chinese
Capital	Beijing
Head of State	President Xi Jinping (2013)
Head of Government	Prime Minister Li Keqiang (2013

A Smooth Transition?

Many political scientists mistakenly assumed that communist countries had a hard time choosing new leaders. It is true that, in most of them, the General Secretary of the Communist Party (as the office was usually known) stayed in power until he died. In those cases, his death did sometimes spark what political scientists called a leadership crisis that included a lengthy power struggle.

As we saw in Chapter 9 following the deaths of Leonid Brezhnev, Yuri Andropov, and Konstantin Chernenko, most communist regimes had come up with established routines for choosing new leaders that avoided protracted succession struggles long before their final crises in the late 1980s. Having broadly accepted mechanisms for conducting leadership transitions did not, however, help Marxist-Leninist regimes in Eurasia survive.

China was—and still is—one of those countries that developed routine procedures for handling the transition from one leader to the next. While they may not be enough to keep the Chinese Communist Party (CCP) in power forever, they do help us understand why communism has survived in China, as its most recent transfer of power in 2012 and 2013 makes clear.

As has been the case since the revolution ended in 1949, a single individual serves as Chairman of the CCP and president of the **People's Republic of China (PRC)**. Since the 1980s, he (so far, they have all been men) has been limited to two five-year terms. In late 2012, **Hu Jintao** (1942–) completed his second term as party secretary; his term as president would end the following spring.

By late 2010, it was already clear that the party leaders had chosen his successor: **Xi Jinping** (1957–). That October, Xi was named Vice-Chairman of the Central Military Commission. His promotion was an all but formal acknowledgment that he would succeed Hu not only as head of that body but of the party and government as well. Xi was only 57 (young by Chinese standards) when he was selected, but he had been on the short list for high office for years.

In fact, in some ways he had been groomed for a top job since birth. His father was a prominent revolutionary and then served as a senior party leader after the CCP took power in 1949. Thus, Xi is a **princeling,** as the children of leading politicians who then rise to prominent positions themselves are known. Like most leaders of his era, Xi is a trained engineer who has spent his entire professional career rising through the CCP's ranks.

As was the case when Hu replaced Jiang Zemin a decade earlier, Xi was powerful enough to install his own team in all top party and government positions. Most of them look a lot like him: late middle-aged career party officials. Almost all are men. That said, Xi did not get everything he wanted. Apparently, his rivals in the party elite insisted that he pick his chief competitor for the presidency, Li Keqiang (1955–), as his prime minister.

Even so, all the signs pointed toward a smooth transition for the new president. Then, while the tradition was well underway, something unusual happened that suggested that the transition might not be quite as smooth as we had expected.

Xi Jinping with Vladimir Putin shortly after he was named China's leader.

ITAR-TASS Photo Agency/Alamy

Chinese Names and Terms

Some features of the Chinese language frequently confuse Western readers and, thus, should be clarified at the outset.

Chinese names are always rendered with the family name first. In other words, Barack Hussein Obama would be written or spoken Obama Barack Hussein.

Failure to remember this can be embarrassing. For example, the first time President Harry Truman met Chiang Kai-shek, he reportedly greeted him, "Glad to meet you Mr. Shek."

There are also two primary ways of transliterating Chinese words. Almost everyone writing about China uses the pinyin system its leaders prefer. People in Taiwan and Hong Kong still use the Wade-Giles version. I have used pinyin for all names and terms other than those associated with Taiwan and the Nationalists who fled there.

In the weeks before Xi formally took over, another princeling, Bo Xilai (1949–) was stripped of all of his government and party positions after it surfaced that his wife, Gu Kailai (herself nearly a princeling) was implicated in the murder of a British business partner, Neil Heywood. The story was filled with politically loaded questions. Were Gu and Heywood having an affair? What was the role of Bo and Gu's son in all of this? The younger Bo was a graduate student at Oxford at the time (after having gone to prep school at London's exclusive Harrow, received his undergraduate degree at Oxford, and started graduate school at Harvard). He was not known as much of a student but gained plenty of notoriety for throwing parties—each of which cost more than his father made in a year from his official salary. Where did the money come from?

Bo could not escape the scandal. He was already controversial because of the populist and some thought neo-Maoist policies he introduced while he was on his way up the party hierarchy. Some thought, too, that he was more popular than Xi and was a potential challenger for the top position himself. Whether or not he was involved, his wife's and his son's peccadillos scuttled his career. He lost all his jobs and was under arrest and pending trial as these lines were written.

To complicate matters further, right after news of Bo's fall from grace broke, the *New York Times* ran a front page story on the up to $2.7 billion amassed by outgoing Prime Minister Wen Jiabao and his family. Like Bo, Wen and his influential wife only drew salaries of about $20,000 a year each.

As is often the case in an authoritarian regime, the immediate crisis blew over. Xi became head of the country and the party. As difficult as the transition turned out to be, President Xi's team seem certain to keep their country on a steady course. In short, we can expect more of the same—for now.

Despite its recent slowdown, Xi and his team have taken power in a country whose economic growth has averaged a bit more than 10 percent a year for thirty years, which means the economy as a whole doubles in size every seven or eight years. Overall, China has the second largest economy in the world in terms of total output. In time, it will join the world's leaders on a per capita basis as well and could conceivably be the richest before this century is over. At the very least, China clearly has earned its spot among the BRICS.

I used the phrase "for now" two paragraphs ago because China's future is not entirely rosy.

If nothing else, all the signs suggest that economic growth cannot continue at the current rate much longer; in fact, it may already have slowed down considerably. Even more importantly for our purposes, political problems loom on the not-so-distant horizon. Will the Communist Party be able to maintain the stranglehold on political power that is the central ingredient of its rule? Will everything from the expansion of private businesses to the use of the Internet undermine its rule?

No one knows the answer to those questions even though almost every analyst of Chinese politics is posing them. One American political scientist recently suggested that China can go in one of two main directions—either move toward further adaptation or atrophy much as its Eurasian counterparts in the former Soviet bloc did.

Over the last thirty years, the CCP has been able to adapt to the demanding changes in its social, political, and economic environment. But, there is also evidence that the party is weaker and could lose even more of its clout if groups such as the newly rich business leaders or the still-impoverished sweatshop workers decide they have had enough.

Again, this chapter cannot provide definitive answers about the China Xi has inherited let alone the one he might leave to his successors. It will, however, present the evidence scholars have used in reaching both of those conclusions.

Thinking About China

There are a lot of question marks in the first three pages of this chapter. And there should be, because almost everything about China seems up for grabs, at least if our time frame extends beyond the decade in which Xi can be at the helm. That said, there are relatively few question marks about either what China has accomplished since the CCP won more than sixty years ago or what the costs of those accomplishments have been.

The Bottom Line

Think Big

The most important thing about China is its size. The People's Republic of China's more than 1.3 billion people amount to about one-fifth of the world's population. The government has effectively limited population growth by prohibiting most women from having more than one child. Nonetheless, a baby is born somewhere in China every two seconds, and demographers now predict that the population will reach 1.5 billion by the middle of this century.

The population is already stretching China's limited natural resources to their limits. Sooner rather than later, China will not have enough water either for people to drink or for farmers to use for irrigation. There are only about two acres of land—or one-eighth of the Asian average—per person, and only one-fourth of that is arable.

We could go on and consider other looming environmental nightmares, but the point would be the same. China is coming close to reaching what environmental scientists call the carrying capacity of its land.

Relative Homogeneity

Unlike any of the other countries covered in the print edition of *Comparative Politics*, China has a relatively homogeneous population. More than ninety percent of its citizens are Han or ethnic Chinese. The rest of the population consists of far smaller groups of whom only the Tibetans and Uighers have been politically important.

There is a single written Chinese language. However, there are dozens of regional dialects, some of which could actually be considered separate languages. A person who speaks only Mandarin, for instance, cannot understand oral Cantonese. Gradually, however, Mandarin is becoming the *lingua franca* and is now spoken by almost all educated Chinese.

Social and Economic Conditions

We in the West probably overstate the degree to which China has become a global power. Its economy is big and getting bigger, but its size pales when its wealth is calculated on a per capita basis. Its military is the largest in the world. Yet, the **People's Liberation Army (PLA)** barely spends a tenth of what the United States does on its military.

The Chinese have made remarkable progress since **Deng Xiaoping** (1904–1997) and his colleagues began to reform the economy in 1979. The average Chinese man or woman can expect to live to be seventy-five. Ninety percent of the population is literate. Only 7 percent of Chinese children are born dangerously undersized.

China ranks higher than the Asian average on all such measures of social well-being. When the CCP came to power in 1949, China was at or near the bottom on just about every such indicator.

At least 100 million Chinese citizens could be considered middle class by anyone's standards. Cities have skyscrapers, malls, and high-tech businesses that have made many young Chinese wealthier than anyone could have dreamed of a generation ago. To cite one minor statistic, the highly selective Grinnell College in Iowa had 200 highly qualified Chinese applicants for its Class of 2016, half of whom scored a perfect 800 on the Math SAT.

Still, China is a very poor country. Per capita income is more than six thousand dollars a year, but, in real terms, more than half of the people have to get by on less than two hundred dollars a month. Over the last few decades, at least 100 million people have moved from the countryside to the cities in search of the prosperity that is out of their grasp at home. All too often, the young migrants end up living in utter poverty in the cities as well.

Key Questions

Xi and his colleagues assumed power in a country that seems to have little in common with what we just saw in Russia. The party can almost certainly continue to follow its current course in the short term and avoid either the end of communism or the uneven development of contemporary Russia. But, we have to wonder if a Marxist-Leninist regime can survive the accelerating rate of social and economic changes and the cultural shifts they are leaving in their wake.

Some students are convinced, of course, that China will go the route of the USSR. However, its now thirty-year-old track record of successful adaptation has kept it afloat and prevented it from atrophying to the point that its institutions and practices degenerated to the point that they were beyond repair. This chapter cannot settle the adaptation versus atrophy or any other major debate about Chinese politics. But what it can do is present evidence that helps clarify the terms of those debates by answering four main questions:

- How did the interaction of China's history, its political culture, and external forces lead to the revolution won by the CCP in 1949?

- How did the Communist Party survive the turmoil of its first thirty years in power?

- How did the party produce an all but total about face in its social and economic policies without undermining its political bases of support?

- Can it continue to do so in the face of what seem certain to be increased pressures both from its own society and from the globalizing economic world which is now vital for its economic future?

The Evolution of the Chinese State

The two characters the Chinese use to write their country's name are best translated into English as middle kingdom. Many countries have cultures that revolve around an exaggerated sense of their own importance. However, calling one's country the middle kingdom may be taking that trend to an extreme.

In some ways, however, it is not an exaggeration. China did lead the world in many respects for most of the last two thousand years. However, China entered a period of protracted decline no later than the beginning of the nineteenth century. It took sixty years of communist government before China could begin to reclaim its place among the world's most powerful nations.[1]

The Broad Sweep of Chinese History

The historical roots of contemporary Chinese politics go back to the dawn of civilization. We can start, however, a mere 2,500 years ago with the teachings of Confucius and other ancient scholars whose ideas have had a remarkable influence to this day (see Table 10.1).

Commonly thought of as a religion in the West, **Confucianism** is actually a code of social conduct that calls on people to accept the social order as long as people in superior positions do what is expected of them. If not (as often happened over the centuries), it was acceptable to rebel (orpheus.ucsd.edu/chinesehistory).

The Chinese developed the world's first centralized state in the third century BC in part on the basis of Confucian values. The militaristic Qin (from which the English word China was derived) defeated most of the other regional kingdoms and established a unified empire covering most of contemporary China. For example, the Qin were able to

---

[1]For an amazing (and occasionally funny) look at this history going back to the dawn of humanity, see Ian Morris, *Why the West Rules—For Now: The Patterns of History, and What They Reveal About the Future.* (New York: Farrar, Straus and Giroux, 2010).

TABLE 10.1 Key Events in the Origins of the People's Republic of China

YEAR	EVENT
551 BC	Supposed birth of Confucius
221 BC	Start of Qin dynasty
1644	Start of Qing dynasty
1839–42	Opium War
1894–95	Sino-Japanese War
1911	Overthrow of the Qing dynasty
1919	May Fourth Movement
1921	Formation of the CCP
1927	KMT attack on CCP
1931	Japanese invasion of Manchuria
1934–35	Long March
1949	CCP victory

© Cengage Learning

mobilize thousands of people to build canals, roads, and the first parts of the Great Wall.

The Qin and subsequent dynasties succeeded in large part because of their remarkable bureaucratic system, which was well established and firmly in place two thousand years before Europeans even thought of the idea. Senior imperial officials were chosen from a small group of young men who passed competitive examinations that tested their understanding of Confucian texts. By the fourteenth century AD, the bureaucracy of some 40,000 members was an indispensable part of a state that included more than forty cities with at least one hundred thousand inhabitants.

But imperial rule had one built-in weakness, which I hinted at above. The system only worked if the country had an effective emperor, which was not always the case. China went through at least twenty-five cycles in which a dynasty declined, rebellions broke out, and a new group assumed power and turned itself into the next dynasty.

By 1900, the Qing dynasty was more than a century into its decline. Population growth outstripped agricultural production, leaving an overstretched peasantry and an often-hungry urban population. Peasant rebellions broke out in many parts of the country. Cultural blinders left the Manchus (as the Qing were also known) convinced that their adopted Chinese traditions were superior to anything the West had to offer.

Early in the nineteenth century, Europe came crashing in. China never became a colony. Nonetheless, much of the country fell under direct or indirect foreign control. The British, who had been smuggling opium into the country, defeated China in the first Opium War (1839–42). The country was then opened up to missionaries and merchants. Only a few areas, like Hong Kong, passed directly into European hands. The Europeans seized much of coastal China and imposed **extraterritoriality**, which meant that their law, not China's, applied to the activities of the Europeans.

Things came to a head after the Sino-Japanese War of 1894–95. Japan had been even more isolated from the West, but once Admiral Matthew Perry arrived in 1854, the Japanese quickly turned their country around and began catching up with the Europeans and Americans. For reasons beyond the scope of this book, the two countries went to war, and China suffered yet another humiliating defeat.

At that point, the Chinese leaders belatedly realized that they, too, had to change. In 1898, for example the emperor issued decrees that did away with many of the traditional practices that had left China so far behind the West. The Confucian examinations were discontinued. Young people were sent abroad to study "modern" subjects, including science and technology, to get the expertise China would need to meet the imperialist challenge.

But as in tsarist Russia, the reforms did not come soon enough and did not go far enough. In fact, the changes in its educational system ended up revealing even more of China's weaknesses and, rather than breathing new life into the dynasty, further strengthened opposition to the imperial regime. Universities that had so recently educated loyal Confucian scholars were now turning out revolutionaries. Disgruntled young people started wearing Western clothes and adopting Western values, including as one of them put it, "Mr. Democracy and Mr. Science."

A Failed Revolution

Also like Russia, China had more than its share of revolutionaries. Between May 1907 and April 1911, there were eleven failed coup attempts launched by the followers of **Sun Yat-sen (1866–1925)** alone.

Sun was one of the first Westernized intellectuals. While still in his twenties, he reached the same conclusion that Lenin did. The situation in China had gotten so bad that he only had one option—to become a full-time revolutionary, although he never came close to becoming a Marxist. In 1895, he was exiled for his role in an abortive plot and spent most of the next sixteen years abroad. In 1905, a group of radicals studying in Tokyo elected him head of what soon became the **Kuomintang (KMT)**, or **Nationalist Party**.

On "double ten" day (October 10, 1911), yet another rebellion broke out in the city of Wuhan. Much to their surprise, the conspirators drove the governor general from the city. Sun was in Denver when he learned about the uprising, and he decided to finish his fund-raising tour rather than return to China right away to join what he assumed would be another failed attempt to oust the Qing.

This time, however, the rebellion spread. When Sun finally returned in December, it was to take over as president of the new Republic of China.

Toppling the old regime was one thing. Building a new one strong enough to take its place was quite another. The empire fell not because the revolutionaries were so strong but because it had become too weak. Little united the revolutionaries other than their opposition to the disasters imperial rule had wrought. Within months, it became clear that they could not govern effectively either.

Unlike Russia, it would be another forty years before a new regime was firmly in place. In a desperate attempt to save the revolution, Sun gave way to the warlord, General Yuan Shikai, whose imperial pretensions simply spawned more rebellions, which continued after his death in 1916.

By that time, China had a national government in name only. In reality, the warlords ran their parts of the country while ignoring the KMT's orders. In short, the political situation was at least as volatile as it had been a generation earlier.

Things only got worse in 1919 when the Treaty of Versailles formally ended World War I. China had entered the war on the Allied side on the assumption that the Wilsonian principles of democracy and national self-determination would lead to the end of imperialism. Nothing of the sort happened. The German concessions were simply transferred to other Allied powers.

The treaty provisions proved to be the last straw for alienated, well-educated young Chinese. The day they were announced, thousands of students took to the streets. Their **May Fourth Movement** railed against Confucianism, the education system, and the family. After May Fourth, the students and their supporters grew more political, but this particular movement was poorly organized and, like so many before it, quickly disappeared.

China Stands Up

Revolutionary fervor did not go away, however. Instead, over the next few years, most revolutionaries became Marxists.

In retrospect, it was not surprising that they did. Even though Marx believed that socialism could only develop after capitalism was firmly established, his ideas began to find an audience in countries like China because Lenin had included imperialism in his critique of capitalism. As a result, alienated and radicalized Chinese students ended up supporting the Soviet cause.

In 1921, twelve delegates, representing fifty-seven members, formed the CCP. The party was made up almost exclusively of young intellectuals and, like the rest of the international communist movement, it quickly fell under Moscow's direct control through the Comintern.

Oddly enough, the Soviets also supported the KMT, because the early Bolsheviks were convinced that they were the one Chinese faction that both could win and would support Soviet interests. Therefore, a generation of KMT officers was trained in the USSR, including **Chiang Kai-shek** (1887–1975), who would become the KMT leader after Sun's death in 1925. The Soviets also ordered their agent in China, Mikhail Borodin, to force the CCP to merge with the KMT in order to unify the country.

The merger did not go well. The communists used their influence among industrial workers to become a major force within the KMT, which, meanwhile, was moving rightward. The CCP maintained its own army, which continued to grow because more and more members of the new working class joined its ranks. The resulting tensions between the CCP and the Nationalists mounted to the point that some communist leaders wanted to end the united front. Borodin refused.

In 1926, the KMT launched its Northern Expedition in yet another attempt to unite the country under a single national government. Workers threw open the gates of a number of cities as communist forces approached. The party's leaders advocated arming workers and peasants under CCP leadership. Once again, Borodin refused.

The differences between the two supposed partners finally came to a head in April 1927, when KMT forces attacked their supposed CCP allies in Shanghai. Nationalist troops slaughtered thousands of CCP members, including most of the leadership. Only ten percent of the fifty thousand CCP members survived.

In the weeks before the attack on Shanghai, the Communists sent one of the few party members from a peasant background, **Mao Zedong** (1893–1976), to investigate conditions in his native Hunan province. The visit convinced Mao that the revolution had to be based in the countryside and waged as a guerrilla war.

Ignoring Borodin's orders to the contrary, Mao began to organize a peasant militia and launched his first attacks on the city of Changsha. Most of his fellow Communists did not share his strategic viewpoint, but Mao persisted and established the first "base camp."

The KMT responded with a series of campaigns to "exterminate the communist bandits." CCP forces survived the first four attacks, but during the fifth they were surrounded by KMT troops, which only reinforced Mao's belief that conventional warfare could not succeed. Therefore, in October 1934, a small group of communist soldiers launched a diversionary counterattack while the bulk of their forces broke through the KMT cordon.

Thus began what became the **Long March**. For the better part of a year, CCP forces fought skirmishes every day and full-scale battles every few weeks against the pursuing KMT and local warlords. The fighting and the difficulties of the march itself took a terrible toll. Only 10 percent of the troops who started out were still alive when the army arrived in Yanan in October 1935. Among the dead was one of Mao's sons.

Strangely enough, the Long March turned out to be a stunning success. All along the way, the party organized. Members talked about a China based on justice and equality. Unlike the bands of marauding soldiers who had come and gone over the centuries, they treated the peasants well. Almost no men were conscripted. Very few women were raped. The CCP paid for most of the food and other supplies it took. Where the party gained control, it expropriated large estates from the gentry and gave the land to the peasants.

In January 1936, the **Politburo** elected Mao chairman of the CCP. With this move, the notion that a Marxist revolution in China could be based on a large, urban proletariat or be run from Moscow disappeared once and for all. Although Mao always paid homage to Lenin, he rejected the core Leninist doctrine that a revolution had to be led by a small vanguard party.

Comparative Emphasis: The Chinese Revolution

Unlike the former Soviet Union and most of Eastern Europe, communists came to power in China as a result of a massive popular revolution. However, this does not mean they did so in the way Karl Marx anticipated.

The revolution succeeded because the Chinese Communist Party could appeal both to the oppressed peasants and to people from other walks of life who wanted to resist the Japanese occupation. As a result, the CCP took China even further from orthodox Marxism than the Soviets. Throughout the forty or so years that Mao ran the CCP, it emphasized mass participation, rural development, and the central role of culture and ideology. ■

Mao Zedong and Zhou Enlai during the Long March.

The communist victory in 1949 cannot be attributed to Maoism alone. In 1931, Japan invaded Manchuria and soon moved into the Chinese heartland. In yet another at least partial break with Marxist orthodoxy, the CCP spearheaded resistance against the Japanese occupiers. Another united front between the CCP and the KMT was cobbled together after a group of disgruntled generals took Chiang prisoner. In practice, the the KMT always had doubts about both the united front and armed resistance against the Japanese. As a result, the CCP led the resistance, which strengthened its anti-imperialist credentials even further and added nationalism to its message of social justice that enabled it to reach out to people from almost every walk of life.

By the time World War II ended, the CCP had gained considerable administrative experience in the one-fifth of the country it controlled. Even more important, the People's Liberation Army had swollen to nine hundred thousand regular troops and two million reserves.

A full-fledged civil war then broke out. Despite the CCP's gains, the KMT seemed likely to win. Its army was much larger, and it received millions of dollars of aid from the United States, whereas Joseph Stalin did little to help the CCP. But in early 1946 the disciplined PLA gained control of Manchuria and started moving south, and the tide turned in favor of the CCP.

Less than two years later, the KMT had been routed. Chiang and the Nationalist leadership fled to Taiwan.

The victory marked the end of one of the darkest periods in Chinese history, something Mao eloquently noted in a speech a week before the PRC was born:

> The Chinese have always been a great, courageous, and industrious nation; it is only in modern times that they have fallen behind. And that was due entirely to oppression and exploitation by foreign imperialism and domestic reactionary government. Ours will no longer be a nation subject to insult and humiliation. We have stood up.[2]

Factionalism

The Communists quickly consolidated control of the entire country other than Taiwan, which the KMT occupied and which remains a bone of contention to this day. Despite its undisputed victory on the mainland, plenty of conflict remained. Now, however, the disputes took place *inside* the CCP in what turned out to be thirty years of intense factional conflict.

Control of the party swung back and forth between more moderate, orthodox leaders and radicals who wanted to make the transition to socialism and communism as quickly as possible. Under Mao's leadership, the radical faction twice took the country to the brink of disaster during the Great Leap Forward and the Cultural Revolution. It was only after the death of Mao that the moderates gained what now seems to be permanent control of the party and state and instituted the reforms they have followed ever since (see Table 10.2).

At first, the CCP seemed united. Neither Mao nor his colleagues considered any options other than adopting a Soviet-style political system at home and following Moscow's leadership internationally. Moreover, Mao himself had the unquestioned support of the entire party. As a result, it started with and continues to use the two key principles common to all Marxist-Leninist systems:

- The party's monopoly on all forms of political power.
- The use of democratic centralism in all internal party decision making.

The PRC's early initiatives confirmed the then common Western conservative stereotypes of a worldwide communist conspiracy, beginning with its participation in the Korean War. In 1950, without any apparent input from the Chinese, North Korean troops invaded the southern half of the Korean peninsula and occupied Seoul. The United States was able to convince the United Nations

TABLE 10.2 Key Events in Chinese History since the Revolution

YEAR	EVENT
1949	CCP takes power
1956	De-Stalinization in Soviet Union begins Hundred Flowers Campaign
1957	Great Leap Forward
1965	Beginning of Cultural Revolution
1972	Opening to United States
1976	Deaths of Zhou Enlai and Mao Zedong; Formal end of Cultural Revolution
1978	Democracy Wall
1989	Democracy Movement and Tiananmen Square
1997	Reversion of Hong Kong to PRC; Death of Deng Xiaoping
2003	Hu Jintao becomes president
2013	Xi Jinping becomes president

© Cengage Learning

to send American-led troops to Korea. The Chinese had little option but to support their fellow communists in the north. As the UN troops approached the Yalu River that separates China and North Korea, the PRC sent in the PLA and fought until the end of the war three years later.

In 1953, the CCP announced a Soviet-style five-year plan that channeled more than half the available investment capital into heavy industry. As in the Soviet Union, the heaviest burden fell on the peasants, who were forced to live and work in huge collective farms that sold their produce to the state at prices it determined.

This Soviet phase of the PRC's history did not last long, however. The CCP's doubts about Soviet leadership that dated from the days of Borodin burst out in the open after Nikita Khrushchev's "secret speech" and his acknowledgment that there could be multiple "roads to socialism."

The CCP used the speech as a pretext for defining its own future and venting its resentment toward the Soviets. Within months the Chinese and Soviets were taking verbal potshots at each other. Mao referred to Khrushchev's reforms as "goulash communism" and blamed it for taking Soviet-bloc countries further and further from Marxist goals.

By the end of the decade, the USSR had withdrawn its advisers, and China had stopped accepting Soviet economic and military aid. During the late 1960s and the 1970s, there were skirmishes along the border separating China and Siberia. It was only in the late 1980s with the rise of reformist leaders in both countries that significant steps were taken toward healing the Sino-Soviet split.

More important for our purposes, the schism between the two allowed the CCP to go off on its own domestically,

---

[2]Cited in Witold Rodzinski, *The People's Republic of China: A Concise History.* New York: Free Press, 1988, 13.

which had the unintended consequence of bringing factionalism to the surface and undermining party unity. Indeed, for the next quarter century, Chinese politics was little more than a battle between the Maoists and the more moderate or orthodox Marxists.

The rift became public during the **Hundred Flowers Campaign** in 1956. Intellectuals were allowed some freedom of expression, much as their Soviet counterparts were during their "thaw" at the same time. In typical Chinese fashion, Mao used a traditional phrase to start the campaign—"Let a hundred flowers bloom and a thousand points of view contend." When they did just that, Mao and the wing of the leadership that was crystallizing into the radical faction clamped down.

Mao shifted gears the next year and called for a Great Leap Forward in order to speed the transition to socialism through massive **campaigns,** one of which encouraged collective farmers to build small backyard furnaces for making steel. In Mao's eyes, intellectuals had become suspect during the Hundred Flowers Campaign. Now, they were expected to engage in manual labor that would bring them closer to the people.

By all accounts, the Great Leap Forward was a disaster. Industrial production plummeted. The backyard furnace and other experimental programs were abject failures. The situation in the countryside was particularly chaotic. During the harsh winter of 1958–59, as many as 35 million people starved to death.

Not surprisingly, the divisions within the party grew more intense, although few people outside the ruling Politburo knew about them. The head of the PLA took Mao to task for the Great Leap Forward. When the Politburo met to consider the critique, Mao threatened to go to the countryside and start another revolution. He was able to fend off the attack in the short run, but he lost much of his influence within the party. The moderates were strong enough to shelve Mao's radical ideas, temporarily demote him, and re-embark on a more orthodox policy of industrial development. Mao's only significant victory in the early 1960s came when he was able to purge most PLA leaders and replace them with his loyalists.

During this time, Mao's own commitment to rapid and dramatic change only got more intense. From his perspective, the CCP was showing signs of the kind of conservative elitism he saw in the Soviet Union under Leonid Brezhnev. Furthermore, a new generation of young people was coming of age that had not experienced the trauma or the exhilaration of the revolutionary struggle.

Almost immediately after his demotion, Mao turned to the PLA, which was also the only real ally he had left. With its support, he launched the Socialist Education Movement in 1963, which returned ideology and cultural change to

PROFILES   Mao Zedong

Mao was not one of the sophisticated intellectuals who led the Chinese Communist Party (CCP) in its early years. His father was a rather unsophisticated peasant who ruled his family with an iron fist. Mao began working in the family fields at the age of six, but because his father wanted to make certain that at least one of his children could read and write well enough to keep the books, he sent his son to school. The young Mao turned out to be an excellent student and graduated from teacher's training college in 1918. He then moved to Beijing, where he took a job at the university library under one of the founders of the CCP. Mao experienced May Fourth in Beijing but soon returned to his home region of Hunan to begin organizing.

Mao might never have become a major CCP leader were it not for the 1927 Kuomintang attack that led the CCP to adopt his peasant-based strategy—a decision that was confirmed by the Long March. Mao's leadership of the party was seriously questioned only once in the next forty years.

As more has been learned about Mao's personal life and the disruption caused by the Cultural Revolution, assessments of his historical role have turned negative. Nonetheless, he will always be thought of as one of the most influential political leaders of the twentieth century. ∎

center stage. Meanwhile, the PLA spearheaded the creation of a cult of personality around Mao that dwarfed the adulation of Stalin by his henchmen. Every imaginable accomplishment was attributed to Mao. His position in Marxist philosophy was put on a par with that of Marx and Lenin as what came to be called Marxism–Leninism–Mao Zedong thought. The ridiculous turned to the absurd when a news story about the seventy-year-old Mao swimming six miles in an hour appeared on the front page of the PLA's daily newspaper.

In March 1966, Mao stepped up the pressure by attacking the Beijing party organization that was dominated by the moderates. His supporters put up the first *dazibao* (big-character posters), urging revolutionary intellectuals to "go into battle" against the party bureaucracy, which brought the conflict within the party establishment into the open, especially in criticisms of moderate leaders, **Liu Shaoqi** (1898–1969) and Deng.

The moderates' counterattack failed. University and middle school students formed teams of **Red Guards** to carry on the work of what was now called the **Great Proletarian Cultural Revolution (GPCR).** Within weeks they had paralyzed the country's schools and universities. Many Red Guard units turned into little more than vigilante mobs after Mao urged them to attack the party hierarchy. In August 1966, Liu was officially labeled "the leading person in authority taking the **capitalist road**" and Deng "the number two person in authority taking the capitalist road." Liu, Deng, and thousands of others were arrested and either went to prison or were sent down to the countryside to perform manual labor. Liu would be the most famous of the countless thousands of Chinese citizens to die. Deng, who was already in his mid-sixties, was forced to work as a machinist on a collective farm. One of his sons was either pushed or fell from a seventh-story window and has been confined to a wheelchair ever since.

New radical groups sprung up all over the country, at least some of them spontaneously. However they were

Protestors during the Cultural Revolution.

Conflict in China

Before 1989, China experienced more open conflict than any other communist country. Its conflict was also different from the disputes discussed in Chapter 8 in three important ways. First, on many occasions, it turned violent. Second, some of it was orchestrated from above as part of the factional dispute within the CCP itself. Third, even as dissatisfaction grew, there was little evidence that the protests and protesters could come together as a unified movement.

There has been less overt conflict in China since the **Tiananmen Square** demonstrations of 1989. Dissidents are occasionally arrested. There have been press reports of strikes in many major cities, and there have also been violent outbursts in minority regions. The Chinese Communist Party (CCP) itself acknowledges that there are, on average, two hundred protests a day.

Widespread resentment toward the CCP and its rule undoubtedly lurks just below the surface. However, China has not seen the development of an independent opposition movement with strong grassroots support ■

formed, they were then manipulated by Maoist **cadres**, including the Shanghai commune, organized by three relatively unknown men—Zhang Chunqiao, Wang Hongwen, and Yao Wenyuan. The three were quickly promoted to positions of national prominence and joined Mao's wife, **Jiang Qing** (together known as the **Gang of Four**) in taking control of the cultural side of the Cultural Revolution by removing everything Western from the theaters and airwaves.

"Seizures of power" became a daily occurrence in schools, factories, and neighborhoods around the country. Jiang urged the Red Guards to take up arms in order to defend themselves. Sometimes the violence was directed at political targets, but on all too many occasions, the young people were simply settling old scores.

It is hard to fathom just how disruptive the Cultural Revolution was. However, Harvard's Ross Terrill offered one anecdote that can at least give you a hint of what it was like. It turns out that even trained circus horses were stripped of their lives of luxury and "sent down" to the countryside. One group of horses was assigned to work at a commune next to a military base, which they dutifully did until the bugles began to play, at which point they returned to the equine version of the capitalist road and performed a few of their old dance routines.[3]

By late 1967, it was clear even to Mao that things had gotten out of hand, and he called on the PLA to restore order. Red Guards were ordered to merge into "three-in-one" committees with the PLA and politically acceptable

---

[3]Ross Terrill. *China in Our Time* (New York: Simon and Schuster, 1992), 65.

CCP members. But in a country that large and in which conditions were that chaotic, the disruption continued.

Over the course of the next few years, order was gradually restored, in particular through the efforts of the one remaining moderate leader, **Zhou Enlai** (1899–1976). In 1973, Zhou announced that China would concentrate on the **four modernizations**—agriculture, industry, science, and the military—that have been at the heart of Chinese public policy ever since. Although already terminally ill, Zhou was politically strong enough to bring Deng back from internal exile and have him named deputy prime minister.

PROFILES Zhou Enlai

Zhou was born into a gentry family in 1899. Like many privileged young people of his generation, Zhou went to Japan to study and returned to participate in the May Fourth Movement. He later continued his studies in France, where he became a Marxist.

Zhou's charm and sophistication enhanced the Chinese Communist Party's reputation with foreigners and Chinese intellectuals alike. Once the People's Republic was established, Zhou became prime minister, a post he held until his death. He was the one leading politician who had the respect of both factions and could sometimes build bridges between them.

Unfortunately, Zhou contracted cancer in the early 1970s and knew he did not have long to live. Still, he was able to gain enough support to launch the four modernizations and bring Deng Xiaoping back into the leadership ∎

Premier Zhou Enlai meeting and dining with President Richard Nixon's envoy, Henry Kissinger.

© Bettmann/CORBIS

All but the most dedicated Maoists realized that China could not afford to continue disrupting "normal" life the way it had for a decade. They increasingly put the economy and administration on center stage, and Zhou personally became more influential.

Zhou died in January 6. In March, a Shanghai newspaper accused him of having been a capitalist roader—an accusation that evoked an unprecedented response. Memorial wreaths began to appear in Tiananmen Square, and demonstrations were held in his honor until the authorities finally broke them up in early April. When Mao died that September, the mourning paled in comparison.

At that time, the succession procedures were not as orderly as they are now. Mao's positions in the party and government were taken over by the politically unknown Hua Guofeng (1921–2008). Hua proved unable to end the still-simmering conflict between Deng, who had become the de facto leader of the moderate faction, and the Gang of Four. In the short run, it seemed the Maoists would win. Deng was demoted again. Hua, however, was no friend of the radicals. In one of his few memorable acts as General Secretary, he simultaneously arrested the Gang of Four and brought Deng back from political obscurity yet again.

The Cultural Revolution was finally over, but its legacy persists to this day in ways that leap out of the pages of popular accounts of political life, such as those included in the list of suggested readings at the end of this chapter. For a decade, scientific and industrial development had been put on hold. In addition, a generation of students had been unable to go to school, so the country lost their potential contributions to social, economic, and cultural development.

Reform

Factionalism has never completely disappeared. Hints of it are to be found in almost all intra-elite disputes, including the one involving Bo Xilai discussed at the beginning of this chapter. That said, factional divisions have not come close to paralyzing the party leadership the way they did when Mao was alive.

Factionalism is less important today for the simple reason that the moderates won, and next to no traces of Maoism remain. In 1978, Deng outmaneuvered Hua and forced him into early retirement. Since then, campaigns, cultural change, grassroots activism, and other hallmarks of the Maoist era have all but disappeared. In their place are the simultaneous pursuit of rapid economic reform and the continuation of as complete political control as possible.

StreetStock/Alamy

The futuristic stadium built for the 2008 summer olympics in Beijing.

As someone who can remember the Cultural Revolution and the first pictures of everyday life that accompanied the American "opening" to China in the 1970s, what seems like a fact of life to young readers today still seems surprising. We tended to look at the new China as just another temporary phenomenon that would join the Cultural Revolution, Great Leap Forward, Hundred Flowers Campaign, and more in what Trotsky and others called the dustbin of history.

Today, there is nothing Quixotic about the new China. The PRC is a major player in most key international markets, and its role is bound to increase unless something utterly unpredictable happens to the world economy.

As we will see in the public policy section below, almost everyone who has played a prominent role in Chinese political life since Mao's death had roots in the faction initially led by Liu and Deng. Most are pragmatists, something that Deng put eloquently—if elliptically—in the statement that starts the chapter.

Together, they have also created smoothly functioning institutions within the CCP of which the transition from one leader to the next is but the most obvious example. It is not the kind of regime we saw in Part 2. It may also not be one that most readers of this book would like to be governed by. Nonetheless, it is hard to escape the conclusion that it *has* been a remarkably effective one.

Deng and his generation were already in their seventies when they returned to power for good. Therefore, they decided not to assume the top formal offices and instead to govern from behind the scenes. The top official jobs were held by their protégés, many of whom had also been

victims of the Cultural Revolution. As Deng's generation continued to age, de facto and de jure leadership passed first to a team headed by Jiang Zemin in 1992 and then to Hu Jintao ten years later. During that time, a number of key milestone events happened surprisingly easily, including Hong Kong's reversion to the PRC when Britain's "legal" mandate to rule the territory expired.

Curiously, the strength of the current regime can perhaps be seen in its most dangerous challenge—the Tiananmen Square protests in 1989. The upheavals that took the Communist world by storm did not spare China. That spring, a spontaneous student-led democracy movement began. Without much formal organization, groups of them decided to occupy Tiananmen Square in the heart of Beijing. The protests spread around the country.

The details of what happened will be discussed later. Here, it is enough to note that the protesters worked on the assumption that democratic institutions could *and should* be built within the existing socialist order. Unlike many of their counterparts in the Soviet Union and Eastern Europe, the students who first occupied Tiananmen Square cast their demands in patriotic terms, arguing that socialist democracy required the party leaders to be open to criticism from the people. After the PLA crackdown, many of the survivors became and remain deeply disillusioned with the regime, although that has not resulted in another massive protest movement—at least not yet.

The brutal repression of the protests revealed an equally important characteristic of the post-Mao leadership. The party was willing to tolerate economic but not political

Political Culture

Some political scientists draw a sharp distinction between political culture and participation. There are certainly places where and periods of time when that makes sense, especially when cultures seem impervious to change.

In China, by contrast, the two tend to blend together more than in most other countries. As long as Mao was alive, cultural change was an explicit goal of the frequent campaigns that swept millions of people into the tumult of political life.

Despite the centrality of culture in Chinese politics after 1945, it is very hard to tell how much success the Maoists had in changing it. In part, that reflects the fact that cultures rarely change quickly, especially when national leaders try to do so from above. In China's case, it is also hard to be precise about anything involving culture, because social scientists have not had access to the kind of public opinion polling or in-depth anthropological studies on which such analyses are normally based. Still, it is hard not to emphasize the importance of continuity rather than change at least until the economy opened.

A Blank Slate? A Cultural Revolution?

Mao's misunderstandings of his own people led to some of his greatest failures. He correctly understood that Chinese values would have to change because he believed that socialist institutions could only be built by a people committed to socialist values. In the early years, the more orthodox and moderate party leaders differed only in degree, arguing that cultural change simply ranked below economic growth on their list of priorities.

However, Mao and his supporters were incorrect in assuming that it would be relatively easy to transform Chinese political culture. Shortly after coming to power, he wrote:

> The two outstanding things about China's 600 million people are that they are "poor and blank." On a blank sheet of paper free from any blotches, the freshest and most beautiful characters can be written, the freshest and most beautiful pictures can be painted.[4]

In one sense, Mao was right about the Chinese people being a blank slate. Prior to 1949, Chinese peasants had no political role other than as taxpayers and soldiers. The gentry, the civil servants, and other members of the elite made the decisions that mattered in a country in which the dominant Confucian values stressed group loyalty,

Students at Beijing's Central Academy of Fine Arts putting the finishing touches on the "Goddess of Democracy," modeled after the Statue of Liberty.

AP Photo/Liu Heung Shing

reform. Whenever economic liberalization threatened to spill over into demands for political loosening, the party was still willing and able to clamp down on dissent.

To use the terminology introduced in Chapter 8, there is nothing "hybrid" about the *politics* of communism in China. The PRC may no longer be a totalitarian regime by any stretch of the imagination, but it is still authoritarian and Marxist-Leninist.

It is hard to see how political authoritarianism can survive given the social and economic changes the regime itself has helped produce. It is also hard to see how the regime could change without something akin to another revolution. How and why that is the case will be the focus of the rest of this chapter and should help explain why Chinese politics remains so fascinating and challenging despite the apparent stability of the last thirty years.

---

[4]Cited in H. Ross Terrill. *China in Our Time* (New York: Simon and Schuster, 1992), 1.

conflict avoidance, and acceptance of one's place in the social hierarchy. In other words, the revolution was fought on behalf of a mostly inactive mass public about which the CCP had huge expectations.

The early CCP tried to replace the hierarchy, resignation, and sullen anger it inherited with a value system based on four main ingredients that were, themselves, filled with contradictions:

- *Collectivism.* The CCP wanted to see group loyalties transferred to a broader and more inclusive institution—the party state.

- *Struggle and activism.* The CCP encouraged the Chinese people to actively participate in what the leadership understood would be a bumpy transition to socialism. However, it did not view participation as something people did voluntarily or out of self-interest but as part of the collectivist goal of serving the people.

- *Egalitarianism and populism.* The CCP tried to end what it saw as the irrational subordination not only of the working class and peasantry but of women and young people as well. On the other hand, the CCP also reinforced hierarchical traditions with its imposition of a Leninist–Stalinist-style party state.

- *Self-reliance.* Finally, the Chinese tried to undermine the hold of traditional values that left most people dependent on the elite, waiting for instructions and leadership from above. As with egalitarianism, their actions belied their words from the very beginning.

The party had tools at its disposal to facilitate change along each of these lines. For example, it had tremendous leverage over all key agents of political socialization. As in the former Soviet Union, the CCP controlled the education system and the mass media, which were used to create what Maoists explicitly called the "new Chinese man." The party also tried to undermine the authority of the family by shifting many child-rearing activities to the *danwei,* or **unit**—the basic body to which most urban Chinese were assigned and through which they received jobs, housing, and social service benefits.

Similarly, the CCP initiated dozens of campaigns from the 1950s through the 1970s to rid the country of physical and social "evils" ranging from flies to homosexuality. Each one included mandatory political study sessions in which people assembled to discuss the issues of the day in the light of some relevant texts by Mao, thereby supposedly deepening their understanding of and commitment to Marxism–Leninism–Mao Zedong thought.

The CCP was almost certainly more successful than the early CPSU was in changing cultural norms. However, its failures had a much longer-lasting and devastating impact.

There was a lot of cynical and self-interested participation in the campaigns. Many of the 17 million young people sent down during the Cultural Revolution came to resent their exile and the system that sent them there, as did the peasants whose lives were disrupted by their arrival.

In retrospect, none of them is more glaring than its failure to "reinvent" one of the most important lingering aspects of traditional thought and action: the role of women. Of all the countries covered in this book, the PRC officially made the most concerted efforts to improve the status of women. Women played a vital role in the revolution, prompting Mao to stress how they "held up half the sky." The 1950 Law on Marriage and other early decrees gave women legal equality and outlawed many traditional practices such as foot binding. Since then, the status of women has largely disappeared from political center stage except for the ban on having more than one child, which few observers ever thought of as a victory for women.

On balance, women in China continue to occupy secondary positions in everything from the politics of the household to the politics of the Politburo. In all, only a few women have played a significant role in the CCP elite, most of whom were the wives of even more prominent men, including Mao and Zhou.

If anything, there are signs that the condition of women may actually be worsening. Women are being discriminated against more in hiring, housing, and the distribution of land. At a recent job fair to recruit government officials, fully 80 percent of the positions were only open to male applicants. Women who are hired are routinely required to promise that they will not marry for at least three years. Furthermore, women are again being bought and sold as wives, a practice that was outlawed in the 1950s.

Cultural Politics since the Death of Mao Zedong

Even after the reformers took control, the CCP's rhetoric still included a commitment to cultural change. That rhetoric all but disappeared before the end of the 1980s and probably would have even if the Marxist-Leninist regimes in the Soviet bloc hadn't imploded.

Since then, analysts have focused not on the speed at which the party would remake China but on whether or not it would survive. The party has all but eliminated its efforts to reshape public opinion and the political culture. Deng's sense of pragmatism, according to which the people were exhorted to "seek truth from facts," left little room for Mao's kind of ideological campaigns. The party has loosened its controls somewhat in recent years, allowing a wider range of views to be expressed in the media and schools and, more important, permitting foreign music, films, and news into China on a scale that would have been unimaginable a generation ago. Despite the limits on freedom of expression to be discussed below, the party cannot hope to dominate public opinion as fully as it did before the reform era.

Women in Chinese Politics: Half the Sky? Or Less?

Several years ago, Nicholas Kristof and Sheryl WuDunn borrowed the title for their book on the global status of women from a speech by Mao in which he urged the CCP to liberate women because they "held up half the sky." However you want to define what half the sky means, there is no doubt that Mao and his successors alike have fallen far short of that goal.

To be sure, abuses such as foot binding were eliminated and it became easier for women to get a divorce. Some would even argue that the one child per family law has eased the burden on women.

There are also some areas in which the status of women has improved in the last few years. About one hundred of the richest one thousand people in China are women, including two of the country's five billionaires. Yet even in this regard the Chinese do not fare all that well. Only about 20 percent of its businesses are owned by women, which is about two-thirds of the global average.

The political status of women is even less encouraging. There are no women on the Standing Committee of the Politburo, which is the most powerful single political body in the country. Only three of the twenty-seven cabinet ministers in late 2010 were women. It is hard to tell whether the CCP or the lingering impact of traditional culture bears the most responsibility here. Nonetheless, it is clear that there is a glass ceiling in Chinese politics that few women can get through.

The modernization of the country has led to the emergence of a number of new social groups. Some, such as the urban entrepreneurs and international traders, are beginning to band together to promote their professional interests. As the number of people who work outside the centrally planned economy continues to grow and the unit and iron rice bowl lose importance, many Chinese who have not benefited from economic growth are angry with the regime. There is little evidence that such anger will have deep political consequences, but most political scientists also failed to see signs that communism was about to fall in the late 1980s in Europe or that the "color revolutions" of the last few years were about to break out.

The protests that do occur (to be discussed in the next section) tend to focus on local social or economic complaints rather than national or political ones. Any number of new social groups could pose challenges for the regime, albeit in very different ways.

First is the new upper middle class with as many as three hundred million members. So far, this group of mostly young and well-educated urban residents has been satisfied with the material rewards of a middle-class life. A decade ago, we wondered if they would be happy enough with knock-off Western videotapes and computers. Now, they are almost as likely to have smart phones and use the Internet as Westerners of their generation.

Second is the larger group of people who have not benefited anywhere near as much from all the social and economic change. China now has one of the highest gini coefficients in the world, which means that its distribution of income is highly skewed. Most attention in the West is paid to millions of poor and unskilled workers who work at companies like Foxconn and make iPads, earn a pittance, and have little or no opportunity for upward social mobility. Just as important are the so-called *yi zu* (ant tribes) of young educated men and women who can neither find jobs in their home towns nor afford housing in the booming cities.

The CCP can almost certainly combine whatever popularity it gets from the new prosperity with the occasional use of repression to prevent major protest movements from growing in the short term. Nonetheless, it is hard to imagine how the regime can keep a lid on things because of the other major change that has occurred in the last thirty years—the Chinese have far greater exposure to the outside world. On this front, nothing has received more attention—or been more controversial—than Chinese policy regarding the Internet. The party has enjoyed some success in limiting free access to it, especially by blocking sites that include material by and about dissidents. Microsoft and Google block access to many websites the authorities find objectionable. The party has banned Facebook and Twitter, but in late 2012 they had 65,000,000 and 35,000,000 users, respectively, because young Chinese netizens have figured out how to get around what has been dubbed "the great firewall."

It isn't just the Internet. More than two million Chinese students attended colleges and universities abroad in 2011, a figure that has grown by over 20 percent per year for the last half decade. In what may be more of a sign of things to come, the number of students returning to China after foreign study increased at an even faster rate. Almost 300,000 foreigners are studying in China in 2013.

We can only say one thing with any certainty. It is hard to imagine how all Chinese citizens could be integrated into a single, uniform political culture for the simple reason that China has diversified while it has grown. We have no way of knowing how much dissatisfaction there is. So far, the limited public opinion polls suggest that the regime still has at least some, grudgingly granted, legitimacy.

Political Participation

Political scientists assume that most participation in democratic regimes is voluntary and therefore best understood from the "bottom up." People get involved in political life because they want to.

Most political participation is decidedly *not* voluntary in authoritarian regimes, as we saw in the discussion of the USSR under communist rule. Therefore, it makes sense to start our discussion with "top-down" participation in China, although we can no longer limit ourselves to it.

Top-Down Participation

For most people in China, participating in politics means doing things that were approved, planned, and organized by others much higher up the CCP hierarchy. This was especially true during the Maoist years, when campaigns were a routine fact of life. In those days, almost everyone in urban areas was assigned to a unit that was managed by local party representatives. Much the same was true of the people's communes in rural areas, which were much like state and collective farms in the Soviet Union.

In fact, mass political participation has only changed in one way since the reforms began. It is still "top down." However, the excitement is gone. Frankly speaking, most forms of activism are downright boring.

Popular participation is still channeled through the CCP, which claimed to have about 82 million members or nearly 10 percent of the adult population in 2011 (www.chinatoday.com/org/cpc/). The work those grassroots members do is hardly glamorous and has little impact—if any—on public policy.

As we will see in the next section, this is one area in which analysts who concentrate on atrophy have the most support. Most party members carry out decisions made by their superiors. Most join the CCP in the first place only because party membership has been the only stepping stone to success in each and every career path. However, as opportunities for accumulating wealth outside of the party have mushroomed, party membership has lost some of its appeal, which has led it to have some trouble in recruiting talented and ambitious young members.

Forced participation does still exist. Most Chinese citizens attend study sessions to consider Xi Jinping's first set of policy pronouncements. Unlike during the Cultural Revolution years, few people go to those sessions with any great enthusiasm—or any great fear.

And Bottom Up?

There is also fragmentary evidence that a growing—but still small—number of Chinese citizens take part in the kind of political participation democratic theorists champion. It is important to underscore the fact that we are only talking about a tiny portion of the population. However, there are signs that those who do take part in the kinds of activities discussed below are placing new kinds of more subtle demands on the system, some of which could reinforce its legitimacy, while others almost certainly will not.

Officially Sanctioned Behavior

The party has allowed some modest forms of "bottom-up" participation.

The most commented on—although perhaps not the most important—are local elections in some rural districts, in which more than one candidate has been allowed to run. The CCP is still the only organization that can nominate candidates. Nonetheless, voters do now occasionally have choices for members of local governments.

In this decade, opportunities for other kinds of voluntary participation also expanded slightly. In 2008, for example, the government passed its first laws that resemble Western freedom of information acts. In the first year, tens of thousands of such requests were filed. The government complied with about half of them. The law's coverage is limited; only people, for instance, who were directly affected by a decision can file a claim. Nonetheless, the new law made it much easier for the Chinese people to learn about what happened in the devastating 2008 earthquake in Sichuan, which occurred a few months after the law went into effect.

Similarly, there were three thousand NGOs in China in 1980. Today, the best estimate is that three million of them are at least tolerated by the authorities. Few of them are political, and those that are rarely do anything in opposition to the Party. Nonetheless, they do exist and *could* lead to more dramatic change in the future.

Dissent

Not surprisingly, Western political scientists have focused on instances of open dissent. Since the end of the Cultural Revolution, there have been a number of waves of protest. Although they never threatened the regime, each suggests that the CCP may not be as powerful as most analysts believe.

As we consider four of them, it's important, again, not to read too much into them. They do reflect what seems to be widespread frustration with the regime. However, almost all of them deal only with local issues and complaints. More important, few have led to the creation of enduring organizations that could be used to mount a serious challenge to either the regime or its most important policies.

Democracy Wall The first was the **Democracy Wall** in 1978. With government approval, people put up big-character posters in Beijing and elsewhere. Many were simply critical of how socialism was being implemented. Others went further and advocated more far-reaching reforms, ranging from freedom of speech to a multiparty system. Soon, Deng's patience ran out and the authorities banned all posters and publications that criticized socialism. The leaders were arrested, many of whom spent years in prison.

Tiananmen Square For the next decade, open dissent came mostly from isolated individuals. In 1989, the situation suddenly changed with the emergence of the **Democracy Movement**, which we have already encountered briefly several times in the course of this chapter.

As with the demonstrations a decade earlier, the Democracy Movement began with spontaneous protests following the death of a respected reformist leader—Hu Yaobang. Within hours of his death, big-character posters appeared on the walls of Beijing University. That evening, politically connected graduate students in its Department of Communist Party History bicycled into Tiananmen Square to place a wreath in his honor. Two days later, five hundred students marched to the square to lay more wreaths. The demonstrations got bigger and bigger. The police chose not to intervene. On the night of April 21, ten thousand of them marched into the square—and stayed. A day later, their ranks had swollen to one hundred thousand.

In early May, the movement spread to other major cities. Journalists defied party discipline and began accurately reporting on what was taking place. The students remaining in the square proved to be an embarrassment to the authorities during Gorbachev's visit to Beijing by making it clear that they were inspired in large measure by the political reforms undertaken under his leadership in Moscow. The demonstrations continued after he left. A small group of students began a hunger strike. By May 17, an estimated two million people filled Tiananmen Square, in the largest demonstration since the Cultural Revolution.

On May 20, the hard-liners started their counteroffensive. They first seized control of the party leadership by replacing Zhao with the anti-reforms mayor of Shanghai, **Jiang Zemin (1926–)**. The standoff continued for two more weeks. Finally, on the night of June 3, PLA soldiers stormed the square. No one knows how many people were killed, but estimates run as high as four thousand. Many student leaders fled the country. In the days and months after the crackdown, the hard-liners solidified their hold on power and made the open expression of dissent impossible. Most movement leaders who stayed in China were arrested.

Little of the hope or momentum of that spring survived the year's end. Occasional demonstrations have occurred since then, including the attempt by dissidents to create the independent China Democracy Party in 1998, all of whose members were either arrested or fled abroad.

Falun Gong In the years after Tiananmen Square, the party made a movement many see as apolitical its prime target. **Falun Gong** is hard to fit into Western conceptual frameworks. On one level, it is nothing more than a series of exercises that practitioners believe lead to spiritual and physical well-being. On another level, it is inspired by Buddhism and, thus, has religious overtones.

It was founded in 1992 by a minor railway official, Li Hongzhi, who had no particular expertise in either medicine or religion. Nonetheless, the movement and its program of exercise and meditation quickly caught on—especially among middle-aged, middle-class Chinese, many of whom had been victims of the Cultural Revolution and were not benefiting from economic reform.

As long as Falun Gong adherents simply went to parks to perform their rituals and exercises, the regime tolerated them. Gradually, however, the authorities came to see the movement as a threat because it was an independent organization with as many as fifty million practitioners that the party did not control.

For the rest of the 1990s, Falun Gong held peaceful demonstrations in Beijing and other cities, some of which were declared illegal by the authorities even though the group's advocates claimed they were not political at all. Finally, the authorities outlawed Falun Gong in 2000, claiming it was an "evil cult." Li went into exile and now runs the movement from New York. The party sent at least five thousand members to labor camps for "reeducation" and arrested several hundred more. A few dozen members committed suicide while in prison. As recently as 2007, there were press accounts of Falun Gong adherents being arrested, persecuted, and even executed for their beliefs.

For our purposes, the importance of Falun Gong does not lie in what its practitioners do or do not believe in. Rather, it lies in the way the authorities respond to it. As the religious sociologist Richard Madsen puts it, "[a]ny organization like Falun Gong, no matter what the content of its ideology, would be a threat to the communist regime."[5] The fact is that a well-organized group beyond

---

[5]Richard Madsen, "Understanding Falun Gong." *Current History* 99 September 2000.

Democratization in China

China and Iran are the only two countries covered in this book where we cannot realistically speak about democratization. Western journalists and human rights advocates seize on whatever evidence they can find of hostility to the CCP, such as the 1998 attempt by dissidents to register an opposition party, as signs of a pro-democratic groundswell. In fact, there is little evidence suggesting that significant support for democratization is lurking just "below the surface."

What will happen in the long term is not as clear. Political scientists are not naïve enough to assume that the emergence of capitalism will necessarily lead to democracy as well. What's more, the regime still seems to be able to quash embryonic movements that do spring up. Still, it is by no means certain that it will be able to stave off democratization efforts in the future or that it will not try to preempt them with gradual, pragmatic reforms of its own. ■

the control of the party is an obvious source of concern for the party elite, who know that the CCP is nowhere near as powerful or as popular as it once was.

Everyday Protest Nothing like Falun Gong exists on a national level in China today. That does not mean that protests have disappeared. Journalists and others estimate that an average of two hundred or more unauthorized strikes and demonstrations take place *each day*.

Typical of these was the Hohhot Nationality Movement that broke out in late May 2011. Hohhot is a city of about 2.5 million people in Inner Mongolia. Despite its location, 87 percent of its population is Han Chinese and thus belong to the PRC's dominant ethnic group.

The protests began after a seemingly minor incident. Two Mongolians who were protesting pollution at a local mine were run over and killed by Han Chinese drivers. Upwards of two thousand ethnic Mongolian students took to the streets to protest the party's failure to prosecute the drivers. The demonstrators didn't stop there, but went on to voice their concerns about what they saw as the central government's assault on their traditional way of life.

The state responded in its typical way, combining positive inducements (carrots) with repression (sticks). By the end of May, they had offered millions of dollars in economic aid for the impoverished region to go along with subsidies for Mongolian cultural initiatives. At the same time, they arrested the ringleaders of the protests, shut down parks and other public spaces the demonstrators congregated in, and threatened to fire any state employee who joined the marches. Students who sent text and other messages on Chinese social media sites were brought in for questioning by the police.

In terms typical of the new China, one of them starkly expressed his frustration. "First, they shut down our Internet, then they interrupted our cellphone service, and finally they imprisoned us at school. The students are afraid, but more than that, they are angry."[6] Their colleagues at Inner Mongolia University threw their Chinese-language textbooks out classroom windows, being locked down on campus.

The Hohhot students were not unique. The unsystematically gathered evidence available to us suggests that sentiments such as the one quoted above from one of the protesters are quite widely held.

Almost all of these start as local disputes. Many take place in minority regions like Mongolia, Tibet, or Xinjiang. As a result, activists have had a hard time turning what happens in places like Hohhot into national movements, while we political scientists have had an equally hard time figuring out what their broader significance is for the regime.

Predicting the Future?

There is no better way to close this section than with a paradox. On the one hand, China is still an authoritarian state in which people can and do have their careers destroyed or spend time in prison because of their political views. On the other hand, the Chinese people have never been as free as they are today. Free political expression does not exist. Censorship is still a fact of life. However, most people have access to new and unsettling ideas coming from sources either at home or abroad.

On the basis of that conflicting evidence, most analysts conclude that China is not on the verge of a major democratic or other protest movement that could threaten the CCP's monopoly on power. But then again, very few political scientists predicted either the collapse of communism in Eurasia or the so-called "color revolutions" in other authoritarian regimes so far this century.

---

[6]Andrew Jacobs, "China Extends Hand and Fist to Protesters." *New York Times*. June 2, 2011, A6.

The Party State

Despite all the forces that are changing the face of China, the CCP is still the only political institution that counts. It has been able to resist all pressure to change the way it governs, if not its public policies. In other words, it is still quite close to the Leninist model laid out in Chapter 8, because the Chinese party and the Chinese state are for all intents and purposes the same.

The CCP in Power

Like all communist parties that joined the Comintern in the 1920s, the CCP adopted democratic centralism along with the rest of Bolshevism. This means that, although the PRC has a government and a constitution, that is not where real power lies. Despite some minor exceptions, which we will encounter later in this section, the central party organization still calls all the political—if not the economic—shots.

The 1982 constitution dropped Article 2, the PRC's equivalent of the Soviet Article 6, which gave the party a monopoly on power. This made little practical difference, because Deng Xiaoping and his successors have never wavered from their commitment to party control of everything that matters.

As in the former Soviet Union, most leading politicians hold key positions in both the party and the government. The Chinese were among the first communist governments to separate party and state leadership below the national level. In practice, however, this has yet to make much of a difference because the CCP's national leadership still controls appointments to both. And, on those rare occasions when the interests emanating from their roles conflict, it is their party "hat" that wins.

Power is officially lodged in the party Congress, which normally meets every five years. The Eighteenth Party Congress took place in November 2012 and ratified the appointment of Xi Jinping as chair of the party and named other key officials to top party organs. Everyone understood that all of them would soon also occupy the top government positions when they officially became vacant early the next year. The Congress also selects the **Central Committee** that supposedly manages party affairs until its next session.

I use the terms *officially* and *supposedly* above because, for all practical purposes, the Congress and Central Committee are powerless institutions in a system still run according to democratic centralism. Party Congress delegates are coopted from above. Its meetings have done little more than ratify decisions already made by the elite. Unlike the former CPSU, there is not much continuity in its membership, with a turnover rate of about 50 percent at each of the most recent Congresses. It also is a massive body that meets only a few times a year because well over half its members live outside Beijing. Although its plenums have often been the site of acrimonious debate over major policy initiatives, the final decisions are invariably made by a tiny, largely self-perpetuating elite.

Similarly, the PRC is officially governed by a massive National People's Congress of well over two thousand members. But, like the Supreme Soviet prior to Gorbachev, the Congress meets infrequently and serves primarily as a rubber stamp for decisions made elsewhere. Similarly, the president and prime minister are powerful primarily because they run the CCP, not because of their governmental positions.

The only significant structural difference between the PRC and other communist governments is the somewhat larger role of provincial and local authorities in China. Even that should not be surprising given China's size. Remember that some Chinese provinces have more people than most European countries. What's more, many politicians, including Deng, Jiang, Hu, and Xi established their credentials as a result of their successes at the provincial level.

Any understanding of the reality of power in the CCP begins and ends with the Politburo (twenty-six members in March 2013) and its **Standing Committee** (nine members), all of whom are senior party leaders. Unlike the CPSU, the Politburo's day-to-day work is the responsibility of its smaller Standing Committee (see Figure 10.1).

In trying to understand how the CCP actually works, Figure 10.1 can be misleading *unless* you realize that all power flows downward, as the dark shading of its arrows suggests. The leadership perpetuates itself through those downward avenues by controlling all major appointments in the vast network of party and state organizations, which is an integral part of all systems using democratic centralism. Thus, like the CPSU, it maintains **nomenklatura** lists of key positions and party members deemed worthy of filling them. If anything, it has allowed the CCP to reinforce the Chinese tradition of authoritarian rule with its emphasis on the top twenty-five to thirty-five officials and the "core leader" at any one time. In that vein, party critics stress the top-down nature of party organization. Some even still use the term *totalitarian* to describe it.

The members of the Politburo and the Standing Committee do not always agree with each other, although we know relatively little about what happens when they do differ. All meetings of the two bodies are held behind closed doors, which is true of elites in almost every country, whatever its political system. However, in authoritarian countries like China, few politicians are willing to discuss what they do and why they do it, and there are relatively few leaks to the

FIGURE 10.1 Decision Making in China

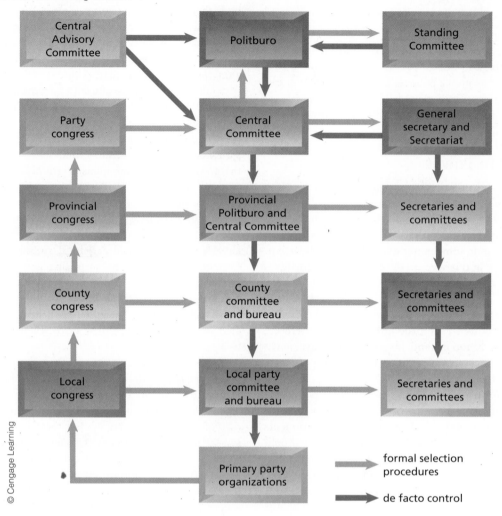

formal selection procedures

de facto control

© Cengage Learning

media, which are a staple of life for journalists and political scientists alike elsewhere.

We (perhaps) gained a unique glimpse into the inner workings of the party with the publication of the *Tiananmen Square Papers* in 2001.[7] Three prominent American sinologists were given copies of what they were told were transcripts of secret meetings of the party's leadership held during the Tiananmen crisis in 1989. Initially, the three doubted that the documents were authentic. However, after months of study and consultation, they decided that they probably were genuine and decided to publish them.

The papers show that the leadership was deeply split, although it is safe to say that similar transcripts from

meetings during the first days of the Cultural Revolution would have revealed even more acrimony. In the end, Deng had the last word and cast his lot with the hard-liners and their desire to force the students and their supporters out of Tiananmen Square.

No one knows how much debate there is under less troubled circumstances. That said, there certainly are signs that the leaders were not completely in agreement about the succession when both Jiang and Hu reached their term limits.

Each time, senior party leaders did act enough as a bloc to solidify the procedures discussed in the beginning of the chapter. Deng and his most trusted advisors were already old men when they came back to power to stay in the late 1970s. Deng himself never held one of the country's top offices and succeeded in convincing his aging colleagues to formally retire with him in the 1980s. Nonetheless, they continued to run the country through the **Central Advisory Committee (CAC)**. In theory, the CAC simply advised the

---

[7]Zhang, Liang, Andre Nathan, Perry Link, and Orville Schell (eds.), *The Tiananmen Papers* (New York: Public Affairs, 2002). Zhang is a pseudonym for the person or persons who leaked the papers.

PROFILES   Xi Jinping

Like most current CCP leaders, Xi is an engineer. What sets him apart from his contemporaries is that his father, Xi Zhongxun, was a senior party official under Deng after his release from forced labor following the Cultural Revolution. That makes him part of what the Chinese call the "princeling party" to describe children of the party elite. In late 2010, he was named head of the **Central Military Commission (CMC)**, which de facto made him the heir designate for President Hu when his second term ended in 2013.

People are already talking about him as the first member of a fifth generation of party leaders (after Mao, Deng, Jiang, and Hu). He is the first leader born after the revolution, yet he has the closest ties to the revolutionary leadership—his father joined the Communist Youth League at age 13. He and his colleagues may well be more open minded than the fourth generation. Given that Xi did all of his university studies in China and has spent his entire career in the party bureaucracy, it remains to be seen how flexible he will be. ■

official office holders. In fact, its members made all the important decisions. With most of its members either deceased or too ill to work even on a part-time basis, the CAC was abolished by the Fourteenth Party Congress in 1992.

Hu Jintao was largely unknown when he was chosen to replace Jiang Zemin in 2002. The outgoing leadership almost certainly wanted to emphasize continuity in its economic policies (see the next section) and opted for someone who was seen as methodical and more of a consensus builder than his predecessors.

It also seems that the leadership disagreed about who should replace him. Hu apparently preferred Yi Keqiang, who is now prime minister. Jiang Zemin still exerts enough behind-the-scenes influence for his favorite, Xi, to get the top position, but his influence is not strong enough to keep Yi from getting the prime ministry.

Fragmented Authoritarianism

The diversity of the country and the differences of opinion that inevitably come with it have led Kenneth Lieberthal to call the PRC **fragmented authoritarianism**. Power in China is not as decentralized as it is in the United States, Germany, and other federal regimes. However, to use an awkward jargon term, power at the top is deconcentrated. That is easiest to see in the informal network of *kou*, or policy gateways, which coordinate decision making regarding party organization, government administration, state security, and foreign affairs.

Nothing shows both the fragmentation and the authoritarianism better than the PLA. As we saw in Chapter 9, the Soviet army stayed away from political controversies until the 1991 coup. The PLA, by contrast, has been an important political actor since the Long March. At that point, the party and the army were for all intents and purposes the same thing. Many of today's party leaders started their careers in the PLA, and army leaders have always held prominent positions in the CCP leadership. Most Western analysts take someone's promotion to the party's CMC as a sign that he is a rising star within the CCP as well as the PLA.

During the 1980s the army was as divided as the party as a whole. Some senior officers sided with the reformers; others became hard-liners. Press reports in spring 1989 suggested that the PLA was so deeply split that units controlled by the rival factions came close to fighting each other. In the end, most of the leading PLA officers came down on the side of the hard-liners.

The PLA today is important for our purposes because it has an independent power base, which cannot be said of other Chinese organizations. It is far less subject to control through the normal mechanisms of party oversight than was the case for the old Soviet army. And it has a vested interest in the future of economic reform because it runs dozens of enterprises, some of which have been converted from military to civilian production and have been accused of using what amounts to slave or sweatshop labor.

Another source of fragmentation is the growing evidence of nepotism and corruption within the CCP that the party now openly acknowledges, as outgoing President Hu did in his speech to the opening session of the Eighteenth Party Congress in 2012. There is nothing new or uniquely Chinese to the way party insiders and those close to them use their connections for seemingly unimaginable personal gain. The Bo Xilai case, however, meant that the top leadership could no longer avoid addressing corruption or the abuse of power.

The existence of the princelings is not a new phenomenon, although the term itself is. Take for instance, Deng's five children. Deng Pufang, crippled during the Cultural Revolution, heads the Chinese Federation for the Disabled. Deng Nan holds a critical position on the State Science and Technology Commission. Deng Lin is an accomplished artist, though many believe that the sixty thousand dollars she commands per painting or tapestry reflects her family name as much as her talent. Deng Rong was her father's secretary and interpreter, who many believe had the most influence over the aging leader. Finally, Deng Zhifang holds an American PhD and is one of China's top entrepreneurs.

The rise of the princelings opens the door to a far broader, but harder to document, concern: the built-in corruption that seems to envelop the entire party elite. Two weeks before Hu's speech, the *New York Times* carried a front-page story claiming that outgoing Prime Minister Wen Jiabao's family controlled assets worth an estimated $2.7 billion.[8] Even if that figure overestimates their wealth by a factor of two or ten or a hundred, it is still an amazing figure. Whatever the real figure is, the Wen's family's asset reflect the fact that the CCP elite sits atop a supposedly socialist country that has one of the most unequal distributions of wealth in the world. In other words, even though China's ranking on the Transparency International Corruption Scale is "better" than that for Russia, Nigeria, or Mexico, all the signs show that it is more politically worrisome because of the way almost everyone at the very top of the party hierarchy has been implicated.

The Future of the Party-State?

The party is not blind to the changes swirling around it. In fact, one of its first reactions to the collapse of communism in Eurasia was to create high-level units that would explore what happened so that the PRC would not suffer the same fate. Surprisingly, much of what the party's analysts—many of whom had lived and worked in the West—determined has been made public.

In the simplest possible terms, they decided that reform had to continue. In the elliptical language that the Chinese use when discussing politics, they still talk about socialism with Chinese characteristics. For all intents and purposes, they agreed that pragmatism as embodied in Deng's famous statements about black and white cats meant the acceptance of private enterprise and market mechanisms as long as they led to rapid growth. However, they also concluded that opening the political system in any meaningful way would leave them far too vulnerable to either another version of Tiananmen Square or the kind of uprisings that killed communism in Eastern Europe. Together, those decisions have led to ever more fragmented authoritarianism and to the all but schizophrenic acceptance of private enterprise and rejection of anything approaching Western-style democracy.

In other words, the party state is now something of a coalition in which far more interests than could be discussed here compete for control of an economy that is still growing at an unprecedented rate. Especially under Hu, the leadership tried to govern through building consensus, which was not hard to do in a country whose economy grew fast enough that it was relatively easy to paper over differences of opinion within the leadership.

That is easiest to see in the party's conscious attempt to expand its membership base. Party membership is still a requirement for a political career. However, for many apolitical young people who are more concerned with making money, there is no need to belong to the CCP. The party does need university graduates (and others whom Maoists would have accused of taking the "capitalist road" during the Cultural Revolution) if it is going to both manage a modern economy, whoever legally owns the means of production, and maintain political control. Therefore, the CCP's pragmatic leaders have consciously recruited university graduates and technicians whose expertise it cannot do without.

In 2001, it allowed business owners to join. Three years later it was estimated that a third of all Chinese entrepreneurs were CCP members. Some hard-liners objected. A regional party official at the time said bluntly: "Capitalists in the Communist Party? You've got to be kidding." Less than a decade later, virtually everyone seems willing and able to live with socialism with Chinese characteristics in which the socialism is hard to detect.

The party is also training the next generation of leaders differently. For example, it maintains more than 2,800 schools where cadres spend at least a year doing what would be considered postgraduate education in the West, the most prestigious of which is the Central Party School, also known as the China Pudong Cadre Academy. The students do learn Marxist theory, but their curriculum looks a lot like one an American MBA student would be studying. Some of their instructors come from very non-socialist firms like Goldman Sachs and Citibank. The journalist William Dobson also points out that its luxurious forty-acre campus is located right off Future Expectations Street in suburban Beijing.[9]

The changing social composition of the party is by no means the only sign of adaptation. The very adoption of term limits guarantees that new leaders—although not necessarily new ideas—will come forward at least once a decade.

On the other hand, the PRC is still an unmistakably authoritarian regime. Those same schools are used to weed out ideologically unacceptable students and keep tabs on

[8]David Barboza, "Billions Amassed in the Shadows by the Family of China's Premier." *New York Times*. October 26, 2012.

[9]William Dobson, *The Dictator's Learning Curve: Inside the Global Battle for Democracy* (New York: Doubleday, 2012), 275.

those who make it through, graduate, and begin their climb up the CCP ranks. Censorship of the media is a fact of life and now, famously, extends to the Internet. China spends about $100 billion a year on internal security operations, almost exactly the same as it spends on the PLA.

Even before the Bo Xilai affair, the party had begun to crack down on the worst forms of corruption. In 2004 alone, 45,000 members were expelled from the party. However, only about 3 percent of the party members charged with criminal offenses are convicted and spend time in jail. We can never pin down just how much corruption there is. However, an average of 15,000 party officials have been accused of malfeasance each year. Not surprisingly, the best source on corruption probably comes from fiction, especially the novels by Qiu Xiaolong, which combine crime solving with insights into the pervasive influence of less-than-honest leaders.

Most importantly, critics who stress the likelihood of atrophy do not deny that the trends discussed above are happening. Instead, they question whether what have only been marginal changes in the party's monopoly on power will be enough to protect the regime from what they believe will be a groundswell of protest from below which will break out in some unpredictable manner sooner rather than later.

Public Policy: *Perestroika* without Glasnost

No country considered in this book so far shows us how government *can* reshape the way people live through public policy as clearly as China after Mao's death. However, in so doing, the CCP's leaders have taken China on a path that is as different from the Marxist ideals discussed in Chapter 8 as one could imagine, all the while justifying their actions in Marxist rhetoric such as socialism with Chinese characteristics.

Economic Reform

The Chinese economy actually did remarkably well during the Cultural Revolution. Industrial production actually grew by an average of 9 percent per year from 1957 to 1976, because most factories were not targeted during the upheaval. Other than at the worst of times, no one starved and everyone had access to at least an elementary education and rudimentary health care.

More importantly, the Cultural Revolution served to paper over economic difficulties, because there were already signs that it was facing many of the same problems the Soviet Union did when it refused to abandon its centrally planned

PROFILES Deng Xiaoping

Like Zhou Enlai, Deng was born into an elite family. At the age of sixteen, he went on a work-study program to Paris, where, among other things, he worked in a factory, became a member of the European branch of the Chinese Communist Party (CCP) that Zhou had formed, and developed a lifelong love of croissants.

After he came home, he joined Mao Zedong in his effort to organize in the countryside and took part in the Long March. He became a leading CCP military figure and by the 1940s was political commissar of the People's Liberation Army (PLA).

After the CCP came to power, he held a number of positions in the party hierarchy and gradually cast his lot with Liu Shaoqi and others seeking a more pragmatic approach to economic policy. For this he was purged during the Cultural Revolution and, again, following Mao's death.

He returned to office for a third time in 1978 and guided Chinese political life until his death. He never officially held any higher position than vice premier of China (and vice president of the Chinese Bridge Club), but, like many of his generation, he exercised power from behind the scenes. He resigned from his last government position in 1989, made his last tour of the country in 1992, and died of Parkinson's disease in 1997.

Deng Xiaoping in 1985—as usual, smoking a cigarette.

© Bettmann/CORBIS

economy and authoritarian party state. Symptoms included inadequate investment in everything but heavy industry, a slow rate of technological innovation, an emphasis on the quantity rather than the quality of production, the inability to respond to consumer preferences, supply bottlenecks, irrational prices, and shortages in food production.

The impact of those problems might well have been even worse in China. Its communication and transportation networks were not very good. The party had spent the previous generation recruiting cadres on the basis of class background and ideological orientation rather than professional competence. Most important of all, the vast majority of the Chinese people were little better off than they were at the time of the revolution despite thirty years of reasonably sustained growth.

Economic reform actually began in 1972 when Zhou announced the four modernizations. It would be another six years before Deng and the other reformists solidified their hold on power. Since then, the CCP has consistently followed an economic reform agenda guided by three very non-Marxist principles:

- Private property can play a useful role in a socialist economy.

- Market forces should be used to allocate goods and services and determine prices.

- Material incentives, including higher wages, profit, and the accumulation of wealth should be used to boost productivity and efficiency.

Those policies have led to spectacular growth that far outstrips that in any other country in this book and perhaps in any country ever. China, however, is not yet a capitalist country if by that we mean one in which the controlling heights of the economy are privately owned *and* market mechanisms determine most important outcomes.

There have been some ebbs and flows in that elite consensus, especially when the pace of reform even began to show signs of threatening CCP hegemony. And, as we will see, even the amazingly broad sweep of these reforms has left China with an economy that is far less capitalistic than anything we saw in Part 2. Still, no country covered in this book has pursued a single, coherent set of public policies with anything like the consistency of post-Mao China.

Before beginning the policies that helped produce that remarkable growth, it is important to stress what they are *not*. The CCP leadership has never endorsed capitalism, even though those policies have led the country in that direction. Rather, the reforms have amounted to a series of pragmatic choices designed to maximize growth in ways that would allow the country to address at least some of its many pressing problems.

Agriculture

Though it receives the least attention today, reform began with agriculture. During the 1980s, the Maoist-era communes were dismantled and replaced by the household responsibility system. The collective farms were divided into small plots that were worked by families that, for all practical purposes, owned them. The state also reduced the share of their crops that farmers had to sell to it and allowed the market to determine almost all agricultural prices.

The new policies worked. Production increased by more than 10 percent per year during the 1980s. Some former peasants are now extremely well off, especially those who live in areas where they can sell their produce in the booming urban markets. In the short run, the gap between urban and rural standards of living was cut by about 30 percent.

Today, the prospects for agriculture no longer seem all that rosy. For a variety of reasons that would take us far beyond comparative politics, there is now an excess of labor in the countryside, and most remaining peasants make less than one hundred dollars a month. That makes even a menial job in a sweatshop attractive because most people make about twice that amount in the cities. As a result, young people are leaving the countryside in droves and heading for seemingly glamorous places like Shanghai even though their lives there end up being anything but glamorous.

Business

Even more dramatic has been the development of private corporations, some owned by Chinese entrepreneurs and others by foreign investors. The party initially moved slowly until it became clear that private enterprise would contribute to its more important goal—modernization. As in the former Soviet Union, the first private businesses were small service-oriented firms, most of which were in the retail trades. The original legislation restricted private firms to eight employees, a figure that was never rigorously enforced.

In 1980, there were only 1,500 privately owned firms in all of China. A decade later there were about 400,000. One million new businesses were registered in 2006 alone. Until the late 1980s, they accounted for less than 1 percent of industrial output. Today their earnings far outstrip those of the state-owned enterprises. In late 2010, the official news agency estimated that the value of all private enterprise had reached $1.4 trillion.

Privately owned industries in the countryside alone employ at least one hundred million people, more than the entire public sector. Most importantly, the private sector firms are far more dynamic and profitable than the state-owned ones and thus attract the attention of the reformers, who are far more interested in maximizing the rate of economic growth than anything else.

There was some concern that hard-liners would slow the pace of economic reform in the aftermath of Tiananmen. By mid-1992, however, it had become clear that Deng had thrown his lot in with the reformers. While on his famous southern tour that summer, he complained that the party had not adequately responded to calls for more rapid economic change.

One indicator of the reforms' early success was the leadership's embrace of foreign investment. Even before Mao's death, his preferred autarchic policies that all but completely isolated China from global markets were eased. Foreign aid and investment came to be seen as ways of speeding up modernization. To facilitate foreign entry into the Chinese market, four **special economic zones** (SEZs), in which foreign investors were offered preferential tax rates and other incentives, were created in 1979. Five years later, Hainan Island and fourteen more cities became SEZs as well. By the mid-1990s, market mechanisms and foreign investment had spread to most of urban China, blurring the distinction between the SEZs and the rest of the country to the point that it has all but disappeared.

Adverse international reaction to Tiananmen Square also did not slow foreign investment, which grew steadily from about $5 billion in 1987 to $27 billion in 1993 to $60 billion in 1999 and then to over $100 billion in 2010. Over half of it came from overseas Chinese communities. Taiwan, which is still officially at war with the mainland, accounts for about 10 percent of the investment, as does South Korea, which has also had a hostile political relationship with the PRC.

Joint ventures have been established in dozens of industries and have turned China into a leading exporter of textiles and other low-tech products. It has also made some, albeit more limited, progress in developing high-tech goods, including a nascent space industry.

China is best known for the rapid expansion of its participation in world markets for lower-technology goods where its growth has become quite controversial. Because labor and transportation costs are low, China is now a world leader in the production and export of clothes, cheap electronic goods, medicine, and other products, from which two of the main criticisms of Chinese enterprise flow.

First, there are problems built into the way the companies operate. Wages are low. Working conditions are often deplorable. The quality of the goods Chinese factories produce often does not meet international standards. There is no shortage of examples—toys contaminated by lead paint, unhealthy food and medical products, sweatshop conditions in Apple factories, and more. Second, it is

often also argued that what looks like China's competitive edge itself gives China an unfair advantage that it used to "steal" Western manufacturing jobs while simultaneously buying up huge portions of the American and European debt.

The Chinese boom is not limited to the low end of the technological spectrum, however. Typical of the new breed of private companies is Huawei Technologies based in Shenzen, one of the original SEZs. The company was founded in 1988 by a former sergeant in the PLA. At the time, it sold telephone equipment made in Hong Kong. Today, it makes world-class computer routers and telecommunications switches that compete with global giants Cisco, Siemens, and Alcatel. It employs eighty-seven thousand people worldwide, and its 2012 sales topped $32 billion, almost two-thirds of its revenue coming from overseas. In 2010 it was added to *Fortune Magazine's* list of the top 500 global corporations

The growth of the private sector does not mean that the party has disappeared from economic life. Most of those firms have had to put on a **red hat** and accept the presence of party units inside the firm, many of which make the decisions that count—and are a source of widespread corruption. That even includes Wal-Mart, which has had to allow party-controlled unions to operate at its stores, something it has not allowed in any other country in which it operates. Chinese law allows a firm's party leaders to attend meetings at which key corporate decisions are made, which, some observers argue, allows the party to control companies in which it has no ownership stake.

State Owned Enterprises

Twenty years ago, the state-owned enterprises (SOEs) were known for their inefficiency, bloated bureaucracy, and indifference to workers and consumers alike. There is no question that the state-sector reform has proceeded more slowly and unevenly than the new private sector which was, after all, created from scratch. There are still about 145,000 enterprises that the state either owns outright or controls.

Serious reform began when SOEs were allowed to sell some of what they produced on the open market. They still had to fulfill state-mandated quotas, but being able to sell anything they produced above and beyond that total turned them into entrepreneurial firms for which profit-maximization was a key incentive. Over time, the party has decentralized political control over inefficient SOEs, sold shares of stock in most of them (including those run by the PLA), and allowed some to go bankrupt. Still, the three Chinese firms near the top of the *Fortune* list of the world's wealthiest companies were all state owned, as are most banks and other financial firms.

Comparative Emphasis: The Rule of 72

Economic growth has an impact much akin to that of compound interest on your savings account. This year's interest builds on what your savings earned in previous years.

It turns out that if you divide the growth rate in a savings account in a given year into 72, that tells you how many years it will take to double your account or the overall economy, assuming that growth rates remain the same.

The "Rule of 72" applies to any economic or social phenomenon in which growth builds on itself, including the rate of economic growth.

With average growth rates of about 10 percent for the last two decades, that means that it has only taken about seven years for the Chinese economy as a whole to double and fifteen years for it to quadruple. ■

At this point, it is hard to tell the private firms and the SOEs apart, because it may not make much difference who officially owns an enterprise in what is a confusing mixture of capitalism and socialism. Whether publicly or privately owned, almost every enterprise is now judged on the basis of how profitable it is. Yet, the CCP still calls most of the shots, and it continues to make certain its own interests play a determining role in a firm's decision-making calculations, which includes making certain that party leaders keep their jobs and get their kickbacks.

Unaddressed Problems

China may not catch up with the United States for decades, but one of the goals it has set for itself, reaching what the leadership calls "reasonable prosperity," is certainly within reach. We should, however, note four ways in which the progress has fallen short of what the most glowing accounts of Chinese economic progress suggest. None poses serious political risks for the CCP at this point, but each of them could do so in the not so distant future.

First, there is little doubt that people with connections (*guanxi*) have benefited the most, often in ethically questionable ways. As we saw in the Soviet Union (and as Orwell predicted in *Animal Farm*), single-party rule almost inevitably leads to the inordinate concentration of wealth and power. Although the specifics may never come to light,

there is no way that the Bo, Wen, and other princeling families could have accumulated their wealth or power without the existence of those connections and informal policy gateways that seem to be an inescapable fact of life in the CCP.

Second, China's newfound wealth is by no means evenly distributed. Growth is concentrated in the major cities near the coast as many of us saw in television coverage of the 2008 Olympic Games. In much of the countryside and much of the interior of the country, living conditions have not changed much—if at all.

Nonetheless, as we will also see in India, there still remain huge pockets of poverty and unemployment even in the booming cities. There are probably two hundred million urban migrants or laid-off state enterprise workers who no longer get the guaranteed housing, health care, and lifelong employment of the old iron rice bowl. That means that few Chinese have enjoyed all the benefits of the hard work they have put in. What, the critics ask, will happen when Chinese consumers demand something like a "fair share" of the growth?

Third, the very success of the reforms is worsening China's already fragile environment. Even its successful population control program is waning. The birth rate has already risen 0.2 percent since the 1980s. The total population will continue to grow by 15 million people per year. Increased agricultural production and industrialization have cost the country more than a million acres of arable land a year. Peasants who want to make as much money as possible have turned to cash crops such as tobacco instead of following their traditional crop rotation practices, which replenished the soil with needed nutrients.

Fourth and most important, the CCP continues to shy away from reforms that could even conceivably jeopardize its hold on power. As recently as August 2013, Xi and other top leas made it abundantly clear that they did not support adopting any kind of Western political institutions, especially those that would allow people to express their grievances or organize in a way that might challenge the party's hegemony.

Foreign Policy

A similar case can be made about Chinese foreign policy. The new PRC followed Mao's lead internationally as well as domestically. Since his death, however, it has pursued pragmatic policies whose goal is to restore the country's status as one of the world's great powers, something it had not been for several centuries.

Maoist Foreign Policy

While Mao was in power, the PRC pursued the kind of foreign policy Marxist theory would lead one to expect. It supported Third World militants who fought against the vestiges of colonialism. The leadership insisted that China had to be independent and self-sufficient on the assumption that the country would have to be ever-vigilant in the face of its hostile and powerful foes.

The PRC was consistently anti-capitalist. Given its role in Korea, Vietnam, and elsewhere, and its failure to recognize the PRC, the CCP singled out the United States for its harshest critiques. Most of the time, their dispute was purely rhetorical. Their two armies did fight in Korea. After that, they only came close to war in 1958 during the dispute over Quemoy and Matsu, two tiny islands in the Taiwan Straits.

Relations with the other great socialist power, the Soviet Union, worsened throughout the forty years between the Chinese revolution and the collapse of Eurasian communism. The rivalry came out in the open during the late 1950s when the Chinese decided that the Soviets had turned their backs on Marx and revolution. Tensions between the two reached a peak in 1969 when the rhetorical battles escalated into skirmishes along their border. Sino-Soviet relations were so bad that Gorbachev's visit to Beijing was the first time the leader of one of the two communist powers had visited the other in decades.

The New China

Since the 1970s, China has pursued a more pragmatic foreign policy in keeping with reform at home, although it has not been either as consistently followed or as far reaching as the shifts in domestic policy. The change in Chinese foreign policy began with its hesitant opening to the West which helped pave the way to economic reform a half decade later. That shift was the result of shifts in the preferences of leaders in both Beijing and Washington.

The Cultural Revolution taught most of the CCP something it probably should have learned from the Great Leap Forward. Mass mobilization and commitment to socialism were not the best way to industrialize the country. During those same years, geopolitical realities also changed. In particular, President Richard Nixon and Secretary of State Henry Kissinger were willing to overlook ideological differences in order to open relations with China as long as doing so advanced what they believed to be in the American national interest.

The first signs of the opening began to appear in the early 1970s. An American graduate student was allowed into the country to claim the body of his recently deceased aunt, Anna Louise Strong, who had spent most of the period since the 1930s in China as a "friend" of the revolution. In 1972, an American table tennis team played in China, lending its name to what soon came to be called "Ping Pong diplomacy." Later that year, Kissinger made a secret trip to China. At that meeting, he and Zhou agreed that the two countries could and should reestablish relations. Before the year was out, President Nixon had visited China, and, virtually overnight, two of the world's worst enemies became friends.

Their relationship deepened. The United States reversed its long-standing opposition to PRC membership in the UN. Formal diplomatic relations were resumed during Jimmy Carter's administration. Currently, no non-Asian country has more invested in China than the United States, and only Japan has more extensive bilateral trade.

Relations between China and the United States have never been smooth. Critics were most vocal in the aftermath of Tiananmen Square, but the rhetorical decibel levels have risen almost any time Washington had to make a decision on which the two countries have differed. Today, American leaders have been highly critical of China's human rights record, its arms buildup, its role in such troubled countries as Sudan, and its alleged attempts to hack into U.S. government computers. By contrast, the Chinese object to American criticism of its human rights record and to what they see as meddling in East Asian affairs. What is critical here is the fact that the variations in Chinese foreign policy have had more to do with shifts in the political winds in Washington than in Beijing.

Comparative Emphasis: Globalization

China is often held up as the political "poster child" of globalization.

No other country has moved so strongly or so quickly onto the global economic stage. Its foreign trade has increased at a faster rate than the economy as a whole, which itself is growing extremely rapidly, as we saw. Some argue that China will become one of the world's economic giants long before the middle of this century.

It is not just the economy. About a million Chinese have studied at Western universities and returned. Western pop culture can be found in all cities—often in bootleg versions. On the other hand, some Chinese films have become cult hits in the West. Although it may not be an important example, when journalist Rob Gifford went to a small city in the Gobi Desert, every room in his hotel had broadband. People he met took him to an An Li meeting. It took him a while to figure out that he was being taken to an *Amway* sales event. ■

Whatever its intentions, China will almost certainly become a more influential force in international relations, largely because of its economic rather than its military might. Depending on how you count such things, it already has one of the largest and best-equipped militaries in the world. Only the United States spends more on its military, although it should be stressed that at 2.0 percent of the GNP, China's military spending accounts for slightly less than the overall global average expressed as a share of total economic output.

However one measures China's massive military, it is hard not to be struck by how restrained the PRC has been in using it. It has made menacing statements about Taiwan, which it still considers to be legally part of China. In recent years, the PRC has laid claim to some islands off the coast of Korea and Japan and has asserted its rights to oil reserves and shipping lanes off its south coast.

China has also been less than a fully cooperative member of the international community at times—in places farther from home. Thus, it has used its power as a permanent member of the United Nations Security Council to block a number of initiatives, most recently stiffening sanctions against both Iran and Syria.

On the other side of the coin, there have been areas in which China has cooperated with the West, although some experts think it could have done more. China was a major participant in the six party talks that convinced the North Koreans to suspend their nuclear weapons and power program in 2007 and has worked closely with its partners since North Korea's nuclear test in 2009. China and the other parties did not always agree, but there is little doubt that the PRC put significant pressure on the regime in Pyongyang.

China may well become a global military power at some point in the not all that distant future, although it will be decades before, for example, it would have reliable long-range missiles capable of reaching Europe or North America. There is no doubt, however, about its international economic power today.

As a newcomer on the global economic stage, China would undoubtedly have stirred up some controversy no matter what it did. Nonetheless, its behavior has produced four main criticisms which could have been more muted had the PRC not pursued policies that so clearly put its own interests first.

First, as we have already seen, China has used its favorable position in global markets to position itself as the world's largest holder of European and North American debt. China holds more of the American debt than any other country. Of a total of $16 trillion in outstanding loans in summer 2012, the United States owed well over $1 trillion to Chinese lenders, most of which are under state ownership or control.

Second, China is often charged with pursuing unfair business practices. Much as Japan was in the 1980s, Chinese firms are accused of selling cheaply manufactured goods at prices below what it cost to produce them

in order to increase their European or American market share. In the Chinese case, that also includes allegations of what amount to slave labor in factories in the private and public sectors alike that hire and supposedly exploit millions of uprooted migrant workers. Similarly, China is taken to task for the poor quality of everything from the toys to the pharmaceuticals it sells because of a lack of regulations and transparency.

Third, China is increasingly dependent on the outside world for a number of products it needs to sustain its economic growth, which it pursues quite aggressively on international markets. Most notably, it has very few proven oil reserves, which helps explain its interest in Sudan and other trouble spots with petroleum deposits. Similarly, China has to important many key agricultural products, including rice and soybeans, which makes it easy to see why it has courted Brazil, which is one of the world's leading agricultural exporters, including of those key commodities.

Finally, critics are concerned that the Chinese manipulate the value of the *renminbi*, which literally means the people's currency. Like most monetary units in countries ever ruled by Communists, it is not fully convertible, which means its value is not completely set as a result of free international trading. Therefore, it is alleged that the government keeps it undervalued in order to artificially lower the price of Chinese exports and increase the price of its exports.

Before concluding, we should put these criticisms in context. After all, just about every country that can engages in a significant degree of economic self-promotion through what international relations experts call mercantilism, and the Chinese no longer do so significantly more or less than other major powers, including the United States.

Moreover, China is increasingly integrated into global international economic decision-making structures, which makes it go along with global rules and norms whatever its official ideology. In 2001, it joined the World Trade Organization (WTO) which has already compelled China to open its markets more to outside investment, abide by international quality and trading standards, and more. Even the decision to grant Beijing the 2008 Olympics brought with it pressure to open its political and social systems.

The Media

There is probably no better indicator of the limits to liberalization in China than the regime's continued leverage over the mass media, which is the primary way people learn about political events. As in the Soviet Union before Gorbachev came to power, the party has long determined who is allowed on the air, what is written in the newspapers, and so on. Some journalists did speak their minds in the weeks before the 1989 crackdown in Tiananmen Square, but they all subsequently lost their jobs. A few independent journals have been able to publish for brief periods, but their circulation has always been extremely small.

The best evidence that the CCP is trying to hold onto these levers of power lies in its policies regarding information technology. In 1989, students used fax machines to keep in touch with each other and with their colleagues studying in the West. Since then, people have tried to feed information into China via the Internet and satellite TV.

Until recently, however, the regime has been remarkably successful at blocking access to foreign-based political websites, including Wikipedia. Private citizens are technically not allowed to own satellite dishes. Cable operators provide as many as thirty foreign channels to their subscribers, including some international news channels. However, cable reaches a very small proportion of the country. As recently as 2002, an Internet service provider was convicted for piping political news into the country via e-mail, which is less susceptible to the filtering technology that keeps people from accessing websites.

But change is afoot, most notably in a deal announced in October 2001 that gave Time Warner the first franchise for a foreign company to operate a cable system in the country. Since then, access to cable has spread, as has ownership of less-than-legal satellite dishes, most of which can receive signals from stations in Taiwan and Hong Kong. One recent report also suggested that the most technologically sophisticated of the one hundred million Internet users have found ways to circumvent the blocks that supposedly keep them from accessing foreign sites.

China is also the world's leader in sales of pirated films, music, and software (not to mention purses and golf clubs). Most Western pop culture is available almost as soon as it is released in Hollywood or London. The underground media community also produces counterfeit as well as real versions of popular Western media, including at least eight fake versions of Harry Potter books with such titles as *Harry Potter and the Chinese Overseas Students at the Hogwarts School of Witchcraft and Wizardry*.

As a result, it seems unlikely that the CCP will be able to slow down an already opening media world. However, if the consumers only want to read real Harry Potter books or watch videos of the Harry Potter movies, maybe the authorities do not need to worry that much. At least not yet.

Conclusion: Is Change the Only Constant?

One could make the case that all of the big questions raised in Chapter 1 other than democratization are issues in everyday political life in China. In tying this chapter together, it makes the most sense to focus on one of them—the pace of change.

Figure 1.1 was drawn to depict the general trend that change on almost every human indicator in almost every country is occurring at an ever-accelerating rate. We do not know how to measure these things, but it is hard to believe that social and economic change are taking place any faster than has been the case in China since the 1980s. Or, as I put it in Chapter 1, change does seem to be the only constant in China.

With one huge exception.

Politics.

One of the key themes in all of Part 2 has been the "disconnect" between political and other forms of change. Even before 1989, pressures from an ever more sophisticated and impatient population and these countries' increasing incorporation in global economic and cultural life weakened all communist states. Some, like the Soviet Union, collapsed in part because the CPSU proved unwilling or unable to apply enough force to stay in power. In China, however, repression has helped keep the CCP in power, at least for now.

But the genie probably cannot be kept in the bottle forever. The Tiananmen Square crackdown in 1989 showed that leaders can still suppress dissident movements, even ones with widespread mass and elite support. Nevertheless, it seems highly unlikely that such movements can be suppressed indefinitely. In part, this reflects the social changes that are leading to a more educated, sophisticated, and ultimately demanding population.

The coercive tools of the command economies in the few remaining communist countries are also imperiled. Again, we do not know precisely what their economic future holds. No one knows if socialist goals of equality, justice, and dignity can be attained using a market-based economy. No one knows, either, how far communist elites are willing to go in sacrificing their political and economic power in exchange for economic growth.

The Chinese communist regime may be able to adapt and hang on to power for some years to come. If it does, it is hard to see how it could do so and retain anything that smacks of totalitarianism.

We could continue to go on to consider more statistics and other "hard" evidence that illustrate these points. However, in closing, it might make more sense to consider two stories, one from the mid-1990s and one from today.

The first comes from a 1990 report on popular fads of the time. One of the "hot" items was the Kadan (the closest Chinese equivalent of Cardin) Model Training School. Apparently, the school had a long waiting list of young people willing to pay the princely sum of forty-two dollars a semester to strive for a new version of the Chinese dream: wealth and fame. Such private training schools that teach everything from modeling to accounting to foreign languages have sprung up around the country to meet the demands of a growing generation of young people who are aware of the outside world and want to be a part of it. The modeling schools have a unique Chinese twist: Both men and women stagger around trying to learn how to walk in high heels. Still, all the aspiring models shared a common goal that one male student expressed well: "I came because I have a dream. I love this. I would love to travel around the world and be the best model of the century."[10]

For good or ill, the Kadan school itself is long gone. Today, the closest equivalent is the nationwide explosion in the number of karaoke bars. Almost every major hotel has one. They are places where hard-driving businessmen (rarely women) get together after work. They are shown into a room reserved for them with a "hostess" who plies them with drinks. After a while, they often start singing songs from Taiwan and force their Western visitors to do the same for top-forty hits from their own countries. Of course, the hostesses are available for other activities for an additional price.

It is not clear how important either Kadan was or karaoke is now. The question I leave you with is simple. Can a regime that has allowed its citizens this much leeway outside the political arena retain its lock on those questions that are the real subject of this book?

KEY TERMS

Concepts
cadres
campaigns
capitalist road
Confucianism
democratic centralism
extraterritoriality
faction
four modernizations
fragmented authoritarianism
nomenklatura
princeling
red hat
unit

People
Chiang Kai-shek
Deng Xiaoping
Hu Jintao
Jiang Qing
Jiang Zemin

Liu Shaoqi
Mao Zedong
Sun Yat-sen
Xi Jinping
Zhou Enlai

Acronyms
CAC
CCP
CMC
GPCR
KMT
PLA
PRC
SEZ

Organizations, Places, and Events
Central Advisory Committee (CAC)
Central Committee
Central Military Commission (CMC)
Chinese Communist Party (CCP)
Cultural Revolution

Democracy Movement
Democracy Wall
Falun Gong
Gang of Four
Great Leap Forward
Great Proletarian Cultural Revolution (GPCR)
Hundred Flowers Campaign
Kuomintang (KMT)
Long March
May Fourth Movement
Nationalist Party
People's Liberation Army (PLA)
People's Republic of China (PRC)
Politburo
Red Guards
Sino-Soviet split
special economic zones (SEZs)
Standing Committee
Tiananmen Square

USEFUL WEBSITES

The Internet itself in China is controversial because the Chinese authorities have tried to block access to overseas sites that carry material critical of the PRC. That is becoming increasingly difficult as the number of regular Internet users approaches 10 percent of the adult population and enterprising Web surfers find ways to get around the firewalls the CCP's censors create. The government itself has created a portal with links to state agencies that have English-language sites.

   www.china.org.cn/english

There are also a number of non-Chinese portals that maintain good resources on Chinese politics and society, including links to other good sites. The University of Heidelberg in Germany continues to operate the Virtual Library site on China. London's Royal Society for International Affairs (Chatham House)

---

[10]James Steingold, "China in High Heels: A Wobbly School for Models," *New York Times*, August 8, 1990, A5.

not only has links but reports emanating from its highly respected projects on China. Finally, Professor William Joseph of Wellesley College has one of the largest and most frequently updated sites on China.

sun.sino.uni-heidelberg.de/e-index.html

www.chathamhouse.org.uk/research/asia/current_projects/china_project/

sites.google.com/a/wellesley.edu/china-politics-links/

Finally, there are some far more specialized sites. The Chinese Leadership Monitor publishes regular reports and updates on the country's elite. Chinese Military Power does the same for national security issues.

www.hoover.org/publications/clm

www.comw.org/cmp/

FURTHER READING

Blecher, Marc. *China Against the Tides: Restructuring Through Revolution, Radicalism, and Reform.* 3rd ed. New York: Bloomsbury Academic, 2009. The best recent overview of Chinese politics, written by one of the few scholars who is still even somewhat sympathetic to socialism and Mao Zedong.

Hua Yu, *China in Ten Words.* New York: Vintage, 2012. As the title suggests, this short book uses ten key terms as jumping off points for an analysis of Chinese politics.

Lee, Jennifer 8. *The Fortune Cookie Chronicles.* New York: 12 Books, 2008. Yes 8 is really her middle name. This is a book about Chinese and Chinese-American food, but I use it to help students take a step back from fortune cookies and General Tso's chicken (neither are Chinese) and have a fun look at some of the most important issues in Chinese culture.

Lieberthal, Kenneth. *Governing China: From Revolution Through Reform.* New York: Norton, 1995. A comprehensive overview of Chinese politics that is especially good at illuminating the informal power relations, which may well be more important than the formal rules and procedures.

Mcgregor, Richard. *The Party.* New York: Harper-Collins, 2010. The best recent book on the CCP, which was written by an Australian journalist who has spent years in China.

Qiu Xialong. *Don't Cry, Tai Lake.* New York: Minotaur, 2012. The most recent of a series of mystery novels that are highly political and fun.

Saich, Tony. *Governance in China.* London: Palgrave, 2004. The best new overview of Chinese politics, including many of the author's personal experiences over the last thirty years.

Santoro, Michael A. *China 2020: How Western Business Can—and Should—Influence Social and Political Change in the Coming Decade.* Ithaca: Cornell University Press, 2009. An eminently readable, short book by a business professor on the legal and other obstacles to working in the Chinese market.

Shambaugh, David. *China's Communist Party: Atrophy and Adaptation.* Washington: Woodrow Wilson Center Press, 2008. One of the best books on change and continuity in the CCP. It draws heavily on internal CCP sources.

Vogel, Ezra. *Deng Xiaoping and the Transformation of China.* Cambridge: Harvard University Press, 2011. A massive biography of China's reformist leader by one of the best American Asianists of this generation.

Zha, Jianling. *Tide Players: The Movers and Shakers of a Rising China.* New York: New Press, 2011. A fascinating set of profiles of leading Chinese entrepreneurs and dissidents.

The Global South

Desmond Boylan/Reuters

© Cengage Learning

CHAPTER OUTLINE

11

Decisions made in Washington are more important to us than those made here in Dar es Salaam. So, maybe my people should be allowed to vote in American presidential elections.

JULIUS NYERERE, FORMER PRESIDENT, TANZANIA

The Global South

THE BASICS

The Richest and Poorest Countries

	LIFE EXPECTANCY (YEARS)	OVERALL EDUCATION INDEX	GROSS DOMESTIC PRODUCT PER CAPITA (GNP)	HDI SCORE[a]
Lowest	59	.39	$1,393	0.46
Highest	80	.89	$37,225	0.89

[a]HDI, Human Development Index, is a statistical measure converting the information from the first three columns in the table to ranges from 0 (least developed) to 1 (most developed).

Source: United Nations Development Program, *Human Development Report*: 2011. hdr.undp.org/. Accessed March 2, 2013.

A Single Slum?

There is no obvious way to begin Part 4 of this book. It could hardly be otherwise, since the Global South includes as many as three-quarters of the world's countries and three-fifths of its population.

Nonetheless, on March 2, 2013, the *New York Times* had one short article on one neighborhood in one Nigerian city that is as good a place to start as any. A few days before, the local authorities in Lagos had demolished Badia East. In a matter of minutes, as many as ten thousand were made homeless when their shanty town that had stood for at least thirty years was leveled. Residents were given as little as ten minutes to pack up their belongings.

The Times Reporter quoted the shocked reaction of one of its former residents:

> I lost everything. We are trying to bring out some sticks, to look for our daily bread. We don't have money to eat. They demolished everything. They didn't give us anything. We are here, suffering. Everything is outside now. We don't have anywhere to go.[1]

The homes of another forty thousand residents of Badia East were in danger of being razed. This wasn't the only slum clearance in Lagos. The summer before, a floating shanty town of thirty thousand residents had been destroyed.

Before moving on, it is important to dash any parallels you might want to draw between Badia East and slum clearance and homelessness in the West. The average displaced residents lived on the equivalent of about one

[1]Adam Nossiter, "In Nigeria's Largest City, Homeless Are Paying the Price of Progress." *New York Times*. March 2, 2013, A4, A6.

hundred dollars a month. Their homes lacked running water, indoor plumbing, electricity, and the other amenities people in the industrialized democracies take for granted.

Badia East is also not the only shanty town we will encounter in *Comparative Politics*. The next chapter begins with an account of life in the still-standing slum of Annawadi, which sits next to the Mumbai airport.

It's not just slums. Almost every indicator you can imagine paints a similarly bleak picture. As the table on the previous page shows, the average person in the world's poorest countries does not live to be sixty, while we in the richest ones can expect to live a whole generation longer. The list goes on and on. The gap between rich and poor continues to grow. The environment is in worse shape. The table at the beginning of this chapter lists the United Nations Human Development Index score, which is a composite of average income, health, and education. By that measure, people in the North are thirty times as well off. Or, just think about perhaps the most devastating statistic that could have been included in such a table. What kind of a life can you expect to lead on an income of $1,393 a year?

This is a book about comparative *politics*. However, if we started this chapter with constitutions, governments, political parties, elections, or even corruption, you would be left with a very misleading picture of just what life is like for upwards of three billion people. In other words, any politically meaningful discussion of the Global South has to start with an all too common theme—lives lived without dignity—which transcends political science or any single social science discipline.

The destruction of Badia East raises two obvious questions.

Why did Badia East and the other indignities we could have begun this chapter with exist in the first place? Finding the answers will force us to go back to the templates first introduced near the end of Chapter 1, especially Table 1.3. The combination of historical conditions at home and imperialism imposed from abroad has left much of Asia, Africa, and Central and South America desperately poor and behind the North on just about every indicator of well-being you can imagine. And, as we will also see, the impact of those historical factors is magnified by more recent pressures arising both at home and from abroad.

For the purposes of this book, examples like Badia East also open the door to four points that will be central to the rest of Part 4.

First, the stakes of political life are much higher in the countries we are about to see than in any of the ones covered so far. In Part 3, we saw that the nature of the regime

SAMUEL JAMES/The New York Times/Redux

Former residents clearing the debris in Badia East.

is still very much up for grabs in many of the current and former communist countries. In most of the parts of the world that we will encounter next, the very existence of the country itself has been debated as well at some point in the not so distant past. To put it slightly differently, the real and potential costs of losing political contests of any sort in any of the countries we are about to consider are a lot higher than in any we have seen so far.

Second, we will also see that few states in the Global South have been able to make much progress in addressing either that historical legacy or the current load of problems they face. There are many reasons why that is the case, all of which revolve around the fact that most of them have relatively weak states that must operate in the face of tremendous expectations about how quickly they could and should develop. One—but only one—consequence of this unbalanced political development is the fact that their states often act in a violent and arbitrary manner when they are able to act effectively at all.

Third, unlike Part 2 and, to a lesser degree, Part 3, the "big questions" are an inescapable and unavoidable part of daily life. People lose their homes from time to time everywhere, not just in Badia. But it is hard to imagine a place where things have changed more rapidly, democracy and equality are harder to realize, or environmental and social conditions are worse than in the slums of Lagos or any other major city we are about to discuss.

Fourth, not all of the news is bad. Badia East was demolished to make room for a new commercial development that the Lagos government determined the city needed to further integrate itself into the globalizing economy. In that sense, Lagos and other parts of Nigeria have something in common with the BRICS—the countries that have made substantial economic and political progress in the last generation or so. Later in this chapter and in Chapter 16, we will also focus on the substantial progress that has been made, but, for now, it is more important to focus on the problems, because they are the key to understanding politics in the South.

Thinking about the Global South

This section has to be longer than the comparable ones in Chapters 2 or 8. That is the case, first of all, because there are three times as many countries and people in the Global South as there are in the rest of the world combined. It isn't just the number of countries and people but the historical, economic, social, and environmental diversity they represent.

Just as importantly, this is the part of the world that the overwhelmingly majority of the readers of this book knew the least about before taking this course. And, to the degree that most students were exposed to life in the Global South beforehand, the odds are high that the accuracy of what they "knew" was limited by stereotypes that are far more distorted than those most of us grew up with about other industrialized democracies or communism.

What's in a Name?

On one level, it is not hard to identify the countries that should be in this final category. It includes all of Africa, almost all of the Americas south of the United States, and most of South and Southeast Asia. About three-fifths of the world's people live there. If we include the poorest countries covered in Part 2 (most notably China), that number leaps to four in five.

There is some ambiguity about which countries should have been colored in gray in the map at the beginning of this chapter. Some analysts believe that some of the non-European countries covered in Part 2 belong here. Others are convinced that some of the more successful southern countries—especially the **BRICS**—should no longer be included in the South. I have decided to use this particular breakdown not because the Global South is some sort of residual category but because these countries have two features in common:

- **Imperialism.** Not all of them were legal colonies that were owned and directly ruled by someone else, and none of them had exactly the same experience as victims of imperialism. Nonetheless, compared to the other countries we have considered, their past as victims of imperialism has gone a long way toward shaping what they can and cannot do today as legally independent countries.

- **Underdevelopment.** We will spend a fair amount of time here and in the chapters to come discussing what this elusive concept means. Whatever definition you end up preferring, there is little doubt either that these countries lag behind the industrialized democracies and most of the current and former communist regimes or that few have them have failed to make much progress in catching up at least until the last couple of decades.

While these countries share those two features and more, their similarities mask tremendous diversity. Some, like India and the other BRICS, are large and have a major impact on global affairs, while others, such as Guinea-Bissau or the island countries in the Pacific, have a minimal international footprint. Given their geographical locations, they also have different cultures, economies, and societies. Most are also deeply divided along ethnic, racial, religious, and linguistic lines, but disputes about identity politics have played themselves out in dramatically different ways.

There is even more uncertainty about what to call this part of the world, which also gives us a first glimpse into why it is both so confusing and controversial. People who live there have chosen to use a number of terms in describing themselves, although it should also be pointed out that not all people who live in the Global South think of it as consisting of a single type of country.

It's not just the people who live there who can't agree. Academics don't either. Sometimes academic debates help clarify matters; sometimes they do not. The debate over what to call the Global South is a good example of one that is intense but *not* particularly helpful.

Over the years, each of the following terms has been in vogue: developing, underdeveloped, less developed, **Third World**, and the Global South. All were tried as part of the search for a term that would convey the plight of most of these countries in a nonpejorative manner.

Although it is currently out of favor, the term Third World is still the one used most often. It was coined more than a half-century ago by a French analyst who wished to distinguish the countries that were then shaking off colonial rule from the Western democracies (First World) and the members of the Soviet bloc (Second World).

The Global South is currently the name most commonly used by the **nongovernmental organizations** (**NGOs**) that belong to the Alliance for Peacebuilding where I work, and I will therefore use that term most of the time. I will use some of the other labels from time to time as well if for no other reason than to make the prose flow more smoothly.

Lives Without Dignity

Chapter 5 on France used the term *syndrome* to describe the interrelated set of political and other problems that led to the collapse of the Third and Fourth Republics. For the Global South, I will use that same word to launch a discussion of issues that stretch beyond the political and, in fact, cover all of society. As with the list of countries, there is no definitive list of what those are, but they typically include the following, reflecting the fact that billions of people lead what can only be called lives without dignity. It is hard to put the differences between the Global South and the rest of the world into words. Any attempt to do so inevitably is gut-wrenching, because literally billions of people lead lives without dignity.

Poverty

That starts with another obvious question. Even after you take into account differences in the cost of living and other factors, what kind of life can someone lead who makes less than $4 a day?

The simplest answer is, "not much." The life of the average resident of any of the countries covered in Part 4 is pretty grim. No smart phone. Or cable TV. Or electricity. Or running water. Or indoor plumbing.

To cite but two examples of countries covered in this book and which are neither the richest nor the poorest in the world, the accounting methods the UN uses show that the United States has a GNP per capita of over $47,000 while the average Nigerian makes little more than $1,000.

In the Global South, almost 70 percent of the rural population lives below the poverty line. More than a third of them do not get enough to eat. In India alone, at least three hundred million people live in absolute poverty, which means they are too poor to buy adequate food in a country that now has a middle class that numbers more than one hundred million.

The average adult in Angola cannot expect to celebrate his or her fortieth birthday. Most Americans will reach eighty. A majority of American children alive today will reach 100.

In Africa and Asia, fewer than half of the people can read and write. Nonetheless, most of these countries have to cope with a "brain drain" because highly educated young people emigrate to Europe and North America because of the widespread unemployment among university graduates at home.

It is not just in the poorest Third World countries that people suffer. In South Korea and Brazil, the infant mortality rates are, respectively, three and six times that of the United States.

Most lack anything approaching a diversified economy. They tend, instead, to rely on the export of a few primary commodities, such as oil in Iraq and Nigeria or coffee and cotton in Nicaragua. Often, prices for these commodities fluctuate. When they fall sharply, there is little hard currency available to pay for food, manufactured goods, or other needed imports. Many Northern banks and companies refuse to accept money issued by these countries because it is not readily convertible into Northern currencies, so they have to use dollars, euros, yen, and pounds to pay for those imports.

The economic crisis of the last few years has made things worse. As we will see throughout the rest of this book, most of the countries we will be covering are so poor and so dependent on wealthier ones for their economic well-being that it could hardly be otherwise. Take, for instance, this statement from MercyCorps, one of the leading **NGOs** that provide humanitarian and development aid.

For families in places like the Central African Republic and Indonesia, rising prices for things like

food and fuel can be catastrophic. It's difficult for most of us to imagine: When we're asked to pay more at the grocery store, it's hard for us—but for those living on just $1 a day, it can be a matter of life and death.[2]

Health

The same pattern exists for almost every indicator of public health. There is one doctor for every 500 Americans, as opposed to one for every 25,000 people in Freetown, Sierra Leone's capital city. In the poorest regions of the country, there is one doctor for every 285,000 people.

In the United States, 6 out of every 1,000 babies die in infancy (and it only ranks thirty-third from the top). For the world as a whole, that number is between 42 and 49 out of 1,000 depending on whose statistics you use. Angola has the worst infant mortality rate—180 out of 1,000. In other words, 18 percent of the babies born in that country will not make it to their first birthday.

Not having a reliable source of safe drinking water is the common—and avoidable—cause of death of more than forty thousand children daily. The United States does not even bother gathering this statistic.

Health conditions are the worst in sub-Saharan Africa which is also the part of the world that still suffers the most from the HIV/AIDS epidemic. Indeed, as Table 11.1 shows, of the estimated 40 million people infected with HIV worldwide, fully 25 million live in sub-Saharan Africa. Between 1981 and 2003, 12 million children in that part of the world were orphaned because they lost both of their parents to AIDS. Even though the cost of the generic versions of the "cocktails" of antiretroviral drugs that routinely keep many patients with HIV alive in the North is down to less than $300 a year in most parts of the world, death rates dwarf those in any other region because even that sum exceeds what the countries where most AIDS victims live can afford.

Put simply, how can either a government or an average citizen afford to pay $300 for antiretroviral drugs when you only make $1,393 a year? If you decide to buy the drugs, what else would you have to give up?

Gender

We are also beginning to pay more attention to the status of women in these countries. In their path-breaking book, *Half the Sky*, Nicholas Kristof and Sheryl WuDunn examine the plight of women and girls who have either been enslaved or turned into sex workers.

That starts with the fact that most women in the Global South earn even less than men. Women are also more

TABLE 11.1 Estimated HIV/AIDS Cases and Deaths, 2007

REGION	PEOPLE LIVING WITH HIV/AIDS	PEOPLE NEWLY INFECTED	ADULT PREVALENCE (IN %)	ADULT DEATHS
Sub-Saharan Africa	22.0 million	1.9 million	5.0	1.5 million
North Africa and Middle East	380,000	40,000	0.3	27,000
Asia	5 million	380,000	0.3	380,000
Oceania	74,000	13,00	0.4	1,000
Latin America	1.7 million	140,000	0.5	63,000
Caribbean	230,000	20,000	1.1	14,000
East Europe and Central Asia	1.5 million	110,000	0.8	858,000
North America, Western and Central Europe	2 million	81,000	0.4	31,000

Source: www.avert.org/worldstats. Accessed July 2009.

likely to not get paid for the work they do. That does not mean that women are unemployed—almost no one in the Global South is. Rather, a disproportionate number of women work outside what is referred to as the cash economy. Although they may not get paid for it, they perform backbreaking chores ranging from gathering firewood to almost all domestic chores, which consume more time and energy because they do not have the labor-saving devices we in the West take for granted. Women are also less likely to be literate, and those who do attend school leave before their male contemporaries everywhere in the Global South.

As the United Nations Division for the Enhancement of Women put it in 2009:

> Long-standing inequalities in the gender distribution of economic and financial resources have placed women at a disadvantage relative to men in their capability to participate in, contribute to and benefit from broader processes of development. Despite considerable progress on many aspects of women's economic empowerment through, inter alia, increases in educational attainment and share of paid work, deeply entrenched inequality persists as a result of discriminatory norms and practices, and the pace of change has been slow and uneven across regions.[3]

---

[2]www.mercycorps.org.

[3]www.un.org/womenwatch/daw/public/WorldSurvey2009.pdf.

Identity and Conflict

Much of the Global South has been wracked by conflict that is ethnic, linguistic, religious, or racial in origin. As we have seen throughout this book, there are relatively few homogeneous nation-states anywhere in the world. What's more, anthropologists and historians have recently proved beyond the shadow of a doubt that national and other broad forms of social identity are relatively recent phenomena.

Identity issues are important enough everywhere for them to be included in the list of big questions that percolate through most of this book. They are particularly pronounced and divisive in the Global South largely because of its imperial legacy. As we will see in the historical section, the European powers typically drew colonial boundaries wherever they made sense to them, whatever the existing alignments of the indigenous population. In other words, "India," "Iraq," "Iran," "Nigeria," and "Mexico" are all, to a tremendous degree, artificial Western creations. This is less true in the Americas, though almost all those countries have significant minorities of Native Americans and people of African descent.

When political scientists started studying the Global South—or whatever we choose to call it—in the 1950s, most of them assumed that the spread of the mass media and Western culture would gradually erode people's attachment to what were then viewed as "primitive" identities. They were wrong. If anything, these identities have become much more important, both in and of themselves, and as a source of conflict within and between countries. There will be plenty of examples of identity-based conflict below, but none rival the genocide in Rwanda.

On April 6, 1994, an airplane carrying the presidents of Rwanda and Burundi was shot down, killing all aboard. This incident set off waves of violence between the majority Hutu and minority Tutsi populations in both countries, which Philip Gourevitch chillingly describes in the very first words of his award-winning book on the genocide that followed:

> Decimation means the killing of every tenth person in a population and in the spring and early summer of 1994 a program of massacres decimated the Republic of Rwanda. Although the killing was low-tech—performed largely by machete—it was carried out at dazzling speed; of an original population of about seven and a half million, at least eight hundred thousand were killed in just a hundred days. Rwandans often speak of a million deaths, and they may be right. The dead of Rwanda accumulated at nearly three times the rate of Jewish dead during the Holocaust.

The crushed skull of a genocide victim is laid into one of the many mass graves to be found in Rwanda . . . and in other places where ethnic conflict has disrupted the peace in the Third World.

It was the most efficient mass killing since the atomic bombings of Hiroshima and Nagasaki.[4]

Rwanda is not unique. At any time, there are twenty to forty wars being fought in the Global South, almost all of which have their origins in identity politics. This has even become at least partially true for the wars the United States began for other reasons in Iraq and Afghanistan after 9/11. Although few societies have had to deal with a conflict anywhere near as bloody as that in Rwanda, all are bitter and intense. In this decade, the most violent examples have been in Darfur and the Democratic Republic of Congo where upward of 10 percent of their populations have been forced to flee and as many as 5 percent have been killed in the most affected regions.

---

[4]Philip Gourevitch, *We Wish to Inform You That Tomorrow We Will Be Killed with Our Families: Stories from Rwanda* (New York: Farrar, Straus and Giroux, 1998), frontispiece.

Environmental Threats

Much of the Global South is an ecological time bomb waiting to go off. Slums like Badia East are environmental nightmares with more than their share of pollution to go along with their unsanitary and crowded conditions.

The key, however, to environmental problems in the Global South is population growth. In the Global South, the youth, rather than the aging of the population, is the most serious demographic problem. Overall, the population in the poorest countries is increasing at three-and-a-half times the rate in the richest ones.

The population crisis is magnified by the fact that most countries have seen massive migration to their cities by people who are desperate for work. Mumbai in India, Mexico City, and Lagos in Nigeria all have populations of twenty million or more. Add to that the up to forty million people who flee conflict each year and end up in refugee camps, and it is hard *not* to see that population growth is fraught with political ramifications.

Birth rates have declined in recent years, but the population of sub-Saharan Africa is still growing at the rate of 2.5 percent per year. But this figure underestimates the problem because population growth is exponential and builds on itself like compound interest on a savings account. At 0.6 percent, it will take 120 years for the population of the richest countries to double, a rate they can easily absorb given projected rates of economic growth. At 2.5 percent, it will take less than thirty years for the sub-Saharan population to double. In Sierra Leone, where the annual increase tops 4 percent, it will not even take a generation. Egypt, with its already overstretched economy and ecosystem, adds two million people to its population every year.

The combination of poverty and population growth has created millions of desperate people who are willing to trade their environmental future for food for themselves and their families today. In Africa, about 15 percent of the land has been severely damaged. Everywhere, development is putting marginally adequate water supplies and irrigation systems at risk. Thus, many—perhaps most—of the people who slash and burn the trees in the Amazon rainforests can only provide for their families by farming that land. In short, throughout the Global South, human action is threatening what environmentalists call the carrying capacity of the land.

The impact of global warming and climate change is harder to predict for the countries in the South than for the rest of the world. Some island countries could end up largely under water. The desertification that has plagued central Africa for decades could well accelerate. Unpredictable epidemics linked to climate change will certainly hit the South harder than anywhere else for no other reason than the fact that they lack the economic and other resources to respond to any profound change taking place around them.

Globalization and Development

Just about every college and university in the North offers courses on political development. Later on, we will see that political scientists and other social commentators have not come close to reaching consensus about what the word *development* means. For now, it is enough to see that development policies all aim to close the gaps and address the issues raised so far in this chapter, which we will explore by considering three interrelated questions in the rest of Part 4.

- **What is development?** We used to think that societies moved from less to more developed conditions. At least implicitly, we assumed that the developing world would become more democratic, industrialized, urban, and affluent. We have since realized that there is no single developmental process and that a "developed" India will not look at all like a "developed" United States. Nonetheless, there is a growing consensus among social scientists that political development involves increasing a country's capacity to meet demands arising from the kinds of problems we will be discussing in Part 4.

- **How do countries develop?** There is almost no agreement on this front. As we will see in the public policy section of this chapter, most answers to that question reflect the ideological predispositions of the person or organization that does the research or issues the policy recommendations. Until the 1970s, most mainstream political scientists assumed that a strong state would be needed in order to develop strong indigenous industries. Since then, the ideological tides have turned and private enterprise and markets are now more often seen as the best route to development. During this century, more and more of us have come to the conclusion that none of the traditional approaches to development have worked anywhere near well enough and that something else—and something largely determined by people in the South themselves—will be needed.

- **How does globalization affect development?** If anything, globalization has sped up the interdependence of North and South. As with everything else, it is hard to pin down exactly how much globalization has heightened the need for concerted action to address what the United Nations calls the Millennium Development Goals (MDGs)—ending poverty, guaranteeing universal access to education,

A refugee camp in Darfur.

AP Photo/Nasser Nasser

ensuring gender equality, improving children's health, sustaining the environment, and building global partnerships (www.endpoverty2015.org/). Globalization is making it harder to meet some of these goals at the very same time that the costs of failing to do so matter more and more.

A Syndrome of Interconnected Problems

It should already be clear that the big questions raised in Chapter 1 are at the heart of everything that happens in the Global South. The only one not mentioned in this chapter already is "Everything 2.0" which is certainly on the political agenda in the countries discussed in the four chapters that follow.

As such, it is useful to think of the big questions as part of an integrated syndrome of problems, which is a term I first used in a very different context in Chapter 5 on France to describe the interrelated set of political and other problems that led to the collapse of the Third and Fourth Republics.

For the Global South, the syndrome involves "maladies" that take us far beyond the political. As with the list of countries, there is no definitive list of what those problem are, but they all reflect the fact that billions of people lead lives with little if any dignity.

The point here is not to add even more depressing facts and figures to an already depressing picture. Rather, think about these as symptoms of deeper problems that cannot be fully addressed separately but have to be examined as

part of one single dilemma—a point we will return to in the concluding chapter of this book.

The BRICS—Mind the Gap

Not all the news from the Global South is gloomy. Overall rates of poverty, disease, illiteracy, and the like have all declined since most of these countries gained their independence a half century or more ago. There is even some evidence that the gap between the richest and poorest countries is beginning to close, although it will take centuries for it to disappear at the rate things are changing today.

The best evidence we have about this comes from an unusual source, the Swedish statistician, Hans Rosling. Rosling is a pioneer in presenting quantitative data that covers decades in order to show broad developmental trends. Most of his TED and other talks feature him using rapidly moving graphic displays to show how many of these gaps are being closed. The one cited here covers two hundred years and two countries in four minutes (www.youtube.com/watch?v=jbkSRLYSojo).

There is more to it than Rosling, and his color-coded graphs. In fact, it would be irresponsible on my part not to at least note the BRICS and a handful of other countries that seem to have escaped the worst clutches of the so-called "development trap."

The term BRIC was coined by Jim O'Neill, an investment banker at Goldman Sachs, to describe countries that "appeared increasingly eager to engage on the global

Comparative Emphasis:
Africa for Norway

One of the newest issues in the dispute over development is a growing call from people in the developing world to have more responsibility for what happens to their country and its people. One recent such initiative is a project based on a video made by South African young people (www.africafornorway.no).

The South Africans who made the video on behalf of Radi-Aid wanted to show that much of the aid and even the sympathy that are given to the Global South come across as paternalistic. Put bluntly, Northern donor governments and other institutions act in ways that give the impression that they—and only they—know what's best for the developing world.

These young activists tried to flip the table. Their video is a delightful take-off on the wildly successful "We Are the World" anthem of the late 1980s. Their tongue-in-cheek song begs Africans to send their extra radiators to help freezing Norwegians. First the narrator introduces Radi-Aid and then the song begins.

A lot of people aren't aware of what's going on there right now. It's kind of just as bad as poverty if you ask me. Sunlight puts smiles on people's faces. People don't ignore starving people so why should we ignore cold people? Frostbite kills too. Africa, we need to make a difference in Norway. We need to collect our radiators, ship them over there, and spread some warmth, spread some light, and spread some smiles.

In Norway kids are freezing.
It's time for us to care.
There's heat enough for Norway
If Africans would share
Yes Africans keep thinking we can contribute
The warmth we've got we'd like to share but we can't distribute
Now the tables have turned
Now it's Africa for Norway
And there's no way we can close our eyes.
We see that they freeze
As Africans concerned
Let's send our heaters all the way
Radi-aid to Norway
With a tropical breeze

Here in Africa
We've had our problems too
With poverty, corruption
With H.I.V. and crime
Norway gave a helping hand
They taught us what to do
And now it's payback time
Now the tables have turned . . .

The second time the chorus is sung, a bouncing icon of a radiator follows the subtitles of the lyrics. ■

stage. Whatever had occurred in their past was over and done with. Globalization was happening and they wanted to be part of it."[5] He and others assumed that the emerging economies of Brazil, Russia, India, China, and (later) South Africa would turn them into major global players. He chose the term in part because he assumed these countries would become the "bricks" for the rest of the developing world to build their own political and economic foundations on.

---

[5]Jim O'Neill, *The Growth Map: Economic Opportunities in the BRICS and Beyond* (New York: Penguin/Portfolio, 2011), Kindle ed., location 265.

They are indeed clamoring for a place among the world's decision makers as part of an expanded Group of Eight (G-8), as the birthplace of the leader of either the World Bank or International Monetary Fund, or as a permanent member of the United Nations Security Council.

We will defer discussion of what made the BRICS different until the policy sections and then the chapters on the individual countries that follow. For now, simply note both that these countries have done far better than most on almost every indicator of economic and social development and that their states have played a major role in that growth. We have, of course, already seen the BRICS in the preceding two chapters on Russia and China. In Part 4, however, we will take the discussion further and see countries in which the turnaround has been even more profound and, in some ways, more surprising.

Political Dynamics

Because we will be discussing almost 150 countries in this part of the book, there is far more diversity in what we will cover in Part 4 than in Parts 2 or 3. Still, with but a few exceptions (including India, which is the focus of the next chapter), the vulnerability of the Global South does mean that there is the one common denominator to politics there—the heightened stakes of political life mentioned above.

As with the BRICS, we will defer discussing the parameters of those stakes until later in this chapter. Here are simply a handful of themes that will appear time and time again in Part 4 but have not been featured much in this book so far.

- Not many countries in the Global South have made much progress toward democratization.

- Instead, almost every country in the Global South has experienced periods of authoritarian rule, sometimes accompanied by widespread corruption.

- At the same time, many of their governments are so weak that political scientists have begun referring to the new phenomenon of failed states.

What Matters Over There Matters Over Here

It is easy to convince students in countries like the United States that they should understand politics in other liberal democracies because doing so can tell them a lot about their own state and its institutions, values, and problems. At first glance, it is less obvious why they should worry about the rest of the world because countries like Nigeria and so many others have so little in common with the West

unless we reconsider the statement by Col. Christopher Holshek that I introduced at the end of Chapter 1: "What Matters Over There Matters Over Here."

To a degree few in the West acknowledge, the South has been a place where the rich countries exported their problems and waged their battles. It was there that Europeans and Americans established most of their colonies. More recently, almost all the wars during and after the end of the cold war have occurred in Asia, Africa, or Latin America, often as a product of First and Second World disputes.

The events of 9/11 drove home the fact that many of these conflicts have a direct impact on life in Europe and North America. This is true only in part because the North is subject to attack by terrorists today and may also be vulnerable to attacks by more conventional forces tomorrow.

Even before 9/11, the South was important because we in the North are dependent on it. Most of our natural resources and more and more of our manufactured goods come from there. As the Organization of Petroleum Exporting Countries (OPEC) oil embargo of 1973–74 and the periodic oil price shocks since then have shown, when Southern commodity producers are able to band together, they can wreak havoc on Northern economies.

In short, we ignore the Global South at our peril. The failure to take its problems seriously has kept us from seeing two seemingly contradictory trends. First, we have been slow to acknowledge the role the rich and powerful countries played in creating and sustaining the economic and political woes in the South. Second, we have been even more reluctant to come to grips with the fact that few Southern countries can solve their problems without significant support from the North.

Key Questions

As was the case in Chapter 8, we will be shifting intellectual gears dramatically in Part 4. We will be able to use the same basic framework developed in Figure 1.1 in the next four chapters. However, as this discussion has already suggested, we will have to go further and ask four more questions to help us understand why so many Southern countries face such serious difficulties:

- Why are global forces so much more influential there than in the rest of the world and how do they contribute to poverty?

- Why have most of them failed to develop?

- Why are so many of these countries deeply divided?

- Why are many of their states weak if not failed?

The Evolution of Politics in the Global South

Imperialism and Its Legacy

With but a handful of exceptions, political patterns in Asia, Africa, and Latin America have deep roots in imperialism. Most were ruled for centuries by white men from Europe and North America. Even the few countries that retained their legal independence (see Chapter 10 on China or 13 on Iran) were not able to escape the corrosive effects of Northern economics and culture.

There were three distinct phases to European colonial expansion. The first came in the sixteenth and seventeenth centuries, when the Portuguese, Spanish, Dutch, British, and French carved up the Americas. These same countries also established beachheads in Africa to support their expanding commercial networks in India and the Americas, including the infamous slave trade. The second wave came mostly in the nineteenth century, when the forts and trading posts were transformed into full-blown colonies in Africa and much of Asia. The third came after World War I when the allies divided up the remnants of the Ottoman Empire (see Table 11.2).

During each of these periods, statesmen, entrepreneurs, missionaries, and adventurers flocked to most of Africa, Asia, and the Americas in pursuit of what the British called the three g's: God, gold, and glory. More often than not, boundaries were drawn to suit the colonizers' wishes and ended up dividing existing political units and lumping traditional adversaries together.

The colonizers looked down on the cultures they encountered and had no trouble convincing themselves that the people they subjugated were primitive in almost every way imaginable. This prompted the arrogance of what Rudyard Kipling called "the white man's burden," according to which everything Western was superior while everything in the indigenous culture was inferior:

Take up the White Man's burden—
Send forth the best ye breed—
Go, bind your sons to exile
To serve your captives' need;
To wait, in heavy harness,
On fluttered folk and wild—
Your new-caught, sullen peoples,
Half devil and half child.

Their arrogance made it easy for the imperialists to ignore the fact that they undermined dozens of highly sophisticated civilizations: the Aztecs, Incas, and Mayans in the Americas; the great kingdoms of precolonial Africa; and the various cultures of India and China. Instead, they turned most of the new colonies into relatively unsophisticated subsistence economies that could no longer produce enough food and other goods to meet their peoples' basic survival needs but had to import them or do without.

The colonizers also insisted that their newly acquired possessions make a profit. The Central American countries became known as "banana republics" because of the way United Fruit and other North American companies concentrated production. Massive coffee and tea plantations were built in the Central Highlands of Kenya. Cotton sent back to factories in Britain destroyed long-established Indian spinning and weaving industries.

Eventually there was some industrialization. Even then, decisions about what to grow, mine, or build were mostly made in Europe and North America. Almost all of the profits from these businesses were sent back there as well.

Even though they all were exploitative, the Europeans and North Americans did not all run their colonies in the same way. In North America, the colonists gained control of relatively sparsely settled lands and then proceeded to wipe out most of the indigenous population. Where large numbers of native peoples survived, they were integrated into the newly dominant Spanish or Portuguese cultures in Central and South America. Most tragic of all, of course, was the forced relocation of millions of Africans, who were brought to the Americas as slaves.

During the nineteenth century, the colonizing powers added most of Africa and much of South Asia to their list of conquests. There, the colonial powers encountered a more serious "numbers problem." Because there were many more Africans and Asians than Europeans, the colonial powers could not hope to govern their new conquests on their own. Therefore, they had to incorporate growing numbers of "locals" into a system of government that the British called indirect rule.

TABLE 11.2 Key Events in the History of the Third World

YEAR	EVENT
1450 on	Exploration and then colonization of the New World
1600 on	Slave trade
1776	United States declares independence
1810–30	Most of Central and South America gains independence
1867	India formally taken over by British government
1880s	"Scramble for Africa"
1919	German colonies pass to Allied powers as League of Nations mandates
Late 1940s	India and other countries gain independence
1960s	Most remaining colonies gain independence
Mid-1970s	Portuguese African empire collapses
1997	Hong Kong reverts to China

© Cengage Learning

Independence

There were three waves of decolonization. The first began during the 1770s, when thirteen of the colonies in British North America became the United States. It spread through most of the rest of the Western Hemisphere during the next half-century. In all of these cases, however, it was not the native peoples—the directly colonized—who rose up and won their independence, but the descendants of the colonizers who had migrated from Europe.

Although one author has described the United States as the "first new nation," most accounts of this first wave of decolonization focus on the Spanish and Portuguese colonies in the Caribbean and in Central and South America. Independence came early there in large part because of the growing domestic weakness of Spain and Portugal, which left them unable to maintain their hold over the colonies.

As Chapter 15 will examine in the case of Mexico, these revolutions settled little. Most of the newly independent countries suffered through at least another century of turmoil in which rival elites vied for power. Meanwhile, they remained on the bottom rung of the capitalist world economy, with Britain and the United States taking over most Spanish and Portuguese economic interests. Many nominally independent Central American states soon had to deal with the United States militarily as well as economically because it sent in the Marines whenever it felt that its financial or security interests were imperiled.

The second wave was also confined to a single region: the Middle East. After World War I, the Ottoman Empire collapsed, and some countries gained at least their nominal independence. Others, such as Iraq, passed under British or French control, though most of them had become somewhat independent before World War II broke out.

The third wave occurred during the second half of the twentieth century. After World War II, protest movements in most of Asia and Africa were able to end legal colonization almost everywhere. The best known of these was the nonviolent movement led by Mohandas Gandhi in India. As we will see in the next chapter, Gandhi and his allies pressured the British into agreeing to grant India its independence after the war in exchange for its at least tacit support during the war. Despite some false starts, the British lived up to their word, and India and Pakistan became independent states within the British Commonwealth of Nations in 1947.

Over the next quarter-century, most of the remaining colonies followed suit. Sometimes the colonial powers hung on, and independence only came as the result of a protracted revolutionary struggle, as in Vietnam and Algeria. In other cases, independence came rather easily, as in Nigeria.

In 1997, Hong Kong was handed back to China, which in many respects marked the formal end of imperialism.

Today, Europe and the United States have only a few, mostly tiny, outposts left.

In a few former colonies, such as India, Israel, Vietnam, and Algeria, the campaign for independence engaged much of the population. When freedom did come, the new regime enjoyed the support of a large proportion of the population, because it was led by the same people who ousted the colonial power. This unity eroded with time, but it gave these countries a number of advantages to start their time as independent countries with, including a well-trained and respected elite.

Most of the other former colonies were not as fortunate. By the late 1950s, it had become clear to most Europeans that their empires could not survive. Although independence itself therefore came more easily in most of Africa and the Middle East, its very ease obscured problems that were to plague these countries soon thereafter. In particular, they lacked either the trained leadership or the unity and commitment on the part of much of the population that figured so prominently in India's nonviolent Congress or Algeria's violent National Liberation Front. Instead, the new leaders only had the support of either the small Westernized elite or their own regional or ethnic constituencies, the benefits of which quickly evaporated once the exhilaration of independence wore off.

Postcolonial Problems

Most of the new countries had internationally respected leaders who ran governments patterned after those in London, Paris, and Washington. Political scientists and political leaders assumed that what they mistook as the enthusiasm of the newly independent peoples along with aid from the outside would lead to a rapid improvement in the quality of life and the development of strong, democratic states.

That almost never happened.

The new leaders' lack of experience and shortage of available resources made reaching broader social and economic goals nearly impossible. Under the circumstances, their many rivals proved willing to toss out whatever democratic institutions they had inherited from their erstwhile colonial masters. More often than not, their fledgling democracies degenerated into military, single-party, or other forms of authoritarian rule.

In many former colonies, identity politics ate away at whatever common ground had been achieved during the struggle for independence. The sense of national identification that had been built before independence gave way to bloody civil wars when the antagonisms between the ethnic groups that the colonial powers had forced to live together came to the political surface.

Far from being helpful, Northern governments and businesses imposed their economic, and sometimes political, will. Regional conflicts often turned into proxy battles between the superpowers, thereby worsening an already difficult situation.

Political Culture

In Part 2, we saw that a political culture based on a common identity, shared values, and a sense of legitimacy plays a vital role in sustaining the established liberal democracies. In Part 3, we saw how hard it is for the former communist countries to sustain that kind of culture. Here, we will encounter even starker evidence of what happens if a peoples' values and assumptions include divisions over basic attitudes about the country's existence and the most basic rules of the political game.

Obviously, there is no way to discuss all the varieties of political culture in the Global South in two pages. However, identity issues are important enough in their own right, as well as being at least an indirect source of the problems already mentioned, that they deserve special attention here.

Colonialism cannot be blamed for all of the cultural problems in the Global South, especially as colonial rule recedes into history. However, imperialism remains an important long-term reason why so many of these countries have been unable to develop anything like a strong sense of national identity.

In Part 2, we saw that most people in the liberal democracies define themselves politically first and foremost in national terms. That is harder for people to do in Africa and much of Asia because of the way the colonial conquerors drew their borders.

In West Africa, for instance, different ethnic groups live in what amount to bands stretching east and west that parallel the Atlantic coast. In the 1880s and 1890s, however, the Europeans established colonial borders that ran from north to south, thereby dividing ethnic, religious, and linguistic groups into two or more separate jurisdictions.

In other words, most Third World countries are artificial entities, with little or nothing that psychologically holds their inhabitants together. To be sure, soccer fans have been treated to the antics of wildly enthusiastic Africans at recent World Cups. However, international soccer is one of the few things that lead them to think of themselves as Nigerians, Ivoiriens, or whatever. More often, their political views are derived from their regional or ethnic identities.

Dozens of African countries have endured bloody civil wars. Even where wars have not occurred, there has been intense conflict. Ethnic divisions have exacted a terrible cost on their own and have also diverted scarce resources that could otherwise be used for economic and social development.

As ethnic conflict erupted in much of the Third World, political scientists began to explore the resilience of the supposedly weak "traditional" societies. Among other things, they found that many institutions reinforcing older values persisted. For example, many countries still have strong informal patron-client relations that have their roots in feudalism. As in Europe during the Middle Ages or in the Mafia today, people are tied together in hierarchical relationships in which they have mutual responsibilities and obligations. Lords, bosses, and patrons are more powerful than their clients. Nonetheless, financial, military, and cultural bonds tie them together in networks that have proven remarkably hard to break.

Similarly, the assumption that the new nations would become more secular as they modernized has proved unfounded. If anything, religion has become more important and divisive. Such is the case in much of West Africa, where long-standing ethnic conflicts are exacerbated by the fact that adherents of traditional religions, Christians, and Muslims were forced together into the same geopolitical units. In other cases, such as India, the conflict is between religious, ethnic, and linguistic groups that have been at odds for centuries.

Some political cultures have also evolved in ways that have left people and leaders strongly preferring *not* to develop along Western lines, most notably with the rise of what we mistakenly refer to as Muslim **fundamentalism**. The Islamic Republic that overthrew the shah and has ruled Iran since the 1979 revolution is based on a rejection of most things Western and modern. The shah's grandiose industrial and commercial projects and his increasingly cosmopolitan society have given way to more traditional customs, including the strict application of Islamic law and the exclusion of women from much of public life.

Iran is not alone in that respect. Throughout the Muslim world, more and more women are wearing the veil that is widely viewed in the West as a symbol of their subordinate status in Islamic society. More generally, Muslim peoples are coming to see their religion and the broader values and lifestyle it embraces as something to have pride in and even as something far superior to industrialization, democracy, and Western culture.

Around the world, new grassroots organizations have been spawned all along the political spectrum—if it still makes sense to speak of a single political spectrum—including many that want to slow down and others that want to speed up the pace of change. In turn, groups have formed within

Comparative Emphasis: Conflict

The first and most obvious conclusion to draw from this chapter is that there is more conflict in the South than in either the liberal democracies or most of the current and former communist countries. In many cases, protesters target not only the government of the day and its policies but also the regime. In some, the existence of the nation-state itself has been questioned. The conflict is all the more remarkable because, in the more authoritarian states, citizens run a major risk by signing a petition, let alone taking to the streets, something we saw in most of the countries where people took part in the Arab Spring.

Not all countries in the Global South are revolutions or civil wars waiting to happen. Still, even in the most stable of them, such as India, deaths during election campaigns are common enough that they rarely draw more than a passing note in the press.

Perhaps most important of all, as the World Bank put it in its 2003 *World Development Report*, conflict in the Global South has a huge social and economic cost, amounting to what its authors called "development in reverse." ■

In other words, some Hindus have modified their cultural norms because they have had to. After all, it is very hard to tell the *jati* of the cooks who prepared their food when a meal is served on an airplane! But these values have not disappeared. In some politically important respects, they are stronger in ways that tend to deepen divisions and hinder the prospects for either national unity or democracy.

Social scientists of all stripes do agree on one important lesson about the relationship between identity and politics—our self-definitions are not in any way "built in" to us. Even before 9/11, there was widespread discussion of how culture and identity were a permanent part of the human condition and were the main reasons behind what the late Samuel Huntington called the "class of civilizations." Research by everyone from anthropologists to neuroscientists has shown that identity in all of its forms is a human creation and a relatively recent one at that.

None of that research, however, should keep us from seeing just how important identity has been as a core common denominator to most political cultures in the Global South.

Political Participation

Political participation is different in the Global South, too. In Part 2, we saw that people in the industrialized democracies resort to the kinds of demands that could threaten the existence of the regime only under the most unusual of circumstances. In the Global South, by contrast, far fewer opportunities exist for any kind of "inside-the-system" participation that allows citizens to vociferously express their views without putting the regime in jeopardy.

In Part 3, we then saw how Marxist-Leninist regimes typically channeled all legal participation through the ruling communist parties. As we will see in the next section, most Southern states are too weak to be able to mobilize participation in anything like these ways.

Hints of Democracy

Many Southern countries have little of the voluntary participation we focused on in Part 2. That's the case both because few of the countries have been able to build and sustain democracies and because much of the participation that does occur includes demands for change at the regime level and not just in an existing government's policies and practices.

In other words, we will only be able to look at some kinds of participation in the Global South using the same kind of analytical lens we used for the established democracies. Thus, political parties, such as Mexico's *Partido Acción Nacional* (PAN), try to forge broad coalitions around a few

elites that are increasingly committed to retaining the status quo and, with it, their own power and privileges.

To make sense of these rather abstract points, briefly consider an example which we will return to in more detail in the next chapter. In India, a Hindu is born into one of four castes or as what used to be called an untouchable. These groups, in turn, are subdivided into smaller communities, or *jati*, on the basis of their member families' traditional occupations such as grocer, tanner, or teacher.

As India has urbanized and industrialized, the historical link between *jati* and profession has declined, and some of the restrictions it imposed on people, such as who they can marry or who can prepare their food, are no longer as important. However, caste and *jati* remain extremely significant politically because the patron-client relationships that sustain them are also the mainstays of the political party organizations at the all-important state level.

key ideological positions. Similarly, India has trade unions, women's movements, and other interest groups reminiscent of those in the industrialized democracies.

However, do not read too much into such examples. Even in countries with reasonably open political systems, a disproportionate amount of the participation "from below" places burdens on decision makers that they find hard to meet, as suggested in the discussion of Table 1.3. That is even true of countries where leaders are normally chosen through elections.

The bottom line is that whatever term we use, much of political life in the Global South revolves around religious, ethnic, linguistic, racial, and other "communities." To be sure, there is some of that in the West, including the all but total loyalty of African Americans to the Democratic Party in the United States. However, such trends pale in comparison with what we will see in the rest of Part 4. If nothing else, it is very hard to assemble a table of Indian election returns like the ones given in Part 2 because only three parties run candidates nationwide. Instead, much of the vote goes to parties that operate only in the one state where their linguistic or religious constituency is clustered.

Participation in Authoritarian Regimes

In countries with authoritarian regimes, patterns of political participation are more reminiscent of what we saw in the former Soviet Union in that it is more "top down" than "bottom up." In countries with single-party or military governments, much of the participation is orchestrated by the regime. For example, in Iraq before and after the first Gulf War, there were large demonstrations in support of the government's intransigence toward the United States, but most commentators wrote them off because they were orchestrated by Saddam Hussein's regime. In Iran, the authorities have used paramilitaries associated with the regime to put down protests like the ones discussed toward the end of this section. The same, of course, was true of the young men who demolished Badai East.

Not all such participation is violent. For example, patron-client relations are more important in the Global South than in the countries considered in Parts 2 and 3 in large part because capitalism and the changes that came in its wake have not gone as far as political scientists first thought they would in destroying traditional social structures. Thus, Mexico's *Partido Revolucionario Institucional* (PRI) was able to stay in power for more than seventy years not because of its ideology or accomplishments but because it built a client-based machine that could turn out—and, if need be, manufacture—the vote through the distribution of jobs and other benefits.

It is a mistake, however, to write off participation in authoritarian or hybrid regimes as nothing more than

cynical manipulation of the masses by the elite. Like the demonstrations in favor of Mao Zedong at the height of China's Cultural Revolution, these activities often reflect genuine enthusiasm and commitment of the people involved.

Similarly, there are many examples akin to the Chinese Communist Party's campaigns in which the state mobilizes people in an attempt to build support for policies that its weak and unreliable bureaucracy cannot implement on its own. These, too, may be portrayed as cynical and manipulative efforts by the state, as in the literacy campaigns of the Iraqi and Nicaraguan governments in the 1980s. In other cases, however, even the most skeptical analysts acknowledge that such campaigns can have a significant and positive impact. Nigeria has few programs it can point to for building bridges across communal lines. However, its National Youth Service Corps sends teams of young people for more or less compulsory service after graduating from college to work in economic and other developmental projects outside their home regions. If nothing else, people in the regions where the volunteers work gain some positive exposure to members of groups toward whom they may harbor antagonistic relations.

Civil Society

There is one final form of political participation that political scientists are just beginning to pay attention to: the role of civil society organizations in general and NGOs in particular. These organizations are unofficial bodies that are independent of governments, political parties, and conventional interest groups such as labor unions and business associations.

Civil society organizations exist in all countries that allow even a glimmer of political freedom, as we saw in the discussion of the growing number of small NGOs in China. Some of them are organized internationally, with paid workers and volunteers who are not from the country in which they work. Others are smaller and only work in a single country or even a single community, as we will see with the organizations that try to stop intercommunal violence in Nigeria.

The most visible NGOs, such as *Médecins sans Frontières* (Doctors without Borders) and Save the Children, are not very political. They concentrate instead on humanitarian relief during what are euphemistically called "complex emergencies." Increasingly, however, even the most apolitical NGOs are recognizing that their work invariably draws them into political life. Those that concentrate on development or conflict resolution gladly acknowledge their political role, including the Alliance for Peacebuilding and our partners in the Global Partnership for the Prevention of Armed Conflict. For countries in which both the state and the formal international community lack resources and credibility, NGOs can play a vital role in efforts to modernize the economy or build civil society from the grassroots level up.

Comparative Emphasis: Women and Politics in the Global South

As part of the new interest in the role of women in political science, their involvement—and often lack thereof—is getting renewed attention. Of course, there are women who play prominent roles in these countries, such as Dilma Rousseff, who was elected president of Brazil in 2011. But they are still few and far between.

More important is the fact that the problems buffeting the Global South normally hit women harder than men. Most domestic chores remain "women's work." Domestic work is becoming ever more burdensome, as in the regions bordering the Sahel desert where women often have to walk for miles daily to find enough firewood to cook with.

Far too many women and teenage girls are raped, and too many are bought and sold into slavery. Teenage pregnancy rates are amazingly high, as is the incidence of often crippling diseases that go along with childbirth among girls who are not physically mature enough to have children. Girls spend less time at school than boys. In poor families, it is not uncommon for fathers to force daughters to drop out and go to work, in far too many cases as prostitutes.

On balance, if there is still a gap between the status of men and women in the North, it remains more like a chasm in the Global South. ■

The Color Revolutions

The Global South (including some of the poorer post-communist countries) has also been the home to a novel form of political protest, often dubbed **color revolutions**. For reasons that no one fully understands, participants and analysts alike started using colors to label popular uprisings, beginning with yellow in the Philippines in 1986. Since then, rose (Georgia), orange (Ukraine), tulip (Kyrgyzstan), cedar (Lebanon), green (Iran), lotus (Egypt), and jasmine (Tunisia) uprisings either brought down long-standing authoritarian regimes or came close to doing so as we will see in Iran. The most famous of them (in this case colorless) occurred in 2000 in Serbia where a group of young people brilliantly organized fellow dissidents to oust the seemingly impregnable dictator, Slobodan Milosevic (www.aforcemorepowerful.org/films/bdd/index.php).

Like civil society organizations, these movements started by organizing men and women who had not previously been active in political life. Drawing on the work of activists like Gene Sharp in the United States, they have developed techniques that allow once powerless people to rise up and challenge powerful regimes without using violence themselves.

The fact that they are known as color revolutions is purely coincidental. However, the fact that they deserve our attention was most evident in recent years in the so-called **Arab Spring** in which youthful protesters toppled authoritarian regimes in Tunisia and Egypt with a minimum of violence and then in Libya after a brief civil war (also see the discussion of Wael Ghonim near the beginning of Chapter 1). Arab Spring protests also broke out in the rest of the region and almost toppled regimes in Bahrain, Yemen, and elsewhere.

Since the heady days of 2011, the Arab Spring has lost some of its luster given sporadic, continuing violence in Egypt and the bloody civil war in Syria that was showing no signs of ending as these lines were written. Still, the Arab Spring and color revolutions suggest that the Global South could become the home of a new kind of political movement in which the powerless can quickly become powerful. We will return to the Arab Spring at the conclusion of the book. For now, it is enough to see that non-democratic and often illegitimate rule, poverty, the uneven distribution of income and wealth, and identity-based differences can turn seemingly stable countries into powder kegs virtually overnight.

Weak and Failed States

Of the three types of states considered in this book, those in the Global South face the most daunting problems and so are most in need of a reasonably strong state. But few have one.

At first glance, this might come as a surprise. After all, the stories we see in the news often stress the excesses of their many authoritarian rulers. But few have been able to do much more than maintain law and order by suppressing dissent, and many have not even accomplished that.

There are some exceptions, such as in India, whose state-sponsored "green revolution" (not to be confused with the political color revolutions) has improved agricultural output so much over the past generation that the country no longer has to import food. Far more common, though, is the disheartening history of Nigeria, where average citizens are worse off now than they were forty years ago despite the billions of dollars the government has earned from the sale of oil.

In the chapters that follow, we will see evidence of this weakness in three overlapping ways.

The first is as a by-product of their poverty. No government in a country with a per capita GNP of less than two thousand dollars per year will have much money to devote to education or health care. Poverty also leaves such a country with a weak infrastructure because it cannot afford to pave roads or erect cell phone towers for modern telecommunications systems.

There is more than just a lack of money involved. In the poorest countries, the government may not "reach" everyone in the ways we in the North take for granted, including enforcing the law and collecting taxes. For example, at the time of independence, there were only thirteen university graduates in all of what is now the Democratic Republic of Congo. Although there have been marked advances since then in education, life expectancy, and other areas of social life, none of these countries benefits from the kind of highly trained workforce that could produce the coalitions of business, government, and bureaucratic elites that have been so important in Europe, Japan, and elsewhere.

Second, many Southern countries have been unable to sustain regimes that last for very long. As we saw in Parts 2 and 3, it takes both time and a degree of political success to develop strong institutions that are not dependent on the power or personality of individual leaders. Time allows people to establish routines and expectations for the institutions that govern them. Success helps build legitimacy.

But this has not happened in most of the Global South. In part, this reflects the fact that their governments have had to deal with very heavy demands in a very short period of time. Many people expect what happened over two or three centuries in the West to be squeezed into two or three decades. Put simply, people run out of patience with states that are not providing results fast enough.

Third, many Southern countries with weak states are also plagued by widespread corruption, which extends far beyond the scarce resource that leaders spirited out of their countries. It is also why the Transparency International Corruption Index is included in the basic table on the inside cover of this book. The corruption often extends far into the bureaucracy, especially in countries that lack a strong legal system and other institutions that could keep state employees in check. Thus, in Nigeria, civil servants are frequently referred to as *lootocrats* or *kleptocrats*.

Democracies

There are only a handful of established democracies in the Third World. In addition to India, they include Costa Rica, most of the island states in the Caribbean, and several of the smallest African states.

Some observers add a few others, like Mexico, that have been able to sustain some aspects of democracy for many years. But Mexico cannot be said to guarantee basic individual freedoms, competitive elections, or the rule of law. Similarly, many of us would like to label South Africa as democratic given the remarkable changes there since Nelson Mandela's release from prison in 1990. However, it is far from certain that its multiracial democracy will survive the many social and economic problems facing the country.

Many countries have taken steps toward democracy since the late 1980s. Indeed, 1990 marked the first time that every country in South America had a government chosen through reasonably free and competitive elections, which most have sustained since then. Democratization has occurred more slowly in Africa and most of Asia, but moves in that direction are occurring there as well, as we will see at the end of the section on public policy.

Authoritarianism

If we use the political criteria for democracy outlined in Chapter 2, almost all countries in Part 4 fall short. If we add the economic ones, we can see why even a country like India merits consideration here rather than in Part 2.

Most of the new nations adopted liberal constitutions with multiparty systems patterned after those of their colonizers. Few lasted.

There are very few purely authoritarian regimes in the Global South today. Most, instead, are a lot like the **hybrid regimes** discussed in Chapters 8 and 9. However, as we saw there, many such regimes only have a thin democratic veneer. In particular, elections may be rigged or conducted in biased ways that ensure that the incumbent wins, something we will see most clearly in Nigeria today and in Mexico before 2000.

Single-Party Regimes

The anticolonial movement was typically dominated by a single movement, which became the most powerful party after the transfer of power. Often, this group quickly abandoned the liberal democratic constitution and made itself the only legal party. In some cases, there were elaborate and plausible justifications for such a move. The late President Nyerere of Tanzania likened competitive party systems to a soccer game in which a lot of energy is expended for only a goal or two—energy a new and poor country like his could not afford. More often, the shift to a single-party regime was little more than a power play by one faction in the country's elite, often representing a single ethnic or religious group.

In Tanzania, attempts were made by Nyerere's colleagues in the Tanzanian African National Union to expand competition within the party in ways that resemble primaries in the United States. In most countries, however, the single party has amounted to little more than political window dressing for a dictatorship. None of the countries considered in the rest of Part 4 currently has a classic single-party regime, because most recent leaders have realized that there are advantages to having at least some of the trappings of democracy.

Military Regimes

Multiparty regimes have also frequently succumbed to military coups. Interstate wars between states almost never occur in the Global South today. Nonetheless, the military has played a prominent political role just about everywhere. Professional soldiers often think of themselves as having a dual role: to protect the country not only from external threats but also from civil unrest. From the military's perspective, multiparty regimes have turned chaotic far too often. Throughout Africa and South America, the twin fears of instability and communist insurrection led the military to seize power time and time again. Consider Nigeria. Under its first two republics (1960–66 and 1979–83), the political parties were organized almost exclusively along ethnic lines, making effective government all but impossible. The ensuing instability prompted the military to intervene to quell ethnic protest and political corruption. As has also often been the case elsewhere, not only has the military overthrown civilian governments but one group of soldiers has also overthrown another on five occasions there as well.

Some military leaders have tried to do more than simply maintain law and order or enrich themselves. During the late 1970s and early 1980s, many political scientists and other observers believed that, for good or ill, these were the only kinds of regimes that could start Southern countries on the road to development. By the end of the decade, however, such governments were in trouble everywhere. Economic growth slowed, making the uneven distribution of its benefits a more significant political issue. Protest over economic conditions combined with opposition to human rights abuses to create powerful movements that removed the military from power throughout South America and, to a lesser degree, in the rest of the Third World.

Personal Dictatorships

Perhaps the most tragic form of government in the Third World is personal dictatorship, the most visible of which, as I write, is the one in Syria. Basher al-Assad has run the country as something like a personal fiefdom since he became president in 2000 after the death of his father, who had run the country for thirty years before that.

The al-Assad family came to power through the Baath Party. Even before the senior al-Assad took power, the values that gave rise to that pan-Arab movement had largely disappeared. Assad—like Saddam Hussein in neighboring Iraq—was able to seize and retain power largely because

President Assad of Syria whose regime was under fire when this book went to press.

he developed networks of supporters who took control of much of the country.

Relatively few of these rulers made it to the end of the twentieth century. Of course, Saddam Hussein was overthrown and later executed after the American-led invasion in 2003. It is entirely possible, too, that al-Assad and other personal dictators such as Robert Mugabe in Zimbabwe, will have been removed from office by the time you read these pages.

Unfortunately, the historical record suggests that the people who succeed them will not find it easy to rebuild their countries. Typically, the leaders take office only to find the treasury looted, the country's natural resources depleted, and the people extremely impatient. In other words, the dictators' impact on their countries continues long after they are thrown out of office.

Failed States

In some parts of the Global South that are most affected by communal violence, we can barely speak of sovereign states. In fact, observers now call them failed states because their governments have lost the ability to carry out the most basic functions. All have governments and officials, but they resemble the Wizard of Oz more than leaders of an effective state. Once we get past the uniforms and the trappings of office, it is easy to see that the leaders are little more than figureheads for a state that has a handle on only a tiny fraction of its crime or other problems.

For reasons of space, we will not cover any of the world's weakest states in this book. However, some observers are convinced that Mexico could become one if its struggle with the drug cartels continues to deteriorate. In other words, in Chapter 15, we will see some of the dynamics that have led to the collapse of governments in such countries as Sierra Leone, the Democratic Republic of Congo, Burundi, Rwanda, and Somalia.

Public Policy: The Myths and Realities of Development

If you conduct a search for "political development" using your favorite search engine, you will find a bewildering array of postings in which only two things will be clear. First, almost everything written about the Global South takes for granted that development is the primary public policy goal. Second, the supposed experts do not agree either on what development is or on how a country can develop.

We will not ignore other policy issues, including democratization, the status of women, or the environment. However, because development is seen as the key to even having a hope of reaching any of those other policy goals, we will focus on it and treat those other issues largely as a subset or even a by-product of development.

Before we dig into development in any detail, it is important to underscore one more common denominator for Part 4 and this book as a whole. Whatever it means, development today does not occur quickly, smoothly, or easily. Economic and political development in Western Europe and North America took the better part of three centuries and is not over yet. In the few cases in which it happened more quickly, such as Imperial Germany and Meiji Japan, it still took decades and required severe repression. And they industrialized at a time when they already were the world's dominant economic and military powers and thus were largely free to marshal needed resources as their leaders saw fit. Quite the opposite is the case today. Southern countries—including those in Latin America that have been independent since the nineteenth century—embarked on their own developmental odysseys only recently and under much less promising circumstances and are playing a frustrating game of political and economic catch-up—at best.

Development

There is a good reason why the literature on development is so confusing. It is by no means a simple concept and is not easy to measure however you choose to define it. For our purposes, the complexity surrounding development falls into two main categories.

Multiple Goals

The first source of confusion exists around what people who are interested in development are trying to achieve.

Given the discussion at the beginning of this chapter, it should come as no surprise that everyone equates development with at least some degree of prosperity. At first, analysts used relatively crude indicators of a country's wealth such as its per capita gross national product. Although some scholars still rely on such simplistic indicators, more and more of us are convinced that measures of economic development have to also take into account the way whatever wealth there is is used. For example, the UN's Human Development Index also tries to tap the quality of life for the society as a whole. Others rely on the gini coefficient and other statistics that provide a snapshot of the distribution of a country's income or wealth.

More and more of us argue that development cannot be measured solely in economic terms, because it is a multidimensional phenomenon, and development on one front does not necessarily mean a country is developed on all of them. Because this is a book about comparative *politics*, we will focus on the ways states enhance their capacity to reach policy goals—or fail to do so as the case may be. Similarly, environmentalists focus on sustainability. Feminists do the same for the status of women. In fact, analysts who use systems theory make the case that observers cannot privilege any single dimension and that real development requires addressing them all more or less simultaneously.

Is There a Single End Point?

Early development scholars naively assumed that societies progressed from undeveloped to developed status. Today, we realize that development does not happen in anything like a linear manner.

Most of us now realize that countries in the South will have to devise their own ways of sustaining growth, adding to their wealth, and improving their people's standard of living. Just about the only thing we know for sure is that not only will their "end product" be different from what we see in the industrialized democracies but they will have to follow their own trajectories for getting there, wherever "there" is.

There is also growing agreement that development does not always proceed in one direction. In other words, countries can also experience periods of decay on any of the dimensions mentioned above. To see that, you don't have to look any farther than Assad's Syria, where everything from economic conditions to the capacity of the government to reach any of its goals has deteriorated since the civil war started.

The Politics of Foreign Aid

Long before the most recent wave of decolonization after World War II, it was clear that the countries of the Global South would not be able to develop on their own.

Therefore, the leading industrial nations—which, of course, included the leading colonial powers—realized that they would have to help.

The same sort of naïve assumptions we saw regarding state building also existed for economic development. The hope was that a limited amount of money and material aid would lead to what analysts at the time called an economic "takeoff" that would propel these countries to become modern industrialized capitalist economies.

However, this occurred only in a tiny handful of them. There are many reasons why this was the case, a number of which have to do with the internal politics of the countries themselves. But the overarching reason was a function of the way the distribution of **foreign aid** evolved after the 1950s.

There are several kinds of foreign aid. Northern governments make some grants and loans directly to Southern governments. In recent years, international agencies and private corporations have become more involved, most notably in providing loans both for long-term investment and to help countries work their way out of the **debt trap**. In a sense, **multinational corporations** (MNCs) also offer a form of aid when they invest in the Third World and create jobs and other indirect economic benefits. Finally, the past few years have seen a growing role for nonprofit NGOs, some of which have been attempting to counter what they see as the negative impact of aid from these other sources.

Foreign aid as we know it today began in 1950 when the British government agreed to the Colombo Plan through which it pledged to provide developmental assistance to its former colonies in South and Southeast Asia. Soon, the United States (1951) and Japan (1954) signed on. Since then, most of the industrialized democracies have been providing some developmental assistance, which, at one point, they agreed should equal at least 0.7 percent of their GNP each year.

TABLE 11.3 Foreign Aid: The Major Donors, 2008, in Per Capita Terms

COUNTRY	OVERSEAS DIRECT ASSISTANCE (IN BILLIONS OF $US)	OVERSEAS DIRECT ASSISTANCE (% OF GNP)
Sweden	4.7	0.98
Luxembourg	0.4	0.92
Norway	4.0	0.88
Denmark	2.9	0.82
Netherlands	0.7	0.80
Ireland	1.3	0.58
Belgium	2.4	0.47
United Kingdom	11.5	0.43

However, few of the industrialized democracies come close to reaching that goal. As Table 11.5 shows, only five of the world's richest twenty-two countries reached that 0.7 percent goal in 2008, all of which are fairly small and can thus have only a limited impact (see Table 11.3).

The United States provides the most foreign aid in absolute terms. Its contributions have increased since the terrorist attacks of 2001, as have those of almost all of the Organization for Economic Co-operation and Development (OECD) member states. Nonetheless, the United States ranks last when it comes to the share of GNP it contributes.

Also the top six recipients of American aid in this decade—Egypt, Russia, Israel, Pakistan, Iraq, and Afghanistan—were chosen because of their strategic importance to Washington rather than their economic need. But it should be pointed out that all the major donors concentrate their aid on former colonies and other countries deemed critical to their national interest.

To be fair, Table 11.3 does not include sources of aid and investment that come from the private sector. Reliable statistics on that score are only available for the United States where corporations and NGOs provide at least twice the amount of aid funded directly by the government.

There are also serious criticisms of what the aid is used for. Much of it goes for large-scale industrial projects that cannot be readily maintained and operated using domestic resources. Similarly, little of the aid is used to help people in the recipient countries develop the skills and other resources that will help them achieve some degree of self-sustained development, thereby reducing the need for aid.

Recipient countries are expected to use the grants or loans to buy material or hire consultants from the donor country. Also a surprising amount of the aid is aimed not at civilian but at military development whose benefits for the economy as a whole are limited. Finally, once all financial transfers and other economic costs, such as agricultural subsidies in Northern countries, are taken into account, some calculations suggest that the rich countries indirectly make more from aid than the South, which is supposed to be the main beneficiary.

Obstacles to Development: Globalization

Development is not coming easily in the Global South for many reasons that have little or nothing to do with what happens politically inside of most of the countries we could have covered in Part 4. In other words, this book's subtitle matters more here than it did in either Part 2 or 3 because, on balance, global forces tend to be obstacles that get in the way of development more than they spur it along.

If nothing else, they limit a state's ability to maneuver. This is the case in large part for the reasons former

Tanzanian president Julius Nyerere pithily laid out in the sentence that begins this chapter. It may be an exaggeration to say that decisions made in Washington, D.C., are more important to Tanzanians than those made in their capital city. Tanzania *is* a sovereign country that passes its own laws, issues its own decrees, and reaches its own judicial decisions. However, what happens in places like Tanzania is largely determined elsewhere. Occasionally, that happens by force as the Western powers have been trying to do by supporting the insurgent forces in Syria. More often, global forces make themselves felt through more subtle and often unintended consequences of actions by power holders in our increasingly interdependent world.

If the World Had One Hundred People

The World Game was an educational organization that helped people understand what it means to live in an interdependent world. Its college version involved laying a massive map of the world on a gymnasium floor on which one hundred people make some basic decisions about allocating the world's natural and human resources. The basic characteristics of these one hundred people reflect current global demographic trends:

- Fifty-one are female
- Fifty-seven are Asians
- Fourteen are from the Western Hemisphere
- Seventy are non-white
- Thirty are Christian
- Seventy are illiterate
- Fifty suffer from malnutrition
- Eighty live in substandard housing
- Six own half the wealth
- One has a college education
- None owns a computer

Unfortunately, the World Game stopped updating its statistics in 1999. Therefore the data shown here are somewhat dated. For instance, as many as two people out of the one hundred would now have a computer. But the stark contrasts remain.

Whether they like it or not, almost all countries in the Global South are now being integrated into the world's economic and cultural systems. However, they are not being brought in as equals. These relationships are hard to document, and their impact varies from country to country and from time to time. Nonetheless, they cannot be ignored, however incomplete our understanding of them may be.

Global links antedate colonialism, but the legacy of imperial ones is the most important one for our purposes because of its role in shaping today's political arrangements in ways that go far beyond the way boundary lines were drawn. Colonial powers, for example, still have considerable economic leverage. In the 1970s and 1980s, left-wing social scientists popularized the idea of **dependency** to describe a situation in which the legal ties of colonialism gave way to informal mechanisms of economic control. Such ideas are far less popular in academic and political circles today than they were a generation ago. The shifting tides of political fashion, however, have not changed the reality of economic weakness in the South and economic strength in the North.

Multinational corporations (MNCs) headquartered in the North dominate the more modern sectors of the economy (see Table 11.4). Going back to colonial times, such companies have always repatriated the bulk of their profits back to their home countries. In recent years, they have tended to relocate operations that require the lowest-skilled labor and produce the most pollution to the South. To be sure, many of the people who work for these companies are better off than they would have been otherwise, and most MNCs do contribute to local economic growth. At the same time, however, these countries are increasingly at the mercy of institutions and events outside their borders. The largest of these companies are so big that they are wealthier than many Southern countries. And as the table also shows, they all have their headquarters in Western Europe, North America, Japan, China, and South Korea. MNCs are often criticized for exploiting the workers and other resources they use in the Third World. In recent years, however, many have adopted corporate responsibility policies that guarantee above-market wages, protect the local environment, and help build the local infrastructure.

Few southern countries are still able to control their own natural resources. That is not universally true as can

TABLE 11.4 The Leading Multinational Corporations by Country of Origin

COUNTRY	NUMBER OF MULTINATIONAL CORPORATIONS
United States	18
China	4
Japan	4
Germany	5
France	6
Great Britain	4
Italy	2
Switzerland	1
South Korea	3

Source: Adapted from "The Fortune Global Five Hundred: The World's Largest Corporations," *Fortune*, money.cnn.com/magazines/fortune/global500/2009/snapshots/10461.html. (Accessed June 2, 2009).

be seen in the obvious case of the OPEC cartel, which forced worldwide oil prices sharply upward in the 1970s and brought untold riches to its member nations. But OPEC is very much the exception to the rule. Economic as well as political power remains concentrated in the North.

From Import Substitution to Structural Adjustment

The ability of Southern governments to control their own destinies has also been constrained by a marked shift in global economic preferences. At first, most Southern governments (with the support of most development experts) followed policies known as **import substitution**, which made the state the primary driver of development. Since the 1980s and the general victory of capitalist approaches to economic management everywhere in the world, most Southern governments have *had* to adopt policies of **structural adjustment** that took power from the state and gave it to the private sector and market forces. The word "had" is italicized in the previous sentence because capitalists rarely have had to even threaten the use of physical force to convince Southern leaders to go along. However, many have had little choice but to follow the wishes of some combination of Northern governments, private corporations, and the **international financial institutions**, which they also dominate.

Import substitution was designed to do just what the two words suggest. If a country could replace expensive imported products with goods made locally, it would conserve much of its hard currency and other scarce resources, which could then be used to speed up development of its own industrial base.

It is easiest to see why such approaches were popular by first exploring **dependency theory**, which helps us understand why countries were eager to pursue what amounted to economic nationalism. Dependency theorists divide the world in two. On one side are the wealthy, capitalist nations of the North. On the other are the poor, underdeveloped countries that remain de facto colonies of the North, whatever their legal status. In other words, dependency theorists focus on the economic rather than the political implications of imperialism and stress how the regions that became the Third World were forced into the global capitalist system.

From this point of view, capitalists restructured local economies for the worse before independence. Instead of encouraging them to grow food or manufacture commodities for domestic consumption, the imperial powers forced the colonies to produce a few primary products for export: coffee and tea in Kenya, bananas in Guatemala, copper in Chile, and so on. In turn, the colonies, and then the new

nations, provided markets for the North's finished goods, which earned massive profits for the already-rich countries.

Dependency theorists do not deny that there has been considerable industrialization in the South in recent decades. Rather, they argue that such development has left them even more dependent on the North than ever. The latter's banks and governments provide aid, but they invariably attach strings to it.

The expansion of world trade in the 1970s and 1980s brought with it unprecedented levels of debt. At the height of the international **debt crisis** in the 1980s and 1990s, Argentina owed Northern banks and governments over $60 billion. For Brazil and Mexico, that figure was well over $100 billion. At the end of the 1990s, the Third World owed Northern banks, governments, and international financial institutions more than $2.8 trillion, or more than $400 per person. In the mid-1990s, countries as different as Brazil, Cameroon, Guatemala, India, Kenya, and Madagascar all paid more in interest on their loans than they spent on social services.

The most important events in this respect were the OPEC-induced "price shocks" of 1973 and 1979. Most countries in the Global South traditionally have to import not only oil but dozens of other products that are made using petroleum and its by-products. Also they have had to pay for these goods in dollars or other **hard currencies**. At best, this meant that they had to export more to earn that money, which, in turn, implied meeting global price and quality standards. At worst, they had to borrow even more from Northern banks, governments, and international organizations, which left many of them so deeply in debt that there seemed no way they could ever pay back even the interest on the loans, let alone the principal.

The debt crisis of the 1980s and 1990s took dozens of countries to the brink of default and beyond. As Table 11.5 suggests, the worst of the debt crisis has passed, but many in the Global South still chafe at the fact that Northern bankers kept them from determining how and if they should develop.

As dependency theorists see it, modern-day capitalism has left most Southern countries with narrowly based

TABLE 11.5 Debt as a Percentage of Gross National Product

REGION	1981	1991	1998	2011
Sub-Saharan Africa	29	108	72	49
South Asia	17	36	29	8
Middle East and North Africa	31	59	35	73
Latin America and Caribbean	36	41	69	16

Source: Data for 1981 and 1991 adapted from R. J. Barry Jones, *Globalization and Interdependence in the International Political Economy* (London: Pinter, 1995), 159. Data for 1998 from World Bank, *World Development Report*, 2001 and 2011, www.worldbank.org, accessed March 4, 2013.

economies that are highly vulnerable to the vagaries of the international market. The industrial development that has taken place benefits only a tiny proportion of the population and has often left everyone else worse off. Foreign investment is increasingly oriented toward industries the Northern countries no longer want because they degrade the environment or cost too much in salaries and benefits. Most important, decision-making power remains overwhelmingly in foreign hands.

Leaders who accepted all or part of this explanation adopted policies that sought to reduce dependency by strengthening their own economy—and their control over it. Most tried to develop a manufacturing base independent of the multinationals in such vital areas as steel, automobiles, clothing, and agricultural equipment. Among other things, they erected tariff and other barriers to trade that made it more difficult for foreign goods and businesses to penetrate their markets so that they could protect their own fledgling manufacturers from competition from cheaper and higher quality imports. Most set up publicly owned or controlled companies, often called **parastatals**, through which the government could steer the development of a domestic industrial base.

Of the countries covered in Part 4, India most consistently pursued import substitution. For the first thirty-five years after its independence in 1947, government after government made it hard for foreign companies to invest there and impossible for them to buy more than a minority share in an Indian corporation. Indian manufacturers, most of which were government owned or controlled, often were granted monopolies in key industrial arenas. The goods they made were rarely competitive in open markets, which meant that India could not export much and that its overall growth rate remained low.

Many countries stuck with import substitution well into the 1980s precisely because it left them with some control over the nature and pace of development. By then, however, three things happened that undermined support for it just about everywhere.

First, it had become clear that the countries using import substitution were growing far more slowly than those that had aggressively tried to build niches for themselves in global markets. In India, it was derisively known as the "Hindu rate of growth"—steady, but very slow.

Second, observers began paying attention to the spectacular growth in the **newly industrialized countries (NICs)**, a term that enjoyed widespread popularity before the advent of the BRICS. Indians, for instance, had to acknowledge that they were far worse off than the Taiwanese, who had been as poor as they were in the 1940s. In short, India may have charted its own development. The problem was that there was just too little of it.

Third, the global center of political gravity shifted dramatically in the 1980s. Everything from the elections of the likes of Ronald Reagan and Margaret Thatcher to the end of the cold war itself sapped import substitution and most other leftist approaches of their political support. They may still have made sense intellectually. However, it was no longer possible for Southern governments to build support for policies that did not mesh with what became known as the **Washington Consensus**.

As was the case in the countries we saw in Parts 2 and 3, almost all Northern governments, MNCs, and independent agencies have opted for liberal, market-oriented development strategies, which the Southern countries have "had" to adopt as well. The word *had* is in quotes because no one put a gun to the heads of leaders in the Global South. Nonetheless, as we will see in the country chapters that follow, they had little choice but to open their borders to foreign trade and investment, export goods for which there is a niche in the global market, and reduce public ownership and other forms of state intervention.

Supporters of structural adjustment assume that these countries will find areas of comparative advantage that spark sustained growth in the long run. In the shorter term, however, these trends are widening the gaps between the rich and poor within these countries and between themselves and the countries of the more affluent North.

There were economic as well as political reasons for the adoption of structural adjustment policies. The World Bank, for example, conducted studies that divided Southern countries according to the degree to which they were "outward" or trade oriented. Contrary to dependency theory's predictions, the countries that traded the most—that is, the countries that played by the rules of the capitalist economic game—grew the fastest. From 1973 to 1985, these countries grew by an average of 7.7 percent per year overall and 10 percent per year in manufacturing. By contrast, the least trade-oriented states grew by only 2.5 percent overall and 3.1 percent in manufacturing.

The evolution of South Korea is instructive. Prior to the Asian economic crisis in 1997, it grew at a rate that exceeded even Japan's and was one of the most trade-oriented countries in the world. At first, the growth was concentrated in low-quality, low-tech industries in ways that mirrored what the dependency theorists would lead us to expect. During the 1970s, however, the nature of that growth changed. Korean companies started making steel, automobiles, and electronic goods, including most first generation cell phones, and became major players in global markets.

There are many reasons why the South Korean economy boomed that had little to do with structural adjustment, including its then strong and often repressive state.

Comparative Emphasis: Globalization

Westerners often think of globalization in their own terms. For the optimists, it is bringing unprecedented riches, instant communication, and affordable global travel. For the pessimists, it is eroding working-class jobs and harming the environment.

When we shift our attention to the Global South, the picture looks less clear—from either the optimist's or the pessimist's perspective. Globalization is drawing more and more people into international networks, commercial and otherwise. However, there are still upward of a billion people whose lives are barely touched by global forces. Moreover, a case can be made that globalization is contributing to a growing gap between rich and poor and is reinforcing traditional values and religions, thereby sparking conflict that people in the Global South can ill afford. ■

Structural adjustment is, in fact, little more than another term for liberalization. Unlike the former communist countries, however, the emphasis in the Global South has not been primarily on privatizing publicly owned corporations. This has occurred in countries like Mexico, which had a large and inefficient state sector, but most banks and agencies have insisted that Southern governments get their countries' macroeconomic life in order in two other ways: reducing inflation and cutting the national debt.

The **International Monetary Fund (IMF)**, in particular, has insisted on **conditionality**, or the acceptance of structural adjustment and other "conditions," before authorizing a loan. Thus, far more than the World Bank, it has had the clout to successfully compel Southern countries to grudgingly adopt these policies, something we will see most clearly in Mexico and Nigeria.

Adopting structural adjustment would supposedly enable them to participate more effectively in the international economy. This may make good sense from the perspective of classical economics. Yet it is less clear whether these countries can use structural adjustment either to catch up with the North or to close the gap between their own rich and poor citizens' standards of living.

It has to be noted that few countries have adopted structural adjustment policies voluntarily. There are exceptions—for example, Chile under General Augusto Pinochet. For most countries, however, liberalization has been urged if not forced on them by Northern governments, banks, and agencies that made adopting structural adjustment a precondition for receiving aid and other forms of support.

Nonetheless, high on any list of explanations for its success has to be the way the state encouraged Korean companies to learn how to operate effectively in international markets.

© John G. Mabanglo/Afp/Getty Images

The first major protest against the World Trade Organization and globalization in Seattle. Dozens more have since been held.

Three international financial institutions are central to any discussion about development—the International Monetary Fund (IMF) (www.imf.org), the **World Bank** (www.worldbank.org), and the **World Trade Organization** (WTO) (www.wto.org). The three are often called the Bretton Woods organizations because the first steps toward creating them occurred at a 1944 meeting at that New Hampshire resort.

The three institutions were created to spur economic recovery in the war-torn countries of Europe and Asia. However, once Europe recovered and as more and more countries gained their independence, their focus turned to the Global South and, after 1989, the former communist world.

In recent years, these organizations have become more controversial than anyone could have imagined when they were created. Each of their major meetings since the protests against the WTO in Seattle in 1999 has been disrupted by demonstrators who accuse the international financial institutions of everything from destroying the environment to reinforcing poverty and sexism in the Third World and beyond.

The World Bank is the largest—and perhaps the least well understood—of the three. Today, it primarily makes loans and also issues a smaller number of direct grants to developing countries. Some of its funds come from member countries, but most now comes from the private financial markets. It is controlled through a system of weighted voting in which the countries that contribute the most funds (the richest ones) have by far the greatest influence.

In its early years, the World Bank supported industrial projects that were consistent with import substitution, but as it has moved increasingly into the private financial sector, it has also made more of its loans along commercial lines. This orientation is one of the reasons anti-globalization critics have attacked the Bank's policies. Those criticisms reached a peak when Paul Wolfowitz, a key right-wing Republican in the United States, served as its president from 2005 to 2007. However, its supporters point to changes in the World Bank's family of institutions, including the creation of units to promote the environment, postconflict reconstruction, environmental protection, and the reduction of poverty.

The IMF has always been more consistently in the structural adjustment camp. It was created at the same time as the World Bank, and the headquarters of the two organizations are located across the street from each other in Washington. The IMF was originally created to stabilize international monetary flows at a time when other currencies were fixed to the value of the American dollar, which, in turn, was pegged to an arbitrary price for the sale of an ounce of gold. In the early 1970s, this system collapsed because of problems facing troubled economies in the Global South and, later, the former Soviet bloc. It is governed in roughly the same way as the World Bank, though the rich countries have even more voting power in the IMF.

The WTO is the newest of the three organizations. Originally, the negotiators at Bretton Woods hoped to create a permanent institution that would work to reduce tariffs and otherwise open up international trade. For reasons we do not need to get into here, that organization was not created at the time. Instead, the far looser General Agreement on Tariffs and Trade (GATT) was formed in 1947. Its original agreement and subsequent "rounds" of negotiations gradually lowered tariffs and eased other

PROFILES   Bono

Aging rock stars rarely find a place in political science textbooks.

Bono is an exception.

Born Paul David Hewson, Bono has been U2's lead singer since he formed the band's predecessor as a teenager in 1975. In this decade, Bono has become the most visible champion for development aid in the Third World along with the academic, Jeffrey Sachs. Today, he is best known for his leadership of the One Campaign (named for one of U2's songs), whose home page reads, "where you were born should not dictate whether you live or die. ONE is a hard-headed network of people around the world fighting the absurdity of extreme poverty" (www.one.org). ∎

Bono at a meeting with politicians of the Social Democratic Party (SPD) in Berlin on May 14, 2007.

© 360b/Shutterstock.com

restrictions on trade around the world. Finally, the leaders of over 130 countries agreed to form the permanent WTO in 1994 and granted it powers to enforce rules that would further free trade and resolve commercial disputes among member states. In other words, the WTO, too, is a strong supporter of structural adjustment and related policies. With China's and Taiwan's accession to membership in 2001, all the world's major economies other than Russia are members.

Structural adjustment's supporters may tend to exaggerate its benefits and ignore its shortcomings, including the fact that it does little to help the plight of the poor. Nonetheless, they are correct in their basic assertion that the countries that have grown the fastest since the 1980s were those that, as the term itself suggests, adjusted their policies to the realities of global economic conditions.

Alternatives

Very few academic analysts and even fewer of my NGO colleagues are satisfied with the progress that has been made on almost any development issue since the last major wave of decolonization in the 1950s and 1960s. That argument holds whether you tend to prefer either import substitution or structural adjustment.

Two alternatives to the traditional approaches to development are beginning to get a lot of attention from practitioners working in the field if not from academics. Both accept the main premise of structural adjustment that solutions today have to involve private enterprise and market mechanisms. However, unlike typical Washington Consensus-based models, both pay more attention to equality of income and the other "big questions" that import substitution advocates have traditionally stressed.

Many rather conservative analysts are convinced that the success of the BRICS shows that the Washington Consensus is the best available route to development. A more dispassionate analysis of them suggests that the picture is far murkier for the simple reason that the four original BRIC countries have little in common other than their size and the fact that they all made decisions to make a clear break with their developmental path at about the same time that the cold war ended.

By the time the word became a household term (at least among development economists), the BRICS had achieved spectacular growth rates (see Table 11.6) on almost all economic indicators. All were poised to overtake some of the leading economies discussed in Part 2 and were clamoring for a greater role in the global political decision-making forums to be discussed in Chapter 16.

Each came up with its own way of finding a comparative advantage in an increasingly globalizing and

TABLE 11.6 BRIC Countries: Selected Indicators

INDICATOR	BRAZIL	RUSSIA	INDIA	CHINA
GDP per capita (2009 US$)	10,500	14,900	3,000	6,800
GDP Growth Rate (1990–2009, in percent)	2.5	0.3	6.3	10.1
Global Rank: GDP Per Capita Growth Rate	15	88	5	6
Percent Change in HDI Score (2000–2010)	7.6	3.8	33.3	44.2

Note: HDI is the UN's Human Development Index.
Source: Adapted from www.globalsherpa.org. Accessed March 8, 2013.

capitalist economy, in keeping with the ideas underlying the Washington Consensus—petroleum production in Russia, manufacturing and construction in China, technology enterprises in India, and agricultural and industrial exports in Brazil. But, unlike what the pro-market supporters of the Washington Consensus would lead us to believe, the state played a major role in sparking that development in ways we have already seen in Russia and China and will see later for India. Just as importantly, we will also see how the relative weakness of the state in Nigeria and Mexico has kept those two countries from meeting BRIC-like standards.

Furthermore, the two Southern BRIC countries (if not Russia and China) have actively sought to combine a more equal distribution of income with rapid economic growth. In fact, the most influential recent book on historical patterns of economic development stresses the importance of political inclusion, which seems to require the acquiescence of potentially disaffected portions of the population.[6]

Even the inventor of the BRIC term has expressed doubts about whether these four or five countries (see the box on the next page) are a model others can follow. As James O'Neill sees it, the BRIC countries have grown this fast in part because they are large enough to influence both global markets and international political relations. A few countries such as Mexico, Nigeria, and Indonesia might be able to follow their lead, but few others are big and powerful enough to do so.

The other popular alternative is **microcredit**. The first and best-known microcredit lender is Bangladesh's Grameen Bank, which was founded in 1976 by Muhammad Yunus, an economics professor at Chittagong University (www.grameen-info.org). Unlike most Western experts, Yunus was convinced that average Bangladeshi peasants could use banking services to create businesses

---

[6]Daron Acemoglu and James Robinson, *Why Nations Fail: The Origins of Power, Prosperity, and Poverty* (New York: Crown Business, 2012).

A new office complex in Bangalore, India, which has become a center for high-tech development.

Comparative Emphasis: BRIC/BRICS

The use of the terms BRIC and BRICS can be confusing. The original acronym (without the S) was coined by James O'Neill, who is an investment banker in the London office of Goldman Sachs. He pointedly left out South Africa because it did not have a big enough economy and was not growing fast enough to meet his criteria.

However, when the BRIC countries themselves decided to organize in order to have more leverage in all international decision-making bodies, they invited South Africa to join, hence the addition of the "S." ■

that they could run and profit from themselves. The success of the Grameen Bank and projects based on it around the world was honored when Yunus was awarded the Nobel Peace Prize in 2006 (nobelprize.org/nobel_prizes/peace/laureates/2006/).

Grameen and other microcredit funders only lend money to destitute people. Their goal is to give them a chance to start their own businesses so that they can develop skills that would allow them to permanently pull themselves and their families out of poverty. Ninety-four percent of Grameen's loans are given to women on the assumption that they are less likely to fritter the money away, for instance, by gambling or drinking.

The Grameen Bank's principles are simple. As Yunus put it just as he was beginning to gain recognition fifteen years ago:

> Their [the peasants'] poverty was not a personal problem due to laziness or lack of intelligence, but a structural one: lack of capital. We do not need to teach them how to survive: they know this already. Giving the poor credit allows them to put into practice the skills they already know. And the cash they earn is then a tool, a key that unlocks a host of other problems.[7]

By mid-2008, Grameen had made seven and a half million loans to people living in more than two-thirds of Bangladesh's villages. The bank does not provide formal business training, but it does expect its borrowers to abide by "sixteen decisions," including a pledge to send their children to school and not to pay dowries when their daughters marry. To obtain a loan, a borrower

[7]Quoted in Alan Jolis, "The Good Banker," *Independent on Sunday Magazine.* May 5, 1996, 15–16.

has to join a group of fellow borrowers who provide support, but also, if necessary, apply pressure to repay the loan. Loans are for a year and may be renewed and extended for up to five years. Repayments are made at weekly meetings in which eight to ten members of the loan groups gather.

In one typical case, a villager could not afford to feed her three children and her blind, unemployed husband. After overcoming her husband's objections, she used her loan to buy a calf. Within a year, she used money from the sale of the cow to pay off the loan and then took out a second one with which she bought another calf and land for banana plants. Within five years, her farm had grown to include a rice paddy, goats, ducks, and chickens. Her family ate three meals a day, and she could afford to send her children to high school. As she put it, "You ask me what I think of Grameen? Grameen is like my mother. She has given me new life."

This is not an isolated example. A World Bank study found that over 95 percent of Grameen loans were repaid on time. Even more impressively, within five years, half of the borrowers had pulled themselves up above the poverty line, and another quarter were close to it. The Grameen Bank's operations have expanded, and it now gives three-hundred-dollar home mortgages to families who have taken out and repaid at least three loans. It also has begun giving its village leaders cell phones, which serve as the only local pay phones. Also, in 1999, the bank became Bangladesh's leading Internet service provider—on the profits from its cell phone business.

**Muhammad Yunus
with a typical group of
Grameen Bank clients.**

Most countries, including the United States, now have some type of microcredit project. In 2006, over two thousand people from 110 countries met in Washington for the second Microcredit summit (www.microcreditsummit. org). At the first summit five years earlier, then American Senator Hillary Clinton and World Bank president James Wolfensohn shared the stage with women from around the world who had taken major strides to improve their living conditions through microcredit programs. By the end of 2011, the growing number of microcredit programs had reached more than two hundred million of the world's poorest people.

Microcredit is not the only innovative program that is seeking ways to blend the benefits of the market with the hope of raising at least a billion people out of poverty permanently. For instance, the late C. K. Prahalad wrote about and later helped fund projects that would entice major multinational companies to develop products that would not only sell to and empower what he calls the "bottom of the pyramid" but make money for those companies as well. A visit to the website set up in his memory and to continue his mission will also show you what a program based on MNCs' desire for profit can accomplish (www.bus.umich.edu/prahalad/).

Democratization?

A generation ago, an introductory chapter on the Global South would have ended with a recap of its economic or environmental woes. It would have been even more depressing than this one. Today, those problems remain,

and most of them are as serious as they ever have been. Nevertheless, we can end this chapter on a slightly more upbeat note.

For the past decade or so, the most exciting trend in the South has been democratization. In 1990, all the Latin American countries south of Mexico had a democratically elected government—the first time this had ever happened—and most have kept those regimes. At the end of the decade, the Nigerian military turned control of the country over to a fourth republic, and a few other African governments are experimenting with competitive elections. This is the first time the momentum has swung in that direction since the early 1960s. A number of the previously authoritarian regimes in East Asia have taken substantial, though still incomplete, steps toward democracy, including the Philippines. Some argue that South Korea has made enough progress on all fronts to be included in Part 2.

Democracy may well be taking root in places that were as far from it as one could imagine a decade or so ago. South Africa, in particular, has made remarkable strides in moving from apartheid to majority rule. Most remarkably, the key leaders of the old Afrikaner regime made their peace (albeit reluctantly) with the African National Congress and served in the government of former president Nelson Mandela for two years before quitting in May 1996. The fledgling South African democracy also made great strides with its Truth and Reconciliation Commission that began the process of healing the wounds of the apartheid era.

For over a decade, political scientists have been focusing more of their attention on why some democracies survive and thrive while others do not. Although they are far from reaching anything like definitive conclusions, they have come to six preliminary ones that offer some reason for hope.

First, much will depend on the attitudes and behavior of average citizens, many of whom are less than forgiving toward dictatorial regimes that have done little or nothing to improve basic standards of living. The experience of South Africa today and India over most of the past sixty years suggests that people may come to support a regime and temper their own demands, not out of a general commitment to democracy but because they are convinced that it is working. In other words, short-term pragmatic accomplishments, which states may actually be able to achieve can be as important in building democracy as the forging of the more difficult-to-reach sense of commitment to the abstract principles and procedures underlying it.

Second, for this kind of "pragmatic support" to build, the state has to be reasonably effective. One of the misreadings of contemporary and historical trends that has accompanied the rightward shift in recent years has been the assumption that if the state merely "gets out of people's lives" then things will improve. The historical record reviewed in Part 2 reveals something quite different. Democratic regimes succeeded in part because their states were capable of making tough decisions about the allocation of resources, the shape of institutions, and the handling of disorder.

Third, timing is important. The first years of any regime are critical because it is new and fragile. Therefore, it seems to be the case that if a democracy can get through the first few elections and, as we saw with France's Fifth Republic, if it can survive the transition from its first leadership to the opposition, it is usually much stronger and more likely to endure.

Fourth, there is a link between democracy and capitalism. However, it certainly is not as simple or as automatic as the advocates of structural adjustment would lead us to believe. Markets are not natural phenomena but have to be created and sustained, reinforcing the importance of a reasonably strong state. Also, the purported benefits of markets do not come quickly—if they come at all—whereas, as the history of all democratic regimes suggests, people tend to be impatient and to expect dramatic improvements in the short run. There is also evidence that democracy may have a good chance of succeeding only after societies have reached a certain level of wealth. The most recent research has put that figure at a per capita income of about five thousand dollars per year, which is well above what most developing countries can dream of.

Fifth, for all the reasons discussed previous[?]tional factors will become more and more importan[t] [as] the world continues to "shrink" (see Chapter 16). There is growing awareness that Northern policy toward the South should be made with more long-term goals regarding development and democracy in mind, which might mean sacrificing some shorter-term profits or market share. However, there are stronger signs that the shift toward market-based policies will continue, which might actually worsen conditions for most people in the politically all-important short run.

Finally, we should definitely *not* expect the democracies that might emerge in the Third World to resemble those in the West. As we saw in Part 2, the Western democracies developed as a result of a long historical process that cannot be reproduced because conditions are so dramatically different today. Indeed, it may well be that democracy in the Third World will not be much like what we saw in Part 2 at all.

At this point, the best way to think about these hypotheses is to consider Iraq and Afghanistan. One of the reasons (but by no means the only one) the United States and some of its allies went to war with both countries was to create democracies. For good or ill that has not happened, in large part because of problems associated with these six conclusions.

The Media

The media, too, are different in the poorest parts of the world in ways that reflect many of the broader themes of this chapter.

Because of poverty, relatively few people have had access to television, which is now the primary source of political information in the rest of the world. Indeed, in 1985, when an American peace group wanted to do a global televised presentation of its annual award, it encountered what seemed to be an insurmountable obstacle. Tanzania, where one of the recipients lived, had no television at all. But it is not just television. Whereas two out of three Americans have access to the Internet at home, that figure is more like one in three hundred in the South.

Many Third World countries also do not have a free press available to their citizens who can read or afford to buy a newspaper or magazine. The authoritarian regimes, in particular, are quite effective when it comes to censoring the news.

There are, however, a number of changes afoot. In the 1990s, a major breakthrough occurred for the world's poorest people who do not have electricity when a British inventor developed an affordable radio that uses a hand crank to generate its own power. They have become so popular that National Public Radio sells them to its American listeners who can use them when their power goes out (shop.npr.org). In the first decade of this century, Michael Negroponte, founder of the innovative Media Lab at MIT, committed himself to developing a laptop that would have wireless Internet access and have a hand crank and other tools for people who do not have electricity—all for one hundred dollars or less (www.laptop.org). People in the North who want one for themselves have to buy two, one of which will be donated somewhere in the Global South.

Last but by no means least, the mass media have often been used to foment ethnic conflict, most notably in the lead-up to the 1994 genocide in Rwanda. Some NGOs like Search for Common Ground (www.sfcg.org) have tried to counter those trends by producing radio programs that document interethnic healing in deeply divided societies, including some that helped ease tensions in Sierra Leone.

KEY TERMS

Concepts

carrying capacity

civil society

color revolutions

conditionality

debt crisis

debt trap

dependency

dependency theory

failed state

foreign aid

fundamentalism

Global South

globalization

hard currencies

Hybrid regime

identity politics

imperialism

import substitution

indirect rule

international financial institutions

microcredit

multinational corporations (MNCs)

newly industrialized countries (NICs)

nongovernmental organizations (NGOs)

parastatal

patron-client relations

structural adjustment

subsistence economies

Third World

underdevelopment

Washington Consensus

Acronym

BRIC

HDI

IF

IMF

MNCs

NGOs

NICs

OPEC

WTO

Organizations, Places, and Events

Arab Spring

International Monetary Fund (IMF)

Organization of Petroleum Exporting Countries (OPEC)

World Bank

World Trade Organization (WTO)

USEFUL WEBSITES

There are not many websites on the Third World, per se. There are, however, many good ones that touch on much of what is covered in this chapter. The best of these is the new site on globalization created by the Center for Strategic and International Studies in Washington.

> **www.globalization101.org**

The Virtual Library also has good sites on sustainable development and on microcredit.

> **www.ulb.ac.be/ceese/meta/sustvl.html**

> **www.gdrc.org/icm/**

The Center for World Indigenous Studies focuses on the status of ethnic minorities in the Third World. The Third World Network is a good left-of-center source for news and analysis on development issues.

> **www.cwis.org**

> **www.twnside.org.sg**

Many international organizations and NGOs issue regular reports filled with analysis and data, including the World Bank, the United Nations Development Program, and the World Resources Institute.

econ.worldbank.org/wdr/

www.undp.org

www.wri.org

FURTHER READING

Acemoglu, Daron, and James Robinson. *Why Nations Fail: The Origins of Power, Prosperity, and Poverty.* New York: Crown Business, 2012. The best recent book on historical trends that makes the case for an inclusive approach to development that does not leave any major social group out.

Beah, Ishmael. *A Long Way Gone.* New York: Susan Crichton Books/Farrar Strauss Giroux, 2007. The best book on child soldiers and maybe the best book to start with in thinking about the less developed world.

Collier, Paul. *The Bottom Billion.* New York: Oxford University Press, 2008. A great overview of problems facing the Third World.

Diamond, Larry. *The Spirit of Democracy.* New York: St. Martin's, 2009. A masterful overview of democratization everywhere, especially in the Global South.

Friedman, Thomas. *Hot, Flat, and Crowded.* New York: Farrar, Strauss, Giroux, 2008. The most recent book by the prolific columnist and author. This one does the most with the downside of globalization in the Global South.

Ghani, Ashraf, and Clare Lockhart. *Fixing Failed States.* New York: Oxford University Press, 2008. The best book on governance in the Global South.

Griswold, Eliza. *The Tenth Parallel: Dispatches from the Fault Line Between Christianity and Islam.* New York: Farrar, Straus Giroux, 2010. A remarkable account of identity politics from Nigeria to the Philippines.

Huntington, Samuel P. *The Clash of Civilizations: Remaking the World Order.* New York: Simon & Schuster, 1996. A highly controversial book, by one of the most respected (and conservative) analysts of the Third World, that focuses essentially on cultural arguments in anticipating the next round of global conflict, domestically and internationally.

Kristof, Nicholas, and Sheryl WuDunn. *Half the Sky: Turning Oppression into Opportunity for Women Worldwide.* New York: Knopf, 2009. By far the best general book on the status of women in the Global South.

Morris, Ian. *Why the West Leads—for Now.* New York: Picador, 2010. Morris has an even longer historical perspective on development than Acemoglu and Robinson because he goes back to the birth of civilization. If you tackle this book, be sure to read the often funny footnotes.

Mohsin, Hamid. *How to Get Filthy Rich in Rising Asia*: *A Novel.* New York: Penguin, 2013. Written in the form of a self-help book, this deceptively funny novel explores almost all the themes—especially the pitfalls—that come with development in the Global South.

O'Neill, Jim. *The Growth Map: Economic Opportunities in the BRICS and Beyond.* New York: Penguin/Portfolio, 2011. The best book on the BRICS, by the inventor of the term.

Prahalad, C. K. *The Fortune at the Bottom of the Pyramid.* Philadelphia: Wharton School Press, 2006. Not an easy read, but the best book on the role of the private sector in fighting poverty.

Sachs, Jeffrey. *The End of Poverty.* New York: Penguin, 2005. Perhaps not the best book on new plans to end poverty in the Global South, but most readable by far. Foreword by Bono.

World Bank. *World Development Report.* Published annually, the best single source of statistics on development issues as well as a topic considered in depth each year.

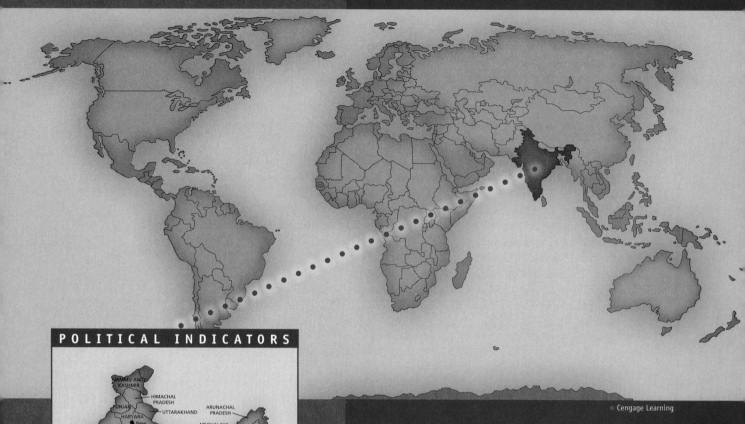

© Cengage Learning

POLITICAL INDICATORS

INDIA

GOVERNANCE (score 0-1)	HUMAN DEVELOPMENT (score 0-1)	DEMOCRACY (rank)	PEACE (rank)	CORRUPTION (rank)
.543	.547	39	142	95

India

As Indian citizens, we subsist on a regular diet of caste massacres and nuclear tests, mosque breakings and fashion shows, church bombings and expanded cell phone networks, bonded labour and the digital revolution, female infanticide and the NASDAQ revolt, husbands who continue to burn their wives for dowry, and our delectable stockpile of Miss Worlds. . . . What's hard to reconcile oneself to, both personally and politically, is the schizophrenic nature of it.

ARUNDHATI ROY

THE BASICS

India

Size	3,287,590 sq. km (About one-third the size of the United States)
Population	1.2 billion
GNP per capita	$3,900
Growth rate	5.4%
Currency	53 rupees = US$1
Ethnic groups	72% Indo-Aryan, 25% Dravidian, 3% other
Religion	81% Hindu, 12% Muslim, 2% Christian, 2% Sikh, 2% other
Capital	New Delhi
Head of State	President Pranab Mukerjee (2012–)
Head of Government	Prime Minister Manmohan Singh (2004–)

A Tale of Two Neighborhoods

As Arundhati Roy suggests in the statement on the previous page, India is a land of contrasts, many of which will preoccupy us, including what she calls its schizophrenic nature. To see that, consider just one of those contrasts as seen through the lens of two typical neighborhoods, both of which tell us a lot about the new, contrast-laden India.

The first is Annawadi, a shanty town next to the airport in Mumbai (Bombay). Like Badia East, which we saw in Chapter 11, it was slated for destruction, in this case to make way for the expansion of the airport and its satellite services. Like Badia East, it was not a place many people reading this book would want to live. Also like Badia East, no one lived in Annawadi legally; even though the town had been there since 1991, all the land technically belonged to the Mumbai Airports Authority.

The residents of Annawadi were not considered poor by official Indian standards. Yet, only six of its three thousand residents had a job that paid a salary. As is the case with 85 percent of the Indian workforce, the rest worked, but as part of the country's informal economy in which people survive through casual labor or jobs for which barter is as common as an hourly wage.

Houses were shacks that people jerry built as material became available. None had indoor plumbing. The few that had electricity stole power from the municipal grid. The village was built next to a lake into which the airport workers throw their garbage, which made dangerous levels of air and water pollution a fact of daily life for the people

INDRANIL MUKHERJEE/AFP/Getty Images

Children playing in Annawadi.

of Annawadi. Most of its residents are an injury or an illness away from utter financial ruin.

To the degree that Annawadi had a leader, it was a woman with close ties to the local neo-racist movement, Shiv Sena, but she was little more than a cog in a political machine that added a heavy dose of corruption to the community's woes. She and her superiors all expected to be paid for the services they rendered, which included helping people deal with the police and the courts any time they had a brush with the law. Bribes were also needed to receive decent medical care or an education that just might lead to a chance for upward social mobility.

Most residents are like the young man who is the "protagonist" of Katherine Boo's recent book on Annawadi, who gathers and sells recyclable trash that could not be reused anywhere in the West. When times were good, he might get 25 rupees ($.50) for a kilogram of used water bottles; after the recession hit in 2008, his income was cut to 10 rupees.

Many female babies were killed at birth because their mothers neither wanted to raise a girl nor had the money to pay for a sonogram that would have led them to have an abortion. Other women entered the sex trade because they were convinced it was the only way they could conceivably get ahead.

About half of the nearly 20 million people in greater Mumbai live in communities like Annawadi. Like so many other slum dwellers throughout India, the village residents "knew" that there was no solution to their problems. As Boo puts it:

> But the slum dwellers rarely got mad together—not even about the airport authority. Instead, powerless individuals blamed other powerless individuals for what they lacked. Sometimes they tried to destroy one another.[1]

Now, consider a prestigious neighborhood in the capital, New Delhi, recently featured in the *New York Times*:

> There is no tennis court, no infinity pool, no Sub-Zero refrigerator or walk-in closet. The paint is chipped, the bathrooms are musty and the ceilings have water stains. The house may ultimately be torn down. Yet when it went up for public auction, the winning bid was almost $29 million. Poor people didn't unite; they competed ferociously amongst themselves for gains as slender as they were provisional.[2]

The house in question is in an unusual neighborhood. Lutyen's Bungalow Zone is located next to the main complex of buildings that houses the national government, which makes it a neighborhood where upwardly mobile people want to live. Most of its homes date from the colonial era, and there are strict limits on construction in the area.

In that sense, the neighborhood is unusual, but the demand for luxury goods by India's nouveaux riches is not. Sales topped $8 billion in 2012 and were expected to double within the following three years. The market is small but growing. About 150,000 Indians now make a total of

---

[1]Katherine Boo, *Behind the Beautiful Forevers: Life, Death, and Hope in a Mumbai Undercity* (New York: Random House, 2012), Kindle edition, pp. 236–7.
[2]Jim Yardley, "Think New York Is Costly? In New Delhi, Seedy Goes for 8 Figures." *New York Times*. March 2, 2013, A4.

$600 billion a year, and many of them are giving the term "conspicuous consumption" new meaning. They spend heavily for weddings and other festive occasions. Much of what they buy is locally made, including the pounds of gold jewelry worn by many brides. Much of it is imported, including goods by such companies as Dior, Gucci, and Armani. The one hundred richest Indian families accounted for almost a quarter of the country's gross national product.

Two years earlier, the same reporter wrote a story about Gurgaon, which is about fifteen miles from New Delhi. The city barely existed thirty years ago. Now it has well over a million people and twenty-six lavish shopping malls. But not all is well in Gurgaon. It has no sewer system, reliable electrical service, sidewalks, decent roads, adequate parking, or public transportation system, all of which are services normally provided by the state. In the boom cities of today's India, that public sector is just not up to speed.

Two obvious questions emerge from these brief accounts. First, which of the two authors is right? The answer to that question is simple. They both are. What looks like two very different narrative snapshots reflect that, at one and the same time, India is one of the most advanced *and* one of the poorest countries on earth.

Second, what does any of this have to do with comparative politics, especially as we have seen it in the first eleven chapters? This question frankly is harder to answer. On one level, the costs and benefits of development reflect nonpolitical dynamics. But, as we will see, everything from India's enduring poverty to its new-found technological boom have profound—if sometimes indirect—political causes, some of whose roots lie in Indian history centuries before it gained its independence in 1947.

Thinking About India

Unlike Parts 2 and 3, there is no obvious country to start Part 4 with.

I chose India for many reasons. It was one of the first to gain independence. If you don't include China in the Global South, it is by far the largest and most influential. If you think democratization is an important criterion for the success of any state, India is at the top of any list of Southern countries.

Most importantly of all, although no single country can exemplify all of the issues raised in Chapter 11, India probably comes the closest. Why is India still so poor? But, at the same time, why is it also a BRIC? Why does it matter that some of the children Boo lived with are Muslim and some are Hindu? Why is the pace of social and economic change disrupting the way Indians live their lives—rich and poor, Hindu and Muslim, urban and rural alike?

The Bottom Line

As the statement by Arundhati Roy that begins this chapter suggests, India is a country of contrasts, if not contradictions. It is one of the most diverse countries in the world, however one chooses to define diverse. It is also changing as fast or faster than all but a handful of much smaller countries.

Enduring Poverty and New Wealth

Depending on how you count, India is one of the most backward or one of the most promising countries on earth. Despite the real estate boom and the size of the luxury goods market, Boo tells us more about the way most Indians live in a country where poverty is such a fact of life that we will devote much of the public policy section to it. As Table 1.2 shows, India's average per capita GNP is a bit more than $3,000 per year, making it the second poorest country covered in this book. Using the World Bank's measure—earning less than $1.25 per day—almost half a billion Indians live in absolute poverty.

Fifty Indian babies out of one hundred die before reaching the age of five, and overall life expectancy is just over sixty years. For most people, health care is rudimentary at best. Although the "green revolution" of the 1960s all but eliminated mass starvation, most Indians eat a diet that does not quite meet the minimal caloric intake people need to lead a healthy life. As a result, little things can matter. In 1998, a doubling in the price of onions took millions of people to the brink of starvation and cost the then ruling BJP control of three states.

At the same time, India is properly touted as one of the Global South's success stories. Almost no one doubts India should be included as one of the BRICS, along with Brazil, Russia, South Africa, and China. It is the world's tenth-largest industrial power. Only the United States and Russia have more scientists and engineers. Even though 60 percent of Indians are illiterate, rural India is connected by a network of satellite stations that have brought television to more than 80 percent of its seven hundred thousand villages.

The middle class of about one hundred million people can afford to buy televisions, refrigerators, and one of the small, locally manufactured, no-frills automobiles. Few Indians can afford a Mercedes or a Lexus. However, many are able to purchase a Tata Nano or one of the other two four-passenger cars that typically come without air conditioning or a radio but sell for the equivalent of $2,500.

There has been a lot of progress beyond the middle class. For example, Hindustan Unilever sells soap, toothpaste, and other personal care products in small quantities that poor people can actually afford. Shampoo, for instance, is sold in a small bottle that has just enough to wash a single person's hair once. In 2012, its products reached one hundred thousand villages and one hundred million customers.

Diversity

Unlike China, India is one of the most diverse countries in the world. Today, those social divisions are perhaps best seen in the gaping inequalities discussed above.

However, most analysts argue that differences over religion, ethnicity, language, region, and **caste** have had a greater impact on Indian politics. At one point or another, each has been a "hot button" issue in Indian politics. Indeed, the fact that all five of them overlap somewhat, but by no means completely, makes identity politics a critical ingredient in the country's often tumultuous political life.

Caste and Class. Traditionally, the most important source of division in India has also been its most distinctive— caste. Historians trace the caste system back nearly four thousand years, when in all likelihood the lighter-skinned Aryans established it to minimize "mingling" with the darker-skinned Dravidians.

The system is incredibly complicated. In the simplest terms, there are four main castes plus a fifth group originally known as outcastes because they were literally outside of the caste system. The Brahmins historically were the priests and the most prestigious caste, the Kshatriyas were rulers and soldiers, and the Vaisyas were merchants. These three upper castes are often referred to as "twice born," reflecting the belief that they are farther along in the Hindu cycle of death and reincarnation. The lowest caste Sudras traditionally were farmers but did "respectable" enough work to warrant their inclusion in the caste system. Below them are the **untouchables**, or *dalits*, who are outside the caste system altogether because their ancestors had "unclean" jobs such as scavengers and collectors of "night soil." Another 20 percent of the population is outside the caste system altogether either because they are Muslims or members of other minority groups that were not a part of this unusual way of segmenting society.

Each caste, in turn, is broken into hundreds of subcastes or *jati*. Each jati has elaborate rules for most social situations, including the clothes people should wear and what food they could eat. Until very recently, people rarely broke out of those restrictions.

The constitution officially abolished the status of "outcaste" and outlawed discrimination against untouchables and other ethnic groups who were never part of the caste system, many of whom are still pejoratively referred to as "tribals."

In practice, caste remains a volatile political issue. Discrimination against those at the bottom of the hierarchy is still as pervasive as racism is in the United States or western Europe. In the summer of 1990, for instance, Prime Minister V. P. Singh proposed reserving about a quarter of all new positions in the civil service for members of the lower or "scheduled" castes in an Indian version of American affirmative action. The proposal so incensed upper-caste young people that some burned themselves alive in protest.

Caste is not as important as it used to be. For generations, upper- and middle-caste Indians had arranged marriages. In the past, parents of the potential bride and groom would meet and agree to the wedding before the couple themselves met. Now, it is common for couples to marry across caste lines. Prospective brides put videos of their cooking or sewing skills on services like "Star Wedding," which its owners call the wedding version of YouTube. Many poorer women insist that their husbands-to-be guarantee that the new family will have a toilet before they agree to wed. Caste is certainly more important than social class, because it makes it hard to organize trade unions and other organizations that appeal to people along such lines.

Religion. India also has three main religious groups. Slightly over 80 percent of the population is Hindu, but each major regional/linguistic group practices Hinduism in its own distinctive way.

About 12 percent of the population is Muslim. Muslims are thus a minority in India, but there are more of them than in any country other than Indonesia and Pakistan. India's Muslims run the full range of belief from fundamentalists to highly assimilated and secularized people who, for all intents and purposes, no longer practice their religion.

Most of the rest are Sikhs. Their religion has roots in an attempt to blend Hindu and Muslim traditions, emphasizing peacefulness and other-worldliness, but Sikhs are now known for their ferocious fighting ability.

Religion has been politically divisive at least since the Muslims first arrived a thousand years ago. Independent India came into existence amid communal violence when millions of Muslims tried to escape India for Pakistan and a similar number of Hindus fled in the other direction. In the 1980s, the most difficult problem involved Sikhs, who sought their own homeland and who saw the national government attack their holiest shrine, the Golden Temple at Amritsar, and kill thousands of believers.

Since then, the most publicized instances of religious conflict have been about the status of the temple/mosque site at **Ayodhya**, which we will examine in more detail later. Here, it is enough to note that the attempt by Hindus to build a new temple there has led to periodic riots in which thousands of Hindus and Muslims have been killed over the last twenty years.

India's second largest political party, the **Bharatiya Janata Party (BJP)**, appeals for votes on the basis of traditional—some would say fundamentalist—Hindu values.

Language. When the Constituent Assembly met to draft the constitution in 1947, one delegate said, "I wonder why Indians do not speak in their own language."[3] The problem is he was speaking Hindustani, which is only one of India's many languages and is itself a combination of Hindi and Urdu. In the end, the assembly ducked language questions as much as possible.

Hindi is as close as the country comes to having an official language. However, all business is also conducted in English because the colonial language is the lingua franca as it is in so much of the Global South.

Nearly 60 percent of the population speaks one of the Indo-Aryan languages used mostly in northern India, of which Hindi is the most common. The 30 percent of the people who live in the south mostly speak one of the Dravidian languages which have nothing in common with Hindi and its variants. About 5 percent of the people (mostly Sikhs) speak Punjabi, an offspring of Farsi and Urdu, the dominant languages of Iran and Pakistan, respectively.

In reality, the situation is far more complicated than Table 12.1 suggests, and as many as one hundred million people speak languages that do not figure on the list because each linguistic family subsumes hundreds of dialects.

The government has drawn the twenty-eight state and seven union territory boundaries so that each has a dominant language and culture. Nonetheless, they all have large minorities that have played a significant and often violent role in political life. Identity issues overlap with state and other regional divisions to such a degree that state and local ones often matter the most in determining winners and losers in national elections.

Democracy, Political Stability, and Change

If India's economic balance sheet is mixed, that is not the case for its political system. As we will see in the rest of this chapter, India is one of the very few Southern countries to have enjoyed political stability throughout most of its history in which it has been able to sustain a reasonably smoothly functioning democratic regime.

As we will see, India was able to win its independence through the efforts of a comparatively large and unified anticolonial movement that was strongly committed to creating a democratic regime. The new regime used the momentum of its mostly nonviolent overthrow of British colonial rule to

TABLE 12.1 India's Principal Language Groups

LANGUAGE	NUMBER OF SPEAKERS IN MILLIONS	WHERE SPEAKERS ARE CONCENTRATED
Assamese	15	Assam
Bengali	67	West Bengal
Gujarati	43	Gujarat, Bengal
Hindi	422	Bihar, Haryana, Himachal Pradesh, Rajasthan, Uttar Pradesh, Delhi
Kannada	35	Karnataka
Kashmiri	10	Jammu and Kashmir
Malayalam	34	Kerala
Marathi	65	Maharashtra
Oriya	30	Orissa
Punjabi	26	Punjab
Tamil	66	Tamil Nadu
Telegu	77	Andhra Pradesh
Urdu	46	Most Hindi-speaking regions
Other	117	--

Source: Adapted from www.webindia123.com (accessed March 10, 2013).

establish a democracy that was able to overcome its massive problems and achieve enough of its goals to survive, overcome difficulties at home and abroad, and then radically reorient its economic policies during the final years of the last century and the first decade of this one.

In other words, if the countries in the "candidates" column of established democracies at the beginning of Chapter 2 listed them in rank rather than alphabetical order, India would have been at or near the top. If our frame of reference, instead, were the emerging democracies in the former communist world, India would outperform all of them on almost every indicator political scientists use to measure the stability and accomplishments of a democracy.

Key Questions

Most of the rest of Part 4 will be an examination of troubled and even failing states. That is not the case for India. Therefore, our attention in this chapter has to be on questions that allow us to see why India has been so different from—and in many ways also more successful than—most countries in the Global South.

- How and why has democracy endured in India but not in most other Southern countries?

- Why is ethnicity based on religion, language, caste, and the like so important in India without seriously putting its democracy in jeopardy?

[3]Cited in Ramachandra Guha, *India After Gandhi: The History of the World's Largest Democracy.* (New York: Harper, 2008), Kindle edition, location 2744.

- Why has India—like most Southern countries—had trouble stimulating and sustaining rapid economic growth?

- Along those same lines, to what degree are domestic and international political forces responsible for India's surprising "membership" in the ranks of the BRICS?

The Evolution of the Indian State

Even though most Southern countries have not been independent for long, the impact of history is, if anything, more extensive than it is in countries with a longer history as sovereign states for one simple reason. Colonialism, which did not figure prominently in Parts 2 and 3, looms over everything.

In exploring that history in India, we could easily go back more than two thousand years. As early as 1500 BC, Aryans from the north began developing what became the Sanskrit language, Hindu religion, and the caste system. Many of the classics of Indian literature and culture antedate the birth of Christ. During the third century, the Mauryan Empire was able to unite almost the entire subcontinent during the reign of Ashoka, who remains an inspiration to many Hindus today.

The Mughals and the Impact of Islam

Until 1000 AD or so, the territory that makes up the Indian subcontinent today flourished. The last thousand years have been a different story. For all but the past seventy years, most of India has been dominated by outsiders.

Oddly enough, the shaping of modern India does not begin in India itself but in the Middle East. After the death of the Prophet Muhammad, Muslim armies set out to convert the world. Their influence extended all the way to the Atlantic coast of Africa and Europe. And more important for our purposes here, the Muslims moved east as well, reaching far beyond India to today's Philippines.

Muslims made their first inroads into India early in the last millennium (see Table 12.2). Note, however, that few of the Muslims who came to dominate modern-day India, Pakistan, and Bangladesh were Arabs. Instead, they came from today's Iran and Central Asia, including, most notably, Mongols from whom the name **Mughal** is derived.

As in most of Europe at the time, there was nothing approaching either a unified nation or state in what we now think of as India. Rather, the region was composed

TABLE 12.2 Key Events in Indian History Prior to Independence

YEAR	EVENT
Circa 1000 AD	Beginning of Islamic impact
1556–1605	Mughal unification of much of the subcontinent
Circa 1600	First significant European impact
1707	Start of Mughal decline
1857	Sepoy mutiny
1858	Government of India Act
1885	Formation of Congress
1919	Jallianwala Bagh massacre
1920	Gandhi's first *satyagraha* campaign
1930	"March to the Sea" against the salt tax
1939–45	World War II
1947	Independence

© Cengage Learning

of hundreds of small states whose borders and ruling elites were constantly in flux. Over the next five hundred years, Muslims extended their domination over much of northern India although the specific areas under their control constantly ebbed and flowed.

In 1526, some of the regional rulers turned to Babur, a descendant of the great Mongol warrior Chinghiz (Genghis) Khan. Babur took Delhi and was named the first *padishah*, or Mughal emperor. Through a combination of negotiation and force, his grandson Akbar united most of the subcontinent into an elaborate and efficient bureaucratic regime. This system was far superior to anything in Europe at the time and allowed the Mughals to run a region that already had over 100 million inhabitants.

The Mughals almost always faced violent opposition, either from rival Muslim claimants to the throne or from Hindus and Sikhs struggling to regain control over their own land. Unlike the areas that came under Arab rule, the Mughals never tried to change popular values or social organization. As a result, Islam remained a minority religion and the Mughals adapted to local conditions, became every bit as much Indian as they were Muslim, and at least tolerated the caste system.

Toward the end of the seventeenth century, the last of the great Mughals, Alamgir, spent the last quarter-century of his life uniting the subcontinent. He assembled an army of unprecedented proportions and traveled with it in a "moving capital" that was thirty miles in circumference and had five hundred thousand "residents." On average, one hundred thousand people died during each year of the campaign, which ultimately ended with the Mughals' conquest of the bulk of India in 1707. It proved, however, to be a Pyrrhic victory. Alamgir himself died two years later, and his empire began to disintegrate almost immediately thereafter.

British Colonialism

The Mughals did not lose power because they were overthrown by other powerful Indians. Instead, India would spend the next 250 years under the domination of other foreigners: Europeans.

Portuguese traders established the first European beachhead in India in 1498. By the middle of the eighteenth century, British and French merchant companies with the support of their own, private armies established beachheads on the coast. Gradually, the British emerged as the most powerful European force in India, largely because of their victories in wars fought back in Europe, not because of what they did in India.

The **British East India Company** began to expand outward from its base in Calcutta. In other words, the first stage in the British takeover was not carried out by a government but by a private corporation—albeit one with strong state support—that was first and foremost looking to make money. As a result, the company was willing to allow local rulers to remain in power if they helped it in its commercial operations. In many respects, their preference was to find or, if necessary, create a class of leaders who would be loyal to Britain and who could themselves profit from the trading networks the British created.

By the early nineteenth century, the company had spread itself too thin to maintain order in India on its own, which meant it had to rely ever more heavily on the British government to the point that it became difficult to tell the two apart. In the meantime, British actions magnified the anger many Indians already felt.

Tensions boiled over in 1857 when the British army (which actually was composed mostly of Indian troops) introduced the Enfield rifle. In order to maintain the guns, the soldiers had to use grease from cows and pigs, which offended Hindus and Muslims, respectively. Tensions boiled over in the first anticolonial "mutiny" in which a number of British soldiers and hundreds of British civilians were killed. The British fought back with what Stanley Wolpert calls "terrible racial ferocity," destroying the social bridges that had been built between themselves and the people.

The mutiny also ended any pretense that India was a privately run colony. The British Parliament passed the **Government of India Act** the next year, which transferred the company's assets and powers to the crown. The British raj was an elaborate bureaucratic system that relied heavily on the cooperation of the Indian elite. It could hardly have been otherwise, given that Indians outnumbered the British by more than ten to one. The British never took direct control of the entire country, but even in the areas where "princely states" continued to exist, the British called the political shots.

At the top of the raj was a secretary of state who served in the British cabinet in London. He, in turn, appointed a viceroy who was based in India and supervised the **Indian Civil Service**, which, despite its name, was chosen on the basis of competitive examinations given only in London until 1923.

© Mary Evans Picture Library/The Image Works

The Enfield mutiny.

FIGURE 12.1 British India circa 1900

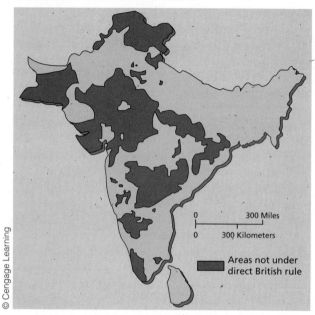

0   300 Miles

0   300 Kilometers

Areas not under direct British rule

© Cengage Learning

The Struggle for Independence

As was the case throughout the empire, colonial rule in India planted the seeds of its own destruction. It wasn't just the way they oppressed the Indian people. Ironically, its need to use Indians in business, education, civil administration, and the military created an ever growing number of people who objected to the raj. What makes India unique is the way opposition to colonial rule came together in a mostly nonviolent movement that achieved independence very early and endowed the new state with a consensus its first generation of leaders used to get the country off to a strong start.

Frustrations with colonial rule came to a head in 1883 when the British enacted a new law that was ostensibly designed to aid Indians by allowing some of them to serve on juries that tried Europeans. The one hundred thousand or so British then living in India forced the government to back down. As Wolpert, again, put it:

> It soon became painfully clear to more and more middle-class Indians, however, that, no matter how well intentioned or powerful individual Englishmen might be, the system they served was fundamentally unresponsive and hostile to many basic Indian needs, aspirations, and desires.[4]

---

[4]Stanley Wolpert, *A New History of India*, 3rd ed. (New York: Oxford University Press, 1989), 56.

In December 1885, seventy-three Indians met in Bombay to form the **Indian National Congress.** They were part of a small group of well-educated, upper-caste Indians who had begun talking about *swaraj*, or self-rule. In addition, Congress demanded reforms that could be met short of independence, such as holding Indian Civil Service exams in India as well as in England so that Indians would have a better chance of gaining admission to the increasingly powerful service.

Meanwhile, the British raj became more ruthless and arbitrary. Costly wars were fought to conquer and then retain land on the frontiers of the subcontinent. In 1905, the British decided to split Bengal into two. This action infuriated the nationalists, leading Congress to launch a boycott of British imports. By 1908, imports had been cut by more than a quarter. Indians, instead, started buying the more expensive *swadeshi* ("of our country") clothes made of Indian cotton and also woven at home.

Congress thus shifted from the polite petitions and requests of its first twenty years and began what would be a nationwide, nonviolent revolutionary movement. The British responded by arresting and prosecuting hundreds of Congress leaders, which further incensed younger activists. Their use of what could only be called terrorist tactics split Congress and enabled the British to temporarily gain the upper hand.

World War I fueled hopes for independence. Most Indian leaders agreed to support the British war effort in the hope that doing so would enhance their chances for freedom.

Those hopes were quickly dashed, however. Proposed political reforms died in the British House of Lords, ending any prospects for a rapid transfer of power. All political meetings were banned, and in April 1919 troops opened fire without warning on a group of Hindus at Jallianwala Bagh. Four hundred were killed and more than a thousand wounded. At that point, thousands more Indians joined the Congress-led independence struggle.

For the next twenty years, the movement was to be dominated by Congress and its remarkable leader, **Mohandas Karamchand Gandhi** (1869–1948). Gandhi rejected all forms of violence on spiritual and religious grounds. He offered a radically new strategy based on two Hindu concepts: *satyagraha* (holding fast to truth) and *ahimsa* (nonviolence).

In the early 1920s, Gandhi led a massive boycott of British goods that landed hundreds of Congress leaders in jail. By the end of 1921, it was clear that the boycott was not going to lead to independence any time soon. Frustration with the Gandhian approach set in, which led to violence between Hindus and Muslims. Gandhi was sent to prison, where he served two years of a six-year term. After his release, Gandhi pulled back from active politics for the rest of the decade, claiming that India was not ready for a nonviolent movement.

Despite those setbacks, two important breakthroughs occurred during the 1920s. First Congress ceased being a movement of upper-caste intellectuals. Gandhi's personal integrity, simple life, and political strategy drew the broad masses of the Indian population into the campaign. Second, a new generation of leaders emerged, which added a more modern approach to Gandhi's traditional spirituality. The most important of them was the young, British-educated Brahmin **Jawaharlal Nehru** (1889–1964), who explored ways of combining socialist ideas with Gandhi's spiritually oriented beliefs.

The independence movement took on new life in early 1930 when Gandhi proclaimed a salt boycott. Salt was one of the few commodities all Indians had to buy and had been heavily taxed by the British. Gandhi and seventy-eight colleagues began a two-hundred-mile march to the sea, where they gathered salt to symbolize their resistance against British rule. The sight of the tiny sixty-one-year-old, half-naked man leading his band inspired millions of other Indians and led to yet another wave of arrests and the imprisonment of both Gandhi and Nehru.

PROFILES   Mohandas Karamchand Gandhi

Mohandas Karamchand Gandhi was born in 1869. His family was upper-caste and his father was the chief minister of a small, unimportant princely state.

Like many privileged and ambitious Indians of his day, Gandhi studied in England. He then spent twenty years in South Africa, where he practiced law and served as a political advisor for the large Indian community there. In 1914 he returned to India and began pressing for independence. By 1920 he was already a prominent Congress leader, and in the aftermath of the violence of the immediate postwar years, the other leaders made him their de facto leader in part because he had such a broad appeal based on his commitment to nonviolence.

Gandhi was a remarkable man whose views, power, and impact cannot be summarized in a few sentences. He was one of the few truly charismatic leaders of the twentieth century, whose power stemmed not from his personality or oratory but from his conduct, in which every action was based on humility and principle.

Gandhi was a devout Hindu. Despite his worldly success, he lived the ascetic life of a Hindu *sadhu*, or holy man, wearing only plain white robes made of cloth he spun and wove himself. Gandhi and his family lived in rural communities known as ashrams, where they forswore almost all modern (that is, Western) human pleasures. Because of his spirituality and devotion, he was known as the Mahatma, or "holy one." ■

Mohandas Gandhi in the simple clothing he always wore, even when, as in this case, he was meeting with top British officials.

AP Photo

To make a long and complicated story short, events in India then moved in three different directions. First, because Britain refused to meet Congress's demand to "quit India," the protests continued. Second, the tensions between Hindus and Muslims that would lead to partition a decade later grew to the point that Congress became a unified movement in name only. Third, the British opened negotiations that led to passage of the Government of India Act in 1935, which expanded the franchise and enabled Congress to win control of eight provinces.

World War II brought an end not only to British rule but also to Gandhi's dream of a united and peaceful India. When the war broke out, most Indians supported the Allied effort on the assumption that independence would finally be achieved after it was over.

By the end of the war, Indian independence was a foregone conclusion, especially after the Labour Party won the 1945 British election. So, too, was its division into a predominantly Hindu India and a Muslim Pakistan. Talks got next to nowhere for the next year and a half. In February 1947, Prime Minister Clement Attlee told Parliament that Britain had decided to relinquish power to "responsible Indian hands" by June of the following year. He dispatched Lord Louis Mountbatten, the dashing commander of British forces in Southeast Asia during the war and Queen Victoria's great-grandnephew, to supervise the transition to independence as India's final viceroy.

Within weeks of his arrival, violence between Hindus and Muslims broke out. By the summer, Great Britain, the Indian National Congress, and the Muslim League had hastily agreed to make about 80 percent of the colony part of a new and independent India and to turn the rest into Pakistan, itself divided in two parts in the northwestern and northeastern (now Bangladesh) corners of the subcontinent. India and Pakistan formally gained their independence six months earlier than planned, on August 15, 1947.

Independence did not stop the intercommunal violence. The new countries were overwhelmingly Hindu and Muslim, respectively. However, fifty million people were caught within the borders of the "other" country. Within days, masses of people began to flee in both directions.

Partition and its accompanying violence occurred over Gandhi's objections. He began yet another fast to try to get people to stop fighting. From almost everyone else's perspective, however, Gandhi and his ideals were a thing of the past. His support for all Indians, including outcastes, Muslims, and Sikhs, had earned Gandhi the enmity of militant Hindus. On January 30, 1948, a member of a militant Hindu group assassinated him. That evening, Nehru announced during a national radio broadcast that "the light has gone out of our lives and there is darkness everywhere."

TABLE 12.3 Key Events in Indian History since Independence

YEAR	EVENT
1947	Independence
1950	Constitution goes into effect
1964	Jawaharlal Nehru dies, replaced by Lal Bahadur Shastri
1966	Shastri dies, replaced by Indira Gandhi
1975	Emergency Rule begins
1977	Emergency Rule ends; first non-Congress government
1979	Congress returns to power
1984	Indira Gandhi assassinated; Rajiv Gandhi succeeds her
1989	Second non-Congress government
1991	Rajiv Gandhi assassinated; P. V. Narasimha Rao becomes prime minister
1996	Congress suffers its worst electoral defeat; the BJP comes in first
1998	BJP elected; nuclear weapons tested
1999	BJP government reelected
2004	Congress returns to power
2009	Congress reelected

© Cengage Learning

The Nehru Years

India and Pakistan were the first countries to break free of colonial rule after World War II (see Table 12.3). The anticolonial movements that led to their freedom were highly unusual. Although it was never as unified, principled, or nonviolent as Gandhi would have wanted, it led to the creation of a regime that enjoyed widespread popular support. It also had dozens of experienced leaders who shared a strong commitment to democracy and who led the country through a generation of stability that has also helped it survive more serious conflict since the late 1960s. As will become clearer in the rest of Part 4, few other countries in the Global South have been this fortunate.

Independent India held its first election in 1952. It was an amazing event. Like every election since then, it became the largest political event ever held. It was all the more remarkable because 85 percent of the people were illiterate and had no direct political experience. Many observers at the time in India and abroad simply assumed that the country could not remain a democracy, if it survived at all.

Yet, somehow India and its democracy worked. In part, the success of its early years had to do with some ingenious strategies used by Nehru and his colleagues. Ads and ballot papers identified political parties with pictures as well as written names. Hindu religious leaders even allowed ads to appear on the sides of the otherwise sacred cows who were allowed to roam freely in the cities as well as the countryside.

India's early success also had deeper roots. Because of the way Congress achieved independence, the new country

TABLE 12.4 Indian Prime Ministers

NAME	YEARS IN OFFICE
Jawaharlal Nehru	1947–64
Lal Bahadur Shastri	1964–66
Indira Gandhi	1966–77
Morarji Desai	1977–79
Charan Singh	1979–80
Indira Gandhi	1980–84
Rajiv Gandhi	1984–89
V. P. Singh	1989–90
Chandra Shekhar	1990–91
P. V. Narasimha Rao	1991–96
H. D. Deve Gowda	1996–98
Atal Bihari Vajpayee	1998–2004
Manmohan Singh	2004–

© Cengage Learning

enjoyed a strong sense of national identity that was at least as important as religious, ethnic, caste, or linguistic ties. People therefore had little trouble thinking of themselves as both Indian and, say, a lower-caste Hindu, which was rarely the case in other new countries.

Congress was also what political scientists call an inclusive party that found a way to appeal to people of all socioeconomic backgrounds and political beliefs. Although the party had opposition, its coalition also included groups representing all major ideological and social groups in Indian society. Thus, when problems arose, Congress was able to take positions that would appeal to the disaffected groups, if not coopt them into the party altogether. That allowed it to win the lion's share of seats in the **Lok Sabha,** the all powerful lower house of Parliament, without ever winning a majority of the vote, by taking advantage of the first-past-the-post electoral system India inherited from the British.

On the policy front, Nehru led the country in two directions, which were shared by most Indians at the time. First, India was an avowedly social democratic country. Unlike most new countries, the constitution explicitly committed the country to planning and state ownership of what socialists call the "commanding heights" of the economy. Internationally, India became one of the leaders of the non-aligned movement, which tried to find a middle way between the Soviet Union and the United States.

Centralization and Fragmentation under Indira Gandhi

Nehru died in 1964. Inclusive politics died shortly thereafter, and political life today bears little resemblance to the consensus-building approach of Congress's first decade in office.

There was no obvious candidate to succeed him. The surviving Congress leaders turned to Lal Bahadur Shastri, who never gained more than the grudging support of his colleagues before he died unexpectedly in 1966.

This time, the leaders, now referred to as the Syndicate, chose Nehru's daughter, **Indira Gandhi** (1917–84), to be prime minister. Despite her married name, she was not related to Mohandas. The Syndicate assumed that they would have less trouble controlling a politically inexperienced woman than any of the other contenders.

To say the least, they were wrong.

After winning reelection in 1971, Gandhi announced a series of egalitarian economic initiatives. Land was given to the peasantry, coal mines were nationalized, and harsh new taxes were imposed on the wealthy. The Fifth Five-Year Plan called for the "removal of poverty" and the "attainment of self-reliance."

More importantly, she adopted an authoritarian leadership style that concentrated power in fewer and fewer hands while alienating many of her colleagues. The appointment of her son Sanjay as head of the new state automobile enterprise catapulted him onto political center stage. Protests against inflation and corruption within Congress became more frequent and strident. Within a matter of months, Congress split when the business-oriented **Morarji Desai** formed a rival Congress party.

Then, in 1975, the Allahabad High Court found Gandhi guilty of two counts of illegal campaign practices four years earlier. Technically, Indian law required her to resign, but Gandhi refused. Two weeks later, she invoked the constitution's provision for **Emergency Rule.** Civil liberties were suspended. Press censorship was imposed. Twenty-six political groups were banned. All major opposition leaders were arrested. Within a month, the remaining Members of Parliament (MPs) passed a law extending Emergency Rule indefinitely, enacted constitutional amendments that banned any legal challenges to it, retroactively cleared Gandhi of any wrongdoing, and "postponed" parliamentary elections.

Democracy was in jeopardy.

On January 18, 1977, however, Gandhi suddenly ended the Emergency, released all political prisoners, and called for national elections in March. The opposition that had borne the brunt of the repression under Emergency Rule was more united than ever. Their new Janata Party beat Congress by 10 percent in the popular vote and won an overwhelming majority of the seats in the Lok Sabha.

For good or ill, Janata was a "negative coalition" which was united only in its opposition to the "Indira Raj." Within two years it collapsed. New elections were held, which Congress won, bringing Gandhi back to power.

Her second term in office was as tumultuous as her first. While she was concentrating power at the national level in her own hands, it was fragmenting outside of New Delhi. National opposition parties, including the predecessors of today's BJP, gained strength by appealing to narrower segments of the electorate. More important, regional parties scored impressive victories, often winning control of state governments and electing up to half of the members of the lower house of parliament from "their" state. Many states elected legislatures hostile to central rule. In several cases Gandhi dissolved those governments and replaced their leaders with officials beholden to her.

Gandhi's most serious challenge was the increase in violent communal riots, which began to occur on a regular basis, especially in Punjab. As we will see in more detail later, Sikhs demanding independence occupied the Golden Temple in Amritsar, their holiest shrine. In May 1984, she imposed martial law in Punjab. The next month Indian troops attacked the Golden Temple, leaving it in ruins and killing hundreds of Sikh activists. Finally, on October 31, Sikh members of her own bodyguard assassinated the prime minister, setting off yet another wave of violence, with Hindus taking revenge against Sikhs who had nothing to do with either the assassination or the wave of protests that led up to it.

Gandhi's domination of Indian politics for nearly a generation remains controversial to this day. There is, however, one point on which her supporters and critics agree. She ended Congress's role as a consensus builder by centralizing power within Congress and driving out politicians who did not go along with her wishes.

She had been grooming her son Sanjay to succeed her. He was tragically killed in an airplane accident, and her other, and previously apolitical, son, **Rajiv Gandhi** (1944–1991), became the heir apparent. No one was surprised when he became prime minister after her death and immediately called for new elections while sympathy for his mother remained high. Congress won an unprecedented 80 percent of the seats in the Lok Sabha.

His victory marked the entry of a new generation of leaders into Indian politics. Rajiv Gandhi and his closest

---

PROFILES   The Nehru Clan

No other democracy has ever been as dominated by one family as the Nehru-Gandhi clan in India.

The patriarch, Jawaharlal Nehru, was one of the two most important leaders of the independence movement, and he also served as prime minister during the new country's formative years. His daughter, Indira, was as influential (although often less constructively so) from the time she became prime minister in 1966 until her assassination in 1984. At that point, her elder son, Rajiv, became prime minister, but only because his younger brother Sanjay had been killed in an airplane crash.

Formally, the Nehru-Gandhi clan has been out of office since Rajiv's assassination in 1991. Instead, they exert power from (barely) behind the scenes. His Italian-born widow, Sonia, has been leader of the Congress Party since 1999. That year, she presided over its third consecutive defeat at the polls. In 2004, she led the party to victory and then surprised the country by declining the prime ministry. Her political future—and that of her children—is uncertain, although her son Rahul is widely expected to be the Congress candidate for prime minister in 2014. ∎

Jawaharlal Nehru, India's first prime minister, holding his grandson Rajiv Gandhi on his knee. Gandhi eventually succeeded his mother and became the third family member to hold India's highest office.

© Bettmann/CORBIS

advisers were young, well-educated, and Westernized. They did not share the older generation's commitment to economic planning and democratic socialism but instead were highly impressed with the market economies in the Western countries where they had studied and worked.

In his five years in office, Rajiv Gandhi introduced the first market-oriented reforms. However, his reputation for honesty was tarnished by a scandal that implicated his government in a kickback scheme in their dealings with a Swedish arms manufacturer. Moreover, to stay in power, the younger Gandhi had to resort to the same kind of centralizing tactics that had led to his mother's death.

Coalition Politics

Rajiv Gandhi's term ended in 1989. Congress was still the only party with a truly national base, but it could not beat another loose opposition coalition, the Janata Dal. Like its predecessor, the Janata Dal was a negative coalition that had been brought together out of joint opposition to Congress but lacked any clear agreement about what it would do in case it won.

That year's election marked the last major turning point in the history of post-independence India. Because Congress lost its traditional role as a hegemonic party, India has been governed since then by broad-based coalitions because no national party has come close to winning a majority of the seats in the Lok Sabha. Furthermore, the balance of power is held by politicians with regional, ethnic, or caste bases of support, a point we will return to in the section on political parties.

The Janata Dal coalition elected in 1989 lasted only months, and after two more weak governments fell, early elections were scheduled for 1991. In the middle of the two-week voting period, Rajiv Gandhi was assassinated by Tamil extremists. The elections were postponed, and Congress desperately sought a new leader. Rajiv's Italian-born widow, **Sonia Gandhi** (1946–), turned down an offer to run for prime minister and keep the dynasty alive. Thus, the party had to turn to the seventy-year-old party loyalist and former foreign minister P. V. Narasimha Rao (1921–2004).

When the elections were finally completed, Congress had come in first, though it fell sixteen seats short of an overall majority. The Hindu-based BJP came in second, well ahead of Janata Dal and the regional parties. Narasimha Rao formed a coalition government with a few of the minor parties.

No one expected the new government to do very well. Surprisingly, however, it lasted its entire five-year term and sped up the pace of economic reform. Narasimha Rao's government did not fare well on other fronts. It was thus

Comparative Emphasis: Democratization

India is one of the few Southern countries that has been able to sustain a democratic regime for an extended period of time. The reasons for this are not clear, largely because we do not understand how democratization takes place anywhere. Nonetheless, we can safely reach three comparative conclusions:

- There is little in Indian history before the creation of Congress to suggest that the new country would be able to sustain a democracy.

- The roots of democratization lie in the independence movement, especially the way Congress mobilized millions of people in an inclusive manner. That gave the Nehru government widespread legitimacy and support for its policies in the vital first years after independence.

- Indian governments have rarely made democratization a central policy goal. Rather, it has emerged more as a consequence of their success in other areas, including political stability, keeping identity politics from becoming too disruptive, and, more recently, economic growth. ■

hardly surprising that Congress went down to a crashing defeat in 1996.

As had been the case the other two times Congress lost, a divided coalition of thirteen political parties won in 1996. No one was surprised when early elections were called in 1998 after two prime ministers fell.

Early elections in 1998 made it clear that India would enter the twenty-first century with little chance of electing majority governments. Now, the lack of a clear majority came with a new and—for some—worrisome twist. This time the BJP came in a strong first and was able to form a government with twelve other parties under Prime Minister **Atal Bihari Vajpayee** (1924–). Many observers feared that the BJP would stress its fundamentalist Hindu roots and deepen the intolerance that had marked Indian politics for the preceding generation. However, Vajpayee and his colleagues understood that they had to govern from the center, both to retain the support of their coalition partners and to have any hope of attracting new voters to the BJP. His government did lose a vote of confidence in 1999, but Vajpayee won the subsequent election, formed an even broader coalition government, and continued the economic reforms begun under Congress.

The BJP coalition could not win three times in a row. In 2004, forty-two parties won at least a single district, and Congress and the BJP barely won half of the 543 elected seats. After Congress was able to cobble together a coalition of thirteen parties, only five of which had at least ten MPs, **Manmohan Singh** (1932–) became prime minister. He was chosen in part because he is an economist who was committed to further integrating India into the global, capitalist economy. Five years later, his coalition was returned to power despite winning only 262 of 550 seats in the Lok Sabha. Enough independents sided with Congress to give him a comfortable majority that will likely endure until the parliamentary term expires in 2014. At that point, Singh will be eighty-two and Sonia Gandhi sixty-eight. The current economic slump and corruption scandals along with its generational challenge leaves Congress a decided underdog as I write in mid-2013.

I ended the comparable section of Chapter 4 with the assertion that you would have to take most of the conclusions about Great Britain as an intellectual leap of faith until you saw the evidence from the other industrialized democracies. The same holds for India in Part 4. Nonetheless:

- The ideas that gave rise to Congress and independence are far less important than they were half a century ago. Most worrisome is the threat to secularism and tolerance posed by the rise of the BJP and other identity-driven groups.

- Support for socialism has all but disappeared. In its place, there is now broad agreement on a capitailst road to economic growth despite the highly unequal distribution of both income and wealth.

- In a country in which no party or firm coalition has a realistic chance of winning a disciplined majority, legislative gridlock is increasingly the norm.

- Despite these problems, the Indian regime is not in any jeopardy.

Political Culture

A first step in understanding why India has enjoyed more success than the rest of the Global South lies in its political culture. Independent India began life with broader support than any other country covered in Part 4. As recently as a generation ago, however, many observers thought that growing intolerance along regional, caste, linguistic, and religious lines might tear the country apart. Now, however, there is general agreement that Indian democracy is secure not because those differences have disappeared but because politicians have found ways to diminish their disruptive potential.

That is an important point which we did not encounter in other countries. There, we saw that supportive cultural norms could enhance national unity and democracy. In the rest of this chapter, we will see that the "causal arrows" can run in the other direction as well. Effective governance itself can also reinforce supportive cultural norms.

Identity Politics

Like most countries covered in Part 4, identity issues have, if anything, grown in importance since independence. Again like them, successive Indian governments have often struggled in trying to keep them in check. However, unlike the others, Congress governments have done enough to keep their most disruptive potential in check.

Identity conflict, in fact, has been important enough that we will consider it explicitly as one of the public policy cases to be discussed toward the end of this chapter. Here it is enough to note that ethnic and regional identification in such different regions as Assam, Kashmir, Tamil Nadu, Punjab, and Gujarat have presented the central state with serious challenges since the 1970s.

The differences independent India inherited from its colonial past have been exacerbated by the rebirth of religious fundamentalism, especially among Hindus. As remarkable as it may seem, many Hindus think of themselves as an oppressed group, even though they make up 80 percent of the population. Politicized Hindu groups have existed since the **Rashtriya Swayamsevak Sangh (RSS)** was founded in 1925. In some states, the Sangh (as it is sometimes known) and similar organizations are pressing for reforms that would put the secular commitment of the country's founders into question. Because the growth of Hindu nationalism has been inextricably intertwined with the meteoric rise of the BJP in the 1980s, we will defer dealing with it, too, in more detail until we cover the party system.

Last, but by no means least, we cannot ignore the continued importance of caste. Although the constitution and subsequent legislation banned discrimination against *dalits* and others formally outside the caste system, it continues to have a major impact on people's daily lives—from what they do for a living to whom they vote for.

Caste can still spark protest if members believe that their interests are in jeopardy. For instance, when the government created a reserved-places (affirmative action for American readers) scheme for untouchables, members of scheduled tribes, and lower castes, it touched off massive protests, including the ritual suicide of hundreds of young Brahmins. In 1994, a mere typographical error led to rioting when an official document included "Gond-Gowari" instead of "Gond, Gowari," which legally meant that there was no Gowari caste eligible for the reserved jobs. Furious Gowaris protested in the state of Maharashtra, where most of them lived. By the time the rioting ended a few weeks later, at least 113 of them had died. One study conducted in the late 1990s found that 200 of India's 534 districts (the administrative unit below the state level) were experiencing intense identity-based conflict.

It is not altogether clear why such issues have not torn the country apart. Two reasons seem to stand out.

First, some nation building occurred even before the creation of the Indian state. This undoubtedly helped India survive the first years after the communal strife at partition, when many observers doubted that an egalitarian democratic political system could be grafted onto a society that was both deeply divided and rigidly hierarchical. Some observers, too, thought that elements of Hindu culture, including its emphasis on harmony, pluralism, and spiritual rather than worldly matters, helped smooth the process. Whatever the exact constellation of causes, there is considerable evidence that by the late 1960s India had developed the kind of political culture that helps sustain democracy in Britain and the United States.

Second, the government redrew state boundaries until each major linguistic group had "its own" state. The officially secular national government has only been willing to do so on religious lines for the Sikhs. Nonetheless, compared with many elsewhere in the South, Indians have little trouble combining a positive identification with the nation-state and those with their caste, religion, or ethnicity.

Regime Success

Despite the divisiveness of identity politics, there is compelling evidence that most Indians support the regime because they are satisfied enough with what it has accomplished. India has had more than its share of other problems, ranging from endemic poverty to incompetent and, even corrupt, leaders. We will consider concrete policy issues later in the chapter. For now, it is enough to see that its electoral successes have built on each other.

India has held fourteen national and countless state and local elections since 1947, and only once—during Emergency Rule—did the democratic process fail to hold. In that case, the Indian people repudiated Indira Gandhi and Congress at the first opportunity.

Simply holding a national election in India is no mean feat given the country's size and diversity. Turnout has averaged 57 percent in each national election, which is a

Comparative Emphasis: Identity

As will be the case throughout Part 4, identity issues are critical to Indian politics. However, they have a different impact in two broad ways:

- India is more fragmented on linguistic and ethnic lines. Given its size and its federal government, identity issues often play themselves out at the state rather than the national level in a bewildering array of subnational coalitions that have little impact on the formation or policy of governments in New Delhi.

- India is also unusual in that many members of the dominant religious group—Hindus—are convinced that they are second-class citizens because the state has granted special privileges to Muslims and other minorities. ∎

bit higher than in the United States. But in India, over half of the electorate cannot read the ballot paper and still has to rely on pictures to identify which party to vote for. Even more remarkable is the fact that the poorest Indians vote at a rate higher than the national average and are remarkably well informed about the issues and the politicians they are voting on.

The Challenge of Modernization

One other cultural question looms on India's horizon—the dislocations produced by the rapid social and economic change we will also focus on for much of the rest of this chapter. Fifty years ago, the economist Mancur Olson wrote a short article that convinced most social scientists that rapid growth could destabilize a society. Olson may have been right about many countries. However, India has done a good job of avoiding the negative consequences of rapid growth.

If anything, the evidence suggests that Indians have adapted quite easily. As India has become wealthier, more and more consumer goods have become available, young middle-class people, in particular, have bought them in record numbers and adopted the Westernized and high-tech life style now open to them. Close to two hundred million people have access to cable or satellite television service, which includes over 350 national channels.

Middle-class Indians have become the world's biggest market for blenders, which they use to grind the chilies and other spices they need to make their traditional dishes. Along similar lines, it seems to take only about six weeks to train English-speaking Indians to sound as if they are from Birmingham, England, or Birmingham, Alabama, so that they can work in call centers operated for businesses in Europe and North America.

This does not mean, however, that traditional values have disappeared. For example, even though the government ruled dowries illegal years ago, many couples who clamor for Western products at the same time submit to arranged marriages with dowries that can top six thousand dollars and include a television, refrigerator, or motor scooter.

Worrisome signs of the persistence of traditional values involve the treatment of girls and women. In most parts of India, male babies still are prized, whereas girls are seen as a burden. Medical care for girls has always been worse because parents do not seek treatment for them as often. If there is a food shortage, boys are more likely to be fed while girls are allowed to starve. The now widespread use of ultrasound tests for pregnant women has added a new twist to the discrimination against girls. There are only about 850 live births of girl babies for every 1,000 boys because parents often choose to abort a fetus if they know it is a girl.

Political Participation

We also have to shift gears in analyzing political participation in Part 4, although we will have to do so less drastically in the case of India. Just as they are in Russia and the countries discussed in Part 2, elections, political parties, and interest groups are the key forms of political participation in India. However, the key concepts of ideology, class, and party identification discussed earlier matter much less in India.

Rather, the Indian party system and politics in general involve many different, overlapping cleavages. As a result, a party that hopes to win enough votes to govern has to be able to balance the interests and demands of enough of the groups spawned by India's many divisions to forge a majority coalition in the Lok Sabha.

In other words, patterns of electoral participation and competition in India seem amazingly complex. However, there have been three trends that help us make sense of much of that complexity.

First, Congress was what political scientists call a dominant party until Emergency Rule. Second, Indira Gandhi's use of emergency powers was at least indirectly a response to the fragmentation in which national parties had already lost votes to those organized along state and identity lines. Finally, for the last twenty years, coalitions headed by Congress and the BJP have competed with each other for the right to lead the government after each election since 1998.

Congress

Along with the Social Democrats in Sweden, the Christian Democrats in postwar Italy, and the Liberal Democratic Party in Japan, Congress is one of a handful of political parties that enjoyed all but nonstop control of a single country for decades on end. Although never able to win an outright majority at the polls, it routinely took advantage of India's British-style single-member-district electoral system and the division of its opponents to win overwhelming majorities in the Lok Sabha until the onset of coalition politics (www.aicc.org.in).

The End of the Congress System

Unlike many other political parties, Congress was able to both stand by its basic principles of unity, tolerance, social democracy, and nationalism and demonstrate remarkable flexibility in dealing with allies and adversaries alike. Once Nehru died and the consensus around those key issues disintegrated, so too did Congress's hegemony.

As we have seen, Indira Gandhi challenged the Syndicate and won, but her victory had tremendous costs for Congress. Over the next decade, the Congress system fell apart in three ways. Its share of the vote declined, its organization deteriorated, and it faced new opposition (see Table 12.5).

The first signs of Congress's decline came in 1967 when its majority in the Lok Sabha was reduced to 54 percent of the seats. Congress also lost six states because it was not as capable of responding to local demands as it had

TABLE 12.5 Congress's Share of the Vote and Seats in the Lok Sabha, 1952–91

YEAR	PERCENTAGE OF VOTE	NUMBER OF SEATS
1952	45.0	364
1957	47.8	371
1962	44.7	361
1967	40.8	283
1971	43.7	352
1977	34.5	154
1980	43.7	353
1984	48.1	415
1989	39.5	197
1991	36.0	226

© Cengage Learning

been before most linguistically defined states were created in the 1950s.

Then, the first signs of Gandhi's heavy-handed leadership led to the schism between her supporters and the Syndicate during the 1969 campaign for the largely symbolic presidency. Against the wishes of the Syndicate, Gandhi supported the incumbent, V. V. Giri, who was running as an independent. The Syndicate then threw her out of the party. Congress MPs, however, voted overwhelmingly in her favor.

The party then split, ironically, during the one-hundredth anniversary of Mohandas Gandhi's birth. Now there were two Congress parties: the Syndicate's Congress (O for organization) and Indira Gandhi's Congress (I for Indira). Because Congress (I) no longer had a working parliamentary majority, the Gandhi government was only able to remain in office by gaining the support of MPs who had been in the opposition.

She made it clear from the beginning that Congress (I) was going to be a new kind of party in at least two respects. First, it would support more radical economic policies in order to appeal to the poor and disadvantaged, especially the scheduled castes, youth, and Muslims. Second, it would be a personalized party organized to support her rule in ways never before seen in Indian politics. The opposition, which now included Congress (O), made her ouster the focal point of its campaign with the slogan *Indira hatao* (Indira out of power).

Gandhi confounded the experts by winning 44 percent of the vote and 352 of 518 seats in 1971 in large part because the opposition was so divided and ineffective. Congress (O) itself soon disappeared (so we can drop the I for the rest of this chapter).

Despite her initial success, Gandhi committed a number of mistakes before and after the Emergency that ended Congress's role as both a dominant and a consensus-building party. For example, she elevated her son to be her heir apparent even though he was viewed as little more than a power-hungry young man. Sanjay used his influence to support such controversial and divisive policies as family planning and forced sterilization. He also controlled access to his mother, the "household" of personal advisers to the prime minister, the Youth Congress, and much of the government's repressive apparatus.

None of her miscalculations was more disastrous than her 1977 decision to end Emergency Rule and hold new elections on the assumption that she would win again. Congress was routed. Both Indira and Sanjay Gandhi lost their seats.

When the Janata coalition government fell, the political pendulum briefly swung back toward Congress. But

Comparative Emphasis: Elections in India

Each time one is held, an Indian election immediately becomes the most massive event in human history.

India is so big that there is no single election day. In 2009, balloting was held in five phases that lasted more than a month from mid-April through mid-May. More than 417 million people or about 60 percent of the electorate went to the polls. That, of course, was a larger number than the population of any country on earth other than China or India itself. The Indian government alone spent more than $200 million to conduct the campaign.

People voted entirely by machine, with 1,368,430 of them distributed around the country. Their use, of course, has rendered the accompanying photograph obsolete. Nonetheless, it is a good reminder of how complicated simply holding an election is in a country as large and diverse as India. ■

Indian election officials counting the vote in May 1996. Because so many Indians are illiterate, ballots have pictures as well as words to identify each candidate's party affiliation.

Gandhi soon alienated many voters and politicians by taking the party even farther to the Left all the while insisting on personal loyalty to herself, her family, and the rest of her inner circle. After Sanjay died in June 1980, Indira Gandhi turned to her elder son, Rajiv, who until then had shown little interest in politics.

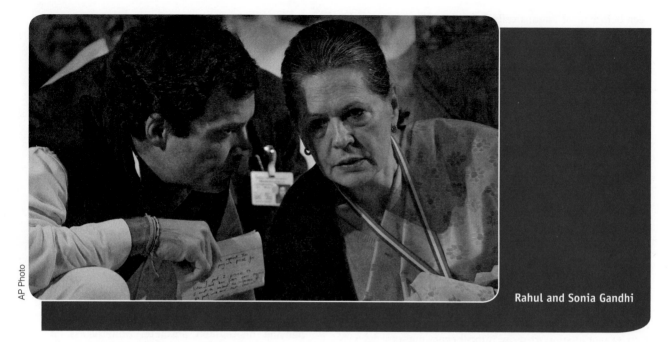

Rahul and Sonia Gandhi

To the surprise of many, he quickly took to political life, and by 1982 he had established himself as his mother's likely successor, a position he assumed following her assassination. Under his government, economic reform barely got off the drawing board given a series of scandals that undermined his image as the "Mr. Clean" of Indian politics. He will probably be better remembered for the ethnic conflict that further eroded Congress's hegemony and ultimately cost him his life, which we will also explore in more depth in the public policy section.

The party's deteriorating fortunes continued after his death, despite the surprisingly effective and reformist leadership initially exercised by his successor, Narasimha Rao. As we saw previously, even he could not stem the public's dissatisfaction with the party, and it went down to the first of two crushing defeats in 1996. That loss and the corruption charges Rao was facing forced him from the party leadership, creating the internal leadership vacuum that still characterizes the party today.

Congress Today

Three themes dominate accounts of Congress today. It is definitely not the Congress of 1947 or 1967. However, it is hard to say definitively what it is other than a party that seeks power while paying homage (and little more) to its core traditional goals.

First, despite making appeals to the poor and minorities and paying homage to the egalitarian goals of its founders, Congress has squarely committed itself to neoliberal reform. Second, it will soon face a leadership transition when its aging and less than charismatic leaders depart.

Rajiv and Sonia's son, Rahul Gandhi (1970–) has long been the presumed heir apparent.[5] Finally, Congress cannot aspire to be more than the strongest member of a loose governing coalition. Now that state issues have become more important than national ones in determining the outcome of Lok Sabha elections, neither Congress nor the BJP can hope to win an outright majority on its own.

In all likelihood, Congress will remain the largest party in 2014 and could well continue as the top party for some time to come. However, there seems to be little or no chance that it could again become the dominant party it was during the first generation after independence.

The Bharatiya Janata Party

Twenty years ago the BJP would not have featured prominently in a book like this. It had topped 10 percent of the vote in 1989 and won eighty-five seats, but few serious observers thought it would ever do much better, let alone become one of the two parties competing for power at the national level (www.bjp.org).

Although the BJP itself is a rather new party, its roots lie in the revival of organized Hindu fundamentalism that began with the formation of the RSS in 1925. In the 1950s and 1960s, the RSS was a fringe movement that led campaigns opposing the slaughter of cows, the presence of Christian

---

[5]In addition to his father, grandmother, and great-grandfather, all of whom had been prime minister, his great-great-grandfather, Motilal (Jawaharlal Nehru's father), was one of Congress's founders.

missionaries, and other alleged evils. Its political party, the Jan Sangh, won more than 7 percent of the vote only one time and was part of the Janata coalition in 1977 and 1979.

At the time, however, most major political figures shared the Congress Party's commitment to a secular India. Politicized Hindus who acted as such were stuck on the political fringes until the decentralizing trends began undermining the country's one-party-dominant system.

At that point, the newly formed BJP began to make inroads in the northern "cow belt," where it won control of four states. It did particularly well among upper-caste young men who felt threatened by affirmative action programs they believed would undermine their social status and economic power.

The BJP's symbolic breakthrough came after a series of violent protests centered on the disputed mosque/temple in Ayodhya. Some Muslims claim it had been built by the first Mughal conqueror, Babur, during the sixteenth century. Some devout Hindus felt just as strongly that the site was the birthplace of one of their major gods, Lord Ram, which made it one of the holiest places in their tradition as well. For most of the past century or so, however, a *modus vivendi* allowed Muslims to use it on Fridays and left Hindus free to pray there during the rest of the week.

After a judge's ruling closed the building to everyone in 1986, the temple/mosque became a political hot potato. The rapidly growing Vishwa Hindu Parishad (VHP), or Worldwide Hindu Brotherhood, which made the freeing of such properties its highest priority, entered the fray. It routinely gathered one hundred thousand devout Hindus along the banks of the river next to the temple/mosque. Within

two years, the VHP had mustered enough support to convince a judge to stop allowing non-Hindus to worship at the site. This, in turn, led to Muslim counterdemonstrations. In one typical incident, a riot broke out in 1989 after the VHP announced that it would add on to the building using specially consecrated bricks. More than 150 people were killed.

Later that year, Congress was defeated and replaced by a government that convinced the VHP to postpone construction of the addition. Pressures around Ayodhya then eased until a Hindu mob destroyed the mosque and started building a new temple in December 1992.

The violence soon spread far from Ayodhya. Hindu revivalist movements, such as the Shiv Sena in Mumbai, took to the streets, attacking Muslims who obviously had nothing to do with the situation in Ayodhya. At least 1,700 died in Mumbai alone.

BJP leaders were already using what can only be described as thinly veiled racist rhetoric. By capitalizing on the associated resurgence of Indian fundamentalism, BJP and its allies were already building a base of support reminiscent of France's National Front.

How that happened is actually easier to see through the career of Bal Thackeray (1926–2012), who was the head of Shiv Sena, the highly popular mayor of Mumbai, and a key, if informal, cog in the BJP machine. He rose to prominence by, among other things, refusing to allow Kentucky Fried Chicken to open restaurants in the state of Maharashtra because there had been some minor health code violations in KFC restaurants elsewhere in the country. It was hard, however, to raise too much of a fuss about a restaurant using excess amounts of MSG or having a dead fly in the batter

© DOUG CURRAN/Staff/AFP/Getty Images

Evidence of the destruction at Ayodhya mosque/temple, which has been in dispute between Hindus and Muslims for a generation.

when street vendors in the same neighborhood were selling cucumbers soaked in water that came from open sewers.

It is easy to not take such actions seriously. However, Shiv Sena and other groups loosely affiliated with the BJP are responsible for widespread violence against Muslims, Sikhs, Christians, and other minorities. Their support base has spread everywhere in Mumbai, including Annawadi. Their armed paramilitaries can mobilize tens of thousands of activists for major protests such as those over Ayodhya.

The BJP also has a strong nationalist streak that has turned it into a strong supporter of India's nuclear weapons system and stiff counterterrorism measures, most notably after the 2008 devastating attacks by Pakistanis in Mumbai. Here, however, it should be pointed out that it differs little from Congress on security issues.

And, now, the same can probably be said for their positions on economic reform, despite the BJP's strong populist rhetoric in the past. In practice, the BJP governments led by Atal Bihari Vajpayee from 1998 until 2004 did little to alter what Congress had done in the previous five years.

The BJP's future will depend heavily on its own leadership transition. As I write in mid-2013, **Narendra Modi** (1950–) has been named as the party's leader in the 2014 campaign. As chief minister of Gujarat since 2001, he has sent mixed messages about his own views and where he would be likely to take the party. On the one hand, he points to a pragmatic track record in which his government has avoided most corruption allegations and helped build up the state's educational, transportation, and energy infrastructure. On the other hand, he is beloved by BJP activists because he essentially turned a blind eye when Hindu mobs retaliated against Muslims after fifty-nine Hindu pilgrims were burned alive on a train by a Muslim mob.

The Other Parties

Congress and the BJP *together* fell short of a majority of the vote in the last two elections (see Table 12.6). In other words, smaller parties, most of which are purely regional, as well as independents got the rest of the vote, reaching almost two-thirds of it in 2009.

Unfortunately, because there are so many of those parties, we cannot hope to cover them all in an introductory text. Thirty-seven of them won 209 seats in 2009 along with nine independents. Almost all of them only run candidates in a single state or appeal to a single ethnic, linguistic, or religious group. This is true even of those whose name or ideology might suggest otherwise.

These small parties can be divided into two main types:

- *The remnants of the traditional Left.* Two parties call themselves communist: the traditional, orthodox Communist Party of India (CPI), which has seen its support dwindle to less than 3 percent of the national vote, and the more radical Communist Party of India-Marxist (CPI[M]), which has support primarily in the state of West Bengal, where it is the largest party. There are also some even weaker socialist parties. In practice, these are all regional parties with no hopes of winning votes nationwide. Their support, however, was needed to keep the Singh government elected in 2004 in power until Congress's sweeping victory in 2009.

- *Regional parties.* Every state that has been subject to ethnic, linguistic, or religious unrest has spawned at least one political party that claims to speak for those interests, including the Akali Dal in Punjab, the DMK and AIADMK in Tamil Nadu, the National Conference in Jammu and Kashmir, and the Telegu Desam in Andhra Pradesh. By 2004, most of them had aligned themselves as part of coalitions with either Congress or the BJP, which won sixty-seven and thirty-seven seats, respectively, from them. Another seventy-four members of the Lok Sabha were elected from the extremely loose All India Forward Bloc.

The Elections of 2004 and 2009

We can see all the trends covered so far in this section in a brief discussion of the last two general elections. As the 2004 campaign neared, all the signs pointed to another victory by the BJP and its partners in the National Democratic Alliance.

TABLE 12.6 The Indian Elections of 2004 and 2009

PARTY	VOTE 2004 (%)	SEATS IN LOK SABHA 2004	VOTE 2009 (%)	SEATS IN LOK SABHA 2009
BJP	22.2	138	18.8	116
BJP allies	13.1	47	5.8	43
Congress	26.8	145	28.55	206
Congress allies	7.8	70	8.7	56
Left Front	7.6	59	21.5	79
Minor parties and independents	22.5	78	6.5	16

Vajpayee's government had muted some of its more nationalistic stands. Polls showed it had gained support among all groups other than the *dalits*, scheduled tribes, and Muslims who had always been among the BJP's strongest opponents. The government even expected to benefit from India's victory against arch-rival Pakistan in that winter's test match series in cricket (www.indian-elections.com).

Congress did find a winning issue by appealing to the three hundred million people who lived in chronic poverty. The lucky people who, for instance, got high-tech jobs outsourced from the West numbered barely a million at a time when nine million young people were entering the workforce each year, most of whom ended up unemployed. Sonia Gandhi and her party appealed to this largely rural voting bloc who passed below the pundits' and pollsters' radar screens. When the votes were counted, Congress and its formal allies had won thirty-two more seats than the BJP but fell short of a majority. Because it could count on support from the Left Front, Congress immediately set out to form a new government. The only surprise was Gandhi's decision not to take the prime ministry, which left the job to Singh, who had been the architect of Congress's first economic reforms in the early 1990s and to whom we will return later.

The 2009 election was even more of a rout than Table 12.6 suggests because dozens of leftist and minor party members of the Lok Sabha supported the new Singh government, giving it an overwhelming majority, which should guarantee another five years of Congress rule and continuity in the economic and other reform policies to be discussed in the public policy section. As such, it brought at least a temporary halt to a period of weak governments and frequent elections.

As I write, plans for the 2014 election are well underway. Congress has made it clear that Rahul Gandhi will be its candidate for prime minister. The BJP has done the same with Nahrendra Modi. In mid-2013, it was not clear which party would win or if either of these men would actually assume the prime ministry if his party won.

Interest Groups

Because India has been a functioning democracy for more than sixty years, it has the full range of interest groups we saw in Part 2—and then some. However, this does not mean that they look and act the same as those in the West.

India has an extensive labor movement with more than twenty-five thousand unions because the labor law allows any group of seven or more workers to organize one. Nevertheless, only about ten million people are unionized. Moreover, the unions themselves are fragmented. Most major unions are extensions of political parties rather than autonomous organizations such as the American AFL-CIO or French

Comparative Emphasis: Conflict in India

At first glance, it might seem as if India's democracy is threatened by the conflicts that kill at least a thousand people during each election campaign. In practice, however, overall conflict is not that serious a problem given the size of the Indian population. Nor does it have as serious implications as the disputes we will see in the next two chapters, largely because even the most outspoken critics of the current government accept the basic "rules of the game" in India. ◼

CFDT. Congress controls the Indian National Trades Union Congress (INTUC). The All-Indian Trades Union Congress (AITUC) is associated with one of the communist parties, and the Congress of Indian Trades Union (CITU) is linked to the other. What's more, few of the unions seem to be gaining strength. The one exception may be the Bharatiya Mazdoor Sangh (BMS), which is associated with the BJP.

The unions have a limited impact, too, because they primarily cover workers in the organized sector of the economy, in which people are paid cash wages. Virtually unrepresented are the poorest people, who work in the informal economy, do not earn regular wages, and are desperately in need of help. Perhaps most important, when unions have chosen to strike, they have rarely been able to overcome the resistance of either the state or private employers.

Similarly, India has no shortage of business associations, the most important of which is the Federation of Indian Chambers of Commerce that counts some forty thousand enterprises among its members. Unlike the unions, business groups do not have formal ties to parties but have historically supported the conservative wing of Congress and its right-wing rivals. Individual business leaders also gain some leverage because of the substantial contributions they make to individual candidates.

Like the unions, business has not been particularly powerful in India. This lack of influence reflects, in part, the traditional Brahmin disdain for commerce. It also grows out of Congress's preference for socialist policies before Rajiv Gandhi came to power. Primarily, though, business traditionally has been weak because the modern sector of the economy has been dominated by the state. This situation is changing as India opens up its economy, as we will see in the policy section, but it is too early to tell how the new generation of entrepreneurs will align themselves politically.

The Indian State

India has more than its share of problems, most of which are typical of the Global South. It is unique, however, in that it has kept its democracy alive—if not always flourishing—for more than a half-century. Accordingly, the section on the state will be longer and more detailed than the comparable ones for Iran, Nigeria, and Mexico, where the personality of individual leaders is often more important than institutions in determining what the state does. India's democracy has endured in large part because Indians have adapted European institutions and practices to create a political hybrid that in some ways very much resembles, and in others markedly differs from, British-style parliamentary democracy.

The Constitution

Like the leaders of most of the new states in Asia and Africa, independent India adopted a system that was based on the one used from their colonial masters as enshrined in their constitution, which went into effect in 1950 (**india-code.nic.in/coiweb/welcome.html**). It is not, however, a carbon copy of the British constitution. For one thing, it is written. Indeed, with nearly four hundred articles and eight schedules, the Indian constitution is one of the longest in the world. And because it can be amended by a simple majority vote in both houses of parliament, it is among the easiest to change. In fact, as of 2012, it had been amended ninety-seven times.

The constitution defines India as a secular republic to ensure a degree of religious and political freedom to the roughly 20 percent of the population that is not Hindu. It also guarantees an extensive list of civil liberties and forbids discrimination along religious, caste, racial, and gender lines.

Although it allows the prime minister to exercise emergency powers during a crisis, these provisions have only been used the one time discussed earlier. During the nearly two years of Emergency Rule, the constitution was drastically amended. After the 1977 elections, however, the government repealed most of those amendments and limited the conditions under which emergency powers could be used to an invasion from abroad or an armed rebellion at home.

As with most new states, India does not have a king or queen. Instead, a president plays the symbolic role of head of state, much as we saw in Germany. Most presidents have readily accepted their secondary roles. The president has had a substantial political impact only during the brief periods when there was no majority party or obvious coalition that could put one together. At those times, the

Comparative Emphasis: Women in Indian Politics

There are plenty of women who have risen to the top of Indian politics beyond Indira and Sonia Gandhi. The previous president, Pratibha Patil, for example, was the first woman to hold that post. Although the presidency is largely symbolic, her election was a sign that women are now playing a more prominent role. A number of women have been chief ministers in some states. Feminists should not be too excited by that trend since at least one of them, Phoolan Devi, was a former bandit and ex-convict who became popular politically largely because of her checkered past.

On balance, however, women are underrepresented in Indian politics. India ranks 97th in the world (tied with Jordan) on the International Parliamentary Union's list of female representation in national legislatures. Fewer than 10.5 percent of the current Lok Sabha members are women.

Indian women have plenty to be concerned about. Above, we saw that dowries are still the norm. So, too, is everything from wife beating and other forms of violence to unequal pay. Middle-class women, who often lead independent lives before they get married, lead the small feminist movement. But once that happens, they fall back into the traditional pattern of male dominance and, in some cases, control by their mothers-in-law. A series of public gang rapes gave sexual abuse crimes new visibility in spring 2013.

All this happens despite the fact that the constitution grants equal rights for all women. ■

president played the role expected of him, helping to find a prime ministerial candidate who could form a government or, if that proved impossible, paving the way for the dissolution of the Lok Sabha and new parliamentary elections.

Parliament

As in Britain, the key to power in India lies in the lower house of parliament, the Lok Sabha. All but two of its 543 members represent single-member constituencies in which elections follow the same kind of **first-past-the-post**, or winner-take-all, system used in the United States and

Great Britain. It should be noted, though, that given the size of the Indian population, the average MP represents close to two million people (loksabha.nic.in).

Nominally, the president appoints the prime minister, but in reality he or she has little or no leeway, because the prime minister must be the head of the majority party or coalition in the Lok Sabha (parliamentofindia.nic.in). As in Britain, the prime minister appoints the other members of the Council of Ministers, who must already be MPs or win election to it in a by-election within six months. The prime minister will invite somewhere between twelve and eighteen ministers to join the cabinet. Because a group even that size can be unwieldy, there is normally a smaller group of cabinet members and other informal advisers (e.g., the "household" of Indira Gandhi's years) that wield the most power.

The legislative process is similar to that in Britain. The cabinet initiates almost all significant legislation (pmindia.nic.in). Other business, including private-member bills, receives less than a day's attention per week during Lok Sabha sessions.

Bills receive the same three readings they do in Britain. The most important is the second, when the Lok Sabha votes on the principles of the legislation after it has been examined by the relevant committee. Voting is almost always along party lines, which all but ensures that the government's bills are passed, except during periods when there is no clear majority.

Party discipline in the Lok Sabha has not been enforced quite as strictly as it is in Britain's House of Commons because the parties themselves are often in flux. Thus, until recently, it was not uncommon for an individual MP to quit his or her party and join a new one during the middle of a term. These defections caused so much uncertainty at both the federal and state levels that MPs who quit their party now have to leave parliament as well unless one-third of their delegation joins them. Not surprisingly, these rather draconian rules have led to a sharp reduction in the number of defections and to less uncertainty in the Lok Sabha.

Once passed by the Lok Sabha, a bill is sent to the upper house, or **Rajya Sabha** (House of the States), which has 250 members. Of those, twelve represent the artistic and intellectual community and are appointed by the president. The rest are elected by the state legislative assemblies. If the two houses do not agree, a variety of consultative mechanisms are used to iron out the differences. If those efforts fail, the two houses meet together and vote on the bill—a vote the Lok Sabha invariably wins, given its more than two-to-one size advantage.

On balance, though, the Lok Sabha is even weaker than the House of Commons. To begin with, there is far more turnover, which leaves it with fewer experienced members than lower houses in most liberal democracies. Even more than in Britain, MPs lack the staff, offices, and other facilities they would need to assume an effective oversight role. Finally, and most important, the opposition has been so fragmented that it has been hard for it to effectively utilize question time and other mechanisms that give oppositions elsewhere a modicum of leverage over the majority party and the executive.

The Bureaucracy

Another British inheritance that is a cornerstone of the state is the **Indian Administrative Service (IAS)**, which sits atop the country's gigantic bureaucracy. The British created the Indian Civil Service in the nineteenth century.

After independence, the service was renamed, but little else changed. The Union Public Service Commission (www.upsc.gov.in) supervises annual examinations through which about 150 extremely talented young men and women are admitted into the IAS and a few other top civil service corps. In all, this bureaucratic elite has about four thousand members.

The rest of the fifteen-million-member civil service is a different story. Below the IAS level, the bureaucracy is generally seen as overstaffed and inefficient. Although bureaucrats have job security, they do not make much money. Many, therefore, tend not to work very hard and/or take bribes. Informal groups of fixers act as intermediaries (paid, of course) between average citizens and the bureaucracy. For instance, it is often only through these intermediaries that Annawadi residents and others gain access to state programs and their financial benefits. In short, in contrast to the impersonal, legally structured civil services in the advanced industrialized democracies, power in the Indian civil service—and, hence, in the degree to which policy is effectively implemented—revolves around personal connections, which are typically based on family, caste, or religion.

Federalism

The British were never able to unite all of India under a centralized government. Their successors never tried. A series of "reorganizations" since the constitution went into effect have left India with twenty-eight states and seven union territories whose boundaries are drawn so that one major linguistic group predominates in each of them (www.india.gov.in/knowindia/state_uts.php). Ten states have more than fifty million residents.

Each has a government patterned after the national one. A governor appointed by the central government is the official head of state. Real power, however, is supposed to lie with a legislature (bicameral in some but not all) and a council of state ministers responsible to the lower house. The exact names of these bodies vary from state to state and language to language.

What matters here is not how these state governments are structured or what powers they do or do not have. Rather, the states are of interest because they are another area of political life in which the importance of caste and other informal social relationships leap to the fore.

At first, Congress dominated at the state level, not losing control anywhere until 1967. Since then, its support has declined even more rapidly in the states than in New Delhi. But even this picture is misleading because much of state politics is not about ideological issues. Rather, the competition is mostly between factions based on **patron-client relations**.

Patrons can be party, caste, or religious leaders (they, of course, overlap) who offer their clients jobs, infrastructure projects, or other benefits in exchange for votes. Local patrons tend to be clients of more prominent leaders who weave networks together into what are all but ideology-free factions. Above all, factional leaders want and need to win to obtain the resources and benefits that keep their clients loyal. Therefore, they can seem quite fickle, casting their lot with one party or leader today but shifting to another tomorrow.

The combination of factional politics and growing linguistic, religious, and ethnic tensions has made most states hard to govern. Few elect clear and disciplined majorities, which means that state governments have often been unstable. Moreover, all too many factional leaders have condoned the use of violence, engaged in corruption, and relied on organized criminals (it is worth noting that *thug* is one of many English words of Indian origin) in seeking power.

In part to maintain their own power, central governments controlled both by Congress and its opposition have been increasingly willing to suspend normal state politics and to use Article 356 of the constitution to impose **President's Rule**, the state-level equivalent of the federal emergency powers.

In December 2003, the federal and state governments reached an agreement that sharply curtailed the use of President's Rule. The prime minister agreed to apply it as a last resort and only if constitutional mechanisms completely broke down. The government would also have to get prior agreement from the Lok Sabha if it was in session (or have it ratify its decision when it next met) and fully explain its reasons for resorting to the use of these extraordinary powers.

Presidential rule has been used three times since 2009, all in Jharkhand. Jharkhand is one of India's newest and poorest states. Less than half of its villages have electricity or are reachable by roads of any kind. It also has tremendous mineral resources. The decision to impose central control also reflected the continued influence of the Maoist insurgency by the Naxalites, which has claimed about one thousand lives nationwide since 2008.

Public Policy

The continuity of India's democracy may be unusual by Third World standards. The travails it has encountered with its public policies are not.

As is the case in most of the Global South, the weakness of India's state is easy to see in virtually any policy area. Lacking economic and other resources to start with, India faces increasing pressures from groups in its own society and from the outside, most notably as the global economy impinges ever more on it. The two sets of pressures are easiest to see in successive governments' attempts to confront ethnic, linguistic, religious, and caste-based conflict and to speed up economic growth.

Confronting Communal Violence

Identity-based conflict has already appeared several times in this chapter, as it will throughout Part 4. What is important to see at this juncture is that violence resulting from such conflict and the state's reaction to it are an all but permanent part of the Indian political landscape.

In the first years after independence, Indian governments succeeded in ensuring that communal conflict fell short of violence. Like every government since 1947, the first Congress leaders never considered any alternatives to a unified Indian state.

However, they were the only ones who tried to work out accommodations with minority regional and linguistic groups who clamored for more autonomy. Given their commitment to India as a secular state, the leadership has never been willing to allow religious groups to stake territorial political claims, which has prompted considerable unrest in many states and union territories after Indira Gandhi solidified her control over the Congress machine. Although specific policies have varied from state to state and group to group, it is safe to say that the net effect of public policy since the mid-1970s has been to exacerbate—not ease—ethnic, religious, and linguistic tensions.

During the Nehru years, Delhi redrew some state borders so that each major linguistic group would have a state it could govern. Once those states were created or restructured, however, the government faced an impasse because the remaining issues generally involved conflict within individual states, pitting the majority linguistic or religious group against a minority or, as in Assam, minorities. Furthermore, these more difficult issues emerged at the same time that Congress's majority was eroding. Therefore, unlike in the 1950s and 1960s, the party had to pay more attention to holding on to its core constituencies, which included key groups that were hostile to further accommodation with minorities.

Ethnic conflict worsened under Indira Gandhi, with her contradictory desires to control as many states as possible but to do so with as weak leaders as possible. To see the general patterns of ethnic conflict and the way public policies contributed to it, we will focus on Punjab, Kashmir, Gujarat, and the terrorist attacks on Mumbai.

Conflict resolution specialists have proposed dozens of ways of stopping communal violence. Some of those policy options involving, for instance, strengthening federal institutions, seemed plausible a generation ago but are now all but completely impractical largely because Indian politicians seem to have lost the Gandhian and Nehruvean ability to support tolerance and consensus building.

Punjab

Punjab lies along the Pakistani border. The original state of Punjab was ethnically mixed. In 1951, a little over half of its sixteen million people were Hindus, but it also had the country's largest concentration of Sikhs. By the 1960s, they were the only large ethnic group that did not have its own state (www.sikhnet.com).

Negotiations to create a majority Sikh state were complicated by the fact that they are a religious as well as a linguistic group, and granting them a state would call the commitment to a secular India into question. Nonetheless, an agreement was finally reached to split Punjab, creating a new state with the same name whose population was about 60 percent Sikh. Some difficulties remained, including the status of Chandigarh, which was to serve as a shared capital for Punjab and the other new state. Still, most people expected this to be another of the largely successful settlements that had marked the history of ethnic conflict in India up to that point.

This was not to happen. In fact, the communal violence there in the 1980s was the most disruptive outburst since partition. Observers are still having a hard time disentangling all the reasons protest increased. Most, though, cite two main factors.

First, the social and economic changes that swept Punjab left many members of its Sikh majority dissatisfied. Punjab had been one of the poorest regions in the country. However, the state-sponsored green revolution and the hard work of thousands of Punjabis had turned it into one of the richest. When this happened, some Sikhs began to fear that their traditional culture and values would be lost. Others remained dissatisfied with the way state borders were redrawn.

To make a long story short, a new generation of militants emerged, the most audacious of whom was a young cleric, **Jarnail Singh Bhindranwale** (1947–1984). Most Sikhs rejected the extremists' demand for an independent state. Nonetheless, tensions mounted as more Sikhs came to demand a larger slice of the political and economic pie, including a greater share of the water from rivers that flowed through the state. In addition, a Sikh party, the Akali Dal, challenged Congress domination of state politics. Finally, Bhindranwale and other leaders used the mass media to spread their message, including their growing hatred of a central government that they thought was ever more pro-Hindu and anti-Sikh.

Second, in keeping with her general centralization of power, Indira Gandhi's government rejected further Sikh demands after the creation of the new Punjab. Gandhi never dealt gently with people who disagreed with her. She took a particularly hard line toward Punjab because the Sikhs and the Akali Dal had been among the most vocal opponents of Emergency Rule.

As support for the Akali Dal grew in the late 1970s, Congress tacitly supported Bhindranwale and other Sikh extremists, but the strategy backfired on Congress once it returned to power. More and more Sikhs endorsed a 1973 agreement that would have drastically reduced Delhi's power vis-à-vis the states. It never went into effect. Sikhs launched attacks against Hindus, some of whom assaulted Sikhs in retaliation. Meanwhile, Bhindranwale and other extremists gained more and more influence, especially among young men.

In 1981, Bhindranwale was accused of murder. Two years later, when it seemed as if the government might finally take him into custody, Bhindranwale and his supporters occupied the Golden Temple in Amritsar, the Sikhs' holiest shrine.

In a typically opportunistic move, Gandhi imposed President's Rule, removing the elected Akali Dal government. Nonetheless, violence continued. Clashes between Sikhs and Hindus threatened to undermine Congress's electoral base among Hindus outside Punjab, who were frustrated by the government's inability to protect their coreligionists.

In March 1984, the All India Sikh Student Federation (AISSF) was officially abolished. One hundred fifty companies of police troops were sent to the Punjab, including ninety at the Golden Temple alone. In response, still active AISSF members occupied more temples. Meanwhile, in neighboring Haryana, the Congress chief minister at the very least condoned organized mob violence against Sikhs who lived in his state.

Finally, in June, Gandhi ordered troops to storm the temple. Bhindranwale and at least five hundred of his supporters were killed. The surviving Sikh leaders, including most prominent Akali Dal officials, were arrested. Sikh soldiers mutinied and rioted in the most serious breach of army discipline since independence.

Then in October, Sikh members of her own security detail assassinated Gandhi. The assassination was followed by nights of rioting in which Hindus killed hundreds of Sikhs around the country, most of whom had nothing to do with Gandhi's murder and probably did not support Sikh secession.

As was the case in most public policy areas, Rajiv Gandhi set out to do things differently. Almost immediately upon taking office, he began negotiations with the Akali Dal. The two sides eventually reached an agreement that, among other things, would have returned Chandigarh to Punjab and given the state some control over the vital water resources its farmers claimed they needed.

In 1987, however, Gandhi backed out of the deal in part because his Hindu constituents throughout northern India were not prepared to accept such sweeping concessions to the Sikhs. Two years later, he played the Hindu trump card in the 1989 campaign in ways designed to maximize his party's support among orthodox Hindus, who were expected to be the swing vote and thus the key to victory. On television, Congress frequently showed footage of Indira Gandhi's funeral pyre with a sobbing Rajiv standing nearby, the implication being that the Sikhs were to blame. The situation in Punjab was so intense following Rajiv Gandhi's assassination during the 1991 campaign that elections there had to be delayed for months.

In the last few years, support for Sikh independence has diminished considerably. Indeed, the most significant protests of the early 2000s in the state came from the BJP, which objected to special benefits supposedly given to Sikhs. Sikh nationalists as such did not launch counterdemonstrations, and the whole question of secession has disappeared from mainstream politics, though many Sikhs remain resentful of what they claim to be thousands of their compatriots who have been killed by Indian authorities and as many as fifty thousand who have been imprisoned since 1984. To cite but the most recent example, in May 2009, rioters protesting against a shootout at a Sikh temple in Austria burned buses and destroyed ATMs in a number of cities.

Kashmir

Over the last decade, the most serious communal conflict has taken place in the state of Jammu and Kashmir. The dispute there is particularly important because the region was a flash point in the conflict between India and Pakistan following the 9/11 attacks on the United States and tensions there could well have led to war between the two rivals.

Kashmir was one of the princely states that were not officially under British rule whose leaders had to choose between joining India or Pakistan. Geography made that choice easy in most cases, but that decision was anything but easy for what became the Indian state of Jammu and Kashmir, which lies in northwestern India along the Pakistani border (www.jammu-kashmir.com/index.html).

It has a substantial Muslim majority, which would lead one to expect that it would have gone to Pakistan. However, its prince was a Hindu who wanted to be in India. In the months after independence, Pakistani troops invaded part of the state and forced the maharajah to flee. He then asked for support from Indian troops, at which point the state formally joined India. Nehru's government agreed to hold a referendum in which Kashmiri voters

The Golden Temple, the holiest shrine in the Sikh religion. It was the site of a bloody 1984 attack by government forces against nationalist rebels.

would choose which of them to join, but it was never held because Pakistan continued to occupy part of the state.

War broke out again in 1965, and Jammu and Kashmir were battlegrounds in the 1971 war that led to the independence of Bangladesh. Afterward, the two sides agreed to a de facto division of the state into regions controlled by India and Pakistan on each side of the last positions their troops had occupied, dubbed the Line of Control.

Over the next few years, opposition to Indian rule grew among Muslims. Some wanted to join Pakistan, and others wanted to create their own country. Tensions reached a peak when many Muslims became convinced that the 1987 state election had been rigged against them.

At about the same time, some militant Muslims went to Pakistan, where they were trained as fighters (many Indians would use the term terrorists). In 1989, the most recent wave of fighting broke out when militant Muslims and allies from abroad started launching attacks on Indian targets. According to Indian sources, over 35,000 people have been killed since then. The Pakistanis put the number at 70,000.

The two sides could not even agree on who did what. Pakistan claimed that it gave only "moral and diplomatic support" to the Kashmiris, and India accused Pakistan of sponsoring "cross-border terrorism." One thing is clear. During the 1990s and the first years of the twenty-first century the opposition became more Islamic than nationalistic and began attracting other *jihadis* who had fought against the Soviets in neighboring Afghanistan.

The outside world paid relatively little attention to the on-again off-again fighting in the region until India and Pakistan both tested nuclear weapons in 1998. At that point, observers realized that fighting there could set off a devastating regional nuclear conflagration. This was readily apparent in May 1999, when Indian artillery began shelling Pakistani positions across the Line of Control, claiming that the government had infiltrated regular troops into the Pakistani region, a charge the government vehemently denied. Tensions were defused when Pakistan submitted to pressure from the United States and redeployed some of its troops.

Jammu and Kashmir made the world's headlines after the 9/11 terrorist attacks. Pakistan quickly agreed to support the American-led war against terrorism. The worst fighting in more than a year began in October 2001 when India started shelling Pakistani positions. Tensions mounted further following an attack on the Indian parliament building in December, for which Vajpayee's government blamed Pakistani and Kashmiri militants for, on the one hand, claiming to oppose the terrorism of al-Qaeda and the Taliban but, on the other hand, continuing to support it in Kashmir. For the rest of 2001 and the first weeks of 2002, rarely a day went by without at least one violent death. Yet another war between India and Pakistan seemed possible.

A brief glimmer of hope occurred in late 2003 and early 2004 when both governments floated peace proposals as part of a general rapprochement between the two countries. Neither succeeded. The most important source of optimism today is the work of Indian and foreign nongovernmental organizations (NGOs) who have been working to get the two sides to the negotiating table.

The most impressive of these has been run by the Washington-based International Center for Religion and Diplomacy (www.icrd.org/projects.html#kashmir). Since 2001, it has sent teams of clergy and laypeople to Kashmir to work on both sides of the Line of Control. By the summer of 2004, it had conducted reconciliation seminars that more than three hundred local Muslim, Hindu, and Buddhist leaders have attended. It helped some of those young men and women establish reconciliation centers in Jammu and Srinagar, which are the winter and summer capitals of the state, respectively. Perhaps most significantly, it identified and helped train a group of leaders who are interested in building bridges between the two communities.

In early 2005, the two governments also forged some small and largely symbolic agreements, the most important of which established bus lines that would carry people across the Line of Control. This may not seem like a major step forward, but any agreement after more than a half-century of frustration has to be taken as a serious move by both sides.

There has been less violence since then. Still, protests flare regularly, most recently when Indians proposed giving a large swath of Muslim-controlled land for a Hindu temple. As we will see, there is reason to believe that at least some of the terrorists who attacked Mumbai in late 2008 were either from Kashmir or had fought there.

Gujarat

The most vicious fighting in the 2000s occurred in the state of Gujarat, which also borders Pakistan. Its population

Next-generation Kashmiri leaders discussing reconciliation at a seminar organized by the International Center for Religion and Diplomacy.

pretty much matches that of the country as a whole. Almost 90 percent of Gujaratis are Hindus; not quite 10 percent are Muslim. Gujarat is also one of the richest states, accounting for 20 percent of India's industrial production and almost half of its exports even though Gujaratis only make up about 5 percent of the population.

The violence began in earnest in 2002 when a Muslim mob allegedly burned fifty-eight Hindus to death while they were riding in a train. Most were women and children. The state's BJP government at best turned a blind eye to a campaign of ethnic cleansing in which tens of thousands of Muslims were forced to flee their homes for hastily constructed refugee camps.

Attacks by Muslims against Hindus and Hindus against Muslims took place in more than half of the state's twenty-six districts. By the middle of that, the violence had become so intense that almost as many Hindus as Muslims had been burned out of their homes. The police did little to try to end the violence, which also got relatively little attention at first from the national government.

Most of the blame for the riots was placed on the VHP and other groups connected to the BJP, whose current leader, Narendra Modi, was already the state's chief minister. Finally, in 2004, an independent commission determined that the initial fire was probably accidental in origin. The state government resigned, and when the national government finally allowed a new ballot, Modi and the BJP won reelection in a landslide.

By that time, 800 Muslims and 250 Hindus were dead. Well over 200 people are still listed as missing. Some advocacy groups put the death toll at closer to 2,000.

The disturbances in Gujarat did not last as long as those in Punjab or Kashmir. As in those two states, there have been sporadic protests since 2004, including a demonstration after police officers killed an election worker who was monitoring a polling place in 2009.

However, because militant Hindus were at the heart of the violence, identity politics in Gujarat is often interpreted as the most dangerous threat to democracy in India. As Martha Nussbaum put it, "Hindus in India have internalized a historical narrative according to which they are a pure and peaceful civilization that has been conquered again and again. When people murder people who have been their neighbors for years, something has gone wrong at a deeper level."[6]

Mumbai

India and the world awoke on November 27, 2008, to one of the most devastating terrorist attacks ever. India had experienced terrorism before, but every other incident paled in comparison with this one.

Home of Annawadi, Mumbai is one of the world's most densely populated cities, historically known for its overcrowding, filth, traffic jams, and poverty. Today, it is also at the forefront of India's economic boom to be discussed in the next section.

About fifteen Muslim terrorists from India, Kashmir, and Pakistan came ashore at the port of Mumbai in rubber dinghies. The terrorists attacked a number of high-profile targets, including a luxury hotel, the city's main commuter railroad station, and an orthodox Jewish center. When the siege ended three days later with the death or capture of all the terrorists, at least 101 were dead and almost 300 wounded. The terrorists seem to have singled out holders of American and British passports.

After the attacks, the Indian and Pakistani governments hurled verbal attacks at each other, though there were few signs that the crisis could take the countries closer to war again.

After a few weeks, the Pakistani government acknowledged that the sole survivor was Pakistani, the plot had been at least partially planned in Pakistan, and at least some of the terrorists were part of Lashkar-e-Taibi, a militant Muslim group that has been active in India, Pakistan, and Kashmir since 2000. It has long been on the list of terrorist organizations that most Western governments maintain. The surviving terrorist was found guilty and executed in 2012.

Stimulating the Economy

Prior to the mid-1980s, Indian governments relied primarily on import substitution and a largely state owned, managed, and planned economy to spur growth and reduce poverty. Since then, outside pressures and domestic frustration with what the Indians themselves often called the "Hindu rate of growth" have led every leader since Rajiv Gandhi to reconsider the social democratic goals and practices that their predecessors had taken for granted.

Indian economic policy before the reforms were introduced was not an abject disaster. There was enough growth to create a new middle class. The **green revolution** and its high-yield crops had all but eliminated famine, if not hunger and malnutrition. It has nuclear weapons and medium-range ballistic missiles, and its computer software was already among the best in the world.

On balance, though, the Indian economy did not fare very well, especially when compared with countries like South Korea, which were almost as poor as India at the end of World War II. Table 12.7 presents comparative data on economic growth for India and some other Southern countries in the mid-1980s that had roughly equal economic conditions in the immediate post-war years.

---

[6]Martha C. Nussbaum, *The Clash Within: Democracy, Religious Violence, and India's Future* (Cambridge: Harvard/Belknap, 2007), 6, 48.

TABLE 12.7 Selected Economic Indicators: India and Comparable Countries before Structural Adjustment

COUNTRY	PER CAPITA GROSS NATIONAL PRODUCT PER CAPITA, 1987 ($)	AVERAGE ANNUAL GROWTH 1965–87 (%)
India	300	1.8
Brazil	2,020	4.1
China	290	5.2
Indonesia	450	4.5
Mexico	1,830	2.5
Pakistan	350	2.5
South Korea	2,690	6.4
Thailand	850	3.9
Turkey	1,210	2.6

India's economy grew by an average of nearly 2 percent per capita per year from the mid-1960s through the mid-1980s. The growth was concentrated in the industrial sector, which import substitution policy made the highest priority. But India did not do very well in relative terms. Of the countries included in the table, none had a slower rate of growth and only China had a lower GNP per capita.

India has since opened much of its economy to the global market, with remarkable success. So far, growth has increased by about 7 percent a year in this century. Like China, it has largely escaped the current economic crisis.

That said, no major dent has been put in the poverty rate and other social problems. In fact, the United Nations Development Project's *Human Development Report* (HDR) for 2011 ranked India just 134th in the world despite the economic reforms.

But unlike China, the state has not been a major stimulus for change. It has changed laws that, for instance, prohibited foreigners from owning India-based companies. But more important, the boom of the last twenty years has almost completely been driven by entrepreneurs in the private sector.

The Nehruvian Model and India's Economic Woes

India's continued poverty obviously has many causes. Atop most scholarly lists is the economic policy of import substitution pursued from 1947 until the mid-1980s. Nehru and his colleagues had been deeply influenced by the British Fabian movement and its democratic version of socialism. This led them to focus on a strong public sector to steer development and to generate a more just and egalitarian society.

The Industrial Policy Resolution of 1948 called for a mixed economy, with government ownership of all munitions, atomic energy, and railroad enterprises. The resolution also gave the government the sole right to start new ventures in such key sectors as iron and steel, telecommunications, aircraft, and shipbuilding. Eighteen other industries remained in private hands but subject to government control and regulation.

Under the leadership of one of Nehru's closest advisers, P. C. Mahalanobis, these "commanding heights" of the economy were to be managed using five-year plans that were more controlling than the French plans but less so than the Soviets' before Gorbachev. At the heart of the system was what the Indians call the permit raj, an elaborate system of tariffs, licenses, and other regulations that kept most imports out and made the ones that did get in so expensive that few people could afford them. In this manner, it protected publicly and privately owned firms alike, which continued making the same products in the same way and earning the same all-but-guaranteed rate of profit year after year.

High tariffs and other regulations protected domestic industry. In 1985, rates ranged from 107 percent on capital goods to 140 percent on most manufactured products. In addition, most industrial goods could be imported only by what the government called "actual users." But even that was not always possible because, for instance, automobile, truck, and bus manufacturers were not allowed to import tires.

There is little question that these economic policies met their initial goals, as India did become reasonably self-sufficient. In 1984 the import of finished goods accounted for only 8 percent of its gross domestic product, compared with an average of over 19 percent in the rest of the Global South. India developed a substantial industrial base with limited interference from or obligations to other countries. But isolation also had its costs. The absence of both internal and international competition was one of many causes of corruption and inefficiency. More important, the economy did not benefit from the capital, technology, and other resources more trade could have provided—admittedly, at the cost of considerable domestic control. Most significant of all, the Indian economy was falling ever farther behind those of many other Southern countries.

Liberalization

Even before the Washington Consensus might have forced reform on them, most Indians came to the conclusion that import substitution was retarding overall growth by depriving the economy of the stimuli a more open market could provide. Since then, India has gradually opened its economy and adopted other promarket policies the international financial institutions and multinational corporations endorsed. It has not done so as quickly as Mexico, nor has international pressure on it to change been as direct. Nonetheless, India's policies in the new century are a far cry from what they were when Rajiv Gandhi took office in 1984.

There are many reasons why he began to tilt the balance away from state ownership, planning, and control. In part, the new policies reflected his own background, which included university study in the West and a career that began in business. In part, they grew out of pressures in the global economy that already inflicted a heavy price on countries that tried to resist the trend toward more open markets and unrestricted international trade.

Gandhi and his youthful colleagues wanted to take India in that direction, and they gradually introduced liberalizing reforms. The forces behind liberalization gained even more support after 1989 and the collapse of the Soviet bloc. Reform efforts peaked early in the Narasihma Rao government, in which reformers like current Prime Minister Manmohan Singh (1932–) and P. Chidambaram (with his Harvard MBA) were given the key economic ministries.

Since then, barriers to outside investment have been cut on the assumption that capital and competition from abroad will give a much needed boost to domestic industries that had stagnated under the permit raj. Foreign direct investment has mushroomed in India even though the government limits the portion of a firm that can be owned by non-Indians. Thus, in 2008, people from outside of India (including a large number of expatriates) invested $27 billion in the country. By contrast, that figure was only $13 million in 1981 and $121 million in 1989. Similarly, foreigners may own as much as three-fourths of the shares in a privately owned bank but only 20 percent in those that are publicly traded.

The government has sold parts of many state-owned industries, including the automobile manufacturer Maruti Udyog, which is now controlled by Suzuki. Air India and Indian Airlines merged in 2011 when the state owned 51 percent of each of them. They are scheduled for privatization at some point in the not-so-distant future.

The most visible change has come in information technology. Because its economic borders historically were so closed, India had not developed a competitive domestic computer industry even though it had long been a world leader in software development. With the newly open economy, it offered outside investors a pool of skilled but low-paid labor, and it held out the promise of a massive new market at some point in the future. "Silicon valleys" have developed around Bangalore in the south and Hyderabad in the north.

In 2011, there were more than ten thousand extremely wealthy people whose fortunes were based in information technology in the Bangalore area alone. More than one-fourth of all outsourced offshore jobs from the United States have ended up in India, with almost half of them in the IT sector.

The government has also encouraged more exports so that India can earn hard currency to buy the goods it has to import. Since the 1990s, exports have grown at the average rate of 20 percent per year, although the country still imports about $100 billion worth of goods and services more than it exports. The biggest growth area, not surprisingly, is in information services.

Prime Minister Manmohan Singh, the surprise choice to lead the government following Congress's surprise victory in 2004.

The dismantling of the permit raj has sped up during Singh's second five-year term as prime minister. Even more importantly, there is little likelihood that subsequent Indian governments will stop the transition, since the BJP is, if anything, even more promarket.

Poverty Most mainstream scholars today estimate that at least three hundred million Indians are poor, a number greater than the total population of every country on earth except for China and the United States. Of the twenty to thirty million Indians born each year, well over half are born into poverty. The bottom 10 percent of the population controls 3 percent of the income; the top 10 percent makes ten times that.

About one-sixth of the population lives in what economists call ultrapoverty, because their incomes fall more than 25 percent below what people need to assure they have access to adequate food, clothing, and shelter. Many of the poor are homeless; the best-off live in substandard housing, with dozens of families crammed into teeming tenements or shanty towns like Annawadi. Many are malnourished, and those who do get the minimum daily caloric intake needed to sustain a healthy life survive primarily on grains. A missed day or two of work can leave a family without enough money to feed itself. Health care for the poor is virtually nonexistent, and life expectancy for those in poverty barely tops fifty years.

Poverty, of course, is not randomly distributed. The lower castes and *dalits* are most likely to be poor.

Comparative Emphasis: Globalization

India is often portrayed in the English-speaking press as one of the most striking examples of how globalization can reshape a country. That has been the case especially in the last decade with the growth of its "silicon valleys" and the export of many Western technology jobs to them.

However, it should be noted that India as a whole has not been all that deeply affected by globalization. It has opened its economic borders more slowly than many countries and continues to try to protect domestic industries, albeit less than previous Indian governments did. To cite but one example, its overall export totals are only about one-eighth those of the Chinese. China ranks third in the world in gross exports. India is twenty-eighth. ■

There are still about six hundred thousand families of outcaste origin who make a living, such as it is, emptying latrines and chamber pots. Poverty is worse in rural areas though the gap between them and the cities is much smaller than it once was. There are thousands of villages without safe drinking water, roads that are passable in all weather, or rudimentary health care services.

Women suffer the most. In poor families, they are responsible for all household tasks, which in rural areas can include the time-consuming and physically draining search for firewood. In urban areas, women are much less likely to receive health care or an education than are men. Overall, not even one-fourth of India's women are literate, and in the poorest, rural areas, only about 2 percent of all women can read and write, thus depriving them of one of the skills they could use to pull themselves out of poverty.

The government has enjoyed some success in reducing poverty. Between 1970 and 1990, the poverty rate was cut by about one-fourth. Still, as a result of continued population growth, the number of poor people actually increased during those same years.

The government also devised a number of successful and innovative approaches to help people improve their lives. The Integrated Rural Development Program (IRDP) was created to give villagers low-level technology and other new skills. For instance, in a number of villages, night soil gatherers were taught how to harness the methane contained in human waste to generate electricity to fuel small-scale industrial facilities. In all, the IRDP reached about 27 million rural families, spending an average of about $500 on each. But this gave no more than 10 percent of the rural poor the ability to escape poverty—assuming the program worked perfectly, which, of course, it did not.

The government has also steered some of its revenues from taxes on the new firms to address the isolation of poor villages. Pilot programs have been conducted in some desperately poor regions near Bangalore where people are trained to use telephone and computer systems that use energy from solar power. The knowledge center in the town of Embalm trained more than six hundred illiterate people how to use the Internet, which saved them significant amounts of time and money that they would have had to spend traveling to find out such basic things as market prices for their crops.

Finally, India's record pales in comparison with most other large Southern countries. India has been able to reduce the size of the population below the poverty line by about 1 percent per year, which is better than Colombia, Morocco, and Sri Lanka have done. But most other countries that started at similar rates of development have done far better, including Indonesia, which is reducing its poor population by about 2.5 percent per year. On another indicator of poverty—reducing the mortality rate for children under five years of age—India ranks last in this same sample of countries.

The Media

As befits its tumultuous and divided political system, India has a lively mass media. Even though barely half of the population is literate, the country has more than two thousand daily newspapers, which are among the cheapest in the world. The papers, of course, are published in dozens of languages, and 12 million out of each day's print run of 68 million are in English. They cover the entire political spectrum, with many of the best papers enjoying reputations for their investigative journalism. Although political news dominates the printed press, the fastest-growing newspapers are the ones that concentrate on financial news; their circulations have tripled since the introduction of economic liberalization.

Until recently, television and radio were completely state owned. Since the mid-1990s, however, cable and satellite television have been introduced, and one journalist estimates that more than two hundred million people have access to one or the other. These people can now watch both the BBC World News and Rupert Murdoch's Star service and, thus, get differing perspectives on political events.

A nationwide network of satellite dishes brings television service to most villages, where the whole community watches together on its one screen.

Conclusion: Democracy in India . . . and Beyond

The obvious "big question" for students of comparative politics to raise about India is why India has remained democratic when so many others have failed to do so. However serious its difficulties may be, India is not likely to disintegrate like the Soviet Union or Yugoslavia let alone see its democracy crumble. It is risky to predict anything during these times of such rapid and unanticipated political change; nevertheless, this conclusion seems warranted if we place India in a broader comparative and theoretical perspective.

In recent years, political scientists have spent a lot of time investigating why some democracies succeed and others collapse. Although these studies are controversial, two themes appear time and time again. First, the more legitimate the regime, the less likely it is to collapse. Second, the more effective the government, the more likely it is to retain that legitimacy and, more generally, to survive. These may not seem like particularly profound conclusions, but if we shift from abstract theory to two comparisons, the reasons we can be reasonably optimistic about India's political future become clearer.

In examining the Soviet Union and the broader collapse of communism in Europe, we saw the dramatic interplay between policy failure and the loss of legitimacy. We may lack systematic evidence that would allow us to directly compare their experiences with India's, but the impressionistic indications available to us reveal a very different situation in the latter country. The Indian government has been more successful in at least some policy areas (e.g., liberalization) than any European communist regime was. And although its population is increasingly angry and polarized, most Indians still view the regime as legitimate. Perhaps most important, Indians on the whole seem to lack the kind of repressed rage ready to erupt when political straitjackets are removed, as happened when *glasnost* was instituted in the Soviet Union and Eastern Europe.

The other comparison is between India and the rest of the Third World. No matter how dire India's situation might have seemed in this chapter, it is in relatively good shape on two levels. First, India's economic performance and, of even more consequence, its economic potential are both superior to most of what we will see in the chapters on Mexico, Iran, Iraq, and Nigeria. Second, its regime has been more effective and retains more legitimacy than most others, some of which are wracked with basic divisions over whether the country itself should even exist.

Whether India is a relative success or a failure in comparative terms should not obscure the most important points for American or European students to learn about this or most other LDCs. First, these are incredibly poor countries that lack some of the basic resources and amenities we take for granted, such as primary education, rudimentary health care, safe drinking water, and shelter. Second, poverty is but one of many factors that make these countries much harder to govern, whatever the strengths or weaknesses of the people who end up trying to lead them.

KEY TERMS

Concepts	Gandhi, Indira	Organizations, Places, and Events
caste	Gandhi, Mohandas Karamchand	Ayodhya
dalit	Gandhi, Rajiv	Bharatiya Janata Party (BJP)
Emergency Rule	Gandhi, Sonia	British East India Company
first-past-the-post	Modi, Narendra	Government of India Act
jati	Nehru, Jawaharlal	Green Revolution
patron-client relations	Singh, Manmohan	Indian Administrative Service (IAS)
permit raj	Vajpayee, Atal Bihari	Indian Civil Service
President's Rule		Indian National Congress
untouchable	**Acronyms**	Lok Sabha
	BJP	Mughal
People	IAS	Rajya Sabha
Bhindranwale, Jarnail Singh	LDC	Rashtriya Swayamsevak Sangh (RSS)
Desai, Morarji	RSS	

USEFUL WEBSITES

As one might expect of a country with such a large high-tech community and such a large diaspora, there are several good portals on Indian affairs, all of which have links to political sites and news feeds. Among the best are:

www.outlookindia.com

www.indiainfo.com

Asianinfo.org is a general site, but it is more focused on making information on Asia (including India) available to the rest of the world.

www.asianinfo.org/asianinfo/india/politics.htm

The Indian government maintains an excellent site about the parliament, federal agencies, and most state governments.

Indiaimage.nic.in

Finally, there are some good sites on Indian politics, including the one run by the government, the Virtual Library, and an India-based site that has material on elections, parties, and public opinion polls. Indian Elections has good, if often too-detailed, data on election results at the national and state levels.

www.india.gov.in

www.indian-elections.com

FURTHER READING

Boo, Katherine. *Beyond the Beautiful Forevers: Life, Death, and Hope in a Mumbai Uncercity*. New York: Random House, 2012.

Brass, Paul. *The Politics of India since Independence*. New York: Cambridge University Press, 2008. The most detailed of the texts on Indian politics. It is especially good on ethnic issues.

Das, Gundcharan. *India Unbound*. New York: Knopf, 2000. A personal and analytical account of India's economic and political transformations by one of the country's leading entrepreneurs.

Dukes, Edward. *Despite the Gods*. New York: Doubleday, 2007. The best recent book on Indian economic growth despite the restrictions imposed by its spiritual traditions.

Giridharadas, Anand. *India Calling: An Intimate Portrait of a Nation's Remaking*. New York: Times Books, 2011. The best and most recent of a series of books on India's economic renewal by one of its leading architects.

Guha, Ramachandra. *India After Gandhi: The History of the World's Largest Democracy*. New York: Harper, 2008. An encyclopedic history of India since Independence.

Kapur, Akash. *India Becoming: A Portrait of Life in Modern India*. New York: Penguin, 2012. The most recent of many great books about India's rise by people who have been part of the story. This time, the author is an Indian-American who returns home after years in the United States.

Kohli, Atul. *India's Democracy: An Analysis of Changing State-Society Relations*. Princeton, NJ: Princeton University Press, 1990.

———, ed. *Democracy and Discontent: India's Growing Crisis of Government*. New York: Cambridge University Press, 1990. Two works that focus on ethnicity and other problems imperiling Indian democracy.

Nussbaum, Martha C. *The Clash Within: Democracy, Religious Violence, and India's Future*. Cambridge: Harvard/Belknap, 2007. An interesting and provocative new book that likens the violence in Gujarat and elsewhere to genocide.

Roy, Arundhati. *Power Politics*. Boston: South End Press, 2001. An impassioned plea against dams, globalization, and their impact on India by a leading architect and writer who gained notoriety after this book was published for criticizing the war against terrorism in Afghanistan.

Wolpert, Stanley. *A New History of India*, 3rd ed. New York: Oxford University Press, 1989. The best single-volume history of India.

———. *Gandhi's Passion: The Life and Legacy of Mahatma Gandhi*. New York: Oxford University Press, 2001. The best recent biography that focuses equally on the man, his politics, and his spirituality.

© Cengage Learning

POLITICAL INDICATORS

IRAN

Tabriz

Tehran

Mashhad

Bakhtaran

Esfahan

Kerman
Zahedan
Bam

Shiraz

Bandar-e 'Abbas

GOVERNANCE (score 0–1)	HUMAN DEVELOPMENT (score 0–1)	DEMOCRACY (rank)	PEACE (rank)	CORRUPTION (rank)
.536	.707	159	128	120

*Your task is very difficult. Not even
Iranians understand Iran.*

ANONYMOUS IRANIAN PROFESSOR

Iran

THE BASICS

Iran

Size	1,648 sq. km. Roughly the size of Alaska
Population	77 million
Average age	27
Ethnic distribution	Persian (61%), Azeri (16%), Kurds (10%), Arabs (2%), Others (11%)
Religion	Shiite Muslim (89%), Sunni Muslim (9%), Other (2%)
GNP per capita	$12,800
Growth GNP	–0.9%
Currency	12,260 rial = US$1 (2008–2012)
Supreme Leader	Ayatollah Ali Khamenei (1989–)
President	Hassan Rouhani (2013–)

A Very Strange Election

For most readers, Iran will be the most controversial country covered in *Comparative Politics*. Its nuclear weapons program. Economic sanctions. Its role in the Middle East, especially Syria. The status of women. Crackdowns on civil liberties and attacks on dissidents. The role faith plays in politics. All of these issues (and more) spark intense debate

both in Iran and around the world, and all of them will feature prominently in the pages that follow. To make matters worse for me as an author, most of the controversies were still raging when my editors made me stop adding new material to this edition of the book!

I had already decided that I would have to wait for the 2013 presidential election before I would have a chance of putting Iranian politics in any kind of meaningful context. That summer, Mahmoud Ahmadinejad (1956–) reached the end of his second four-year term. As is the case now in most countries, he was constitutionally barred from running for a third consecutive mandate.

The elections were going to be an important turning point even though it did not seem as if the results would matter all that much when popular attention turned to the election campaign early that winter. Almost everyone assumed, at least, that the elections would not have as momentous an impact as the one four years earlier when Ahmadinejad was reelected after having almost certainly rigged the vote count. Protests against the alleged fraud broke out around the country and led to the formation of the Green Movement which the authorities brutally repressed.

In the four years that followed, the religious leaders who truly run the country grew displeased with Ahmadinejad as well as the reformers whom he had "defeated." Therefore, most observers assumed that the clerics led by

Supreme Leader Ali Khamenei (1939–) would use their powers to deny both reformers or an Ahmadinejad supporter the opportunity to run, which is exactly what they did.

That is why most observers expected the election to come down to a choice among a group of conservative candidates who would do what Khamenei wanted. That is not what happened.

Two months before election day, we did not even know who would be running. It was only then that 686 candidates (all men) declared their candidacy (the government pays a stipend to all candidates who express a desire to run) by the deadline that came little more than a month before election day. That did not mean that they all actually made it as far as the final ballot. The **Guardian Council** has to approve all candidacies. As in the past, they ruled out most of the frivolous ones. This time, they also banned Ahmadinejad's preferred successor, Esfandiar Mashaei, and former President **Hashemi Rafsanjani** (1934–).

Eight candidates were allowed on the ballot for the three-week-long campaign, but two of them dropped out before election day. All the signs were that it would not be an exciting race. Most of the candidates were closely tied to Khamenei and his team. There were no dramatic ideological differences among the candidates, most of whom seemed remarkably dull for this day and age of telegenic candidates—even by Iranian standards.

Suddenly, however, in the last few days, the one cleric in the race, **Hassan Rouhani** (1948–), made a sudden surge in public opinion that caught the authorities so much by surprise that they ran out of time to find a way to rig the results. Rouhani rode that wave of support to a shocking first ballot victory. Although he barely won a majority of the vote, he did well enough to avoid a runoff ballot at which the authorities might have been able to "win" by hook or by crook.

Typical was the reaction of the Iranian-born political scientist Ray Takeyh in an article published in the *Washington Post* minutes after the final results were announced:

> This was supposed to be a well-regulated, well-crafted election, and then the wheels came off. It appears that the leadership miscalculated on Rouhani's appeal, and also miscalculated on the ineptness of its preferred candidates and the impact of the divisions among the conservative coalition.[1]

The election itself may not prove to be all that important, because the president is by no means Iran's most important office holder. The constitution gives that role

---

[1]www.washingtonpost.com/world/iranians-await-presidential-election-results-following-extension-of-polling-hours/2013/06/15/3800c276-d593-11e2-a73e-826d299ff459_story.html?wpisrc=al_national.

to the unelected Supreme Leader, who has to be a leading member of the clergy. In fact, given the frequent flare-ups between Khamenei and Ahmadinejad, there was even discussion of abolishing the presidency altogether as these lines were being written the day after Rouhani's victory.

In other words, Iran provides us with yet another example of the mixed or **hybrid regimes** that have figured so prominently in Parts 3 and 4. As we will see, Iran has some quasi-democratic features with its competitive elections. Indeed, one could make the case that it was the most democratic country in which Muslims make up the overwhelming majority of the population at least until the Arab Spring brought new leaders to power in Egypt and Tunisia earlier in this decade. On the other hand, the power of the Supreme Leader and other clerical officials suggests that Iran falls far short of any definition of democracy even hinted at in Chapter 2.

Thinking About Iran

The Bottom Line

Iran is one of the world's oldest countries. Despite that fact, almost everything about the country is a subject of ferocious debate.

What's in a Name?

The debates start with what the country should be called. It was most commonly referred to as Persia by most Western observers until recently. That name comes from the region's dominant language, Farsi. **Reza Shah**, the first of the two **Pahlavi** monarchs, officially changed the country's name to Iran, which had long been the term most people who lived there chose to call it. That term, too, is significant because its origins are the same as the word *Aryan*, which that shah wanted to stress as a key theme in the country's history, which stretches back to the time of its first great emperors, Darius and Cyrus, about 2,500 years ago.

The two names also reflect the country's two most powerful cultural traditions, Persian culture and Shiite Islam. It is not too much of an overstatement to say that Iranian politics since the late nineteenth century has been a struggle over which of the two would predominate. As we will see in the section on Iranian history, the Pahlavis and other modernizers wanted to downplay the role of Islam and thus stressed the more secular aspects of Persian history, ranging from the poetry of its intellectuals to the world-famous wine made from Shiraz grapes. By contrast, the clergy emphasized the country's Shiite tradition and the role of faith.

The **Islamic Revolution** in 1979 tilted the balance toward religion to such a degree that Iran is one of the few theocracies left in which religious and political power are legally fused in what is officially called the **Islamic Republic**. Officially, Iran is governed according to Muslim principles largely as they are interpreted by clerics, most notably its Supreme Leader, who constitutionally has to be a leading member of the clergy. As such, **Sharia** (Muslim law) is far more influential than in most other heavily Muslim countries as we will see in the next chapter on Nigeria. At the same time, we will see that events such as the emergence of the Green Movement in 2009 have put the debate over what the role of religion should be very much on center stage.

To make matters even more confusing, Iran is not an overwhelmingly Persian country because they make up less than 60 percent of the population. Almost a quarter of all Iranians are Azeris. The rest come from a number of ethnic groups, including Kurds and Arabs, none of which make up more than 8 percent of the population. Only three in five Iranians are native Farsi speakers. As we will see later, more than 2,500 years of common history have enabled Iranians to put their ethnic differences in perspective and develop a strong sense of national identity that is missing, for example, in Nigeria. However, one of the politically important misconceptions foreigners often have is that Iran is a homogeneous country whose people share a common culture and belief system.

Shiite and Sunni

Iran is an *Islamic* republic. However, its version of Islam is by no means the same as the one practiced in Saudi Arabia or espoused by groups like al-Qaeda. What's more, the common Western misconception that all Muslims are the same has led to a series of political blunders over the last half-century, many of which have taken a terrible toll on Iran and its people.

As is true of all the world's major religions, Muslims have been divided into rival sects for centuries. About 90 percent of all Muslims are **Sunnis**, who are politically predominant everywhere except for Iran and now Iraq. Most of the remaining 10 percent are **Shiites**, who are widely and often mistakenly viewed as the most militant Muslims despite the fact that almost all followers of al-Qaeda and related groups are Sunnis.

The Sunni/Shiite split dates from the death of the Prophet Muhammad in 632. He did not designate a successor to head the rapidly expanding faith and empire he had given birth to. Almost immediately, his followers split into two camps. Those who became Sunnis felt that the most prominent members of the community should select the caliph on the basis of personal attributes such as piety, wisdom, morality, leadership ability, and competence.

Others, however, contended that only members of the prophet's family should lead the Islamic community. They also believed that Muhammad had designated his cousin, son-in-law, and close companion, Ali, to be his successor. They were called Shiites or Shi'a, a word derived from the expression "Shi'at Ali," or "the partisans of Ali."

To make a long story short, the Sunni won the debate with the establishment of the Umayyad dynasty in 661. The Shiites never recognized Umayyad rule and continued to insist that only Ali's direct descendants had the right to lead the Islamic community. In 680, Ali's son, Hussein, led his followers in an armed uprising against Umayyad rule. Hussein was defeated and killed at Karbala in what is now southern Iraq. The story of Hussein's defeat lies at the heart of Shiite culture and its emphasis on martyrdom and sacrifice.

Over the centuries, what began as a disagreement over who should succeed the Prophet turned into a full-fledged religious and political schism that still reverberates throughout the Muslim world. The differences between Shi'a and Sunni reflect their histories and their religious practice more than their basic belief. Like all Muslims, Shiites believe in one god, Allah, whose teachings were revealed in the Qu'ran, Hadith, and other sacred texts, pray five times a day, are expected to make the hajj or pilgrimage to Mecca at least once in their lives, and fast during Ramadan.

Shiite rituals, however, reflect their minority status and the fact that they have been repressed by Sunni leaders over the centuries. In particular, they believe that the martyred twelfth imam will return to life and reunite the Muslim community. Also unlike Sunni Muslims, they have an established and hierarchical clergy which, in Iran, is led by senior **Ayatollahs**, who have also been expected to be political as well as spiritual authorities since the revolution.

To this day, it is easy for outsiders to see the importance of tradition within the Shiite clergy. Regardless of rank, clergymen who can claim direct descent from the Prophet's family are allowed to wear black turbans.

Fundamentalism and Other Misnomers

Because of its traditions, many conventional interpretations of Shiism overstate its **fundamentalism**, which is itself a term one should normally avoid when talking about any religion, not just Islam. The word was initially coined to describe nineteenth-century American Protestants who interpreted the Bible as literally as possible.

In that sense, the late Osama bin Laden, the Taliban, and many of the early leaders of the Islamic Revolution in Iran could well be considered fundamentalists. However, others, including the reformers in Iran, are better thought of as **Islamists**, because they are trying to find a way to

Comparative Emphasis: Arab and Muslim

Westerners often make the mistake of assuming that Arabs and Muslims are one and the same.

Arabs are the dominant ethnic group from Morocco in the west to Iraq in the east. Not all Arabs are Muslims. Large numbers of Lebanese and Palestinians, for example, are Christians.

And by no means are all Muslims Arabs. Most Iranians are Persians who have little in common culturally with Arabs and do not speak Arabic. In this case, we will soon see that Arabs and Iranians have frequently been enemies of each other. In the world as a whole, Islam is the dominant religion as far as western Africa (see Chapter 14 on Nigeria) and Indonesia in East Asia. In fact, the countries with the largest Muslim populations, India, Pakistan, and Indonesia, have no Arabs to speak of. ■

blend the tenets of their faith with the needs and complexities of a modern, industrialized, and globalizing world.

The same misgivings exist about another commonly used label, *fanatics*. It is true that some of the people we will encounter in this chapter and the next one are furious with the West in general and the United States in particular. But fanaticism is a pejorative word, one that could be used to describe anyone who deeply espouses and publicly demonstrates extreme beliefs. My colleagues in the conflict resolution and peace-building fields shy away from terms like fundamentalism that tend to obscure the complexities of life anywhere, especially in a country as diverse as Iran. Fundamentalism is also a pejorative and misleading word to the extent that its connotations of fanaticism lead us to understate the differences among Iranians—or any other group of people. Thinking along such lines often leads us into what psychologists call the **image of the enemy** and the stereotypical view that people who disagree with us are completely evil and impossible to work with.

Social and Economic Conditions

Iran has tremendous economic potential because it sits atop almost one hundred billion barrels of proven oil reserves. Overseas markets for its oil have largely dried up because of the embargoes imposed by the international community as part of the U.S.-led campaign to stop its alleged plans to develop nuclear weapons. Even so, it still produces almost four million barrels a day, much of which finds its way into the global market and provides the state with most of its income.

That said, oil has not made Iran as rich as Saudi Arabia, Kuwait, and the other oil-producing states in the Persian Gulf. Hard statistics are not easy to come by, but most analysts estimate that its gross domestic product per capita is only about $11,000 a year. Additionally, the distribution of income and wealth is highly skewed toward a rather small upper middle class that coexists with as much as 20 percent of the population living in poverty.

It should also be noted that Iran's population is younger than that of any other country covered in this book. In the early years of the Islamic Republic, the leadership encouraged people to have as many children as possible, which has turned into an unexpected burden on an economy that cannot offer meaningful jobs to most of its young people who are entering the work force in droves.

Last but by no means least, note that, like India, Iran has a large diaspora or people who were born there but now live abroad. Unlike India where most people leave in search of better economic opportunities, most Iranians who live abroad have left for political reasons. Only a few of them are officially classified as refugees, but there is no doubt that members of the diaspora have featured in the various dissident movements to be discussed below—and have been the authors of several of the books included in the list of suggested readings.

A Note on Transliteration

As is the case for all languages that do not use the Roman alphabet, there are many ways of rendering Iranian terms in English. The task is particularly difficult for Iran because scholars, the American government, journalists, and others do not agree on the best one to use. The United States government uses a complicated one that converts each Persian-Arabic letter into its closest English equivalent. Most scholars and journalists use one of several other systems. Usually, the reader has no trouble figuring out the person or place being referred to. Thus, as I was looking for results on election day in 2013, I found the new president referred to as Ruhani, Rohani, Rowhani, and Rouhani. When the choice does seem to make a difference, I have used the English version of the Farsi term most commonly used in quality Western newspapers and magazines, for the simple reason that they are the most familiar to most readers.

The Status of Women

After its nuclear program, the status of women is arguably the most controversial feature of Iranian politics both in the country and elsewhere.

Under the shah, women were granted the right to vote. Wearing veils was prohibited. More than half of the university students were—and still are—women. Trendy stores in chic neighborhoods of north Tehran sold the same clothes that were on sale in Paris or London or New York.

Everything changed after the revolution. Since then, the Iranian authorities have limited women's rights as much or more than any Islamic regime other than the one in Saudi Arabia or in Afghanistan under the Taliban.

Women have to wear at least a head scarf and veil, and the regime prefers that they include a *manteau* (coat) that covers their entire bodies. Most schools are segregated by gender. In those that are still coeducational, women have been arrested if parts of their ankles were revealed while they were running up stairs. Stonings and other forms of violence against women are common.

As the box about *Reading* Lolita *in Tehran* points out, middle-class and educated Iranian women can find ways around those restrictions. By the late 1990s, some middle-class women were testing the rules by wearing makeup under their *manteaux* or allowing wisps of hair to appear from their head scarves. Women, who were not allowed into the stadiums where soccer-crazed men watched Iranian teams play, took to disguising themselves as men (*manteaux* do have their advantages in that respect) and sneaking in.

Only men are allowed to run for president. Fewer women hold other high-level positions in Iran than in any other country considered in this book. Although it drew the support of many well-known intellectuals and creative artists, the small but growing women's movement was one of the major victims of the crackdown following the 2009 election.

Nothing illustrates the second class status of women better than the case of **Shirin Ebadi**, who was awarded the 2003 Nobel Peace Prize. She had been named a judge before becoming an enthusiastic supporter of the revolution. Shortly after the fall of the shah, she lost her job because the new authorities ruled that women should not be allowed to interpret Islamic law. She then decided to specialize in cases involving alleged human rights abuse, for which she won the award. As a devout Muslim, she covered herself in public in Iran but did not when accepting the Nobel Prize as a sign that many Iranian women sought change (nobelprize.org/nobel_prizes/peace/laureates/2003/ebadi-lecture.html).

Reading Lolita *in Tehran/Lipstick Jihad*

Iranians at home and in the diaspora have written dozens of books deploring the status of women in contemporary Iran. Two very different and nonacademic memoirs have shed a lot of light on what has happened—for good and for ill.

The first is Azar Nafisi's *Reading* Lolita *in Tehran*. Vladimir Nabokov's *Lolita* is controversial everywhere because it deals with a middle-aged teacher's obsession and affair with a thirteen-year-old student. But nowhere is it more controversial than in Iran, where women face unprecedented levels of discrimination. Nafisi is an American-educated literature professor who went back to Iran to take part in the revolution and later taught at a number of universities. Eventually, she lost her job because she would not conform to the many restrictions on women. In the year before her family decided to return to the United States, she invited her best women students to take an independent study course in her own home. The curriculum included *Lolita*, but that's not what her book is about. Instead, she chronicles how these young women handled themselves in public and in private, where they took off their veils and *manteaux* to reveal Western clothing, makeup, and anything but traditional Iranian values.

Lipstick Jihad is a very different book. Its author, Azadeh Moaveni, is a young journalist who has dual Iranian and American citizenship. She was studying in Egypt when the reform period under Mohammad Khatami was coming to an end. She also found that she was one of the few American journalists who could actually cover events in Iran firsthand because she has an Iranian passport. Her book focuses on the culture shock that hit a totally Westernized young woman professionally and personally. Among other things, she was shocked that most people she met did not fast during Ramadan.

Key Concepts and Questions

At first glance, it may seem as if Iran is a case unto itself that has little to offer to comparative analysis. After all, it is one of the few countries that is still a theocracy, is ruled by Shiite Muslims, and escaped direct colonial rule. However, once we scratch the surface, it will be easy to see how Iran helps us understand some of the broader themes raised in Chapter 11, including:

■ How have countries that were never formally colonized dealt with the legacy of imperialism?

- Why is Iran one of the few countries left in the world that is run by religious leaders?

- Why has the Islamic Republic had so much trouble developing effective, noncharismatic leadership and effective state institutions since the death of the Ayatollah Khomeini?

- Why is Iran having a hard time developing its economy, especially given its oil reserves and other natural resources?

- How does its isolation since the 1979 revolution and the hostage crisis affect the way the Iranian government is structured and limit the prospects for democracy?

The Evolution of the Iranian State

Before Islam

Many features of Iranian politics today have important roots that go back more than 2,500 years and thus long antedate the arrival of Islam (see Table 13.1). Those roots are both religious and political in nature and begin with the Prophet Zoroaster, who lived between the ninth and seventh centuries before the birth of Christ and created one of the world's first monotheistic religions (www.iranchamber.com/history/historic_periods.php).

The region's political evolution dates from the accession of Cyrus the Great to the throne of Medes in 550 BC. At that time, the people who lived on the Fars plain took up agriculture and moved into fixed settlements that required protection. By the time his son in law, Darius, and his grandson, Xerxes, died the empire had spread as far as parts of today's Bulgaria and Greece in the northwest, Libya in the southwest, and India and Pakistan in the east. Most members of their dynasty drew on the Zoroastrian

tradition that rulers were expected to establish good relationships with those they governed and could not rule solely by force.

Their dynasty did not last long. In 332 BC, Alexander the Great defeated the Persians and occupied their large and glorious capital, Persepolis. Shortly after Alexander's death, an Aryan tribe established the Parthian dynasty which was able to wall Persia off from the Roman Empire and restore a degree of independence.

They were followed by the Sassanian dynasty (208–637 AD), which also adopted most of what was by then a millennium-old Persian culture and began calling their ruler *shahinshah*, or "king of kings." The last of the great Sassanian shahs, Khosrow I, took power in 560. He restored Persian power and began to move its influence and borders westward again. He also built a new capital at Ctesiphon, where the floor of his immense palace was covered with a remarkable ninety-square-foot carpet known as the Spring of Khosrow.

Islamic Iran

The Christian Byzantines forced the last Sassanids from Ctesiphon in 626, but they would not end up being the group that next dominated Persia. At that same moment, the new religion of Islam was taking root on the Arabian Peninsula. Following the Prophet's death in 632, his followers fanned out in all directions to convert people to the new faith. Previously, Persians had never had any reason to fear the relatively underdeveloped Arabs. Thus, when their far larger and far better equipped army faced the Muslims at Qadisiya in present-day Iraq, they expected a swift and easy victory. But when the battle began, the dispirited Sassanian troops crumbled. The next year, the Arabs occupied Ctesiphon. In a sign of things to come, they shipped the Spring of Khosrow back to Mecca, where they cut it into pieces.

It was not hard to incorporate Islam into Persian culture given the Zoroastrian belief in a single God. However, Persians had a hard time adjusting to the fact that they were now far less powerful and that their tradition of strong kings had been undermined. Persian Muslims did help turn the Middle East into one of the cultural centers of the world during the first few centuries of the last millennium. However, Persia itself fell into decline in part because Islam downplayed the role of kingship, which had been at the heart of its society for almost one thousand years.

As we saw earlier, the Islamic world split between Shiite and Sunni after the Prophet's death. However, it would be eight hundred years before the Persians became the first people to accept Shiism en masse—and then only following another debacle that would shape their culture for centuries to come.

TABLE 13.1 Turning Points in Iranian History before 1900

YEAR	EVENT
550 BC	Cyrus comes to power
332	Defeat by Alexander the Great
560 AD	Accession of Khosrow I
638	Arab victory; introduction of Islam
1219	Invasion by Mongols
1501	First Safavid shah named
1896	Assassination of Nasir ed-Din Shah

In 1219, Chinghiz (Genghis) Khan and his Mongol army overran Persia. Among other atrocities, they decapitated and disemboweled every resident of Naishapur, then one of Persia's intellectual centers. Chinghiz's grandson, Hulagu, rampaged through Persia forty years later, stayed, and went on to rule much of southwest Asia as an independent Mongol territory. The last invasion from the northeast came in 1394 under Tamerlane, who called himself a Tatar rather than a Mongol. These repeated invasions gave birth to an understandable fear of outside intervention that continues to this day.

During this time, some Iranians created the Sufi mystical tradition, in which holy men whipped up religious frenzy, promising that the faithful would reach spiritual unity with God. One of the Sufi orders, the Safavid, came to the fore under Junayd, who turned it from a religious into a political movement. In 1501, forces loyal to his grandson, Ismail, took control of the city of Tabriz and proclaimed their leader **Shah**. Ismail and his followers fought back the Sunni Ottoman Empire founded by the Turks who originally came from what is now western China and Mongolia. As they solidified their rule over a land that is about 20 percent larger than today's Iran, they also turned to Shiism, in part to set themselves apart from the Ottomans and Arabs.

For the next four centuries, the Safavid and Qajar dynasties blended the Persian acceptance of strong kingship with Shiite beliefs to bolster an authoritarian state in which monarchs with absolute power dominated a hierarchical society in which religion was central and social and economic change were all but impossible to achieve. To cite but one example, Abbas Shah was convinced that his closest advisors were conspiring with his sons against him. So, he ordered one of his sons killed in 1615 and another blinded six years later. Authoritarian rule was reinforced by Shiism, which provides tremendous respect to the most learned scholars, especially those who are descendants of the Prophet. Together, these long-standing values led to the widespread expectation that the king would be charismatic and powerful, but they also required that his rule be just and in keeping with religious beliefs.

By the end of the nineteenth century, the failure of generations of kings to live up to that ideal did the traditional line of dynasties in. The shahs of that era were not wholly without accomplishments. The Qajars, in particular, sat atop a reasonably integrated state that used networks of local warlords and potentates to forge at least a rudimentary sense of national identity and escape direct colonial rule.

However, Persia had no hope of completely escaping Western influence. Many middle-class Iranians studied in Europe and North America. Foreign companies had established a foothold in Iran long before oil became its leading export, often as a result of direct grants or concessions handed to them by the Qajars. Russian military advisors provided the only semblance of training and discipline the army received. Most telling of all, the military and economic power of the West drove home just how weak the Qajar dynasty had become.

Opposition to the regime mounted throughout Iranian society. Orthodox Shiites objected to secularization. The *bazaaris*, or small businessmen who owned stalls and shops in the country's marketplaces, wanted the opportunity to make more money while reducing competition from outsiders. The secular middle class demanded political reforms that would lead to the rule of law, if not to democracy (see Table 13.2).

The late 1800s and early 1900s were hard on Iran. There were protests against almost everything the leadership did, including its extremely unpopular ban against smoking tobacco.

The most important of the protests led to the short-lived **Constitutional Revolution** of 1905. It succeeded initially because it promised all things to all people, including

© Courtesy of Search for Common Ground

The ruins of the ancient city of Persepolis.

TABLE 13.2 Iran: 1900–1979

YEAR	EVENT
1905	Start of Constitutional Revolution
1911	End of Constitutional Revolution
1925	Reza Khan becomes shah
1941	Mohammad Reza Pahlavi becomes shah
1953	Overthrow of Mossadeq government
1979	Islamic Revolution

© Cengage Learning

firming up the legal status of Islam, strengthening the state, instituting economic reforms, and codifying the legal system. On January 12, 1906, a huge protest convinced Muzaffar ed-Din Shah to dismiss his prime minister, give up absolute rule, and create the first **Majlis** or parliament.

Unfortunately, conditions deteriorated further in a matter of weeks. In June, soldiers fired on demonstrators and killed a cleric. As many as twenty thousand protesters sought sanctuary in the British embassy. The situation became even more tumultuous when the shah died and was replaced by his son, Muhammad Ali, who was described by one American advisor as "perhaps the most perverted, cowardly, and vice-ridden monster that had disgraced the throne of Persia in many generations."[2] He finally backed down and accepted the Constitution of 1906, marking a short-term victory of the secular and Westernized portion of the population. By 1907, proclerical forces had begun criticizing the Constitution in the Majlis, insisting, for instance, that a council of clerics be given the right to review all legislation passed by the parliament before it went into effect.

In the meantime, the Russians and British divided the increasingly ungovernable country into two zones of influence. In 1908, Russian-led troops attacked and destroyed the Sepahsalar Mosque, which had been the symbolic home of the protest movements associated with the Constitutional Revolution. For the next three years, Russian troops reinforced those of the shah, who dissolved the Majlis and brought the Constitutional Revolution to an end in 1911.

The Pahlavis

Royal authority had all but evaporated. The shah controlled Tehran and a few other cities, while tribal leaders ran the rest of the country to the degree that it was run at all.

The British filled some of the ensuing power vacuum. Following its navy's decision to switch from coal to oil to fuel its ships, British demand for Iran's oil spiked. As a result, the British all but formally occupied the southern part of the country while the Russians stepped in as well, taking over the north, leaving Iranians in control of only a narrow strip in the center that did not include Tehran or most other major cities.

Things got even worse after the Bolshevik Revolution when Marxists briefly set up a Soviet Republic in northern Iran. In the short run, Iranian forces overthrew the Marxist republic and, in the process, produced the first serious nationalist movement.

One of those nationalist leaders was a mid-level officer, Reza Khan, who would establish Iran's final dynasty a decade later. Born in 1878, he quickly rose in the ranks of the Cossack troops (named for their Russian leaders) and led the military campaign that overthrew the Soviet-backed regime. He then led three thousand Cossacks into Tehran and went on to subdue many of the tribal leaders who were still in charge in most of rural Iran.

The British threw their support behind him because they were convinced that this tall, tough soldier could restore order nationwide. For the next four years, Reza Khan was the de facto leader of the country. But it was only in 1925 that he had himself crowned shah and chose the dynastic name Pahlavi, after the language spoken before the Arabs arrived.

Reza Shah took power in the name of nationalism and Shiism. However, he soon turned his back on Islam and focused his attention on modernizing his poor and weak country. His government built the first national railroad system, introduced the first modern factories, and expropriated land from rural elites. The Majlis continued to exist, but it did little more than rubber-stamp decisions he had already made.

Most important of all, the shah turned on the clerics, taking two steps that proved to be anathema to orthodox Muslims. Women were no longer allowed to wear the veil and men had to shave their beards. He also closed religious schools, replacing them with free, state-run institutions that stressed science and other modern topics.

The Pahlavi regime stressed the country's Persian origins and its historical glories before the arrival of Islam. He even changed the name of the country from Persia to Iran on the dubious historical claim that it was the one used under Cyrus and Darius.

Reza Shah was able to preserve the country's territorial integrity by maintaining a complicated pattern of international alliances. In the 1930s, he cast Iran's lot with Germany because of his support for the Nazis' Aryan policies. After Germany attacked the Soviet Union in 1941,

---

[2]W. William Schuster, "The Strangling of Persia", cited in Sandra Mackey, *The Iranians: Persia, Islam, and the Soul of a Nation* (New York: Plume, 1996), 149.

the British decided that they could not risk having the Iranian oil fields come under Nazi control. Therefore, the British navy captured southern Iran, and the Soviets marched into the north. Claiming that he could not remain as the head of a country under foreign occupation, the shah abdicated and went into exile.

Assessments of his generation in power are mixed. There is little doubt that Reza Shah brought much-needed social and economic change to a country he treated as a personal fiefdom. That said, he definitely lost touch with most of the people, provoking widespread anger because he failed to live up to the Persian tradition of "just rule."

Mohammad Reza Shah (1919–1980) succeeded his father shortly before his twenty-second birthday. Most observers thought of him as a playboy who preferred dancing and drinking in Europe to managing the affairs of state. The second Pahlavi shah did little to alter his reputation for the first twelve years he sat on the Peacock Throne. After World War II, the new shah faced even more serious difficulties, two of which are critical here.

First, diplomatic pressure from the United States and the United Kingdom led the Soviets to withdraw from northern Iran. In 1949, the growing communist party (Tudeh) tried to assassinate him. One bullet hit his cheekbone and emerged under his nose. Three more went through his hat. Somehow he survived.

Some observers think that the shah decided that his recovery from his wounds was a sign that he had a divine right to rule and to do so in an absolutist manner. Moreover, he governed in a way that reflected his lack of trust, even in the men who were supposedly his most valued advisors. Consequently, he provoked more intense opposition than his father ever had seen in the years after Mossadeq's overthrow.

Second and more important in the long run, the charismatic **Mohammad Mossadeq** (1882–1967) served as prime minister from 1951 to 1953, and his years in power set in motion the political dynamics that would lead to the shah's ouster a quarter century later. Mossadeq led the National Front, a broad coalition of political groups that included many of the secular leaders of the early days of the future Islamic Republic as well as the more politicized clerics.

Over the shah's objections, he ordered all British employees of the British-controlled Anglo-Iranian Oil Company (AIOC) to leave the country before nationalizing the firm that was the most visible symbol of foreign influence over Iranian affairs. The British only owned 51 percent of the company's shares, yet Iran earned more from the export of carpets than it did from its much more valuable oil.

Because Iran did not have workers who could run the production and refinery facilities, chaos ensued. In July 1952, the Majlis granted Mossadeq emergency powers in a law including nineteen clauses that enumerated areas in which he was authorized to act with only limited oversight.

The nineteenth was simply "et cetera."

Mossadeq was the most popular Iranian politician in decades, but he went too far and lost the support of the clerics and the Tudeh. He also dissolved the upper house of the parliament, suspended the supreme court, confiscated royal property, and expanded the scope of martial law, all of which ate away at his support.

The shah then tried to fire Mossadeq, who refused to resign. At that point, the United States intervened. Kermit Roosevelt (son of President Theodore Roosevelt) organized a Central Intelligence Agency (CIA)-led coup. In the ensuing fighting, at least three hundred people were killed. The shah fled the country. Finally, the United States succeeded in forcing Mossadeq to resign, which enabled the shah to return but also laid the groundwork for his overthrow a quarter-century later.

He started by alienating most Shiite clerics. Despite the stereotypes that have arisen since the 1979 revolution, most Shiite scholars and clergymen traditionally shunned politics and only became politicized in the 1960s after the shah instituted the **White Revolution** in 1963 and created the notoriously brutal **SAVAK** to enforce his rule.

The White Revolution was a revolution in name only. In truth, it was little more than an attempt to modernize the country while increasing the shah's power. Like his father, the shah made a point of attacking the clergy. He gave the peasants land that belonged to the clerics and reduced their impact on daily life in general. Women's rights were extended, as the shah increasingly equated modernity with a secular society.

SAVAK (a Farsi acronym for Intelligence and Security Organization of the Country) was formed in 1957. It not only arrested and tortured dissidents at home, but it spied on and even killed students and others living abroad who dared to oppose the shah. SAVAK and the military both benefited from massive American aid, and Iran came to be seen as Washington's most vital ally in the turbulent Middle East other than Israel.

In retrospect, the most important change in the 1960s and 1970s came from the religious community, especially from **Ayatollah Ruhollah Khomeini** (1902–1989). Khomeini had long been one of the leading clerics in Qom. When he gained the title of ayatollah in 1960, he was not actively involved in political life. That would change in a matter of months.

The tall, austere Khomeini had built his reputation and his **charisma** largely on the basis of his expertise in the legal aspects of Islam and had mostly stayed out of politics. The White Revolution proved to be the last straw. He argued that the clerics had an obligation to make certain that Islamic principles were upheld in Iran. In so doing, he shifted the center of gravity of opposition to the shah from the secular left to orthodox Shiites.

The government cracked down. Troops broke into the most famous theological school in Qom and killed two unarmed students. Others escaped and immediately sought Khomeini's support because he was already the symbolic heart of the opposition. When he later went to preach at that same school, the authorities cut off electricity throughout the city. Khomeini and more than sixty other clerics were arrested. His followers rioted after he was detained, and it took the imposition of martial law in a number of cities to end the disturbances.

Khomeini was released from prison the following spring. The shah and his supporters tried to convince him to stay out of political life, but he gave what became his standard response: "All of Islam is politics." In 1964, he was arrested again and sent into exile in Iraq. He later moved to the outskirts of Paris. For the next fifteen years, he galvanized opposition to the shah. Even though he was ignored by the official media, his supporters were able to smuggle in audiotapes of his messages, which were copied and distributed around the country.

Practicing Shiites were not the only Iranians to oppose the shah. In fact, the unintended consequences of land reform may have done him the most harm. Most peasants were illiterate and ill-prepared to run the farms they were given. Many, for instance, had to take out huge loans that they could not repay, lost their land, and ended up flocking to the cities, where they lived in dreadful slums. Tehran's population doubled in the 1970s, and urban residents made up half of the total population by the time of the revolution.

Meanwhile, the shah failed to see that his power was evaporating. He grew ever more distant from the population as a whole, while he concentrated more and more power in his own hands. All opposition political parties were abolished. The SAVAK monitored the opposition at home and abroad and is widely believed to have assassinated a number of leading dissidents and tortured thousands more at its infamous and enormous Evin Prison.

The shah's alliance with the United States was also problematic. The overthrow of Mossadeq made the United States and the CIA rather than the United Kingdom the main focus of anti-imperialist sentiment in Iran. Americans doing business in Iran did not help their country's image because they acted as if they ruled it and failed to even notice that their drinking or sexual openness insulted the sensitivities of many Iranians. Nonetheless, the shah acted as if nothing had changed, using the country's newfound oil wealth to buy billions of dollars worth of weapons.

PROFILE Mohammad Reza Shah

The last Pahlavi king was born in 1919, two years before his father took power. He received his initial education in Switzerland but later graduated from a military academy in Tehran.

His first years on the throne were marked by turmoil. Communists tried to assassinate him in 1949. In 1951, he fled the country after the creation of Muhammad Mossadeq's reform government and was able to return only after the Central Intelligence Agency (CIA) orchestrated a coup d'état that forced the nationalist prime minister from office.

By the 1960s, the shah had solidified his rule and embarked on the White Revolution that continued the secularization and modernization begun by his father. He provoked even more opposition from both the secular Left and the religious Right and was forced from office and the country in 1979. He died the following year (persepolis.free.fr/iran/personalities/shah.html). ∎

A soldier bends to kiss the feet of Mohammad Reza Shah as he leaves the country in 1979.

The revolution occurred so quickly that it took many contemporary observers by surprise, even though Iran watchers had been paying attention to the dissidents for at least a decade. Massive protests broke out in Tehran and other cities at the same time that the shah was diagnosed with terminal cancer. All of a sudden (or so it seemed), the all-powerful regime seemed to lose all of its power and collapsed when the shah left for medical treatment abroad. He never returned.

The Islamic Republic

The rest of the chapter will deal with the institutions and policies of the Islamic Republic. Much of what it has done seems irrational to Western readers. Therefore, it is important to see how it has evolved chronologically so that we can analyze the ways in which its actions have *not* been as outlandish in the ways its most strident critics have alleged.

Typically, scholars divide the history of the Islamic republic into four periods that coincide with the influence of the four men who have dominated political life in post-revolutionary Iran in which its basic political patterns were solidified (see Table 13.3). Given the results of the 2013 presidential election and the looming succession after Supreme Leader Khamenei dies, we could well soon enter a fifth.

The Khomeini Years

Not surprisingly, the first period covers the decade when Khomeini was Supreme Leader. Despite the initial popularity of the revolution and Khomeini himself, these were not easy years. To begin with, the coalition that toppled the shah was too diverse to govern. Early on, Khomeini indicated that he favored having a mixed government in which the clerics might not dominate. During those years, he shared power with prominent politicians who had opposed the shah but had serious doubts about an Islamic state.

In retrospect, it is clear that Khomeini always planned to create an Islamic regime. In ways reminiscent of purges in totalitarian regimes, people from every other major political faction were purged. Some prominent politicians

TABLE 13.3 Key Events in the Islamic Republic

YEAR	EVENT
1979	Khomeini becomes Supreme Leader
1980–88	War with Iran
1989	Death of Khomeini
1997	Election of Khatami
2004	Victory by conservatives in Majlis election
2005	Election of Ahmadinejad
2013	Election of Rouhani

PROFILE Ayatollah Ruhollah Khomeini

The Ayatollah Ruhollah Khomeini was born in 1902 in the isolated town of Khomein. As was the norm in those days, he did not have a family name, something Reza Khan Shah imposed on the country in 1926, at which point Khomeini became known as Ruhollah Mustafavi. His father, also a cleric, was killed when Ruhollah was a baby, and the boy (whose name means "soul of God") reportedly completed his first reading of the Quran when he was only seven.

In Shiism, an ayatollah has reached the highest level of spiritual awareness. Those who are descended from the Prophet are allowed to wear a black turban; others wear a white one. In Iran, they also usually use their hometown as their family name, which is why he became known as Ayatollah Khomeini rather than Mustafavi.

Khomeini emerged as a leader for two main reasons. First, he developed the notion that senior clerics had the obligation and right to rule to ensure that Iran remained Islamic. Second, he became one of the leaders of the opposition to the increasingly secular regime of the shah, especially after he was forced into exile, first in Iraq and later in France.

As Supreme Leader of the Islamic Republic, Khomeini struck a stern and often angry pose in his dealings both with his own people and with the United States (www.asiasource.org/society/khomeini.cfm). ∎

Ayatollah Khomeini addresses an audience in the airport building in Tehran, Iran, February 1, 1979, after his arrival from fourteen years of exile.

at the highest levels were accused of crimes and executed as were thousands of supporters of rival political movements ranging from the communists to moderate Muslims.

By the early 1980s, Khomeini had succeeded in creating an Islamic republic. Members of the laity continued to hold important positions in the Majlis, the bureaucracy, and the executive, but all decisions that mattered were made by senior clerics. Khomeini's power was then reinforced by the three most important events and trends of his decade in power.

First was the 444-day occupation of the U.S. embassy by a group of young Islamic militants. Young people who had earlier occupied the embassy had been denounced by Khomeini, which led them to withdraw.

Now, the United States allowed the dying shah to enter the country for medical treatment. That act deepened anti-American sentiment and led to the second occupation of the embassy. On November 4, 1979, Khomeini and other hard-line leaders gave the action at least their tacit approval. The occupation deepened the divide between Washington and Tehran, which have not had diplomatic relations ever since. It also made it easier for Khomeini and the other clerics to force out the remaining secular revolutionaries with whom they had overthrown the shah.

Second was the long and brutal war with Iraq, which raged from 1980 to 1988. In 1979, the longtime second-in-command in Iraq, Saddam Hussein, forced his mentor and predecessor from power. He and Khomeini viewed each other as threats both to their respective regimes and

to their dreams of hegemony in the troubled Middle East (www.crimesofwar.org/thebook/iran-iraq-war.html).

The eight years of fighting degenerated into a stalemate. The front lines barely moved. Yet by the time the two sides accepted a cease-fire, there were more than five hundred thousand killed and wounded on each side. The Islamic Republic used the war to bolster grassroots support and as justification in repressing the last dissenting voices from secular Iranians. The war also solidified American hostility toward the Islamic republic, which led it to give at least indirect support to Saddam's regime, something most American policy makers came to regret following the Iraqi invasion of Kuwait in 1990.

The third was less obvious at the time but is of central importance to Iranian politics today. The war put the very existence of the new republic in jeopardy and heightened pressure on Khomeini to clamp down on potential as well as real opponents. On one level, that introduced new institutions like the **Iranian Revolutionary Guard Corps (IRGC)**, which sought to supplant the less than loyal military inherited from the shah. Even more worrisome is the fact that the regime imprisoned or executed thousands of people in an attempt to solidify support for the regime and its war with Iraq.

The Rafsanjani Presidency

For the last third of a century, secular and religious authorities have vied for power, with the balance tilting toward the clerics once Ayatollah Khamenei solidified his

An Iranian protester sets fire to a United States flag, while other demonstrators give a clenched-fist salute during an anti-American protest in Tehran, Monday, November 5, 1979. The demonstration came after students stormed the United States Embassy in Tehran and held the staff hostage against the deportation of the former Shah of Iran from the United States.

AP Photo/Mohammad Sayad

position as Supreme Leader. When Khomeini died in 1989, Khamenei was elevated from the presidency to be the new Supreme Leader even though he had only become an ayatollah in the weeks before Khomeini died, and it was suggested that he was only promoted to that post so that he would be eligible to succeed the Islamic Republic's founder.

Ayatollah Hashemi Rafsanjani won the presidential elections held six weeks later with 95 percent of the vote. He was a leading cleric and an integral member of the revolutionary leadership who was held in high esteem especially after he survived an assassination attempt while he was speaker of the Majlis. Rafsanjani was and still is a pragmatist who has always wanted to concentrate on Iran's mounting domestic policy concerns. Chief among them at the time was the slumping economy whose performance was hurt by the theological commitments of the Khomeini years, the costs of the war with Iraq, and the boycott of Iranian goods by the United States and some of its allies.

The first signs of the split between the moderate and hard-line factions began to appear during his term as president. He enjoyed widespread support throughout his presidency because he had the backing of the vast majority of his fellow clerics.

The more conservative Khamenei spent his first eight years as Supreme Leader trying to keep the spirit of the revolution and the purity of the theocracy alive. Because his own clerical credentials were at least somewhat suspect, he was significantly less influential than Rafsanjani and would remain so during the first few years of Khatami's presidency.

At the time, many believed that the balance of power was shifting away from the clerics. Time proved them wrong.

Khatami and Reform

The constitution limits presidents to two consecutive terms, and Rafsanjani had to step down in 1997. Early on, pundits expected the conservative Ali-Akbar Nateq-Nouri, who had been the speaker of the Majlis and had the implicit support of Khamenei, to win. Instead, the reformer **Mohammad Khatami** (1943–) won, with almost 70 percent of the vote. Despite being a cleric, Khatami was known as a moderate who had, among other things, fought against censorship when he was a newspaper editor. During his election campaign, he openly supported extending the rights of women and members of religious and ethnic minority groups and strengthening civil society more generally.

Reformists did even better in the 2000 legislative election, winning 189 of the 290 seats. When Khatami ran for reelection the next year, he won 78 percent of the vote against what amounted to only token opposition.

During the first six years of his presidency, Khatami was a reasonably effective reformist leader. It became easier for

Former president Mohammad Khatami.

people to organize political groups, there was less press censorship, and some open protests were permitted. The government also began to try to improve relations with the United States and even allowed some inspections of its nuclear facilities by the International Atomic Energy Agency.

In retrospect, the surge in support for reformist politics was more illusion than reality. Although Khatami had widespread popular support, the hard-liners fought back through what I will later call the unelected half of the state.

The very different fourth period actually began in 2003 before Khatami's second term ended. In essence, Khamenei and his more conservative colleagues began to reassert their influence and bolster support for the Islamic Republic's initial goals and values. Forces loyal to the clerics struck back at the limited political reforms of the early Khatami years. For example, armed thugs operating with government support routinely attacked demonstrators. Most important of all, the clerics refused to allow about

2,500 moderates and reformists to run in the 2004 Majlis election, thereby guaranteeing a conservative landslide.

Ahmadinejad: Hardening the Lines

The conservative ascendancy continued with the surprise election of Ahmadinejad over the far more widely known Rafsanjani in 2005. Since then, both the secular and the clerical wings of the state have become far more hostile to both the West and reform at home, even with the recent election of the reformist-leaning Rouhani.

As we will see in the next section, the 2009 election serves as a metaphor for almost all of the Iranian state's strengths and weaknesses. The election itself had many of the democratic and nondemocratic features of any hybrid regime. The official campaign was reasonably free and even had Iran's first-ever televised presidential debates. At the same time, the Guardian Council denied a number of potentially strong candidates the opportunity to run.

PROFILES   Shirin Ebadi

The hopes for an improvement in Iran's human rights record and in the status of women in the country were given a major and unexpected boost when Shirin Ebadi was named the Nobel Peace Prize winner in 2003. Ebadi was a surprise pick because she was little known outside Iran.

Ebadi was, however a highly visible figure, in Iran. She was the first female judge in Iran but was forced to resign after the 1979 revolution on the assumption that women should not be permitted to interpret Islamic law. Since then, she has been a champion of human rights and democracy. After being forced out of the judiciary, she became a professor and set up an organization that tried to reform laws on inheritance and divorce and defended dissidents, and she was banned from practicing law in 2000 for her political beliefs and activities.

The Nobel Prize committee said in announcing her award, "As a lawyer, judge, lecturer, writer and activist, she has spoken out clearly and strongly in her country, Iran, and far beyond its borders." And, in a rare political statement, the committee also made it clear that its choice

The Nobel Peace Prize winner and human rights lawyer, Shirin Ebadi.

AP Photo/Hasan Sarbakhshian

was designed to aid the movement for democracy and human rights in Iran.

In the first hours after the announcement, no mention of Ebadi's honor was made in the state-run Iranian media. When informed of her award, Ebadi said, "I'm a Muslim, so you can be a Muslim and support democracy. It's very good for human rights in Iran, especially for children's rights in Iran. I hope I can be useful." ■

More importantly, the authorities almost certainly rigged the election, and their fraud set off the Green Movement, which will be the focus of the section on political culture and participation.

Of equal concern, at least outside Iran, is its nuclear program, which we will explore in more detail in the public policy section. Despite almost universal opposition from the international community, Iran has continued developing its nuclear capabilities in ways that *could* enable it to build a bomb within a few years at most. Iran insists that it only plans to use its reactors and stockpile of enriched uranium to generate needed electricity.

The United States has taken the lead in imposing far-ranging sanctions in an attempt to stop Iran from getting "the bomb." There is no question that the sanctions have taken a toll on the Iranian economy and the standard of living of its people. It is not clear, however, if the sanctions have had their desired impact on its policy makers. In fact, recent studies suggest that the sanctions have so angered Tehran that they have only strengthened the leadership's resolve to go ahead with its nuclear efforts.

In the longer run, the ever-growing tensions between Ahmadinejad and Khamenei may have an even more lasting effect on Iran. The two men did not disagree on most issues. However, they had very different styles, and some suggest that Ahmadinejad threatened clerical control of the Islamic Republic despite the fact that he is a devout Muslim himself.

The dispute was intense and personal and had as much to do with the balance of power among conservatives after Ahmadinejad stepped down. However religious he may be, it cannot be stressed enough that Ahmadinejad is the first person from outside the clergy to hold a key post in Iran since the early 1980s. That has led many to focus on the influence of institutions that the clerical authorities do not directly control, such as the Revolutionary Guard (where Ahmadinejad began his career) and the vigilante gangs of *basiji*. Their feud reached a head in the run-up to the 2013 presidential election. The Guardian Council refused to authorize the candidacy of Ahmadinejad's protégé, Esfandiar Mashaei. The outgoing president then threatened to disrupt the election and lead protests after it if the winner was someone he did not approve of. Neither threat materialized.

Rouhani

It is hard to predict what will happen during the Rouhani presidency. As we will see later on, he has close ties to *both* the reformers and the clerical leadership of which he is a member after all. The key will probably be the way the new government and the Supreme Leader handle pressure from the United States and the rest of the international community. One possibility is that Rouhani will be able to draw on his experience as a leader of the Iranian negotiating team a decade or so ago to begin negotiations toward an agreement. It is, however, just as likely that the conservatives will win and that the very office of the presidency will be abolished in a new round of constitutional reform.

The People and Politics

Other chapters covered political culture before political participation. We can't do that here. Because culture and participation are so inextricably intertwined in Iran, it makes more sense to start with the stunning protests after Ahmadinejad's reelection and then work back to culture and more conventional forms of participation.

The Green Movement

When President Ahmadinejad ran for reelection in June 2009, most remaining questions about the democratic nature of the Iranian regime were answered in the negative. As is always the case in Iran, the campaign was an unusual one by Western standards. Because the constitution strictly limits campaign activity, the list of candidates was not known until a few weeks before people went to the polls—other than Ahmadinejad of course. Everyone also understood that the Supreme Leader and most of the other clerics in the government supported the incumbent. As it would also do in 2013, the Guardian Council did not allow any of the well-known reformist candidates to run.

Nonetheless, one well-known alternative to Ahmadinejad was on the ballot, although no one initially gave **Mir Hossein Mousavi** much of a chance. Most members of the opposition, including Khatami, united behind Mousavi, who had impeccable revolutionary credentials. He had been prime minister in the 1980s before that post was abolished. Both he and his wife are from minority ethnic groups. His wife, Zarah Ranavard, is a well-known academic and cultural figure who became the first woman to actively take part in a national political campaign.

There is no professional polling industry in Iran, which means we do not know when, how, or why his campaign suddenly took off, but it did. By polling day, it was obvious that he could win. It was just as obvious that Ahmadinejad and Khamenei would make certain that he didn't. Before 2009, it had taken a few days for election officials to count the votes. This time, the "results" were announced almost as soon as the polls closed.

Table 13.4 presents the official election results. I almost decided to leave it out—and not because it is by far the

TABLE 13.4 2009 Presidential Election

CANDIDATE	PERCENTAGE OF THE VOTE
Mahmoud Ahmadinejad	62.6
Mir Hossein Mousavi	33.8
Others and invalid votes	4.6

smallest table in *Comparative Politics*. Instead of what the table shows, most observers in Iran were convinced that Mousavi had at least won enough votes to force a runoff and had probably even come in first.

The authorities refused to authorize a recount or consider holding a second election. In fact, all key religious and civil bodies determined that the election had been run fairly and that the results were more or less accurate.

Many middle-class and young Iranians had never liked Ahmadinejad to begin with. They were outraged and refused to accept the results. Building on existing groups of critics among women, intellectuals, and others, they launched a spontaneous wave of protests that came to be known as the Green Movement. The color green is often associated with Islam. Mousavi had had most of his campaign material printed in it. Perhaps most revealing of all, green is also the dominant color in the Iranian flag. Protesters, thus, dressed in green both as a sign of their piety and their acceptance of the regime and turned their demonstrations into one of the first color revolutions against authoritarian rulers whose participants decide to use some color as a symbol of their outrage.

Over the following few weeks, hundreds of thousands participated in demonstrations. Theirs was also a new kind of social movement. Participants relied heavily on then little known social media software like Twitter and Facebook to organize their demonstrations. Iranians living in the diaspora also participated in the planning to such an extent that Western analysts had a hard time telling which tweets came from Los Angeles and which from Tehran.

For good or ill, the movement was short-lived. The government and the revolutionary guard found ways to keep demonstrators out of the broad boulevards where large numbers of people had gathered. Many participants in the movement were arrested. The notoriously vicious *basij*, or semilegal vigilantes affiliated with the Revolutionary Guard, played a leading role in the crackdown. On July 9, the authorities allowed *basijis* to attack a dormitory. At least one person was killed and several others were hurled out of fourth-story windows. Hundreds of protesters were killed, including the recent college graduate and previously apolitical Neda Agha-Soltan, who became a global celebrity after her killing (recorded on a smart phone) was shown on YouTube and

other Internet outlets worldwide. Larger protests followed in the next few days, but the movement quickly lost momentum as the regime made it clear it would use arrests and the *basijis* to quell the protests.

Many participants in the movement were arrested. Those who survived were convicted in show trials that were reminiscent of those in the Soviet Union under Stalin. Even an Imam who blogged ended up in court where he confessed to crimes that he did not commit but that the state alleged. One of Rafsanjini's daughters was arrested and one of Mousavi's nephews was killed.

As exciting and as hopeful as they are, we should not read too much into protests like the Green Movement. The Bush administration and Iranian émigrés saw them as signs of an imminent revolution, yet there is no reason to believe that such is the case (but also see the conclusion to this chapter). While the few available public opinion polls show widespread support for reform, almost everyone wants it to occur within the framework of the system created in 1979. Indeed, most dissidents who have been interviewed by Western television networks and newspapers insist that their country has been through too much turmoil since the revolution and that any regime change would almost certainly make a bad situation worse.

Yet, despite the repression, signs of dissatisfaction have never disappeared. While there is almost no chance that the Green Movement will reappear in anything like the form it took in 2009, there is also almost no chance that the Islamic Republic can continue in its current form without facing significant dissent, especially as people who remember the shah and the events of 1979 leave the political scene.

No one has defined this complex situation better than the British political scientist Ali Ansari did long before the 2009 election and the birth of the Green Movement:

> **Far from the monolithic totalitarian state described by some commentators, Iran's politics reflect an intensely complex, highly plural dynamic characteristic of a state in transition that incorporates the contradictions and instabilities inherent in such a process. Democratizing moderates confront authoritarian conservatives; a secularizing, intensely nationalistic society sits uneasily next to the sanctimonious piety of the hard-line establishment.[3]**

As is often the case with protest movements against repressive governments, the Green Movement quickly disappeared, and there have been few public signs of dissatisfaction with the regime since 2009. However, Rouhani's

---

[3]Ali Ansari, "Continuous Regime Change from Within," *Washington Quarterly, 26* (Autumn 2003): 53.

People protesting the death of Neda Soltani, who was killed in the demonstrations after the 2009 presidential election.

surprising victory was accompanied by isolated gestures of protest against the clerical leadership demonstrating, at least, that the sentiments that gave rise to the Green Movement have not completely disappeared.

Political Culture

Foreign scholars have not been able to do field research in Iran since 1979. Among other things, that means that there are tremendous gaps in what we know about its political culture, which can only be analyzed through in-depth and direct observation of the link between people's core beliefs and what they actually do politically.

The lack of information, of course, has not kept academics and journalists from speculating. Nonetheless, any statement that tries to assess the importance of cultural norms with any degree of precision needs to be taken with many grains of intellectual salt.

One thing is clear. Iran does not have a homogeneous political culture. Given its history, the Iranian people are quite nationalistic, perhaps increasingly so.

After that, however, any sense of homogeneity disappears in a welter of somewhat overlapping subcultures,

the size and importance of which are hard to define, but which extend to religious beliefs and practices. Although most Iranians are Shiites, they approach their faith in a number of ways. Many people do support the conservative and even puritanical version of Islam adopted by the ruling clerics. But there is also an Islamic Left, which is best reflected today in the reformist groups. Finally, there are Iranians like Azar Nafisi and most of her students, who are secular and do such forbidden things as drink alcohol, wear makeup, and watch foreign television shows and films, albeit in the privacy of their own homes.

The religious subcultures also overlap with others that grow out of the country's social and economic divisions. Orthodox Shiites tend to live in poor and rural areas. The bazaaris have mostly cast their lot with clerics like Rafsanjani who have supported them, for instance, against foreign competition. Well-educated and affluent Iranians are most likely to have had ongoing contacts with the West and to be secular. Those differences are so pronounced that the words "north Tehran" conveys an image of secular modernity in much the same way that "Silicon Valley" means technology and start-ups for Americans.

The Lizard

At times, one of the ways Iranians have been able to express their dissatisfaction is through film, and no better example exists than *The Lizard (Marmoulak)*, which was produced in 2004 with the approval of the authorities.

The film's lead character (Reza, played by famous comic actor Parvis Pathui), has been jailed again as a chronic thief and finds himself in a hospital ward in a bed next to a *mullah* (we are not told why they are in the same prison hospital). When the mullah goes to take a shower, leaving his robes behind, Reza dons them and walks out of the prison. After all, who would question a mullah in a theocracy?

He tries to hail a cab. Because most cab drivers do not like mullahs, no one picks him up. Eventually one does—and drives him twenty miles in the wrong direction.

At the end of the film, Reza is trying to get out of the country and finds himself in a village near one of Iran's borders. Worshipers at a local mosque see him (still in mullah's robes, of course) and demand that he come lead Friday prayers. He does his best, but, as is often the case in modern Iran, people fall asleep as soon as he starts his sermon.

The most significant uncertainty about Iranian culture is the way today's youth will evolve. Almost two-thirds of all Iranians are under thirty and have no memories of the revolution or the early years of the Islamic Republic. Instead, they have grown up in tough economic times. Half of their generation is chronically unemployed, and few members of their cohort have any hope for a meaningful or lucrative career.

Outside observers have focused on the upper-middle-class background of many dissidents, who are also suffering through the country's economic downturn. Support for the clerics and Ahmadinejad is greatest among poor Iranians. Many Iranian expatriates, however, have pointed out that the regime can no longer take their support for granted. The protests after the 2009 election may have marked a turning point in this respect, because the protesters came from all walks of urban Iranian society.

These differing and even conflicting values are also reflected in Iranian attitudes toward the United States. Many Iranians despise the United States—and the West as a whole—for the way their country was treated before the overthrow of the shah as well as their troubled relationships since then. But others are fascinated by American culture, especially those aspects of it that are formally forbidden by the clerics. In fact, one public opinion poll conducted in 2007 showed that Iranians were more pro-American than citizens of any other country in the Middle East. That sentiment is also reflected in statements by Western doctors, scientists, filmmakers, and others who have been able to visit Iran as part of cultural exchanges and who have been amazed at how warmly they have been welcomed by their Iranian colleagues.

Elections and the Ayatollahs' Democracy

Nothing shows the liberal side of Iranian politics more clearly than the fact that Iranians have voted in regular, reasonably fair, and competitive elections since the 1980s. The Islamic Republic is far from being a democracy in any meaningful sense of the term. Nonetheless, elections have had a significant impact on Iranian politics in an uneven way that Hooman Majd touched on with the title of his recent book, *The Ayatollahs' Democracy*.

He makes the case that some of the revolutionary leaders in 1979 wanted to create what they saw as an Islamic—or perhaps better, Iranian—form of democracy. As we will see in the rest of the chapter, the senior clergy would call all of the major shots but there would also be a role for citizens as well. In short, as we will see more clearly in the section on the state, they had enough leverage to turn the new Iran into a hybrid system in which a strong authoritarian regime permits a noticeable albeit varying amount of democracy.

The Conduct of Elections

The democratic side of the electoral process leaps out at you at first glance. Iranians have voted in ten presidential and eight Majlis elections since the revolution. All citizens over the age of fifteen were eligible to vote until the voting age was raised to eighteen following the 2005 presidential election.

Almost any man can declare his candidacy for president, and almost all men and women can put their name forward for the Majlis. In the weeks before the 2012 Majlis campaign officially began, 5,400 people filed papers to run for one of the 290 seats, most of which are chosen from geographically defined districts. The initial list of candidates was so big in part because the government actually pays candidates to run, not the other way around.

There are a few unusual conditions candidates have to meet to officially stay on the ballot. Women are still not allowed to run for president. Except for a handful of seats reserved for minorities, candidates must attest to a "belief in and commitment in practice to Islam and the sacred system of the Islamic Republic of Iran" and not have a "notorious reputation," although neither of those criteria has ever been clearly defined. Today, Majlis candidates have to be between 30 and 75 years old, attest to being in good health, and have a university degree (incumbents are exempted).

In some ways, elections are conducted in what seem like a conventional manner given what we saw in Part 2. For both presidential and Majlis elections, the law provides for two ballots in much the same way that legislative elections are conducted in France. In presidential races, if no candidate wins a majority the first time out, a runoff ballot is held in which the top two finishers at the first round square off against each other. Majlis elections rarely get that far, because three quarters of the races are normally decided at the first ballot.

Many typical campaign tactics in the West, such as putting up posters, are forbidden. Candidates are allowed to hand out campaign literature, but no piece of paper can be larger than roughly four by six inches. Candidates are allowed to circulate lists of colleagues they support to help voters reach decisions, but elections are effectively nonpartisan. When they arrive at the polls, voters see a ballot with a long list of names without any labels.

Doubts about the democratic nature of Iranian elections center on the role of the Guardian Council, which has to rule on the eligibility of all candidates. In some elections, it has done little more than screen out candidates who were too radical in one form or another along with those who had no chance whatsoever of winning. In 2000, it was particularly lenient, only preventing 11 percent of the candidates from running, including just a handful of prominent reformers.

After the success that the reformists had during the first two-thirds of the Khatami election, the Guardian Council decided to clamp down on who could run in the 2004 contests for the Majlis. It kept most prominent reformists from running, including many incumbents. In all, at least one thousand names were kept off the ballot.

Since 2005, the electoral process has become even less democratic. Because he was at the end of his second term, Khatami could not run again. The reformists tentatively planned to present a ticket that would have included his brother as the vice presidential candidate. However, the Guardian Council denied all potential reformist candidates the right to run while also overturning a court ruling that might have allowed women to run for the presidency.

That left the field to clerics and others who were committed to maintaining the core values of the Islamic Republic.

At the last minute, former President Rafsanjani decided to run at a time when he was hardly beloved by reformist voters. Almost all experts expected him to win, but he narrowly lost at the second ballot when almost all supporters of other candidates from the first ballot threw their support behind Ahmadinejad.

The Guardian Council's impact was felt in a different, but no less worrisome, way in 2009. The likelihood that it would refuse to allow reformists to run had the chilling effect of convincing people like Khatami (who was again eligible to be president) from even testing the waters. As a result, the reformists were represented by Mousavi, whose career had been in eclipse since the late 1980s. Although he proved to be a much stronger campaigner than anyone had expected, it was clear to most observers from the outset that neither the lay nor the clerical power holders were going to allow him to win.

The Guardian Council continued to have a disproportionate impact on the Majlis and presidential elections of 2012 and 2013, respectively. In 2012, it again kept most reformist candidates with a legitimate chance of winning off the ballot. As we saw earlier, it did the same the following year for Rafsanjani and Mashaei.

That time, however, it made a mistake if its real intentions were to guarantee the victory of someone who supported Supreme Leader Khamenei. Of the eight candidates who were allowed to run (two of whom later dropped out), three openly and strongly supported the clerical leadership. None were popular nor did any of them wage a rousing campaign. As a result, the far better known and somewhat reformist Rouhani snuck up on the three erstwhile front runners and just broke the fifty percent barrier, thereby removing the need for a second ballot (see Table 13.5)

Political Parties or the Lack Thereof

Readers of earlier chapters may be surprised that there has been no discussion of political parties in Iran given the role they play in organizing elections and providing voters cues

TABLE 13.5 Iranian Presidential Election of 2013

CANDIDATE	PERCENT OF THE VOTE
Rouhani, Hassan	50.7
Ghalibaf, Mohammad Bagher	16.6
Jalili, Saeed	11.4
Mohsen, Rezaee	10.6
Velayati, Ali Akbar	6.2
Gharazi, Mohammad	1.2
Blank or invalid votes	3.3

© Cengage Learning 2015

on how to cast their ballots in democratic regimes. That has not been the case in Iran.

Political parties that support the principles of the revolution are supposedly allowed to exist. A political party system of sorts began to form in the more open aftermath of the revolution. Early regime supporters created the Islamic Republican Party, but it was disbanded at Khomeini's urging in 1987. More generally, as the regime tightened the controls on the opposition, organizations that Westerners would think of as political parties fell by the wayside.

The few groups that call themselves parties are tiny and poorly organized. Because Majlis and presidential elections are at least nominally nonpartisan, the closest one comes to them in most campaigns are loose coalitions of candidates who more or less run together and are more or less associated with the same broad points of view on the big issues. In practice, Majlis candidates run their own campaigns as what Americans would call independents, but they make it clear where they stand vis-à-vis the broad ideological groupings in the population as a whole regarding the pace and extent of political reform. The situation is so confusing that the Wikipedia sites on elections and political parties in Iran often have dramatically different lists, not because one or the other of them is inaccurate but because the situation is so fluid.

Since Khatami's presidency, there have been two *very* loose groupings of candidates (see Table 13.6, which includes the official results as tabulated by the Ministry of the Interior).

In 2012 and 2013, Khamenei's supporters were typically lumped together as principlists. A few years ago, the reformists had an embryonic party, the **Second of Khordad Movement** (named for the day of Khatami's first, landslide election—Khordad is a month in the Iranian calendar). Given the Guardian Council's actions after 2005, most reformists who made it onto the ballot officially ran as independents who took easily identified reformist positions on the issues.

Comparative Emphasis: Conflict

Iran has been beset by conflict for a century or more. In the first years of the twenty-first century, much of the conflict revolves around the differences between religious conservatives and reformers. Public support for the latter would undoubtedly be greater in a more open political system, especially among young people. However, conservative clerics control enough of the country's critical political positions that they were able to ensure victories in the most recent elections.

In 2012, one of the most visible forms of conflict included a series of squirt-gun fights among young people. They claim they are not being political. However, a number of the participants have been arrested and hard-line critics worry that this could turn into an opening "salvo" for the next presidential election. ■

The Women's Movement

Every other chapter has a box on the political role of women. I use them as vehicles for emphasizing broader comparative implications of the experience of the country or type of regime under consideration. There is no such box in this chapter for the simple reason that gender issues, per se, are so central to Iranian political life that they had to be woven into the main narrative of the chapter.

It could hardly be otherwise given both Iran's history under the Pahlavis and the Islamic Republic. Recall that the last two shahs banned wearing of veils and downplayed the role of religion in general, in the process "liberating" more women than anywhere else in the Muslim world. Recall, too, that the clerics associated with the 1979 revolution interpret Islam, regarding the status of women, in a very traditional way, which they turned into laws after they overthrew the shah.

Many women chafe under the restrictions imposed by the regime, especially those in the middle class who had benefited personally, professionally, and politically from the more open atmosphere before the revolution. It should thus come as no surprise that women's movements have bubbled to the surface regularly since 1979 or that most of them have been repressed by the regime.

TABLE 13.6 The Majlis Election of 2012

COALITION	VOTES (IN PERCENT)	SEATS
Conservative	59.7	182
Reformist	35.5	75
Religious minorities	4.8	14
Independents	2.5	19

© Cengage Learning 2015

As Sanam Vakil puts it in beginning her book on women and politics in Iran, the Islamic Republic has at least one built-in contradiction. The state came into existence in large part to stop the emergence of what it perceived to be a sacrilegious civil society. Yet, the regime cannot turn all of the political clocks backward, because the very social and economic changes the authorities seek add to the pressures on it from below. As she puts it for the country as a whole:

> The nature of politics, religion, and society has evolved. In effect, these changes have been circular. The government has been forced to adjust to the changing nature of society.[4]

Despite what the "principlists" might prefer, they have had no choice but to allow women to play a more prominent role in most aspects of life. More women than men attend universities. Women are found in almost every profession other than the judiciary . About ten percent of Majlis members are women.

In fact, Vakil argues that there are three kinds of women's movements in Iran today—secular, Islamic feminist, and traditional.

The secular feminists are easiest for Western readers to come to grips with. They are the people who are featured in the press and in books like *Lipstick Jihad* and *Reading Lolita in Tehran*. They want an Iranian version of the same rights and opportunities that Western women's movements have been fighting for since the 1970s. For example, they have had to push hard for reforms in the divorce laws, which have historically privileged the former husband in matters such as child custody or alimony support. Much of their effort has been concentrated on obtaining a million signatures in favor of Iran's endorsement of the United Nations Convention for the Elimination of Discrimination Against Women (CEDAW) and other goals (www.we-change.org/english/).

But, what some Western observers have failed to notice is that most Iranian feminists are also practicing Muslims, many of whom played a prominent role in the Green Movement. In other words, even if they get what they want, Iran would remain some sort of Islamic republic and the status of women would not likely return to what it was under the shah.

Islamic feminists try to carve out a new role for women within the theological boundaries of Shiite Islam. As should have been clear from the first few pages of

this chapter, Islam is no more theologically monolithic than Judaism or Christianity. Some Iranian clerics still interpret sharia in a literal way that they believe is in keeping with what was written 1,300 years ago; many Muslims think that the practice of Islam has to reflect the realities of modern life. Thus, Islamic feminists may not argue for exactly the same rights as men, as their secular colleagues do, but they do insist on equal rights with men defined in ways that are consistent with Islam. Thus, Islamic feminists tend not to treat wearing a veil or headscarf as a political issue and argue, instead, that a woman should be free to make her own choices about what to wear and do so for reasons of her own choosing.

At times, the two groups of feminists have been able to work together, including in the Green Movement. And they have enjoyed some success. Family law now gives more rights to divorced women. Stoning of women accused of adultery has been "suspended."

Traditional Iranian women are a different story. They do tend to accept restrictions on women's rights and opportunities more than the members of the other two groups do. Nonetheless, they have been quietly urging the authorities to create more schools in which women can obtain religious training. There are, for instance, also women in the police and even in the *basij* groups who have been used to put down and infiltrate some of the women's groups. However you choose to count them, their numbers are declining given the country's changing demographics and openness to the outside world.

Whatever progress women seemed to have made under Khatami ground to a halt under Ahmadinejad for many of the same reasons and in many of the same ways that the entire reformist movement suffered a setback. If anything, his government tried to reverse what progress women's groups had achieved. The proposed Family Protection Law reduced the legal age of marriage for women to thirteen, made it easier for men to take multiple wives without the consent of their first wife, and all but prohibited the marriage of Iranian women to non-Iranian men. By the time this book went to press, only the parts of the bill regarding "temporary marriages," which is a code word for polygamy, had passed.

In the end, it would be safe to say that the various women's movements have lost far more than they have won since 1979. Especially under Ahmadinejad, many women's organizations have been banned and their media outlets shut down. Activists and prominent women such as Shirin Ebadi and Zarah Ranavard are rarely featured in any mass media that average Iranians have access to.

---

[4]Sanam Vakil, *Women and Politics in the Islamic Republic of Iran: Action and Reaction* (New York: Continuum, 2011), 3 (Kindle edition).

Below the Surface of Some Very Murky Political Waters

Of all the countries covered in *Comparative Politics*, it is probably the hardest to make a firm assessment of what the people think and the impact of what they do for Iran.

One thing is clear, however. Unlike many authoritarian regimes, Iran has had an often vibrant and visible opposition for much of the time since the Islamic Revolution.

As we saw, the coalition that overthrew the shah was quite diverse, and it took several years before the clerics could completely solidify their rule and remove most members of the Islamic Left from office. Ever since then, there has been simmering discontent among a number of groups in Iranian society that have periodically spilled out as they did in the Green Movement.

The most obvious and widely discussed groups are the well-educated, secularized young people for whom the term North Tehran is a convenient shorthand designation. These are people who have gotten the most publicity in the West not only for their political views but for their lifestyle choices which, of course, often have political overtones. Thus, these are the kinds of people who wear makeup, make wine in their bathtubs, and watch expatriate television that comes to them from barely hidden satellite dishes on their roofs.

On the other side of the coin are the loyalists, who seem to be splitting into two camps. Despite what the Western press and the expatriate community tries to say, there are plenty of devout Muslims who agree with conservative clerics on the role of religion and its implications, including limits on the rights of women and the widespread use of censorship. In the other camp are many of the Revolutionary Guards and the basiji for whom religion is increasingly a secondary concern coming after the maintenance of their social and economic status on their list of their personal and political priorities.

Last but by no means least, as hopeful as they may be, we should not read too much into the Green Movement or the sentiments that swept Rouhani into office. We certainly should not treat them as signs of an incipient popular revolt as dissidents in Iran and critics in Western capitals have a tendency to do. While the few available public opinion polls show widespread support for reform, almost everyone wants it to occur within the framework of the system created in 1979. Indeed, most dissidents who have been interviewed by Western television networks and newspapers insist that their country has been through too much turmoil since the revolution and that any regime change would almost certainly make a bad situation worse.

Comparative Emphasis: Identity

Iran does not suffer from divisions along identity lines as seriously as most other countries in the Global South.

As we have seen, it is by no means homogeneous ethnically or religiously. There have been times in Persian/Iranian history when identity-oriented tensions have divided the country. And, there is no doubt that the Islamic Republic has cracked down on some minorities, especially Jews and Baha'is.

That said, because of its long history as a sovereign state and because of its resentment toward the West, most Iranians feel a strong sense of national identity which transcends the issues that divide them—at least for now. ■

The Iranian State

The ambiguities in Iranian politics are easiest to see in the way its state operates. That said, this section is relatively short, because we have already discussed several features of Iran's version of a hybrid state.

The main provisions of the constitution written after the 1979 revolution remain in place despite passage of some significant amendments in 1989 (e.g., abolishing the prime ministry) (iranonline.com/iran/iran-info/government/constitution.html). In different ways from the hybrid regimes in post-communist countries, it blends elements of democratic and authoritarian (in this case, clerical) rule.

On the one hand, by relying on elections conducted using universal suffrage to elect the Majlis and president, it is by far the most democratic constitution Iran has ever had. On the other hand, it was written to ensure that ultimate authority rests in the hands of senior Shiite clerics through a series of unelected and often repressive institutions. Over the years, the clerics have certainly lost some prestige and possibly some of their power, but almost all events in this century suggest that they have no intention of giving up their dominant role in the Iranian state. Indeed, how the balance between the elected and authoritarian elements of the state evolves will almost certainly determine the political direction the country takes.

The order in which this section is written is itself a telling statement about Iranian politics. Had it been written a decade ago when the reformists were in office, the elected parts of the state would have come first. There were signs then that the rule of law and other aspects of democracy were gaining support under the leadership of President Khatami. But writing in the aftermath of the 2013 presidential election, it is clear that Supreme Leader Khamenei, the Guardian Council, the Revolutionary Guard, and other unelected components of the Iranian state have reasserted their influence and that the future of reform and of the elected parts of the state are very much in doubt.

The Unelected Institutions

For all intents and purposes, Iran has two chief executives. The first is the elected president. The second is the Supreme Leader—a senior ayatollah named for life by other senior clerics—who has veto power over almost everything elected officials want to do.

The original rationale for the position of Supreme Leader can be found in the writings of Ayatollah Khomeini. As his opposition to the shah intensified, Khomeini added political recommendations to his preaching, most notably in a series of nineteen lectures he delivered in Najaf, Iraq, in early 1970, which were subsequently published as *Velayat-e Faqi*, or the Guardianship of the Jurist.

Before then, most Shiite clerics stayed out of politics, because they believed that it was inappropriate for members of the clergy to take part in mundane political affairs before the twelfth imam reappeared. In other words, Khomeini sparked a major shift in Shiite thinking when he argued that senior clerics had a moral responsibility to provide leadership in political as well as religious matters. Because the jurist carried with him the ethical concern about faith and justice, he would be a more legitimate ruler than anyone drawn from the secular community. That relatively new line of thinking became the cornerstone of the Islamic Republic and its reliance on a Supreme Leader who epitomizes both religious and political authority.

The Supreme Leader himself is appointed by the Assembly of Experts, a body of senior clerics who are elected by the people. The leader then serves for life and is more powerful than any world leader today considered in this book. He controls the military, much of the media, the judiciary, and the clerical hierarchy. Both Khomeini and Khamenei have spoken out on any issue they deemed important and, thus, largely set the agenda for the country as a whole.

While he was alive, the charismatic Khomeini was the unquestioned leader of the entire political system. At first,

PROFILE Ayatollah Ali Khamenei

Supreme Leader Ali Khamenei was born in Mashhad in 1939 and began his theological studies in elementary school. At eighteen he moved to the holy city of Najaf in Iraq, but he returned to Qom the following year to continue his studies under Khomeini and others.

He joined the growing Islamic resistance movement against the shah in the early 1960s and was arrested along with many others in 1963. After his release, he continued to teach and preach. He was arrested again in 1977. After his release, he helped found the Combatant Clerics Association, which became the Islamic Revolutionary Party after the fall of the shah.

Following the assassination of President Muhammad Ali Rajai in 1981, Khamenei was elected to that post with about 95 percent of the vote. He was named an ayatollah in early 1989, which made him eligible to replace Ayatollah Khomeini when he died later that year. ■

Supreme Leader Ayatollah Khamenei.

AP Photo/Vahid Salemi

Khamenei suffered by comparison. As is almost always the case for leaders who follow a charismatic figure, he could not command the same degree of authority Khomeini did. It did not help that Khamenei had just been named an ayatollah at the time of his selection, and his appointment drew some criticism from more senior colleagues. By the end of the 1990s, though, he became the focal figure for conservatives who resisted the reformist movement that was based among President Khatami's supporters.

The most powerful theological body is the Guardian Council. It consists of six senior clerics appointed by the Supreme Leader and six judges named by the Majlis from a list compiled by the Supreme Judicial Council, the members of which are appointed by the Supreme Leader.

Today's Guardian Council consistently supports the conservative and theocratic elements of the regime. It has to approve all legislation and has blocked reform proposals on numerous occasions as when it vetoed the loosening of restrictions on the media in the late 1990s. As noted a few paragraphs ago, it was the body responsible for barring thousands of candidates in Majlis and presidential elections since the dawn of this century, thereby ensuring a string of conservative landslides.

To help resolve the frequent conflicts between the Majlis and the Guardian Council, Khomeini created the **Expediency Council** in 1988. The Expediency Council meets with the leaders of the other two appointed bodies and generally tries to anticipate procedural and other problems not foreseen by the Constitution. Its members are appointed by the Supreme Leader for five-year terms. All major factions have representatives on it. It is led by Rafsanjani, and former opposition candidate Mousavi is a member. However, Khamenei's followers currently far outnumber the reformers. Almost half of its members in 2012

were either ayatollahs or hojatoleslams (the second highest rank in the Shiite clergy).

The judiciary is probably more important than its equivalents in most Southern countries. In addition to the kinds of criminal and civil courts one finds elsewhere, Iran also has clerical courts with vast powers not only to adjudicate but also to prosecute cases that involve alleged offenses against Islamic law.

The constitution adopted a highly restrictive version of Sharia. Conviction for offenses such as adultery or homosexuality can lead to the death penalty. Until recently, the courts could call for stoning or the amputation of fingers as punishments for various crimes. And, initially at least, banks were not allowed to charge interest. The courts have loosened up a bit as the regime has solidified, but it is still one of the major conservative forces in the country.

The final unelected institution is the IRGC. As noted earlier, it was created because Khomeini and his colleagues doubted the loyalty and competence of the military they inherited from the Shah's regime. The IRGC has since become a linchpin of the regime, especially because it served as Ahmadinejad's political base. Despite only having loose ties with clerics, the Revolutionary Guard is one of the most conservative elements of the regime and is widely rumored to manage the *basij* vigilante groups that were so in evidence in putting down the demonstrations after the 2009 election. The IRGC also plays a major role in managing the economy.

Comparative Emphasis: Democratization

The uncertainties about democratization in Iran are reflected in the two types of state institutions. On the one hand are the offices that are directly elected and that seemed to be gaining in importance under President Khatami. On the other hand, with the resurgence of the conservative clerics before and after the 2004 election, nonelected and nondemocratic institutions regained their central place in Iranian politics. It seems likely that these institutions will keep their influence given the results of the Majlis and presidential elections held in 2012 and 2013, respectively. It is not clear, however, if that can remain the case indefinitely. ∎

The Elected Institutions and the Balance of Power

Since Khomeini's death, the balance between religious and other leaders has ebbed and flowed, albeit not in ways that lend themselves to easy description. As noted earlier, the presidency was in the ascendancy in Khamenei's first years as Supreme Leader. Given the way conflicts between his office and the presidency played themselves out during the Khatami and Ahmadinejad administrations, it seems safe to claim that the Supreme Leader is by far the more powerful of the two offices today, to such a degree that there were rumors during the 2013 campaign that the presidency itself would be abolished.

Since 1979, Iran has had seven presidents (see Table 13.7). The first two are barely worth mentioning. Abolhassan Bani-Sadr, an Islamic leftist, was removed from power by Khomeini within a year of taking office and still lives in exile outside of Paris. He was succeeded by Muhammad Ali Rajai, who was assassinated the following year. After that, three clerics were president: Khamenei, Rafsanjani, and Khatami. Ahmadinejad was elected in 2005

TABLE 13.7 Presidents of Iran since 1979

NAME	YEARS IN OFFICE
Abolhassan Bani-Sadr	1979–80
Muhammad Ali Rajai	1980–81
Ali Khamenei	1981–89
Hashemi Rafsanjani	1989–97
Mohammad Khatami	1997–2005
Mahmoud Ahmadinejad	2005–13
Hassan Rouhani	2013–

PROFILE Hassan Rouhani

Hassan Rouhani came out of nowhere to win the 2013 presidential election.

Although he is a cleric who was born into a religious family, Rouhani is the most westernized of the Islamic Republic's leading officials. In addition to his religious studies, he has an Iranian law degree and a PhD from Glasgow Caledonian University in Scotland.

While a young man, he changed his family name to Rouhani which can be translated as either "clerical" or "religious."

Rouhani experienced the revolution as a young man and spent the two years before the ouster of the shah in exile. After returning to Iran, he became active in politics and held a succession of elected and appointed offices, including service as the country's chief negotiator on nuclear issues.

Although he was the only candidate deemed acceptable by most reformists, he is not as critical of the clerical regime as either Khatami or Moussavi. Thus, in his initial press conference after his election, he hinted at a willingness to encourage a loosening of some political restrictions at home while insisting that Iran retain the right to develop its own nuclear program without interference from the international community. ■

despite not being a cleric. As we saw earlier, he was replaced by Rouhani who was the only member of the clergy to run in 2013.

The other important elected institution is the Majlis, whose formal title is the Islamic Consultative Assembly. The title itself suggests that it is not a parliament with formal decision-making authority. The Majlis can force individual ministers and governments out of office through the kind of votes of confidence we saw in Part 2. However, given the dominance of conservatives following the last three Majlis elections, that rarely happens.

For the reasons discussed throughout this section, the balance of power has been shifting away from the elected officials back toward the unelected ones for at least the last decade. That was particularly clear during Ahmadinejad's presidency. He and Khamenei agreed on broad policy initiatives such as continuing the nuclear program and purging secular professors and other moderate leaders. But their differences frequently were aired in public, and Khamenei routinely won.

There is no better example of this than Khamenei's successful effort to force Ahmadinejad to fire his recently appointed senior vice president, Esfandiar Rahim Mashaie, the very same man who was denied the right to run in 2013. Mashaie may be more moderate than most of his fellow leaders, having once said that Iranians and Israelis are friends. After his appointment (which was the president's right), Khamenei sent Ahmadinejad a letter stating that the appointment was "against your interest and the interests of the government. It is necessary to announce the cancellation of this appointment."

The balance seems to have swung even further in Khamenei's direction during the run up to the 2013 election when all candidates seen as critical of the Supreme Leader were kept off the ballot. On the other hand, Khamenei was in his mid-seventies when these lines were written, and it is an open question how long he will be able to stay in power or what might happen if Rouhani turns out to be more assertive than most observers expect him to be.

President Rouhani at his inauguration in 2013.

Public Policy

In every other chapter the public policy section begins with domestic issues. Not this one.

Most readers of this book will be more interested in Iran's troubled relations with the West that are currently focused on its nuclear program than any aspect of its domestic political life, including the status of women. What's more, the difficulties Iran faces internationally constrain what it can do at home, which explains why we cannot understand its social and economic policies without first putting them in their global context.

Toward the Next War?

Any discussion of Iranian public policy has to start with its at best troubled relationship with the West in general and the United States in particular, which has existed at least as long as oil has been an important global commodity. The United States itself became the foe of Iranian nationalists no later than the CIA-led overthrow of Mossadeq in 1953. Anti-American sentiment grew hand in hand with opposition to the shah, who was widely seen as little more than a tool of Washington and its cold war politics.

Today, many analysts in both countries are convinced that all of the bad blood since 1979 has put Iran and the West on a collision course. For some, Iran is not only trying to expand its influence but wants to export its style of Islamic revolution throughout the Muslim world and, perhaps, beyond. Many in Iran worry that the United States remains committed to ousting its regime and that their country will become the next battleground in what critics around the world are now calling the "permanent war."

As always, the causes of difficult relations between two countries over the long-term lie on both sides, as can be seen in this case from the very first days of the Islamic Republic. For many Iranians, the Carter administration's decision to allow the shah to come to the United States for medical treatment was the last straw, which prompted the occupation of the American embassy on November 4, 1979. Needless to say, the hostage crisis infuriated most Americans, an anger that was reinforced by Iranian action and rhetoric during the fifteen months of the standoff. Formal diplomatic relations between the United States and Iran were broken off during the hostage crisis and have not resumed since.

During and shortly after the crisis, Khomeini and his colleagues used inflammatory language, including calling the American government "the great Satan." Even its few humanitarian gestures, such as releasing the women and people of color it held, were accompanied by self-serving and anti-American statements. The authorities reacted to the failed attempt by American forces to rescue the hostages in mid-1980 as yet more evidence of Washington's evil designs on Tehran. Finally, many saw the timing of Iran's releasing the hostages the day President Reagan was inaugurated as a sign of their hatred of President Carter, whose chances for reelection were destroyed by a crisis he was unable to solve.

Iranians next demonstrated their deep dislike of the United States during its eight-year war with Iraq, which began before the hostages were released. The United States never officially supported Iraq. Nevertheless, its antipathy toward Iran led the Reagan administration to rebuild its relationship with Baghdad, while Khomeini's government kept up its anti-American rhetoric, especially during the second half of the war.

Relations between the two countries remained tense for the rest of the century. Despite some attempt to ease the tension, the United States passed a law during the Clinton administration that prohibited American companies and their subsidiaries from doing business with Iran, thus beginning the imposition of sanctions, which has escalated ever since.

American-Iranian relations turned even worse in the aftermath of the terrorist attacks on the United States on 9/11 largely because of decisions made in Washington rather than in Tehran. President George W. Bush sought to link Iran to al-Qaeda and the global terrorist network, even though there was little or no evidence to link the two. If anything, Iran played a minor, and even constructive, role in the defeat of the Taliban in Afghanistan and did nothing to oppose the war that toppled Saddam Hussein's government.

Nonetheless, President Bush included Iran with Iraq and North Korea as part of the axis of evil in his 2002 State of the Union address. Since then, American leaders have consistently criticized Iran's nuclear energy and weapons program and its alleged support for terrorist activities, especially those aimed at Israel.

The relationship has continued to deteriorate under President Obama in large part because of American objections to both the nuclear program and Iran's seemingly menacing posture toward Israel. His administration did initially make some overtures toward Iran, most notably in a speech the new president gave in Egypt during the first weeks of his administration. Some analysts believe that the international community and Tehran came close to reaching an agreement that would have slowed the nuclear program and allowed more inspections until the United States backed away from the deal in 2010.

Iran's nuclear program currently seems to have the two countries locked on a collision course. The issues are complex, but few facts are in dispute. Iran continues to develop its capacity to enhance nuclear material, which it insists it will only use to generate electricity. The United States and its allies point out that the same enrichment technology is needed for building the nuclear weapons, which they adamantly insist they will not allow Iran to add to its arsenal.

Iran continues its enrichment program. Experts differ, but most assume that Iran could develop a bomb and the means for delivering it at least as far away as Israel in no more than a few years.

The difficulties between Washington and Tehran have been compounded by Israel's understandable, but less than constructive, position. Publicly and privately, Prime Minister Benjamin Netanyahu has made it clear that Israel cannot accept a nuclear Iran and that his government would do everything in its power—including launching a preemptive strike—to keep it from deploying weapons of mass destruction.

It isn't just rhetoric. Under American pressure, the United Nations has extended the economic sanctions it has imposed on Iran. Unanimity in the Security Council has been hard to achieve given Russian and Chinese objection to the sanctions. Nonetheless, UN sanctions today prohibit almost all sales of Iranian oil on the world market.

Sanctions are always controversial, and it is never easy to tell whether they work or not. In this case, they definitely have had an impact on the Iranian economy and have hit the already struggling working class particularly hard. Nonetheless, if the remarks made by Supreme Leader Khamenei in his sermon at Friday prayers on the Iranian New Year's day (*Nowruz*) are any indication, sanctions and the rest of Western policy may only have strengthened Tehran's resolve.

Today, it has been thirty-four years that whenever the word 'enemy' has been mentioned, the people of Iran have been reminded of the US government.

[Audience chants: Death to America]

It is best for the US officials to pay attention to this issue and understand that in the past thirty-something years, the Iranian nation has seen certain things and passed through certain stages that as soon as the word 'enemy' is mentioned, their minds are drawn to the USA. This is a very important matter for a government that seeks to maintain a good reputation in the world.

Americans are constantly sending messages to us through different ways to let us talk about the nuclear issue. I am not optimistic about these talks. Why?

Americans do not want the nuclear talks to finish and the nuclear conflict to be resolved. Otherwise, if they were inclined to the completion of the talks and to the resolution of the conflict, the means of the solution

would be very close and simple. In the nuclear issue, Iran just wants its right for the enrichment [of uranium], which is its natural right, to be accepted by the world.

Relations between the two countries are bad not only because they have conflicting interests and conflicting values. Both have engaged in a practice psychologists call "the image of the enemy," which is a common theme in most of the world's hot spots. From this perspective, each side tends to view the other in stereotypical terms, typically stressing what it sees as the negative characteristics of the other. Use of terms like "axis of evil" or "the great Satan" only deepen already deep divisions and lead to misperceptions and mistakes in judgment about the other side's behavior and the intentions underlying it. Most problematical of all, when both sides invoke the image of the enemy, each waits for the other to take the first steps to improve the relationship, which means that it almost never happens.

It is too early to tell if Rouhani's election will help break this vicious cycle in U.S.-Iranian relations.

In fact, there has only been one area in which some progress has been made through what the conflict resolution community calls track-two diplomacy. Such negotiations involve private citizens who have no official authority and cannot represent their governments in discussions that could lead to binding treaties or other agreements. Instead, track-two processes can involve people with close ties to decision makers or simply try to improve the relationships among people in the societies involved at a time when formal, traditional diplomatic initiatives are not likely to prove fruitful.

There was, in practice, very little track-two contact between Americans and Iranians before the late 1990s. It was difficult for people to get permission to visit the other's country, and there were relatively few contacts between people from the two societies, except through Iranian émigrés, who are for the most part vocal opponents of the Islamic Republic.

The first significant opportunities for track-two work began after newly elected President Khatami called for a "dialogue of civilizations." Search for Common Ground, an organization founded with the purpose of finding cooperative rather than adversarial ways to resolve conflict, has been a leader in those efforts ever since (www.sfcg.org). In 1998, it arranged for the American national wrestling team to participate in a major international tournament, the first time the American flag had been displayed by Americans in Iran since the hostage crisis. The American athletes were greeted warmly by the Iranian wrestlers and by the huge crowd that turned out for the event; wrestling is one of the two most popular sports in Iran.

Since then, other athletic opportunities have been seized, including a soccer match between the two national teams

Comparative Emphasis: Globalization

Iran is one of the few countries in which globalization is not primarily an economic issue. To be sure, the government is eager to see restrictions on its oil sales abroad end, especially given the on-and-off but still dramatic rise in oil prices since the start of the Iraq war in 2003. However, it is probably the case that its overall isolation from the rest of the world will prove a more vexing problem. The conservatives' recapture of control of the presidency in 2005 led to more radical rhetoric, if not more radical policies, toward the West. That said, the authorities will have a harder and harder time keeping Western influences out of the country, influences that have already had a profound impact on at least the younger members of the middle class. ∎

that was watched by over one hundred thousand fans, all men. Search for Common Ground and other NGOs have also arranged exchanges of scientists, filmmakers, and artists, arranged for the Iranian ambassador to the United Nations to meet with two leading Republican members of Congress, and helped host an Iranian cultural festival and the visit of a leading ayatollah to Washington. In 2004, at the request of Iranian officials, Search for Common Ground sent a group of American educators to Tehran to begin negotiations on long-term exchanges of students and faculty.

One should not overestimate the impact these unconventional and unofficial diplomats have had either in Iran or in Nigeria (see the next chapter). On this front, neither government has helped the NGOs accomplish much of anything, beginning with the difficulties activists from one face in getting visas for entry into the other.

The Economy

As noted at the beginning of this section, foreign policy comes first in the case of Iran because what it does internationally sets the stage for what happens domestically, although not necessarily in the ways suggested in Figure 1.3. Nowhere is that clearer than in the difficulties the Islamic Republic has had in invigorating its economy. As with every other issue covered in this book, Iran's economic sluggishness has many causes, ranging from the

lingering impact of its war with Iraq a generation ago to the widespread corruption that even touches members of the clerical elite, including former President Rafsanjani. Nonetheless, the sanctions and other policies that have served to isolate Iran have kept it from reaching its economic potential.

There is another way in which global forces affect domestic politics. It is the only country covered in Part 4 where the debates over development strategies do not matter much, simply because their potential importance is dwarfed by the impact of the sanctions.

Iran is by no means a poor country. Its per capita income of about eleven thousand dollars a year in purchasing power parity terms makes it almost as wealthy as Mexico or Russia. However, sanctions and the leadership's own policy choices have left Iran no better off than it was when the shah was overthrown.

Much of Iran's wealth comes from a single resource: oil. It has 7 percent of the world's proven oil reserves, and only Russia has a larger untapped supply of natural gas. The spike in oil prices after the 9/11 terrorist attacks is largely responsible for Iran's recent growth spurt, which stood at about 7 percent for most of the first years of this century. As is true in Russia and Nigeria as well, dependence on the export of a single commodity is not a recipe for economic success in the long term. It may prove to be what economists call the "Dutch disease," a term based on the Netherlands' unhealthy reliance on the export of tulip bulbs three hundred years ago.

Yet, above and beyond its dependence on a single commodity whose price is vulnerable to global fluctuations and bursting economic bubbles, the Iranian economy faces problems that are political in origin. Even at its peak, the oil boom did not help the government address poverty, inflation, and youth unemployment. To find work for all of its young people, Iran needs to add eight hundred thousand jobs a year, a figure it has never come close to reaching. The standard of living of most Iranians is below what it was in 1979. The inflation rate routinely hovers around 20 percent. Even oil production is only about two-thirds what it was under the shah.

Public policy experts do not agree on what the most important economic problems are let alone what should be done about them, but they do agree that the state's economic priorities for the last quarter-century have been largely misguided. Especially during periods like the current one when the conservative clerics have been dominant, the economy has not been at the top of the leadership's list of priorities. When asked by an assistant about the difficult state of the economy, Ayatollah Khomeini once said, "This revolution was not about the price of watermelons."

In short, economic growth and prosperity have never been at the top of the conservatives' list of political priorities. That does not mean, however, that its actions have little or no economic impact. Depending on how one counts, the state owns or controls as much as 80 percent of the economy, far more than is the case in any other country covered in this book.

Iran's private sector was never a model of either efficiency or transparency under the shah. After 1979, the new leaders confiscated the property of the shah's family and almost every other industrial leader who had cooperated with the old regime. Those resources were turned into *bonyads*, a form of Islamic charity that the clerics control. The evidence is sketchy, but it seems certain that most *bonyads* are corrupt money losers. Some even charge that former President Rafsanjani has become the wealthiest man in Iran because of the money he rakes in from them. Overall, the concentration of power in a narrow elite plus the absence of an enforceable system of commercial law help explain why only Russia and Nigeria rank below Iran on Transparency International's Corruption Index among all the countries covered in *Comparative Politics*.

Ultimate responsibility for what they do and how they operate rests with the Supreme Leader, not the marketplace. Generally speaking, there are few incentives for entrepreneurial behavior, especially in invigorating the private sector because the constitution denies the government the right to privatize many state-run enterprises.

The government has been willing to issue low-interest loans and grant so-called "justice shares" in state-run enterprises. These developments should not be scoffed at since almost $3 billion worth of shares have been handed out, which have already resulted in over $50 million in dividends. Similarly, when the Khouzestan Steel Company was privatized in August 2007, 5 percent of its stock sold within minutes of its initial public offering (IPO).

Yet, as one economist put it recently,

> This government believes in supply side economics. It knows there is excess capacity in the country that could be harnessed with a cash injection. Unfortunately, the business climate is so bad that people only want to invest in hard assets such as property—and that fuels inflation.[5]

Rafsanjani and many of his colleagues became extremely wealthy men through their control of the shah's former property and other assets. Ahmadinejad, too, has been accused of giving his supporters in the Revolutionary Guard, as well as members of his family, sweetheart deals.

The leadership has also been reluctant—and is now unable—to open the economy to outside investment or involvement. In 2002, the government signed a contract with a Turkish firm to run the Imam Khomeini International Airport in Tehran. When the company arrived to set up operations, it found that the government had decided to break the contract, arguing that foreign management of the airport would be an insult to Iranian national pride.

Today, such opportunities only exist when Iran finds a way to skirt the restrictions imposed by the international sanctions regime.

The potential for growth is there. Like Nigeria, Iran is a major oil exporter but has to ration gasoline sales to its own citizens. In the long term, the key is to create jobs for the hundreds of thousands of young people who join the workforce every year and have next to no chance of finding a steady job. But frankly, in the current international context, there is relatively little the Iranian government can do to jump start the economy.

The most recent example was a series of reforms (really reductions) in subsidies the government underwrote that went into effect in early 2011. Until that time, the government had been spending about $100 billion a year—or almost a third of its total budget—to keep the cost of gasoline, food, and other daily consumer purchases artificially low. As a result of the sanctions, the government could no longer afford them, and its new policies gradually phased them out and had the direct effect of sharply increasing the price of key commodities. In early 2013, President Ahmadinejad continued to support subsidy reform as a vehicle to breathe new life into an economy that had seen its currency lose almost a third of its value in the preceding three years. Even his conservative critics argued that reducing the subsidies took cash out of the economy that could have been used for investment and the creation of new jobs.

As with everything else in Iran, much will depend on what the Rouhani government does. In his first statements after the 2013 election, he made it clear that he would make economic recovery a higher priority than it has ever been under the Islamic Republic. It is also clear that the Iranian electorate will judge him on his government's economic performance as well as the way it handles the ongoing tensions with the United States.

It is not yet clear whether his team will have the skills or the international community will allow it to have the resources to make that recovery possible.

---

[5]Cited in Angus McDowell, "Immunising the Economy Faced with Further Sanctions and a Confrontation with the United States." *Middle East Economic Digest*, 51 (24 August, 2007).

The Media

The state-controlled IRIB (Islamic Republic of Iran Broadcasting) has a legal monopoly on the country's airwaves. Its television and radio operations are usually known by the translation of part of its formal title in Farsi, Voice and Vision. The system has a staff of over forty-five thousand and a budget that approaches one billion dollars a year. Needless to say, clerics supervise almost all of its programming. In announcing the appointment of its current chief executive, Supreme Leader Khamenei defined its role as promoting "morality, religion, and hope [by] promoting ethical and religious values and increasing public awareness."

At times, the government has allowed critics to publish newspapers and magazines. But they tend to crack down whenever these publications are perceived as having gone too far. Since 2000, the government has shut down almost all of them, and virtually no dissenting periodicals were being published in 2011.

Despite these controls, the state does not have anything like a monopoly on what people see and hear. Iran has not tried to control Internet access to anywhere near the degree that China has (see Chapter 10) despite some significant attempts to do so since the Green Movement. More important, the state itself acknowledges that about half of the population watches foreign television on illegal satellite dishes. The dishes themselves cost about $150 and are programmed to receive international channels like CNN or the BBC as well as Farsi-language programs beamed from Dubai and elsewhere in the Muslim world, as well as Los Angeles, which is home to a huge Iranian émigré community.

Conclusion: Uncertainty

I revised this chapter last in preparing the ninth edition of *Comparative Politics* in the hopes that the 2013 election results might have offered a clearer sense of where the country is heading. Despite Rouhani's surprise victory and the initial optimism it prompted in Iran and in Western capitals, the easiest conclusion to reach about Iran is that it faces an uncertain future for all of the reasons discussed so far in this chapter and in the rest of Part 4, which can be summarized in the following:

- How will the political dynamics between the slightly reformist Rouhani government and the more hard-line clerical authorities evolve, especially if the aging Khamenei has to step back from political center stage?

- How important will economic and domestic issues be in determining what Rouhani and his team try to do?

- In the week after the election, there were already hints that something like the Green Movement might reappear. If so, what form would it take? More generally, what will the millions of Iranians who have at least some qualms about the Islamic Republic do?

- Will the new government be able to capitalize on initial welcoming signals from Washington and other Western capitals to ease international tensions in ways that could give it more room to maneuver in setting social and economic politics?

- Assuming these first four questions are answered in some sort of constructive way (which is, of course, a huge assumption), how will the government respond to the developmental challenges discussed in the other chapters in Part 4 of this book?

KEY TERMS

Concepts
charisma
fundamentalism
Guardianship of the Jurist
image of the enemy
Islamists
Pahlavi
sanctions
Shah
Sharia
Shiite
Sunni

People
Ahmadinejad, Mahmoud
Ebadi, Shirin

Khamenei, Ayatollah Ali
Khatami, Mohammad
Khomeini, Ayatollah Ruhollah
Mossadeq, Mohammad
Mousavi, Mir Hossein
Rafsanjani, Ayatollah Hashemi
Rouhani, Hassan
Shah, Mohammad Reza
Shah, Reza

Acronyms
IRGC
SAVAK

Organizations, Places, and Events
Assembly of Experts
Ayatollah

basij
bonyads
Constitutional Revolution
Expediency Council
Green Movement
Guardian Council
Hybrid regime
Iranian Revolutionary Guard Corps
   (IRGC)
Islamic Republic
Islamic Revolution
Majlis
principlists
Second of Khordad Movement
Supreme Leader
White Revolution

USEFUL WEBSITES

There are not a lot of reliable websites that provide information on Iran. The Iranians themselves have very few sites with information in English, and most Westerners treat them with skepticism because they are directly or indirectly controlled by the government. However, there are four Western sites that provide good sets of links to sites on Iran as well as news feeds on a daily basis.

The Middle East Research Information Project (MERIP) is a somewhat left-of-center publication. The website includes its own material plus op-ed pieces and other items that originally appeared elsewhere. Columbia University's School of International and Political Affairs is also one of many sites that provide in-depth news on the country. The Iran Chamber is one of the best general portals for information on Iranian life in general and not just politics. Finally, the Italian Scuola Superiore Sant'Anna maintains the best data sets on Iranian elections.

www.merip.org

gulf2000.columbia.edu/iran.shtml

www.daraee.com/iran.html

www.iranfocus.com/modules/news

www.iranchamber.com

www.sssup.it/context_eng.jsp?ID_LINK=7927&area=47&lang=UK

FURTHER READING

Ebadi, Shirin. *Iran Awakening: A Memoir of Revolution and Hope.* New York: Random House, 2006. By the Nobel Peace Prize–winning jurist.

Ignatius, David. *The Increment.* New York: W. W. Norton, 2009. A novel by the *Washington Post*'s best foreign policy editorial writer. Examines both the American intelligence community and the Iranian nuclear program better than any academic has.

Keddie, Nikki. *Modern Iran: Roots and Results of Revolution.* New Haven, CT: Yale University Press, 2003. Probably the best book on Iran by an academic historian; covers the period from the late eighteenth century to the present.

Majd, Hooman. *The Ayatollahs' Democracy.* New York: W. W. Norton, 2010. By a cousin of Former President Khatami. Immensely readable.

Moaveni, Azadeh. *Lipstick Jihad. A Memoir of Growing Up Iranian in the United States and American in Iran.* New York: Public Affairs, 2005. A very funny and insightful book by an American journalist of Iranian origins who goes to Iran to cover events in her "home" country while still in her twenties.

Nafisi, Azar. *Reading Lolita in Tehran.* New York: Random House, 2003. A stunning look at gender and politics in contemporary Iran through the lens of a small, informal American literature seminar run by a former Iranian professor.

Pollack, Kenneth. *The Persian Puzzle.* New York: Century Books, 2004. By the provocative author of one of the best books on why the United States should have gone to war with Iraq. He argues the opposite here.

Sciolino, Elaine. *Persian Mirrors: The Elusive Face of Iran.* New York: Touchstone, 2000. The most readable overview of Iran written by the veteran *New York Times* correspondent who has spent a lot of time covering Iran.

Takeyh, Ray. *Guardians of the Revolution: Iran and the World in the Age of the Ayatollahs.* New York: Oxford University Press, 2009. Probably the best book by a policy wonk on Iran. Very readable.

Vakil, Sanam. *Women and Politics in the Islamic Republic of Iran: Action and Reaction.* New York: Continuum, 2011. A remarkable book by a young Iranian-American scholar who was able to get into Iran and interview women activists for this book.

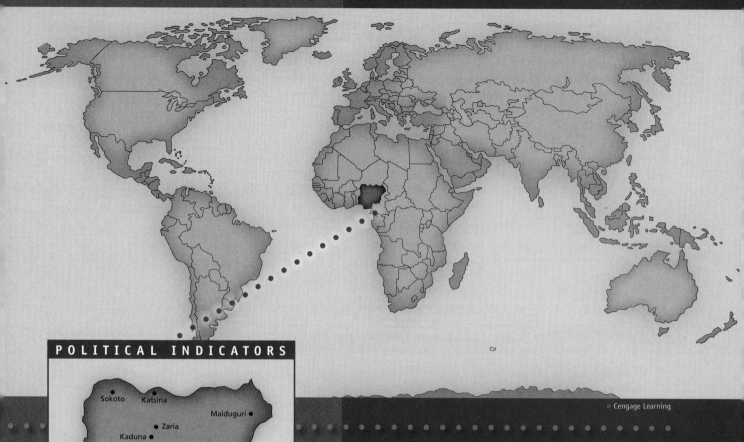

© Cengage Learning

POLITICAL INDICATORS

NIGERIA

- Sokoto
- Katsina
- Maiduguri
- Zaria
- Kaduna
- Jos
- Abuja
- Ibadan
- Lagos
- Port Harcourt

GOVERNANCE (score 0-1)	HUMAN DEVELOPMENT (score 0-1)	DEMOCRACY (rank)	GLOBAL PEACE INDEX (rank)	CORRUPTION (rank)
.489	.459	119	146	143

14

Nigeria

The trouble with Nigeria is simply and squarely a failure of leadership. There is nothing basically wrong with the Nigerian character. There is nothing wrong with the Nigerian land or climate or water or air or anything else.

CHINUA ACHEBE

THE BASICS

Germany

Size	823,770 sq. km (about twice the size of California)
Population	155 million (estimated)
Population growth	2.6%
GDP per capita (purchasing power parity)	$2,700
Growth GDP	7.1%
Currency	157 naira = US$1
Major religions	About 50% Muslim, 40% Christian, 10% indigenous religions
Literacy	61%
Life expectancy	52 years

Goodluck, Jonathan

On April 8, 2011, Nigeria reelected the incumbent president with the unlikely name of Goodluck Jonathan (1957–) in its fourth national election since the military once again handed power back to civilians. As a politician, Jonathan was already the beneficiary of a good bit of good luck. Already vice president, Jonathan became acting president in early 2010 when his predecessor, Umaru Musa Yar'Adua

(1953–2010), had to leave the country for medical treatment. When Yar'Adua died later in the year, Jonathan formally assumed the presidency.

Jonathan also had his share of bad luck. His problems actually began when Yar'Adua was elected to succeed Olusegun Obasanjo (1937–) as head of the country's fourth republic. Obasanjo had run the country twice, first as a military dictator and then as an elected president.

As we will soon see, Nigeria is deeply divided along ethnic and religious lines. There is an unwritten agreement that the presidency will rotate between the largely Muslim north and the heavily Christian south. Yar'Adua was a Muslim and succeeded the Christian Obasanjo. He was under sixty years old when he was elected, and most pundits assumed that the presidency would stay in the north until he had to step down after completing his two terms in office, which is all the constitution allows.

Jonathan's problems began with the fact that he is a southerner and a Christian. Yar'Adua had named Jonathan as his vice presidential candidate to balance his ticket. The president's unexpected death disrupted the rotation between the two communities and alienated most politically active Muslims who thought they had the "right" to choose the next president. Given provisions in the constitution, however, the vice president automatically succeeds the president if he (so far, they have all been men) either becomes incapacitated or dies in office.

AP Photo/Pablo Martinez Monsivais

Goodluck Jonathan with Barack Obama at the White House.

When he had to run on his own the following year, Jonathan and the **People's Democratic Party (PDP)** swept the south. The Muslim-dominated parties did the same in the north where they make up the vast majority of the population.

Nigeria also has had more than its share of political violence, which extends far beyond disputes between Christians and Muslims. Indeed, as the presidential campaign was heating up in early 2011, protests led by the Movement for the Emancipation of the Niger Delta (MEND) broke out in the state of Bayelsa where Jonathan had been governor before moving to Abuja, the national capital, upon becoming vice president.

It wasn't just Bayelsa. Since 2009, a previously little-known sect, **Boko Haram,** has been conducting a campaign of terrorist attacks that killed hundreds of Christians and what its leaders considered to be less-than-observant Muslims.

His string of bad luck went beyond ethnicity and religion. Transparency International (www.transparency.org) includes former President Obasanjo as one of its cofounders. Despite that fact, it ranked Nigeria as the 143rd most corrupt country in the world in 2011. Some would go so far as to argue that Obasanjo himself was one of the leading contributors to the country's low score, because it was revealed that millions of *naira* slated for hospitals, schools, and other development projects "disappeared" into private hands during the course of the 2011 campaign.

Furthermore, Nigeria is by far the poorest country included in *Comparative Politics*. That need not have been the case. By all rights, Nigeria should be the wealthiest country in Africa, because it is the biggest producer of oil and natural gas on the continent and is in the top fifteen in the world, ranking barely below Kuwait and Iraq.

Yet, it has so few functioning refineries of its own that it actually has to export crude oil and import gasoline which is then sold at inflated prices, with rich Nigerians often raking in huge profits along the way. Meanwhile, 70 percent of the population lives in poverty.

Over the decades, Nigerian governments have tried every populist strategy imaginable to help their country achieve some degree of sustainable development. It is only a slight exaggeration to say that all of them have failed. Even the profits the country makes from its oil exports seem to have disappeared into thin air—or, more likely, into the foreign bank accounts of the country's elites.

Last, but by no means least, Jonathan has the good or bad fortune of heading a country in which civilian rule of any sort is the exception to the rule. Yar'Adua was the first civilian to succeed another civilian as president. Twice before, military officers staged coups that overthrew civilian leaders. A third time, they launched a coup before the third republic even had a chance to get off the ground. No one expected the uncertainties of the transition to Jonathan's presidency to spark what would be the tenth coup in Nigerian history, but no one was willing to rule one out either.

In short, of all the countries covered in this book, Nigeria comes closest to being what political scientists call a **failed state**. Unlike the case forty years ago, Nigeria is unlikely to splinter into a number of separate and antagonistic countries. In few other ways can Nigeria be considered a success.

Thinking About Nigeria

Names aside, Nigerian politics is not about luck. It is about all the problems that Goodluck Jonathan inherited that together leave the country seemingly locked in what is arguably the most difficult set of vicious cycles we will consider in *Comparative Politics*. The country itself does not seem on the verge of falling apart as it has at other points in the fifty years since independence. However, there are few optimistic signs that any of the social, economic, or political "corners" hinted at above will be turned in the near future.

Any discussion of Nigeria, therefore, has to revolve around three overlapping themes:

- It is blessed with abundant human and natural resources.

- Those resources have not been used well by anyone's definition, leaving the country with those problems I have already mentioned and more.

- As a result, the stakes of Nigerian politics are extremely high, including a history of conflict and instability that stretches back at least to its independence more than a half-century ago.

The Bottom Line

As the world-renowned novelist Chinua Achebe (1930–2013) suggests in the statement that begins the chapter, Nigeria has had more than its share of trouble. Whether run by civilians or the military, the state has never lived up to either popular expectations or its potential. There have been times, as during the civil war of 1967–70 over **Biafra**, when it could be argued that there was no viable Nigerian government that could meet such basic social needs as maintaining law and order.

Resources

That said, Nigeria does have a lot going for it.

Almost one in five Africans is Nigerian. The country is blessed with some of the most fertile soil on the continent. Compared with the rest of Africa, it has a well-educated population with at least two million university graduates.

Most important of all, its oil and gas deposits have brought Nigeria more money than most other African nations can dream of. It is the sixth leading oil producing country in the world. The petroleum industry alone accounts for 90 percent of Nigeria's export income or about $600 billion in 2012. The government retains almost all of the profits earned from its oil, which make up at least 75 percent of its total revenue.

Other than the oil, those assets were available to Nigeria as soon as it gained its independence in 1960. Therefore, most observers expected Nigeria to help lead the continent in building strong states, democratic regimes, and modern economies.

That is not what has happened.

Poverty

Nigeria's problems begin with its basic social and economic conditions. Despite those resources, Nigeria remains desperately poor. Definitions of poverty vary, and statistics about countries like Nigeria are notoriously unreliable. Nonetheless, it is hard not to be depressed about the quality of life there.

It ranks in the bottom fourth of the world's countries on almost every indicator measuring social and economic development. Forty percent of its children are either malnourished or suffer from other poverty-related deficiencies that stunt their growth. One international agency ranked the Nigerian health care system 187th in the world.

According to the National Bureau of Statistics, 60.9 percent of the population was poor in 2010, up 6 percent from 2004 even though the economy as a whole had grown significantly. The poverty rate is 60 percent in the *richest* parts of the country. It tops three-fourths in the regions where Boko Haram has had the most support. In perhaps the most revealing statistic, more than one hundred million people have to survive on the equivalent of one dollar a day or less. Even at the more generous purchasing power parity (PPP) rate, GDP per capita is barely $2,400.

Seven percent of Nigerian children do not reach the age of one. Fourteen percent die before their fifth birthday. Most of those children succumb to malnutrition or diarrhea that could easily be treated or prevented if the country could afford basic medications that are sold over the counter in the West.

The life expectancy of the average Nigerian is barely fifty. Only 20 percent of the people have access to safe drinking water. There are only 0.4 doctors for every thousand Nigerians. Mexico has four times as many. To make matters worse, there are almost as many Nigerian-born physicians practicing medicine in the United States as in Nigeria itself. About two-thirds of the population is literate, but barely three in five women can read and write.

As is the case in most of Africa, Nigeria has to cope with population growth of monstrous proportions which is likely to make Nigeria poorer as it is forced to spread its already limited resources even further. During much of the 1980s it averaged over 3 percent per year. About 45 percent of the Nigerian population is under fifteen, while only 3 percent is over sixty-five. At the current average growth rate of nearly 3 percent, the size of the population will double in barely twenty-five years. At that rate, Nigeria will have nearly four hundred million inhabitants by the middle of the twenty-first century, which will be roughly one-and-a-half times larger than the *total* African population today.

Nigerians are already in more or less constant danger of famine. In 2009, the *Washington Post* reported that almost 40 percent of Nigerian children are malnourished. Two-thirds of the population is what the United Nations calls food insecure. The year before, when food prices soared, authorities feared the outbreak of rioting in most cities. The government agreed to import more food and then had to renege on its promise because it would take longer to bring food into the country than to grow it at home in a country that has millions of acres of land that could grow crops with only minimal irrigation. Only 7 percent of that land is currently farmed.

Add to these other problems the rapid urbanization that Nigeria shares with most countries in the Global South. Over half of its population now lives in cities, whose growth is fueled by millions of young people who leave the country-side seeking jobs.

The population of Lagos, for instance, reached one million by the mid-1970s, and many people were surprised when the 2006 census showed it "only" had eight million people. Its metropolitan area is estimated to have nearly seventeen million people today, which would make its region one of the largest cities on the planet.

Lagos also provides a good picture of the twin realities of urban life in Nigeria and beyond. Miles of shantytowns in neighborhoods like Badia East (see Chapter 11) surround a central city whose wide boulevards and gleaming skyscrapers remind one of New York or London. For most urban Nigerians, life is restricted to the shantytowns with their ethnically segregated neighborhoods, houses without indoor plumbing or electricity, dead-end jobs (if they have paying jobs), endless traffic jams (called "go slows"), and tensions with people from different ethnic groups.

Pedestrians and shoppers make their way through a crowded street in Lagos.

The economy as a whole has grown. From 1965 until 1980, Nigeria's gross national product (GNP) grew by an average of 6.9 percent per year because of the income it was able to realize from low-level industrial development and oil exports. From 1980 to 1987, however, the economy shrank by more than 40 percent because its industries ceased being productive and oil prices collapsed. In the decade between 1992 and 2002, the shrinkage continued at a pace of about half a percent per year. Growth has picked up in the last decade, but not enough to make Nigeria anywhere near as well off as the other countries considered in this book.

Identity

Very few countries in the South have been able to avoid identity-driven conflict. That is especially the case in Nigeria where the two overlap all but completely as we saw in the regional results for the 2011 presidential election. As a Christian, Jonathan carried all but one state in the south, where most Christians live. His Muslim opponent Muhammedu Buhari won every state in the north where his co-religionists dominate.

Nigeria has about four hundred ethnic groups, each of which has its own language and customs. Politically, the three largest ones matter the most, although combined they only make up about two-thirds of the population.

The **Hausa-Fulani** make up the largest group, with about 30 percent of all Nigerians, the vast majority of whom live in the north. Most are Muslims. Almost all Nigerian Muslims are Sunni, but only a small fraction of them are devout, however one chooses to define that term. The Fulani, who had Northern African or Arabic roots, gradually moved into the north and, beginning in 1804, gained control of the region and its predominantly Hausa-speaking population. Since then, the two have intermarried so frequently that they are virtually indistinguishable.

The region to the west of the Niger and Benue rivers is dominated by the **Yoruba**, that on the east by the **Igbo**. Many Yoruba and Igbo have converted to Christianity, but there are sizable Muslim and non-Christian minorities among the Yoruba. Together, they account for 60 to 65 percent of the population. Both regions are more prosperous than the north, and the Igbo are known for their entrepreneurial skills.

Not surprisingly, the **middle belt** is in the center of the country, where no single ethnic group or religion dominates. Perhaps as a result, it has been home to many of the leaders who have been least preoccupied with religious and ethnic issues. In an attempt to create a symbol of national unity during the 1980s, the government moved the capital from Lagos in the heart of Yoruba territory to the new city of Abuja in the middle belt.

Divisions over identity issues begin with a seemingly simple issue: how people communicate with each other. In the rather homogeneous rural areas, almost everyone still speaks the dominant local group's traditional language. The elite usually speak English, which is the official language of the national government and used in most mass media. In the cities, where poorly educated people from different groups have to communicate with each other, new languages have emerged that combine simple English terms and African grammatical structures. Then *Washington Post* correspondent Blaine Harden provides the following example from a rap song about corrupt politicians: "If him bring you money, take am and chop. Make you no vote for am," which means, "If he tries to buy your vote, take the money and buy food. Then vote for somebody else." *Chop-chop politics* is the common Nigerian term to describe what Americans call log-rolling or pork-barrel politics.

As we will see in the rest of the chapter, Nigeria's identity issues go far beyond the trouble people have in communicating with each other. They determine where people live, what they believe in, how they conduct their lives, how jobs are allocated, and who they support politically. And, more than any other factor, ethnicity has made democratic government difficult and led to the coups of 1966, 1983, and 1993, countless riots, and the civil war of 1967–70.

As should already be clear, ethnicity and religion overlap. About half the country is Muslim and 40 percent is Christian. The rest of the population practices religions that antedate the arrival of the Arabs and Europeans.

Not all Nigerians are devout, whatever religion they believe in. And there are traces of traditional faiths in the way both Christians and Muslims practice their religion. However, both religion and ethnicity are critical components of **identity politics** in Nigeria. And, as we have seen throughout Part 4, it is hard for people to find compromise solutions on identity-based issues because they tend to be cast in all-or-nothing terms.

In the Nigerian case, the differences between Muslims and Christians have equally important social and political implications. Muslim regions, for example, are still governed using traditional institutions that blend secular and religious leadership, some of whose roots can be traced back even before the arrival of Islam. Nigerian Christians, on the other hand, are increasingly drawn to Pentecostal and other non-mainstream denominations whose missionary zeal worries Muslims of all stripes.

Nigeria is not unusual in having important identity-based divisions. What makes it unique among the countries included in this book is the overlap among these divisions that make it all but impossible to tell where religious issues end and those other ones begin.

The Tenth Parallel

The tenth parallel north of the Equator is an informal but important border between two worlds. In Nigeria, it separates the part of the country where the Sahara has an impact on the climate and the south whose topography is defined more by its jungles. It also marks what the journalist Eliza Griswold calls the "fault line between Christianity and Islam" in almost all of Africa and South Asia.

People on each side of the parallel tend to portray their disputes in religious (if not always theological) terms. As practiced in Nigeria, both faiths are dominated by their evangelical wings, which focus on spreading the faith among "unbelievers."

But, as Griswold is careful to point out, all of the other problems these countries face are inextricably intertwined with those over religion, because they invariably raise economic, environment, ethnic, and gender issues, many of which are portrayed in zero-sum terms by participants on all sides. If Griswold is right, most of the conflicts do not *start* with religious differences, but they almost always become part of the mix and, for good or ill, tend to intensify the disputes.

As she puts it about hard line believers in Nigeria, "*Tolerance* is a word of which both sides are wary, since to them, it smacks of a moral relativism to which they do not subscribe. To them, it suggests they should tolerate heresy and falsehood."[a]

[a]Eliza Griswold, *The Tenth Parallel: Dispatches from the Fault Line between Christianity and Islam* (New York: Farrar, Straus and Giroux, 2010), 66.

Zero-Sum Politics

These problems and more have turned politics in Nigeria into a very high-stakes or **zero-sum** game. More people have been killed by repressive regimes elsewhere. Nonetheless, its politics is highly charged because people have great and growing expectations about what their government could and should do. The fact that successive civilian and military governments alike have met so few of them has left the country mired in as wrenching and as self-perpetuating a vicious cycle as we will see in this book.

People tend to view all political choices as leading to clear winners and losers. In as poor a country as Nigeria, winning might not bring tremendous benefits to the individuals or groups who end up on the "right" side. However, almost everyone believes that the costs of losing are so severe that it is never worth running the risk of doing so.

The political stakes are easiest to see in the alternation between civilian and military governments, none of which have been able to make much headway on any of the problems Nigeria faces. Whatever institutional forms it takes, Nigerian politics is a struggle which all the key groups desperately want to win or, at the very least, prevent their adversaries from doing so. The spoils of office are high, as the rampant corruption attests. And any time the stakes get high, all concern about the national interest seems to disappear.

Key Questions

All of this makes Nigeria harder to study than most of the other countries covered in this book. Because of the shifts back and forth between civilian and military rule, Nigerian institutions have not been in existence for very long and therefore do not have much of an impact on the way politics is structured. As a result, the sections on the state and parties will be shorter than those in other chapters. On the other hand, the next major section on the history of the alternation between civilian and military rule has to be relatively long because without understanding those twists and turns you will not be able to see why the stakes of politics are so high.

In the process, we will be asking questions about Nigerian politics that both mirror those posed in the chapters on other countries in Part 4 and focus on conditions unique to Nigeria.

- How does the legacy of colonization continue to affect Nigerian politics?

- What role does identity politics play in reinforcing the country's difficulties?

- Why does political culture seem more important here than in other chapters?

- Why does Nigeria remain one of the poorest countries in the world despite its massive oil and natural gas reserves?

- How has the alternation between civilian and military rule exacerbated the country's many social and economic problems?

The Evolution of the Nigerian State

Critics are quick to point out the faults of Nigeria's leaders. They are right to do so, because leaders of all political stripes have made damaging mistakes, many of which seem, in retrospect, to have been easily avoidable.

However, the incompetence or venality of these men by no means tells the entire story. Whatever the leaders of independent Nigeria had been like, they would have inherited a tremendous burden of problems from colonial times that continue to trouble it today in three main ways:

- The Atlantic slave trade cost the Nigerians and their fellow Africans countless millions of people from the sixteenth through the nineteenth centuries.

- Colonization disrupted traditional social and political systems when Europeans created new borders that suited their own purposes but did not take existing regional alignments into account.

- The very drawing of the boundaries, as well as the nature of colonial administration, made ethnic conflict all but inevitable after independence. The anticolonial struggle, the political arrangements made at the time the former colonies became independent states, and the informal pattern of neocolonial relations that was established afterward left the new state in a poor position to develop politically, socially, and economically.

Before the British

For many years, the conventional wisdom was that precolonial Africa was "primitive" and lacked anything approaching civilization or government. That was not the case (africanhistory.about.com). A number of rather advanced civilizations existed in what is today's Nigeria. None had a written language, but, otherwise, many of them had well-developed political, cultural, and economic systems.

It actually does not make sense to talk about precolonial Nigeria because no such place existed. What is today known as Nigeria was created by the British for their own reasons which had little or nothing to do with what happened there before colonization began in the late nineteenth century.

Outside influence on life in what became Nigeria actually began long before the Europeans arrived (see Table 14.1). The spread of both the Sahara Desert and Islam brought the Hausa-speaking peoples into contact with the Arab world about a thousand years ago, when it, not Europe, was the center of world civilization. By the thirteenth century, most Hausa had converted to Islam.

By the thirteenth century, a king, or *mai*, had gained control of dozens of Hausa states. Although the kingdom's power ebbed and flowed over the centuries, it had well-developed bureaucratic, judicial, and imperial institutions.

Power in the north was further centralized in the early nineteenth century when Usman Dan Fodio led a Fulani takeover of the northern region, established a caliphate under Islamic law, and transformed the old Hausa states into emirates. When the British arrived, they found extensive mines, factories that made elaborate ceramics, over thirty types of cloth sold by merchants who relied on sophisticated financial and monetary systems, and an elaborate trading network that extended at least as far as Baghdad.

The Yoruba developed a very different—but no less complex—political system. They trace their history back more than two thousand years and initially came together in the Oyo empire in the twelfth century in the capital city of Ife-Ife. Over the centuries, people spread out from there and established at least sixteen other kingdoms, all patterned along similar lines. By the end of the eighteenth century, a single kingdom had expanded to include today's Yoruba regions of Nigeria and virtually the entire country of Benin.

The Igbo had a different, but still elaborate, social and political system. Little attempt was made to forge a centralized regime atop a network of what were largely self-governing villages, all of which shared a widely accepted, if unwritten, constitution that specified clearly defined policy-making, administrative, judicial, and military roles as Chinua Achebe brilliantly described in *Things Fall Apart*. Power and prestige went to those elders who had accumulated the most wealth, shown the most bravery in battle, and demonstrated the strongest commitment to village values. In short, life among the Igbo was based more on merit and less on the accident of birth than for the British who colonized them.

Europeans arrived in the late fifteenth century when Portuguese explorers landed on the coast and its merchants started exchanging gold for slaves. There had long been an intra-African slave trade, but it took on its well-known and tragic proportions during the seventeenth century when huge sugar plantations dependent on imported labor were established in the Caribbean. At that point, the British, French, Dutch, Spanish, and Swedes joined the Portuguese in creating the infamous slave trade that was centered along what is now the Nigerian coast.

The Europeans did not establish settlements away from the coast. African rulers were too strong and malaria and other diseases too deadly. Instead, they bought millions of people from African merchants, who captured, kidnapped, or purchased them.

No one knows how many people were enslaved before the practice was finally brought to an end, but the most reliable estimates range from eleven to twenty million. Of those, upward of one million were Nigerian. At least two hundred thousand slaves a year were sent westward from 1827 to 1834 from the Bight of Bonny alone.

The impact of slavery cannot be measured by the numbers of people taken into captivity alone. At the same historical moment that new discoveries sparked by human initiative and curiosity were propelling European civilization forward, African development was being stunted as generations of its best and brightest youth were ripped out of society and sold into slavery.

Colonial Rule

The slave trade wound down in the years before the American Civil War. That did not mean that European involvement in Africa ended. Far from it.

Historians still debate which of the "three G's"—god, gold, and glory—was most important in leading Europeans to take over all of Africa. What is clear is that by the end of the nineteenth century, almost the entire continent was ruled by Europeans.

A permanent European presence was made easier by the discovery that quinine cured malaria. Still, there was little

TABLE 14.1 Events in Nigeria before Independence

YEAR	EVENT
Eleventh century	Arrival of Arabs
Sixteenth century	Beginning of slave trade
1884–85	Berlin Conference on Africa
1914	Unification of Nigeria as a single colony
1920	Creation of National Congress of British West Africa
1923	Formation of Nigerian National Democratic Party
1938	Nigerian Youth Charter issued
1948	Nigerianization of civil service begins
1951 and 1954	Interim constitutions go into effect
1960	Independence

thought of colonizing all of Nigeria or the rest of Africa. Instead, in 1865, a British parliamentary commission went so far as to advocate phasing out all British activity along the Nigerian coast.

The industrial revolution prompted Britain and the other European powers to seek new sources of the raw materials they needed for their manufactured goods. The most lucrative Nigerian export was palm oil, which was used to lubricate the machines in the new British factories. During the nineteenth century, annual sales of palm oil grew from 450 to 50,000 tons per year.

The British also used economic pretexts to justify expanding their political control. Of particular importance were the actions of a private corporation, the United African Company, and its leader Sir George Goldie. His quest for "gold" and "glory" led him to convince the Foreign Office to appoint him chief agent and vice-consul of the Niger, which allowed him to offer British military protection on behalf of the UAC. By the mid-1880s, Goldie had negotiated more than two hundred treaties, which the British government then used as the basis for its claim to the north.

Meanwhile, events in Europe transformed the way the great powers thought about Africa. During the 1870s, the newly unified Germany and Italy disrupted the balance of power that had been so delicately carved out after the Napoleonic Wars. Those pent-up pressures did not erupt in Europe itself at the time. However, they had to be released somewhere, and that somewhere turned out to be Africa, setting off the "scramble for Africa."

Explorers and soldiers spread across the continent and staked claims to territories for their governments back home. Often, representatives of two or more countries claimed the same places, which only magnified the tensions in Europe itself. In part to avoid another continental war, Germany convened the International Berlin West Africa Conference, which lasted from November 1884 to February 1885. For all intents and purposes, it finished the carving up of the continent that was already well under way.

To complicate matters further, English missionaries were appalled by the values and customs of the Africans they encountered. The new sense of nationalism combined with the Europeans' moral certainty to create an unfortunate blend of arrogance and ignorance. The missionaries in particular failed to even notice that they had encountered well-developed—albeit very different—civilizations.

The British used their coastal enclaves as staging grounds for the conquest of the interior. Pacification campaigns destroyed the power of local leaders. Though vastly outnumbered, the British used their technological superiority and exploited divisions among the Africans to subdue their opponents during the rest of the century.

Finally, in 1906, British forces destroyed the remnants of the Fulani Empire and took full control of the north. Eight years later the British combined the north with the south and east to create the single entity that they called Nigeria, which was not even an African word. It was, in short, an artificial name to describe an artificial entity that people who lived there almost certainly would have never created had the choice been left to them, which, of course, it was not.

There is very little positive to say about colonial rule in Nigeria or anywhere else. The first colonial administrator, Frederick Lugard, spoke of Britain's **dual mandate**. On the one hand, colonial administrators had to serve the interests of imperialists and industrialists back home. On the other hand, they had to improve the lot of what he called the "native races." In reality, the "benefits" of British rule went all but completely in one direction.

Colonial rule was also racist and exploitative. The British argued that Africans were inferior and had to be "civilized," thereby justifying the actions of missionaries and others who undercut traditional African ways of life.

Things Fall Apart

No one has shown how colonialism disrupted cultural, economic, and political life in Nigeria (or elsewhere) any better than Chinua Achebe did in *Things Fall Apart*.

Most of us would not want to have lived in traditional Igbo society. Women were second-class citizens. Twins were killed.

But theirs was a society with a distinctive culture and values in which people led lives of dignity as portrayed in the successes and failures of Okonkwo, the novel's protagonist, and his village's leader.

Toward the end of the book, a British missionary arrives to convert the village residents. He starts with its weakest links, including one of Okonkwo's children who could not or would not live up to the cultural norm that men had to prove themselves as warriors.

Seeing his way of life slip away, Okonkwo ultimately kills the minister, knowing full well that his act will bring British soldiers in pursuit. He knows, too, that not only his life, but also his people's way of life, are about to be destroyed. Okonkwo kills himself in a final act of desperation. The novel ends with a British soldier writing his memoirs, tentatively titled *The Pacification of the Primitive Tribes of the Lower Niger*.

Imperialism's economic toll is the easiest to see. The British assumed that their colonies had to pay for themselves while simultaneously financing industrial development at home. That was not possible given the economic systems the British inherited with the consolidation of colonial rule. Therefore, as in India, they embarked on a series of changes that "undeveloped" Nigeria.

Up to that point, Nigeria had produced enough food to feed its people and had the trade and manufacturing networks noted earlier. The British destroyed almost all of that. They introduced cash crops Nigerians could export to help cover the costs of administering the colony. Each region specialized in a different crop: palm oil in the east, cocoa in the west, and peanuts in the north. As a result, Nigerian agriculture no longer produced enough for local consumption and became dependent on imports.

The British also seized tin mines that Nigerians had worked for more than two thousand years. By 1928, they were employing upwards of forty thousand Nigerians in larger and more technologically sophisticated mines, but now the Nigerians were poorly paid wage laborers, not independent producers.

The political situation only made things worse for most Nigerians. In 1914, the British created a single Nigerian colony, the very existence of which flew in the face of all traditional political arrangements. Northerners had little in common with either the Igbo or the Yoruba in the south. Economic policies magnified regional differences. The north experienced slower economic growth and enjoyed fewer of the so-called benefits of colonial rule, including education, which we will discuss in a few paragraphs. Meanwhile, groups were arbitrarily divided across colonial lines, with substantial numbers of Igbo forced to live in Nigeria and the Cameroons.

The vastly outnumbered colonial administrators had no choice but to hire local officials. As late as 1938, there were no more than 1,500 British officials in the entire colony. The British, therefore, had no choice but to rely on **indirect rule**, in which local leaders ostensibly governed subject only to the limited supervision of imperial officials. The British thus enhanced the power of traditional local leaders, whom they dubbed "kings" and "emirs" in the north and "chiefs" in the south. However, it cannot be stressed strongly enough that these local leaders had no role in determining basic colonial policies, which were set by white men in London and Lagos.

Last but by no means least, colonial rule may not have been as ruthless as it was in other countries, but the years of British rule laid much of the foundation for the problems the Africans would have to deal with once the country gained its independence by exacerbating whatever ethnic and religious differences already existed. Thus, people began to consciously define themselves as Yoruba, Igbo, or Hausa-Fulani.

Independence

As was the case in India, British colonial rule was doomed from the outset. It had too many built-in contradictions, although many of them were not obvious at the beginning of the twentieth century. Over the next thirty years, those flaws made colonial rule increasingly untenable so that by the end of World War II, Nigerian independence was all but inevitable.

The difficulties began with the fact that the British had to educate Nigerians in order for indirect rule to work. The "civilizing mission" side of Lugard's dual mandate required Nigerians who could read and write and who also prayed to the Christian God. One unintended but inevitable consequence of the expansion of Nigerian education was the exposure of young people to what the British claimed to be their core values, including freedom and democracy, which, in due course, led many of them to question whether they wanted or needed the British in the first place.

By 1926, there were about 4,000 elementary and 18 secondary schools. In 1934, the first "higher college" that concentrated on technical education was opened, followed by a full-fledged university in Ibadan in 1948.

Even though only a tiny fraction of the colonial population received even an elementary education, expanding educational opportunities especially at the secondary and university levels had two important and unintended side effects that were to hasten independence and a third that which trouble the new country.

- It created a new elite that would form the core of the independence movement.

- The growing number of literate Nigerians turned into an audience for an active and often critical press.

- The fact that almost all of the secondary schools and universities were in the south meant that southerners filled almost all of the key jobs the British created, which bred considerable resentment in the north.

World War I made the weakness of British rule even more apparent. To help pay for it, the British imposed heavy taxes on and drafted some Nigerians to serve in the British army. The war and the reasons the British gave for fighting it led a few members of the still tiny educated elite to see the contradiction between the colonizers' democratic principles and the harsh realities of their rule.

British misconceptions about African life also helped sow the seeds of their own destruction. They were convinced that most Africans lived as part of tribes and that indirect rule should therefore rest on the power of chiefs. That led them to create tribes and chiefs in areas where none had previously existed. Gradually, the practice took hold. As chiefs began to consolidate their authority over communities that came to see themselves as unified peoples, the tribes became vehicles Africans could use to see and defend their common interests. Of course, they would later serve as the support base for the ethnicity-based parties that helped undermine civilian rule in independent Nigeria.

Organized opposition to colonial rule first appeared in the 1920s, most notably with the creation of the Nigerian National Democratic Party (NNDP) by Herbert Macaulay (1864–1946) in 1923. The NNDP and similar organizations drew most of their support from the still small group of Western-educated lawyers, teachers, and merchants in Lagos. Only a few members of the old elite like Sir **Ahmadu Bello (1909–66)**, the Sardauna (ruler) of Sokoto, supported these movements that were created by men who were not part of the British-inspired indigenous leadership.

The costs of Nigerian dependence on international markets became clear after the October 1929 stock market crash in New York. Demand for colonial goods evaporated. That left not just the Nigerian elite but also workers painfully aware of what colonial rule was doing to them.

Although Macaulay was more radical than earlier opponents of colonial rule, his movement stopped short of demanding outright independence. During the 1930s, that changed with the formation of the Nigerian Youth Movement (NYM). In 1938, it issued the Nigerian Youth Charter, which was the first call for self-government. The British ignored the charter, which heartened and radicalized the educated elite, which now included a growing number of young people living outside of Lagos. Perceptive British observers also realized that irreversible changes were occurring that, sooner or later, would lead to the end of colonial rule in Nigeria and beyond.

World War II made independence inevitable. This time, around one hundred thousand Nigerians served in the British army. Many saw combat. Unlike their parents in 1914, these soldiers returned with a heightened desire for independence, democracy, and equality—all those things they supposedly had been fighting for. In other words, the war that had begun as an antifascist struggle became an anticolonial and antiracist one as well. In 1944, Macaulay and **Nnamdi Azikiwe (1904–96)** formed the National Council of Nigeria and the Cameroons (NCNC), which went beyond the small steps advocated by earlier nationalists and demanded independence.

Social change continued at an ever more rapid pace. The closure of many European and American markets deepened

poverty in the countryside. The cities filled with un- and underemployed young men. Hundreds of new schools and universities were opened. Trade unions were formed.

Events outside Nigeria also hastened independence. In 1941, American President Franklin Delano Roosevelt and British Prime Minister Winston Churchill issued the Atlantic Charter, which declared that the Allies would "respect the right of all peoples to choose the form of government under which they will live" after the war. Shortly after it ended, Britain granted India, Pakistan, Burma, and Ceylon (now Sri Lanka) independence, giving Nigerians new hope for their own future. The war had weakened the British, leading many politicians to conclude that they could no longer afford the empire. In 1946, the new Labour government committed itself to reforms that would give colonies like Nigeria responsible government without either defining what that meant or establishing a timetable for the transition to self-government.

Everywhere on the continent, support for nationalist movements mushroomed. Nigerian leaders raised the stakes by demanding meaningful political power immediately and independence in the not very distant future. They recognized that a mass movement in support of independence had to extend beyond the urban intellectuals. The easiest way to do that was to organize regionally, which led to the formation of parties that recruited support largely along ethnic lines. Nationalist leaders built much of their support among the "old boy" networks of high school and university graduates and the ethnic associations that emerged among the new urban migrants. They also used a relatively free press to publicize their attacks on British policy and to claim that they would do a better job if they were in charge of an independent Nigeria.

The British did not reject their demands out of hand. In 1946, they promulgated a constitution that established elected regional assemblies, solidifying the borders that would later create problems for the independent Nigeria. In 1948, the British started the "Nigerianization" of the civil service. During the 1950s, they helped the Nigerians write two more constitutions, which established a federal structure in which the national government shared power with the three regions.

By that time, electoral politics had already taken on a decidedly regional and ethnic tone. The NCNC organized the Igbo, including some in the neighboring French colony of the Cameroons. The relatively conservative Northern People's Congress (NPC) and more radical Northern Elements Progressive Union (NEPU) did well among the Hausa-Fulani. The Action Group (AG) dominated among the Yoruba, while the United Middle Belt Congress (UMBC) organized the various groups in the center of the country. A federal election under universal suffrage (except for women in the north) was held in 1959.

Nigeria finally became an independent country within the British Commonwealth of Nations on October 1, 1960, with Tafawa Balewa (1912–66) as prime minister and Azikiwe as governor-general. Azikiwe would later become the symbolic president when Nigeria declared itself a republic three years later.

But as independence neared, two of the problems associated with high-stakes politics emerged as well. In their desire to spur development and to gain the support of voters, politicians began dispensing "favors," the first step toward the corruption that no Nigerian regime has been able to overcome. Similarly, sharing power within a largely regional framework intensified the already serious ethnic differences. Until it became clear that Nigeria was going to become independent, its people had a common enemy: the British. But once independence was assured, their internal differences began taking center stage. Nigeria was united in name only.

The First Republic

Like most former British colonies, Nigeria inherited a traditional parliamentary system based on the Westminster model. It had a bicameral parliament, but only the directly elected House of Representatives had any real power. Executive authority was vested in a cabinet and prime minister, all of whom were members of the parliamentary majority. The government could remain in office until its five-year term ended as long as it maintained the support or confidence of that majority (see Table 14.2).

The new Nigerian regime differed from classical parliamentary arrangements in only one significant way. It was a federal system in which the national government shared power with three (later four) regional governments whose boundaries roughly followed ethnic lines. The creation of a federal system marked the early recognition that high-stakes politics in this highly diverse country would make governing from the center impossible without fanning ethnic tensions that long antedated the arrival of the British but that they had magnified.

In retrospect, it is easy to see why adopting a parliamentary system was a mistake. In such regimes, politics tends to be adversarial and pits a unified majority against an equally united opposition. It "works" in a country like Great Britain because everyone accepts the rules of the game. The opposition accepts the fact that it is not going to have much of a say in determining the content of legislation and that its main role is to criticize the government to try to turn the tables at the next election.

TABLE 14.2 Nigerian Regimes and Leaders since Independence

YEAR	HEAD OF STATE	TYPE OF REGIME
1960–66	Tafawa Balewa	First republic
1966	J. T. U. Aguiyi Ironsi	Military
1966–75	Yakubu Gowon	Military
1975–76	Murtala Muhammed	Military
1976–79	Olusegun Obasanjo	Military
1979–83	Shehu Shagari	Second republic
1984–85	Muhammadu Buhari	Military
1985–93	Ibrahim Babangida	Military
1993	Ernest Shonekan	Third republic and military
1993–98	Sani Abacha	Military
1998–99	Abdulsalami Abubakar	Military
1999–2007	Olusegun Obasanjo	Fourth republic
2007–2010	Umaru Yar'Adua	Fourth republic
2010–	Goodluck Jonathan	Fourth republic

That is not how things turned out in Nigeria. The regional and ethnic basis of political life was reinforced. The main leaders of those years—Azikiwe (NCNC), Obafemi Awolowo (AG), and Sir Ahmadu Bello (NPC)—tried to gain support throughout the country, but they enjoyed next to no success outside their own ethnic community (see Table 14.3). Each party won overwhelming victories in its "home" region. The Muslim-based NPC came in way ahead of the other parties but fell nineteen seats short of an absolute majority and therefore had to form a coalition with the Igbo-based NCNC, with which it had formed a loose alliance.

Political life turned into a vicious cycle in which politicians convinced themselves that every contest was a zero-sum game. The Yoruba-Hausa coalition feared that losing would entail far more than simply spending a few years out of office. The Igbo-led opposition, in turn, resented its powerlessness and grew more convinced that the incumbents would do everything possible to stay in power. At the regional level, Nigeria was a collection of one-party fiefdoms where leaders bullied their opponents, which only served to heighten ethnic conflict and raise the stakes of national politics.

Only one thing united these politicians: the pursuit of power. The new state had a lot of resources at its disposal, including the aid money that poured in after independence. Leading politicians became enthralled with the wealth, status, and privileges that came from holding office. Members of each faction sought to control the government so that they could distribute the lion's share of

TABLE 14.3 Political Parties and Leaders in the First and Second Republics

REGION	FIRST REPUBLIC PARTY	SECOND REPUBLIC PARTY	ORIGINAL LEADER
North	Northern People's Congress (NPC)	National Party of Nigeria	Ahmadu Bello
West	Action Group (AG)	United Party of Nigeria (UPN)	Tafawa Balewa
East	National Council of Nigeria and the Cameroons (NCNC)	Nigerian People's Party (NPP)	Nnamdi Azikiwe

© Cengage Learning

the money to their clients—above and beyond what they kept for themselves.

To make matters more complicated, the north, although it was dominant politically, lagged economically. Traditional Islamic rulers and values remained important, which led to limited educational development (only 2.5 percent of northern children were attending school), the exclusion of women from civil and economic life, and something approaching the rejection of "modern" society.

The crisis that ultimately destroyed the republic started in the west. Awolowo had gradually moved to the Left and began criticizing the fancy lifestyles politicians were beginning to lead. In the process, he alienated both the national and the regional governments headed by his erstwhile colleague-turned-rival Akintola. Their Action Group split in two.

Problems also mounted at the national level in 1963 when the government tried to conduct a census. In most countries, administering a census does not provoke deep divisions. In Nigeria, it was controversial because the results would determine how parliamentary seats would be allocated to each region and how government revenues and outside development aid would be distributed.

Consequently, the three sets of regional leaders doctored the results. Preliminary counts showed that the populations of the east and west had grown by 72.2 percent and 69.5 percent, respectively, in the ten years since the last census. Demographers easily showed that women cannot physically bear children fast enough to reach that level of growth. Meanwhile, the north reported a more or less accurate increase of 33.6 percent, which meant it would see some of its political power eroded. Therefore, northern officials mysteriously "found" 8.5 million people who had been left out of the initial count, which restored them to the same share of the population they had before the census began. The census sparked so much distrust that no government has been able to conduct a credible one to this day.

The census debacle fed the next crisis over the parliamentary and regional elections held in 1964 and 1965. On the surface, the party system seemed to be realigning into two broad coalitions, around the outgoing government and most of the opposition, respectively. The politicians expressed lofty goals. In reality, the campaign was marked by fraud, intimidation, and violence that made a mockery of the democratic process.

Even though a candidate needed the support of only two fellow citizens to get on the ballot, sixty-one seats in the north went uncontested because NPC operatives "convinced" their opponents to withdraw. Violence during the campaign was so widespread that the vote had to be delayed in fifty-nine constituencies. Contests in many others were rigged to such a degree that district-by-district results were never published and would not have been believed had they been made public. In the end, the NPC-led coalition swept to victory, confirming the regionalization of Nigerian politics. The NPC won 162 of 167 seats in the north and none anywhere else. All the NNDP victories were in the west, where it won 36 of 57 seats. The opposition carried every seat in the east, in the new midwestern state, and in Lagos.

Regional elections in the west proved to be the last straw. The campaign was so violent that the federal government banned all public gatherings and sent half the federal police force into the region to maintain order. When results came in, they showed an overwhelming NNDP (Akintola) victory, even though most experts thought the UPGA (Awolowo) had actually won. The UPGA decided that it could not find a legal way to redress its grievances, so it, too, turned to violence. On the night of January 14, 1966, Akintola met with Bello and Balewa in a desperate attempt to try to restore order. By morning, the military had intervened, overthrown the republic, and killed all three of them.

Military Rule I

That night's events, unfortunately, are hardly unusual in the Global South. At one point or another, well over half of the sub-Saharan African countries have had military rulers, and almost all of the rest have had some other type of authoritarian regime.

Nigeria's case was typical, too, in that the military had two reasons for intervening. They spoke about the obvious one: the need to restore order. But there were ethnic reasons as well, because the Nigerian military was by no means neutral in the ethno-partisan battle that was the downfall of the republic.

Like everything else in Nigeria, the army changed rapidly after independence. In 1960, 90 percent of its officers were British expatriates. By 1966, 90 percent were Africans. Most of the officers, in other words, were young and had risen through the ranks very quickly. A disproportionate number of them, too, were Igbo and resented the way easterners were being treated.

After some initial confusion, Major General J. T. U. Aguiyi Ironsi, an Igbo, took control of the new military regime. He moved quickly against corrupt officials and promised a rapid return to civilian rule. At the same time, Ironsi also suspended most civil liberties and established the **Supreme Military Council (SMC)** and the **Federal Executive Council (FEC)** and handed them the power to govern the country for the next thirteen years.

Ironsi, however, made a terrible mistake. That June, he announced plans for a new constitution that would have centralized power, which confirmed northern fears that the coup leaders' real goal was to secure Igbo control over the entire country. Hundreds of educated Igbos, who had been recruited to take jobs in northern cities, were killed. In July, another set of officers staged a second coup that brought Lieutenant Colonel Yakubu Gowon (1934–) to power.

The new military leaders faced a new challenge—keeping the country intact. The eastern region's governor and military commander, Colonel Chukwuemeka Ojukwu, refused to recognize Gowon's government. Riots broke out. A million Igbo refugees hastily returned to their region. Ojukwu and his supporters then created the independent Republic of Biafra, plunging Nigeria into a bloody civil war. Over the next thirty months, hundreds of thousands of people were killed before federal troops finally put down the revolt.

In sharp contrast with the events of the preceding decade, Gowon was generous in victory. He announced that the military would remain in power another six years and then hand the government back to civilians. It used money it made selling oil at inflated prices following the 1973–74 Organization of Petroleum Exporting Countries (OPEC) embargo to ease the east's reintegration.

Nonetheless, things were not going well. Many officers proved to be as corrupt and arrogant as their civilian predecessors. In October, Gowon announced that the return to civilian rule would be postponed indefinitely. Finally, nine years to the day after he seized power, Gowon was overthrown in a bloodless coup and was replaced by General Murtala Muhammed and a group of fellow officers who claimed to be committed to reform. The governors of the now twelve states, one hundred fifty military officers, and ten thousand civil servants were summarily fired. A year after taking power, he outlined a four-year plan for the restoration of democracy. Unfortunately, Murtala also incurred the wrath of many of his fellow officers, who assassinated him in early 1976.

He was replaced by Lieutenant General Obasanjo, who continued the preparations for a return to civilian rule. Over the next three years, Obasanjo was a model of integrity and made certain that progress toward the new regime went smoothly. Freedom of the press and other liberties were extended, a new constitution was drafted, and seven more states were created in the vain hope of easing ethnic tensions. A Federal Electoral Commission (FEDECO)

Four starving Biafran children sit and lie around a bowl of food in the dirt during the Nigerian-Biafran civil war.

Hulton Archive/Getty Images

was established to end partisan manipulation of the way elections were conducted. In July 1978, civilians replaced military officers as governors of the now nineteen states. In 1979, Obasanjo gracefully gave up power.

The Second Republic

Obasanjo and his colleagues tried to draft a constitution that they felt would give the country the best chance of avoiding a repeat of 1966. The parliamentary model was rejected in favor of a presidential system based on the one in the United States. They hoped that a directly elected president would be a source of national unity. To give the president an opportunity to break down the ethnic stranglehold on the first republic's party system, they decided that a winning candidate had to win a majority of the vote and at least a quarter of the ballots cast in at least two-thirds of the states.

The president nominated a cabinet that was neither drawn from nor responsible to the Parliament, whose two houses had equal powers. The House of Representatives was elected from single-member districts drawn up on a one-person-one-vote basis, although, of course, no census had been conducted to provide accurate population figures. There would also be a senate with five members chosen in each state. All first republic parties were banned. To be licensed, a new party had to demonstrate that it had a national, not just a regional, organization.

Problems began before the new republic came into existence. The military government waited until September 1979 to lift its ban on partisan politics, which meant that the new organizations would only have three months to organize, establish national offices, and file the required papers with FEDECO.

Not surprisingly, four of them were direct descendants of first republic parties in large part because only the surviving politicians had well-established networks that would allow them to put together even the semblance of a national organization in so short a period. Each party tried to broaden its base of support, and each had some success in doing so. Nonetheless, because they had so little time to prepare for the first elections, all the politicians found it easy to return to the rhetoric of first republic days.

Five separate elections for state and federal offices were held in July and August 1979. Although there were quite a few charges of fraud and unfair campaign practices, the first elections were conducted relatively freely and honestly. The mostly northern and Muslim National Party of Nigeria (NPN) won 37.8 percent of the house and 37.4 percent of the senate vote, respectively. Its candidate, Shehu Shagari, won 33.8 percent of the presidential vote, 4.6 percentage points more than his chief rival, Awolowo, who once again represented a mostly Yoruba party.

Awolowo challenged the results, claiming that Shagari had not met the constitutional requirements for victory because he had won only 25 percent of the vote in twelve of the nineteen states. FEDECO ruled that Shagari had won the 25 percent in twelve and two-thirds states, thereby giving him the minimum required.

Dissatisfaction with the new regime spread quickly once it became clear that politicians were not going to be any more honest this time. Ministers were accused of accepting bribes. A governor was arrested for allegedly trying to smuggle millions of naira to his private British bank account. The national telecommunications center was burned down to keep evidence about fraud and mismanagement from being made public.

Meanwhile, world oil prices collapsed. Well over 90 percent of Nigeria's foreign earnings already came from oil sales, so when its income dropped by nearly 60 percent from 1980 to 1983, the government found itself in desperate straits. The federal and state governments lost the money they needed to pay civil service salaries or complete development projects. That did not stop them from continuing to take kickbacks from development grants, foreign investment, and what oil revenues remained.

The second round of elections was held in 1983. All observers assumed that it would be a make-it-or-break-it event for the republic. Both Awolowo and Azikiwe insisted on running for president. Unfortunately, the campaign proved even more violent and fraudulent than the one four years earlier.

Most observers expected that the divided opposition would guarantee Shagari's reelection. But, fearing the worst, the NPN passed out thousands of already completed ballots, bribed election officials, and refused to allow opposition poll watchers to do their jobs. When the votes were counted, Shagari and the NPN had won a landslide victory. The official—and unbelievable—figures gave him nearly 48 percent of the presidential vote, an almost 50 percent improvement over his 1979 tally. The party also took advantage of the electoral system based on single-member districts to turn its slim plurality into a two-thirds majority in the House of Representatives.

To no one's surprise, the military stepped in again on New Year's Eve 1983. Like its predecessor, the second republic was not to survive its second election.

Military Rule II

At first, the military coup was widely accepted as inevitable given the level of corruption. The new military government, led by Muhammadu Buhari, was a lot like the old one. The SMC was reconstituted. The military rulers cracked down, arresting hundreds of politicians, including the president, vice president, and numerous ministers and governors. Soldiers found vast quantities of cash in the homes and offices of those arrested, lending even more credibility to the rumors of corruption in high places.

Decree Number 2 gave the government broad powers to arrest anyone thought to be a security risk, which it interpreted to mean anyone who criticized the military. Decree Number 3 created military tribunals to try former politicians and government officials. Decree Number 4 banned any publication or broadcast that inaccurately criticized any government official or policy.

Support for the regime was not to last. The officers were far less vigilant in prosecuting former NPN leaders than other politicians. The economy continued to flounder as the oil-induced crisis sent unemployment, inflation, and the foreign debt skyrocketing. There were few signs that the government was preparing a transition back to democracy.

Few were surprised when Buhari was overthrown in 1985 in yet another coup led by General **Ibrahim Babangida** (1941–), who is now known mostly by his initials, IBB. Babangida sent mixed signals. On the one hand, he immediately repealed Decree Number 4 and declared that his government "does not intend to lead a country where individuals are under the fear of expressing themselves." Journalists were released from jail. On the other hand, Babangida banned serving politicians from public life for a decade. Babangida renamed the SMC the **Armed Forces Ruling Council (AFRC)**, but in practice there was little difference between the two.

Then, in 1986, the regime seemed to tilt the balance toward reform. First, the AFRC accepted **structural adjustment**, including fiscal austerity and a shift toward the use of markets and other capitalist practices. Second, it announced a phased plan for democratization to be completed by 1990. Both will be discussed in more detail in the section on public policy.

Critics had come to doubt any general's commitment to civilian rule and greeted the political reforms skeptically. Their suspicions grew as the government announced a series of delays.

Nevertheless, the military plugged ahead. A constituent assembly drafted the constitution for a third republic. The next year, it began rebuilding the political parties. All politicians who held office in the first and second republics were banned from at least the first group of elections. Thirteen groups asked to be certified as political parties, but all were rejected. Instead, the government created two new ones, the National Republican Convention (NRC) and the Social Democratic Party (SDP), which were, in Babangida's own terms, "one a little to the left, and the other a little to the right of center."

Presidential elections were finally scheduled for 1993. Both parties nominated rich business leaders with close ties to the military regime to be their candidates. And despite the regime's attempt to cast politics in national and economic terms, ethnicity remained on center stage. The NRC's candidate, Bashir Tofa, a Hausa-Fulani banker, chose an Igbo Christian as his running mate. The SDP, in turn, nominated Yoruba **Moshood Abiola** (1937–96), a well-known shipping magnate, publisher, and owner of soccer teams. Because he was a Muslim, the SDP thought Abiola might have an appeal in the north as well.

Neither candidate would have made an American campaign manager happy. Tofa was so unknown he did not even appear in Nigeria's *Who's Who*. His commitment to democracy was suspect because he had publicly urged Babangida to stay in power until the turn of the century. Abiola was better known than Tofa, in part because of Afro-Beat star Fela Kuti's song about him and the publicity he received in 1992 for demanding that Britain and the other colonial powers pay reparations for the damage they did to Africa.

The election campaign had little of the violence that marred previous contests. But that is about the only positive thing that one can say about it. Only about 30 percent of the population cast a ballot. Voting patterns once again broke along ethnic lines, as Abiola ran far better in the south and Tofa in the north.

Unofficial results showed that Abiola won 55 percent of the vote. But even before the election took place, a shadowy group close to Babangida called on the general to stay in power. On June 23, the military nullified the election. Babangida insisted the military still intended to return the country to democratic and civilian rule in August, but it was hard to see how that could happen.

Abiola and his supporters publicly defended their all but universally acknowledged victory, sued the government, and announced their boycott of any subsequent election. On August 26, Babangida decided to forgo another election and turned power over to a handpicked civilian government headed by Ernest Shonekan, who was little more than the outgoing president's puppet.

Civilian rule was to last eighty-three days, which makes it hard to even talk about a third republic. In November, the military ousted Shonekan and replaced him with yet another military leader, **Sani Abacha** (1943–1998), who had been a coconspirator with Babangida in 1983 but had since become one of his fiercest critics.

Military Rule III

Abacha's rule turned out to be the most repressive and the most corrupt in Nigerian history. The government arrested Abiola and dozens of others. All civilian political organizations were disbanded by the Provisional Ruling Council, which was made up exclusively of officers.

P R O F I L E S   **Sani Abacha**

Sani Abacha was the military ruler of Nigeria from 1993 until his death in 1998. He was born in the northern city of Kano in 1943. After graduating from high school, he joined the army and received further training at some of the most prestigious military academies in Great Britain. He then rose through the ranks very quickly and was promoted to general in 1980, at which point he received further training in Monterey, California.

There is some debate about his role in General Ibrahim Babangida's coup in 1983 or in his subsequent government. By the early 1990s, Abacha had become one of the regime's most vocal internal critics. When the 1993 election led to another coup, he was the obvious person to lead the next military government.

His was probably the most ruthless and certainly the most corrupt of Nigeria's military governments. It is estimated that Abacha's family alone spirited $5 billion out of the country, a sum probably equaled by what his colleagues stole. Abacha died at his villa in June 1998.

His legacy endures. One of the most popular Nigerian Internet scams comes from someone claiming to be his widow who seeks help in obtaining their funds, which are supposedly frozen in foreign bank accounts. ∎

Nigerian President General Sani Abacha at the airport of Abuja shortly before he died of cardiac arrest.

The opposition did not capitulate. It launched a wave of strikes in the petroleum industry. The regime continued to crack down on dissidents—real and imagined—culminating in the execution of the writer and environmental activist **Ken Saro-Wiwa** (1941–1995).

Then the government cracked down harder than ever to keep its real, potential opposition cowed. Abacha purged the cabinet, fired trade union leaders and the military, and shut down all government institutions other than the elementary school system. More worrisome for most was the repression of dissidents, including the Nobel Prize–winning author Wole Soyinka, radical lawyer Gani Fawehinmi, and former President Obasanjo, who was sentenced to death shortly before the military government fell.

Strange things happened toward the end of Abacha's rule. First, Abiola died in prison under mysterious circumstance. Then, Abacha died in even more mysterious circumstances. Among the *least* scandalous versions have him dying with three Indian prostitutes after taking a potentially fatal overdose of Viagra.

We could consider here why military rule unraveled under Abacha and how that helped pave the way for the creation of the fourth republic. But it makes more sense to see those details in the context of the broader prospects for democratization included in the section on public policy.

The Fourth Republic

After Abacha died, another general assumed the presidency, **Abdulsalami Abubakar**. In the face of considerable pressure at home and from abroad, he announced plans for a speedy return to democratic rule. The transition occurred so quickly that there was not enough time to write a new constitution. Therefore, the fourth republic has the same basic institutional arrangements as the one overthrown in 1983.

Most uncertainty about the future ended with the election of Obasanjo as president. He took office with more popular support and enthusiasm than the country had seen since the first heady days right after independence.

Though once a military dictator, Obasanjo had become one of the continent's leading advocates for reform and democracy in the twenty years after he had turned over power to the civilian leaders of the second republic. Critics argue that he was just about as corrupt as the civilian and military leaders he replaced, a point we will come back to at length in the rest of this chapter.

Obasanjo and his successors have provided plenty of evidence for optimists and pessimists alike. The state has tried to crack down against dissidents both in the north and in the oil-producing states. Obasanjo's administration was based on people who were politically beholden to him, a tradition Yar'Adua and Jonathan have continued. Corruption

PROFILES Olusegun Obasanjo

Olusegun Obasanjo was born in 1937 in the largely Yoruba southwest. Like many soldiers of his generation, he won swift promotion in part because Nigeria had to replace the British expatriate officers who had run the military during the colonial era.

At age thirty-three, he was already a general and accepted the surrender of Biafran forces that ended the bloody civil war. Six years later, he was part of the group that staged a military coup that made him the country's de facto ruler for the next three years.

Unlike most other military rulers around the world, Obasanjo relatively willingly and relatively graciously presided over the return to civilian rule with the creation of the second republic in 1979, at which point he retired from active political life and returned to his home region to set up a poultry and pig farm.

He never fully withdrew from politics, serving on a number of ad hoc groups dealing with broader African issues, including apartheid in South Africa. He also was the founding president of Transparency International.

In 1995, he and forty-three other former soldiers were arrested by the Abacha government. Obasanjo was sentenced to death and expected to be executed before Abacha suddenly died in 1998 and all political prisoners were released. He instantly became the favorite to win the presidency of the new republic, an election he won in a landslide the next year.

Nigerian President Olusegun Obasanjo, *left*, shakes hands with outgoing military ruler Gen. Abdulsalami Abubakar after a ceremony to hand over power to civilian rule in Abuja, Nigeria, on Saturday, May 29, 1999. Promising that "we shall not fail," Obasanjo became Nigeria's first civilian president in fifteen years, ending a string of military regimes that crippled this west African nation.

Most observers think that Obasanjo was one of the most honest and effective elected leaders in recent African history. His critics, on the other hand, point to the fact that at least ten thousand Nigerians died because of their politic views in the first term of his presidency and also because of accusations of corruption among the people surrounding the president. ■

remains so widespread that civil servants are often referred to as lootocrats. International observers found enough irregularities in the way the 2003, 2007, and 2011 elections were conducted to cast doubt on their outcomes.

Optimists point to equally incontrovertible facts. Whatever the problems with the last three presidential elections, Obasanjo was the first civilian leader to be replaced by another civilian. Now, a second civilian-to-civilian transition has occurred. Despite the violence that has continually afflicted the country (including on the day I wrote these words), there seems to be little chance of yet another military coup. Not even the most diehard optimist

would argue that democratic rule is secure in Nigeria. They can, however, accurately point out that the country has made a few key steps in that direction since 1999.

Political Culture

Of all the countries covered in this book, nowhere is the connection between political culture and everyday politics clearer than it is in Nigeria. That does not mean that we fully understand it. Public opinion polling is not very reliable. If nothing else, analysts doubt how honest survey respondents are when asked about the kind of values we will focus on in this section. As a result, we have to depend on the studies by anthropologists and the stories filed by journalists, neither of which can be readily extrapolated to any attitudes or behaviors at the national level.

However, the core beliefs one sees at the grass roots and among members of the elite have clear historical ties in the litany of events and trends covered so far. And, even more important, cultural norms and the social structures they are based on go a long way toward explaining why Nigeria has not broken out of the downward spirals that have characterized its political and economic life since independence, if not before.

In some chapters, we have seen how cultural values can be at the heart of a virtuous circle that worsens over time. Thus, in France, Germany, and India, prolonged periods of effective government led to tangible benefits that average citizens could actually see and led them to support parties and politicians at that particular moment. Furthermore, if those benefits continued for a longer period of time, that support translated into acceptance of a new regime (Fifth Republic France, the Federal Republic in Germany, and post-independence India).

By contrast, we have seen signs of an opposite trend. Other things being equal (which, of course they never are), if a state performs poorly over time, the ties that bind a people to their leaders *can* begin to fray. If that continues for a long enough period of time, support for the regime and the system as a whole *can* be put in jeopardy as well.

Note that the word "can" was italicized in the previous two sentences. In other words, poor performance does not always erode supportive values in a culture, but, as we are about to see, they have done so for the most part in contemporary Nigeria.

The Ties That Don't Bind

It cannot be stressed strongly enough that Nigeria suffers from a syndrome that is all too common in the Global South. Rather than helping tie a population together, cultural norms in Nigeria tend to stress differences and divisions even when they do not seem to be on the verge of tearing the country apart.

The available impressionist evidence suggests there is little that Nigerians like about their political system. In the 2008 Afrobarometer survey, 55 percent of those sampled felt either that Nigeria was not a democracy yet or that its democracy had major problems, while almost two-thirds expressed dissatisfaction with the way democracy operates in practice.

Things did not start that way. Polls conducted in the early 1960s suggested that Nigerians had a greater sense of national identity and pride than did most people in what we then called the Third World. One 1962 survey, for example,

found that only 16 percent of those sampled had trouble thinking of Nigeria in national terms. Similarly, three-quarters of that same sample felt that Nigeria had "made progress" over the previous five years, and two-thirds thought it would continue to do so in the five years to come.

Within a matter of months, people began to worry about whether Nigeria itself would survive. Thirty years later, any reasonable observer had to harbor doubts about whether the fourth republic would be any more successful than its ill-fated predecessors. Today the existence of Nigeria is not in question. And there are no credible alternatives to the fourth republic, however imperfect its performance has been.

There is some evidence that the situation may not be as bleak as it seems at first glance. Thus, in the months before and after the 2011 elections, poll after poll showed that a huge majority of Nigerians professed support for democracy and the progress their country had made in reaching it. Most, too, agreed that the **Independent Nigerian Election Commission (INEC)** had done a good job of preparing for the national and state elections that year.

Nigeria is also not deeply divided along ideological lines in the ways that Western political scientists have focused on the most. In particular, despite the country's widespread poverty, class issues are not and have never been particularly important, despite efforts by Marxists, trade union organizers, and others to promote them.

Nonetheless, two major roadblocks stand in the way of anything approaching a widespread sense of legitimacy or national unity. The first of these has already appeared several times in this chapter; the second one, however, has only lurked below the analytical surface.

Identity Politics

Nigeria is still fragmented along various lines that all deal with identity issues in one form or another. Nigerians think of themselves at least as much as believers in a particular faith, residents of a particular region, or members of a particular ethnic group as Nigerians.

Identity issues are qualitatively different from most others precisely because people feel so strongly about them. They are almost always seen by participants in zero-sum terms because they involve such questions as "who am I?" A gain for one side means a loss for the other. It is much easier to "split the difference" on issues involving money than on issues involving race, language, or ethnicity, which raise powerful emotional divisions and do not lend themselves to finding common ground.

Naive observers once assumed that what they referred to as "parochial" identities would give way to a national one soon after independence in all of the newly independent states in the Global South. That has not been the case. If anything, subnational identities have become more, not less, important both as a source of pride (e.g., we Igbo) and, even more important, as a source of dislike and division (e.g., you Yoruba).

The three largest ethnic groups have virtually nothing in common politically, socially, or historically other than the fact that the British forced them to be part of a single colony—and now nation-state. The overwhelming majority of Nigerians only speak their "home" language. If they learn another one, it is English and not one of the other African tongues. The different groups live separately, either in their traditional regions or in ethnic enclaves in other parts of the country which are referred to as *sabon gari*, literally "strangers' quarters."

Closely paralleling ethnicity is religion. Religion is nowhere near as important as ethnicity in most of the south, where, for instance, Yoruba Muslims tend to act politically as Yorubas more often than as Muslims. In the north, however, it is hard to disentangle the impact of religion and ethnicity because so much of Hausa-Fulani culture is defined in terms of Islam.

Finally, there is the region itself, which transcends both religion and ethnicity in the even broader fears the north has about the south and vice versa. As we saw earlier, many northerners are afraid that southern (or modern) cultural values and economic practices will undermine their way of life. Southerners, by contrast, fear that a northern majority could seize power and leave them a permanent and aggrieved minority.

In short, region, religion, language, and ethnicity overlap so much that social scientists have not learned how to disentangle them analytically. In her book on the often violent interaction between Islam and Christianity, Eliza Griswold argued:

> Being a citizen in Nigeria means next to nothing: in many regions, the state offers no electricity, water, or education. Instead, for access to everything from schooling to power lines, many Nigerians turn to religion. Being a Christian or a Muslim, belonging to the local church or mosque, and voting along religious lines have become the way to safeguard seemingly secular rights.[1]

Other observers put the emphasis on ethnicity rather than religion. However, the overlap between religion and ethnic identification is so close that it is impossible to tell where one ends and the other begins.

The Politics of Patronage and Identity

There is one cultural norm that is common to each identity group—the seeming contradiction between the all but universal complaints about corruption and the all but universal acceptance of it. To see that, we have to take an analytical step back from the issues political scientists traditionally have worried the most about and explore **patron-client relationships**, which anthropologists understand far better than we do because their research focuses on the often contradictory realities of daily life. In this case, on the one hand, the country has all the trappings of a modern state. On the other hand, the lives of most of its citizens, especially the poor and rural residents, are embedded in these other relationships that operate in ways that tend to undermine the legitimacy and effectiveness of the state.

The key here is the fact that most aspects of life revolve around hierarchical, reciprocal relationships. They are hierarchical in that patrons almost always have more wealth and power than their clients. They are reciprocal because patrons and clients both exchange goods and services with each other from which grow duties and responsibilities toward each other.

Comparative Emphasis: Social Structure, Identity, and Culture

One reason students have trouble mastering the material in *Comparative Politics* is that the links between the parts of the system as shown in Figure 1.3 are not always easy to follow. That is certainly the case of Nigeria.

To some degree the identity issues described in this section can be traced back long before the British arrived and set up the self-reinforcing dynamic discussed on the previous page.

Of the countries covered in this book, Nigeria is the most obvious one in which there is a long-term link between historical trends and current political dynamics that is translated through the intermediary of cultural values, but it is not the only one. In the chapter on Russia, for example, we saw evidence of how that country's long history of authoritarian and later totalitarian rule can be seen today in a society in which many—if not most—individuals are reluctant to take personal initiatives, especially ones that entail significant risk. ■

[1]Eliza Griswold, *The Tenth Parallel: Dispatches from the Fault Line between Christianity and Islam* (New York: Farrar, Straus and Giroux, 2010), 19.

In other words, "connections" are still important for getting everything from a job in a country with massive poverty and unemployment to admission to a university or to a party's nomination in an election campaign. Patrons cannot do without clients and vice versa. As Daniel Jordan Smith put it,

> to be without a patron is to be without resources, but to be a patron is to be under great pressure to accumulate and share wealth, including through corruption.[2]

He goes on to document how corruption is built into almost all aspects of Nigerian life because of the power embedded in these patron-client relationships which both antedate and were reinforced by colonialism.

We will discuss corruption itself in the section on the state. Here, it is enough to note that almost all Nigerians (including Smith's own Nigerian family) take part in a system in which bribes are the norm. Participation in patron-client relationships also leads to the deeply held cynicism and alienation that rarely shows up in public opinion polls.

Elite Culture

In every country, elites think and act differently from average citizens. In few places, however, are the differences as pronounced and as potentially politically explosive as they are in Nigeria.

The political and economic elite there has been what amounts to a bourgeois class, if not quite in the way Karl Marx had in mind. Its wealth stems from its control of the state and is reinforced through patron-client relations that operate from the top to the bottom of Nigerian society. This situation has given rise to a category of political and bureaucratic officials who have used their positions for personal gain and who have been able to protect their wealth and power under civilian and military rule alike.

With few exceptions, members of the Nigerian elite were willing to violate the rules of the democratic game under each of the republics and overstepped normal bounds of authority when the military was in power. Their greed and their willingness to subvert the democratic process were not the province of any particular ethnic, religious, or regional group, but seem to have been shared by leaders throughout Nigerian society.

These kingpins who sit atop patron-client relationships are known by the Yoruba word for master, *oya*, which is

Comparative Emphasis: Women

Women play a relatively minor role in Nigerian politics.

Women in the north only gained the right to vote in 1975, and it is still often the case that they have to cast their vote in voting booths that are separate from and perpendicular to those used by men.

In 2011, only 5.3 and 6.4 percent of the winning candidates for the House of Representatives and Senate, respectively, were women. The International Parliamentary Union ranks Nigeria 113th of the 129 countries for which it has adequate data.

There are a number of reasons why this is the case. In the Muslim-dominated north, there are still places where it is difficult for women to vote, let alone run for office. The patron-client networks at the heart of this chapter rarely include women in prominent positions. Similarly, elections are expensive affairs, and few women have access to the supply of money needed to win.

There is a women's movement. The most prominent of its organizations is Women's Rights Advancement and Protection Alternative (WRAPA—wrapanigeria.org). Formed in 1999, WRAPA casts its net widely to cover all areas of public and private life in which women are discriminated against. The other major women's group is Baobab for Women, which tries to promote women's rights under traditional as well as statutory law (www.baobabforwomen.org). ∎

now found in all major Nigerian languages, including English. The oyas manage access to the spoils of patronage mentioned above and use their control over scarce resources to buy the support of their clients. Many, too, have been willing to resort to force to rein reluctant clients in.

At the national level, most of the oyas are retired generals, including Obasanjo. At the state and local levels, they come from other walks of life. Many, in fact, are part of the traditional elite of emirs and chiefs who were at least partially created as part of colonial rule. Again as we will see later, it is relatively easy for men (there are very few women oyas) to amass huge fortunes as well as political power.

[2]Daniel Jordan Smith, *A Culture of Corruption: Everyday Deception and Popular Discontent in Nigeria* (Princeton: Princeton University Press, 2001), 13.

Political Participation

In Nigeria, ethnicity and the issues eddying around it trump almost everything else for many of the same reasons that they are central to its political culture. In short, it goes a long way toward determining what they do as well as what they think about political life.

Before examining the ways people do participate, it is important to stress one intellectual trap many analysts have fallen into. There is nothing inevitable about the role that either identity politics or patron-client relationships plays in Nigeria or anywhere else.

In fact, there is considerable evidence that political leaders have manipulated attitudes and social structures that both serve their own interests and heighten their impact. Most obviously, the British imperial authorities made identity an issue by the very way they drew the colony's boundaries, in particular by combining the north and the south in a single unit. More recently, civilian and military elites alike have reinforced the financial and other incentive structures that make it hard for Nigeria to build alternatives to patron-client relationships and the illicit centers of power they lend themselves to. And, as we will see in the discussion of MEND and Boko Haram at the end of this section, elites have fomented ethnic and religious antagonisms in ways that have made seeking, let alone finding, consensus-based solutions to national problems all but impossible.

Political Parties

Political parties and competitive elections are accorded a privileged place in theories of democracy. Their very existence is part of the definition of liberal democracy itself. How they operate in practice goes a long way toward determining whether or not democracy will endure.

There is no need to spend any more time on the bewildering array of parties that competed for power under the first and second republics. It is enough to note here that they did more to undermine than to sustain democracy precisely because they magnified ethnic tensions. Thus, after the ill-fated presidential election of 1993, the Abacha government outlawed all political parties, and it was only after his death that the caretaker military government authorized the creation of new ones.

The new parties that sprang to life in 1998 seemed to have little in common with the old ones. In all, nine political parties won legal recognition. Of the nine, only three did well enough in state and local elections to be eligible to nominate candidates for the 1999 legislative and presidential elections. Each at least voiced their intention to forge large, nation-wide coalitions, but in reality, each one tried to ensure victory in its "home" area and gather enough support elsewhere to piece together a majority.

One issue does seem to have been settled. As part of the negotiations that led to the latest transition to civilian rule, the civilian and military leaders agreed to the Nigerian Charter, which calls for **zoning**. The assumption since 1999 has been that the presidency would pass from south to north. A Christian incumbent (like Obasanjo) would be replaced by a Muslim and vice versa. That seems to have been the case in 2007 when the Muslim Yar'Adua replaced Obasanjo.

In keeping with the charter's provisions, he ran with a Christian, southern vice presidential candidate, Jonathan. As we saw earlier, Yar'Adua died in office, propelling his Christian vice president into office, and at least temporarily leaving zoning in tatters. Jonathan put at least some concerns to rest when he agreed not to seek a second full term in 2015 when, presumably, all the major parties will nominate a Muslim again.

That does not mean that they have escaped the problems of the past. Identity may be less divisive a force than it was before 1999. In its place, however, patronage politics has, if anything, become more important.

The two parties that have won the lion's share of the vote since 1999 both have close ties to the military. Obasanjo and his allies formed the PDP (People's Democratic Party). The smaller All Nigeria People's Party (ANPP) was initially led by politicians who were close to Abacha, including Muhammadu Buhari, who was its standard bearer in 2007 and 2011. Only the small Action Congress (AC) had anything approaching unambiguous democratic credentials because its founders had been close to Abiola.

The parties all have weaker but noticeable ties to the ethnically based parties that dated back to the first republic. Although he is a Yoruba and a Christian, the roots of Obasanjo's PDP can be traced back to the dominant Muslim-based parties of the north during the 1960s and 1970s. Similarly, the ANPP has an Igbo stronghold, whereas the AC draws its support primarily among the Yoruba.

They have had to expand their base beyond their core ethnic constituency. No presidential candidate can win unless he or she has captured at least one-fourth of the votes in two-thirds of the states. As we saw previously, officials in the second republic manipulated a similar requirement to ensure a victory in 1979. So far, that has not been a problem in the fourth republic.

Zoning has not eliminated identity issues from electoral politics. As we saw at the beginning of the chapter, Jonathan swept the south; his opponent did the same in the north. That election may prove to be the exception to the rule on the assumption that zoning is restored in 2015 and only Muslims are nominated by the major parties.

More worrisome is the fact that it is hard to tell where the parties stand on national issues. Their goals and ideologies are rarely mentioned in their own literature or in the press. The PDP claims to support a market-based economy but has also pioneered a national health service that would eventually cover all Nigerians. The ANPP is, in reality, a northern and thus Muslim-based party (all party websites can be accessed at the official Electoral Commission site www.inecnigeria.org/index.php?do=political&id=34). The AC defines itself as left of center. It, too, has ties to the military and has gained the most support because its 2007 candidate, Atiku Abubakar, had been Obsanjo's vice president but split with the PNP largely over the question of whether the constitution should be amended to allow a president (i.e., Obasanjo) to run for a third term.

Elections Under the Fourth Republic

If there is reason to worry about what the parties and politicians stand for, there is even more to do so about with the way elections are conducted, which is where patronage politics most comes into play, which is one of the reasons why democratization is one of the public policy issues I focus on later in the chapter. Tables 14.4 and 14.5 present the results for the four national elections held under the fourth republic. Those official statistics should be read with a hefty grain of salt, because they do not and cannot show how much fraud occurred. The winner undoubtedly got the most votes each time. However, they could not realistically have won as many votes as the official tallies suggest. If anything, international election observers and domestic critics alike suspect that the results have been distorted more and more each time.

The PDP handily won each of those contests. However, there is no need for a further table with a breakdown of the vote that suggests why people voted the way they did because identity, patron-client relations, and outright fraud would have made those figures meaningless.

Nigeria is not on the brink of becoming a single-party-dominant country like India was under Congress until the

TABLE 14.4 Presidential Elections in Nigeria: 1999–2011 (percent of vote)

PARTY	1999	2003	2007	2011
PDP	63	63	70	59
APP/ANPP	37	32	19	31
Action Congress	—	—	7	5
Others	—	—	4	5

APP/ANPP, All Nigeria Peoples Party; PDP, People's Democratic Party.

Note: The APP and ANPP ran a single candidate for president in 1999 and Action Congress did not run one in 2003.

© Cengage Learning 2015

TABLE 14.5 House of Representatives Elections in Nigeria: 1999–2011

	1999	2003	2007	2011
PDP	206	223	263	199
APP/ANPP	74	96	63	27
Action Congress	68	34	30	69
Others	12	7	4	65

© Cengage Learning 2015

1970s. Nonetheless, there is little reason to believe that the PNP will lose—or let itself lose—an election in the foreseeable future. It probably is the most popular party in the country because of its ties with Obasanjo and the transition from military rule. But, it also has the strongest network of patron-client relations *and* the closest ties to the military. In other words, it has done the best job of attracting important oyas from around the country.

Nonelectoral Participation

If we looked at culture alone, it would be tempting to conclude that Nigeria is a devastating civil war or revolution waiting to happen. Yet, ironically, neither seems imminent.

The most surprising trend is that relatively few people participate in political life other than by voting, despite the severity of the country's problems. To the degree that they do, we should highlight two trends, one of which is encouraging, the other of which definitely is not.

Interest Groups and Civil Society Organizations

Nigeria does have some interest groups that are similar to the trade unions, business associations, and grassroots movements discussed in other chapters. Their most striking feature is their weakness that grows out of the fact that most of them are organized along patron-client lines and only gain support from people from a single identity group.

That said, there is one exception to the rule: the growing number of groups that monitor elections and otherwise promote democracy. Some of them have roots going back to the struggle for independence. Others sprung up in response to the abuses of military rule, such as the Transition Monitoring Group, which brought to light a number of violations of the electoral law during the 1999 legislative and presidential campaigns.

Since then, most of them have had the support of foreign governments and international NGOs in drawing attention to solutions that could enhance democratization. After the 2011 election, Human Rights Monitor proposed creating a new authority that would have the staff and financial resources to prosecute voting fraud and other abuses that INEC cannot handle. Similarly, Youngstar produced and distributed a video on how young people can more effectively interact with elected officials that focused on techniques that would allow new activists to avoid taking part in patronage politics.

Identity-Based Conflict: MEND and Boko Haram

Despite these encouraging efforts, most Nigerians and international observers have focused on the upsurge in identity-based violence. Although only a small minority of the population is involved, there are widespread fears that the protests could grow and, if they do, disrupt what is still a fragile regime.

The first group of protesters is based in the Niger Delta where Jonathan grew up. The region has been a political hot spot ever since Ogoni activists, including Saro-Wiwa, were executed for their opposition to alleged environmental devastation and human rights abuses by the Abacha government in the 1990s.

More recently, opponents of the oil industry have come together as MEND (Movement for the Emancipation of the Niger Delta; www.mendnigerdelta.com). Officially, the organization's goal is to give local residents more local control over the oil industry, including protecting the environment and ensuring that a larger share of the profits stays in the region. MEND has also been accused of using violence, ranging from siphoning oil from the pipelines to destroying the infrastructure that allows multinational corporations to get the oil to market.

In 2010, MEND agreed to a cease fire, one provision of which called for its activists to take courses in conflict resolution, which have been anything but a success. The young men who enrolled in the program got stipends of about $400 a month, which is six times the average regional salary, which had the unintended consequence of heightening the antagonism of their nonviolent contemporaries. Furthermore, most of the former fighters were so poorly educated that they could not complete the exams they had to take to pass the course. As the 2011 elections neared, the local oyas used them as enforcers to control the vote, thus reinforcing the incentives for young men to turn to violence.

At about the same time, a hitherto unknown group, Boko Haram, staged its first attacks in the northern city of Maiduguri where it was founded in 2002 by Mohammed Yusuf. Its name is best (but loosely) translated as "Western education is forbidden." Boko Haram supporters have adopted traditional versions of Islam in part out of frustrations with both southern economic domination and what they feel as the failure of Muslim political leaders to put their faith into practice when they have been in government.

Before 2009, however, Boko Haram was best known for running a Muslim complex, which included a school that attracted students and families from around the country. Despite advocating an Islamic state and the use of Sharia law, Boko Haram was mostly apolitical.

However, in 2009, its activists carried out attacks on government offices that killed over a hundred people in Maiduguri, most of whom were shot by young men riding on motorbikes. The state responded with violence of its own and killed at least one thousand activists, including Yusuf.

Comparative Emphasis: Conflict

Almost every outburst of popular protest in Nigeria since independence has revolved around religion, language, or ethnicity. No single incident reflects that fact better than a bizarre series of protests that broke out in the northern city of Kaduna in 2002.

Although no one quite knows why they did it, the leaders of the Miss World pageant decided to hold the 2002 finals in a city where almost everyone is a devout Muslim, many of whom were deeply offended by the notion of scantily clad young women parading across the stage of their local civic center. Anger mounted when an English-language newspaper criticized the anti–Miss World activists and jokingly suggested that the Prophet Muhammad would have chosen someone like the contestants for his wife.

At first, the protests were not a cause for alarm. Crowds did chant *Allahu Akhbar* (God is great) and "Miss World is sin," but that was about it. Without much warning, however, things turned violent. People that members of the mob thought were Christians were pulled from cars and beaten. Dozens were killed. Churches were burned; Christians later retaliated and burned mosques. More than one hundred people were killed and five hundred more injured.

The organizers of the Miss World contest moved it to London. A Muslim Turk won.

One of the few recent incidents of conflict that did not involve ethnicity occurred in the summer of 2004 when urban residents, who are pretty much the only people who own cars, rioted after the government announced that gasoline prices would be set by the market and not fixed at an arbitrarily low level by the government. ∎

Boko Haram's influence spread and its violence intensified. Among other things, it blew up the UN's headquarters in Abuja in August 2011, killing at least twenty-one people, destroyed churches there that Christmas day, and has reportedly begun developing ties with Islamist insurgents in Mali, which was in the midst of a civil war as these lines were written.

Systems Theory, Inputs, and Vicious Cycles

Optimistic analysts who use systems theory view inputs as an important way to constructively link average citizens and decision makers. In everyday life, grassroots organizations, elections, and beyond giving support and making demands can create ties that cement bonds between people and the state.

That has rarely been the case in Nigeria. Instead, as we have seen in the last two sections, political participation has mostly had the opposite effect in two main ways. To the degree that it reflects patronage politics, it has served largely to reinforce the status quo, which, among other things, leaves the country stuck in the policy-making rut we are about to explore. To the degree that it revolves around identity, political participation has helped turn the country into what some analysts fear is a political time bomb waiting to explode.

The Nigerian State

Nigeria is the one country in *Comparative Politics* that comes close to being a failed state. That might seem surprising at first glance. After all, military rulers ran the country with an iron fist for many years.

To use Ian Morris's simple definition of social development, an effective state has the ability to "get things done." In those terms, the weakness of military as well as civilian rule in Nigeria is all but inescapable.

No government has been able to provide basic services that people living in more successful states take for granted. Foreign diplomats and business executives rarely leave their homes without armed escorts. It is not just the rich and powerful people who live in fear for their lives. The bodies of people killed in traffic accidents are frequently left by the side of the road because the officials who are supposed to collect them are afraid of being attacked by gang members or being held until they pay a bribe to the police.

To be fair, the Nigerian state is short on resources. More than 90 percent of its revenue comes from the sale of oil and taxes on the profits made by multinational petroleum companies. As we all know from our own countries, the price of oil is volatile, which does leave Nigerians at the mercy of fickle global markets. But the problems run deeper. Nigeria also has to import most of the oil it needs for domestic consumption, because it does not have enough refineries of its own. The ones it does have are frequently out of service because the government either cannot afford to buy replacement parts or lacks the trained personnel to fix the broken machinery. In other words, the inability to get things done has political roots.

Nigeria's problems cannot be attributed to a shortage of talented people or to constitutional flaws and poorly written laws. Rather, Nigeria's problems rest with the behavior of the people who fill key positions rather than with its constitutional framework. Whoever controls the state puts friends, relatives, and clients on government and corporate payrolls, and they then direct scarce resources to other favored clients. To complicate matters further, there have been so many regime changes that almost all state institutions other than the military and the civil service are no more than fifteen years old.

In creating the fourth republic, President Obasanjo and his colleagues hoped to end nearly half a century in which Nigeria had a weak, corrupt, and often repressive state and to replace it with one that is both more effective and more responsive to Nigeria's people. The initial signs were not all that encouraging. For example, the new constitution was not published until after the 1999 legislative elections took place, and many of its provisions were not known until after Obasanjo was inaugurated. In the years since then, however, the new institutions have demonstrated considerable staying power if not the capacity to create a state that can enact and implement public policy nationwide (www.nigeria.gov.ng).

The Station

Some people are trying to break down the barriers among Nigerians. One intriguing effort is *The Station*, which was finishing its first year on national television as these lines were written. Produced by Search for Common Ground, *The Station* revolves around the work of journalists at Nigeria's and Africa's first 24/7 news channel. In all, 1,800 Nigerians have been involved in producing the series.

Search for Common Ground is the world's largest producer of conflict-resolution soap operas. None beat the viewer or listener over the head with their political message. They simply show people solving their everyday problems. The episode on identity is particularly useful. It is also available on YouTube (www.sfcg.org/programmes/cgp/ cgp_station2.html).

The Branches of Government and the Personalization of Power

The centerpiece of the new state is its American-style presidency, which dates back to the second republic. The constitution gives the president wide-ranging powers, but, like his counterpart in Washington, his is largely the power to persuade in a system built on the separation and division of powers. However, given Obasanjo's popularity and the PDP's continued overwhelming majority, the first three presidents have been able to get what they want through the legislative process almost all of the time. Whether that can continue under Jonathan's successor obviously remains to be seen.

The president is responsible for managing the day-to-day operations of the state and is also commander-in-chief of the armed forces, an important power in a country with such a long history of coups and military rule. As is the case in most such systems, the president is not a member of the legislature, but he (or she, presumably, at some point in the future) can make statements to it at the request of either body.

The president can only serve two terms. As noted earlier, the Senate rejected a proposed constitutional amendment that would have allowed Obasanjo to run for a third term in 2007. It is not clear if Jonathan's first year on the job should have counted as a term, but he has already declared that he will not run for reelection in part to resume zoning between northern and southern leadership at least in the PDP.

The National Assembly has two houses, a 360-member House of Representatives elected from single-member districts and a 109-member Senate composed of three people elected from each state plus a single member from the capital region of Abuja.

As in the United States, the president is not responsible to the Assembly, which therefore cannot remove him from office through a vote of no confidence. Nonetheless, given the size of the PDP's majority and the nature of patronage politics, the two houses have gone along with the president's wishes, with the possible exception of Obasanjo's less than open campaign for the constitutional amendment on term limits.

On paper, the National Assembly's powers are similar to those of the American Congress (www.nassnig.org). Each house must agree on the same version of a bill before it is submitted to the president. The president has to give his assent before a bill becomes law, which is, for all intents and purposes, equivalent to the American president's veto power. If he refuses to assent or fails to act within thirty days, the bill is returned to the legislature. If each house passes it again with at least a two-thirds majority, it becomes law without any further action by the president.

The Assembly does occasionally try to flex its muscles. Thus, in 2012, a committee chaired by a northern legislator investigated alleged kickbacks of oil profits to southern leaders. Its report was sent to President Jonathan, after which it was never heard of again.

Nigeria also has a fairly standard judicial system for a country with strong Anglo-American legal roots. It retains the previous regimes' network of local and state courts and reinforces the power of a Supreme Court whose authority was often honored in the breach during Nigeria's first thirty years of independence (supremecourt.gov.ng). The court is not a doormat today. It has heard some key cases, including suits seeking to overturn the 2007 presidential election. However, the court has been better noted for its failures to act than for decisions that could have reshaped the country's history.

The one important new feature is an appellate court for Sharia law in Abuja and any individual state that chooses to create one. If a case involves issues that touch on Islam,

PROFILES
Goodluck Jonathan

Jonathan is an unusual politician by Nigerian standards.

He was born in 1957 and grew up in the Niger Delta in the southern part of the country, where his family made canoes. Unlike most members of his family, he went to school and ultimately earned a PhD in biology from the University of Port Harcourt, which is not far from his home village. Before entering politics in 1998, he was a college professor and an environmental safety inspector.

His political career started fairly late when he joined what became the PDP in 1998 when he was already 40 years old. The next year, he was elected lieutenant governor of Bayelsa state and assumed the governorship six years later. The then unknown regional politician was chosen as the also little known Dar'Adua's running mate in 2007. When he died, Jonathan became president.

Jonathan has an unusual political style. For example, he announced his 2011 reelection campaign on his Facebook page which then had more "friends" than British Prime Minister Cameron, German Chancellor Merkel, and South African President Zuma *combined*. He is also renowned for his hats, and he even broke social convention when he wore one the first time he met President Obama in the Oval Office. ■

either the plaintiff or the defendant can refer it to these religious courts rather than to a civil one.

As is true of much of the Global South, one should not read too much into the formal language of the constitution and other legal documents because individual leaders can bend them to their own "needs" far more often and far more easily than is the case in the countries covered in Part 2.

Federalism

Like most other large, ethnically diverse countries, Nigeria has always been a federation in which national, state, and local governments have somewhat independent responsibilities. At independence, the country was divided into three regions whose borders gave each of the main ethnic groups the opportunity to dominate one of them. Since then, the country has been subdivided in an attempt to blunt the impact of ethnic conflict. Today, there are 36 states and 774 local government authorities, which, as in India, means that every substantial ethnic group can control the government of its "home" territory.

On one level, the creation of so many local government bodies has been a success. Having so many smaller states has made local politics less a part of the all-or-nothing game played primarily at the national level. In other ways, however, federalism is at the heart of Nigeria's problems in two familiar ways.

First, 58 percent of state oil revenues are distributed on a per capita basis to the states. The oil-producing states receive a further 13 percent of the central government's income, although MEND and others do not think that figure is anywhere near high enough. In typical Nigerian fashion, there are few rules that require state authorities to account for how they spend that money, which helps produce the corruption and lack of transparency at all levels of government.

Second, state and local governments are part of the national system of patron-client relations. The patterns are complicated and have changed over time. Basically, state and local officeholders arrive in their jobs through networks that permeate the major parties and their oyas at the national level. State and local leaders are oyas in their own right in their own communities, which means that they take part in distributing the perks of office to the clients whose votes put them there in the first place.

Corruption

Patron-client relations and the personalization of power are key contributors to Nigeria's widespread corruption, which may be the most visible and intractable feature of its political life. Of course, there is much we do not know about its magnitude because corrupt officials rarely talk about their ill-gotten gains.

Other countries have leaders who have raked off even more money, as we saw in the chapters on Russia and China. Corruption is particularly important politically in Nigeria, however, because it is woven into every aspect of Nigerian society. As the anthropologist Daniel Jordan Smith sees it,

> **Ordinary citizens are ambivalent about corruption. They recognize that it undermines the country's democratic institutions, economic development, and global reputation, yet they also realize that wealth, power, and prestige in Nigeria are commonly achieved through practices that could easily be labeled as corrupt. For Nigerians, the state and corruption are synonymous.[3]**

Smith, for example, writes that his in-laws felt (perhaps accurately) that they needed to offer substantial bribes to get their children into college or get a job. He also writes about the roadblocks where drivers had to pay "tolls" (again, bribes) before they could continue on their way.

In that sense, corruption in Nigeria can be little more than a petty annoyance, which everyone endures. However, it also defines much of national political life in ways that help us understand why governments don't seem to get things done and how an estimated eight billion dollars disappears each year from the state's coffers.

To see that, consider the 2012 conviction of Delta state governor James Ibori. Ibori began his career as a shop clerk where he first dabbled in criminal activities and later entered the lucrative political world in 1991. Over nearly twenty years, he bought multimillion-dollar homes in London and South Africa along with a million-dollar fleet of automobiles. After he was indicted in Nigeria, he had the trial transferred to his home state, where one judge (who happened to be his brother) threw out all 150 charges against him. At his subsequent trial—which not coincidentally was held in a British court—he admitted to having embezzled at least $70 million, a figure the judge said was probably closer to $300 million.

The Nigerian anticorruption agency indicted fifteen former governors from 2005 to 2012. As amazing as it might seem, Ibori was the only one to stand trial. It seems as if only prominent leaders who have fallen from power are prosecuted for the simple reason that just about everyone else is implicated.

---

[3]Daniel Jordan Smith, *A Culture of Corruption: Everyday Deception and Popular Discontent in Nigeria* (Princeton: Princeton University Press, 2007), 4, 14.

419 Scams

Particularly notorious are what are commonly known as 419 scams, which were named for the article in the penal code under which people are (rarely) prosecuted.

The Internet versions are the best known. Before the days of spam filters, I would get dozens of emails a week from Nigerians. Many claimed to be President Abacha's widow. Here is an excerpt from one I received while I was looking for the "best" Abacha one I had in my archive of 419 emails. The request obviously is not legitimate, but I am being honest about when it arrived! The grammatical mistakes were in the original.

Dear Friend,

This is a censored information presented to you for your consideration, I request that it should remain absolutely off the record. Please bear with me for using this channel to contact you. I know you will be surprised to read from me. I got your detail through a close contact with the UN database Administrator, apart from being bolt from the blue, you may be skeptical to reply based on what happened to my family.

It's me Muhammad Muammar Al-qaddafi. I want you to assist my family to protect and capitalize the summation of £650million Pounds Sterling, the said reserves are in safety depository {name withheld}

Entertain undisclosed information to anyone, my contact will handle the whole arrangement and ensure the e-relocation to you successfully after we have signed covenant, however if you think you're not capable of handling this don't bother and delete this email.

Muhammad Muammar Al-qaddafi
Allah guard us all.

We know enough about 419 schemes to know that this one was almost certainly written by a Nigerian.

The 419 scams have a common pattern. You—and only you—can help. If you, "dear friend," are kind enough to do so, you will make millions of dollars if you start the process by wiring a few hundred thousand dollars to a numbered bank account. Before the days of the Internet, a surprising number of people were duped. There are dozens of websites that document 419 scams, including *www.419scam.org*.

Corruption is so common because patron-client relationships pave almost all routes to power. It is worsened by the fact that there are almost no tools average citizens or transparency advocates can use to hold officials accountable. It should come as no surprise that the national budget is often called the "national cake" that any rational political or economic actor wants to get his or her "slice" of.

That includes former President Obasanjo who, ironically, based his reputation on his efforts to block arbitrary rule and corruption. Obasanjo was not one of the worst economic offenders, although he and his family were rumored to be under investigation toward the end of his second term. Instead, critics point to the network of oyas he constructed, the way he tried to use them to prolong his term, and his desire to be the "power behind the throne" even after he left office.

The Military

Nigeria has had an elected, civilian government since 1999. That does not mean that the military has completely withdrawn from politics. To be sure, military officers no longer govern, and the worst human rights abuses of the Abacha years are far behind us. However, the military is still an important force in Nigerian politics in two interrelated ways.

First, in many respects, retired military officers hold tremendous amounts of power even if they exert it largely behind the scenes. As we have already seen, Obasanjo is arguably the most important PDP politician. Babangida plays a similar role in the opposition. Muhammadu Buhari, Jonathan's only serious competitor in 2011, is also a former military leader.

Second, senior serving and retired officers have been implicated in some of the most glaring instances of corruption since the return to civilian rule. Chukwudifu Oputa, a former Supreme Court justice who led a commission that considered human rights violations under the military put it this way. "During the period of military rule, most of our rulers' principal motivation and preoccupation were not service to the country but the accumulation of wealth and personal gratification."

At this point, the military does not seem eager to return to power. That does not mean that some officers will not do so at some point in the future should either national stability or their own pocketbooks become threatened.

Public Policy

Two issues have dominated policy making in Nigeria since independence: **democratization** and **development**. No Nigerian government—civilian or military—has made significant progress on either front, giving rise to the widespread sense of futility that is the heart of the chapter so far.

Democratization

Nigeria is the only country discussed in Part 4 that has consciously tried to create and sustain a democratic regime. And it has done so three times. As we have seen, the first two times Nigerian policy makers failed. The fourth republic has outlasted the first three combined, although it is hard to make the case that it has survived because democratization has succeeded.

The third and fourth republics deserve our attention as public policy issues because they were the products of intentional policy choices made by the politicians who created them. In that sense, the abject failure of the former and the weakness of the latter go a long way toward helping us see why the country has had so much trouble solving any and all of its problems.

The Third Republic

When General Babangida seized power in 1985, he endorsed what he called the custodial theory, which held that military rule can only be justified on a temporary basis and only to prepare for the return to civilian rule. Many observers then and now have cast doubts on his motivations, which we have no way of knowing. However, assuming he took his commitment seriously, it is easy to see that he and his colleagues may have done a good job of diagnosing the problem that destroyed the first two republics but fell far short when it came to designing the next one.

They did understand that ethnic divisions lay behind the country's fragmented multiparty system. They therefore decided to bar leading politicians from holding office and planned to rebuild the party and electoral systems from scratch. In particular, they intended to only allow new political parties that would require cross-ethnic support in order to win. The federal government would also fund the parties so that they would not be dependent on local bosses or corrupt officials. A neutral federal election commission would be set up to manage the way elections were held.

Problems with the plan surfaced almost immediately. The government rejected all thirteen of the potential parties that applied for licenses and created two of its own practically out of thin air. Then it rejected the presidential candidates the two parties initially nominated.

When the 1993 presidential election actually occurred, it was the most honest and least violent in Nigerian history up to that point. Nonetheless, the government rejected the results and arrested the apparent winner, Abiola, thereby paving the way for the coup led by Abacha later that fall.

One obvious lesson to be learned from the sad history of the third republic is one we saw about more effective democratizing efforts in Part 2. No matter how accurate their authors' diagnoses of a country's problems may be, writing a new constitution is never enough. In this case, we will never know what the outcome would have been had the military regime fully played by the rules they themselves created. In other words, leadership matters, and, in this case, it was sorely lacking.

The Fourth Republic

So far the fourth republic has been more successful, but only modestly so. To be sure, the military has not intervened in what would be the ninth successful military coup in little more than half a century. Otherwise, it is hard to be sanguine about the state of democracy or its future prospects.

Unlike the stillborn third republic, this one was born with almost no prior planning. After Abacha died, General Abubakar almost immediately announced that new elections would be held and that he would leave politics, which he did the following May.

Ironically, the lack of planning may actually have helped democratization in the short run. It was a foregone conclusion that Obasanjo would be overwhelmingly elected president of the new republic. Given his reputation and support in all parts of the country, that seemed to bode well for democracy.

However, there were already signs that the return to civilian rule would not necessarily lead to true democratization, however one chooses to define that term. There were enough reports that the military acted improperly on Obasanjo's behalf that former U.S. President Jimmy Carter left Nigeria rather than certify that the election had been fair. Doubts about the three subsequent elections have been even more widespread to the point that few take the published results of Yar'Adua's's 2007 victory seriously.

There is little doubt that Jonathan actually won four years later. However, there is widespread suspicion that there was enough fraud in the casting and counting of ballots to allow him to avoid a runoff. We do not know if these accusations are correct, but there are dozens of YouTube videos purportedly showing people casting dozens of votes in districts Jonathan and his supporters carried handily.

At this point, all the themes raised so far in this chapter come into play. Nigeria's failure to sustain a viable democracy has little to do with the expertise of its lawyers and other experts who have drafted its constitutions. Rather, if the political scientists who have studied successful transitions are to be believed, democracy in Nigeria is not likely to take root until the problems discussed so far are addressed and until the state can point to some success on the other big area of public policy failure which we are about to address—economic development.

Comparative Emphasis: Democratization

Nigeria is one of many countries that have made the transition from authoritarian to democratic rule a top priority, though few have had as many frustrations along the way.

Although some of the signs are positive for the fourth republic, it still has a long way to go before we can feel reasonably certain that democratization will succeed. Whatever his faults, because Obasanjo did have to leave office because of term limits, the new regime lost its most effective leader. Not surprisingly, his successors lack his charisma and track record. It is also by no means certain that the military will stay as politically neutral as it has been since Obasanjo took office. Nigeria has yet to experience the transition to a leader elected from the opposition. Last but by no means least, it is hard to imagine democracy gaining widespread public support unless the government can address many of the social and economic problems that plague the country. ■

Economic Development and Structural Adjustment

As has been suggested throughout this chapter, the Nigerian economy is in disarray. There have been periods when it grew at a respectable rate and the future seemed promising, but the country has not been able to take any significant steps that would improve the living conditions of its impoverished population.

Nigeria has been caught up in the global debate between supporters of **import substitution** and structural adjustment. Even more important for our purposes are the way political instability and corruption have impeded any significant progress toward economic development, despite the country's abundance of natural resources.

For the first twenty years after independence, Nigerian governments pursued import substitution policies, which were the orthodoxy of the day. In order to reduce its dependence on imported goods, civilian and military rulers alike depended heavily on foreign aid and loans for the investment capital that Nigeria could not provide on its own. Over the years, Nigeria received considerable aid from both governmental and private sources, and it used that money to build universities, factories, and modern urban amenities in its major cities either on its own or through the more than ninety partially private and partially public organizations known as **parastatals**. Few of those projects worked.

Typical was the Delta steel complex in Aladja, which opened in 1982. Creating a locally run steel and iron industry has always been a high priority of any Southern government because they are components of almost all modern industrial products. The Aladja mill was to provide steel rods and other products for factories that would produce finished "rolling" steel.

Like so many other projects, the Aladja mill fell far short of expectations. It never operated at more than 20 percent of capacity, which means that other factories that depended on its products went underutilized as well. Another project, the Adjaokuta steel mill, was projected to be Africa's largest steel factory when plans for its construction were made in the boom years of the 1970s, but it was a decade behind schedule when it came on line and ended up costing $4 billion more than originally projected.

By the late 1980s, the bottom line was clear. After two decades of import substitution, Nigeria could not meet its domestic demand for industrial products. In iron and steel, that shortfall reached about 6 million metric tons in 1990, but even if all its plants that were either in operation or under construction worked at full capacity, it would only have been able to produce 1.3 million metric tons. The same was true in every other industrial sector.

There were problems with agriculture as well. After independence, Nigerian officials emphasized industrial development at the expense of agriculture to the point that farm products made up only 3 percent of total exports, while the country was ever more dependent on imported food.

The government adopted ambitious-sounding programs to modernize agricultural technology with titles like "Operation Feed the Nation" (1976–79) and "Green Revolution" (1979–83). Despite new roads into farming regions and expanded irrigation, most farmers still used traditional agricultural techniques, and their output did not increase appreciably.

The economy went into a tailspin in the mid-1980s from which it is yet to recover. To a considerable degree, the crisis of the late 1980s was the result of forces beyond the government's control.

Declining oil prices after the price shocks of 1973 and 1979 produced a crisis of massive proportions. In the second half of the 1980s alone, plummeting prices led to a more than 80 percent fall in GNP which only rebounded slightly in the early 1990s. That sharp drop cost the Nigerian government almost a third of the export revenues it had been counting on to pay for imports and to finance industrial and other development projects.

Meanwhile, the naira's value dropped by about half, a decline that continued through the 1990s. To complicate matters further, there was an enormous black market on which the elites traded their naira and made millions in profits—in foreign currencies. The drop in the naira's value is one of the reasons the country's total debt rose by about 1,000 percent.

Under the best of circumstances, the Nigerian government would have been in trouble. Everything from skilled labor to replacement parts was in short supply. The country also received less foreign aid than it expected.

Although there is no way of demonstrating how big their impact was, the corruption of Nigeria's military rulers made a bad problem substantially worse. There is little doubt, for example, that government officials siphoned off hundreds of millions of dollars in foreign aid and oil profits long before the Abacha regime turned corruption into an art form. After all, the first serious stories about 419 scams surfaced in the 1980s, years before the invention of the Internet and spam email.

In the late 1980s the political and financial tide began the shift in the capitalist world. As we saw in Chapter 12, the **International Monetary Fund (IMF)**, the **World Bank**, and other international financial institutions abandoned the socialist-leaning import substitution in favor of structural adjustment which gave free markets a far higher priority in charting development strategies. That shift also coincided with the victory of conservative politicians in the industrialized North, most notably Ronald Reagan and Margaret Thatcher.

In the simplest terms, public and private sector donors began to insist that countries like Nigeria dismantle the tariffs that had been used to protect young, domestic industries, such as iron and steel. Governments throughout the Global South were required to balance their budgets and reduce subsidies on the prices of imported goods.

At first, Nigeria's military government tried to resist. The leaders of the second republic actually introduced higher tariffs and other policies that would make imports more expensive and thus give a boost to domestic producers. Economic conditions did not improve, which was one of the reasons the military overthrew the second republic.

The new military regime initially tried to retain existing policies and encourage people to buy needed goods domestically. Sooner rather than later, they had to give in—on paper at least.

Government spending was cut and new projects frozen, which led to thousands of layoffs. The price of oil continued to collapse. As it did, the country's debt spiraled upward, at which point the international financial institutions that "owned" the debt stepped in. The government had to apply to the IMF's Extended Fund Facility for a loan

to cover its immediate shortfall and restructure its long-term debt. The IMF agreed to a new loan and to negotiate new terms for the outstanding debt only if the government agreed to very different macroeconomic policies, conditions that have come to be known as **conditionality**. The IMF's conditions were part of the reason for Babangida's 1985 coup. Officially, his government decided to reject the IMF loans under its proposed terms, but it did agree to do whatever was necessary to restructure Nigeria's economy in a more profitable direction, which, in the end, meant acceding to Northern demands.

Comparative Emphasis: Globalization

Nigeria shares many of the problems that all less developed countries are facing as they struggle to integrate their economies into the increasingly interdependent world economy. That has been true since before Nigeria gained its independence, but it has become particularly burdensome in the last thirty years, when the debt crisis and other problems led international financial leaders to require that governments adopt structural adjustment plans in order to receive loans and aid. These programs typically include reductions in tariffs, the encouragement of foreign investment, the greater use of markets in domestic economic life, privatization of state-owned enterprises, and fiscal restraint on the part of the government.

The logic behind structural adjustment is that, in time, Southern economies will find profitable niches that will stimulate rapid growth in general. The problem is "in time." So far, the benefits of structural adjustment have gone to relatively few Nigerians, most of whom were wealthy to begin with.

In other words, the gap between rich and poor has widened considerably in the last generation. There is no better example of this than the riots that occurred when the government tried to change gasoline prices so that they better reflected market conditions. In fact, the protests were so intense that the government had to cancel many of the increases it had intended to implement. ■

Babangida introduced a structural adjustment program of his own, which has been extended in one form or another ever since. Its goal was to expand exports other than oil, reduce the import of goods that could be manufactured locally, achieve self-sufficiency in food production, and, most notably, increase the role of the private sector. Tariffs were reduced and import-license procedures simplified or, in some cases, eliminated altogether. In 1986 alone, seventeen parastatals were privatized, and by 1990, sixteen more had been as well. Another thirty have been sold since then.

Foreign investors can now own 50 percent of existing enterprises and a controlling ownership or, in some cases, even total ownership of new ones. In summer 2010, for instance, the government announced plans to attract $10 billion in foreign investment to take over the decrepit electrical generation industry. That same year, the government began negotiations to sell the Nigerian National Petroleum Company, which has a monopoly in the domestic market. In all, dozens of industries from cement to the national airlines to a number of banks are at least in the process of being sold.

So far, structural adjustment's record is mixed. At first glance, things are improving. GDP doubled between 2005 and 2010 without counting the underground economy. On balance, however, the transition has been difficult. Debt remains high, and interest on outstanding loans continues to consume a third of the government's annual budget.

Most important of all, whatever the benefits of structural adjustment, economic control is concentrated more than ever in two places—in foreign hands or in the hands of the wealthy domestic elite. Economic inequalities have increased, since structural-adjustment plans in general provide few incentives for the beneficiaries of economic growth to deal with poverty and other social problems.

The Media

As is the case almost everywhere, most Nigerians learn about political life primarily through the mass media. For most of its history, Nigeria has had a reasonably free press. Its hundreds of newspapers and magazines reflect a wide range of opinions on almost every issue. To be sure, the various military regimes cracked down on the press and even closed some outlets at moments of the highest tensions, as was the case after Saro-Wiwa was executed. But in general Nigerians have had access to a free press.

The problem is that relatively few Nigerians are literate enough to read a newspaper or wealthy enough to afford to buy one. Therefore, the key to feedback in Nigeria is radio and television, which civilian and military authorities have tried to control through the Nigerian Broadcast Commission (NBC).

Since the creation of the fourth republic, the NBC has struggled to find a balance between a desire to foster national unity and the new constitution's provision that states could establish and even own radio and television stations, which most of them now have done. The contradiction between those two positions became clear in 2001 when the state of Zamfara created a radio station, Voice of Islam, that infuriated Christians already worried about what they saw as the extreme use of Sharia in the state. Zamfara's leadership, for example, had authorized the beating of a woman who conceived a child out of wedlock and banned women's soccer as un-Islamic. The media, especially television, has spread largely through cable and satellite services, but their impact is limited by the fact that there are a total of seven million sets of any kind in the country.

Conclusion: The Imam and the Pastor

At this point you might well be asking a question that has lurked below the surface throughout this chapter. Why should there even be a Nigeria? After all, Nigeria as we know it began as an artificial creation of the colonial powers, and its history has at best been a rocky one ever since. It has never come close to creating an effective government or a modern economy despite all the human and natural resources Achebe alluded to in the statement that begins this chapter. In other words, it may well be the case that the Nigerian people would be better off if the country split up into at least three parts representing the main geographic and ethnic divisions of the first republic.

But there is some hopeful news.

In the late 1980s, Pastor James Wuye and Imam Muhammad Ashafa ran rival militias in the northern city of Kaduna, which is one of the few places were Muslims and Christians live side by side. It is also where the initial rounds of the Miss World contest were held in 2002.

Early in this century, the two men decided that their rivalry no longer made sense. They began reconciling their personal differences and then embarked on a larger project on interfaith understanding, that resulted in the highly acclaimed film, *The Imam and the Pastor*, at least some of which is available for free on the Internet (www.fltfilms. org.uk/imam.html). Like *The Station* mentioned earlier, this film is a sign of what could go right in Nigeria.

We can only hope so.

KEY TERMS

Concepts
conditionality
democratization
dual mandate
failed state
federalism
Hausa-Fulani
identity politics
Igbo
import substitution
indirect rule
Middle Belt
oya
parastatals
patron-client relations
structural adjustment
Yoruba
zero-sum

zoning

Acronyms
AFRC
FEC
IMF
INEC
PDP
SMC

People
Abacha, Sani
Abiola, Moshood
Abubakar, Abdulsalami
Azikiwe, Nnamdi
Babangida, Ibrahim
Bello, Ahmadu
Jonathan, Goodluck
Obasanjo, Olusegun

Saro-Wiwa, Ken
Yar'Adua, Umaru Musa

Organizations, Places, and Events
Armed Forces Ruling Council (AFRC)
Biafra
Boko Haram
Federal Executive Council (FEC)
Independent Nigerian Election
  Commission (INEC)
International Monetary Fund (IMF)
National Party of Nigeria (NPN)
Nigerian Republican Convention
  (NRC)
People's Democratic Party (PDP)
Supreme Military Council (SMC)
World Bank

USEFUL WEBSITES

The Nigerian government now has a very good portal with links to its main offices and departments:

www.nigeria.gov.ng

The International Crisis Group does the best research on crisis-burdened countries. Its work on Nigeria is state of the art. Go to the website and then search on Nigeria.

www.crisisgroup.org

There are now a number of portals that include general information about Nigeria and its politics. These include:

www.nigeriamasterweb.com/Politics.html

www.nigeriaworld.com

FURTHER READING

Aborisade, Oladimeji, and Robert Mundt. *Politics in Nigeria, 2nd ed*. New York: Addison-Wesley, 2002. The best textbook on Nigeria, although now somewhat dated.

Achebe, Chinua. *The Trouble with Nigeria*. London: Heinemann, 1984. Although very dated, this book addresses many of the problems Nigeria still faces today, especially its leadership.

Campbell, John. *Nigeria: Dancing on the Brink*. Boulder, CO: Rowman & Littlefield, 2010. By far the best recent book that was written for a general audience.

Davidson, Basil. *Modern Africa*. New York: Longman, 1983. One of the best overviews of modern African history that puts Nigeria in perspective.

Dike, Victor. *Nigeria and the Politics of Unreason*. London: Adonis-Abbey, 2003. One of the highly critical books on the Obasanjo government.

Falols, Toyin, and Matthew M. Heaton. *A History of Nigeria*. New York: Cambridge University Press, 2008. The best single-volume text on Nigerian history.

Griswold, Eliza. *The Tenth Parallel: Dispatches from the Fault Line Between Christianity and Islam.* New York: Farrar, Straus and Giroux, 2010. Not just on Nigeria, but this is by far the best book on the intertwined tensions between Christians and Muslims.

Smith, Daniel Jordan. *A Culture of Corruption: Everyday Deception and Popular Discontent in Nigeria.* Princeton: Princeton University Press, 2007. An insightful and often funny (tragically so) book on Nigerian social structure, culture, and corruption.

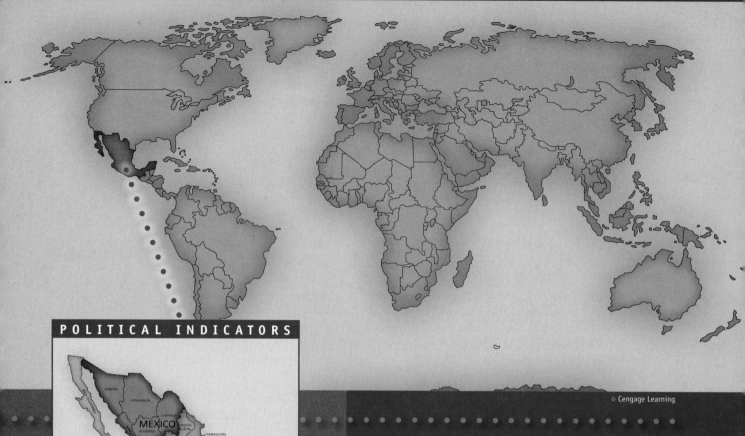

© Cengage Learning

15

Mexico

> The pervasive sense that something has gone terribly wrong extends beyond the beheadings and the employment deficit and reflects a much broader phenomenon of weak and malleable state institutions.
>
> JO TUCKMAN

THE BASICS

Mexico

Size	1,972,550 sq. km (roughly three times the size of Texas)
Population	116 million
GNP per capita	$15,300
GNP growth rate	3.8% (2010)
Out migration	3.24 people per 1,000 per year
Currency	13 peso = US$1
Religion	76% Catholic, 6% Protestant, 17% unspecified or none
Capital	Mexico City, Federal District
President	Enrique Peña Nieto (2012–)

They're Baaaaaaaaaaack

The title for this section was originally a line (with seemingly that many a's) in the popular 1986 film, *Poltergeist II*. The film itself was not a memorable one, but the scream uttered by a frightened little girl announcing the return of evil spirits to her home took on a life of its own.

"They're back" is a good way to begin this chapter, because they—in this case the PRI (Institutional Revolutionary Party)—are back after twelve years out of office. That might not seem surprising for readers who live in democracies where shifts in power between one party and another happen all the time. Not in Mexico.

Before 2000, the PRI and its predecessors had not lost an election since the end of the most recent Mexican revolution and the adoption of the current constitution in 1917. Although the term had not been coined yet, the PRI's Mexico certainly was a hybrid state.

Mexico had regular and seemingly competitive elections. However, the PRI always won, by "hook or by crook," which all too often meant by crook toward the end of the twentieth century. Even when elections were reasonably free and fair, the PRI stacked the political deck so dramatically in its favor in ways we will explore in the rest of this chapter that the opposition never really had a chance.

The PRI in power was never a model of either efficiency or honesty. More often than not, the Mexican economy failed to perform up to its potential, and almost all lists of the reasons why that was the case had the PRI's role at or near the top. It used its monopoly on political power and unusual political practices (e.g., not allowing

ZUMA Press/ZUMA Press, Inc./Alamy

President Peña Nieto at his inauguration.

any office holders to run for reelection) to secure its political position but in the process built a system that left widespread nepotism and accusations of corruption in the massive state-dominated sectors of the economy in its wake.

In addition, Mexican political life unfolded in the shadow of its giant neighbor to the north. The United States has had tremendous leverage over Mexico literally since the day it declared its independence from Spain. Today, American influence is easiest to see in its economic clout, ranging from its use of cheap Mexican labor to produce industrial goods to the fact that Walmart is now the largest retailer "south of the border."

As the twentieth century drew to a close, the PRI's hold on power evaporated. It only "won" the 1988 presidential election by rigging the vote. It gradually lost support to opposition parties to its left and right. New civil society organizations and a vibrant private sector took root in an increasingly middle-class society that was no longer as dependent on PRI patronage and other benefits.

Finally, the impossible happened. **Vicente Fox** (1942–) and **Felipe Calderón** (1962–) of the opposition **PAN (National Action Party)** won the presidential elections in 2000 and 2006. Fox, at least, was elected with great fanfare and great expectations, as one would expect of the first non-PRI president in three quarters of a century.

The PAN's time in power, however, was anything but a success. Neither president ever had a majority in Congress which made passing legislation difficult and left Mexico with its own version of Washington's gridlock. Then the economic crisis hit early in Calderón's presidency, which had the double effect of slowing Mexico's economy and convincing millions of immigrant workers to return home and thus deprive the country of billions of dollars in **remittances**. Last but by no means least, Mexico's internal drug war, which years of effort had done little to end, escalated to the point that it had taken at least fifty thousand lives before Calderón left office.

In other words, if the 2000 election was about democratization delayed, the campaign twelve years later revolved around unkept promises and unmet hopes. In fact, the results were a foregone conclusion even before the campaign began. The PRI candidate **Enrique Peña Nieto** (1966–) was considered a shoo-in the day he was nominated, and he swept to victory in the election.

Unfortunately, Peña and his team took over under less than auspicious circumstances. Despite the progress we will discuss later in the chapter, the economy continues to flounder. Drug violence persists.

Mexico's problems are nowhere as severe as those we saw in Nigeria or Iran. Nonetheless, many analysts think they are serious enough to worry about Mexico turning into a **failed state**. Those fears may not be warranted, since it is hard to imagine the Mexican state become as weak as those in Sudan or Somalia. Nonetheless, we will see plenty of support for more nuanced arguments about the troubled Mexican state like the one made by the journalist Jo Tuckman that begins this chapter. At the very least, Mexico will need a lot more than "just" alternation in power between the PRI and the opposition before it can overcome the social, economic, and political problems that will be at the heart of this chapter.

Thinking About Mexico

Most people reading this book live in the United States and will therefore probably be more interested in Mexico than the rest of the Global South. But just because people in the United States and Mexico share a long border, that does not mean that Americans know much about their southern neighbor. That ignorance often leads to stereotypical images about what Mexico is like.

The Bottom Line

Diversity

Mexico's diversity begins with its geography, which may come as a surprise to generations of Americans raised on Westerns, with their scenes of an arid, wide-open country of mountains and deserts. That image applies only to the northern part of the country. Southern and coastal regions are hot and humid, but as you move inland and into the mountains, the climate turns more temperate.

The stereotypes are right in one respect: Mexico is a rugged country. Between the mountains, deserts, and jungles, only about 12 percent of its land is arable, and much of Mexican agriculture is marginal at best.

The Mexican population is also extremely diverse. Relatively few Spanish women came to New Spain, as Mexico and other Spanish holdings north of Panama were known during the colonial period. Moreover, unlike the situation in what became the United States and Canada, the Spaniards did not kill off most of the people they encountered on their arrival. In short, marriages and nonmarital sexual relations between Spanish men and Indian women were common, so that now the largest group of Mexicans are *mestizos*—part Indian and part white. A substantial number of Africans also were brought to Mexico as slaves. To this day, many observers think that the state of Veracruz along the Gulf coast feels more Caribbean than Mexican.

Terms like Indian or *mestizo* are no longer in everyday use when describing people's physical appearance. Indian is primarily used to describe the 5 percent or so of the population that only speaks an indigenous language and is thus not very well integrated into what is predominantly a Spanish-speaking culture. The very term "Indian" is controversial. Some scholars refuse to use it, preferring what they think is the less value-laden term "indigenous." Whichever term you use, Mexicans, like Brazilians, are a racial mélange.

The very name Mexico reflects the country's diversity. It is derived from either Mexica, one of the Aztec tribes, or Mexitl, an Aztec epithet for God. Mexico's rich and diverse traditions can still be seen in everything from the way many Mexicans dress, to the food they eat, to the way they practice Catholicism.

Mexican Names and Places

There are two linguistic issues to keep in mind while studying Mexico.

First, names. As in most Spanish-speaking countries, Mexican names have the following structure: first or Christian name (Enrique), father's family name (Peña), mother's maiden name (Nieto). Some Mexicans (e.g., Felipe Calderón) do not routinely include their mother's family name. If there are three names, it is usually the middle one that denotes the family, as with President Peña.

And, like most writers, I will regretfully use the term American to refer to people from the United States. Anyone who lives in either North or South America is, of course, an American. However, given the way the English language has evolved, there is no other stylistically acceptable adjective, to describe things and people from the United States.

A Tale of Two Countries

Mexico is not as poor as most of the Global South. Although it is not one of the BRICS, the World Bank ranks Mexico's economy ahead of Russia's. Similarly, according to most statistical indicators, Mexico is one of the world's fifteen leading industrial powers.

Mexico does have a lot going for it, starting with its abundant natural resources. Its minerals became an important industry the minute the Aztecs greeted the *conquistadors* with what must have seemed like mountains of gold artifacts. Today, Mexico ranks seventh in the world in oil production, with petroleum products accounting for about 40 percent of its GNP.

Yet, for much of the past forty years, stagnation rather than progress has been the economic norm. Growth in per capita GDP only averaged about 1 percent per year in the 1980s, although it has been higher since **NAFTA** (the **North American Free Trade Agreement**) went into effect in 1994. Along those same lines, the inflation rate often ran between 30 and 50 percent per year before the government began to get it under control in the late 1990s.

One consequence of that mediocre economic track record is widespread poverty. Housing and health care are not very good. More than 20 percent of Mexicans do not have access to either safe drinking water or indoor plumbing. In the decade after NAFTA went into effect, the number of people in extreme poverty (with an income more than 25 percent below the poverty line) grew from 17 to 26 million. Eight percent of the population lives on less than the equivalent of two dollars a day today. The widespread despair about ever rising above a subsistence standard of living, of course, contributed to the flow of immigrants to the United States.

Mexican poverty has been compounded by a long history of international debt. The government borrowed heavily during the 1960s and 1970s on the assumption that it could use oil revenues to pay back Northern banks and governments. When prices fell after the oil crisis of 1979, Mexico's debt skyrocketed, reaching more than $100 billion in the late 1980s. Although it declined somewhat in the early 1990s, total debt leaped back toward late 1980s levels as a result of the peso crisis in 1995. For the bulk of this century it has been $210 billion a year.

To complicate matters further, Mexico's second largest source of foreign income comes in the form of remittances from its citizens living in the United States, amounting to about $25 billion in 2008. That figure dropped 14 percent in 2010 and 2011 because the American recession hit Mexicans living and working there particularly hard. Some Mexicans who have lived in the United States for decades have returned home (no one knows exactly how many there are), adding to already severe pressures on the domestic labor force and denying the country the money it used to get from the money they send to relatives back home.

Finally, Mexico has to cope with the violence associated with the drug trade. About 70 percent of the illegal drugs entering the United States come by way of Mexico, although few were produced there. That trade is controlled by a handful of powerful cartels whose rivalries with each other and with the government have taken at least fifty thousand lives. Ironically, the drug war has occurred in a country that does not itself have a serious addiction problem and that makes it all but impossible to legally buy firearms—there is only one legal gun store in the entire country.

Despite its historical woes, some observers are beginning to describe Mexico as a middle-class society. Even though about three quarters of the population are in the bottom two categories used by Mexican marketers (which means, among other things, that they cannot afford to buy a car), almost every indicator of the standard of living has shown noticeable improvement since the turn of the century. About half of all Mexicans own their homes. The number of children graduating from high school and university is skyrocketing.

Big Brother Is Watching

Another unusual feature of Mexican politics is its relationship with the United States. All countries in the Global South have had a long and not always pleasant relationship with the industrialized democracies. Mexico's connection to the United States is exceptional in two main ways. First, although the United States never colonized Mexico, it did seize one-third of its territory in the middle of the nineteenth century. Second, no other Northern country has

as wide ranging an impact as the United States does on almost everything that happens in Mexico.

For the two centuries Mexico has been an independent country, the United States has exerted a massive and often unwanted influence on its politics, which began with the first U.S. ambassador to Mexico, Joel Poinsett, who insisted that the new Mexican government heed Washington's wishes.[1] As recently as 1914, American troops invaded Mexico. And although the United States no longer engages in that kind of direct intervention, its indirect leverage—ranging from the tens of billions of dollars Mexico had to borrow in recent years to the impact of its popular culture—may be no less overwhelming.

Many Mexicans speak of their "dependent psychology," or the sense that the American big brother is always watching. With its wealth and freedom, the United States is highly regarded by most average Mexicans. At the same time, many are envious of what North Americans have and resent their often arrogant, high-handed interference in Mexican affairs.

The United States and Canada shared the world's longest unguarded border until 9/11. As the seemingly never-ending controversy over immigration reform suggests, the U.S.-Mexican border, in contrast, is one of the most closely patrolled because of the flow of illegal immigrants and drugs heading north. Indeed, some pundits refer to it as the border between the First and Third Worlds. U.S. concern about the porousness of the frontier only heightened after the 9/11 attacks, even though Mexico had nothing to do with what happened.

If anything, the two countries are more dependent on each other economically than ever. Mexico is the United States' third leading trading partner, trailing only Canada and China. The United States is even more important for Mexico because two-thirds of all Mexican exports are sold there. Even prior to NAFTA, there was significant U.S. investment, especially in the *maquiladora* factories that dot the border and use poorly paid Mexican workers to produce goods destined for foreign markets. The agreement allowed similar enterprises to open in most of the rest of the country.

More important politically is the migration of Mexicans to the United States. There is nothing new to this. The American Southwest has long been a "safety valve" providing jobs for unemployed Mexicans, who, had they not traveled north, might have fomented protest at home. The Department of Homeland Security estimates that there could be as many as eleven million Mexicans living legally or illegally in the United States, and they send more than twenty billion dollars a year back to family members at

---

[1]Incidentally, Poinsett brought back from Mexico the Christmas plant that bears his family name, the poinsettia.

home, adding more money to the economy than Mexico makes from its agricultural exports.

Many people in the United States believe that Mexican immigrants are a burden, a belief that led to the passage of the Immigration Reform and Control Act of 1986 and other restrictive measures since then. Many Americans, too, are worried that the presence of so many Spanish-speaking immigrants (not all of whom are from Mexico, of course) is diluting and threatening American culture.

Immigration reform is again on the political agenda in the United States as I write in mid-2013. Most Americans are finally convinced that their country needs new legislation that includes a way for most of the millions of illegal immigrants to remain if not become citizens. It is not clear, however, that the legislation will pass.

What is important here is to note that Mexicans will have little to do with future American immigration policy. The key decisions will all be made in Washington.

Key Concepts and Questions

The most important questions about Mexican politics cannot be answered yet. As these lines were written, Mexico had just begun Peña's *sexeño* or six-year term. President Fox had initiated sweeping reforms, many of which died in Congress. President Calderón faced a similar predicament especially after the PRI made gains in the 2009 mid-term legislative elections. Now that the PRI is back in power with a clear legislative majority, the government should face relatively smooth sailing on a day-to-day basis, although it is far too early to tell how successful the new government will be in reaching its policy goals.

Above and beyond that uncertainty, other long-standing and often divisive questions remain, including:

- How did the PRI stay in power for so long?
- How and why did forces undermining PRI rule emerge?
- Has the defeat and then return to power of the PRI helped or hindered the prospects for democracy in Mexico?
- Why did three successive administrations in the 1980s and 1990s reject Mexico's long-standing commitment to *import substitution* and embrace structural adjustment as fully as the leaders of any country in the Global South?
- How much have those reforms addressed Mexico's poverty and other pressing needs?
- How have the events of the last few decades affected Mexico's all-important relationship with the United States?

The Evolution of Mexican Politics

Mexican political history shares a number of features with most other Central and South American countries—colonization by Spain or Portugal, independence in the early nineteenth century, and a rather tumultuous history ever since (see Table 15.1). There is one way in which Mexico's political history is dramatically different. As should be clear already, the United States has had a massive impact on Mexico at least since its first years as an independent country (www.mexconnect.com/mex_/history/historyindex.html).

The Colonial Era

Not that much is known about the people who lived in what is now Mexico before Hernán Cortés and his *conquistadors* arrived in 1513. The best accounts suggest that there were at least four distinct indigenous civilizations, the most important of which historically were the Mayans, who lived along the Gulf coast. Until about one thousand years ago, they had one of the most advanced civilizations in the world, but it had begun to decline for reasons no one fully understands centuries before the Spaniards arrived. By that time, the Aztecs had come to dominate dozens of other tribes from their capital of Tenochtitlán (now Mexico City), where they were able to establish a centralized empire with an elaborate administrative system.

Despite fierce resistance from Moctezuma (Mexicans prefer this spelling rather than Montezuma as usually used in English) and, later, his nephew Cuauhtémoc, Cortés was able to overcome Aztec resistance within two years. His victory is often ascribed to Spanish military superiority, but that could not have been the only cause, since there were very few Spaniards in his expedition. At least as important were the diseases the Spaniards unknowingly brought with them. The Aztecs had never built up any

TABLE 15.1 Key Events in Mexican History

YEAR	EVENT
1519	Arrival of Hernán Cortés
1810	Declaration of Independence
1836	Loss of Texas
1848	Mexican-American War
1864	Emperor Maximilian installed
1876	Beginning of Porfirio Díaz's reign
1910	Revolution
1929	Formation of PNR, which renamed itself PRI in 1946
1934	Election of Lázaro Cárdenas

immunity to smallpox, syphilis, and other diseases they had never been exposed to before. Something on the order of 90 percent of the people who were alive when Cortés arrived were wiped out, after which the Spanish gradually extended control over New Spain, which stretched from what is now northern California well into Central America.

Spanish and British colonial practices had next to nothing in common. The Spaniards encountered well-established civilizations, not nomadic tribes. They thus had to incorporate the native population into the colonial system in an elaborate hierarchy that placed native Spaniards at the top, their mixed offspring below them, and the massive indigenous population at the bottom. New Spain became part of an exploitative mercantilist empire that sent resources back to Spain but gave little politically or economically to the colonies in return. The Spaniards forced the indigenous population to convert to Catholicism, and the Church became an integral part of the colonial administration. They did allow the Mexicans to maintain some non-Spanish traditions, most notably the veneration of the dark-skinned Virgin of Guadalupe who "appeared" in 1531 and has been a central part of Mexican Catholicism ever since.

Hints of problems to come soon appeared. New Spain was never allowed self-government, which was already well established in British North America long before the Revolutionary War. The church owned one-third of the land, most of which was divided into huge estates or *haciendas,* and the prior owners became indentured servants to their Spanish overlords.

The Spanish were also not very effective colonial administrators, especially the farther away one went from the major cities. Nonetheless, there was one common theme to their approach to colonization: Not many people liked it, especially when the Spanish had to clamp down in order to extract even more resources to pay for their participation in the European conflict that spanned the end of the eighteenth and the beginning of the nineteenth centuries.

Independence

Although Americans rarely think about it in these terms, the thirteen colonies gained their independence in large part because the British were too preoccupied by events in Europe to commit the resources needed to hold onto a distant, troublesome, and not very important part of their empire. Independence for Spain's American colonies occurred for similar reasons. Involvement in the Napoleonic wars sapped Spain of much of its wealth and power. As a result, it could not or would not pay the price to hold onto its colonies in the Americas.

The bloody, decade-long revolutionary struggle began in 1810 when the *mestizo* priest Miguel Hidalgo y Castillo first proclaimed independence and raised an army of more than one hundred thousand soldiers. Hidalgo proved to be something less than a brilliant military strategist. Within a year, his forces were routed, and he was captured and executed, a fate that befell many others before the decade was out. In what came to be a national tradition, his surviving soldiers fled to the countryside and kept fighting.

In the end, it was the lay and clerical elite that finally won Mexico's independence. Many of them felt squeezed between the demanding Spaniards and Hidalgo's nationalist successors and decided they could best protect their financial interests in an independent Mexico. But their victory settled very little.

For more than a hundred years, Mexico careened from crisis to crisis and from *caudillo* (strongman) to caudillo while social and economic problems festered. No historical figure exemplifies independent Mexico's early difficulties any better than Augustin de Iturbide (1773–1824). Iturbide was a rather unscrupulous opportunist who manipulated Spanish emissaries into granting Mexico its independence and making him the head of the first government in 1821. But pressures quickly mounted. When Spain rejected their agreement, Iturbide responded by having himself declared Emperor Augustin I. Within two years, he had been overthrown and sent into exile. It should be pointed out that U.S. intervention in Mexican politics began in these years, too, when Ambassador Poinsett made it abundantly clear that the Monroe administration did not approve of the Iturbide regime and helped ruin it financially.

During the next thirty years, the most important political figure was General Antonio López de Santa Anna (1794–1876), best known in the United States for his 1836 victory at the Alamo at San Antonio, Texas. At home, Santa Anna has a considerably worse reputation, which Daniel Levy and Gabriel Székely describe as follows:

> In 1848, Mexico's most despised, traitorous, duplicitous native son presided over the loss of roughly half of Mexico's territory in a war with the United States. Santa Anna's most consistent preoccupation was self interest. Among his favorite self-designations were Most Serene Highness, Father of the Country, Savior, and Perpetual Victor. It is a sad commentary on Mexico's political instability from the 1820s to the 1950s that the last title had some validity. Almost no one could establish a viable government and a viable economic base.[2]

---

[2]Daniel Levy and Gabriel Székely, *Mexico: Paradoxes of Stability and Change,* 2nd ed. (Boulder, CO: Westview Press, 1987), 23.

Santa Anna came to prominence in 1823 by forcing Iturbide into exile and then having him executed when he tried to return. He dominated Mexican politics for the next quarter-century. Most of the time he operated behind the scenes as a series of weak elected presidents and military officers tried to govern. Meanwhile, the country grew ever more divided largely over the economic and other powers of the church.

Santa Anna held onto power primarily because of his reputation for defending Mexico's threatened sovereignty, though it must be said that he was not very good at it. He led Mexican troops in overcoming Spanish forces attempting to regain their lost colony in 1830, but after that he fared less well. Despite his victory at the Alamo, he could not keep Texas from gaining its independence. He also could not prevent the United States from annexing Texas and then seizing most of northern Mexico during the Mexican-American War in 1848. After the war, Santa Anna was exiled to Jamaica. Remarkably, he was brought back five years later to help restore order. This time he sold parts of what are now Arizona and New Mexico to the United States and clung to power for two more years before he was finally overthrown and exiled for good.

He was replaced by a loose coalition of liberals whose 1857 constitution stripped the church and military of virtually all of their wealth and civil power. Within months, conservatives tried to oust them, which sparked a new civil war. In 1861, liberal forces led by General Benito Juárez entered Mexico City, making him the country's first indigenous president though he was unable to consolidate his power, because the years of war, intrigue, and chaos had taken their toll.

British, Spanish, and French forces took advantage of the resulting power vacuum to take over, ostensibly to make Mexico pay for their financial losses. At first, Mexican forces defeated the invaders in 1862. But the Europeans eventually forced Juárez out of Mexico City and in 1864 installed the Austrian prince Maximilian as emperor. Quickly, Maximilian and the French forces that really held power realized that there were few riches to be had and that the Mexicans were not going to accept new foreign rulers. Within three years, Juárez was back in Mexico City and Maximilian was executed.

As the 1871 election neared, political leaders cast their net for someone to replace the aging Juárez. Attention shifted to one of his most successful generals, **Porfirio Díaz** (1830–1915), whose campaign for the presidency was based on the idea that no president should be allowed to run for reelection. When no one won a majority of the votes, the nation turned to Juárez yet again. His death the next year touched off more violence that culminated in a coup by Díaz in 1876.

Thus began the longest period of dictatorial rule in Mexican history, which, ironically, was led by the very man who had introduced the principle of non-reelection to political life. To his credit, Díaz brought more than thirty years of stability after a half-century of tumult. With it came considerable foreign investment and the first steps in the development of a modern economic infrastructure. Thousands of miles of railroads were built, as were oil refineries, sugar mills, and electricity-generating facilities. Nevertheless, growth came with a price. Order in the countryside was maintained by the ruthless mercenary *rurales*. Perhaps as many as five million peasants were forced back into servitude on the *haciendas*, many of which were bought by foreigners.

The Revolution

By the early 1900s, Diaz's rule had touched off the same kind of broad-based opposition that had toppled earlier strongmen. At first, the revolution did not seem all that different from the previous upheavals. However, by the second decade of the new century it had sunk deeper roots in Mexican society and provoked an unusually fierce response from Diaz and his supporters.

Peasant bands led by the legendary Emiliano Zapata (1879–1919) and Pancho Villa (1878–1923) took up arms in the countryside. In the cities, the ever more frustrated liberals found a rallying point in the meek Francisco Madero, who wrote *The Presidential Succession of 1910* in which he pointedly used Díaz's own theme of non-reelection against the aging dictator. Meanwhile, the new labor movement organized a series of crippling and often violent strikes in the mines and mills.

Tensions came to a head with the 1910 presidential election. Madero was the nominee of the Anti-Reelectionist Party which he had helped form. Toward the end of the campaign, however, Madero was arrested on trumped-up sedition charges. Díaz was declared the winner despite evidence of widespread fraud.

Right after the election, Madero's family bribed the government to secure his release on the condition that he would stay out of Mexico City. He took to the countryside and drew the support of the United States and most populist leaders, including Zapata and Villa. In early 1911, forces loyal to him took up arms, met surprisingly little resistance from the federal army, and negotiated an agreement through which Díaz would resign in favor of Madero.

The revolution, however, was far from over. Many populists stopped supporting him and resumed fighting him within a matter of weeks and took up arms again only two and a half weeks after the new president was inaugurated.

In 1913, pitched battles erupted. After his initial military leader was wounded, Madero appointed the untrustworthy General Victoriano Huerta as his new commander-in-chief. Within ten days, Huerta had defeated both Díaz and Madero. Madero was arrested on February 18, resigned the next day, and was shot three days later. Huerta, too, was not to survive. A number of regional leaders, including Venustiano Carranza, refused to accept his presidency and joined a rebellion led by Zapata and Villa.

While all this was happening, the Woodrow Wilson administration in Washington entered the fray. Worries about European influence on the Mexican oil industry led it to send an expeditionary force that occupied Veracruz for most of 1914. Between them, the U.S. invaders and Mexican rebels drove Huerta from office before the year was out, leaving behind yet another power vacuum. Marauding armies on all sides killed about 1.5 million people in a country that at the time had only 14 million inhabitants. In the end, Carranza and the so-called Constitutionalists, who had the support of most large landowners, were able to gain control of the army and then of the country.

By year's end, Carranza defeated both Villa and Zapata and occupied Mexico City, which prompted President Wilson to recognize his government. That fall, elections were held to choose a new constitutional assembly, which brought the bloodiest six years of the country's bloodiest century to an end.

Institutionalizing the Revolution

On several occasions in the course of this book, we have seen that new constitutions do not invariably lead to sweeping political change. That was definitely the case in Mexico. Given the instability and violence of its history in the century after 1810, no reasonable observer could assume that a new constitution alone would settle much of anything.

Surprisingly, the constitution of 1917 not only survived its crucial first few years but has structured Mexican political life ever since. None of the social, economic, or political problems have disappeared, but Mexico has largely been spared the widespread violence that characterized its first century of independence.

The new constitution drew heavily on the ineffective but popular one adopted in 1857. The president and most other officeholders were not allowed to run for reelection. The power of the church was sharply limited. Foreigners were barred from owning Mexican land or mineral resources. Articles 27 and 123 legalized the breakup of the largest haciendas, though not without compensation for their owners.

At first, there did not seem to be much of a chance that this constitution would be any more successful than earlier ones. Above and beyond the immediate difficulties that came with putting the new institutions in place, the new regime had to deal with lingering opposition from those who did not think the revolution had gone far enough in promoting social equality. To make matters more complicated, the Carranza government turned on its former allies who had turned into opponents, in particular by assassinating Zapata in 1919. His forces retaliated by killing President Carranza the following year.

He was succeeded by another general, Alvaro Obregón, who had risen to prominence by defeating Villa in 1915. He tried to "complete" the revolution by expanding public education and introducing land reform that gave ownership of about three million acres of land to the peasantry. After putting down a rebellion by Huerta's forces in 1923, Obregón turned power over to Plutarco Elías Calles when his term ended in 1924. Calles, in turn, attacked the church, provoking a right-wing and clerical counter-revolution from 1926 to 1929. Then the succession issue reared its ugly head once again. Obregón declared his candidacy for the presidency in 1928 in clear violation of the Constitution's non-reelection provision (Article 23). He won the almost certainly rigged election anyway, but he, too, was assassinated before he could be sworn in to start a second term.

For once, an assassination did not lead to a new outburst of violence. To make a long story short, having realized that presidential succession was not going to be an option, Calles and his supporters found another way to provide sorely needed but sorely lacking continuity: create a political party that could control who became the next president. The first convention of their National Revolutionary Party (PNR) was held in 1929, and after several name changes, it became the PRI in 1946.

The new leadership also put the brakes on social reform. The redistribution of land, in particular, ground to a halt even though Mexico still had the largest number of rich landowners in the world. In short, despite the revolution, most Mexicans still lived in misery, albeit less violent misery.

These were important years, nonetheless, precisely because Calles and his colleagues accomplished something that had eluded their predecessors. By regularizing and controlling the transfer of power from one president to the next, they were able to extend their control over the entire state. The single party controlled selection not just of the president but of all political office holders.

Cárdenas and His Legacy

The Great Depression that began with the U.S. stock market crash in October 1929 hit Mexico hard and gave rise to a new populist protest and then what turned out to be a final period of left-leaning reform. Disgruntled party leaders convinced Calles (who remained the behind-the-scenes kingmaker) not to select another conservative to run for president in 1934 but to turn instead to the populist Indian and minister of war **Lázaro Cárdenas** (1895–1970).

Cárdenas had gained experience in reaching out to the masses when he was governor of Michoacán in the 1920s. He drew heavily on populist themes in blaming Mexico's problems on capitalism at home and abroad. In this, he was not terribly different from many of his contemporaries. Unlike them, however, he was able to translate the rhetoric into concrete accomplishments. About fifteen thousand villages and a quarter of the population benefited from agricultural reform in which roughly half the cropland was taken from the *haciendados* and given not to individual peasants but to collective or cooperative farms known as *ejidos*.

Cárdenas is best known for nationalizing the oil industry. Mexico produced about a quarter of the world's oil in the 1920s, most of which was controlled by foreign firms. In 1938, Mexico took over the oil wells and refineries, placing them under the control of a state-owned firm, **PEMEX**. In addition, it became illegal for foreigners to own rights to most natural resources and, even, most forms of real estate. Although not the only firm to be nationalized, PEMEX was the key to the Cárdenas-era reforms. Until the 1950s, about three quarters of the oil was sold to businesses at subsidized prices, which helped make rapid industrialization and economic growth possible.

Cárdenas was neither a radical nor a revolutionary. However, his presidency was not all that democratic either. The inspiration for his policies did not come as a result of pressures from below. Potential opponents, including former president Calles, were exiled to the United States. Moreover, it was during the Cárdenas presidency that the party established an official trade union, the **Confederation of Mexican Workers (CTM)**, and two peasant organizations, which became the main cogs in the PRI's corporatist machine.

Problems mounted during the second half of his presidency. The nationalizations cost the government support from Britain and the United States, among other countries. Most ominously of all, the reforms provoked enough opposition that there was talk of another armed uprising. Perhaps as a result, Cárdenas slowed down the pace of reform and turned his attention to building the party and planning for his own succession, choosing the moderate Catholic minister of war Manuel Avila Camacho instead of another reformer. Unlike many of his predecessors, Cárdenas withdrew from politics after he left office, thereby starting a practice that all subsequent Mexican presidents have followed.

Cárdenas's reforms were not an unqualified success even by his own standards. Land redistribution did little to eliminate poverty or inequality. The *haciendados*, for instance, were able to use loopholes in the law to hold on to most of the productive land. Still, considerable progress was made toward some of the revolution's goals, and Cárdenas richly deserves his reputation as one of the most revered leaders in Mexican history.

An Institutional Revolutionary Party

Most analysts argue that Cárdenas's retirement marked the end of the revolutionary period in Mexican history and set the stage for what political scientists call the **pendulum effect**. Even though the PRI was the only party that mattered and always had its own left and right wings, an unwritten rule eased the transfer of power between the two factions most often as the result of who was chosen to be the next president.

The key to this process is what Fox's first foreign minister and political scientist, Jorge Castañeda, calls the "peaceful and well-choreographed transfer of power" through which the revolution was institutionalized.[3] Between 1940 and 2000, Mexico has had ten presidents (see Table 15.2). The first two, Manuel Avila Camacho and Miguel Alemán, were far more conservative than Cárdenas. Alemán, in particular, shifted away from Cárdenas's policies and leadership style. Placing land reform on the back burner, he pursued rapid industrialization, assuming that it would eventually provide a better standard of living for all Mexicans through what is known as trickle-down economics. The Alemánista model was not based on market forces. Rather, his approach stressed state ownership of a few key industries such as PEMEX and substantial state control over the private sector, which was largely controlled by the PRI.

He was followed by the rather bland Adolfo Ruiz Cortines, who said he wanted to strike a balance between the Cárdenistas and Alemánistas but is often called the Mexican Eisenhower because so little happened during his administration. Then, in 1958, the pendulum swung marginally leftward with the next three presidents, Adolfo López Mateos, Gustavo Díaz Ordaz, and Luis Echeverría. All three stuck with the Alemánista approach to economic development. Even more important for our purposes, each was willing to repress groups that raised objections to PRI rule, including the bloody crackdown on student demonstrators in 1968.

[3]Jorge Castañeda, *Perpetuating Power: How Mexican Presidents Were Chosen* (New York: Free Press, 2000), xi.

TABLE 15.2 Presidents of Mexico

NAME	START OF TERM
Venustiano Carranza	1917
Adolfo de la Huerta	1920
Alvaro Obregón	1920
Plutarco Elías Calles	1924
Emilio Portes Gil	1928
Pascual Ortiz Rubio	1930
Abelardo Rodríguez	1932
Lázaro Cárdenas	1934
Manuel Avila Camacho	1940
Miguel Alemán	1946
Adolfo Ruiz Cortines	1952
Adolfo López Mateos	1958
Gustavo Díaz Ordaz	1964
Luis Echeverría	1970
Jose López Portillo	1976
Miguel de la Madrid	1982
Carlos Salinas de Gortari	1988
Ernesto Zedillo	1994
Vicente Fox	2000
Felipe Calderón	2006
Enrique Peña Nieto	2012

© Cengage Learning 2015

As was the case in most of the world, 1968 was a year of turmoil in Mexico. Although many of the young people who took part in the demonstrations that year returned to the PRI fold as adults, the existence of widespread disillusionment with the party could no longer be denied.

At the same time, evidence of chronic economic problems surfaced. Growth slowed, debt accumulated, and the peso had to be devalued. Echeverría's successor, Jose López Portillo, was able to stabilize the economy for most of his administration.

But then the Alemánista model collapsed toward the end of the López Portillo presidency. Because of the steep drop in oil prices, Mexican debt skyrocketed from not quite $49 billion in 1980 to over $72 billion the following year. The government had to cut its budget and the subsidies it provided to industry and consumers alike. Austerity measures led to sharp conflict over wages and prices as government, business, and labor all found themselves strapped. The flight of capital out of the country accelerated. Rumors about corruption began to implicate the president's office.

The government had no choice but to turn to the International Monetary Fund (IMF) and private banks for help. The conditions they attached to their eight-billion-dollar loans included putting pressure on the Mexican government to begin shifting away from its state-dominated approach and moving toward economic development.

As it had done so many times in the past, the PRI followed the shifting political and economic winds and, in 1982, nominated a new kind of presidential candidate, **Miguel de la Madrid** (1934–) who led the party—and therefore the country—in a new direction. Before he became the candidate, most prominent PRI politicians had built their careers in the military, labor, or the interior ministry. De la Madrid represented a new generation of politicians, dubbed the *tecnicos*, most of whom had studied at prestigious American universities and had established their careers in one of the economic ministries.

The new president spoke of "moral renovation," democratic reform, and a more market-based economy, but he was only able to make progress in the latter. Foreign investment was encouraged. Public enterprises were sold, especially those that were losing money. Public subsidies were cut. Thousands of bureaucrats were fired. Unfortunately, because interest rates remained high and the price of oil low, very little economic growth occurred, especially after the middle of his term.

Midterm congressional and state elections showed that the PRI was losing its grip. The conservative, business-oriented PAN grew, won some local elections, and probably captured two governorships that the PRI managed to hold onto through fraud.

Nonetheless, his administration continued to pay lip service to democratic and economic reform with the selection of another young *tecnico*, **Carlos Salinas de Gortari** (1948–), as its presidential candidate for the 1988 election, which he won only through fraud. Salinas continued the generational change begun under de la Madrid. Eight of his twenty-two cabinet secretaries, for instance, had advanced degrees in economics or management and were in their early forties or younger, earning them the nickname "smurfs" to contrast them with the older "dinosaurs." The new market-oriented policies de la Madrid and Salinas so enthusiastically endorsed were as far removed as one could get from the egalitarian ideals of the revolution or of the Cárdenas years. So, too, were the corruption and repression that some observers believe included the use of torture and occasional killings by the authorities.

The Salinas administration was able to keep a lid on the most serious problems. However, his retirement opened the proverbial floodgates.

Ernesto Zedillo (1951–) almost certainly won the 1994 presidential election legitimately. As soon as he took office, however, he was greeted by another financial crisis that required even more foreign loans. Soon, scandals reached the top ranks of the party, including the Salinas family. His government's popularity and that of the PRI plummeted.

The most important event demonstrating that Mexico was nearing the end of a political era came with the 1997 congressional election. The PRI only won 38 percent of the vote and 48 percent of the seats. Cuauhtémoc Cárdenas (1934–) of the Party of the Democratic Revolution (PRD) was elected mayor of Mexico City in the first election for that post.

The End of the PRI(?)

By 2000, electoral reforms (to be discussed in the section on political parties) had progressed too far for the PRI to blatantly steal another election. Not surprisingly, the Fox presidency began with tremendous expectations about a new, more democratic, and more capitalistic Mexico.

For good or ill, most of those expectations were not met. The fact that Fox and Calderón never had a majority left them dependent on cooperation from the PRI or PDR, which rarely materialized. Then, at about the time that Calderón assumed the presidency, the drug war escalated, further sapping his administration of the momentum it could have used to add to the reforms initiated under Fox.

Therefore, it came as no surprise that Peña began the 2012 campaign with a huge lead which he never relinquished. The title of this section ends with a question mark for a good reason and not simply because Peña had only been in office for a few months when these lines were written. The question mark is not there because I expect the PRI to disappear; its success in 2012 suggests that that is not going to happen any time soon. However, the PRI's hegemony is almost certainly a thing of the past. As we will see in the rest of this chapter, Mexico may be a far cry from being a democracy, but it does seem that the alternation of power between the PRI and the opposition will become a regular phenomenon, if not the norm.

Political Culture in Mexico

Mexico has an important place in the history of scholarship on political culture, because it was the only Southern country included in Gabriel Almond and Sidney Verba's pathbreaking *Civic Culture*. Since then, unfortunately, the study of Mexican political culture has not received anywhere near the attention it deserves, because analyses based on individual attitudes about authority and the regime do not readily lend themselves to some of the most important themes in Mexican culture that emerge more readily from anthropological field work. Despite the gaps in our database, it is hard to deny the importance of the values that follow especially in keeping the PRI in power

even if some of the social and economic changes of the last forty years have eroded some of them.

Cultural Norms

In so doing, it makes sense to focus on the following six values, knowing that none is held by all Mexicans and that political scientists disagree about the importance of all of them.

First, in stark contrast to Nigeria, almost all Mexicans feel a strong sense of national identity. There is a common language and history from which only a few non-Spanish-speaking people who are descended from the indigenous population are excluded. And, even they share a common religion that is a powerful unifying force despite the anticlericalism of many Mexican regimes. This national identity rests, too, on what some scholars have more speculatively seen as the blending of Spanish and Aztec cultures starting in the sixteenth century.

Second, in many, often-surprising respects, most Mexicans believe that the regime is legitimate. If nothing else, the revolution remains a source of pride no matter how most Mexicans feel about the way the PRI ruled in its name. Populist revolutionary figures like Hidalgo, Juárez, Zapata, Villa, and Cárdenas are still widely viewed as heroes. Before 2000, the term *revolution* was used to describe almost anything held in high esteem, and the PRI tried to cloak most of what it did in revolutionary symbolism. Nationally approved textbooks had positive passages about the Soviet Union and Cuba, not because the PRI was in any way Marxist but because their revolutions helped legitimize Mexico's own revolutionary past.

Third, although anthropologists warn us not to overstate their importance, there have been trends toward and toleration of authoritarian leadership throughout Mexican history. Its frequent turns to charismatic and, according to some, even messianic leaders has at the very least reinforced those broader cultural traditions. Undoubtedly, all this made it easier for the PRI to build support for a strong presidency that, though shorn of the messianic, repressive, and even charismatic aspects, is highly reminiscent of those leadership styles from its past.

Fourth, many observers doubt how strongly Mexicans support democracy. The World Values Survey, which tracks people's commitment to democracy and other beliefs around the world, suggests that Mexicans tend to have less respect for either democracy or human rights than people in all major parts of the world except for the post-communist societies (see Table 15.3).

A more recent but less globally comprehensive study found that 49 percent of Mexicans preferred democracies over all other forms of government. That figure left Mexico

TABLE 15.3 Satisfaction with Democracy and Respect for Human Rights*

COUNTRY/ REGION	SATISFACTION WITH DEMOCRACY	RESPECT FOR HUMAN RIGHTS
Mexico	37	43
Advanced democracies	63	74
Latin America and the Caribbean	53	41
Africa	50	54
East Asia	45	59
Post-communist	35	45

*Percentage saying they were very or somewhat satisfied with democracy, and human rights matters a lot or some.

Sources: Adapted from Alejandro Moreno and Patricia Mendez, "Attitudes toward Democracy: Mexico in Comparative Perspective." *International Journal of Comparative Sociology* 29 (December 2002), 350–369.

Comparative Emphasis: Identity

Identity is one of the most important but least researched aspects of Mexican politics.

Identity issues have been at the heart of the most serious uprisings there since the protests of 1968—the movements eddying around the Zapatista uprising that began in 1993. There is little doubt, too, that people with dark skin color and who are not highly integrated into Spanish culture are discriminated against.

However, identity does not define Mexican political life to the extent that it does in India, let alone Nigeria. Despite the publicity that the Zapatistas got and the fears they provoked, there seems to be next to no chance that disputes over identity could destroy either the country or the regime in the foreseeable future. ∎

in sixteenth place among the twenty countries included in the 2010 Latinobarometro survey. The pollsters also created an overall index of support for democracy on which Mexico came in eighteenth. Perhaps more worrisome is that support for democracy and democratization had actually declined in the decade the PAN had been in office.

Reinforcing those potentially anti-democratic sentiments are Mexico's amazingly durable **patron-client relations**, or *camarillas*. The PRI in particular drew heavily on networks that bound the party elite to vote-mobilizing and patronage-dispensing organizations all around the country. As we will see in the next section, the influence of the *camarillas* has eroded, taking with it much of the support for the PRI.

Fifth, Mexicans' deeply ambivalent feelings about the United States are powerful and long-lasting enough that they should be included as part of its culture. We will wait to discuss them in depth until the section on U.S.-Mexican relations toward the end of the chapter. For now, simply note that, on the one hand, most Mexicans are drawn to things American ranging from their love of American values to their love of baseball. On the other hand—and not surprisingly—most Mexicans resent what they see as American interference from the days of Poinsett on.

Sixth, along with most of Latin America, Mexico is also known for male dominance in all areas of life, not just politics. Historians debate why this exists. Some cite the Spanish *conquistadors*, and others stress aspects of precolonial social structures. Whatever the cause, women have historically played a relatively minor role in Mexican politics—they only got the right to vote in federal elections in 1953—which many observers are convinced is a sign of how strong values associated with machismo still are.

But as is so often the case with stereotypes, the reality is much more complicated. As Mexico urbanizes and

women become better educated and enter the formal or wage-based workforce (they currently make up only one-third of it), more and more women are beginning to reject the macho side of Mexican culture and to demand a more equal role in social, economic, and cultural as well as political life.

Subcultures

In addition to these general trends, we should also at least briefly mention four distinct Mexican political subcultures. So little research has been done on them in recent decades that we have to use dated language in describing them.

A handful of people—certainly less than 10 percent of the total population—are what Almond and Verba called parochials. Most of them live in the countryside, do not speak Spanish well, are not integrated into the dominant national culture, and have not traditionally been active in politics. However, small groups of them have been involved in on-again/off-again uprisings in such poor states as Chiapas and Guerrero.

Second, impressionistic evidence suggests that the biggest bloc of Mexicans are what they called "subjects." That is, they are reasonably aware of what the government is doing, but they are not directly engaged in trying to influence what it does. Instead, they tend to tolerate the system and assume that there is little they can do to change what they take to be a powerful, corrupt, or evil government. In one observer's words, they are "stoically fatalistic." They are disproportionately older, poorly educated, lower class, and female.

Third, there are also quite a few people who clearly supported the PRI and the system as a whole for the same reason that there were comparable people in Brezhnev's Soviet Union. Some Mexicans undoubtedly still believe in the revolution and the party's commitment to carrying out its ideals. But they are few and far between. Rather, the PRI's supporters tend to be people who were most fully tied into (and benefited from) the PRI-based patron-client networks which, as we will see in the next section, blanketed much of Mexican society.

Finally, even before 2000, there were clear signs that an overtly anti-PRI subculture was growing. The regime always had its critics. Although very few people were willing to take up arms against it, anti-PRI opposition grew from the 1960s onward and hastened its defeat. Although this segment of Mexican society continues to grow (and the others shrink) as a result of social, economic, and political change, it is hard to tell how this final subculture will evolve. If the PRI becomes a party much like the one it was before 2000, this group could continue to grow. By that same token, if the new PRI government turns out to be no more effective than the PAN administrations it replaced, some in this group of voters could turn against the entire regime.

Political Participation

Democratic Rights, Sort Of

A generation ago, the focus in this part of the chapter would have been on the PRI's ability to manipulate the way the public participated in political life. Then, as now, there were few legal restrictions on what people could do. There was little or no interference with an individual's ability to exercise a religion, travel, own property, or choose a school for his or her children. There was also open and heated debate in the press and the legislature on almost every significant issue.

At the time, political scientists often called Mexico only "semi-democratic" because the PRI routinely violated democratic principles. Elections were always officially competitive. However, everything from the PRI's willingness to buy votes to its stuffing of ballot boxes made it impossible to think of Mexico as anything like the kind of democracy we see in a country like India, let alone the countries discussed in Part 2 (www.pri.org.mx).

The right to protest was all too often honored in the breach. Strikes by railroad engineers in the 1950s and by telephone workers in the 1970s were forcibly suppressed. The government expelled peasants from land they had occupied. Most notoriously, government forces killed at least three hundred students in the so-called Tlatelolco massacre of 1968. During the infamous "battle of the streets" in 1980, Mexico City police officials "convinced" dissidents that their demonstrations clogged traffic and posed a danger to public safety, and so had to be stopped even though everyone understood that this ruse was nothing more than a threat from a government that was fully prepared to take more drastic actions. Some even claim that PRI members were responsible for the assassination of their own candidate during the early stages of the 1994 presidential election.

In comparative terms, however, the Mexican regime was never as repressive as the ones in China or Iran today. Instead, the PRI was able to stay in power by turning its clientelistic networks into an umbrella organization that shaped what most people did politically most of the time. It usually did not have to rely on force to keep the opposition at bay and out of office by drawing on its exceptional skills at rigging elections.

In the end, it was this disconnect between the relative freedom of individual expression and the sharply limited opportunities that led political scientists to scoff at claims that Mexico was democratic. To be sure, civil society has grown considerably since protest movements that were put down from the 1960s through the 1980s. And, the PRI did have to acquiesce to reforms that made elections fairer and vote counts more honest and transparent.

However, focusing on the "new Mexico" now puts the empirical horse before the analytical cart. In other words, were we to do so, you would not have any kind of context in which to make sense of the changes that have swept politics twice so far in this century.

The PRI's Hold on Power

Prior to 1988, the PRI never won less than 72 percent of the reported presidential vote or less than 65 percent of that for the Chamber of Deputies. Through the 1985 elections, it never lost a governorship or failed to win all but a single Senate seat. Even after its support began to erode, it was still able to maintain control of more than 95 percent of the country's two thousand municipalities.

The PRI looked like a "normal" political party in many ways. It had a formal institutional structure and regular meetings at which national issues were debated. That said, it never was a classical democratic party whose main goal is to build support at the polls around a reasonably coherent set of political values (see Tables 15.4 and 15.5).

Comparative Emphasis: Democratization

Under the PRI, Mexico had what some political scientists call a "semiauthoritarian state" that had the trappings of democracy, including competitive elections and constitutional guarantees of basic civil liberties. In practice, access to power was highly limited because power itself was monopolized by the self-perpetuating oligarchy atop the PRI. There were concerns, too, about how much those civil liberties were honored, especially with the upsurge in crime and corruption involving the police in recent years.

As a result, the 2000 election that swept the PRI from power for the first time in three quarters of a century marked a sea of change in Mexican politics. However, it will take years of expanding democratic practices before we can have any real assurance that Mexico has become democratic with any degree of certainty. ■

TABLE 15.5 Mexican Chamber of Deputies Election Results, 1976–2012: Main Parties Only

YEAR	PRI	PAN	PRD AND ITS PREDECESSORS
1976	85.2 (%)	8.9	–
1979	74.2	11.4	5.3
1982	69.3	17.5	4.4
1985	68.2	16.3	3.4
1988	50.4	18.0	4.5
1991	61.4	17.7	8.3
1994	50.3	26.8	16.7
1997	38.0	25.8	25.0
2000	36.9	36.9	18.7
2003	48.0	23.1	17.6
2006	28.2	33.4	29.0
2009	39.3	28.7	12.9
2012	31.2	25.9	18.5

© Cengage Learning 2015

The party's base of support was rooted in Mexico's version of **corporatism** which itself was based on the *camarillas*. In Germany, we saw that corporatism was used to smooth economic policy making. In Mexico, the PRI used it, instead, to secure its control.

Recall that an official trade union and two peasant organizations were created by the Cárdenas administration. Afterwards, others were formed for railroad, electrical, and telecommunications workers. Eventually, they grew to the point that they incorporated almost every profession and played an important role in solidifying PRI support in three main ways.

First, some theorists think that the tangible benefits they bestowed on millions of voters did more to tie them to the regime than the values we normally think of as underlying political legitimacy. For example, more than two million families benefited from land redistribution during the 1950s alone. Government-sponsored health care programs were administered through these organizations. Photographers could buy inexpensive film only through their professional—and PRI-controlled—association. The bottom line was simple. The PRI made certain that people remembered who was responsible for providing such benefits.

Second, by tying poor and powerless Mexicans to the regime, the PRI was able to reduce the amount and severity of the protest it might otherwise have faced. Put simply, these organizations provided another example of the "causal arrow" running "downward" from state to society.

Third, these organizations gave the PRI a pool from which to recruit grassroots leaders. This, in turn, meant that workers or peasants who saw themselves as potential leaders built their careers more by being part of the PRI machine than by being advocates for those they supposedly represented.

Instead, the traditional PRI was an elaborate network of *camarillas* and had as many as ten million members. These patrons and their clients were drawn to politics less by their ideological beliefs than by their desire for power and, sometimes, wealth.

The Machine

At the grassroots level, the PRI's organizers rarely talked about pressing national issues. Votes were won—or manufactured—in ways reminiscent of the American urban political machines of the early twentieth century. Votes were often bought outright or support obtained in exchange for benefits offered to a given neighborhood, village, or social group.

TABLE 15.4 Mexican Presidential Election Results, 1988–2012: Main Candidates Only (in percent)

YEAR	PRI	PAN	PRD
1988	50.7	16.8	31.1
1994	48.7	25.9	16.6
2000	36.1	42.5	16.6
2006	22.7	36.7	36.1
2012	38.2	25.4	31.6

© Cengage Learning 2015

That said, the PRI campaigns before 2000 were not merely pork barrel politics in action. The PRI also used them to legitimize its rule by building broader awareness and support in ways the opposition parties could not match. In 1982, de la Madrid made nearly two thousand campaign appearances. PRI symbols were everywhere—on posters, walls, T-shirts, and plastic shopping bags. Party leaders in Oaxaca gave prizes to workers who did the most to make the party known.

The PRI's hold on these organizations and their voters did erode. In the late 1980s, in particular, the CTM called strikes at some of the *maquiladora* factories, apparently against government wishes. More important, the PRI found it harder to incorporate well-educated urban voters into its networks.

Fraud

The PRI probably would have won most elections it contested had they been conducted honestly. The more important point here is the fact that it was also able to win even when it stood a reasonable chance of losing. Because the party also controlled the **Federal Election Commission (CFE)**, which was responsible for counting and validating election returns, it could manipulate the results. Polling places were moved after they opened. Mysteriously, only likely PRI voters knew where they had gone. Some people voted more than once, and PRI supporters stuffed the ballot box with fistfuls of premarked votes. The vote count often bore little or no resemblance to the actual tally. Once the votes were in, *alquimia electoral*—literally, **electoral alchemy**—took place. A few days later, the CFE would report the official results, which were widely viewed as fraudulent. As one PRI governor put it, "If it is fraud, it is patriotic fraud."

Electoral fraud became a serious issue in 1988 when, it is all but universally assumed, the PRI stole the presidential election. After the 1989 municipal elections, opposition groups seized over a hundred town halls to protest alleged electoral fraud. At least twenty protesters were killed. After that, elections were conducted more honestly, but the corruption did not disappear. In the months before the 1991 elections, about 8 percent of the registered voters discovered that the CFE "lost" their enrollment cards. In the state of Guanajuato, Fox, then the PAN's gubernatorial candidate, claimed that more PRI votes were cast than there were registered voters at several hundred polling stations. He also alleged that voting credentials were withheld from his supporters and used by others to cast multiple ballots for his PRI opponent. In this case, the corruption was so blatant that the PRI candidate had to step aside and cede the state to the opposition. Fully 5 percent of the people who took part in the first-ever primary election to choose the PRI's candidate for the 2000 presidential campaign *admitted* that they had been paid for their votes. Loyal and effective party workers were rewarded with jobs that are abundantly available given the rules on non-reelection.

Reform and Defeat

Even before its partial defeat in 1997, the PRI had weakened considerably. In addition to the social changes discussed above, the PRI's growing weakness was a by-product of changes in the electoral system that made voting more honest, gave opposition parties more seats, and offered people more of an incentive to vote for them. In all, the PRI went from winning 85 percent of the vote in the Chamber of Deputies election in 1976 to not even half that in 2009.

Over the years, the PRI had to accept changes in the way elections were run that helped make the results more transparent and the results harder to fix. Like Germany, Mexico now uses an electoral law that combines single-member districts and proportional representation for the Chamber of Deputies. Out of a total of five hundred seats, three hundred are elected from single-member districts. The rest are drawn from party lists using a complex formula that brings each party's total representation closer to its share of the vote.

Prior to 1997, no opposition party ever won more than nine single-member districts, which meant that the proportional side of the voting had no practical impact because the PRI had already won an overwhelming majority before the winners of those two hundred seats were determined. By the mid-1990s, the PRI had been forced to accept sweeping reforms that made the 1997 elections by far the most honest since the revolution. A truly independent **Federal Electoral Institute (IFE)** was created to supervise the balloting. Voters were issued registration cards with their photographs on them. Workers at polling places were given at least rudimentary training, and independent observers monitored the voting at most of them. Most important, the IFE developed a mechanism for reporting the vote tallies the same night as the election, leaving the ruling party with little time to engage in electoral shenanigans.

There are still charges of fraud during each election campaign. In fact, complaints about vote rigging continued at least until 2006 when Lopez-Obrador claimed that that year's presidential election was stolen (see the section on the PRD).

However, electoral reform combined with the social and economic problems facing the country to launch the most dramatic changes in Mexican electoral history. In 1997, the PRI lost its majority in the Chamber of Deputies.

The first election of the twenty-first century finally saw the PRI suffer a complete loss. The campaign went badly for the PRI from the beginning. The outgoing president, Zedillo, did not handpick his successor, although it was fairly clear that he supported Francisco Labastida, who ultimately won the nomination. Labastida turned out to be a lackluster candidate who had to support an administration that had had little success in dealing with Mexico's economic difficulties or with the rebellion in Chiapas. As we will see, the PRI also faced a formidable opponent in Fox, who had been on the political scene for more than a decade. Although many observers called Fox's victory an upset, it probably was not, because the polls showed that voters were looking for change.

The New PRI?

By early 2002, the PRI had begun something of a political comeback that had more to do with the PAN's inability to govern effectively than it did with the PRI's own rejuvenation. It staged a hotly contested election for its new leader in which Roberto Madrazo edged out Beatriz Paredes in a ballot that was open to all voters, irrespective of party. After forming broader alliances than ever before, the PRI won close to half of the vote in the 2003 election for the Chamber of Deputies and continued to do well in state elections through 2004. But, then, the bottom fell out for the PRI, culminating in Madrazo's disastrous campaign in 2006.

That said, the legislative elections in 2009 saw a surprising recovery by the PRI. It became the largest party in Congress by far, which allowed it to block most of Calderón's legislation.

Its 2012 victory soon became almost a foregone conclusion. As suggested in the introduction to this chapter, Peña Nieto turned out to be a very strong candidate. Even though he comes from a family that has produced many senior PRI leaders, he cut a more honest, youthful, and reformist image than his main competitors or his own PRI predecessors.

There are signs that internal changes within the PRI are not purely superficial. Even before the campaign, the leadership signaled that it was willing to reconsider some of its traditional clientelistic ties with the trade unions. Before the old parliament adjourned, it announced support for legislation that would have stripped the CTM of its collective bargaining and other rights. Despite the close ties some CTM leaders have to the PRI, the union rejected the bill out of hand. Protests by the unions and their supporters blocked the proposed legislation in April 2011 because it probably would have made the unions weaker than they ever had been since they were legalized in 1917.

The PRI's 2012 presidential choice and victory may be nothing more than one of its periodic shifts in direction in response to social changes much like the one that led to Cárdenas's ascendancy in the 1930s and that of the tecnicos in the 1980s. However, there is no reason to believe that Mexico will return to the times when a corrupt PRI dominated the entire political system.

The Other Parties

The PAN

Unlike the former Soviet Union, Mexico has always had more than one party. However, none of them had a realistic hope of unseating the PRI before 1988. In fact, some of the parties that claimed to be in the opposition were actually funded by the PRI (most likely including the PAN) in a peculiar attempt to give the outside world the impression that Mexico was a viable democracy.

By the mid-1980s, the PAN had grown to the point that it was one of two parties that could claim to be a viable candidate to win the presidency. It was formed in 1939. Most of its first generation of leaders were practicing Catholics and business executives for whom Cárdenas's reforms went too far. Its earliest support was concentrated in the north.

The PAN gradually built on its base and then received a boost of support from the Reagan administration, which had more than its share of doubts about what it thought was a left-leaning and financially irresponsible PRI. The bottom line, however, is that the PAN's support grew mostly because it was not the PRI (www.pan.org.mx).

The PAN's first real breakthrough came in the 1983 election when its candidate was elected governor of Baja California Norte. Its progress was blunted somewhat by

Comparative Emphasis: Conflict

Observers who call Mexico democratic often cite the relative lack of violent conflict to support their claims. It is true that, by the Global South's standards, Mexico has relatively little "outside-the-system" protest and little of the racial, linguistic, and ethnic strife that is so common in the Third World.

However, there are two countertrends. First, there has not been very much of it in part because the state has made it hard for potential opponents to organize, let alone express their discontent. Second, the amount of dissatisfaction with the PRI had been mounting for years, whether measured in the number of attacks by guerrillas in Chiapas or Guerrero or in the number of votes won by opposition parties. ■

the PRD's arrival on the scene (see the next section) and by the PRI's continued reliance on fraud.

The PAN kept building on its gains. It won a full quarter of the vote in 1994 and 1997, which set the stage for its breakthrough in 2000 and the election of Calderón six years later.

The PAN's growth had a lot to do with the personality of former President Fox. The six-foot, five-inch Fox is the most charismatic leader Mexico has had since Cárdenas. He had a broad appeal because he could present himself as an earthy farmer (he has been known to give the finger to PRI politicians) and a savvy business executive given his U.S. education and career at Coca-Cola. And in 2000, he decided to try to unify the opposition by appealing both to the Left and to traditionally conservative PAN supporters. He did this, for instance, by agreeing with Mexico's small Green Party to form the Alliance for Change and by associating himself with left-of-center intellectuals such as Jorge Castañeda and Adolfo Aguilar Zinser, who became his foreign minister and chief economic adviser, respectively. Electoral reforms in the 1990s also gave candidates ample public funds, which meant that the telegenic Fox had plenty of money to run Mexico's first "modern" campaign.

Fox swept to victory in 2000, riding a groundswell of support from people who told pollsters that their primary reason for voting was a desire for change. He did particularly well among middle-class voters, women, and others who are at the core of the growing civil society. Finally, he convinced about 30 percent of the people who had voted for Cárdenas in 1994 to switch, thereby eliminating the possibility that the PRI could sneak into power against a divided opposition.

As the 2006 presidential campaign opened, it seemed that the PAN would lose to the PRD or the PRI. It had done poorly in the 2003 legislative elections in part because of the gridlock in policy making to be discussed below. The PRD's candidate, **Andrés Manuel López Obrador**, began the race with a significant lead in the polls until Calderón nosed ahead in most surveys during the final few weeks of the campaign.

The election results were so close that both Calderón and López Obrador declared themselves the winner. Eventually Calderón was declared the victor, and despite months of protests, he eventually was able to take office. Unfortunately for the PAN, his government was not a popular success for reasons that will become clear in the public policy section below. As a result, its 2012 candidate, Josefina Vázquez Mota, faced an uphill battle that was not made any easier by the fact that she was the first woman to be nominated by a major political party. She came in a distant third, although the party won the second largest share of the votes in each house of the legislature. It remains to be seen whether the party can restore its lost luster.

PROFILES Vicente Fox Quesada

Vicente Fox's victory removed the PRI from office for the first time in seventy-one years. Born in 1942 to a wealthy farmer and a devout Catholic, Fox was educated at a Catholic university in Mexico City and then at Harvard. He returned home to work for Coca-Cola, helping the company beat out Pepsi for the number-one spot in the Mexican soft drink market. When he ran for president, he was divorced, but shortly after taking office he married his public relations advisor.

Fox is a political veteran. He was first elected to the Chamber of Deputies in 1988. He ran for governor of Guanajuato in 1991 and probably would have won had the votes been counted honestly. He did win the seat four years later and almost immediately began his campaign for the presidency.

Fox is both charismatic and controversial. Although he claims to admire "third way" politicians such as Bill Clinton and Tony Blair, Fox has strong right-wing roots. He also tries to strike an earthy, populist tone despite his family's wealth. He was also close to President George W. Bush. He came to Washington for a state visit on September 4, 2001. Immigration reform was on the agenda but never got anywhere after the attacks on New York and Washington a week later.

He rarely wears a suit, preferring blue jeans and a belt with a massive buckle bearing his name. He also does not shy away from controversial statements. During the campaign, he even made personal attacks on his opponents that would have been considered unacceptable in most democracies. ∎

Vicente Fox holding a press conference wearing traditional Indian clothing.

AP Photo/Victor Camacho

The PRD

In 1988, it looked as if the more serious challenge to the PRI's hegemony would come from a new and unlikely source—Cuauhtémoc Cárdenas, son of the last radical president, who had named him for the symbol of Aztec resistance to the Spanish conquest. The elder Cárdenas had criticized the PRI's conservative, antirevolutionary turn in diaries that were published after his death in 1970, which served to crystallize left-wing dissatisfaction with the government. Internal dissatisfaction intensified after de la Madrid introduced his liberal reforms in the 1980s, when the younger Cárdenas emerged as the leading advocate of the increasingly disgruntled Left.

Initially, they organized as a faction within the PRI. As soon as Carlos Salinas's nomination was announced, Cárdenas and labor leader Porfirio Muñoz Ledo left the PRI to form the PRD. Cárdenas then declared his presidential candidacy and stressed many of the same populist themes raised by his father nearly a half-century earlier.

The PRD did surprisingly well in 1988. Cárdenas "lost" only because of the most extensive voting fraud in Mexican history. Almost all outside observers were convinced that he won a plurality of the vote and that the PRI "manufactured" or "discovered" enough votes to deny him victory.

The PRD also came close to winning in 2006. In fact, its candidate, Andres Manuel López Obrador, has always claimed that he won in another stolen election, this time by the PAN. The official tally declared Calderón the winner by less than half a percentage point. López Obrador disputed the government's refusal to count 9 percent of the ballots, most of which the PRD's candidate claimed would have gone to him. Like Cárdenas, López Obrador did well among disaffected voters the PAN had little hope of reaching—the poor, intellectuals, and others who believe they have been ignored by the PRI.

It stumbled badly in 2009. Despite its reputation for honesty, the PRD was implicated in its share of scandals. One videotape shows many of its top leaders gambling at a high-stakes table in Las Vegas. A number of its officials (including Cuautemóc Cardenas's son) are alleged to have ties to the drug cartels. Several PRI activists infiltrated the party and ran under its banner that year. All in all, it lost about a third of its vote and came in a distant third. Many observers assumed its decline would continue in 2012 especially once it became clear that López Obrador planned to run again despite the fact that most pundits thought that his failure to concede six years earlier had undermined whatever sympathy voters had once felt for him.

Then during the campaign, the PRI adopted new welfare and social service programs in a clear attempt to eat away at some of the PRD's support. To the surprise of

A November 20, 2006, rally of political supporters of Andés Manuel López Obrador in Mexico City.

many, López Obrador came in a respectable second. His success, however, did not translate into votes or seats in the legislative election, and most observers think that the PRD is likely to remain a distant third at a time when the Left everywhere is losing support.

Toward a Three-Party System?

In this book, we have seen many kinds of party systems. The Mexican one is unique in that it now has three parties, each of which could conceivably win most elections but none of which can win a legislative majority on its own. This kind of outcome makes governing difficult for two reasons. First, it can easily lead to gridlock in policy making. Second, it encourages parties not to take risks or strong positions on controversial issues to the point that the first PAN government passed a constitutional amendment banning negative campaigning.

That is what President Peña Nieto has to look forward to at least until the mid-term legislative elections in 2015. The new president did cut a deal with the opposition known as the Pact for Mexico that so far has allowed him to begin overhaul education and law enforcement and even break up long-standing monopolies in telecommunications and oil exploration.

The PRI is also only eleven seats short of a majority in the Chamber of Deputies and four in the Senate. It is possible that the PRI will regain those seats and control both elected branches of government in the next national election. Still, all the signs point to a future in which an increasingly centrist PRI will have to fend off competition from its left and right from parties which, themselves, will find it difficult if not impossible to cooperate with each other enough to govern.

Civil Society

It is safer to predict that Mexico is unlikely to return to corporatist, *camarilla*-based PRI dominance despite its victory in 2012 because of the changes in Mexican society that have led to the emergence of a reasonably vibrant civil society. There are now dozens of human rights, environmental, labor, and other associations that one could mention as evidence of this trend. Given the macho aspect of Mexican culture, however, there probably is no better single example demonstrating how much the country is changing than its burgeoning women's movement.

The modern Mexican women's movement is new. In the 1960s and 1970s, it appealed almost exclusively to wealthy, educated women who had been influenced by feminists from the United States and Europe.

Since then, it has broadened its appeal considerably. It started with one of those "historical accidents," which so often play an important role in political change. In 1975, Mexico City hosted a United Nations–sponsored conference to kick off International Women's Year, itself the beginning of a decade-long effort. It was hard for either the foreign participants or Mexican women to ignore the inequalities between men and women in Mexico when such an event was taking place there.

The rather elitist women's movement began to give way to what has been called "popular feminism," which organizes poor and middle-class women in both the cities and the countryside. There is no single popular feminist movement. Rather, it is an informal collection of organizations that coalesce mostly around local and national issues, ranging from reproductive rights to the lack of safe, drinkable water or decent schools in small towns.

These organizations combined protests over the kinds of issues we see in feminist movements in most countries (e.g., abortion, violence against women, and unequal pay), with concerns for the poor in general. Meanwhile, the economic changes of the past generation have created more employment opportunities for women at all levels, from manual and clerical workers to corporate executives.

No one knows how strong these loosely organized movements are. Nonetheless, it does seem safe to assume that women's groups will grow dramatically as Mexico democratizes and economic developments further erode traditional social structures.

As strong as the women's movement has become, it should be noted that the PAN remains quite conservative on gender-related issues and opposes both legalized abortion and gay rights. Therefore, feminists are likely to shift their support ever more to the PRD whose legislative assembly passed a law in Mexico City in 2007 to permit abortion during the first twelve weeks of pregnancy.

The Mexican State

An examination of the Mexican state will help us revisit two of the most important themes raised throughout this book.

First, it provides us with one final example of the way that constitutional theory and political reality are so often at odds with each other. As the revolution was drawing to a close in 1917, the victors wrote a constitution that was supposedly based on the one used in the United States. Indeed, there are a fair number of parallels between the two—at least on paper. Like the United States, Mexico has a bicameral legislature. Both are federal systems in which state and national governments are supposed to share power. Both call for the clear separation of powers, so that the legislative, executive, and judicial branches of the national government can "check and balance" each other. In practice, the Mexican state has next to nothing in common with the American one (historicaltextarchive.com/sections.php?op=viewarticle&artid=93).

Second, we will see that much about the Mexican state is in flux and may be more susceptible to dramatic change in the next few years. Still, we will concentrate on the way the state operated under the PRI, because there have been no basic changes in state structures and procedures since 2000. Even if the two PAN presidents had wanted to do so, they could not count on enough votes in Congress to pass major constitutional amendments. There is little doubt that the government became more open under the PAN, but it remains to be seen if the likelihood of regular alternations in the partisan composition of the government will do anything to make the state either more efficient or more accountable. What's more, constitutional and other major reforms are for all intents and purposes off the table now that the PRI is back in office.

Comparative Emphasis: Women

Mexico's tiny feminist movement got a boost when the United Nations held its conference to start International Women's Year there in 1975. But it is safe to say that women are just now beginning to play a significant role in main-stream political life.

Thus, in 2012, the PAN's Josefina Vázquez Motato became the first woman to run for president with the support of a major political party. More generally, women are becoming more visible in political movements across the political spectrum.

Calderón had already named three women to key positions in his cabinet, including foreign relations, energy, and education. Some observers think that the central role of women is now so firmly established that the conservative Calderón's conservative wife, Margarita Zavala, does not bristle when she is called a feminist.

Plenty of discrimination remains. The business tycoon, Jorge Hank Rhon, once declared, without jeopardizing his career, that women were his favorite animal. A prominent woman doctor was offered a job at half the salary as the man she would replace even though the two had virtually identical resumes. Many businesses still have unwritten rules against hiring young married women out of fear that they will stop working in order to have children.

About the only feminist issue that reaches the front pages is abortion. In 2008, the Supreme Court ruled that the states should have decision-making authority on abortion policy. Most now permit abortion under some circumstances, but only Mexico City allows it "on demand." More important, just as is the case north of the border, very few states provide extensive abortion services. Also, few enforce the laws on their books. For good or ill, doctors who conduct safe but illegal abortions are rarely prosecuted.

Mexico City passed a law in 2009 permitting gay marriage and adoption. The next year, the Supreme Court ruled that all states had to enforce the law despite objections from Calderón and the Church. Other bills on civil unions are working their way through about 20 percent of the states. ■

Non-Reelection and Presidential Domination

As we have seen, no Mexican official has been allowed to run for reelection for more than a century, which Mexicans have used as a way of preventing any leader from amassing too much power. As Frank Brandenburg pithily put it, Mexico has been able to "avoid personal dictatorship by retiring their dictators every six years."[4]

As a result, an incoming president starts with a blank slate because he takes over a government that does not have any incumbents. All legislators and cabinet members are new to their jobs. The president also appoints people to all key bureaucratic and judicial positions because their office holders also normally resign at the start of each new presidential term. During the PRI years, almost all of them were also dependent on him for gaining the nomination for their positions in the first place. The way the PRI used the system to reward its friends and punish its enemies gave it a compliant Congress and state governments for almost all of its more than seventy years in office. But, as we will see in the rest of this section, this peculiar system also left Mexico with a weak state precisely because every six years the leadership had to rebuild almost everything from scratch.

The president probably is more powerful than his counterpart north of the border, however. Virtually all bills of any importance are drafted in the executive branch. He can issue decrees on a wide variety of subjects, including the way a law is implemented, the transfer of funds from one account to another, and even the authorization of expenditures above original appropriations.

But the president's real sources of power are informal.

Although there was considerable variation in the way PRI presidents led, they all followed a common pattern driven by the constraints of the single, six-year term. For all intents and purposes, the president's term began the day it became clear that he would be the PRI nominee. Because it did not have any impact on who ended up winning, the candidate used the election campaign to lay out his own agenda and style.

Upon taking office, the president enjoyed a period of consolidation that lasted as long as a year and a half, during which he put his own team in place. It was primarily in the next two years or so that the president could implement substantial new policies of his own. In the last two years, his attention had to turn to the succession, and even before the election occurred, power began to shift to the next president.

Even though the president was already a lame duck, he could still have an impact on the policy process after his retirement through the selection of his successor.

[4]Frank Brandenburg, *The Making of Modern Mexico* (Englewood Cliff s, NJ: Prentice-Hall, 1964), 141.

Until Zedillo's administration, the outgoing president chose the next PRI candidate from the cabinet secretaries in office during the middle of his *sexeño*. The president was thus drawn from a very small and narrow pool of candidates.

A little more than a year before the election, the party chair (himself a client of the president) released a short list of about a half dozen possible candidates to the press, beginning what was known as *el dezdado* or the "fingering" of the candidate. Supposedly, the list was the result of a wide consultation within the party, which rarely happened. The "fingered" candidates could then be subjected to broader scrutiny in the population as a whole. Within a few months, the president made his final choice known, even though he had probably made up his mind before the short list was made public and all the other potential candidates jumped on his bandwagon. Only then did the party hold a convention to officially nominate the president's choice. The president-designate then began his campaign by exercising the first of his many informal powers: determining who the party's candidates for the Chamber of Deputies and the Senate would be.

By the 1980s, most potential candidates were relatively young men who were sons of PRI politicians, Mexico City–based, American-educated, and part of the outgoing president's personal network of supporters. Salinas, for example, had been associated with de la Madrid since his student days, when he took a course from the future president.

This pattern was already eroding before the PRI lost in 2000. In March 1999, President Zedillo announced that he would not personally designate his successor. Instead, the PRI would hold an American-style campaign with debates among the contenders and then a primary election. Critics doubted Zedillo's sincerity and the openness of the primary process. However, all three major parties now have primaries for their nominations which are at least as hotly and openly contested as those in the United States.

Despite the institutional changes since the 1990s, the incoming president still has tremendous latitude, especially in placing people in jobs. The president directly appoints thousands of people to positions in the twenty-four cabinet-level departments and the hundreds of quasi-independent agencies and public corporations. Normally, only about 35 percent of those appointees have held high office in any prior administration, thereby providing the new president with an ample opportunity to assert his independence.

Research on changes on presidential appointments and control over what people in the United States would call the executive branch since 2000 has been sketchy at best. Nonetheless, all the signs suggest that the last three presidents have used the massive turnover in administrative and policy-making personnel to recast the governmental machine in their own light.

PROFILES
Enrique Peña Nieto

Enrique Peña Nieto became president of Mexico at the end of 2012, becoming the first PRI member to hold that office in twelve years.

In many ways, Peña is a product of the PRI machine. Although his parents were not all that politically active, he joined the party as an undergraduate along with many of his closest friends who did come from politically prominent families. Unlike most of the *tecnicos*, he completed all of his studies in Mexico other than a year in junior high school learning English in Maine. His early career resembled that of many PRI leaders before the emergence of the *tecnicos*, rising through the ranks as a state legislator and governor.

In others, he is atypical, especially because he is personable and telegenic. In other words, he seems to be the kind of leader the PRI will need in order to have a chance of winning in a more competitive electoral arena. ■

Presidents Pena Nieto and Obama.

The Cabinet, the Bureaucracy, and the Judiciary

The principle of non-reelection actually applies to senior appointed officials as well, most of whom resign their posts at the start of each new presidential term. That means that the president's power of appointment extends to the entire state and gives him tremendous leverage over the way policy is implemented as well as made.

Under the PRI, most important positions in the cabinet and bureaucracy were filled either from the new president's personal *camarilla* or from a small group of other politicians whom he trusted. Virtually every officeholder owed his or her job to someone higher up in the hierarchy and, thus, ultimately, to the president. Ambitious politicians enhanced their careers by exchanging favors with their patrons and clients, not by campaigning on their record or the issues (www.mexonline.com/mexagncy.htm).

The way the PRI used these powers did change over the years. At first, the PRI was little more than a loose coalition of revolutionary leaders held together by military officers turned politicians. Not surprisingly, the most important cabinet position and the source of future presidents was the minister of defense. As the regime became institutionalized, the center of gravity shifted to **Gobernación**, the ministry responsible for internal security and public administration. With the debt crisis and the emergence of other complex economic issues, the *tecnicos* came to dominate the PRI, and the various economic ministries became the key stepping-stone. But this should not obscure the basic point. The *tecnicos*, like everyone else, rose to prominence because of their personal connections in the shifting PRI constellation of patron-client relations.

As with the electoral system, presidential domination of the appointment process loosened. Fox's original cabinet included longtime members of the opposition, including some who were neither longtime PAN members nor part of Fox's personal entourage. Calderón's initial cabinet was made up mostly of pro-business economists and prominent PAN leaders, which made sense given the fact that, unlike Fox, he was a party insider.

Peña Nieto's cabinet even includes one member who served in the outgoing Calderón administration. However, in keeping with long-standing Mexican tradition, his two closest advisors got the most important jobs at *Gobernación* and the Ministry of Finance.

Mexico's peculiar system of personnel management has another worrisome feature. Its bureaucracy bears less resemblance to a classic civil service than any of the others considered in this book. Most Latin America countries have not historically had a strong, professional civil service that is recruited on the basis of merit, that willingly serves any government no matter what its ideology, and that provides career-long opportunities to the men and women who join it.

Mexico has never come close to that model, because the entire government bureaucracy, which employs about one out of every five Mexicans, was also part of the PRI machine. Individual civil servants tend to move from agency to agency with their bosses, who, in turn, move more frequently than politicians in other Latin American countries. As with the Congress, there is so much turnover that it is hard for anyone to develop the expertise that years of experience brings.

These bureaucratic weaknesses may not have been a serious problem when the demands on Mexican government were not very great. Now, however, they are a major contributor to Mexico's woes.

Presidents Fox and Calderón faced another constraint that limited what they could accomplish. Some of Fox's advisors wanted him to purge the civil service of PRI loyalists who did not share the new president's commitment to reform. However, the PAN had few experienced men and women to take their places in senior executive positions. Therefore, he opted to keep many senior civil servants, in essence choosing a hefty dose of corruption over inexperience.

His government did secure passage of a reform law that supposedly will professionalize the hiring and promotion of the civil service. Even under the best of circumstances, it will take a generation before the entire federal government is restructured. And early signs are that the Peña Nieto government has returned to the old system of appointing PRI cronies at least to the most important and visible jobs.

Mexico also has a Supreme Court that officially has the power of judicial review. But, unlike its counterpart in Washington, it almost never overruled an important government action or policy under the PRI. That was the case because even the judiciary is subject to presidential control. Judges are nominated by the president and must be approved by the Senate. They can serve one fifteen-year term, although many resign each time the presidency changes hands, giving the new chief executive yet another way to shape the state. The court has been somewhat more assertive and independent since the 1990s, including its decisions certifying that Calderón had won the disputed election in 2006.

Congress and the Legislative Process

As noted earlier, the constitution provides for a bicameral legislature. Members of the Chamber of Deputies are elected for three-year terms. Senate terms last six years, with half its members chosen every three years.

Although the Congress has to approve all legislation, it was little more than a rubber stamp under the PRI. There is no Mexican version of cabinet responsibility that obliged the PRI's members in the Chamber of Deputies and Senate to fall in line behind their president, but they consistently did so because of the way power politics worked.

The roots of congressional weakness lie in the same peculiar feature of Mexican presidential rule that has been at the heart of this section so far. Members of each house can serve only a single term. Therefore, it is impossible for them to develop the expertise or the seniority that makes U.S. congressional committee chairs, for instance, so important.

Even more important, PRI members of Congress were subservient to the president, who chose the party's slate of nominees. Ambitious politicians could only advance their careers by building personal connections with more influential power brokers, not by making one's own mark on legislation.

Before the PRI's partial defeat in 1997, all significant legislation was initiated by the president and passed the Congress as easily as in parliamentary systems. Thus, the PRI voted as a bloc to confirm the questionable results of the 1988 election. The next year, it again voted unanimously to endorse President Salinas's bill to privatize the banks.

The 1997 election did change things. Even though the PRI still held the presidency and a majority in the Senate, the PAN and the PRD held the balance of power in the Chamber. That left Mexico with a version of gridlock that students of the U.S. Congress would find familiar. Because no party has had a majority in either house since 2000, neither PAN president could get much of what he wanted enacted as legislation.

The parliamentary arithmetic is complicated by the fact that Mexico has little history of finding common ground on controversial issues. As far as relations with Congress were concerned, President Fox did allow congressional committees to gain a bit more autonomy, and party discipline was relaxed somewhat. But that did little to either provide legislators with the kind of expertise one finds in countries that have not adopted non-reelection or that have a more fully developed tradition of compromise decision making.

Federalism

Much the same can be said for state and local governments. Mexico is a federal country, officially known as the United Mexican States. The country is divided into thirty-one states plus the Federal District (Mexico City). The states, in turn, are subdivided into more than two thousand municipalities, which are more like American counties than cities. Each state has a governor and unicameral legislature. Each municipality has a mayor and municipal council.

In practice, the states and municipalities were all but powerless because the PRI controlled everything at that level as well. As late as 2000, the PAN and PRD only controlled 15 percent of the municipalities and a third of the governorships. Not only did the president select the PRI's candidates, but he could also remove governors or mayors from office. Again, as with the members of Congress, governors and mayors could build their careers only by strengthening their position in the PRI machine. In short, it did not pay to rock the party boat. In addition, every national ministry maintained a federal delegate in each state to deal with overlapping jurisdictions and to make certain that the president's preferences were carried out.

As we have seen, the PAN and PRD both rose to national prominence largely on the basis of footholds they established at the state and municipal levels. Along those same lines, Peña first gained national attention while he was governor of the State of Mexico, which surrounds Mexico City. His first cabinet also included several other former governors, who came from some of the most corrupt states that were still controlled by the PRI machine. In short, there is little reason to believe that subnational institutions will become significantly more important as long as the PRI remains in power.

Corruption

For what obvious reasons, there is no way to accurately measure corruption in Mexico—or any other country for that matter. All we know is that corruption is widespread and all but built into the system.

Corruption touches just about everyone and everything in Mexico. Almost all big business deals depend on connections, some of which are unethical if not illegal. The police and the military both have ties with the drug cartels. More often than not, the authorities turned a blind eye to the *coyotes* who smuggled immigrants into the United States. Transparency International estimates that Mexicans as a whole spend well over two billion dollars in bribes per year.

No party or politician appears to be corruption free. Calderón's administration was almost certainly the least corrupt in recent years if for no other reasons than the fact that he and his family were already extremely wealthy. However, just one of the scandals during his *sexeño* involved alleged bribes given by Americans to the chief operating officer of the state-controlled electrical power monopoly. Court documents unsealed in 2010 revealed that he had received a two-million-dollar yacht, a Ferrari, and almost two hundred thousand dollars to pay credit card bills.

Since 2000: Democracy Interrupted

Many observers thought that the 2000 election would lead to sweeping change in Mexican politics. For the most part, that hasn't happened. This chapter begins with a statement by Jo Tuckman who subtitles her book *Democracy Interrupted*, which is a fitting phrase to describe what has—and has not—changed since then.

To be sure, pressures to democratize Mexico continue to mount. However, a preliminary balance sheet of the two PAN administrations and of the first few months of the PRI's new one suggests that the term "interrupted" might be giving Mexico the benefit of the doubt, because the informal workings of Mexican politics have not disappeared. Indeed, they persist in ways that also serve as a good introduction to the country's policy dilemmas, which will be the focus of the rest of the chapter.

Critics argue that neither Fox nor Calderón was a particularly effective leader. Fox's supporters cite problems largely beyond his control, most notably the economic downturn that began just as he took office, the effects of the terrorism attacks on 9/11, and the renewed controversy over immigration in the United States. Calderón was also saddled with the violence surrounding the drug trade, which he almost certainly had nothing to do with starting.

Both of them led minority governments and thus needed the negotiating and bargaining skills an American president has to use in getting legislation through Congress. We should not be surprised that Fox and Calderón were not very good at that. Like everyone else in Mexican politics, they had had little or no opportunity to hone such skills before taking office. Although their career paths were quite different, they had succeeded in winning the presidency in large part because of their intransigent opposition to the PRI with which they ended up having to cooperate in order to get almost anything done.

The first initiatives of the Peña Nieto government also reinforce the conclusion that not that much has changed. In this case, the fact that the PRI controls both the legislature and executive could lead to a return to the political practices that helped keep the party in power for almost a century.

In other areas, the changes since 2000 have probably had a lasting impact. Most Mexicans now understand that divided government does not inevitably lead to chaos and that the regime can live with policy-making gridlock, at least in the short run. Put in terms used throughout the book, the difficulties since 2000 do not seem to place the regime in jeopardy in any way.

For now.

In the worst-case scenario, Mexico *could* become a failed state ten or twenty years from now. The country itself almost certainly would not fall apart, but its regime could. Military, nationalist, and left-wing populist leaders are among the possibilities we should be concerned about.

Public Policy

Debt and Development

Had this book been written forty years ago, this section would have focused on the so-called "Mexican miracle," which was the way many observers referred to its steady growth. However, the miracle turned into a house of cards as a result of the debt crisis in the 1980s and 1990s.

Until then, PRI governments had smoothed the transition from revolutionary egalitarianism to state-sponsored industrialization and an improved standard of living. Even more importantly, Mexico seemed to be breaking the bonds of dependency by building its own industrial base and relying less on imports.

The Mexican miracle is long gone. The sharp decline in oil prices in the early 1980s sparked a general downturn that left no part of the economy untouched. In particular, the last three twentieth-century PRI presidents had little choice but to open the economy up to foreign investment and to adopt a strategy in line with structural adjustment as demanded by the World Bank, IMF, and other Northern financial institutions.

Early Success

High wartime demand for Mexican manufactured goods, minerals, and labor in the United States spurred industrialization in the 1940s. That allowed the PRI to reinforce their existing preference for policies consistent with **import substitution** as we have discussed throughout Part 4.

At the heart of the state-led sector was NAFINSA, the National Development Bank, which supplied about half the total investment funds (and still exists but with a different mission). Much of its money went to the public sector, beginning with the nationalization of the railroads and PEMEX in the 1930s. By the end of the 1970s, the government owned all or part of more than a thousand companies, including smelters, sugar refineries, hotels, grocery stores, and even a shampoo factory. The wave of nationalizations ended in 1982 after the banks were taken over during the last weeks of López Portillo's presidency.

Tax rates were kept low, and the price of oil and other key commodities was subsidized to spur investment. Tariffs on imported goods averaged about 45 percent, and importers who were willing to overcome that hurdle also had to pay hefty fees for government licenses, which in turn also required substantial bribes.

At first, the corporatist structures and import substitution policies paid off. The economy as a whole grew by more than 6 percent per year from 1940 to 1980 without much of the inflation that was plaguing many other Latin American economies. Industrial production rose even faster. Development was concentrated in labor-intensive, low-technology industries, such as food, tobacco, textiles, machinery, iron and steel, and chemicals. Exports grew tenfold. Agriculture's share of total production dropped to 11 percent, while that of manufacturing accounted for a third of the economy. The peso was one of the world's most stable currencies because the government kept it pegged at 12.5 to the dollar from 1954 to 1976.

Don't be misled into thinking that everything was fine. Despite its revolutionary heritage, the PRI paid relatively little attention to inequality and social justice. For example, there was no unemployment insurance of any kind. Mexico's income distribution was (and still is) highly skewed. Rapid industrialization brought with it traffic congestion and pollution.

The Crisis

Although few economists or politicians paid much attention to it at the time, the economic boom began to slow during the 1970s. Neither the private nor the public sector could spark the next stage in Mexico's industrial revolution, in which it would make more sophisticated, higher-technology products.

Meanwhile, the mismanagement of key industries became a problem. It was estimated, for instance, that PEMEX employed three or four times the number of workers it needed. Rapid population growth meant that the number of young people entering the workforce far outpaced the number of available jobs. There was a dramatic increase in government spending brought on by the last wave of nationalizations and a belated attempt to deal with social problems. To make matters worse, government revenues lagged behind its spending, creating budget deficits that, in turn, led to a sharp increase in the national debt.

The government then made a costly mistake. López Portillo based his economic strategy on the assumption that oil prices would remain high in the aftermath of the OPEC oil embargo of 1973–74, which occurred at the same time that Mexican production capacity increased. Then, after the Iranian revolution in 1979, oil prices shot up again. As a result, Mexico began selling massive amounts of oil. From 1979 to 1981 alone, Mexican oil revenues increased from $3.9 billion to $14.5 billion and accounted for almost 75 percent of its exports and for 45 percent of government revenues.

Oil revenues, however, papered over underlying economic problems. Budget deficits and overseas borrowing continued to mount. The cost of imported consumer goods outpaced growth in exports. Inflation broke the 20 percent barrier for the first time. The low value of the peso and high interest rates abroad accelerated capital flight by the so-called *sacadolares* (dollar plunderers).

When oil prices began to fall in 1981, the government assumed that the decline would be temporary. It was wrong. By 1982, the Mexican economy was on the brink of collapse.

The various fiscal shortfalls were met through extensive loans extended by northern banks and governments. Because of the role debt had played in causing Mexico's nineteenth century economic woes, the first PRI governments had borrowed very little. In 1970, the total debt was only $6 billion. In 1987, it reached a peak of more than $107 billion or 70 percent of its annual GNP, making Mexico one of the most heavily indebted countries in the world.

The **debt crisis** was just the tip of the iceberg. Whether it wanted to or not, Mexico was being drawn into the global economy, which made it harder and harder to retain import substitution. The peso's artificially low exchange rate made it difficult for Mexico to import the new technologies it needed to continue its development. This, in turn, made foreign investment by rich Mexicans ever more lucrative, leading to massive capital flight in the second half of the 1970s.

Once the crisis had reached its peak, government closed the foreign exchange markets and nationalized the banks. Still, the economy remained out of control. By 1983,

Walmart is Mexico's biggest retailer, with over 150,000 employees.

inflation had topped 100 percent, reaching a peak of 159 percent in 1987. The peso was allowed to float freely, and the exchange rate went from 56.5 pesos to the dollar in 1982 to 1,460 in 1987. This had devastating consequences for a country that was now dependent on imports that had to be paid for in ever more expensive dollars. The economy suffered yet another jolt in 1985. A devastating earthquake in Mexico City cost the government $5 billion it could ill afford. Meanwhile, the price of a barrel of oil dropped another 50 percent, which cut export earnings from $16 billion in 1985 to only $9 billion the following year.

Reform

The economic crisis led to two fundamental and related shifts in Mexican politics: the election of de la Madrid and his government's shift toward structural adjustment as demanded by the country's international creditors. The PRI choice of a free market supporter like de la Madrid did not come out of political thin air.

Under the best of circumstances, Mexico would have had trouble competing in the global market with its inefficient industries, limited investment capital, and overvalued currency. Despite forty years of import substitution, the country found itself more dependent on the outside world than ever. Its difficulties were compounded by the fact that the crisis occurred at precisely the time that import substitution models were losing favor in international circles and being replaced by structural adjustment with its emphasis on debt reduction and unrestricted trade in free markets as the best "engine" for economic growth.

It is only a slight exaggeration to say that the massive borrowing left the Mexican economy hostage to its creditors, who held the upper hand in negotiating deals to restructure the debt. No foreign bank or government issued commands to Mexican policy makers. Rather, the size of the debt and the need for outside help in repaying it left the Mexican government with far fewer options than it had had prior to 1982.

As a result, the last Mexican governments of the twentieth century had little choice but to follow a path similar to the ones we saw in India and Nigeria. In short, the combination of the new leaders' values and the crisis conditions led to one of the most dramatic economic about faces in modern history. Quickly, the government adopted four overlapping policies that the Salinas and Zedillo administrations continued and added to.

Debt reduction. Even before he took office, de la Madrid began negotiations with the IMF, the World Bank, Northern governments, and private banks, which led to a multinational agreement that consolidated some loans, turned others into bonds, and reduced Mexico's annual interest payments by one-third. The agreement included mechanisms for keeping up to seven billion dollars in capital in the country for future investment.

Mexico suffered a second fiscal crisis in the first weeks of Zedillo's term when investors removed about five billion dollars in capital from the Mexican market, which sparked a run on the peso and forced Mexico to accept another expensive bailout package. As in Nigeria, it would be another decade before the debt crisis stabilized, but even then, Mexico remains vulnerable to Northern financial institutions.

Spending cuts. In 1983, Mexico and the IMF agreed to a severe austerity plan. Government spending would be sharply reduced in order to cut the deficit by half within three years. Subsidies would be cut and the prices charged by such government agencies as CONASUPO, which provided basic foodstuffs at below-market prices, would be increased. The Salinas and Zedillo administrations slashed government spending and raised taxes even further. They were able to keep the deficit under 5 percent per year and bring inflation under control. However, the social service programs, which were never very good to begin with, were seriously compromised.

Privatization. To give market forces a greater role in the Mexican economy, the government decided to sell many of its nationalized enterprises, especially those that were a drain on the budget. In February 1985, the government announced that 237 parastatals would be sold, and privatization has continued apace since then. Of the 1,155 firms the government controlled in the mid-1980s, only about 100 remain in state hands today. The government does, however, retain control of some of the largest and most important ones, including most of PEMEX. The most significant privatization came in 1990 when the Salinas government returned the banks to private ownership. Actually, the first steps in that direction had begun within months of the initial nationalization, when the de la Madrid government allowed Mexican investors to buy 34 percent of the shares in any bank and foreign investors to purchase some nonvoting stock. Although the details are complicated, the state retained only a limited, minority interest in some of the banks. The $6.5 billion it raised was supposed to be used to provide basic services, including drinking water, sewers, electricity, schools, housing, and health care, but little of it ended up there. All the signs are that PRI insiders were able to gain control of these companies and become wealthy overnight to the point that Mexico had twenty-four billionaires in 2000, more than half of whom earned their wealth in the newly privatized banking system.

Opening up the economy. The United States and the other creditors also insisted that Mexico open its economy to more foreign investment. This began as early as the 1980s but reached its peak with the 1994 implementation of NAFTA, which gradually removed barriers to trade. The government also agreed to join the General Agreement on Tariffs and Trade (GATT) and its successor, the World Trade Organization (WTO), which also forced the government to move in a promarket direction. Only 6 percent of imports now require government licenses. Tariffs have been reduced to an average of 10 percent, the lowest rate in Latin America.

To some extent, opening the economy has paid off. A mini "silicon valley" has been created in Guadalajara, where IBM, Hewlett-Packard, and other high-tech U.S. firms assemble computers for the Mexican and export markets. Most of the new industrial development originally was concentrated in the north, where special laws had long allowed foreign firms to open *maquiladora* factories that use duty-free imported components, assemble intermediate or final products, and export what they manufacture. In 1990, more than fifteen hundred of them were shipping GI Joe and Barbie dolls, televisions, and automobiles for American and Japanese firms. The rules have since been loosened so that similar establishments can be opened elsewhere in the country. Mexico is attractive to foreign firms because wages are about an eighth of what they are north of the border. In fact, wage costs are so low that some Nissans built there are actually being shipped back to Japan. One American consultant estimated that it would make sense for any American firm that spends as little as 30 percent of its total budget on wages to relocate its manufacturing operations to Mexico.

Reform Under the PAN

It should come as no surprise that structural adjustment policies were retained by the PAN. Although attention has focused on the drug cartels (see the next section), the party's economic track record has drawn its share of praise. Inflation remained low, and although debt levels fluctuated, there has been nothing like the crisis—and panic—of the 1980s. Growth rates were respectable, and the middle class has expanded dramatically.

The PAN accelerated the privatization of industries that had begun under the PRI. For instance, American firms, one of which has the distinctly un-Spanish name of Kansas City Southern de Mexico, now dominate the freight rail networks connecting Mexico to the United States. The government presided over the privatization of entire sectors, including the 2010 decision to sell its water pipelines, sewers, and dam construction industries. As was the case before 2000, privatization increased foreign investment and at least partial ownership of Mexican firms, including in the development of new oil fields, which PEMEX could not afford to pay for on its own.

Overall growth has been sustained enough that some optimistic analysts think Mexico could be one of the next BRICS. Such development, however, works on the assumption that global markets will continue to recover and that trading patterns will favor a country with Mexico's location, pattern of industrial development, and labor force, none of which seems certain in these uncertain economic times.

Combatting Poverty

Despite the last two decades of substantial if intermittent growth, Mexico has had little success overcoming the uneven distribution of income and wealth we find in the supposedly successful economies in the Global South. Mexico's income distribution remains, in the World Bank's estimation, one of the world's worst. Average real wages have declined by about half. Forty percent of the workforce is either unemployed or underemployed, and the same proportion of the population suffers from some form of malnutrition. To complicate matters further, jobs have to be found for the million or so people who enter the workforce each year.

The PRI tried to soften the impact of the economic reforms on the poor by creating the Program for National Solidarity (PRONASOL) and other welfare projects. In classic Mexican corporatist style, however, PRONASOL was administered through the president's office and was used as a way to solidify support for the PRI. In many people's eyes, it turned into little more than another stage agency that distributed consumer goods to buy support for the PRI.

President Zedillo abandoned that approach, especially for the rural poor, when he created the *Progresa* program in 1997 which Fox renamed *Oportunidades* in 2002, that differed from traditional Mexican antipoverty policy in two main ways. First, the program's benefits are cash transfers given directly to mothers with children, giving women a degree of financial independence from their husbands. *Oportunidades* provides enough money so that women now make about as much money as their husbands. Second, families receive the funds only if their children stay in school, the family gets regular medical care, and the mothers attend workshops on health, education, and personal finance. About one-fourth of all Mexican families are enrolled in the program. All in all, the number of rural Mexicans living in absolute poverty declined from 37.4 percent to 13.8 percent little more than a decade later. Though that reduction in poverty cannot be wholly attributed to *Oportunidades*, improvement under it has far outpaced the overall rate of growth. At least thirty other countries are experimenting with similar programs, and a pilot program has been established in New York City.

Still, inequality is the rule rather than the exception in Mexico. The richest 10 percent of the population makes 26 times as much money as the bottom 10 percent. The average gap in Organization for Economic Co-operation and Development (OECD) countries is only nine to one.

The Bottom Line

When all is said and done, only one thing is clear. Mexico is losing control of its development. It may turn out that the reforms lead to substantial growth and generate a lot of wealth. But much of it—and the concomitant political power—will lie in the hands of the foreign investors who supply the capital and attach conditions to their loans.

After more than a decade of NAFTA (www.ustr.gov/Trade_Agreements/Regional/NAFTA/Section_Index.html), Mexican dependency on the United States has probably increased, although the impact of the trade agreement is a subject of tremendous controversy on both sides of the border. As NAFTA's supporters projected, trade between the United States and Mexico grew by a factor of four after the agreement went into effect. However, it also exacerbated differences within Mexico as the states closest to the U.S. border saw their economies expand while those elsewhere in the country grew poorer.

For instance, the American government and private American firms are putting pressure on the government to allow outside investment in PEMEX (www.pemex.com/index.cfm), even though it is a symbol of Mexican national independence and pride. In 2008, Calderón said that the core of PEMEX would not be privatized after a law was passed that allowed some foreign investment in the new oil fields mentioned earlier. Although the high-tech firms that have built factories in Guadalajara provide jobs and other benefits for people in the area, it is also true that the Americans control how those factories are run and repatriate almost all their profits back to the United States—just as they do with the *maquiladoras* along the border.

U.S.-Mexican Relations: Immigration and Drugs

In the first six editions of *Comparative Politics*, this section dealt almost exclusively with the immigration of Mexicans to the United States, legal and otherwise. The related issue of the drug wars was introduced in the seventh edition. Now, the two have to be given equal treatment, because, in different ways, both illustrate the imbalance between the two neighbors that has been the hallmark of their relationship since Mexico gained its independence.

Imbalance of Power

Legally speaking, Mexico has always been able to do what it wants in global affairs. However, it is hard to make the case that it has ever really been free to do so because of the overwhelming power the United States wields in all aspects of Mexican life.

Since the beginning of the twentieth century, the United States has rarely tried to explicitly tell Mexican governments what to do. However, because of its size, wealth, and geopolitical power, Mexican policy makers follow U.S. wishes the vast majority of the time, especially when the issue at hand matters a lot to their counterparts in Washington.

Washington has never held all the power, because there have always been aspects of the relationship that work in Mexico's favor. For example, many industrial workers in the United States have seen their jobs transferred to Mexico. Nonetheless, when all is said and done, the relationship is much the same as it has always been. The United States shapes Mexican affairs to a degree that far exceeds the impact of any one country on any other covered in this book.

There has always been a strong undercurrent of wariness regarding the United States even under the PAN. Virtually no Mexicans take U.S. declarations that its policies are altruistic at face value. Put simply, Mexican leaders realize that they must get along with their powerful neighbor to the north, and life in the United States is attractive to most Mexicans. On the other hand, most Mexicans remain highly suspicious of U.S. policies and intentions.

One former U.S. ambassador recently summed it all up when he remarked that he had once apologized to the

PROFILES   Carlos Slim

There is no better example of how wealthy some Mexicans are than Carlos Slim Helú (1940–) who is one of the three richest people in the world.

Slim comes from good entrepreneurial stock. His father emigrated to Mexico from Lebanon (the family name was originally Salim) and established a small store. He soon started buying real estate.

After getting a degree in engineering, the younger Slim also went into business. He has been most active in telecommunications, controlling the leading landline, cell, and telephone equipment companies. In 2009, he loaned the financially troubled *New York Times* $250 million. He already owned almost 7 percent of the company; he could end up with 17 percent of it by 2015.

Slim is also a philanthropist supporting Mexico's largest technical university and development projects throughout Central and South America.

He is not without his critics, however. In 2011, for example, his company was accused of charging four times what it cost the firm to establish a cell phone account, and it has something approaching a monopoly on the service. ∎

Carlos Slim, perhaps the world's third richest man.

REUTERS/Henry Romero/Landov

Mexican foreign minister for having to raise a trivial matter. The minister told him not to worry because about 85 percent of his time was devoted to U.S.-Mexican relations anyway. U.S. intervention affected the course of the Mexican revolutions of 1810 and 1910 and almost everything in between. As the nationalist journalist Gastón Garcia Cantú put it:

From the end of the eighteenth century through 1918, there were 285 invasions, incidents of intimidation, challenges, bombardments of ports, and subtractions of territory out of which seven American states were carved. No people in the world have had their territory, wealth, and security as plundered by anybody as Mexico has by the United States.[5]

By the time Cárdenas won the presidency in 1934, U.S. interests controlled more of the Mexican economy than ever. In the second half of the twentieth century, however, relations improved to the point that the United States never again contemplated direct intervention in Mexican affairs. Given Mexico's stable, non-communist regime, it receded from center stage in U.S. foreign policy concerns.

Hostilities never completely disappeared. Even the most accommodating PRI governments criticized U.S. interventions in Latin American affairs which were prompted by American fears of communism. Relations between the two grew frostier during the 1980s in part because of resentment toward the U.S. role in "renegotiating" Mexico's debt and other policy shifts discussed in the previous section. In part, too, it had to do with the Reagan administration's open courtship of the PAN, which it saw as a conservative and procapitalist alternative to the PRI.

U.S.-Mexican relations improved considerably after the PAN's victory. Improved relations, however, should not obscure the main point being made here. At all times this has been an unequal relationship, controlled by a United States that has actively pursued its own interests, often without paying much attention to what the Mexicans wanted, as we will see in the case of immigration and drug policies in which what happens in Washington is at least as important as what happens inside Mexico.

Immigration

No issue in recent years has revealed the unequal power in U.S.-Mexican relations more than the migration of millions of Mexicans to the United States.

Mexicans have been moving to the United States since colonial times. Immigration only became a serious political issue, however, after World War II. The United States had encouraged Mexican workers to work there during the war. However, with the demobilization of millions of U.S. soldiers in 1945, the Mexicans became "excess" labor, and the United States began sending them home.

For the next forty years, U.S. policy ebbed and flowed. When the American economy was expanding, limits on immigration were loosened and U.S. officials turned a blind eye to the hiring of illegal or "undocumented" aliens. But when unemployment rose and Americans began to complain that illegal Mexicans were taking "their" jobs, pressure to end or curb immigration rose.

Historically, there have been four major crackdowns—in 1947, 1954, 1964, and 1986. Whether economically justified or not, each was handled in a way that was bound to anger Mexicans. The 1954 program, for instance, was known as Operation Wetback and was directed by an army general as a military operation.

The 1986 Immigration Reform and Control Act created an amnesty program for Mexicans who had been in the United States illegally for five years, limited further immigration, and, for the first time, imposed penalties on U.S. employers who knowingly hired undocumented workers. The act, of course, applied to all illegal immigrants, but it was widely perceived as an anti-Mexican act because something on the order of two-thirds of all undocumented immigrants were Mexican. Despite the law and the efforts of the Immigration and Naturalization Service (INS) to close the border, an estimated seven million undocumented Mexican immigrants were living in the United States in 2011.

Immigration has been a controversial issue north of the border for most of this century. Fears about the cost of providing immigrants with social services, as well as the "dilution" of American culture, led to demands for tighter restrictions on immigration and even sending all or most of the undocumented aliens "back home." Attempts have been made to define English as the only language to be used in official business and in education in a number of states. Young people who are not in the country legally are ineligible to receive financial aid or in-state tuition to help pay for a university education in all but a handful of states.

The most notable initiative along these lines was Arizona's highly restrictive 2010 law, which limits what illegal immigrants can do. Similar legislation is pending in at least five other states. It does not affect the border, which is a federal responsibility. However, it introduced draconian policies, including allowing (practically forcing) the police to check on someone's immigration status whenever they are picked up for even a minor traffic violation. All but a few of its provisions have been upheld by the U.S. Supreme Court.

Given the 2012 American election and other trends, U.S. immigration policy could well change in the next few years. Whatever happens on that front, however, the emphasis in this section will still hold. As in the past, future policy will reflect American more than Mexican political dynamics. Immigration *is* important to Mexicans. The United States has long offered an economic safety valve for workers who could not find work at home. In the state of Michoacán

---

[5]Cited in Robert Pastor and Jorge Castañeda, *Limits to Friendship: The United States and Mexico* (New York: Vintage Books, 1988), 123.

alone, migrants send about $2.5 billion a year to relatives back home. Nationally, the figure is ten times that amount even after taking into account the fact that remittances have declined in recent years because tens of thousands of Mexicans have returned home and the number of Mexicans who are trying to "go North" is down to a trickle.

Most Mexicans believe that U.S. immigration policy is biased and shortsighted. Although most Mexicans will admit that migration strains U.S. educational, social service, and health care systems, they argue that U.S. politicians overstate the problem. They point out that few undocumented Mexicans are taking jobs from Americans. Instead, most work in jobs that Americans are no longer willing to take. They also point out that the migrants themselves are not a threat to American society in any significant way. If anything, the immigrants disproportionately come from the most talented and dynamic sectors of Mexican society, including ten to fifteen thousand professionals a year. And they complain that the racism and indignity that everyone of Mexican origin is subjected to are not even on the U.S. policy-making agenda.

Drugs

There is no question that the United States has a serious drug problem. There is also no question that many of the drugs Americans consume enter the country from Mexico.

Drugs became politically important on the Mexican side of the border during the last decade because of the drug-related violence that had taken sixty thousand Mexican lives by the end of 2012. As strange as it may seem, Mexico does not have a serious drug problem of its own, and few of the drugs it exports were grown or manufactured in Mexico. In other words, Mexico serves primarily as a transshipment point for drugs made elsewhere and then sold in the United States.

The drug trade is run by a series of cartels that have close ties with the police, the army, and the government. In all, the cartels are estimated to control 90 percent or more of the cocaine, methamphetamines, and synthetic drugs that are imported across Mexico's porous border and then sent north across the only slightly less porous one with the United States.

The cartels went to war with each other because they all wanted to control more of the drug business. By 2010 they had gone beyond targeting each other, and their victims included innocent civilians who, for instance, might have been riding in a bus hijacked by a cartel. Hostages who were not killed were held for ransom that often reached hundreds of thousands of dollars.

The drug networks also have close ties with each of the three major parties and fill their ranks with former police officers and military veterans. That makes a crackdown on them all the more difficult. The Mexican government claims it has confiscated more than three hundred thousand weapons in the last decade, most of which were smuggled into Mexico from Arizona, Texas, and other border states, where the cartels are the strongest.

La Familia, which was based in Michoacán, has drawn the most attention because it is both one of the largest and most unusual of the cartels. The cartel has its headquarters in the port city of Lázaro Cárdenas, ironically named for the last great reformist PRI president. The port, and much of the state, sits on the Pacific coast and contains a number of transportation links to the United States. In one form or another, La Familia has existed for years, but only went off on its own in 2006 when its members tossed five decapitated heads into a night club.

In 2010, it probably had about four thousand full-time members. In order to join, they have to pass an alcohol and drug rehabilitation program based on models developed by conservative American Evangelical Christians. It counts at least ten mayors and countless local officials, plus a member of the Chamber of Deputies, in its ranks.

La Familia's operations are extremely profitable. Its commitment to a drug-free workforce notwithstanding, it controls a huge share of exports to the United States. It has also set up "legitimate" businesses, including hotels and restaurants.

Like many criminal networks, *La Familia* itself was always an unstable and fluid organization. By the end of 2009, it had both split into a number of competing (and warring) factions and spread its activities throughout northern Mexico.

The Calderón government made ending the escalating drug violence one of its most important priorities, with *La Familia* as one its main targets. Thus, it sent at least eight thousand military and police personnel into Michoacán with the twin, but contradictory, goals of wiping out and negotiating with *La Familia,* although it is hard to tell with whom it could negotiate. At first, the crackdown only served to add to the bloodshed and seemed to implicate more officials. By the end of his term, however, there were signs that the combined police and military operations had killed or arrested enough middle-level cartel members to put a dent in the violence. Still, mass graves are routinely uncovered while seemingly innocent people are taken as hostages who are often never heard from again. As the journalist Javier Valdez Cárdenas put it,

> **Narco here is not a military problem. It isn't even a police problem. It is a way of life. We have allowed it into our homes, our kitchens, our dining rooms, our bathrooms, our bedrooms and under the sheets. I am pessimistic whether we can get it out again.[6]**

Law enforcement and military officials in the United States are also paying more attention to the cartels. Most of those who study them think a viable strategy has to

---

[6]Cited in Jo Tuckman, *Mexico: Democracy Interrupted* (New Haven, CT: Yale University Press, 2012), 43.

AP Photo/Jose Luis Magana

Marijuana seized by Mexican authorities in 1996. Many Americans argue that the Mexican government is not doing enough in the war on drugs.

address the root causes of the trade, which lie in the United States and its demand for drugs, not in Mexico. Nonetheless, most American politicians continue to focus on "simply" stopping the flow of drugs across the border.

There is little doubt that American policy on this front is dated and inadequate. During the 1980s, the U.S. government decided that it would concentrate less on reducing the demand for drugs and more on cutting the supply in what the first Bush and Reagan administrations called the "war on drugs." And as with immigration, this has led some Americans to blame Mexico for much of the drug problem. Also, after the murders of U.S. Drug Enforcement Agency (DEA) officers, U.S. officials were highly critical of Mexican authorities for their failure to do much about the problem and for their involvement in drug trafficking itself. Such criticisms surfaced again in the mid-1990s with the scandals implicating the Salinas, Hank, and other leading PRI families.

There is now considerable cooperation between policy makers and enforcement agencies on both sides of the border. The CIA, FBI, and other U.S. agencies train Mexican officials, though they are skeptical of the commitment south of the border.

In this case, the tension emerges less from misunderstanding than from the different national interests regarding the drug issue. As noted above, Mexico itself does not have much of a drug problem. Moreover, even though the money is never included in official statistics and is never taxed, the profits from the drug trade amount to at least two billion dollars in additional income for Mexicans. Despite the efforts of the Calderón administration, thousands of

police officers at least turn a blind eye toward the cartels, while hundreds have been accused of actively participating in and profiting from their efforts.

As the drug cartels have moved into the southwest to get guns, they have brought their rivalries along with them. In short, although Mexico may not yet be a failed state, it may become one soon if these drug wars continue to escalate. At the very least it has what the late student of revolutions Crane Brinton called "dual sovereignty," which means that official authorities have to share power with rivals in much of a country.

Peña has made two things clear. First, he is more interested in Mexico's domestic problems than the drug trade and has therefore signaled that his administration will make stopping it a lower priority than it had been under his predecessor. Second, to Washington's chagrin, he has centralized all national security programs—including the war on drugs—in the Interior Ministry, thus trying to undercut the rivalry between the army and the police while reducing the impact of the United States.

As with immigration, the key point about drug policy for the purposes of this book is not that U.S. policy is wrong per se. Rather, the problem is that it has contributed to the weakening of Mexican sovereignty. The Mexican government really has had no choice but to allow the DEA to operate inside Mexican territory, something Americans cannot ever imagine allowing another government to do on their soil. The Mexicans have been able to block some U.S. proposals, including one that would have allowed Air Force jets to pursue drug suspects into Mexican airspace. However, U.S. policy makers have largely turned a deaf ear to Mexican requests to pursue policies that address Mexican needs, particularly ones that would provide marijuana and poppy growers with the opportunity to make a decent living raising other crops.

The Media

The same ambiguity regarding democracy and Mexico that we have seen throughout this chapter exists with the press as well. Newspapers, magazines, and television stations are ostensibly free of government control. The mass market press, however, rarely took the PRI governments on, failing to report on electoral fraud and other flagrant violations of the law because the government had considerable leverage over it. The PRI, for example, had a virtual monopoly on the supply of newsprint. It supplied chronically underfunded and understaffed papers with substantial amounts of information that often found its way into their pages with next to no investigation by journalists. The largest newspaper chain and, until recently, the one television network with a national audience were controlled by PRI loyalists.

Despite the control it already had, PRI governments did clamp down, as when they engineered the firing of the editorial team at the independent and often critical magazine *Excelsior* in 1976. But, more often, the press censored itself. Mass circulation dailies and television news provided bland coverage and tended to avoid controversial stories altogether. Instead, they presented government proclamations and covered the actions of its leaders in ways that made them seem like little more than propaganda outlets for the PRI.

That said, pressures to open up the media have been building for years and have already had an impact. While there are more independent outlets, most of these still only reach the relatively well-educated and affluent.

As in most countries, the most important media outlet for political purposes today is television. Until recently, Mexico only had two networks that were closely tied to the PRI. Since 2000, Televisa and TV Azteca have tried to strike a more independent tone. In all likelihood, the situation regarding the media will change even more dramatically in the near future with the opening up of the economy and the technological revolution that has brought in more media that are not controllable by the government, including satellite access to CNN and the U.S. networks' Spanish-language services.

Conclusion: Democracy Interrupted and the Big Questions

Jo Tuckman subtitled her recent book on contemporary Mexico, *Democracy Interrupted*, and there is no better term to pull this chapter together or provide us with a link to the "big questions" that will be the focus of the next one.

The most important theme in the last few pages is the erosion of national sovereignty. Countries like Mexico remain *legally* sovereign, but its de facto erosion is occurring everywhere. It is especially evident in Mexico and the other countries covered in Part 4.

I do not want to overstate this point. Few countries are giving up their legal sovereignty. Still, the growing interdependence of the world's economic and other systems is sapping all countries of at least some of their ability to determine their own destinies. This trend is especially marked in the Global South where governments lack the wealth and other resources of the liberal democracies in the North.

It may be that this "globalization" is inevitable and irreversible. However, this should not keep us from thinking about the ways in which it is reinforcing existing imbalances in the distribution of wealth and power or from worrying about what the consequences could be as globalization continues, including a growing number of failed or failing states.

KEY TERMS

Concepts

camarillas

corporatism

debt crisis

electoral alchemy

failed state

import substitution

maquiladora

mestizo

non-reelection

patron-client relations

remittances

sexeño

structural adjustment

People

Calderón, Felipe

Cárdenas, Cuauhtémoc

Cárdenas, Lázaro

de la Madrid, Miguel

Diaz, Porfirio

Fox, Vicente

Lopéz Obrador, Andrés Manuel

Nieto, Enrique Peña

Salinas de Gortari, Carlos

Santa Anna, Antonio López de

Zedillo, Ernesto

Acronyms	PRD	Immigration Reform and Control Act
CFE	PRI	Institutional Revolutionary Party (PRI)
CTM		National Action Party (PAN)
IFE	**Organizations**	North American Free Trade Agreement
NAFTA	Confederation of Mexican Workers (CTM)	(NAFTA)
PAN	Federal Election Commission (CFE)	Party of the Democratic Revolution
PEMEX	Federal Electoral Institute (IFE)	(PRD)
	Gobernación	

USEFUL WEBSITES

There are plenty of websites on Mexican politics. The problem is that surprisingly few of them have English-language material, including those of the Mexican government and political parties. The sites listed here all have at least some material in English.

The President's Office now has a fairly extensive website in English, though there is far more in Spanish. The Chamber of Deputies' site is only in Spanish, but we have included it anyway on the assumption that many readers of this book will speak some Spanish.

> www.presidencia.gob.mx

> http://www.diputados.gob.mx/inicio.htm

Washington's Center for Strategic and International Studies and its Woodrow Wilson Center are good sites on the Americas in general.

> www.csis.org/americas

> www.wilsoncenter.org/program/mexico-institute

The left-of-center North American Conference on Latin America (NACLA) provides periodic analyses of events in Mexico and throughout the region.

> www.nacla.org

The Latin American Network Information Center (LANIC) at the University of Texas has the best set of links to all aspects of Mexican life for academic use.

> lanic.utexas.edu/la/mexico/

The Latin American Public Opinion Program at Vanderbilt is the best single source for survey data throughout the region.

> http://www.vanderbilt.edu/lapop/

FURTHER READING

Bazant, Jan. *A Concise History of Mexico: From Hidalgo to Cárdenas*. New York: Cambridge University Press, 1977. The best short history concentrating on the century and a half when Mexican politics was most turbulent.

Camp, Roderic Ai. *Mexico: What Everyone Needs to Know*. New York: Oxford University Press, 2011. A very short book organized around short answers to one hundred questions rather than chapters.

Castañeda, Jorge. *Mañana Forever*. New York: Knopf, 2011. An overview by Mexico's preeminent political scientist, who was foreign minister in Fox's government.

Grayson, George. *La Familia Drug Cartel*. Carlisle, PA: Strategic Studies Institute/Army War College, 2010. The first of two books by a professor at William and Mary. A broader and more popular book is due out soon.

Megaloni, Beatriz, *Voting for Autocracy: Hegemonic Party Survival and Its Demise in Mexico*. New York: Cambridge University Press, 2006. An insightful study of the PRI's ability to hold onto power but then lose it that many comparativists use as a framework for studying other semiauthoritarian regimes.

Morris, Stephen. *Political Corruption in Mexico: The Impact of Democratization*. Boulder, CO: 2009. The most rigorous examination of corruption in Mexico.

Shirk, David. *Mexico's New Politics: The PAN and Democratic Change*. Boulder, CO: Lynn Rienner, 2005. The best recent book on the first years of the transition.

Tuckman, Jo. *Mexico: Democracy Interrupted*. New Haven, CT: Yale University Press, 2012. An insightful new book by a journalist who has spent years covering Mexico for British and American newspapers.

Wright, Lawrence. "Slim's Time" *The New Yorker*. June 1, 2009. By the best journalist working on terrorism, who also plays in a blues band.

Conclusion

PART 5

CHAPTER 16
Global Challenges and Domestic
Responses

CHAPTER OUTLINE

16

Power itself has become more available—and, indeed, in today's world more people have power. Yet its horizons have contracted, and once attained it has become harder to use.

MOISÉS NAÍM

Global Challenges and Domestic Responses

Most textbooks summarize the conventional wisdom in their disciplines. For "mature" fields that have what I called a **paradigm** in Chapter 1, that is good enough, because almost all analysts and researchers agree on the key questions that define the field. In that case, introductory courses could and should be designed to give students an overview of what they need to master before they move on to more advanced study.

Comparative politics does not have anything like a paradigm. When I took my first graduate seminar, the professor began by stating, "comparative politics is in a pre-paradigmatic state." He is still correct today.

Those of us who study comparative politics for a living do not agree on what the questions—let alone the answers—are. In other words, because comparative politics is so open-ended and so much of it is controversial, a textbook *has to* at least touch on the open questions, especially those we disagree about. To be perfectly blunt, there probably has not been a time in my career when the gap between pressing issues in real life and the preoccupations of comparative politics specialists have been more at odds.

No textbook on comparative politics would be complete without paying at least some attention to those burning issues that are at the heart of both academic and "real world" debates. That is what this chapter will try to do by

going beyond the facts, figures, names, dates, and places that have been at the heart of the first fifteen chapters.

I have been working in the "trenches" of comparative politics since my undergraduate days in the late 1960s. Since then, we have learned a lot, especially about places that were barely on the academic radar screen at the time. We have also had to reconfigure our field in response to such unanticipated events as the end of the cold war and the aftermath of 9/11.

But the progress we have made is by no means enough to make sense of the world we live in let alone reach the broad agreement that could become the basis for a paradigm. Doing that requires thinking about bigger and more controversial issues than one normally finds in a textbook and considering approaches to comparative politics that are dramatically different from those covered so far in this book.

Strangely enough, the best way to do that is to return to two points I made in Chapter 1 but which have largely been off intellectual center stage since then.

■ The five big issues discussed in Chapter 1 that have received scant attention from political scientists as well as politicians, especially in the countries covered in Part 2.

- Systems theory, which has fallen out of favor among political scientists despite the fact that it is particularly well suited for helping us come to grips with globalization at a time when the disciplinary lines of academic life seem to make less and less sense.

Focusing on those two topics also allows me to incorporate perspectives from my work in peacebuilding. It would be easy to assume that there would be a huge overlap between peacebuilding and comparative politics. After all, the issues that lead to violent conflict around the world today have their roots in the kinds of dynamics discussed on virtually every page of the first fifteen chapters. However, I find that my colleagues in the two fields often talk past each other. The insights I have gained in my career as a peacebuilder have rarely made their way into comparative politics—to the detriment of both.

None of this is designed to be critical of a field I have worked in for my entire career. Rather, I simply want to suggest that comparative politics—or political science as a whole or economics or anthropology or ecology—is not broad enough to give us an understanding of the people, places, and events discussed so far.

In the process, we will have to look for answers in ways that take us far beyond comparative politics. Chapter 1 made the case that comparative politics is like the tip of an iceberg. Most of its "mass" lies below the surface of its "water," which in this case means exploring other fields of inquiry.

I will also be crossing an important but ill-conceived line most textbook authors avoid. Especially when there is a paradigm, we typically concentrate on the **empirical** side of our fields by analyzing and explaining the evidence and interpretations just about everyone accepts, because the scientific canon suggests that we leave the **normative** or ethical issues aside.

It should be clear by now that we cannot omit controversial issues while studying comparative politics. In fact, one or more of them led most of us to become interested in the subject in the first place.

It would also be irresponsible of me to do so here. Therefore, I will be presenting you with my reading of the evidence presented so far in this book.

My goal is not to convince you that I'm right. In fact, it would be unethical of me to do so. What I have tried to do is present my reading in such a way that it is easy for you to reach your own conclusions, especially when they are different from mine.

The Big Questions Revisited

The big questions raised in Chapter 1 did not recede from center stage in the rest of this book because they are unimportant. Rather, as often happens in a constantly changing world, political leaders—and political scientists—have not paid that much attention to them. Now, however, they return to the "starring role" as the first step in pulling this book's content together.

Change Is the Only Constant

The case about change being the only constant in political life today was the easiest one to make in Chapter 1. Therefore, we will not have to spend much time on it here. But, as was the case at the beginning of the book, it makes sense to first see it in trends that frankly are not very political.

Every academic year, Beloit College publishes a list of things that faculty members should bear in mind about that year's first-year students. In 2012 when many people reading this book would have been starting their undergraduate careers, they pointed out that those incoming students:

1. Have always lived in cyberspace.
2. Can watch reruns on YouTube if they miss that day's *Daily Show*.
3. Think of Bill Clinton as a senior statesman because they were seven or eight when he left office.
4. Have never seen an airplane ticket.
5. Have had a woman serving as U.S. Secretary of State for most of their lives.
6. Have what must look like obsolete icons of floppy disks (save), telephones (ring), and snail mail envelopes (email) on their tablets and smart phones.
7. Rarely watch television on a television.

None of those statements would have made any sense when I took my first comparative politics course and the original *Star Trek* was in the middle of its run on NBC.

Comparative politics has, of course, changed, too. My first course was typical of those taught at the time. It only covered Europe, and my instructor did not bother including Russia (then, of course, the Soviet Union).

Those courses do now include countries from all over the world, but otherwise the subject matter is largely the same. We still focus on national governments, the pressures they face, and the policies they make. And often without being aware that we are doing so, we tend to emphasize continuity rather than change, especially in the developed world.

To some extent, there is every reason to organize our courses and our research that way.

Citizens of the United States, Great Britain, and Canada all take justifiable pride in their long and reasonably stable political histories. Regime change has not been on the agenda for well over a century. Politicians from those days might be baffled by the Internet or by machines that can "read" an entire bill "out loud" in a matter of seconds,[1] but they would have little trouble following the ways their descendants enact legislation.

What's more, regime changes are never easy. We saw that, too, since every other country covered in this book (except for Mexico) has had to go through at least one of them during the lifetime of many people still alive today.

Nonetheless, in a world of constant and accelerating change, one should at least think twice about any country that does not question its traditional ways of doing business. Indeed, the widespread dissatisfaction with the political status quo we see in so many polls and in the American Tea Party or Occupy protests suggests that at least some people would like politics to be in the mix when we talk about change being the only constant.

Democratization

Political life, of course, is not stagnant. When I took that comparative politics course nearly half a century ago, a democratic Soviet Union, China, or Nigeria was not something a realistic person even dreamed of. Today, **democratization** has become one of the most exciting research topics in comparative politics.

However, acknowledging that democratization is now a central issue in our field actually raises more questions than it answers. Indeed, what a democratic regime entails and what it takes to sustain one are more open for debate than ever before in three overlapping ways.

First is the often unspoken assumption that democracy is something that all countries could and should aspire to. That may seem obvious to most readers of this book who have spent much if not all of their lives in established democracies. That is by no means true for millions of people in much of the rest of the world. Some people and politicians reject democracy altogether, as we saw with many members of the ruling elites in China or Iran. Others who claim to be democrats give at most lip service to the ideal, as the discussion of hybrid regimes in Parts 3 and 4 attests.

Second, what democracy means can be controversial once one begins exploring what I called "thick" rather than "thin" definitions of it in Chapter 2. The American Tea Party and Occupy movements have almost nothing in common other than their shared conviction that a real democracy has to give average citizens like themselves more power over the decisions that shape their lives than the guarantee of civil liberties, competitive elections, and the rule of law alone provide. However, the evidence presented in this book so far just as clearly shows that thicker versions of democracy are harder to engineer than thinner ones.

Third, because conscious attempts to create democratic societies are so new, there is a lot we do not know about the trajectories such societies take. As we have seen repeatedly since Chapter 6 on Germany, no one set out to create a democracy before the end of World War I. And as I at least indirectly suggested several times in Parts 3 and 4, there is no reason to believe that emerging democracies will not end up looking like existing ones because there is no single path toward democratization.

Identity

The first fifteen chapters have demonstrated how divisive identity issues can be. Many political scientists, in fact, think that they have become an all but permanent feature of political life and are the primary causes of what peacebuilders call **intractable conflicts** (www.beyondintractability.org).

However, recent research has begun to suggest that our identities may not be set in stone. If our frame of reference is the last thousand years, people have learned to identify with ever "larger" political units.

To see that, it is useful to reflect on two sources political scientists rarely refer to—The Bible and the epic poem, *Beowulf*. In the Old Testament, the Jewish kingdom is attacked dozens of times by Hittites, Edamites, Baalites, and other groups that have not existed for centuries. Similarly, *Beowulf* pits North Danes, South Danes, and East Danes against each other (and Grendel the dragon), which means that people who think of themselves as one and the same today were archenemies a thousand years ago.

Similarly, most of the seemingly ironclad ways we have of defining ourselves are actually quite new. As we saw in the introductory chapters to Parts 2 through 4, the modern nation-state itself is a new phenomenon, which most political scientists date from the Treaty of Westphalia in 1648.

Well into the twentieth century, national identities were fluid. It was even hard to speak of national languages. Before the advent and spread of radio, most people spoke regional dialects, and only some members of the elite either spoke or understood "national" language.

Values such as nationalism and patriotism seem to be nineteenth-century creations in most of Europe and emerged even later in the rest of the world. People did

---

[1]This is not a joke. At the end of the 2013 session, Democrats in the Florida state legislature exercised their legal right to have all bills read aloud in their entirety before they were voted on. The Republicans were ready for what the Democrats thought of as a stalling maneuver. Their Auto Reader machine (who was nicknamed Mary and had "her" own Twitter account) "read" over 1,000,000 words in a 24-hour period (www.npr.org/2013/05/01/180361645/florida-legislature-at-an-impasse-over-expanding-medicaid). Obviously, this is an experience better heard than read about.

think of themselves somewhat as Serbs or Catholics or Whites, but even these definitions are relatively recent phenomena as defining parts of peoples' identities. Thus, in 1916, the prominent conservationist and founder of the Bronx Zoo, Madison Grant, published a bestselling book, *The Passing of the Great Race*, in which he decried the fact that Italians, Slavs, and Greeks were now being thought of as white.

Along the way, we also learned how to live together more peacefully. As the psychologist Steven Pinker points out, we have learned to overcome Thomas Hobbes's fear of the "war of all against all" by creating larger institutions that allow us to govern ourselves despite our social and cultural differences.[2]

In this respect, Benedict Anderson refers to national and other forms of identity as "imagined communities." Thus, in a recent examination of the flexibility of the way people think about race, class, gender, religion, and ethnicity, the historian David Cannadine focuses on the ever-changing variety and overlapping nature of them which he claims:

> helps explain why identities are not like hats, which can only be worn one at a time, to the exclusion of any or all others. Most people in the past, like most people in the present, maintain several loyalties, attachments, and solidarities simultaneously, and any one of which might at any one time be foremost in their minds, as occasion suggested and circumstances required.[3]

The last standing fragment of the World Trade Center towers in New York.

Globalization

Of the five questions, globalization will get the most attention here in part because it is an outgrowth of the other four. As noted in Chapter 1, it is one of the hottest buzzwords in the social sciences today, even though there is not much agreement about its political implications.

Some observers think that globalization will help enrich the poor around the world and usher in an era of unprecedented progress and connectivity. Others denounce it for causing everything from the destruction of traditional cultures to the continued poverty of billions of people.

The only thing beyond dispute seems to be that globalization is shaking up almost all aspects of our lives, especially politics. Unfortunately, few national leaders have put these social and economic trends on center stage in building their own political careers.

Economics

Globalization may not be a new phenomenon economically. Some globalization skeptics properly point out that international trade accounted for more of the major powers' GNP in the early twentieth century than it does today. By most indicators, however, the economy is far more "global" today than it ever was before, because borders matter less when it comes to both the production and consumption of goods and services.

Almost all companies have a home country, but **multinational corporations (MNCs)** have sales, workers, and management teams, all of which straddle national boundaries. If you own any Apple device, you might think of it as an American product. After all, Apple's home office is in Cupertino, California. But, most of the parts in your device were made and (until recently) assembled in Asia.

A generation ago, MNCs like Apple were routinely criticized for exploiting workers and markets in the Global South. Protests against my beloved Apple's labor policies with its Chinese suppliers suggest that many of those criticisms are still valid. Nonetheless, there are also signs that at least some of them (including Apple) are beginning to

---

[2]Steven Pinker, *The Better Angels of Our Nature: Why Violence Has Declined* (New York: Viking, 2011).

[3]David Cannadine, *The Undivided Past: Humanity beyond Our Differences* (New York: Knopf, 2013), 91 (Kindle edition).

implement corporate strategies that emphasize the long-term consequences of what they do everywhere they make or sell their products.

Not all do so eagerly or even willingly, as one particularly worrisome incident made clear while I was writing this chapter. In 2013, a textile factory in Bangladesh collapsed, killing over one thousand workers. Almost everything the factory produced was exported to North America and western Europe, and the major brands who bought the clothing manufactured there immediately came under pressure to improve the working conditions in their factories located almost exclusively in the Global South. One could argue that those companies should have acted years earlier, but the fact of the matter is that dozens of companies learned that they have a vested interest in the treatment of workers halfway around the world.

Stories like the one about the Bangladeshi factory do draw needed attention to the continued problems associated with globalization. But there are hopeful ones as well, even if they rarely make it into the headlines.

If you had been able to travel from the United States to Europe over the span of the last forty years as I have, the homogenization of goods and services on both sides of what the British call "the pond" would have leaped out at you. Unlike the 1970s, hip young people wear the same clothes and enjoy the same music as their "pond mates."

That is less true if you go to the Global South. But even there, people who can afford them tend to buy the same computers that use the same operating systems and have installed the same social networking software that mine do. The gap between the North and the rest of the world is closing fast in this regard. At the end of 2012, more than six hundred million Africans had cell phones and far more had access to them. Those phones increasingly tie people in the South into global networks through which they learn about the larger world and, more importantly for our purposes, have an impact on it. To be sure, there is still a digital divide that separates the North and South as well as the rich and the poor everywhere, but it is rapidly disappearing as the cost of technological products continues to plummet.

It's not just technology. Although the poverty discussed in Part 4 is real, so, too, are the antipoverty campaigns. Between 1990 and 2010, the number of people living in extreme poverty (defined as living on less than the equivalent of $1.25 a day) was reduced by half, and some projections suggest it could be eliminated altogether in another generation.

People live longer and healthier lives. More people can read and write. More people, too, have access to running water, electricity, and other "consumer comforts" that we in the West take for granted. I could continue and present more data, but there is no better way to see them than to go on line and watch any of the riveting data-driven videos by the Swedish mathematician, Hans Rosling (www.gapminder.org).

The Environment

Contrary to what many people think, globalization is far more than just economic. Nothing demonstrates that better than the environment and the highly controversial issue (at least in the United States) of **climate change**.

Climate change is not the only environmental issue to worry about. What happens to the solid waste I generate does matter, but it is often hard to see the worldwide implications of a problem that can probably be solved locally or regionally.

What makes climate change (which is also sometimes inaccurately referred to as **global warming**) different is that it has global causes and almost certainly will require global solutions. There *is* widespread agreement that the average world temperature has risen by about half a degree Centigrade over the last century. There is also little doubt that the changes in global temperatures are accelerating. Most scientists—including those funded by climate change skeptics in the United States—accept the **International Panel on Climate Change** (**IPCC**; www.ipcc.ch) estimate that temperatures will rise by 1.5 to 2.5 degrees Centigrade during the course of this century.

At this pace, the scientific models predict that some currently frigid places will get warmer and more livable. That would not be true for most of the planet where, on balance, the consequences of climate change will not be beneficial, to say the least. The average sea levels will almost certainly rise enough that the Maldives Islands (and their three hundred thousand inhabitants) would be underwater, as would many of the monuments on the Washington, DC, mall. Seacoasts would be in danger of regular flooding. Agriculture and fishing would be disrupted. There would almost certainly be extinctions.

There is some evidence that climate change has contributed to the extreme weather events of the last few years. Already, the twenty-first century has seen ten of the twelve warmest years on record, the two most damaging tsunamis ever, unusually powerful tropical storms, extended periods of drought and flooding in much of the world, the worst outbreak of tornadoes in modern American history, and the rapid melting of the polar icecaps.

Climate change is controversial because some politicians and a tiny handful of scientists still disagree about its causes and therefore what should be done about it. The vast majority of scientists agree that people emit billions of tons of carbon dioxide and other "greenhouse gases" each

Burning the rain forest
in the Amazon basin.

©iStockphoto.com/Brasil2

year as a byproduct of such everyday human activities as driving our cars, heating our homes, and growing our food.

Those gases rise to the upper reaches of the atmosphere. In simple terms, they get trapped and block heat generated on earth from escaping the earth's natural "air conditioning" system, which leads to rising temperatures in most parts of the world.

Other "natural" phenomena that have nothing to do with human behavior also affect global temperatures, including the actions of other species (e.g., cows emitting methane as part of their digestive process) and other periodic fluctuations in global weather patterns. However, only the most diehard climate change skeptics still doubt that human activity has had the most to do with the changes in the last century or that those of us who live in the industrialized North emit by far the most greenhouse gases.

If the extent and causes of climate change are controversial, what to do about it makes those discussions seem like the clichéd tempest in a teapot. An introductory textbook on comparative politics is not the place to critique the dozens of proposed solutions to climate change, all of which have more than their share of drawbacks.

Some transnational policy changes have been introduced. Most notably, the 1997 Kyoto Protocol (which the United States never signed) required signatories, who were both affluent and major polluters, to reduce their CO_2 emissions to 1990 levels by 2012, a goal few of them reached. There are also interesting proposals that would

add voluntary programs, such as the various voluntary "cap and trade" options that could bypass national governments altogether. But, on balance, it is more important to note how much difficulty the world's people and their leaders are having finding a *global* solution to the world's most ominous global problem, a point we will return to in other ways on other issues during the rest of this chapter.

Human Security

Despite the welcome reduction in poverty rates, globalization has also made it hard for us to ignore the fact that millions of people around the world still live lives without dignity. Part 4, in particular, discussed how wide the gap in living standards is between the suburbs of Washington, DC, where I live and the slums of suburban Mumbai or Lagos, not to mention the slums of downtown Washington where I work.

That has also led some scholars and a larger number of activists to broaden what the word *security* means. Until the last few years, almost all comparativists relied on a concept of security that we borrowed from our colleagues in international relations. *National* security was defined in geopolitical terms and was measured by countries' control over population, territory, wealth, and other tangible resources.

Impressionistic research suggests that many citizens and national leaders view security in sharply different terms. When asked about security, political leaders are more likely to talk about protecting their people and their country from hostile acts. Average citizens, by contrast, cite economic, health, and personal issues far more often.

In 1988, in a remarkable speech to the **United Nations**, then Soviet President Gorbachev anticipated that our definition of security might have to change:

> Today we have entered an era when progress will be based on the interests of all mankind. Consciousness of this requires that world policy, too, should be determined by the priority of the values of all mankind. The history of the past centuries and millennia has been a history of almost ubiquitous wars, and sometimes desperate battles, leading to mutual destruction. They occurred in the clash of social and political interests and national hostility, be it from ideological or religious incompatibility. All that was the case, and even now many still claim that this past—which has not been overcome—is an immutable pattern. However, parallel with the process of wars, hostility, and alienation of peoples and countries, another process, just as objectively conditioned, was in motion and gaining force: The process of the emergence of a mutually connected and integral world. The formula of development "at another's expense" is becoming outdated.[4]

Five years later, the 1994 United Nations' *Human Development Report* introduced human security, which views the idea in more holistic terms, including political, economic, social, nutritional, environmental, physical health, personal safety, gender, mental health, and more.

In the thirty years since the idea of human security first surfaced as a serious concept, globalization has driven home the understanding that these dimensions of security are interconnected. As Gorbachev said more than thirty years ago, it is hard for a person to feel secure in *any* of these areas if he or she does not feel so in *all* of them.

Events like 9/11 remind us that traditional security concerns still matter even if threats come in new and hard-to-address forms. However, globalization also suggests that we have to deal with all of those other aspects of security simultaneously and in an integrated way.

Domestic Responses to Global Challenges?

The section on globalization could have been much longer because I could have added literally dozens of other issues. But you have already seen enough to see an intellectual disconnect that I alluded to in Chapter 1 but asked you to put on hold until now.

Even though the problems we face are increasingly international if not global in scope, we still start by seeking domestic solutions for them, as this book's subtitle suggests. As we have seen in almost every chapter so far, however, few domestically oriented policies have shown much potential for making significant headway in solving any of them.

That is in part the case because few politicians build careers on the basis of their positions on global issues. There are some, such as France's former Foreign Minister, Bernard Kouchner, who first rose to prominence as founder of *Médecins sans frontières* (Doctors Without Borders), but politicians like him are few and far between.

If we listen to our colleagues in international relations or to most mainstream political commentators, it would be easy to conclude that nationally based solutions to today's problems are the best we can hope for. Realists and other leading international relations theorists make the often unstated and/or unproven assumption that the state is the most advanced political unit we could realistically create.

However, the research on identity and other issues mentioned above suggests otherwise. We don't have to think about the fantasy world of *Star Trek* where everyone shares a common language and culture to imagine a world in which identity politics takes very different forms than it does today or that some unit or units other than the nation-state make most of the key decisions that matter. In fact, toward the end of the chapter, we will see signs that some of the most promising answers to our global challenges are being incubated in almost all institutions *other than* national governments.

Toward a New Paradigm?

Our collective inability to solve today's problems using today's political tools suggests we should at least consider moving toward a different approach to politics that builds on what we have seen in the first fifteen chapters *and* uses them to sketch some plausible alternatives to our domestically based status quo. Doing so, in turn, forces us to go back to the role theory could or should play in comparative politics, which I also raised in Chapter 1 but have largely left hanging since then.

Paradigms and Paradigm Shifts

Chapter 1 defined a paradigm as an overarching theory that structures an entire discipline. In that chapter, I also suggested that there was no such paradigm for comparative politics, which is one of the reasons studying comparative politics can be so complicated and even confusing.

---

[4]legacy.wilsoncenter.org/coldwarfiles/index-34441.html.

That statement about comparative politics lacking a paradigm is only partially accurate. It is true that we do not have models that are as comprehensive and as widely accepted as the periodic table of elements is for chemistry or neoclassical theory is for economics. That said, comparative politics does have at least two common denominators that approximate one, because almost everyone:

- uses the nation-state as its primary unit of analysis.
- defines power as "A's" ability to get "B" to do something that B does not want to do.

In 1962, the historian of science, Thomas Kuhn, fundamentally changed the way we think about science and scientific change when he wrote a book about what he called scientific revolutions, which are now popularly referred to as **paradigm shifts**. As he saw it, real steps forward in what we know do not happen through what he called "normal" science, in which researchers work in their laboratories and publish their findings in obscure journals. Instead, profound progress is only made when a scientific community adopts a wholly new world view that covers an entire discipline.

It is not clear how much he was influenced by Karl Marx and others who thought about political revolution. Nonetheless, the pattern Kuhn laid out parallels Marx's theory of how political and economic revolutions occasionally occur and why most of them fail.

First, discrepancies or anomalies appear in the old paradigm. Thus, when Galileo invented the telescope, he and his fellow scientists realized that their predictions about the movement of heavenly bodies were wrong. Second, because they all "knew" that the old paradigm was "correct," they adjusted their calculation about the movement of heavenly bodies to "fit" their preconceptions by adding epicycles (or curlicues) to their orbits so that the moon, the planets, the sun, and the other stars still revolved around the earth. Third, Nicolaus Copernicus realized that the accepted wisdom itself was wrong and devised a new paradigm with the sun rather than the earth at the center of the solar system. Fourth, in the process, Copernicus touched off a political struggle between supporters of the heliocentric (sun-centered) and geocentric (earth-centered) paradigms. It took two centuries, but Copernicus' disciples finally won. But by that time, Copernicus himself was, of course, long dead.

This book includes one obvious example of an attempted paradigm shift, admittedly one that did not succeed—Mikhail Gorbachev's campaign to restructure political and economic life in the Soviet Union. Indeed, his six years in power show how quickly a seemingly strong and stable system can collapse.

I took a group of students to the Soviet Union a year after Gorbachev became General Secretary of the CPSU. There were no signs that the country had less than six years to live.

We did see some signs that the economy was in trouble and that the party elite had already lost some of its all but total grip on power. Nothing seemed to work. At least half of the hotel elevators were *na remont* (under repair). My students discovered that they could all but pay for their trip by selling their college sweatshirts on the black market, because quality consumer goods were simply not available. The food we were served in what were supposed to be the best hotels was dreadful. Things we took for granted like photocopying machines and direct-dial long distance phone calls were not available because the authorities feared that they would be used to organize dissent.

We also learned that the Soviet Union was no longer as closed as we thought (or as I had taught). We were taken to a disco that, despite the censorship of the media, played all the world's top hits. Young people in the USSR and Eastern Europe had a reasonably good idea of how badly off they were compared to their counterparts in the West.

Gorbachev did seem securely in charge of a country that seemed unlikely to change in any profound way. After all, Gorbachev was only able to make it to the top of the party hierarchy because the Soviet Union faced a number of international and domestic difficulties that could not be successfully handled using the top-down leadership and management style of the party-state as described in Chapters 8 and 9.

Little did we know that he would soon introduce reforms that would tear the country apart. At first, Gorbachev attempted to get the economy moving by working incrementally within the party-state paradigm, for example, by making people work harder or by limiting the sale of alcohol. When that failed, he and his colleagues decided on a wholesale transformation of politics and society with *glasnost'*, *perestroika*, and his other reforms. Taken together, they came as close to the outlines of a full paradigm shift as one ever finds in the "real world" of political life. And as has often been the case with other paradigm shifts in political history, Gorbachev's reforms ultimately failed.

Embedded in this brief review of material presented in more detail in Chapter 9 are three more conclusions about paradigm shifts, each of which suggests how difficult they are to accomplish and why the historical evidence is rarely on their side.

First and most obviously, not all paradigm shifts succeed. Even if opinion leaders reach the conclusion that something is profoundly wrong, someone has to devise a new way of thinking and popularize it, which has not happened yet with any proposed responses to either climate change or the stagnant global economy. Then, once the new paradigm becomes a "contender" for power, its proponents have to wage and win a political and intellectual struggle, which Gorbachev and his supporters, of course, lost.

Second, people rarely consciously set out to design or implement a paradigm shift. In that respect, Gorbachev was very much the exception. So, too, are activists like me who are trying to produce profound changes in the way we all deal with such big issues as climate change, conflict resolution, or equality across racial, gender, and other identity-related lines.

Third, paradigm shifts never happen as smoothly or as completely as the paragraphs at the beginning of this section might have led you to expect. They are always messy. What might look like four discrete stages in fact blend inextricably into each other. Along those same lines, paradigm shifts are never fully complete. American readers can see that by thinking about the line in their declaration of independence that reads "all men are created equal." Over the last two centuries, Americans have dramatically expanded what they mean by both "men" and "equality." Men now means all people, and equal includes more than just legal equality before the law but some degree of social, economic, and cultural parity as well.

Einstein and His One Liners

Most people think of Albert Einstein as the greatest scientist of the twentieth century. Far fewer think of him as a political commentator. Far fewer yet turn to him as a source of one liners. Yet, a quick tour of the Internet reveals dozens of his pithy quotes, two of which are especially useful in considering political paradigm shifts.

The first one never actually made it into his collected writing and thus can be found in a number of slightly different forms online. This is the version one finds most frequently.

**We can't solve problems
by using the same kind of thinking
we used when we created them.**

That statement suggests why a paradigm shift should at least be on the agenda today politically. Our list of pending problems is huge and shows few signs of shrinking. At the same time, our "toolkit" for solving them does not seem to be working very well. If Einstein is correct, that is the case because we are trying to do so using political instruments or kinds of thinking we used in creating the modern state *and* the range of problems discussed at the beginning of this chapter. In some ways, it is hard to imagine solving our problems without something akin to a paradigm shift

because, as Tim Hurson put it in a book for corporate leaders, "there is no way to turn a desk calculator into an Excel spreadsheet."[5]

In one of his more famous (and, in this case, accurately transcribed) statements, Einstein also suggested that a paradigm shift begins when people consciously adopt new ways of addressing their problems. To that end, he included the following sentence in a telegram he sent to two hundred prominent Americans shortly after World War II urging them to stop the nuclear arms race in its tracks.

**The unleashed power of the atom
has changed everything
save our modes of thinking
and we thus drift
toward unparalleled catastrophe.**

Einstein's statement has four interesting components, which are reflected in the way I presented it here. The first appears at the beginning and the end of the sentence and is the part we tend to gloss over today because the "unparalleled catastrophe" of an all-out nuclear war is not likely to occur in the foreseeable future. Second, Einstein said "everything" had changed, not just warfare. Even within a few weeks of Hiroshima and Nagasaki, he realized we were entering a new era in all areas of life and not just in politics. Einstein died before the word *globalization* was invented, but he knew that something like it was coming. Third, he used a remarkable verb to describe our condition that is powerful because of the very weakness it conveys: "drift." In old western movies, a drifter was a cowboy who rode aimlessly from town to town. A sailboat is adrift if there is not enough wind to allow the person at the helm to steer it. Finally, he went on to say that everything had changed except for "our modes of thinking" or the values and assumptions that shape our lives.

Over the next half-century, Einstein's statement became one of the most widely quoted political one liners. His words did not, however, lead many people to address the middle part of either statement—the ways of thinking we use in tackling the vexing problems in our lives, politically and otherwise.

But that may be the crux of the matter. If you decide that the gap between our ways of thinking and the demands being placed on us politically is not all that wide, you could and should conclude that no paradigm shift is needed. If, however, you decide that the gap is really a chasm, then you should at least consider a paradigm shift, because, in Hurson's words, you can't turn a mechanical calculator into a spreadsheet.

---

[5]Tim Hurson, *Think Better: An Innovator's Guide to Productive Thinking.* (New York: McGraw Hill, 2007).

Systems Theory Revisited

A consideration of the five big questions and paradigm shifts next leads us to systems theory, which I introduced in Chapter 1. There and in subsequent chapters, I used it largely as a lens through which you could make sense of the thousands of events, dates, people, and places introduced since then. Now, we return to systems theory and view it in another light because it *could* be an alternative to state- and power-centered models of political life.

It allows us to reconfigure elements of the old paradigm—including the state and power—into a new lens just like the Copernicans came to the understanding that the earth and the other planets circled around the sun. As the Copernican revolution did for astronomy, basing political analysis and activity on systems theory leads us in qualitatively different directions, an exploration of which will take up the rest of this chapter.

Although systems theory is currently not widely used in political science, it is at the heart of most other social and natural sciences, because **feedback** is the key to understanding how any organization or organism changes over time. In that sense, it is particularly important because it draws our attention to the often convoluted feedback loops among the component parts of a country's or any unit's political system (see Figure 1.1 on page 4) and how they move a society in one of three main directions. Thus, a system can:

- **Stay in balance.** A homeostatic system remains stable in much the same way that a thermostat regulates the temperature in a house. Incidentally, the people who brought systems theory into political science thought that this was the best we could do.

- **Decay or degenerate.** Many of those same political scientists had lived under totalitarian regimes or fought in World War II, which led them to search for ways of avoiding the kind of collapse that led to World War II and all of its horrors.

- **Grow.** Business executives, in particular, tell us that systems can improve their performance and learn over time, whatever one means by "improve" and "learn." This was the aspect missed by the scholars who pioneered the use of systems theory in political science in the 1950s and 1960s. It may also be what we need to focus on more in this age of globalization.

But the most important reason to focus on systems theory is that it uses interdependence as its starting point. Each component of a system is connected directly or indirectly to every other one in a complex and complicated network. If you change one piece of a system, everything and everyone else will change with it. As the cliché puts it, "what goes around comes around."

Two Perspectives

To see how systems theory can lead us in new directions both normatively and empirically, think about (or better yet do it with some of your classmates) an exercise I have used in hundreds of classrooms and public workshops. I divide the participants into small groups and ask them to discuss why instances of interpersonal, national, and international conflict they know about did not turn out well. Then, I reassemble the larger group and have someone from each group sum up what they had talked about.

No group I ever worked with had trouble coming up with long lists of causes for each type of conflict. As I write their ideas down on a whiteboard, the participants see that they can be collapsed into a handful of clusters that are strikingly similar for all three levels, which are summarized in the left-hand column of Table 16.1. They give us a good first glimpse of our political problem-solving paradigm or, in Einstein's terms, our "modes of thinking."

In one form or another, the scarcity of resources underlies almost all instances of conflict that matter to political scientists and average citizens alike. Because there is not enough money or prestige or clean air to go around, we compete with each other for them.

The rest of the entries in that column reflect a rather consistent and common mindset most people use when confronting most conflicts most of the time. If you have taken an international relations course, you have probably encountered ways of thinking that parallel the first column. What is instructive for our purposes as students of comparative politics is how widespread these values and assumptions are for *all* types of contentious issues and the conflicts they spawn.

The people who have taken part in this exercise over the years assume that the parties to the dispute are all trying

TABLE 16.1 Contrasting Values and Ways of Thinking

CURRENT VALUES	NEW THINKING
Scarce resources	Scarce resources
Separate	Interdependent
Short term	Long term
Self-interest = "me" first	Self-interest = good of the whole
We versus they, image of the enemy	We with they thinking
Power over	Power with
Power = force and violence	Power = cooperation, working together
Conflict is bad	Conflict can be good

© Cengage Learning

to get as many as they can of those scarce resources. If not, they are trying to prevent the other side from doing so.

We also see ourselves as independent or separate actors who "merely" pursue their self-interest in competing for those scarce resources. Table 16.1 portrays that as putting "me" first. However, me is a metaphor that covers not only me personally, but the groups I belong to and identify with. In that sense, we assume that conflict always involves an "us" and "them," however we define those terms in any single event.

Although it does not have to turn out this way, we often demonize our adversaries, as we have seen time and time again in these pages in heated conflicts over identity issues. At those times, we use what psychologists call the "image of the enemy" that seemingly turns conflict (and hence politics) into a life-or-death struggle.

It is hardly surprising that we also assume that our dispute will have a **zero sum** outcome in which only one side can win and one side has to lose. Under the circumstances, winning is important, but not losing is even more so.

Under those circumstances, we have little choice but to think of power the way I defined it earlier—my ability to get you to do something *you otherwise wouldn't do.* Because those italicized words are central to the way we think of power, we assume that exerting it will involve at least the threat if not the actual use of force, which I can use physically or in less violent ways, for instance, by deducting points from your grade if you hand your paper in late. In other words, power is something I exert *over* my adversary and is something that carries with it the real possibility of harm for all participants. In other words, more often than not, even contemplating using "power over" someone else can mark the start of a vicious cycle filled with all sorts of self-reinforcing feedback loops.

After the large group works through the left-hand column, I put them back into their small groups to think about disputes that had significantly better outcomes at each of the three levels. It only takes them a few seconds before they have their first insight. They have a much harder time coming up with examples. But, once they do, they develop different clusters of values and assumptions that are listed in the right-hand column of Table 16.1.

That list, too, starts with scarce resources, but after that the two differ all but completely in part because when people operate in the right-hand column, they are already thinking in systems terms without being aware of the fact that they were doing so, which is why I invented the exercise in the first place.

These conflicts worked out "better" because the parties to the dispute treated them as if they were part of an interconnected whole, whether that "whole" was an entire country or simply a family. In an interdependent world, it makes sense to think of our differences as something we share as well as something that divides us. That is the case because anything I do affects you and vice versa. And, if I exert power *over* you and force you to do what I want, the odds are good that you will react in a way that comes back to haunt me and could well do us both harm.

People tend to act in ways that are consistent with the right-hand column that do not seem likely to maximize their short-term self interest, especially when they see a shared or common interest in doing so. When that happens, our goal—and often the outcome we reach—is what conflict resolution theorists call a **win-win** or **positive-sum outcome** that benefits everyone involved, including ourselves. It is by trying to meet both of our shared interests and adapt to their successes and failures through feedback that the system improves over time.

To that end, the technology and organizational behavior expert Clay Shirkey asks us to think about such mundane events as picnics more than politics to help us see that we cooperate all the time, because they happen when a group of people decide that it is in their common interest to share a meal outdoors.[6] If he is right, it becomes easier and easier to cooperate once they see that they share common interests and problems and act accordingly, which he argues is increasingly the case as a result of globalization and the new technologies that it has helped give birth to. He goes on to suggest that conflicts leading to the use of "power over" one's adversaries are very much the exception to the rule in most areas of life—other than politics.

From this perspective, the often gloomy assumptions we make about human nature should not be taken for granted. Yes, we all have a self-interested side that leads us to try to assert power over others *some* of the time. But we also have other built-in motivations that include a desire to cooperate and do good things for others, especially if we do well ourselves in the process, which is what win-win outcomes are all about.

Under those circumstances, power itself takes on new meaning. Power is now also something I exert *with* you. In fact, in French, the word for power (*pouvoir*) when used as a verb simply means *to be able.* In that sense, we can talk about empowering or enabling others to accomplish things.

Conflict can actually even be a good thing.

There is a growing body of research that suggests people do not use the motivations, values, and assumptions listed in the left-hand column all of the time even when the stakes are high and the conflict is intense. Instead, we cooperate for the good of the whole a lot more often than

---

[6]Clay Shirkey, *Cognitive Surplus: How Technology Makes Consumers Into Collaborators.* New York: Penguin, 2011.

social science theory (especially mainstream economics, on which so many of our assumptions are based) would lead us to expect.

Political scientists may not have looked at power in that sense very often, but social psychologists have. Thus, Adam Grant distinguishes between what he calls givers and takers.[7] The traditional definition of power shares a lot with the way he describes the taker, because such a person or institution enters relationships trying to win or "take" something from another individual or organization. Grant shows that givers use power in a way that helps others reach their goals and succeed because they reap benefits for themselves over time as well.

As Shirkey, Grant, and I would be the first to acknowledge, people and governments today tend to operate using the values and assumptions laid out in the left-hand column most of the time when they have to deal with political issues. In fact, one of the lessons of this book (and of Shirkey's) is that we have far more experience competing against than cooperating with each other, especially as the size of the unit making decisions grows or the stakes of their actions increase.

Shirkey's bottom line is a call for us to develop institutions and practices that benefit the entire system and create what he calls opportunities and cultures through which the collaborative side of our human nature can come out and then build on itself in what he calls cooperative spirals. Through them, it is at least possible to encourage the kind of interpersonal trust and sharing that is so critical for successful problem solving but has been so lacking in the countries and crises covered in this book.

For our purposes, one of his most surprising conclusions is about the cultural changes that are already occurring as a result of the spread of new technologies. What's more, evidence that we can and do cooperate readily and occasionally easily comes from the technology world itself in the success of open source software, such as the UNIX operating system, Apache web servers, and crowd sourcing tools such as Wikipedia.[8]

As with everything else in this chapter, I do not mean to seem like a pie-in-the-sky idealist. Whatever you think about the argument that I derived from Table 16.1, it is hard to deny that the realities of the way we lead our political lives have not kept pace with the challenges of globalization. There is little doubt, too, that our political patterns are deeply ingrained to the point that they have become

hard to change as is the case with any habit. However, as the *New York Times* journalist Charles Duhigg notes in his recent book, history is filled with examples of people breaking habits and opening new possibilities for themselves in politics as in all aspects of our lives.[9]

There is little doubt, too, that the kinds of behavior Shirkey likes are found least often when people have to make the tough political decisions discussed in the first fifteen chapters. Yet, sometimes they do.

The best example we can point to was not covered in this book, because South Africa is rarely included in introductory courses in comparative politics. After years of repression and struggle, the leaders of the National Party and the African National Congress realized they had to live together. Otherwise, the country would slide into deeper difficulties and, perhaps, fall apart. At that point, then-president F. W. de Klerk, Nelson Mandela, and their colleagues began the negotiations that led to power sharing, the transition to democratic rule, the end of apartheid, the creation of the Truth and Reconciliation Commission, and a whole series of less visible bridges between the white and black communities.

In the course of this book, we have seen examples of at least partial paradigm shifts that produced qualitative changes in political life at least partially toward the kind of inclusive and power-sharing networks that Shirkey and his colleagues have in mind. The transition from the Fourth to the Fifth Republic in France included a dramatic expansion of inter-elite cooperation. Deng Xiaoping's economic reforms succeeded in large part because they encourage CCP and new innovative elites in the public and private sectors to work better together. Finally, the reduction in global poverty levels discussed earlier in this chapter all involved cooperation among the international financial institutions, parts of the private sector, NGOS, and the governments of the countries involved.

It is important to stress one note of caution. Whatever happens, we will almost certainly live the rest of our lives in a world in which people and institutions operate using the values and assumptions in *both* columns. And, it is certainly true that the larger the organization and the higher the political stakes, the more difficult it is for individuals or their leaders to find or build on common ground. Especially under those circumstances, we have little experience in building institutions that offer meaningful incentives or opportunities for people to cooperate when the political going gets tough, which is when we are most likely to use those values that are part of what Einstein meant by our unchanged "modes of thinking."

---

[7]Adam Grant, *Give and Take: A Revolutionary Approach to Success* (New York: Viking, 2013).

[8]This was clear to at least some political scientists as long as a decade ago. See, for example, Steven Weber, *The Power of Open Source* (Cambridge: Harvard University Press, 2004).

---

[9]Charles Duhigg, *The Power of Habit: Why We Do What We Do in Life and Business* (New York: Random House, 2012).

A newly arrived refugee family from the Sudan region of Darfur crosses into Chad on January 27, 2004, in the direction of the three improvised refugee camps in Tine, Chad. Something like 250,000 people have been killed. Ten times that number have been forced into exile (www.savedarfur. org).

MARCO LONGARI/AFP/Getty Images

The End of Power?

The discussion so far has been rather abstract and removed from the issues I focused on in the first fifteen chapters. I will bring it down to earth and the mainstream of political science in the rest of this chapter by drawing heavily on yet another new book by someone who is not a political scientist, Moisés Naím's *The End of Power*.[10] Although he rarely uses the term itself, his is one of the most complete explorations of systems theory and its implications for political life today.

A Networked World

Naím thinks of our world as a **network** of networks. For most of us, that word immediately brings the Internet to mind. It *is* a network of millions of interconnected computers and other devices that share information across cyberspace. However, it is not the only network. If Naím and observers like him are correct, networks are the defining organizational structure of our time.

As we have seen time and time again in this book, the world still has its share of hierarchical institutions and relationships, most notably whenever power and wealth

[10]Moisés Naím, *The End of Power: From Boardrooms to Battlefields and Churches to States, Why Being In Charge Isn't What It Used to Be* (New York: Basic Books, 2013).

are involved. However, as he sees it, the ties that bind us together are just as important in a world that is changing as fast as ours is, because today's networks share four common features:

Volatility Naím uses the term *volatility* to describe a world in which change is the only constant. In fact, it is probably a better single image than the graph on p. 4 implies, because in a volatile world, things are changing in unpredictable and, seemingly, uncontrollable ways.

Uncertainty For good or ill, the traditional approaches to comparative politics raised in Chapter 1 rest on the assumption that scholars can boil political life down to reasonably simple explanatory propositions. After reading this book so far, that should seem like an overly ambitious if not delusional goal. Most specific events—if not most general trends—are hard to predict, including such memorable ones as the 9/11 attacks. If network theorists are correct, the number of all but unpredictable events is increasing along with every other indicator of change.

Complexity Complexity is a fancy word some scientists use to convey the idea that everything is interconnected. In other words, if you turned each chapter in this book into a flow chart (which is, in fact, the way I outlined them), you see that everything is connected to everything else, which is why paying attention to feedback loops is so important. And, because the world is uncertain, we can't always anticipate what those links are like. Complexity scientists also focus on the way systems adapt to changes in their complicated networks or their environments.

Ambiguity It should come as no surprise that very little in a volatile, uncertain, and complex world can be seen in simple "either/or" terms. Statements like "capitalism is good" or "most whites are racists" cry out for nuances. And, nothing illustrates the ambiguous nature of modern life more than comparative politics! In some ways, this is the hardest of Naím's characteristics for readers of this book to deal with, because research on college students has shown that learning to deal with ambiguous problems is one of the biggest challenges of an undergraduate's career.

The Three M Revolutions

In addition to networks, Naím stresses what he calls three revolutions, each of which begins with M.

More Colleagues on the political left like to argue that real wages in most countries have not gone up appreciably since the late 1970s. On the one hand, that is statistically accurate.

On the other hand, it is also misleading. Most people live more comfortable lives than they or their parents did at the height of the cold war. The number of people living in what the United Nations calls extreme poverty has been cut by about two billion people since 1990.

It isn't just that we are wealthier. Fewer people starve to death or succumb to easily treatable diseases liked diarrhea. About two billion people had access to the Internet in 2010 and more than half of the world's population has regular access to and uses a mobile telephone.

We have learned to make things that cost less and work better, faster, and easier than anything we had a mere generation ago. This paragraph is a shining example of that. I "wrote" it in a few seconds using voice recognition software that did not exist 20 years ago.

We shouldn't exaggerate here. The fact that a few hundred million people now live on two dollars a day rather than one does not mean that they are anywhere near the lap of luxury. To see that, all you need to do is consider the stories of the slums I described at the start of several of the chapters in Part 4. Still, there are few people for whom today's world much resembles the one I was born into in 1947, as the cheeky list by the Beloit College professors mentioned earlier so clearly shows.

Mobility The world's people are increasingly in motion. No matter how you choose to measure it, we go more places and see more things.

In a typical year, about forty million people move from one country to another. Some are refugees, while others emigrate in search of a better life for themselves and their families.

Most of us also travel more. When I was an undergraduate, only foreign-language majors studied abroad. A half-century later, almost all students at the college I attended spend at least a month studying off campus.

And of course, we have also become more mobile virtually. We see that in everything from today's 24/7 news cycle to the way that the Internet seemingly brings the world to our screens and smartphones. The new technologies are not only useful for entertainment purposes. Smartphones and social media software did not make the protests in Iran after the 2009 election or the rapid response to the 2010 earthquake in Haiti possible, but they certainly made them easier to organize and in so doing opened new avenues for implementing social change.

Mentality Naím's most controversial—but perhaps most important—contribution is his suggestion that our mentalities or ways of thinking are changing as well. On issue after issue, core cultural values have changed dramatically, although sometimes it appears as if we are being pulled in multiple and often conflicting directions.

On the one hand, much of today's younger and more mobile population is becoming more cosmopolitan and egalitarian. Although plenty of inequalities still exist, women and members of minority groups have seen their rights and their influence expand in the last half-century. In my youth, everything from the end of apartheid to the acceptance of same-sex marriage seemed like impossible dreams. Today, millions of people take them for granted. To cite but one example, the neighborhood I live in had segregated schools fifty years ago. In 2008 and 2012, more than 70 percent of my neighbors voted for an African-American president.

On the other hand, many people resist those changes, especially the ones that stress humanity's common bonds. There is no clearer example of this trend than the rise of militant Islam which long antedates the terrorist attacks on 9/11. More generally, millions of people find the social and cultural changes that accompany globalization to be threatening traditional values, including many of those same shifts that led to the breakdown of racial, religious, and gender barriers alluded to in the previous paragraph.

Being in Charge Isn't What It Used to Be

Like most analysts who use networks as a starting point, Naím believes that everything is up for grabs, including power. Here, his understanding of our networked world leads him to reach three unusual conclusions, all of which are reflected in his subtitle. The second and third of them may come as a surprise given what we have seen so far in this book.

Power Is Concentrated In some important respects, fewer people seem to be in meaningful positions of power than ever. There is no question that wealth and the power that comes with it are held by fewer people and smaller groups in the industrialized democracies. In that sense, the Occupy and Tea Party movements on the Left and Right, respectively, lash out against the perception as well as the reality that "they" have too much power, in ways that have echoed throughout Europe as well.

It's not just true of the established democracies. Political power is more concentrated in other kinds of countries as well, as we saw in the strengthening of hybrid regimes that have at most a veneer of democracy.

The concentration of power is occurring even more rapidly outside of politics. Massive corporations dominate what are increasingly global brands. A generation ago, we might have focused on General Motors or Volkswagen or Toyota. Today, our attention and our critical eye are more likely to be drawn to Google or Apple or Microsoft. But the point is the same. The economic as well as the political decisions that matter seem to be made by fewer and fewer people representing fewer and fewer interests.

Analysts debate just how much power is being centralized. For our purposes, it is probably more important that a growing number of people are convinced that it is and that those perceptions give rise to much of the anger "from below" first hinted at in Table 1.3.

Power Is Fleeting Paradoxically, one can also make the case that people on the top of all those hierarchies are less powerful than they used to be for at least two reasons.

The first is an outgrowth of the dynamics depicted in Figure 1.3 and reflected in this book's subtitle. Individual countries and their institutions are less and less masters of their own destinies. Power within them may be concentrated in fewer and fewer hands. However, those "hands" are less and less able to determine what happens, whether at the national (ending the recession), local (stopping urban violence), or nonpolitical (preventing people from sharing copyrighted files on the Internet) level.

Second, being influential in one area does not make one as powerful in others. When Naím argues that power is hard to hold on to, he is also suggesting what economists mean when they say that power isn't fungible because it cannot easily be transferred from one policy area to another or from one time to another or from one place to another.

To cite but the most obvious example, the United States may be the wealthiest country in the world and have by far the best-equipped military, but neither its riches nor its weapons have done much to help it defeat terrorism or slow climate change. Even corporate giants like Dell and General Motors have seen their market shares plummet in the face of competition from Samsung and Toyota, and even they have found it hard to transfer their clout from one economic sphere to another *or* to protect themselves from upstart companies who challenge their prominent positions.

Power Isn't Only About Today Thinking in terms of networks leads us to focus more on the longer-term implications of power than we used to. Network and systems analysts often use the analogy of a spider web to describe power relationships in which changing any one node will directly or indirectly produce additional effects that reverberate throughout the entire system often over an extended period of time. That leads many of them to consider indirect, unexpected, or "second-order" effects of any action. In particular, we tend to underestimate the ways in which exerting one's power over someone or something else might only lead to "victories" in the short run and come back to haunt the "winner" in the long run.

This is where feedback most obviously comes into play. You don't have to dig far between the lines of the last fourteen chapters to see that what happens today affects what happens tomorrow and usually does so in a frankly messy way.

Our inattention to the longer-term impact of our activities has always come with its share of costs. Today we have to consider the implications of everyone's actions over time because therein lies the reasons power seems so fleeting.

Systems theory is particularly important in this respect because it encourages us to look at power as a multidimensional phenomenon whose exercise varies from time to time as well as from issue to issue.

However, most mainstream definitions of political power emphasize the short-term effects of power in which it is fairly easy to distinguish winners from losers the way we do after an election. The impact of the exercise of power does not end immediately after election day or a victory on the battlefield, and that is where the volatility, uncertainty, complexity, and ambiguity normally come stampeding in.

New Politics: Three Examples

As noted above, one of the misconceptions about paradigm shifts noted above is that they happen cleanly and clearly. As the two-centuries-long struggle over the Copernican model makes clear, that is almost never the case even when the evidence clearly points in the direction of a new way of doing things, as I certainly feel is the case today.

In other words, we are likely to spend the rest of my lifetime and probably the rest of yours in a political world that relies on both columns of Table 16.1 depending on the circumstances. All I can reasonably claim is that there are ways in which people and the institutions they form already draw on some aspects of the second column, which I will illustrate with three brief examples.

International Regimes: The EU

Almost all international relations experts agree that supranational governing bodies are among the weakest institutions on the planet. In fact, one of the most obvious lessons to take away from our analysis of the most powerful of them—the EU (see Chapter 7)—is that their impact pales in comparison with all but the weakest failed states.

However, we should consider what international relations scholars call **international regimes**, which come in many forms. Some were created by a treaty or other binding international legal document. Others are informal and are based on widely accepted international norms. Despite their variety, international regimes all provide us with a degree of international if not **global governance**. Some of them involve routine mechanisms for managing matters that transcend national boundaries, such as the all but universally accepted rules governing the flow of international mail, telecommunications, and travel.

These regimes have little in common with the international state many world federalists, for example, lobby for. That is the case for many reasons, perhaps the most important of which is the fact that they cannot overcome the anarchy of international relations that gives rise to the "war of all against all" that Thomas Hobbes feared. They do, however, provide alternatives to aspects of the "dog eat dog" world Hobbesians of his day and ours rightly worried about.

Before proceeding to two examples we have already discussed, note that international relations experts do not use the term *regime* in the same way comparativists do. As they see it, an international regime consists of "principles, norms, rules, and decision making procedures around which actor expectations converge in a given issue-area" that member states agree to follow.

Whatever you think of the future prospects for global governance in general, there is little doubt that the European Union is the most advanced example of it today. As we saw in Chapter 7, the postwar creators of what became the EU thought of unification as a vehicle to achieve peace in Europe and reach other **superordinate goals** that individual states could not meet on their own.

A half-century later, the EU stands alone as an international organization to which states have explicitly handed over some of their national sovereignty "upward" to a supranational body. Although the individual governments rarely come right out and say it, they ceded control over a large part of what used to be national policy-making responsibilities to "Brussels." In most areas of economic policy making, what happens there has more of an impact on their citizens than any law passed or decree enacted in their capital cities.

Unlike most international regimes, the EU has some tools it can use to make certain its decisions are carried out, which international relations experts rightfully criticize international regimes for not having. To be sure, realists and other critics of international regimes are right in pointing out that the EU lacks either an army or a police force and thus lacks what Max Weber called a monopoly on the legitimate use of force. However, international regimes work either because they have other legal remedies (in this case, the various European courts) or because they create the expectation that their policies will be implemented without the threat of force but by dint of the authority they have created over the years.

The EU is also interesting for our purposes because it illustrates that power can be shared "downward" as we saw in its exploration of the concept of subsidiarity, which overlaps considerably with the use of federalism at the national level. Starting with Jacques Delors near the end of the twentieth century, European leaders have tried to assign tasks to that level of government that seemed best suited to carry it out. That has even allowed some urban areas that straddle national boundaries to begin developing transnational governing bodies at the metropolitan level.

Peacebuilding

The second example is the one I work on when I am not writing new editions of *Comparative Politics*, which also illustrates how the scope of comparative politics is likely to expand in the near future. Peacebuilding itself is one of the most casually used terms in all of political science. It can refer to everything from what happens as a war is winding down to conscious efforts to create conditions in which we can avoid war from starting in the first place. Despite our fascination with questions of war and peace, political scientists have done little to explore what you would think would be the closely related field of peacebuilding.

For our purposes, peacebuilding is useful precisely because it is hard to imagine reaching a lasting peace agreement, in any of the countries beset by conflict, that doesn't involve the international community, business leaders, **nongovernmental organizations (NGOs)**, as well as the parties to the dispute itself. There definitely is nothing approaching an international peacebuilding regime. However, the dozens of approaches to peacebuilding are all based on the assumption that actors at multiple levels can find ways of cooperating with each other.

Interest in peacebuilding is not new. Its roots can be traced all the way back to most of the world's great spiritual traditions. It entered Western political thought no later than Immanuel Kant's 1795 essay "On Perpetual Peace," which over time ushered in the theory that democracies do not go to war with other democracies.

But modern peacebuilding also has newer and somewhat different roots. There is no agreed-upon date for its beginning, but most of us point to the early 1980s when three then-unrelated events occurred. Roger Fisher and William Ury published *Getting to Yes*, which has sold well over two million copies and has been translated into dozens of languages. A group of professors at George Mason created what is now the School for Conflict Analysis and Resolution, which was the first degree-granting program that combined conflict resolution and peacebuilding. Finally, a former Foreign Service Officer, John Marks, created Search for Common Ground (**www.sfcg.org**), which initially worked on easing cold war tensions and now has programs in more than forty countries.

Most pioneer peacebuilders started out as mediators who rarely addressed explicitly political issues because they started out by helping divorcing parents, healing dysfunctional families, and assisting judges and lawyers so that they make more productive decisions. Soon, however, peacebuilding scholars and activists alike learned that mediation was not enough. As we saw, for instance, with the 1995 Oslo Accord between Israel and the Palestinians, protracted political conflicts take a long time to settle and require a wide variety of tools before anything approaching long-term reconciliation among the disputants can be achieved.

In the absence of some equivalent of a state that can settle disputes, peacebuilding has so far mostly tried to assemble ad hoc coalitions of local, national, and international actors that are often quite different from those focused on in this book. But over time, they have come to see that identity-based and other conflicts have system-wide causes and therefore will require system-wide solutions.

Thus, the Alliance for Peacebuilding (where I work; www.allianceforpeacebuilding.org) recently decided to base all of its own projects on explicitly systems-based approaches. I am personally responsible for a project that brings peacebuilders and current and former military officers together to help societies make the transition from conflict and war toward peace and stability. We have assumed from the beginning that neither of us can reach such goals on our own and that we have to forge coalitions of actors at all levels from the grassroots up to the leading national authorities in all countries that are party to a dispute. Consequently, we also assume that reaching some kind of stable peace will also require addressing identity, equity, gender, environmental issues, and more as part of the process.

That means exploring all the feedback loops connecting potential causes and effects of peacefulness. Our various projects proceed on two levels. The first incorporates the perspectives of multiple disciplines in diagnosing the problems facing the world's most troubled countries—including my own. By a similar logic, we understand that peacebuilding efforts "on the ground" have to address the many-faceted realities of human security as discussed earlier in this chapter and that peacebuilding itself will not always be at the top of our list of priorities.

The Gendered Nature of Globalization

Unlike peacebuilding, the role of women is now a central focus in academic political science. That has not always been the case. When I was a student, the women's movement was in its infancy, there were very few women among my fellow students, and only a few of them were studying gender and politics, which was not seen then as a ticket to a promising academic career.

The extent to which times have changed was hard to miss while I was writing this chapter. Hillary Clinton stepped down as U.S. Secretary of State and began contemplating a presidential candidacy in 2016. Margaret Thatcher, Britain's first woman prime minister, died. On that day, Amazon.com listed 32,339 books that dealt with women and politics.

Over the course of my career, feminism and feminist scholarship have each made major contributions to our understanding of new social movements. But, even so, my colleagues who focus on gender and politics are just beginning to see we have not fully considered the ways the changing role of women affects entire political systems and their feedback loops. In other words, just like peacebuilding, the politics of gender today touches at least all of the social science disciplines if not more as it has become a global political issue.

Despite vocal criticisms from the Right, the study of gender and politics need not take one to the left end of the political spectrum. In fact, most political scientists use the term *feminism* in a fairly bland way that overlaps with the United Nation's definition agreed to at a 1985 summit in Nairobi, Kenya.

> Feminism constitutes the political expression of the concerns and interests of women from different regions, classes, nationalities, and ethnic backgrounds. There is and must be a diversity of feminisms, responsive to the different needs and concerns of different women. Contrary to the best interests of "sisterhood," not all women share identical interests.[11]

Women have made considerable progress in most of the industrialized democracies, but their status has not improved as much in the rest of the world, where, in fact most people live—men and women alike. It isn't just the lack of a Margaret Thatcher or a Hillary Clinton among most countries' political elites. Few countries outside the industrialized democracies have seen any significant increase in the number of women in any professions, whereas in the United States women now constitute the majority of all law and medical students.

Along those lines, many feminist scholars have begun to think of gender issues as a central component of the political agenda in our globalizing world. As such, they are like students of international regimes and peacebuilding in shifting their attention from "government" to "governance" because the latter "includes not just institutions but a set of gendered social relations in a system of rules and regulatory norms and mechanisms that are translated through the discourses of law and policy."[12]

In short, many feminist scholars are convinced that bias along gender lines is all but built in to globalization. There have long—perhaps always—been gendered roles and gender-based distributions of power and authority in everything from families to national political systems. However, to the degree that these analyses are on target, the trends discussed so far in this chapter may be turning gender into a global issue. To see why, consider the overlapping examples of women's forced labor and migration.

If anything, women in the Global South suffer worse forms of discrimination and have fewer opportunities for improving their condition than their counterparts in the North. For instance, no one knows how many women are sold into the sex trade when they are too young to bear

children yet become pregnant and come down with debilitating and, at times, life-threatening diseases.

More generally, we often think that phenomena such as the forced labor of women happen "somewhere else." Not true. On the day I finished drafting this section for the last edition of *Comparative Politics*, the *Washington Post* reported that a couple had been arrested in that city's suburbs for having held a Filipina woman in slave-like conditions for about a decade. She was paid a pittance and rarely allowed to leave the house. The "owner" (a retired doctor) claimed that he supported the woman's family by renting a small apartment in the Philippines where her nine children lived. Because almost no one is actually convicted of human slavery in the United States, the couple never faced even a day of prison time.

That case was just the tip of a much larger iceberg. The Philippines is the second-largest recipient of remittance funds sent by its citizens who work abroad, half of whom are in the United States. Altogether, remittances accounted for 12.5 percent of the Philippine GDP in 2007. In Latin America and the Caribbean, those funds make up more of the GDP than foreign direct investment and foreign aid combined.

Discrimination against women is not limited to the sex trade. There are more women than men in the global, transient workforce of migrant laborers, both because they are not protected as well by national and international laws and because they are generally paid less. Most migrant workers in general are women. In fact, Mexico is the rare country in which men make up the majority of those who move to work abroad, legally or otherwise. The gendered wage gap makes women more attractive to hire in "private" areas, such as the home, and makes the phenomenon somewhat lower on the radar screen of most mainstream politicians. In other words, governments in the Global South send women to work abroad so that they can earn wages that are much higher than they could hope to make in their home country, at least some of which will be sent back to their families.

There is growing realization that in order to truly hold up half the sky, as Chairman Mao and, later, Nicholas Kristoff and Sheryl WuDunn put it, there will have to be some sort of global attempt to address gender issues, just as there will be in peacebuilding. That initiative began with the merger of four previously separate divisions of women's policy making in the UN in 2010 to form "UN Women," short for the UN Entity for Gender Equality and the Empowerment of Women (www.unwomen.org). The new agency has designated a number of policy areas as its top priorities, which parallel those identified by the World Bank and the regional international organizations, including preventing violence against women, enhancing their role in

---

[11]World Conference to Review and Appraise the Achievements of the United Nations Decade for Women: Equality, Development and Peace. Nairobi, Kenya, 1985 (www.un.org/womenwatch/daw/beijing/nairobi.html).

[12]Shirin, Rai, and Georgina Waylen, eds., *Global Governance: Feminist Perspectives* (London: Palgrave, 2008), 6–7.

peacebuilding, empowering women leaders, and reaching the UN's broader Millennium Development Goals.

National governments are beginning to do their part as we saw with France's law requiring that women make up half of each party's nominees in elections run under proportional representation. Even Iran, which is not known as a bastion of women's liberation, has seen the emergence of a variety of independent women's movements that the regime has not been able to fully suppress during its periodic political crackdowns.

As with peacebuilding, we have also seen a dramatic increase in the number of innovating NGOs, many of which bridge the divide between the public and private sectors, which is still a roadblock for many conflict resolution groups. One of the most intriguing initiatives in that respect is Vital Voices (www.vitalvoices.org), which began as an experiment by then U.S. Secretary of State Madeleine Albright and then First Lady Hillary Clinton. It has since become an independent NGO and is one of the few that explicitly tries to build partnerships with the private sector, with partners including firms without a significant feminist track record, including Bank of America, Walmart, Exxon/Mobil, Nike, and Ann Taylor.

Student and Citizen

There is one final reason I decided to set off in a different and, frankly, complicated direction in this chapter. It is also one of the reasons I study and worry about comparative politics—your future. If my experience is any indicator,

very few of you will become professional political scientists and use the material covered in this book in your professional lives.

You will, however, all be citizens of a world of constant and accelerating global challenges. Whether you accept the arguments made in this chapter, you will be asked to help make decisions about the issues discussed throughout this book and this course.

My colleague Colonel Christopher Holshek is right in making the remark I used to end Chapter 1: What happens over there matters over here. Your political decision will not be just *whether* you get involved but *how* you do so.

I am lucky. I chose a career (well, actually two of them) that enabled me to integrate my profession and my politics. Not all of you will share that luck (if it is, indeed, luck). Nevertheless, the future of the world will be placed in your hands as you get older, and you will need to find some way to assume that responsibility.

I initially agreed to write *Comparative Politics* to help pay for my step-daughter's college tuition and therefore dedicated the first eight editions of the book to her. Since the eighth edition came out, she has given us a grandson to whom this book is dedicated, because I want him to inherit a far better world when he reaches his mother's age.

Although Evonne is a generation removed from her high school days, I still find the coffee mug she gave me for our first Christmas/Hanukkah together (which I still use) to be the best way to end this book. In its short and simple way, it conveys the message it took me almost five hundred pages to get to.

It has a picture of a tabby cat holding up the world The simple caption reads. "Fragile. Handle With Care."

KEY TERMS

Concepts
climate change
feedback
global governance
international regimes
network
nongovernmental organizations

(NGOs)
paradigm shift
positive-sum
superordinate goal
systems theory
United Nations
win-win

Acronyms
EU
IPCC
NGOs

Organizations, Places, and Events
International Panel on Climate Change

USEFUL WEBSITES

Globalization 101 is by far the best single site on globalization. It has links to material on most topics covered in this chapter—but not on peacebuilding. In keeping with the pace-of-change argument we have made, it has "moved" three times since it was created in 2000.

   www.globalization101.org

The International Panel on Climate Change not only does the best work but it has the best site on the topic.

   www.ipcc.ch

UN Women focuses on its own work, but it has plenty of links to other sites and covers a lot of ground.

www.unwomen.org

The best site on peacebuilding amounts to an online handbook on the subject.

www.beyondintractability.org

The Institute for Peace and Economics conducts the annual Global Peace Index, which has a ton of good analysis as well as the results.

www.visionofhumanity.org

FURTHER READING

Collier, Paul. *The Bottom Billion.* New York: Oxford University Press, 2007. The best book on globalization, poverty, and their implications.

Franzway, Suzanne, and Mary Margaret Fonow. *Making Feminist Politics: Transnational Alliances between Women and Labor.* Champaign: University of Illinois Press, 2011. To my mind, the most thoughtful and accessible recent book on the role of women in all aspects of political life.

Friedman, Thomas P. *Hot, Flat, and Crowded.* New York: Farrar, Straus, and Giroux, 2009. Arguably the best and most optimistic book on globalization.

Grant, Adam. *Give and Take: A Revolutionary Approach to Success.* New York: Viking, 2013. By a social psychologist who teaches in a business school, this book discusses the circumstances under which people who do not put their immediate self-interests first tend to succeed.

Hauss, Charles, and Richard O'Neill. *Security 2.0.* Lanham, MD: Rowman and Littlefield, 2015. Builds on this chapter. Prepublication drafts will be available by summer 2014.

Naím, Moisés. *The End of Power: From Boardrooms to Battlefields and Churches to States, Why Being In Charge Isn't What It Used to Be.* New York: Basic Books, 2013. This Libyan-born former Venezuelan cabinet minister turned Washington pundit has written by far the most sweeping book on the way power is changing at the state and other levels.

Pinker, Steven. *The Better Angels of Our Nature: Why Violence Has Declined.* New York: Viking, 2011. A remarkable reading of the last few hundred years of history that suggests that we have come a long way in undermining Hobbes's pessimistic conclusion.

Shirkey, Clay. *Cognitive Surplus: How Technology Makes Consumers Into Collaborators.* New York: Penguin, 2011. One of the most thoughtful books on technology and cooperative problem solving. Other authors address politics more than Shirkey does, but his book has the widest-reaching implications for comparative politics and the social sciences in general.

Glossary

Concepts, Organizations, Places, & Events

Action Congress (AC) Political party in Nigeria. Third in most recent election.

Action Group (AG) A Yoruba-based political party in post-independence Nigeria.

Akali Dal The Sikh-based party in Punjab, India.

All Nigeria Middle Belt People's Party (ANPP) The leading opposition party in Nigeria today.

Alliance Coalition of British Liberals and Social Democrats in the 1980s that became the Liberal Democrats of today.

American exceptionalism The theory that the United States occupies a special niche in the world in terms of its national credo, historical evolution, political and religious institutions, and unique origins.

Anticlerical The belief that there should be no link between church and state.

Arab Spring Series of protests that rocked much of the Middle East in 2010 and 2011.

Armed Forces Ruling Council (AFRC) Formal title of the military government during the second period of military rule in Nigeria.

Assembly of Experts An informal body in Iran that has de facto veto power over all major political decisions.

Austerity Economic policies that stress controlling inflation and balancing budgets. Normally endorsed by conservatives.

Autogestion A version of self-managed socialism popular in France in the 1970s and 1980s.

Ayodhya Site of a disputed mosque/temple that sparked communal violence in India for much of the 1990s.

Backbenchers Members of a parliament who are not in the government or shadow cabinet.

Base Marxist term to describe class and other economic relations that define the "means of production" and the distribution of wealth and power.

Basic Law The German constitution.

Basij Semi-legal vigilantes in Iran.

Beveridge Report Published in the 1940s; set the stage for the British welfare state.

Bharatiya Janata Party (BJP) The Hindu party that won the 1998 election; often referred to as fundamentalist.

Biafra A secessionist state in southeastern Nigeria.

Bloc vote French practice that requires a vote on an entire bill without amendments.

Boko Haram Violent Islamic militants in Nigeria.

Bolsheviks Lenin's faction of the Russian Social Democratic Party; later came to mean anyone who subscribed to his views and/or organization.

Bonyad Islamic charities in Iran, many of which are controlled by the government.

Bourgeoisie Among other things, a Marxist term to describe the capitalist class.

BRIC(S) Large countries undergoing rapid economic growth, including Brazil, Russia, India, China, and, sometimes, South Africa.

British East India Company Private company that colonized much of India until the 1850s.

Broadening Support for expanding EU membership.

Bundesbank Germany's central bank, replaced by the European Central Bank in 1999.

Bundesrat The upper house of the German parliament.

Bundestag The lower house of the German parliament.

Bureaucracy The part of the government composed of technical experts and others who remain from administration to administration.

Cabinet responsibility Principle that requires a prime minister and government to retain the support of a parliamentary majority.

Cadre Term used to define the permanent, professional members of a party, especially in the communist world.

Camarilla In Mexico and elsewhere in Latin America, a politician's personal following in a patron-client relationship.

Campaign In China, policies in which the party seeks to reach its goals by mobilizing people.

Capitalism An economic system in which the means of production are privately owned and prices, wages, and profits are determined by private industry.

Capitalist roader Derogatory term used to label moderate CCP leaders during the Cultural Revolution.

Carrying capacity The amount of development an ecosystem can bear.

Castes Groups into which Hindu society is divided, each with its own distinctive rules for all areas of social behavior.

Catch-all parties Term devised in the 1960s to describe a new type of political party that plays down ideology in favor of slogans, telegenic candidates, and the like.

Central Advisory Committee (CAC) Informal group of senior Chinese Communist leaders in the 1980s.

Central Committee Supposedly the most important body in a communist party; its influence declined as it grew in size and the party needed daily leadership.

Central Military Commission (CMC) The political leadership of the Chinese military.

Chancellor democracy Germany's informal system of political domination by the prime minister.

Charisma A style of leadership that emphasizes the personal magnetism of a single individual.

Checks and Balances Informal American term denoting the fact that one branch of government can normally act with the consent of one or more of the others.

Cheka The Soviet Union's first secret police.

Chinese Communist Party (CCP) The only legal party in China, which has run the country since 1949.

Christian Democratic Union (CDU) Germany's leading right-of-center party; similar parties exist elsewhere where there is a large Catholic population.

Civic culture Culture characterized by trust, legitimacy, and limited involvement, which some theorists believe is most conducive to democracy.

Civil society The web of membership in social and political groups that some analysts believe is needed to sustain democracy.

Cleavage Deep and long-lasting political divisions.

Climate change Also known as global warming or the greenhouse effect, in which the Earth's temperature increases incrementally due to carbon dioxide release.

Coalition An alliance of parties that are close enough to one another ideologically to stay together for the duration of a parliamentary term.

Codecision A cooperation procedure that obliges the EU's Council and Commission to consult the Parliament in two stages and gives the Parliament more influence.

Codetermination German system that gives unions half the seats on boards of directors of all companies with more than two thousand employees.

Cohabitation In France, a period in which one party or coalition controls the Parliament and the other has the presidency.

Cold War Rivalry between the superpowers from the end of World War II to the collapse of the Soviet Union.

Collective responsibility The doctrine that all cabinet members must agree with all decisions.

Collectivist consensus Cross-party British support for the welfare state that lasted until the late 1970s.

Colored Revolution Term used to describe uprisings referred to by a color, such as the Green Movement in Iran.

Comintern The interwar coalition of communist parties directed from Moscow.

Command economy A centrally planned and controlled economy. This kind of economy operated in the former Soviet Union and other communist countries.

Commission, European The executive of the European Union.

Committee of Permanent Representatives European Union civil servants who are sent by and work for the member states rather than the EU itself.

Common Agricultural Policy (CAP) The EU's agricultural policy, blamed for many of its economic troubles and likely to be changed as it adds new members.

Common Foreign and Security Policy (CFSP) EU goal of creating a single foreign policy for its fifteen member states; one of the three pillars.

Common Market Colloquial name used to describe the European Union, especially in its early years.

Communal group Racial, ethnic, or linguistic groups that today are often the source of political violence.

Communism/Communist Has many meanings, but usually used to describe policies and institutions derived from the works of Marx, Engels, and Lenin that were adapted and used in such countries as China and the former Soviet Union.

Communist Party (PCF) French Communist Party.

Communist Party A political party inspired by Marxism-Leninism, usually as developed in the former Soviet Union.

Communist Party of the Russian Federation (CPRF) The new incarnation of the CPSU for Russia.

Communist Party of the Soviet Union (CPSU) The party that ran the Soviet Union until its collapse in 1991.

Compromise Decision-making procedure in which all sides make concessions in order to reach an agreement.

Concerted action Cooperation involving the government, business, and labor in Germany.

Conditionality The imposition of stipulations before the granting of loans by the IMF, World Bank, and other international financial institutions.

Confederation of British Industry (CBI) The leading British business interest group.

Confédération Française Démocratique du Travail/French Democratic Confederation of Labor (CFDT) Socialist-leaning trade union federation in France. Once Catholic.

Confédération Générale du Travail/General Confederation of Labor (CGT) Trade union federation in France affiliated with the communist party.

Confederation of Mexican Workers (CTM) The trade union affiliated with the PRI.

Confucianism Chinese philosophical and religious tradition stressing, among other things, order and hierarchy.

Consensus policy making Decision-making procedures that emphasize win/win outcomes.

Conservative Party Britain's most important right-of-center party, in power more often than not for two centuries.

Constitution A basic political document that lays out the institutions and procedures a country follows.

Constitutional Council French council created in 1958 with the power to supervise elections and rule on the constitutionality of bills passed by the National Assembly before they formally become law.

Constitutional Revolution Begun in 1906, the first attempt to bring anything like democracy to Iran.

Constructive vote of no confidence In Germany, means that a chancellor can be removed in a vote of confidence only if the Bundestag also agrees on a replacement.

Contradictions Marxist notion that all societies based on inequality have built-in flaws that will eventually lead to their destruction.

Corporatism/corporatist In Europe, arrangements through which government, business, and labor leaders cooperatively set microeconomic or macroeconomic policy, normally outside of the regular electoral legislative process; in Mexico and elsewhere in the third world, another term to describe the way people are integrated into the system via patron-client relations.

Council of Ministers A generic term used to describe the cabinet in many countries.

Crisis A critical turning point.

Cult of personality In communist and other systems, the excessive adulation of a single leader.

Cultural Revolution The period of upheaval in China from the mid-1960s to the mid-1970s.

Dalit Term to describe untouchables in India.

Debt crisis The massive accumulation of loans taken out by third-world countries and owed to northern banks and governments from the 1970s onward.

Debt trap The inability of third-world countries to pay back their loans to northern creditors.

Decision making The way governments (or other bodies) make policies.

Deepening Expansion of the EU's powers.

Demand Inputs through which people and interest groups put pressure on the state for change.

Democracy/democratic A system of government in which sovereignty resides in the people.

Democracy Movement Protests by Chinese students and others that culminated in the Tiananmen Square disaster of 1989 in Beijing.

Democracy Wall Literally, a wall on which Chinese dissidents wrote "big-character posters" in the late 1970s.

Democratic centralism The Leninist organizational structure that concentrates power in the hands of the party elite.

Democratic deficit The lack of an effective democracy in the EU.

Democratic Party U.S. political party that is more likely to propose expansion of social service programs and tax rates that tend to demand more of richer Americans.

Democratization The process of developing democratic states.

Dependency/dependency theory A radical critique of mainstream economic theory that stresses the continued power the north has over the third world.

De-Stalinization The shift away from Stalinist policies and practices beginning with Khrushchev's secret speech in 1956.

Devolution The process of decentralizing power from national governments that stops short of federalism.

Dialectic The belief that change occurs in dramatic bursts from one type of society to another.

Dirigisme French belief in a centrally planned and managed economy.

Dual mandate In Nigeria and elsewhere, the notion that colonial powers had to rule on their own and through local leaders at the same time.

École Nationale d'Administration (ENA) Grande école for training France's bureaucratic elite

Electoral alchemy The way Mexican governments have used fraud to rig elections.

Electoral system Mechanisms through which votes are cast and tallied, and seats in the legislature are allotted.

Emergency Rule A provision in some constitutions that allows cabinets to rule in an all but dictatorial way for a brief period, as in India from 1975 to 1977.

Environment In systems theory, everything lying outside the political system.

EU Committee of Permanent Representatives (COREPER) In the EU, permanent representatives of the national governments.

Euro The new European currency, introduced in 1999.

European Central Bank (ECB) Leading bank for the EU, replaced national central banks.

European Coal and Steel Community (ECSC) One of the precursors of the European Union, formed in 1951.

European Community (EC) The formal name of what became the EU in the 1970s and 1980s.

European Court of Justice (ECJ) The EU's judicial body, with sweeping powers.

European Economic Community (EEC) The precursor of the EU.

European Monetary System (EMS) The first attempt to link the EU member states' currencies.

European Monetary Union (EMU) Created in 1998; includes a central bank and the euro.

European Parliament The EU's legislature.

European Union (EU) The current name of the "Common Market."

Euroskeptic People opposed to expansion of the EU's power.

Eurozone Shorthand term used to describe the EU members that use the euro.

Events of May 1968 French protest movements that almost toppled the Gaullist government.

Expediency Council A half lay and half clerical body designed to smooth relations between those two communities in Iran at the highest levels.

Extraterritoriality Portions of China, Japan, and Korea where European law operated during the late nineteenth and early twentieth centuries.

Faction A group organized on ideological or other lines operating inside a political party.

Failed state System in which the government loses the ability to provide even the most basic services.

Falsify testing/falsify Contradicting a theory by finding at least one example in which it does not hold true.

Falun Gong Chinese spiritual movement suppressed by the government since the late 1990s.

Fascism Right-wing regimes, often drawing on racist philosophies in countries such as Germany and Japan between the two world wars.

Fatherland-All Russia One of the leading opposition parties in Russia in the 1999 Duma elections.

Faulted society Germany from the late nineteenth century to the rise of Hitler, reflecting the unevenness of its social, economic, and political development.

Federal Constitutional Court (FCC) Constitutional court in Germany with significant powers of judicial review.

Federal Election Commission (CFE) The old (and corrupt) body that supervised elections in Mexico.

Federal Electoral Institute (IFE) Created before the 1997 election to provide more honest management of elections in Mexico than its predecessor, the Federal Election Commission.

Federal Executive Council of Nigeria (FEC) Leadershp of the first Nigerian republic.

Federal Republic of Germany (FRG) Formal name of the former West Germany and, now, the unified state.

Federalism/federal Constitutional practice in which subnational units are granted considerable power.

Federalist Papers Key documents written in support of the U.S. Constitution during the debate on ratification in the 1780s.

Federation Council The largely powerless upper house of the Russian parliament.

Federation of German Labour (DGB) The leading German trade union.

Feedback How events today are communicated to people later on and shape what people do later on.

Fifth Republic French regime since 1958.

First-past-the-post Electoral system based on single-member districts in which the candidate who receives the most votes wins.

Five-year plan In the former Soviet Union and other communist countries, the period for which Gosplan developed goals and quotas.

Force ouvrière Workers' Force, France's second largest and most dynamic trade union federation.

Foreign aid Money or goods provided by richer countries to help poorer ones develop.

Four modernizations A policy first introduced by Zhou Enlai and championed by Deng Xiaoping, focusing on developing industry, the military, agriculture, and science in China.

Fourth Republic Current Nigerian regime.

Fourth Republic French regime from 1946–58.

Fragmented Authoritarianism Term used to describe the internal differences within the CCP-led Chinese state.

Free Democratic Party (FDP) Germany's Liberal party.

Freedom Charter The ANC's proposals from the 1950s that led to its being banned.

Führer German term for "leader," used by Hitler.

Fundamentalism Religious beliefs of a literal nature that often lead to right-wing political views.

FY Fiscal year.

Gang of Four Radical leaders in China during the Cultural Revolution, led by Jiang Ching, Mao's wife.

Gaullists General term used to describe supporters of General Charles de Gaulle and the parties created to back his vision for the Fifth Republic.

General secretary Term used to denote the head of a communist party.

German Democratic Republic (DDR) Formal name of the former East Germany.

German question A series of questions used to study Germany's unique circumstances: why did Germany take so long to unite; why did the country's first attempts at democracy give way to Hitler; how did the division of Germany and other events after World War II help create the prosperous and stable democratic FRG in the west but also the stagnant and repressive DDR in the east; and why did unification occur with the end of the Cold War in Germany?

Glasnost Under Gorbachev, Soviet policies that opened up the political system and allowed for freedom of expression.

Global warming The well-supported theory that the earth is getting warmer due to the trapping of certain gases in the atmosphere.

Globalization Popular term used to describe how international economic, social, cultural, and technological forces are affecting events inside individual countries.

Global governance The goal—and to some degree the reality—of making political decisions internationally.

Global South The underdeveloped and largely poor countries in the world. Often called the third world.

Gobernación The ministry in charge of administration in Mexico; until recently, a post often held by politicians before becoming president.

Good Friday Agreement A practical peace agreement reached by the major parties in Northern Ireland with the British and Irish governments on, not surprisingly, Good Friday 1998.

Gosplan The Soviet central planning agency.

Governance The exercise of political authority and use of institutional resources to manage society's problems and affairs.

Government Either a generic term to describe the formal part of the state or the administration of the day.

Government of India Act The 1858 law that turned most of India into a formal British colony.

Gradualism The belief that change should occur slowly or incrementally.

Grand coalition A cabinet that includes all the major parties, not just a bare majority.

Grandes écoles Highly selective French universities that train top civil servants and, hence, much of the elite.

Grandeur Gaullist goal for France.

Great Leap Forward Failed Chinese campaign of the late 1950s to speed up development.

Great Reform Act Law passed in 1832 that expanded the suffrage; widely seen as a key step toward democracy in Britain.

Green Revolution In India and elsewhere, the technological improvements that drastically improved agricultural production and eliminated widespread starvation.

Greens Political parties that emphasize environmental and other "new" issues, and radical change. In Germany, the first major environmentally oriented party; a junior partner in government until 2006.

Gross domestic product (GDP) A measure of the total output of goods and services in a country.

Gross national product (GNP) The total value of the goods and services produced in a society.

Guardian Council The leading theological body in Iran for political purposes.

Guardianship of the Jurist Developed by Ayatollah Khomeini, supports the notion that senior clerics have the best capacity to rule in a Muslim society.

Gulf War The war between the UN coalition and Iraq following the latter's invasion of Kuwait in 1990.

Hard currency Currencies that can be traded openly on international markets.

Hausa-Fulani The leading Muslim group in northern Nigeria.

Historical materialism Marxist belief that the class divisions of a society determine everything else that matters.

House of Commons The all-important lower house of the British Parliament.

House of Lords The weaker upper house of the British Parliament, slated for reform or abolition.

Human Development Index (HDI) The UN's best indicator of social development.

Human security The belief that security includes all areas, not just the military.

Hundred Flowers Campaign Reformist Chinese campaign in the mid-1950s.

Hybrid Regime Term used to describe regimes that combine elements of liberal democracy and authoritarianism in post-communist and other countries.

Identity How people define themselves in racial, linguistic, ethnic, or religious terms.

Igbo The leading ethnic group in southeastern Nigeria. Often also spelled Ibo.

Image of the enemy Psychological concept that focuses on stereotyping one's adversary.

Immigration Reform and Control Act U.S. law, passed in 1986, that limits the rights of immigrants, especially those from Mexico.

Imperialism The policy of colonizing other countries—literally, establishing empires.

Import substitution Development strategy that uses tariffs and other barriers to imports, and therefore stimulates domestic industries.

Incompatibility clause French constitutional provision that bars people from holding a seat in both the National Assembly and a cabinet.

Incrementalism Used to describe policies that make limited, marginal, or minor changes in existing practices.

Indian Administrative Service (IAS) The bureaucratic elite today.

Indian Civil Service The bureaucratic elite during colonial rule.

Indian National Congress The leader of the struggle for India's independence and the dominant party since then.

Indirect rule British and other colonial procedures through which "natives" were used to carry out colonial rule.

Individualism The belief that emphasizes the role of the individual voter or consumer, typically associated with the rise of democracy in the West.

Industrialized democracy The richest countries with advanced economies and liberal states.

Input Support or demand from people to the state.

Institutional Revolutionary Party (PRI) The party that governed Mexico from 1927–2000.

Integrated elite In Japan, France, and Germany, refers to cooperation among government, business, and other interest groups.

Interest group An organization formed to work for the views of a relatively narrow group of people, such as a trade union or business association.

Intergovernmental Panel on Climate Change (IPCC) An international body working on the threat of climate change. Endorsed by the UN.

Interim government Generically, any government that serves for a brief period as part of a transition. In Iraq, the government chosen in the 2005 election whose one main mission was to draft a new constitution.

International Criminal Court (ICC) A new international tribunal that deals with alleged crimes against humanity.

International financial institutions (IFI) Transitional bodies that are charged with regulating trade and investment.

International Monetary Fund (IMF) International agency that provides loans and other forms of assistance to countries with fiscal problems.

International organizations (IO) Formal transnational governing institutions. Some, like the EU, have considerable power.

International political economy The network of economic activity that transcends national boundaries.

International Regime Often informal bodies that have some of the characteristics of a transnational state.

Interventionist state Governments in industrialized democracies that pursue an active economic policy.

Iranian Revolutionary Guard Corps (IRGC) Elite military unit set up after the 1979 revolution. Some claim it runs the country.

Iron triangle A variety of close relationships between business leaders, politicians, and civil servants.

Islamic Revolution The overthrow of Iran's monarchy under Shah Mohammad Reza Pahlavi and its replacement with an Islamic republic under Ayatollah Ruhollah Khomeini, the leader of the 1979 revolution.

Islamicists Muslims who are convinced that their faith should dominate politically.

Janata An early political party in India.

Janata Dal Loose coalitions that unseated Congress in the late 1970s and 1980s in India.

Jati In India, a subcaste with its own rules, customs, and so forth.

Judicial review Power held by courts in some countries that allows them to rule on the constitutional merits of laws and other policies.

Just Russia A Russian political party created in 2006 under Putin.

KGB Soviet secret police.

Kuomintang (KMT) The Chinese Nationalist Party, which was nominally in power from 1911–49; now on Taiwan.

Kurds Minority ethnic group in Iraq and other countries in the region.

Labour Party The leading left-wing party in Britain, in power from 1997 to 2010.

Laissez-faire Economic policy that stresses a limited government role.

Länder (*land*) German states.

Law for Promoting Stability and Growth in the Economy Passed in 1967, a key provision in Germany's economic consensus.

Left Party A German political party formed in 2005 that brought together dissident SPD members and the remnants of the East German Communist Party.

Left Political groups favoring change, often of an egalitarian nature.

Legitimacy A key concept stressing the degree to which people accept and endorse their regime.

Less Developed Countries (LDC) A classification of countries marked by poverty; often the inability to forge functioning courts, bureaucracies, and other institutions; and have often experienced military coups and other forms of political upheaval that have sapped regimes of the popular support needed for the long-term strength.

Liberal In the United States, it refers to people who support the left and an interventionist government. Everywhere else in the world, however, it means opposition to government interference in the economy and any other area in which individuals can make decisions for themselves.

Liberal Democratic Party In Britain, the number-three party and in some ways the most radical; in Russia, the neofascist and racist opposition party led by Vladimir Zhirinovsky.

Lok Sabha The all-important lower house of the Indian parliament.

Long March Retreat by the CCP in the mid-1930s, which turned into one of its strengths in recruiting support.

Maastricht Treaty Created the EU and EMU; signed in 1992.

Magna Carta An English charter signed in 1215 that marks the first trend toward democratization.

Majlis The Iranian parliament.

Manifesto In Britain and other parliamentary systems, another term for a party's platform in an election campaign.

Maquiladora Factory in Mexico (initially on the U.S. border, now anywhere) that operates tax-free in manufacturing goods for export.

Marshall Plan U.S. funds provided for reconstruction of Europe after World War II.

Marxism-Leninism The philosophy adopted by ruling communist parties, which combined Marxist analysis with Leninist organizational structures and tactics.

Mass line Chinese Communist principle that stressed "learning from the masses."

May Fourth Movement Chinese protest movement triggered by opposition to the Treaty of Versailles; a major step on the path leading to the creation and victory of the CCP.

Means of production Marxist term designating the dominant way goods are created in a given society.

MEDEF The leading interest group representing French business.

Member of Parliament (MP) Elected members of the British or other parliament.

Mensheviks The smaller and more moderate faction of the Russian Social Democratic Party before World War I.

Mestizo Term used to describe Mexicans of mixed racial origin.

Microcredit Lending and development strategy that stresses small loans for new businesses, developed by the Grameen Bank in Bangladesh.

Middle Belt Ethnically mixed region of central Nigeria where the capital, Abuja, was built.

Modell Deutschland Term used to describe the political approach to German economic growth after World War II.

Movement of French Enterprises (MEDEF) Leading French business association.

Mughals The Muslims who invaded and dominated India beginning in the sixteenth century.

Multilevel analysis A way of looking at politics that includes several layers of government at once.

Multilevel governance A form of decision making that involves national, regional, and/or local governments together.

Multinational corporation (MNC) Company operating across national boundaries.

Nation As used by political scientists, primarily a psychological term to describe attachment or identity rather than a geopolitical unit such as the state.

Nation building A process in which people develop a strong sense of identification with their country.

National Action Party (PAN) The leading right-of-center opposition party in Mexico.

National Assembly In France and South Africa, the lower house of parliament.

National Congress of British West Africa (NCBWA) One of the leading groups advocating Nigerian independence.

National Council of Nigeria and the Cameroons (NCNC) An Igbo-based movement for Nigerian independence.

National Democratic Party (NPD) Germany's most powerful neo-Nazi party since the end of World War II.

National Front (FN) France's racist right-wing party.

National Party of Nigeria (NPN) A Muslim-based political party during the Nigerian Second Republic.

National Republican Convention (NRC) A leading independence movement in colonial Nigeria.

National Socialist Democratic Workers Party (NSDAP) Political party of Hitler and the Nazis in Germany.

Nationalist Party The Kuomintang, the ruling party in China before the CCP victory.

Nationalization Philosophies or attitudes that stress the importance of extending the power or support for a nation; government takeover of private business.

Nazis Hitler's party, which ruled Germany from 1933–45.

Near abroad Russian term to describe the other fourteen republics of the former Soviet Union.

Network A sociological term used to identify "nodes" in an interdependent system.

New Left Radicals from the 1960s.

New Right Conservative political movements in industrialized democracies that have arisen since the 1960s and stress "traditional values," often with a racist overtone.

Newly industrialized countries (NIC) The handful of countries, such as South Korea, that have developed a strong industrial base and grown faster than most of the third world.

Nigerian National Democratic Party (NNDP) One of the regionally based political parties in post-independence Nigeria.

Nigerian People's Party (NPP) One of the major parties in post-independence Nigeria.

Nigerian Youth Movement (NYM) A leading pro-independence movement in colonial Nigeria.

Nomenklatura The Soviet system of lists that facilitated the CPSU's appointment of trusted people to key positions, adopted by other communist regimes.

Nongovernmental organizations (NGO) Nonprofit, private groups that exert political influence around the world and are playing an increasingly important role in determining developmental and environmental policies.

Non-reelection Principle in Mexican political life that bars politicians from holding office for two consecutive terms.

North American Free Trade Agreement (NAFTA) Agreement linking the economies of Canada, Mexico, and the United States.

Northern Elements Progressive Union (NEPU) A left-of-center Muslim party in the Nigerian second republic.

Northern People's Congress (NPC) One of the Muslim-based political parties during post-independence Nigeria.

Oligarch Business and political leaders with what some think is undue influence in Russia.

Operation Desert Shield the mobilization of American troops into Saudi Arabia at the time of the Gulf War.

Organization of Petroleum Exporting Countries (OPEC) Cartel of oil-producing countries; responsible for the 1973–74 embargo.

Ossi German who grew up in the former East Germany.

Ottoman Empire Islamic empire based in present-day Turkey; collapsed with World War I.

Our Home Is Russia New political party chaired by former prime minister Viktor Chernomyrdin.

Output Public policy in systems theory.

Pacting A process in which leaders from opposing sides cooperate.

Pahlavi dynasty The father and son who ruled Iran for most of the twentieth century, until the revolution of 1979.

Pantouflage The French practice of leaving the bureaucracy to take positions in big business or politics.

Paradigm A theory that covers an entire discipline.

Paradigm shift A change in basic assumptions and theories in science, including political science.

Parastatal Companies owned or controlled by the state in the third world.

Parity Law Recent French legislation guaranteeing seats in the parliament for women.

Parliamentary party The members of parliament from a single party.

Party of Democratic Socialism (PDS) The successor to East Germany's Communist Party.

Party of the Democratic Revolution (PRD) The leading left-of-center opposition party in Mexico.

Party of power A kind of Russian political party created to support the current leadership.

Party state The notion that the CPSU and other ruling communist parties dominated their entire political systems.

Patriotic Union of Kurdistan (PUK) One of the leading Kurdish opposition groups in Iraq and beyond.

Patron-client relations Neofeudal relations in which "patrons" gain the support of "clients" through the mutual exchange of benefits and obligations.

PEMEX Mexico's nationalized petrochemical industry.

Pendulum effect The notion that policies can shift from left to right as the balance of partisan power changes; in Mexico, reflects the fact that the PRI can move from one side to another on its own as circumstances warrant.

People's Democratic Party (PDP) The current ruling party in Nigeria.

People's Liberation Army (PLA) China's military.

People's Redemption Party (PRP) A leading political party in Nigeria's second republic.

People's Republic of China (PRC) Official name of the Chinese state.

Perestroika Ill-fated program to reform the Soviet economy in the late 1980s.

Permit raj In India, the system of government rules and regulations that required state approval of most enterprises.

Politburo Generic term used to describe the leadership of communist parties.

Political culture Basic values and assumptions that people have toward authority, the political system, and other overarching themes in political life.

Political participation Opportunities for citizens to take part in their country's government, such as voting in competitive elections, joining interest groups, and engaging in protest.

Political party Organization that contests elections or otherwise contends for power.

Politics The process through which a community, state, or organization organizes and governs itself.

Positive-sum outcome Conflict resolution in which all parties benefit. Also known as win-win.

Postindustrial society Society in which the dominant industries are in the service and high-tech sectors.

Postmaterialism/postmaterialist Theory that young middle-class voters are likely to support environmentalism, feminism, and other "new" issues.

Power As conventionally defined, the ability to get someone to do something he or she otherwise would not do.

Power ministries The most important departments in the Russian government.

Prefect Until 1981, the central government appointee who really ran France's departments.

Presidential Administration The term used to describe the formal and informal network of leaders surrounding the Russian president.

Presidential Rule In India, the government's power to remove elected state officials and replace them with appointees from Delhi.

Princeling Chinese leaders who are the sons (and occasionally daughters) of key figures in the revolution or early CCP.

Principlists Loose term to refer to the most conservative politicians and clerics in Iran.

Privatization/privatized The selling off of state-owned companies.

Proclerical The belief that the church should play a leading role in government.

Proletariat Marxist term for the working class.

Proportional representation (PR) Electoral system in which parties receive a number of seats in parliament proportionate to their share of the vote.

Provisional government Generic term used to describe temporary governments formed until a new constitution is written; also, the government in Russia between the two 1917 revolutions.

Public policy The decisions made by a state that define what it will do.

Purges The systematic removal of people from party, state, or other offices; especially common in communist systems.

Qualified majority voting The EU voting system in which the Council of Ministers does not need to reach unanimity on most issues.

Radicals People to the left of center; in France, the liberals who were radical only in nineteenth-century terms, which is to say they favored democracy, capitalism, and anticlericalism.

Rajya Sabha The weaker upper house of the Indian parliament.

Rally for the Republic (RPR) The former name of the Gaullist Party in France.

Rashtriya Swayamsevah Sangh (RSS) A fundamentalist Hindu group and a precursor of the BJP.

Realignment A shift in the basic electoral balance of power in which substantial groups in a society change their longterm party identification.

Red Guard Radical students and other supporters of Mao Zedong during the Cultural Revolution.

Red hat A slang term used to describe CCP influence in formally privatized enterprises.

Red versus expert Debate in China pitting ideologues against supporters of economic development.

Regime The institutions and practices that endure from government to government, such as the constitutional order in a democracy.

Remittances Money sent "home" by immigrants working in other countries.

Reparations Payments demanded of defeated powers after a war, especially important in Germany after World War I.

Republican party/Republican One of the two main contemporary political parties in the United States whose political platform is considered center-right and supports business interests.

Resiliency An organization's ability to return to health and strength after a setback.

Right Political forces favoring the status quo or a return to earlier policies and values.

Rule of law In a democracy, the principle that legal rules rather than arbitrary and personal decisions determine what happens.

Russian Federation Formal name of Russia.

Sanctions Policies designed to limit or end trade with a country to help force it to change its policies.

Satellites The countries in eastern and central Europe that came under communist rule after World War II.

SAVAK Iranian intelligence service under the shah.

Second of Khordad Movement The political party organized to support the reform efforts of then-president Khatami in Iran. Named for the day he was first elected.

Secret speech Given by Khrushchev in 1957; seen as the start of the "thaw."

Secretariat Generic term used to denote the bureaucratic leaders of a communist party.

Senate Upper house of the legislature in the United States, France, Mexico, and South Africa.

Separation of powers Formal term for checks and balances in a system like that of the United States.

Sequestration American policy of across the board budget cuts that began in 2013.

Sexeño The six-year term of a Mexican president.

Shadow cabinet In systems like Britain's, the official leadership of the opposition party that "shadows" the cabinet.

Shah Title of the rulers of Iran before the 1979 Islamic revolution.

Sharia Islamic legal code that many argue should supersede civil law in countries such as Iran and Nigeria.

Shiite Minority Muslim sect, usually seen as more militant than the Sunnis.

Shock therapy Policies in formerly communist countries that envisage as rapid a shift to a market economy as possible.

Single European Act (SEA) Act that created the truly common market in 1992.

Single-member district Electoral system in which only one representative is chosen from each constituency.

Sino-Soviet split Tensions between the USSR and China that rocked the communist world.

Social Democratic Party (SDP or SPD) Germany's left-of-center party, in power since 1997; Britain's former Social Democratic Party; also, one of the political parties in Nigeria during the very short-lived third republic.

Socialism A variety of beliefs in the public ownership of the means of production and an egalitarian distribution of wealth and income.

Socialist Party (PS) France's Socialist Party, created in 1971.

Solidarity The anticommunist union formed in Poland in the 1980s.

Sovereign Debt Crisis A key part of the recession that began in 2007 and 2008 that has especially been a burden in the EU.

Special Economic Zones (SEZ) Cities and regions in China in which foreigners are allowed to invest.

Standing Committee The subcommittee that runs the Politburo in China.

State All individuals and institutions that make public policy, whether they are in the government or not.

State Duma The lower house of the Russian parliament.

Strong state One with the capacity and the political will to make and implement effective public policy.

Structural adjustment Development strategy that stresses integration into global markets, privatization, and so on. Supported by the World Bank, IMF, and other major northern financial institutions.

Subsidiarity In the EU, policy that devolves decision making to the lowest appropriate level.

Subsidy In Iran and elsewhere, policies that compensate or help individuals or groups overcome economic problems.

Subsistence economy One in which peasants predominate and grow food and other crops primarily for domestic consumption.

Suffrage The right to vote.

Sunni Majority Muslim sect, usually seen as more moderate than the Shiites.

Superordinate Goal A political or other goal that can only be met through cooperation.

Superstructure Marxist term for the government, religion, and other institutions whose primary role is to help support the dominance of the ruling class.

Support In systems analysis, popular input that tends to endorse the current leadership and its policies.

Supranational Authority that transcends national borders.

Supreme Leader Title given to the ayatollah who sits atop all Iranian political institutions.

Supreme Military Council (SMC) A title used during the two most important periods of military rule in Nigeria.

Swaraj The Indian movement for independence and self-rule.

Syndicate Indian Congress leaders who ended up opposing Indira Gandhi.

System A group of interacting, interrelated, or interdependent elements forming a complex whole in comparative politics, inputs, decision making, outputs, feedback, and the environment within a state.

Systems theory A model for understanding political life:; examining how a state's components interact over time and how nonpolitical and international forces shape what it can and cannot accomplish.

Tea Party Loosely organized American political movement which was largely responsible for GOP gains in the 2010 election.

Theory Explanatory statements, accepted principles, and methods of analysis.

Third International Moscow-dominated organization of communist parties around the world between the two world wars.

Third way A term used to describe the new and more central left-wing parties of the 1990s, most notably Britain's "New Labour."

Third world Informal term for the poorest countries in Asia, Africa, and Latin America.

Three line whip In a parliamentary system, statements to MPs that they must vote according to the party's wishes.

Three pillars Informal term denoting the main areas in which the EU has worked since the Maastricht Treaty.

Tiananmen Square Symbolic heart of Chinese politics; site in Beijing of protests and a massacre in 1989.

Tories Informal name for Britain's Conservative Party.

Totalitarian/totalitarianism Regime in which the state has all but total power.

Trades Union Congress (TUC) Britain's leading trade union confederation.

Treaty of Amsterdam Minor 1998 agreement that added some limited powers to the EU.

Treaty of Lisbon A 2007 EU treaty that balances big and small states, old and new members but does not serve as a constitution and has not been fully ratified by Fall 2009.

Treaty of Nice EU's December 2000 treaty that opened the door to the broadening of the EU in 2004 and 2007 and outlined provisional plans for reforming the EU's institutions so they could function effectively with as many as thirty members, including the possibility of enacting a constitution.

Treaty of Rome Created the EEC in 1957.

Treuhand The agency responsible for selling off formerly state-owned East German companies.

Troubles Informal term describing the violence in Northern Ireland in the late twentieth century.

Tutelle In France, central government control over local authorities.

Twentieth Party Congress Occasion of Khrushchev's "secret speech" launching de-Stalinization.

Two-ballot system An election system in France in which any number of candidates can run at a first ballot, and if one of them wins a majority, he or she wins the seat. If not (which is usually the case), a second ballot is held one week later.

Two-party system Countries in which only two parties seriously compete for power.

Unanimity principle Formerly required for all decisions in the EU, now only for major new policies.

Underdevelopment The status of poor countries in the Global South.

Union for a Popular Majority/Movement (UMP) Center-right French political party that was founded in 2002, has an absolute majority in the National Assembly and a plurality in the Senate, and elected Nicolas Sarkozy as their candidate for president in 2007.

Union for French Democracy (UDF) The number-two right-of-center party in France under various names since 1962.

Union of Right Forces A Russian democratic opposition party associated with free market reforms and privatization.

Unit The basic body assuring work, housing, and welfare to which most urban Chinese were assigned before economic reforms took hold.

Unitary state Regimes in which subnational units have little or no power.

United Middle Belt Congress (UMBC) A powerful force during the Nigerian second republic.

United Nations (UN) The world's leading international organization.

United Party of Nigeria (UPN) The main Yoruba party in Nigeria's second republic.

United Russia The political party led by Russian president Vladimir Putin.

Untouchable Indians outside of and "below" the caste system; abolished legally with independence.

Vertical of Power Russian term to describe the centralization of power in the hand of the president and his closest associations.

Vicious Cycle System that deteriorates over time.

Virtuous Circle System that improves over time.

Vote of confidence In a parliamentary system, a vote in which the members express their support for (or opposition to) the government's policies; if it loses, the government must resign.

Warlord Prerevolutionary Chinese leaders who controlled a region or other relatively small part of the country; also a term used in other countries such as Afghanistan.

Warsaw Pact Alliance that was the communist world's equivalent of NATO.

Washington Consensus Informal agreement in support of structural adjustment policies.

Weapons of mass destruction (WMD) Biological, chemical, and nuclear weapons.

Weimar Republic Germany's first and failed attempt at democracy.

Westminster system Term used to describe the British parliamentary system and others based on it.

White paper In Britain and elsewhere, a government statement that outlines proposed legislation; the last stage before the submission of a formal bill.

White revolution The term used by the shah to describe reforms in Iran between the end of World War II and the downfall of his regime in 1979.

Win-win outcome Conflict resolution in which all parties benefit; also known as positive-sum game.

World Bank A major international lending agency for development projects based in Washington.

World Trade Organization (WTO) International organization with wide jurisdiction over trade issues; replaced the General Agreement on Tariffs and Trade.

Yaboloko One of the leading reformist parties in Russia.

Yoruba The leading ethnic group in southwestern Nigeria.

Zapatistas Informal name for Mexican revolutionaries in Chiapas.

Zero-sum game Political outcome in which one side wins and the other loses.

Zoning Informal Nigerian policy through which the presidency alternates between.

People

Abacha, Sani The military ruler of Nigeria until his death in 1998.

Abiola, Moshood The apparent winner of the 1993 Nigerian presidential election; died in prison of unexplained causes five years later.

Abubakar, Abdulsalami Interim military leader of Nigeria in 1998.

Adenauer, Konrad First chancellor of the German Federal Republic (West Germany).

Ahmadinejad, Mahmoud President of Iran.

Awolowo, Obafem A leading Igbo politician and head of Biafra during the civil war in Nigeria in the late 1960s.

Azikiwe, Nnamdi The leading Yoruba politician in post-independence Nigeria.

Babangida, Ibrahim Military ruler of Nigeria in the 1990s and potential candidate in 1997.

Balewa Tafawa One of the leaders of early independent Nigeria; killed in the first coup.

Barroso, José Manuel The Brazilian-Portuguese eleventh president of the European Commission, since 2004.

Bello, Ahmaedu One of the leaders of early independent Nigeria; killed in the first coup.

Berezovsky, Boris Russian oligarch who put together United Russia.

Bhindranwale, Jarnail Singh Radical Sikh leader killed during the attack on the Golden Temple in 1984.

Bismarck, Otto von Chancellor and most important founder of unified Germany in the last half of the nineteenth century.

Blair, Tony British prime minister, 1997–2007, and architect of "New Labour."

Bové, José An outside-the-system French protester and well-known critic of globalization.

Brandt, Willy First Socialist chancellor of the German Federal Republic.

Brezhnev, Leonid General secretary of the CPSU, 1964–82; largely responsible for the stagnation of the USSR.

Brown, Gordon Prime Minister of Great Britain from 2007 until 2010.

Bush, George W. 43rd president of the United States.

Calderón, Felipe President of Mexico from 2007 to 2012.

Cameron, David Prime Minister of Great Britain since 2010.

Cárdenas, Cuautémoc Son of Lazaro Cárdenas, founder of the PRD, and first elected mayor of Mexico City.

Cárdenas, Lazaro President of Mexico, 1934–40. The last radical reformer to hold the office.

Castro, Fidel President of Cuba since 1959.

Chen Duxiu Founder of the Chinese Communist Party.

Chiang Kai-shek Nationalist president of China before 1949 and later of the government in exile on Taiwan.

Chirac, Jacques Career French politician; president from 1995–2007.

Chubais, Anatoly Russian reformer committed to promarket policies; created the Union of Right Forces.

Clegg, Nick Leader of British Liberal Party and current deputy prime minister.

De Gaulle, Charles. Hero of the French resistance against German occupation; founder and first president of the Fifth Republic.

De la Madrid, Miguel President of Mexico, 1982–88; introduced structural adjustment reforms.

Debré, Michel Primary architect of the constitution of France's Fifth Republic; also its first prime minister, from 1958–62.

Delors, Jacques Prominent French Socialist politician who was president of the European Commission, 1985–95.

Deng Xiaoping De facto ruler of China from the late 1970s to 1997.

Desai, Morarji First non-Congress prime minister of India.

Diaz, Porfirio Introduced the principle of nonreelection into Mexican politics; ironically, de facto dictator of the country for a quarter century in the late nineteenth and early twentieth centuries.

Ebadi, Shirin An Iranian woman who won the Nobel Peace Prize for her work as a lawyer defending cases of alleged human rights abuses in Iran.

Engels, Friedrich With Karl Marx, the creator of communist theory.

Fang Lizhi Physicist and leading Chinese dissident, now living in exile in the United States.

Fischer, Joska Green member of parliament; foreign minister in the Schroeder government in Germany.

Fox, Vicente First non-PRI president of Mexico, elected in 2000.

Gandhi, Indira Prime minister of India, 1966–75 and 1979–84; daughter of Nehru and mother of Rajiv Gandhi; assassinated in 1984.

Gandhi, Mohandas Karamchand Leader of the Indian National Congress in the twenty years before independence.

Gandhi, Rajiv Prime minister of India, 1984–89; assassinated in 1991; son of Indira and grandson of Nehru.

Gandhi, Sonja Head of the Congress Party; turned down the prime ministry in 2004.

Giscard d'Estaing, Valery Moderate president of France, 1974–81.

Gorbachev, Mikhail Head of the CPSU and last president of the Soviet Union.

Gore, Al Former American vice president. Author of *An Inconvenient Truth.*

Hitler, Adolf Nazi leader of the Third Reich, 1933–45.

Hobbes, Thomas British social theorist of the seventeenth century who emphasized a strong state.

Hollande, François President of France, elected in 2012.

Hu Jintao Former president of China.

Ironsi, Aguiyi The military ruler of Nigeria during the Biafran war.

Jiang Qing Fourth (and last) wife of Mao Zedong and one of the leaders of the Gang of Four, a radical faction in the CCP during the Cultural Revolution.

Jiang Zemin Former President of China and successor to Deng Xiaoping.

Jonathan, Goodluck Current president of Nigeria.

Jospin, Lionel Socialist prime minister of France, 1997–2002.

Kano, Aminu A Muslim leader of early Nigeria.

Khamenei, Ayatollah Ali Supreme Leader of Iran since the death of Ayatollah Khomeini.

Khatami, Mohammad Reformist president of Iran, 1997–2005.

Khodorkovsky, Mikhail Russian tycoon arrested on corruption and tax evasion charges in 2003.

Khomeini, Ayatollah Ruhollah Muslim cleric who led the 1979 revolution in Iran and was leader of the country until his death in 1989.

Khrushchev, Nikita Successor of Josef Stalin as head of the CPSU and Soviet Union from 1953 until he was ousted in 1964.

Kohl, Helmut Longest-serving chancellor of Germany, 1982–98; oversaw unification.

Le Pen, Jean-Marie Founder and main leader of France's racist National Front.

Lenin, Vladimir Architect of the Bolshevik revolution and first leader of the Soviet Union.

Lin Biao Head of the PLA and designated successor to Mao Zedong; died in mysterious circumstances after a failed coup attempt in 1972.

Liu Shaoqi Moderate CCP politician and designated successor to Mao Zedong; died during the Cultural Revolution.

Locke, John Leading democratic and liberal theorist who stressed "life, liberty, and the pursuit of property."

Lopéz Obrador, Andres Manuel A Mexican politician who was the mayor of Mexico City from 2000 to 2005, before resigning to contend the 2006 presidential election representing the PRD.

Louis XIV French king from 1643 to his death in 1715, popularly known as the Sun King.

Macaulay, Herbert The most important leader of the struggle for independence in Nigeria.

Major, John Former Prime Minister of the United Kingdom and leader of the Conservative Party. He held these posts from 1990 to 1997.

Mao Zedong A Chinese revolutionary, political theorist, and Communist leader. He led the People's Republic of China from its establishment in 1949 until his death in 1976.

Marx, Karl With Friedrich Engels, the leading nineteenth-century communist theorist.

Medvedev, Dmitri Third and current president of Russia.

Merkel, Angela Chancellor of Germany since 2006.

Mitterrand, François Resuscitated the French Socialist Party; president, 1981–95.

Modi, Narendra Current leader of BJP in India.

Monnet, Jean Primary architect of the EU and the French planning system.

Mossadeq, Mohammad Left-of-center prime minister of Iran, overthrown in a CIA-led coup in 1954.

Mousavi, Mir Hossein An Iranian reformist politician who served as the fifth and last prime minister of the Islamic Republic of Iran from 1981 to 1989 and was a candidate for the 2009 presidential election.

Narasimha Rao, P. V. Prime minister of India, 1991–96.

Nehru, Jawaharlal Indian leader before independence; prime minister, 1949–64.

Nieto, Enrique Peña President of Mexico elected in 2012.

Obasanjo, Olusegun President of Nigeria since 1999.

Pompidou, Georges Second president of the Fifth Republic of France, from 1969 until his death in 1974.

Putin, Vladimir President of Russia from 2000 to 2013.

Rafsanjani, Ayatollah Hashemi Second president of Iran after the 1979 revolution.

Rouhani, Hassan President of Iran elected in 2013.

Royal, Ségolène A prominent French politician who is a member of the French Socialist Party.

Salinas de Gortari, Carlos President of Mexico, 1988–94; continued structural adjustment reforms; currently living in exile because of his family's involvement in scandals.

Santa Anna, Antonio López de Nineteenth-century general and dictator responsible for Mexico's losing more than a third of its territory to the United States.

Sarkozy, Nicholas President of France from 2007 until 2012.

Saro-Wiwa, Ken Nigerian activist executed by the military government in 1996.

Schmidt, Helmut Chancellor of West Germany, 1974–92.

Schröder, Gerhard SPD chancellor of Germany from 1998 to 2006.

Shagari, Shehu President of Nigeria; overthrown in 1983 coup.

Shah, Muhammad Reza The second and last Pahlevi shah of Iran; deposed in 1979.

Shah, Reza First Pahlevi shah of Iran.

Singh, Manhoman Prime minister of India since 2004.

Spaak, Paul-Henri Belgian politician who was one of the leading architects of the early Common Market.

Stalin, Joseph Leader of the CPSU and Soviet Union, 1924–53.

Sun Yat-sen President of China after the 1911 revolution.

Thatcher, Margaret Conservative and first female prime minister of Great Britain, 1979–90.

Vajpayee, Atal Bihari BJP prime minister of India, 1998–99.

Walesa, Lech Most important leader of Solidarity and then president of Poland.

Wei Jingsheng Major Chinese dissident, now in exile in the United States.

Xi Jinping President and head of the Chinese Communist Party since 2012.

Yar'Adua, Umaru Musa President of Nigeria since 2007.

Yeltsin, Boris Former reformist communist leader and president of Russia, 1991–2000.

Zedillo, Ernesto President of Mexico, 1994–2000.

Zhirinovsky, Vladimir Leader of the right-wing and racist Liberal Democratic Party in Russia.

Zhou Enlai Number two to Mao Zedong in China from 1949 until his death in 1975.

Zyuganov, Gennady Head of the Russian Communist Party.

Name Index

Italic page numbers refer to photographs, illustrations, tables, or figures. Boldfaced page numbers refer to biographical profiles.

Subject Index

Italic page numbers refer to photographs, figures, and tables.